India, China, and the World

India, China, and the World

A Connected History

Tansen Sen

ROWMAN & LITTLEFIELD
Lanham • Boulder • New York • London

Published by Rowman & Littlefield
A wholly owned subsidiary of
The Rowman & Littlefield Publishing Group, Inc.
4501 Forbes Boulevard, Suite 200, Lanham, Maryland 20706
https://rowman.com

Unit A, Whitacre Mews, 26-34 Stannary Street, London SE11 4AB,
United Kingdom

British Library Cataloguing in Publication Information Available

Library of Congress Cataloging-in-Publication Data
Names: Sen, Tansen, 1967– author.
Title: India, China, and the world : a connected history / Tansen Sen.
Description: Lanham : Rowman & Littlefield, 2017. | Includes bibliographical references
    and index.
Identifiers: LCCN 2017024077 (print) | LCCN 2017037323 (ebook) | ISBN
    9781442220928 (electronic) | ISBN 9781442220911 (cloth : alk. paper) | ISBN
    9781538111727 (pbk. : alk. paper)
Subjects: LCSH: India—Foreign relations—China. | China—Foreign relations—India.
Classification: LCC DS450.C5 (ebook) | LCC DS450.C5 S43 2017 (print) | DDC
    327.54051—dc23
LC record available at https://lccn.loc.gov/2017024077

Printed in the United States of America

To my parents, Namita Sen and Narayan Chandra Sen

Contents

Foreword

Wang Gungwu

This is a book of many fresh insights. I have followed Tansen Sen's writings for over ten years and continue to be stimulated by his quest to understand the ancient and exceptional relationship between the entities that we refer to as India and China. It began when I read with admiration his study of *Buddhism, Diplomacy, and Trade: the Realignment of Sino-Indian Relations, 600–1400* (2003). That work filled a huge gap in our knowledge. Since then, Tansen Sen has not only been adding to that store of knowledge but has also done new research on people and events since Asia came to be dominated by the European powers. We are now rewarded with this splendid attempt to connect the early cultural and commercial contacts with some key developments of the past two centuries.

I am struck by the way Sen has used the ideas of circulation and connection to divide the book into two halves. In the first half, he shows how it was the attraction of cultural goods and enlightening knowledge that induced people to travel long distances to keep exchanges going. And he never fails to remind us how multi-directional the contacts were. By focusing on how ideas, artistry, and objects were circulatory, he makes the earlier encounters more meaningful and comprehensible.

For the second half, Sen explores several archives and various vernacular writings to trace some of the multifarious connections between past and present during the period when Asia was modernizing and being globalized. The connections enabled individuals and groups, ranging from journalists, soldiers, artists, poets, teachers, and philosophers to diplomats, politicians, itinerant traders, and contracted coolies, to engage in ways never possible before. Among them were many who each learnt to see the emergence of a new India and a transformed China from a different perspective.

Here I am reminded of my personal experience of how this was possible in the world in-between, in British Malaya where hundreds of thousands of Indians and Chinese were thrown together in the nineteenth and twentieth centuries. It meant that Chinese school children could have teachers who came from Bengal, Punjab, Madras and Jaffna. They could connect with the idea of being Asian that was first inspired by Japan as a modern nation-state ambitious to have its own colonial empire. But they could also disconnect with this pan-Asianism when their friends joined the Indian National Army to fight with the Japanese while their brothers joined the Malayan Communist Party against brutal Japanese treatment.

After 1945, when almost every polity was embarked on building nation-states out of former colonial states, the forces of ideology and national interests swirled around us with greater intensity. The Chinese and Indian leaders who wrote the promising slogans and images of Asian brotherhood were the same ones who led their countries to a Himalayan war. Most Indians and Chinese could only contemplate further disconnects thereafter. For me, I recall the excitement when, still only an undergraduate, I first visited Delhi in December 1952 to attend the United Nations Students Association meeting. We were delighted when Prime Minister Jawaharlal Nehru came to address us. Among other uplifting thoughts, he spoke passionately of a new Asia where India, China and the new postcolonial nation-states would be united and change the world. That memory, however, also leads me back to the disappointments by the end of the decade followed by the cruel end of those dreams after 1962.

This book also stands out when Sen boldly introduces the idea of "imperial connections" in chapter 3 to link the first half (chapters 1 and 2) with the second (chapters 4 and 5). He opens up the larger historical question of what was "imperialism." This is a complex issue that urges us to examine the nature of the Roman imperium and the various pre-modern feudal and territorial expansions that are now also called empires, including those that originated in India and China and also those of the Turks, Mongols, and Manchus of the steppe and the desert. They need to be carefully compared to the two new varieties of maritime commercial and colonizing "empires" that emerged after the fifteenth century. These led to long-distance and large-scale peopling across the Atlantic and then into the Indian and Pacific Oceans.

In particular, two distinctive features of the new empires across the Atlantic are significant. They enabled two modern developments to change the course of world history: I refer to industrial capitalism, and the nation-states that established their own empires. Together, these global empires of resources and markets, and of national colonies, gave rise to the spectre of modern imperialism.

It is interesting to try to link the many kinds of pre-1500 empires to the development of what is identified as imperialism, and Sen's chapter raises many tantalizing comparisons. His work will stimulate further detailed studies of the phenomenon, and could help us eventually to arrive at an agreed understanding of the imperialism that has turned scores of colonies into the nation-states now engaged in the global market economy.

Sen's fascinating book confirms that no simple narrative about the two millennia of India-China relations is possible. It was never that kind of story. What was India and what was China depended on the people who at different times sought to discover and define the two. There were multiple differences in perspective and whatever contacts there were between the two entities were largely scattered and unplanned. Some of us thought that would change after the age of colonialism. We saw two new countries emerging out of decades of distress and turbulence and there was hope that a beautiful new start would follow. That is yet to happen, but Sen's study encourages us to think that, in the context of a rapidly changing world, it is increasingly possible to gain a deeper understanding of this complex relationship.

It is in that spirit that I feel honored to be asked to write this foreword for a book that all who are concerned for the future of Asia should read.

Wang Gungwu, National University of Singapore
August 2017

Acknowledgments

Academic research is essentially a collaborative work. By the time a book manuscript is completed one has to draw on and becomes indebted to numerous people who either directly assist in the research and writing or indirectly do so through their pioneering publications. The bibliography at the end of this book is an acknowledgment to many in the latter group. Here I would like to express my gratitude to all those who have assisted me on my journey through the various libraries and archives, field research, writing and re-writing of the chapters, and the comforts of conversations and discussions.

My father Narayan Chandra Sen is one of the most knowledgeable persons I know on issues relating to China and India-China connections. There are several sections of this book that originate in his recounting of events and episodes, many of which he personally participated in as an Indian scholar of China. I thank him for introducing me to all things China and for being a vital source of information on twentieth century India-China interactions. I am proud to be his son.

Prasenjit Duara, Victor H. Mair, and Geoff Wade have been close friends and mentors for a long time. Prasenjit da was instrumental in helping me to conceptualize the idea of circulatory connections between India and China. His comments and suggestions at many stages of writing have helped improve all the chapters in this book. And while we don't share the same appreciation for Indian classical music, we agree on many aspects of intra-Asian interactions. Victor Mair was the ideal doctoral advisor who saw me through my PhD and has continued to guide me through the subsequent twenty years of academic research. I thank Victor for his continued guidance and support, and for always being there for consultation. I worked with Geoff Wade in Singapore at a unique institution known as the Nalanda-Sriwijaya Center (NSC) for over a four-year period between 2009 and 2012. We soon realized that we shared a common passion for intra-Asian interactions and Zheng He. Together we built the NSC, initiated and edited an academic series on intra-Asian relations, and organized numerous conferences and seminars. Geoff has been extremely generous in reading and commenting on the drafts of my publications. I am truly grateful to him.

Several other people in Singapore contributed to the research undertaken for this book. The former director of the Institute of Southeast Asian Studies Amb. K. Kesavapany, the visiting fellows as well as the staff at NSC, including Jayati Bhattacharya, Rinkoo Bhowmik, Jayani Bonnerjee, Herman Kulke, Lu Caixia, Lu Xi, Pierre-Yves Manguin, Tony Reid, Nilanjana Sengupta, Joyce Zaide, and Zhang Xing have all been great friends and most helpful in my academic pursuits. I worked on the Chinese communities in Kolkata together with Zhang Xing and some of the materials and findings on the community that appear in this book come from the joint research we undertook in India, China, and Singapore. Also in Singapore, I need to thank Puneet and Sukanya Pushkarna, who have made my every stay on the island fun, exciting, and a gastronomic pleasure.

I have been fortunate to have taught at the History Department of Baruch College, The City University of New York, with a fabulous group of colleagues. The former chairs of the Department, Myrna Chase, Stanley Buder, and Cynthia Whittaker, as well as the current chair Kathy Pence have guided and supported my research and teaching career over the last twenty years. Jed Abrahamian, Charlotte Brooks, Thomas Desch-Obi, Vincent DiGirolamo, Johanna Fernández, Bert Hansen, Thomas Heinrich, Veena Oldenburg, Murray Rubenstein, Clarence Taylor, and Randy Trumbach made the two decades at the Department a stimulating place for intellectual activity and pedagogical development. The more recent hires to the Department, Anna Boozer, Elizabeth Heath, Martina Nguyen, Mark Rice, and Andrew Sloin have maintained this tradition.

I have been affiliated with four other institutions during the researching and writing of this book. Serving on the Nalanda University Governing Board from 2007 to 2016 with Prapod Assavavirulhakarn, Sugata Bose, Meghnad Desai, Susumu Nakanishi, Amartya Sen, N.K. Singh, Wang Bangwei, Wang Gungwu, and George Yeo was a unique learning opportunity in terms of institution building and the intellectual discourse of higher education. Working with the former vice chancellor Gopa Sabharwal and the former dean Anjana Sharma also provided insights into the vicissitudes of academia and an understanding of Indian bureaucracy. I am extremely grateful to Professor Wang Gungwu for gracing this book with a foreword.

Over the last three years, Shanghai has become a site of research and writing for me. First a fellowship at the International Center for Studies of Chinese Civilization (ICSCC) at Fudan University, and then a visiting professorship at NYU Shanghai allowed the incorporation of the nineteenth and early twentieth centuries phases of India-China interactions into this book. For this, I thank Jin Guangyao, Li Tiangang, Sun Yinggang, and Zhang Ke at ICSCC, and Joanna Waley-Cohen, Zhao Pan, and Chen Fuyue at NYU Shanghai. Also in Shanghai, my old friend Chen Jinhua and new comrades, including *mingtianjian* buddies Xiao Wu, Wu Shengqing, and Xu Bin, as well as Celina Hung, Selina Ho, and Duane Corpis, provided much needed distraction from research and writing. The presence of Amitav Ghosh at NYU Shanghai and his talks given around China were also inspirational in my writing about the colonial connections between India and China.

The affiliation with the fourth institution was serendipitous in many ways. I had passed through the small German town of Halle previously, but never thought that I would one day come here to write the acknowledgments to my book. I met Burkhard and Conny Schnepel at a conference on Zheng He in Victoria, Canada, in 2014. Since then Burkhard and I have become close friends and collaborators on studies of the Indian Ocean World. I have benefited from several conferences he has organized in Halle, the summer school program that we jointly offer, and the seminars and colloquia at the Martin-Luther University and the Max Planck Institute of Social Anthropology. Burkhard was instrumental in my appointment as the Christian-Wolff Visiting Professor at the Zentrum für Interdisziplinäre Regionalstudien right when I needed time to check the copy-edited version of this book, write the acknowledgments, and wait for the page proofs to arrive. My sincere gratitude, Burkhard. Special thanks also to Mareike Pampus, Burkhard's PhD student, who, despite her busy research schedule, helped me track down Chinese temples in Kuala Lumpur and Ipoh in Malaysia. In Halle, Mareike has assisted with numerous personal and logistical issues. Xiexie!

The later chapters of this book use archival material from many regions of the world. My archival research began with the files on the Chinese communities in West Bengal housed at the West Bengal State Archives in Kolkata. Hari Vasudevan and Ananda Bhattacharya were the key figures who made it possible for me to start working on over 200 files at that location. It became clear then that the archival material told a very different story about India-China interactions and that similar files may also exist in China and elsewhere. Fortunately, Brian Tsui, a scholar of mid-twentieth century India-China interactions, now at the Hong Kong Polytechnic University, was also thinking on the same lines. Brian and I successfully applied for a Chiang Ching-kuo collaborative grant. The grant allowed us to bring together a group of scholars to work on the archival materials of early twentieth century India-China interactions. Liao Wen-shuo, Kamal Sheel, Madhavi Thampi, Anand Yang, and Zhang Ke participated in the project as core members. I have benefited from reading the materials that they have collected and listening to the presentations they made during the course of the project. I thank them and the Chiang Ching-kuo foundation for making it possible to examine and use these neglected sources on India-China interactions.

My search for archival material took me to many institutions and resulted in indebtedness to many people. The British Library and the National Archives in Kew, England; the National Archives and the Nehru Memorial Museum and Library in Delhi; the Shanghai Municipal Archives in China; Academia Historica in Taipei; the International Institute of Social History in Amsterdam; and the Swarthmore Library Peace Collection were just some of the major institutions from where I gathered the materials used in this book. However, this was only possible through the dedicated assistance I received from the staff at these institutions and from Barnali Chanda, Rebecca Fu, Faith Hahn, Namrata Hasija, Nirmola Sharma, and Kailun Wang. Murali Ranganathan transcribed the correspondence of the Parsi trader Jamsetjee Jejeebhoy, several of which are used in this book.

While much of the funding for archival research came from the Chiang Ching-kuo Foundation grant, an earlier fellowship from the National Endowment for the Humanities (in 2009–2010), sabbatical and research fellowships from Baruch College, and travel grants from PSC-CUNY also supported the research for and writing of this book. I acknowledge these various foundations as well as Jeff

Peck, the former dean of the Weissman School of Arts and Sciences, for the financial aid and the time I was allowed for research.

There are numerous other people who have contributed to this project. I hope that these friends and well-wishers will not mind that their names do not appear here. All your contributions, no matter how minor, are appreciated. I profoundly thank you all for your help and support. I do have to single out the team at Rowman & Littlefield for the attentive and smooth process of turning a manuscript into a book. I am grateful to Morris Rossabi for connecting me to Susan McEachern, vice president and executive editor at Rowman & Littlefield. Along with Susan, assistant editor Rebeccah Shumaker, production editor Alden Perkins, and copyeditor Matt Evans guided the editorial process in a courteous and timely manner. Indeed, it has been an immensely satisfying experience.

A part of chapter 3 was published in the *Bulletin of the School of Oriental African Studies* as "The Impact of Zheng He's Expeditions on Indian Ocean Interactions." Similarly, a portion of chapter 4 has appeared in the edited volume *Buddhism in Asia: Revival and Reinvention* as "Taixu's Goodwill Mission to India: Reviving the Buddhist Connections between China and India." I thank the reviewers and editors of these publications for their input and suggestions.

Finally, I am indebted to my wife, Liang Fan, for her tolerance of my itinerant academic lifestyle. Neither the research nor the writing of this book would have been possible without your understanding and support. My deepest appreciation to you.

I must also claim sole responsibility for any errors, mistakes, or serious blunders that might appear in the pages that follow.

Tansen Sen
Halle, Germany
17 June 2017

Introduction

Those who come between or dare
Tamper with us. We reply:
Hindi-Chini bhai-bhai
—Harindranath Chattopadhyaya (1898–1990)

Between 25 April and 1 May 1924, the renowned Chinese intellectual Liang Qichao 梁啟超 (1873–1929) delivered several talks in Beijing to welcome the Indian Nobel laureate Rabindranath Tagore (1861–1941) to China. In one of these talks, titled "The Fraternal Relationship between the Cultures of India and China," Liang outlined the various ways in which Chinese culture was indebted to India in the realms of philosophy, literature, music, architecture, art, astronomy, and medicine.[1] Calling India the "elder brother," Liang ([1925] 2002: xiii) emphasized that what China received were "gifts of singular and precious worth, which we can never forget." He also noted that Chinese and Indians were separated for "at least one thousand years" after these influences spread through the transmission of Buddhism. Indirectly blaming the European colonial powers for being "threatened," "mocked," and "trampled upon," he observed that India and China had begun to lose a "sense of self-respect" during this period of "separation" (Liang [1925] 2002: xxvi–xxvii). However, the ancient traditions and values of

1

Indians and Chinese, he believed, would eventually rescue the two civilizations and prevent them from being separated again. He (Liang [1925] 2002: xxx) concluded the talk by saying, "The responsibility that we bear to the whole of mankind is great indeed, and there should be, I think, a warm spirit of cooperation between India and China. The coming of Rabindranath Tagore will, I hope, mark the beginning of an important period of history."

Rabindranath Tagore's visit to China in 1924 did indeed turn out to be a watershed for the interactions between Indians and Chinese as the subsequent three decades witnessed vibrant interactions and collaborations between various groups of people, including artists, intellectuals, Buddhists, and political leaders. New sites of interactions, such as Cheena Bhavana (Chinese Hall) in Shantiniketan, emerged to foster these collaborations. The visit also led to the burgeoning of writings about the historical exchanges between India and China within the monolithic scheme of civilizational discourse founded on anticolonial and nationalist agendas. The diversity of people and places and the multiregional networks of connections to the past eventually became subsumed under the rubric of nation-states, the Republic of India (ROI) and the People's Republic of China (PRC).

This book challenges the above rubric by examining the *longue durée* connections between the regions that now constitute the ROI and the PRC in the broader geographical settings of Asia and the world. In doing so, it makes the following four arguments. First, the pre-twentieth-century interactions between these two regions should not be construed within the framework of modern nation-states. That is to say, the historical exchanges should not be claimed to inevitably imply a connection between the ROI and the PRC for over two thousand years. These two entities did not exist before the 1940s, the geographical contours that make up these two states were never under one political regime, and some of the peoples who have now been incorporated into the ROI and the PRC

Figure 0.1. Rabindranath Tagore and Liang Qichao in Beijing, 1924. Courtesy of the Liang family

long had their own distinct political and cultural identities and pursued their own external relationships. Second, the connections between these two regions, from the early phases (as can be discerned from the networks of the Austronesians in the second millennium BCE outlined in chapter 2) to the contemporary period, have been intimately linked to people living in several other regions, including locations outside the Asian continent. These people, their networks and self-interests, facilitated, hindered, or transformed the connections between the two regions. It is, therefore, important that India-China connections also be seen in the context of the roles of people who were not native to these two regions and in terms of linkages to and entanglement with other parts of the world. Third, the presence of European colonial powers in Asia did not terminate these connections. Rather, the exchanges witnessed significant growth and diversification with the emergence of new sites of interactions; more intensive circulation of knowledge, goods, and people; and close intellectual collaborations between Indians and Chinese. Fourth, the formation of these territorialized nation-states in the mid-twentieth century created wedges in the relations between the ROI and the PRC that eventually resulted in an armed conflict in 1962 and the subsequent contraction of the broader linkages that had defined and fostered earlier connections between the two regions.

Material exchanges, transmissions of knowledge and ideas, contacts between individuals, varied forms of imperialism, and the creation of new sites of interactions are some of the main themes examined in this book. The analysis of these issues makes it evident that the past connections and encounters cannot be constrained within either neatly defined borders, vague notions of civilizations, or contours of geography. Rather, in order to fully comprehend the interactions between India and China, a wide canvas of space, people, objects, and time frame is needed. Consequently, the connections between India and China must be placed within the context of Asian and world history, and the relationship in contemporary times analyzed with reference to global interdependencies.

CONNECTIONS AND CIRCULATIONS

The connections between India and China were at multiple levels, not only across time and space but also among various groups of people, some of whom lived in these two regions and others who operated from intermediary areas or distant parts of the world. The connections were sometimes imaginary, deliberately generated to legitimize a past event (such as the transmission of Buddhism), create new histories (the legend of the bodhisattva Mañjuśrī on Mount Wutai, for example), initiate a movement (as in the case of anticolonial pan-Asianism in the early twentieth century), or celebrate geopolitical relationships (evident in the rhetoric of "Hindi-Chini bhai-bhai" ["Indians and Chinese are brothers"] of the 1950s). The connections took place at monastic institutions and imperial courts, in port and oasis towns, on plantations, and even at the United Nations headquarters in New York City. Many of these connections either sustained existing circulations of people, ideas, and products or created new networks of transmission and movement. Wars and other disputes, ecological changes, and unseasonal monsoon winds contributed to temporary disconnections, which were also integral features of India-China interactions.

This volume contends that the connections between India and China took place across several different regions of the world, the specific extent of which changed over time. While the spaces across the Himalayan ranges, the Taklamakan Desert, the mountainous terrain of Burma (now Myanmar), and the maritime regions of the Bay of Bengal and the South China Sea formed key intermediary areas, connections between Indians and Chinese were also established in Japan, Africa, Europe, and the Americas at different periods. Each of these regions facilitated and contributed to the interactions between India and China through trade and commerce, intellectual discourse, and, in recent times, geopolitical contention and global financial partnerships. At the same time, direct exchanges between India and China had a notable impact on intermediary regions as well as areas more distant.[2] The Buddhist exchanges between India and China, for instance, influenced societies in Southeast Asia, Korea, and Japan. The seminomadic polities such as Liao (916–1125) and Xixia (1038–1227), the Sogdian traders traveling across the Indian Ocean or the Taklamakan Desert, and the artists and manufacturers of Buddhist images were all influenced by and participated in these exchanges. As a result, the Buddhist connections were not merely between India and China, as some studies written within the rubric of national histories would imply,[3] but involved most of Asia.

Similarly, the early commercial exchanges between the two regions involved a larger geographical space that extended to Africa and Europe. They formed part of the Afroeurasian networking from the late first millennium BCE, when Roman goods (especially glass products) were exchanged for Chinese silk. These connections became more integrated and interdependent with the participation of Arab and Persian Muslim traders in the seventh and eighth centuries and the occupation of maritime spaces by the European colonial enterprises in the sixteenth and seventeenth centuries. The trade in bullion, tea, and opium and the financial mechanisms that sustained these commercial ventures in the eighteenth and nineteenth centuries eventually intimately linked the exchanges between India and China to the Americas. Also during the colonial period, the transfer of indentured labor from India and China by the British to plantations in places such as Mauritius and Guiana/Guyana resulted in the creation of new sites of interactions between Indians and Chinese that were located outside the Asian continent.

The post–World War II period led to geopolitical alliances, the emergence of regional and transregional organizations, and the formation of global financial institutions. India and China have been, as a result, connected through the East Asia Summit (EAS) forum, which has eighteen member countries, including ten Association of Southeast Asian Nations (ASEAN) states, the United States, and

Russia. BRICS, the more recent grouping, consists of Brazil, Russia, India, China, and South Africa. These forums give the state leaders and officials opportunities to connect with each other and discuss issues around the world. Despite this, however, the contemporary phase of India-China connections, particularly in the aftermath of the 1962 war, has largely involved disconnected polities focused more on promoting bilateral exchanges under state guidance.

Prior to the mid-twentieth century, the most impressive aspect of India-China connections was the circulation of people. This movement of people—including traders, missionaries, pilgrims, diplomats, soldiers, refugees, migrants, and tourists—further facilitated the circulations of products, ideas, technologies, and animals. The tribute carriers from South Asian polities to the Chinese courts; the transmitters of Buddhist doctrines; traders of horses, spices, tea, and opium; Chinese diplomats and pilgrims; the Cantonese migrants to Calcutta (now Kolkata); and the Sikh guardsmen in Shanghai all constituted aspects of the connections and circulations between India and China at different periods of time. Sogdian and Arab traders, Korean Buddhist pilgrims, Southeast Asian sailors, Jesuit missionaries, and even peace activists from the United States also played important roles in connecting India and China. The national histories of the past encounters and studies of contemporary relations often neglect this multidimensional aspect of India-China connections.

Several individuals who played unique roles in these connections stand out over the *longue durée*. Their travels and contributions to India-China interactions exemplify the interconnectedness of multiple regions of the world. Before the Common Era began, the Han diplomat Zhang Qian 張騫 (167?–114 BCE) traveled to Central Asia, where he learned about the routes that connected Han China and the place the Chinese called "Shendu" 身毒 (River Indus and its vicinity). His report about these routes inaugurated the cir-

culation of knowledge between India and China. The activities of
the Sogdian monk Kang Senghui 康僧會 (fl. 250 CE), born in what
is now northern Vietnam and active in the present-day Nanjing
region of China, epitomized the roles of people who were not of
Indian or Chinese origin. Kang's ancestors were traders dealing in
horses and other commodities between the Indian and Chinese regions before his father decided to settle in Jiaozhi 交趾 (northern
Vietnam). The defection to Yuan China of a Muslim named Buali
不阿里 (Abū 'Alī?) who lived in the Ma'bar polity on the Coromandel coast and whose father had migrated from West Asia, as
well as his subsequent marriage to a Korean woman (see chapter 1),
is an illustration of the intra-Asian connections that intensified during the Mongol period. The Venetian Marco Polo (1254–1324) and
the Moroccan Ibn Baṭūṭah (1304–1368) are further examples of
individuals from other regions of the world involved in the interactions between India and China.

The expeditions of Zheng He 鄭和 (1371–1433), the networks
of the Parsi opium trader Jamsetjee Jejeebhoy (1783–1859), and the
artistic tradition transmitted by the British painter George Chinnery
(1783–1859) are similarly cases of individuals from various regions who played notable roles in fostering the connections between India and China during the period of imperialism. Some
individuals did not have to travel to have noteworthy influence.
Bertrand Russell (1872–1970), for example, in the aftermath of the
India-China war of 1962, acted as an interlocutor between the Chinese premier Zhou Enlai (1898–1976) and the Indian prime minister Jawaharlal Nehru (1889–1964). He communicated with the two
leaders from his home in England and made a tremendous effort to
achieve a peaceful settlement between the two countries. His participation in India-China connections as well as the roles of Zheng
He, Jamsetjee Jejeebhoy, and George Chinnery are examined in
more detail later in the book.

Objects, which Bruno Latour (2005) has argued have agency as constituents of social networks, also served to connect India and China by instigating the movements of people and the transmissions of ideas and knowledge. These objects ranged from commercial goods to ritual items, as well as books and souvenirs. Chinese silk, porcelain, and tea; pepper from the Malabar coast; textiles from Bengal; and opium from Bihar and Malwa were some of the major commodities traded between India and China. Additionally, there were foreign products that transited through India, such as cowries, horses, and frankincense. The spread of Buddhism to China triggered the circulation of images, texts, ritual goods, relics, and other material objects (Liu 1988; Kieschnick 2003; Sen 2003). While in the first few centuries of the spread of Buddhism these items entered various regions of China, during the second half of the first millennium certain Buddhist objects, such as images of the bodhisattva Mañjuśrī, circulated back to India as souvenirs (Sen 2003). Moreover, in the late nineteenth and early twentieth century, Chinese migrants brought Buddhist images and artifacts to adorn their temples in India (Zhang 2014). And in 1954, Chinese premier Zhou Enlai presented a relic bone of the monk Xuanzang 玄奘 (602?–664) to Jawaharlal Nehru as a gesture to renew the ancient connections.

Similar to movements of people, the transmission of objects not only linked India and China but also integrated several other regions of the world. These included places that produced and supplied the commodities, those that consumed them, those that relayed them, and those that financed these transactions. Also important to note is the fact that the objects, as they moved from one location to another, acquired lives of their own,[4] taking on new meanings, uses, and shapes. The example of Buddhist texts is perhaps most pertinent in the context of early India-China connections. The Indic texts written in Sanskrit on palm leaves were rendered into Chinese and transcribed on paper in China. As these texts circulated in China, commentaries were composed to interpret the main teachings contained in them. Together these translated texts and commentaries formed part of the Chinese Buddhist canon, which were, in the tenth and eleventh centuries, printed and distributed (or sold) to neighboring polities such as Japan and Korea (Sen 2003). In the late 1930s, efforts were made, particularly at Cheena Bhavana founded by Rabindranath Tagore in Shantiniketan, to translate these Chinese texts into English and Indian languages for Indian readers.

India and China were also connected through the means of imagination. This included imagination of sites and events associated with the life of the Buddha that most Buddhists in China were unable to visit, visions of moving or translocating objects, and the imagination of past encounters.[5] Each of these imaginations served different purposes, but they were all associated with the connections between India and China created by the transmission of Buddhism. The holy land of Buddhism inspired awe among Buddhist monks, the readers of Buddhist texts and travelogues, and the observers of cave paintings living in China. These imaginations resulted in an elevated perception of the Buddhist homeland in Chinese texts. It also triggered a sense of distance and longing among the Chinese clergy, leading to the creation of Indic spaces in China, with either stories of an entire mountain translocating or existing mountains retrofitted with Buddhist paraphernalia. The Feilaifeng 飛來峰 ("the mountain that came flying") in Hangzhou and Wutaishan 五台山 in Shanxi Province of the PRC are respectively such examples of establishing Indic spaces within China (Sen 2003).

The above connections between the Chinese Buddhist clergy and the Buddhist holy land became the model for twentieth-century advocates of pan-Asianism and subsequently those calling for solidarity between the ROI and the PRC. The India and China of the first millennium thus became transposed upon the India and China of the present day. This resulted in the domestic periodization of

India-China connections into a Buddhist era of intimate relations, a colonial phase of forced separation, and a Tagoreian period of revived brotherhood. This periodization overlooked the complexities of Buddhist interactions, the political and cultural diversification of the two regions, the role of Muslim traders and preachers after the decline of Buddhism, and the intensification of exchanges during the colonial period.

In the 1950s, when the nationalist civilizational narrative prevalent in the early twentieth century developed into nation-state-based discourse of past encounters, the leaders of the ROI and the PRC attempted to recreate these connections through the exchange of delegations, invocation of the "Hindi-Chini bhai-bhai" slogan, and the composition of India-China friendship songs and poems. Missing from all this was the key element of the past encounters: the extensive participation and contribution of people who did not belong to the two regions. The narrative of the past encounters written during this period reflected or deliberately promoted this contracted connection. The works of P. C. Bagchi (1898–1956), a member of the Greater India Society, and Jin Kemu 金克木 (1912–2000) laid the foundation for the narrative of a "thousand years of cultural relations" and civilizational bonding and friendship for the ROI and the PRC. In the preface to the first edition, published in 1944, of his classic *India and China: A Thousand Years of Cultural Relations*, Bagchi ([1950] 1981: xiii) wrote, "Perhaps we are not yet fully aware of the magnitude of this gratitude which we should feel for our ancestors who had sacrified [*sic*] themselves for the selfless work of building up a common civilization for the two largest agglomerations of people in Asia. The accounts of their efforts may be an inspiration to us, their descendants, in the twilight of a new age."

This inspiration and the search for common civilization ended in 1962 with the armed conflict between India and China. Connections were severed for almost two decades, and a new discourse of rivalry and dispute took root. As part of the attempt to normalize bilateral relations, the nation-state-based discourse of past encounters was revived, and exchanges of cultural delegations were resumed in the 1980s. The connections, however, despite the emergence of multiregional forums mentioned above, remained overwhelmingly bilateral. In fact, the ROI and PRC governments have deliberately tried to limit these exchanges to the citizens of the two countries who reside in the respective countries. The aim, according to joint statements released by political leaders, is to create deeper understanding between the people of India and China. The recent coining of the term "Chindia" is also intended to invent an artificial linkage between India and China and promote the notion of agelong affinity, a shared past, and a belief in a utopic future (see chapter 5).

Such reconstructed narratives of the past within the nation-state framework reflect the many differences between the connections, circulations, and complicated transregional entanglements prior to the mid-twentieth century and those of the present, where demarcated territories, political and national security interests, and the regimes of visas and emigration rules inhibit connections. The connections of the past, therefore, should be examined as a distinct historical phenomenon that evolved over time until the formation of decolonized nation-states in the mid-twentieth century. Given the diversity of cultures, societies, and polities involved, the connections between the past and the present cannot be framed, it is argued in this volume, either as nation-to-nation interactions or as "dialogue" between two civilizations.

The circulatory nature of India-China connections must also be emphasized here. Traders, Buddhist monks, and commercial goods, as well as news and information, frequently moved between India and China. This movement back and forth of people, objects, ideas, and knowledge is one aspect of circulation highlighted in this study. Sometimes these circulations were directly between India and China. Often, however, they involved several other regions of Asia or even the world. There were also instances when these movements were circulatory in nature, with people, objects, ideas, or knowledge returning to their places of origin. On some instances, this took place within a short span of time, and at others it entailed several decades or even centuries. I have used the term "circulatory connections" to describe such specific instances. Circulatory connections, especially over the *longue durée*, do not necessarily imply that the exact same object, person, or idea had to rotate between two places. Rather, objects could be modified, transformed, or redesigned, or they could attain new symbolic meanings if and when they returned to their place of origin. The circulation of Buddhist texts mentioned above is an example of this. The visit to India by Xuanzang, his return to Tang China, and the appearance of his bodily remains at Nālandā, the site where he studied, is also an illustration of circulatory connection. The Chinese transformation of Mañjuśrī into a Buddhist divinity residing on Mount Wutai, the transmission of the legend to South Asia, and the subsequent pilgrimages to the mountain by South Asian monks similarly embodies the circulatory movement of ideas, knowledge, people, and objects. Contemporary circulatory connections manifest in new ways. In the news media of the two countries, for example, reports about the disputes and contentions between the PRC and the ROI move back and forth creating a distinct pattern of circulatory connection that is framed within the context of nation-states. Circulations were often an integral part of transregional and cross-cultural interactions and as such need to be adequately addressed in both historical and contemporary studies of India-China interactions. And while the connections of the past and those of the present are distinct, circulatory connections between geographical regions could at times bridge the temporal differences. Thus, while the connections between India and China during the first millennium should not be transposed upon the India and China of the present day, the examples above of Buddhist texts and Xuanzang illustrate that circulatory connections could take several centuries before they are completed irrespective of the changes in the political structure.

THE COMPLEX IDENTITIES OF INDIA AND CHINA

Some of the issues of terminology, connectivity, periodization, and sources that are pertinent to the above issues and arguments need to be clarified at the outset. It is also important to outline the contribution this book intends to make to conceptualizing and understanding the interactions between "India" and "China" and to the field of connected history in general.[6] Indeed, the connections between the two regions were invariably important parts of Asian and world history, as Buddhism, commerce, imperialism, and disputes over territorial claims triggered circulations of people, ideas, technologies, and objects and also led to trepidation and diatribes that drew together peace activists and organizations based as far away as London and New York City.[7] However, the complexity of the terms "India" and "China" has to be addressed since a conscious effort has been made in this book to delink the contemporary nation-states from the historical interactions that took place between the two geographical regions. This effort has led to the use of distinct terms for these places in the next few chapters that could be confusing and conflicting at times. These are necessary distractions because an unqualified usage of the terms "India" and "China" negates, as argued above, the multidimensional, multidirectional, and sometimes muddled temporal progressions that define the *longue durée* connections between the geographical spaces that are now within and beyond the borders of the ROI and the PRC.

The title of this book (and this introduction) uses the terms "India" and "China" due to what Arif Dirlik (2008) has called the "limitations of modern vocabulary." Dirlik explains the problems of mapping and assigning distinct geopolitical identities to cultures and civilizations that encountered each other in the past. "These encounters," he writes (2008: 4), "are not just between politically identifiable units but involve the encounters of many social and cultural spaces. They are, therefore, overdetermined, subject to the dialectics of the parts of which they are constituted. They need not be atomized to the level of the individual, because individual encounters take place within contexts that seek to reproduce themselves, creating the possibility of continuity (or, better still, reproduction) but also of disruption, depending on circumstances." The limitations of the modern vocabulary of nations and regions, according to him (2008: 14n.28), attests to "the power of modern ways of mapping history as well as to the dilemmas presented by the very vocabulary of historical and cultural analysis."

Indeed, it creates a dilemma to use either "India" or "China" in studying the individual histories of these regions or the encounters between the two. Early foreign travelers used the terms "Indica" and "Tianzhu" 天竺 to vaguely designate the regions located east of the Indus River. However, these were not the designations that the polities located within those regions used or were cognizant of. Similarly, the term "Chin" in Indic sources is supposed to describe regions of the present-day PRC, but the exact geographical contours were never specified. The contemporary emic terms "Bharat" and "Zhongguo" 中國 did not in the pre-twentieth-century period correspond to the territories that today define the ROI or the PRC. Therefore, an unqualified use of the terms "India" and "China" fails to provide, as Dirlik insinuates, an adequate sense of the complexities that existed in the regional and cross-regional encounters of the past.

The qualifications are not easy to make. In the case of "India," one could imply, as is done in this book, the regions that now comprise the ROI, Pakistan, and Bangladesh. "China," however, referred to a constantly shifting geographical terrain based on the expansion and contraction of various dynasties. As a result, the term "China" is best qualified with dynasty names, such as Han China, Tang China, or Three Dynasties China, in reference to the areas over which these dynasties exercised political control. Similarly, using names of specific polities in "India," such as the Chola, Kāmarūpa, or Harṣa's Empire, might be more appropriate in some instances. Although cumbersome, such distinctions and specifications are important in order to understand the role of specific regions and polities, the intermediary peoples and regions, the modes of transportation, and the diversification and limitations of the past encounters.

Those who compiled the Chinese dynastic histories, as well as other authors, including Chinese Buddhist travelers, made a distinction between what they called Tianzhu and the polities of Shiziguo 獅/師子國 (i.e., Siṃhala, or Sri Lanka/Ceylon) and Nipoluo 尼婆羅 (Nepal). However, all three entities were part of Chinese Buddhist narrative as places to acquire texts and relics. Buddhist monks, diplomats, and traders from various Chinese courts interacted with all of these places at one time or another. Thus, the past encounters included much of what is now considered "South Asia," a term that is employed in chapters 1 and 2. With the expansion of maritime commercial connections in the eleventh and twelfth centuries, the coastal polities of South Asia become more relevant to the Chinese dynasties. As a result, names of specific polities in South Asia are used when the sources are explicit about the polities and regions involved.

Arif Dirlik's apprehension about assigning distinct geopolitical identities to past encounters is relevant for another reason. As noted in chapters 4 and 5, pan-Asianists and subsequently scholars and governments in the ROI and the PRC have consciously attempted to link the exchanges of the late and post-colonial periods to the encounters of the first millennium CE. While the objective of the pan-Asianists was to create an idealized perception of peaceful and harmonious Asia interrupted by European colonial powers, the two

nation-states tried to, in addition to representing themselves histori-
cally (Duara 1995: 4), incorporate the past encounters with neighboring polities into their nationalist histories. Thus, in recent years
for instance, the past encounters have been invoked in Pakistan-
PRC and Bangladesh-PRC diplomatic overtures using phrases such
as "two thousand years of China-Pakistan relations." The cumbersome use of terms for the two regions in this book, therefore, is also
intended to dissociate this analysis from the pan-Asianist, nationalist, and civilizational projects.

With the entry of European colonial powers, the connections
between the two regions become significantly more complicated.
While the use of Ming and Qing China and "British India" may be
appropriate for some regions and periods, it should be noted that
there were intimate connections between "Portuguese India,"
"Dutch India," and Ming and later Qing China. There were also
strong ties between Portuguese Macau, British Hong Kong, the
other treaty ports, and "British India," as well as with the adjoining
Princely States. Even after the foundation of the Republic of China
in 1912, a state that did not fully control many of its peripheral
regions, the designation "China" might be considered inadequate.
The connections between Indian and Chinese intellectuals during
the first half of the twentieth century, nonetheless, resulted in the
more frequent use of the terms "India" and "China," both as political and civilizational designations. Accordingly, the past interactions were not only between an India and a China, but also between
"Indian civilization" and "Chinese civilization."[8] In chapter 4,
where issues related to these intellectuals are discussed, the terms
"India" and "China" are employed, but neither as strict geopolitical
constructs nor as civilizational states. Rather, they imply vaguely
the same region that we refer to as "India" in the first millennium
CE and the areas that the ROC attempted to govern as "China."

It is only in the late 1940s that the geopolitical contours of India
and China were fixed with the emergence of the ROI and the PRC.

Thus, in chapter 5, the designations "ROI" and "PRC" are used in examining the relations between these two countries, which for the first time shared a common yet contested border.

These variations in the names of entities examined in this book are befuddling at times. However, in the study of *longue durée* connections, especially where nation-states use past encounters as part of their national histories and international diplomacy, such clarifications and qualifications of geopolitical terms are essential. It is important also for explicating the four arguments outlined at the beginning of the chapter. The connected history between India and China, as already emphasized above, was both temporal and spatial. It was also multilateral, with people of diverse ethnic, cultural, linguistic, and occupational affiliations participating in fostering the linkages. Indeed, within this context, the changes in political configurations, the variations in networks that connected the two regions, the participation or interventions by people and polities from elsewhere, and the imaginations that connected the past to the present all mattered. Therefore, the terms "India" and "China," whenever they appear in this book, embody the complexities of history, time, and space.

PERIODIZATION AND SOURCES

In my earlier book *Buddhism, Diplomacy, and Trade*, I argued that the ninth and tenth centuries were a watershed in the connections between India and China, when the interactions between the two regions shifted from those that were dominated by Buddhism to exchanges that were fostered through commercial contacts. That periodization is reaffirmed in the first two chapters of this book. It is argued that the subsequent transition takes place not with the expansion of European colonial powers in Asia, but with the expeditions of Zheng He in the early fifteenth century. These expeditions created new sites of interaction, vastly expanded the maritime linkages between polities in South Asia and coastal China, and introduced the factor of state monopoly into the circulation of commodities. The early Portuguese used many of these networks and channels established through the Zheng He expeditions to enter and subsequently dictate the connections between several regions of India and China.[9] The first Opium War (1839–1842) precipitated significant changes to these connections. The circulation of people, objects, and knowledge not only grew significantly, but there was also a notable reduction in the length of time needed to travel between the two regions with the introduction of steamships. Additionally, with the global migrations of Chinese and Indians in the second half of the nineteenth century (Amrith 2011: ch. 1), the interactions between people originating from these two regions now started taking place beyond the Asian continent.

The twentieth century is not easy to periodize. The end of World War II is usually perceived as a major demarcating point for Asian and world history, especially with the onset of the Cold War. For India-China connections, however, 1924, 1947, the late 1950s, and 1988 could all be considered important years/phases of transition. The visit of Rabindranath Tagore to China in 1924, as noted above, led to the establishment of new networks of cross-cultural connections. The year 1947 witnessed the emergence of Tibet as an issue of contention between the Guomindang (GMD) government and the soon-to-be-independent India. The late 1950s, especially 1958, marked a deterioration of India-China relations, leading to the war of 1962. The year 1988 is usually considered the year of détente with the visit of the Indian prime minister Rajiv Gandhi to China. In a broader Asian context, the early 1930s, when the expansion of the Japanese in China and Southeast Asia ended the idealized vision of pan-Asianism, could be noted as a divide between multiregional connections of India-China exchanges and the period thereafter when the bilateral relationship attained more prominence.

The objective of the chapters that follow is not to offer a meticulous periodization of the connections but to challenge the existing tripartite division of the connections into Buddhist, colonial/decline, and revival. Similar to the problems with using "India" and "China" for the past encounters, delineating phases does not serve us in understanding the complexity of connections that spanned over time and space and involved people from different parts of the world. Rather, the aim is to demonstrate the changing nature of these connections and the impact they had more broadly. Likewise, the book does not aim to be a comprehensive listing of the events and connections that occurred over several centuries. Instead, it attempts to highlight some of the neglected aspects, episodes, and individuals that contributed to these connections. It also tries to bring to light some of the archival sources and writings in Indian vernacular languages that have not been fully utilized in examining the connections and encounters between India and China.

A majority of the sources for the study of the connections between India and China prior to the sixteenth century are found in Chinese records.[10] These sources range from the dynastic histories to travel records of Chinese monks visiting South Asia. These sources often give the impression that the connections between the two regions were unidirectional, from India to China, and primarily driven by Chinese monastic institutions, dynasties, and merchant groups. However, a detailed examination of these sources also indicates the agency of Indian Buddhist institutions, rulers, and traders. They confirm that the connections and circulations were multidirectional and involved many different groups of people. Indeed, it is evident from these sources that objects, ideas, and people also frequently moved from China to India. Chapters 1 and 2 offer evidence of such circulations through to the mid-second millennium CE by analyzing the Chinese sources, but also the notices of Arab merchants, the writings of Persian historians, and the travelogues of Ibn Baṭūṭah and Marco Polo. Archaeological findings, especially for the pre–Common Era period, have also been used in these chapters.

After the sixteenth century, the sources for India-China connections become voluminous and wide ranging. These include diaries, letters, and other writings of European missionaries and officials; Indian and other private traders; and new compositions on the maritime world by Chinese writers. A significant increase in sources on these connections took place after the first Opium War. There are reports of Chinese officials and surveyors visiting India, the writings of Chinese and Indian intellectuals about each other, reports collected by intelligence officers, and statistical accounts of the trade in opium, tea, and other commodities. Newspapers, magazines, and propaganda pamphlets also emerge as important sources for the study of India-China exchanges and interactions in the aftermath of the Opium War. Chapters 3 and 4 use many of these sources to examine the vibrant connections and the multifaceted circulations of people, ideas, and knowledge between India and China during this colonial period.

In chapters 4 and 5, special attention is given to archival sources that relate to the experiences of "subaltern" individuals and the role of international peace activists. Reports of the Indian Intelligence Bureau (IB) housed in the West Bengal State Archives in Calcutta, documents in the National Archives in Delhi, and the documents and letters pertaining to peace groups and activists stored in Delhi, Amsterdam, and Swarthmore are some of the sources used in this chapter. Also discussed are the diaries and travelogues of Indians who visited the People's Republic of China in the early 1950s, as well as newspaper articles, from both India and China, that reported on the vicissitudes of India-China relations in the late 1950s and early 1960s.

These sources (and even their wide locations) are all indicative of the multiple evolving, changing, and complicated levels of connections between India and China. They also corroborate the involvement of groups of people, organizations, and polities from around the world. At the same time, however, these sources have their biases and exaggerations and contain information that is either incorrect or deliberately manipulated. Wherever necessary these issues are noted in the chapters.

OUTLINE

The book consists of five chapters that are organized in chronological order, from the pre–Common Era to the contemporary period. All of them deal with issues of connections and circulations, paying special attention to neglected topics, the roles of individuals, and the wider linkages and impact of India-China interactions. Not detailed are *all* the specific events and issues, such as the 1962 war and border negotiations, that have been the focus of numerous other studies. There are several other aspects, such as the Islamic networks that connected the two regions, the role and contributions of the Indian surveyors of the frontier regions during the British rule of India, and the intellectual discourse on India and China that took place in Japan in the early twentieth century that merit detailed discussion but cannot be included here due to constraints of space. The main aim of this book with regard to coverage, therefore, is to fill some of the gaps in knowledge about the *longue durée* connections between India and China and to explain the four arguments outlined above.

The first chapter focuses on the circulations of knowledge, specifically with regard to geography, manufacturing technologies, astronomy, and medicine, between South Asia and China from before the Common Era to about the fifteenth century CE. It demonstrates the mechanisms through which these aspects of knowledge circulated between the two regions, the ways in which they were adapted locally and, in some cases, transmitted further to other regions and societies. The roles of these neighboring and intermediary regions are also examined to illustrate the multiple methods and agencies involved in these circulations. The connections clearly were not just between South Asia/India and China but entailed entanglements with several other regions and peoples. Also argued in this chapter is that knowledge transmitted or acquired at some point could become dated or lost. This pertains to the Chinese knowledge of South Asian geography, which changed over time and became confused and perplexing during the second millennium CE. The reasons for this loss of knowledge are explained in the chapter.

The second chapter deals with the circulations of objects and the routes and networks that facilitated these exchanges prior to the arrival of the European colonial enterprises. The overland and maritime routes; the mercantile networks of Persians, Southeast Asians, Indians, and Chinese; and the principal goods that circulated between South Asia and China are examined in this chapter. Buddhism, the Chinese tributary system, and the demand for bulk products were some of the key motivators for the exchanges of goods, which ranged from ritual items to exotic animals. The role of relay centers and transit hubs is also explained in this chapter. It is argued that the circulation of objects indicates a closely connected Afroeurasian world integrated through mercantile networks, interlinked ports and oasis towns, roads and river channels, and the knowledge of demand and supply chains. The South Asia–China circuit of exchanges was part of this wider world of Afroeurasian connections.

The third chapter contends that the seven expeditions of the Ming admiral Zheng He between 1405 and 1433 had a significant impact on the circulations of people and goods between India and China. By creating new hubs in the Indian Ocean, fostering linkages between coastal South Asia and Ming China, and stimulating the circulation of goods such as pepper and porcelain, these expeditions set in motion maritime connections between Indian and Chinese traders that would define the subsequent five centuries. The chapter also questions the narrative that the period between the sixteenth and twentieth centuries was a "sluggish" and inconsequential phase in India-China connections. The networks established by the Portuguese and the Dutch in the early phase of European colonialism resulted in extensive commercial and missionary activity between India and China. The British expanded these linkages by transforming tea and opium into the most lucrative commodities of Indian Ocean trade. The British initiated contacts with Tibet and were also instrumental in creating the oppressive regime of indentured labor that brought Indians and Chinese to plantations in Guiana and Mauritius. The latter development led to the intermingling of Chinese and Indians in places that were, for the first time, located outside the Asian continent. Rather than a phase of disconnect between India and China, the colonial period, from the sixteenth century to the end of the nineteenth century, witnessed the development of new networks and sites of exchange, an unprecedented increase in the movement of Chinese and Indians across the Indian Ocean, and a tremendous growth in commercial activity between the two regions.

The response to European colonialism by Asian intellectuals by forging a sense of solidarity, which resulted in the emergence of new forms of connections and new sites of interactions between India and China, is studied in chapter 4. The chapter analyzes the idea of pan-Asianism, its evolution and its failure. It contends that the Japanese invasion of China in the 1930s and the dispute between India and China over the status of Tibet ended this hope for Asian solidarity. Additionally, the chapter examines the period after World War II, when the civil war in China and the anticipated victory of the Communists led to contemplations of new connections among Indian intellectuals and officials. This transitional phase also had a significant impact on the intelligence community in India, which tried to monitor potential disputes between the two new states, the ROI and the PRC, now with a common and largely undemarcated border separating them.

The final chapter of the book explores some of the lesser-known aspects of India and China connections during the tumultuous second half of the twentieth century. The 1950s, it is argued, was a period of failed opportunities, when the leaders of the two countries, well aware of the various problems in their bilateral relations, chose instead to celebrate the rhetorical notion of brotherhood and ageless affinity. To demonstrate the underlying tensions and apprehensions of this period, the chapter focuses on the writings of Indian reporters and commentators in the 1950s and the experiences of a Chinese resident of India who was the target of surveillance by the intelligence community throughout the decade and was eventually arrested and deported on the charge of espionage. It also examines the attempt by an international group of peace activists as well as the British philosopher Bertrand Russell to mediate between India and China in the aftermath of the 1962 war. It is proposed that one of the reasons for the tumultuous nature of this period was the overt focus on the bilateral relationship, perhaps necessitated by the constraints of nation-states. The state-sponsored bilateral exchanges in the sphere of cultural or people-to-people exchanges, for instance, were managed and directed by the two governments more for celebratory purposes than to make any real contribution to mutual understanding of the complexities of the relationship. Even with regard to resolving the border dispute, bilateral negotiations have not yielded any major breakthroughs in the past three decades. The emphasis on bilateral exchanges and negotiations, and the constraints of this strategy, also prevents innovative subregional cooperation initiatives, such as the BCIM, which promotes connectivity in the subregions of Bangladesh, China, India, and Myanmar (thus the acronym BCIM), from succeeding.

Together these chapters demonstrate that India-China exchanges were connected and integrated into the broader circulations of ideas, people, and objects within and beyond the Asian continent. While these interactions expanded or at times contracted due to these broader connections, they often drew new groups of people to participate in these exchanges. Thus, Sogdian traders, Parthian monks, Southeast Asian polities, European colonial enterprises, global peace activists, and multinational companies were, at different times, attracted to the prospects of riches and wealth, fresh philosophical and technical knowledge, or the chance to implement new ideas about conflict resolution or to venture into new markets that emerged from the interactions (or conflict) between India and China. These new entrants created distinct types of connections and circulations. Even during the contemporary period of competing nation-states, where national interests and bilateral exchanges are accentuated, these broader connections, and indeed interdependencies and global impact, form important aspects of India-China relations.

NOTES

1. "Yindu yu Zhongguo wenhua zhi qinshu de guanxi" 印度與中國文化之親屬的關係. The talk was translated into English by Xu Zhimo 徐志摩 (1897–1931) and appears as the introduction to Tagore's ([1924] 2002) *Talks in China*. There are several studies on Tagore's visit to China. The most useful of these are Hay (1970) and Das ([1993] 2005).

2. See, for example, Sen (2014d) on how Buddhist connections between South Asia and China prior to the fifth century may have resulted in the introduction of Buddhism to maritime Southeast Asia.

3. Such studies, produced mostly by Indian and Chinese scholars, became prevalent in the twentieth century and include the works of Bagchi ([1950] 1981), Jin (1957, 1958), and Tan and Geng (2005).

4. See the essays, especially the introduction and the contribution by Igor Kopytoff (1986), in Appadurai (1986).

5. On early Chinese imagining of India, especially through the prism of Buddhism, see the essays in Kieschnick and Shahar (2014).

6. See the various works by Sanjay Subrahmanyam (2004, 2005) collected in the *Explorations in Connected History* volumes published by the Oxford University Press. Most pertinent is his essay "Connected Histories: Notes towards a Reconfiguration of Early Eurasia" that appeared in 1997.

7. The concept of circulatory history in the Eurasian sphere has been high-lighted recently in Duara (2015: 71–90). The issue of circulations, in the context of South Asia, is also examined in detail in Markovits, Pouchepadass, and Subrahmanyam (2003).

8. Subrahmanyam (2016: 21–24) in his critique of K. N. Chaudhuri's *Asia before Europe* has noted the shortcomings of using the term "civilizations" in the study of Indian Ocean interactions. He writes (2016: 22), "[U]sing the concept of 'civilization' tends to lead here down to the path to reification and essentialism." The same applies to the case of the past encounters between India and China.

9. Subrahmanyam (1997: 737) has already alluded to the importance of the Zheng He expeditions in the connected history of Eurasia in his seminal essay. However, he errs in his most recent article with regard to India-China connections, when he states (2016: 27), "In some crucial sense, the thirteenth century was thus a moment when India and China turned their backs on each other." Subrahmanyam probably implies an end to the cultural exchanges between the two regions, because material exchanges, as evidenced by this book, continued through to the India-China war of 1962. In fact, cultural contacts also continued, as can be seen from the record of Islamic networks existing between Quanzhou and Delhi mentioned by Ibn Baṭūṭah in the fourteenth century, from the Yongle emperor's interest in Buddhist artifacts and regions in the early fifteenth century, and from the transmission of the Bengali language to Ming China perhaps also at the same time (see Sen [2016c]). The use of India as a point of reference by Portuguese missionaries in Ming China (see chapter 3), the composition of the Ming novel *Journey to the West* in 1592, and the translation into Chinese and printing of the Bible in Serampore in the early nineteenth century (Kitson 2013: 58–65; Cutts 1942) are perhaps indications that the cultural connections persisted both in imagination and in reality.

10. For an overview of Chinese sources on South Asia, see Sen (2015).

Chapter One

The Circulations of Knowledge

By reading this *Record*, you may visit
the five parts of India with a few steps
without taking the trouble to
move even one foot.
—Yijing (635–713)

The circulations of knowledge, including such wide-ranging aspects as geographical knowledge, astronomy, medicine, manufacturing techniques, market demands, and grammar and linguistics,
were key components of the historical interactions between South
Asia and China. These circulations were linked to several broader
facets of cross-regional connections, including the travels of Buddhist monks, the trade in luxury and nonluxury commodities, diplomatic exchanges, migrations, the translation of religious texts, and
the composition of records on foreign regions. The processes and
mechanisms of the circulations were intensely complex because of
the involvement of multiple intermediaries, varied cultural traditions and languages, diverse worldviews, and the changes associated with the passage of time. The aim of this chapter is to examine
the ways in which knowledge was acquired, transmitted, translated,
transformed, imagined, and in some cases rejected or lost as it
circulated between South Asia and China from the second century

BCE to the sixteenth century CE. It will argue that South
Asia–China interactions did not comprise linear, evolutionary processes founded on the continuing accumulation of knowledge over
time. Rather, changes, perplexities, and loss of knowledge were
important elements of these interactions. A second objective of the
chapter is to demonstrate, through the study of the circulations of
geographical and technical knowledge, that the interactions between South Asia and China were intimately tied to broader intra-
Asian connections through the participation of diverse peoples and
the involvement of locations across the vast continent.

The chapter first outlines the complexities as well as the agencies of knowledge circulation between South Asia and China. Then
the circulations of geographical knowledge between South Asia
and China and the ways in which perceptions and sources of information changed over time are examined. The third section of the
chapter is devoted to the disseminations of multiple forms of "technical" knowledge associated with astral science, medicine, and
manufacturing technologies. The conclusion to the chapter sum-
marizes the key aspects of these circulations within the context of
intra-Asian interactions.

As noted in the introduction, Chinese records, which constitute
the main sources for South Asia–China interactions prior to the
sixteenth century, often insinuate a unidirectional, South
Asia–to–China movement of ideas and influences. However, within
these Chinese records, there are also indications, as discussed below, of flows in the other direction. In fact, they confirm the circulatory nature of these movements.

THE COMPLEXITIES OF KNOWLEDGE CIRCULATION

There are multiple meanings, categories, and forms of knowledge,
which can differ based on linguistic groups, regional variations,
belief systems, and so forth. There could be empirical and nonem-

pirical/theoretical/conceptual aspects to knowledge also determined by numerous factors and settings. Immanuel Kant, for example, was deeply concerned with such complexities of knowledge. The Greek philosophers, Kant points out in his *Groundwork for the Metaphysic of Morals*, had three branches of knowledge: Physik (natural science), Ethik (ethics), and Logik (logic). He explains that there are two kinds of "rational knowledge": material knowledge, which concerns some object, and formal knowledge, which pays no attention to the difference between objects and is concerned only with the form of understanding and of a reason and with the universal rules of thinking. For him, these classifications eventually led to distinctions between empirical and a priori knowledge. Views on knowledge and ways to classify them also existed in other religious, philosophical, and intellectual traditions, including Brahmanism/Hinduism, Jainism, Buddhism, and Confucianism.

A recent volume on various facets of knowledge and its global circulations edited by Jürgen Renn (2012) is relevant to our discussions of South Asia and China. Defining the concept of knowledge, Renn and Hyman in the introduction to the volume write (2012: 20–21),

> [F]rom the historical and social viewpoint, it is necessary to consider knowledge as something that moves from one person to another: something that may be shared by members of a profession, a social class, a geographic region or even an entire civilization. From this perspective, knowledge and its movement may be mapped. Shared knowledge is especially important to the artistic, religious, legal and economic systems that constitute cultures; and knowledge travels along with artifacts and artistic styles, myths and rituals, laws and norms, goods and wealth.

Hyman and Renn later explain the multiple ways in which knowledge circulated across the globe, noting that the process may have been as "old as Homo sapiens itself" (2012: 75). The migrations of early humans, the spread of agriculture and animal husbandry, the diffusion of languages, urbanization and the invention of writing, the emergence of sciences, and the attempt to organize "historical material systematically" all contributed to the circulations of knowledge. Knowledge transmission processes, they argue, had three basic dimensions: mediation, directness, and intentionality. For each of these dimensions, they suggest that specific questions have to be asked: "Is the knowledge transmitted through direct personal contact or through external representation?" "Was [sic] knowledge transmitted directly from end to end, or were there relays?" And "Is knowledge transmitted intentionally or accidentally?"

The circulations of knowledge between South Asia and China examined in this chapter respond to some of these questions. They suggest the existence of several different types of knowledge, as well as distinct methods/dimensions of acquiring, transmitting, and employing it. Indeed, the circulation of information and knowledge between South Asia and China was also a complicated process that took multiple forms and involved diverse agencies. During much of the first millennium CE, Buddhism facilitated the circulation of knowledge about geography, linguistics, science and technology, medicine, art and architecture, fate prognostication, and so forth. There were also transmissions of ideas that pertained to the realm of imagination, such as artistic motifs describing different levels of heavens and hells, the life in paradise, and the contours of the sacred Indic continent Jambudvīpa that centered on the mythical Mount Meru/Sumeru. Ideas and knowledge circulated through both personal contact and external representation, directly and through relays, and they were transmitted intentionally as well as accidentally.

Raw information transmitted between places did not always immediately result in the formation of knowledge. The example given below which examines the report by the Han envoy Zhang Qian on the polity known as Shendu 身毒 did not lead to knowledge about South Asia until a century or two later after more information filtered into China through traders and diplomats. Similarly, there is the possible transmission of aspects of Chinese elixir therapy into South Asia, which had little or no impact on generating knowledge either about Chinese medical practices or China itself. In fact, frequently the knowledge circulating between South Asia and China was jumbled, conflicting, incomplete, or deliberately manipulated. Reality and imagination often mixed as knowledge was carried across vast distances. Moreover, transmitted knowledge went through various degrees of interpretation and eventually shaped perceptions and understanding.

It is important to note that the transmission of knowledge usually involved multiple intermediaries, who incubated and transformed it before passing it on to either South Asia or China. The knowledge gained was of course not always accurate. This is clearly illustrated in the discussions of geographical knowledge below. Distortions and manipulations of knowledge were also common. Buddhist monks, both Chinese and foreign, often manipulated translated texts to argue their case for the legitimacy of the foreign doctrine in China, to promote South Asia as a sophisticated and advanced civilization, or to offer arguments about the ideal relationship between the ruler and the Buddhist community. Even in the cases of firsthand knowledge, supplied, for example, by Chinese Buddhist monks who traveled to South Asia, the biases and intentional misrepresentations of the region to promote the Buddhist (and sometimes sectarian) cause in China are evident. Similarly, the example given later in this chapter about the Southeast Asian polity of Śrīvijaya illustrates how intermediaries could also distort specific knowledge for commercial reasons. These transmitters of knowledge contributed to the formation of distinct types of understanding about South Asia in China. While the first group tried to advance the image of South Asia as a civilized region inhabited by sophisticated people, the Śrīvijayans attempted to portray the Chola (c. 850–1279) polity in South Asia as militarily weak and under their subjugation. As the Chinese records indicate, both groups were successful in their efforts.

The role of intermediaries, such as the Śrīvijayans, in transmitting and shaping knowledge was indeed significant. These intermediaries included not only those who occupied the geographical space between South Asia and China but also those who lived in several other regions of Eurasia. In the thirteenth century, paper- and gunpowder-making technologies, for instance, reached South Asia not directly from China but through Arab and Persian intermediaries. Elements of South Asian astronomy likewise seem to have mixed with Greek traditions in Central Asia before entering China. Also significant is the fact that these circulations did not end with either South Asia or China. As noted below, knowledge about South Asian geography gathered by the Chinese was passed on to the Koreans and the Japanese, who created their own imagined maps and perceptions of the Indic lands based on Chinese writings. Later, during the colonial period, the British in India experimented with tea plantation techniques imported from China, which were eventually transmitted from South Asia to Kenya, now the third-largest producer of the commodity. The broader Asian, or even the Afroeurasian, context is therefore necessary to understand the intricacies of the circulations of knowledge between South Asia and China.

Another important aspect of the circulation of knowledge was the ways in which it was employed. With regard to astronomy, for example, Indic methods for observing and calculating the movements of stars, planets, the sun, and the moon, which entered China primarily through translations of Buddhist texts, were employed in different spheres in China. While the officials working at the court used these methods to compile calendars for agricultural and political purposes, those interested in the prognostication of fate applied some of the same ideas to designing horoscopic charts intended for the common people. The local Buddhist clergy, on the other hand, produced their unique forms of stylistic ritual diagrams of the cosmos known as *maṇḍala*s. Such multiple applications of Indic ideas and concepts also existed in the spheres of Chinese medicine, pharmacology, and manufacturing techniques.

The complexities with regard to the circulations of knowledge were, moreover, shaped by the nature of long-distance interactions. The tenth–eleventh centuries marked a watershed in South Asia–China interactions with the breakdown of Buddhist connections and a shift toward exchanges dominated by merchant groups (Sen 2003). As detailed below, the decline of Buddhist interactions may have resulted in a significant loss of knowledge about the hinterland areas in South Asia, creating great confusion about South Asian geography among the Chinese. Plotting the numerous South Asian polities, the coastal regions, and other geographical determinants within the larger landmass that was called Shendu, Tianzhu, or Yindu 印度 in earlier sources became an impossible task for many Chinese writers after the eleventh century. [1]

Finally, a significant hindrance in examining the circulations and knowledge between South Asia and China is created by the lack of sources in Indian languages. It was noted above that some of the extant Chinese sources offer clues as to how the South Asians might have received their information and generated their own knowledge on China. Many of the conjectures presented in this respect below are necessarily speculative. However, the existence of networks that facilitated the movement of Buddhist monks, merchants, and diplomats suggests that knowledge, distorted or otherwise, regularly reached South Asia from China. The complexity here is to assess whether these translated into South Asian knowledge about China and Chinese methods and practices.

The Facilitators of Knowledge Circulations

It is difficult if not impossible to pinpoint when and how circulations of knowledge commenced between South Asia and China. Archaeological evidence and analysis of textual records suggest that certain regions of South Asia and the Central Plains of China were connected through various intermediaries prior to the spread of Buddhism to China sometime in the first century CE (Mair 2004). Initially, however, geographical and ethnographical knowledge must have been limited or entirely lacking even though ideas and goods had started circulating between the two regions. The Chinese concept of twenty-eight lunar lodges (*ershiba xiu* 二十八宿) and the comparable Indic *nakṣatra* system of representing the ecliptic may have circulated between parts of South Asia and the Central Plains of China in the second millennium BCE. The existence of similar concepts in the two regions does not, however, imply that the Chinese and South Asian interpreters of the sky were aware of each other's existence at this point in time.[2] Similarly, the trade in Maldivian cowries, which took place through Bengal, Assam, and Yunnan to the Shang capital of Anyang in the first millennium BCE (Vogel and Hieronymus 1993; Yang 2004), is not proof of awareness about South Asia among the people living in the Central Plains of China.

Similarly, the mention of commodities with the prefix *cīna* in the Brahmanical work *Mahābhārata* and a work on statecraft named *Arthaśāstra* is not indicative of direct contact between South Asia and China. These commodities, which include *cīnasī* (hides), *cīnapiṣṭa* (vermilion), *cīnaka* (camphor), and *cīnāṃśuka/cīnapaṭṭa* (silk) (Sen 2003: 182–183), most likely entered South Asia through various conduits and intermediaries. Although the word *cīna* commonly indicated China in South Asian sources,[3] it is likewise not conclusive proof of knowledge about the Central Plains among South Asians. If Bruno Latour's (2005) contention of objects having agency is correct, then these early items of trade may have at most contributed to the circulations of some fragmentary knowledge between South Asia and China. The early circulations clearly suggest linkages as well as the active participation of unknown intermediaries occupying the spaces between South Asia and China. These intermediaries, such as the various nomadic groups in Central Asia and the people inhabiting the region Willem van Schendel (2002) and James C. Scott (2009) call "Zomia" in the modern Yunnan-Burma borderlands, were most likely the facilitators of the movement of goods, ideas, and knowledge between China and South Asia during much of the first and second millennia BCE.

With the establishment of the Mauryan Empire (322 BCE–185 BCE) in South Asia and the expansion of the Han Empire (206 BCE–220 CE) some two centuries later, rudimentary knowledge, connected to geography, military prowess, commodities, and in particular the existence of Indic and Sinitic realms, may have started to circulate between South Asia and pre-Han and Han China. Warfare, migrations, and brisk long-distance commercial exchanges in the centuries prior to the spread of Buddhism to China facilitated such circulations of knowledge, perhaps initially among those living in the frontier regions and subsequently spreading to the urban centers in the hinterland areas. In fact, these factors clearly contributed to the composition of the earliest Chinese accounts of South Asia found in *Shi ji* 史記 (Records of the Grand Historian), the first Chinese dynastic history.

The Han court's interactions with the Xiongnu 匈奴 confederacy during the first and second centuries BCE, which included diplomatic and commercial exchanges as well as military conflict, had wider implications across Eurasia. They resulted in the circulation of commodities, the diffusion of ideas, and the migration of people. One of the famous episodes associated with the Xiongnu–Han China interactions relates to the strategic mission of the Han emissary Zhang Qian. Dispatched by the Han emperor Wu in 138 BCE,

Zhang was asked to probe the prospect of a military alliance with the Yuezhi 月氏 people in Central Asia against the Xiongnu. Zhang, however, was captured by the Xiongnu and held as a prisoner for about a decade. We are told in the detailed record of the episode found in the *Shi ji* that Zhang Qian eventually managed to escape and find his way into the territories occupied by the Yuezhi people somewhere near the Ferghana Valley (in present-day Tajikistan). The Yuezhi, most likely an Indo-European group, were forced to leave their original homeland around the Tianshan mountain ranges and move to the Ferghana Valley due to the westward expansion of the Xiongnu. While Zhang Qian failed to convince the Yuezhi leader to form a military alliance with the Han court, he came to know of an alternative route to Central Asia, which in Zhang's opinion could be used to launch a surprise attack on the Xiongnu. [4]

At a market in Bactria (Daxia 大夏), Zhang Qian saw what he believed to be cloth ("*Shu bu*" 蜀布) and bamboo sticks ("*Qiong zhuzhang*" 邛竹杖) from the southwest region of the Han Empire. Upon inquiring about the route through which the products reached the local market, Zhang was told that they arrived through a polity in the south called "Shendu" (*Shi ji* 123: 3166). This is the first mention in Chinese records of a name that for the subsequent centuries remained associated with India. Although unsuccessful as far as the main objective of his mission was concerned, Zhang Qian nonetheless acquired elementary information about the neighboring regions of Han China, including South Asia, with the aim to eventually use this alternative route to counter the Xiongnu threat.

Zhang Qian is also credited for inaugurating the so-called Silk Road that linked the markets of Han China to those in Rome. [5] While it is unlikely that Zhang Qian's visit to Central Asia contributed to the launching of the silk trade or even led to a growth in long-distance commercial interactions, it is obvious that scribes at the Han court started paying more attention to the peripheral regions of the Han Empire after he returned in 125 BCE. The collapse of the Xiongnu confederation in 55 BCE not only resulted in the further penetration of the Han Empire into Central Asia, but also a rapid growth in trade with, and knowledge about, South Asia. The records relating to tribute missions from the South Asian polity known as Jibin 罽賓 (indicating, at that time, the region around present-day Afghanistan and northwest Pakistan)[6] contained in *Han shu* 漢書, the second dynastic history compiled by Ban Gu 班固 (32–92) in the first century CE, are important for identifying the agents responsible for the circulation of knowledge a few decades before Buddhist doctrines reached the Han capital. The tribute carriers from Jibin who appeared at the Han court were clearly merchants trying to exploit the tribute system. As tribute carriers they were exempted from paying duties on goods they brought with them, some of which they offered as gifts and others they sold at the local markets. The records of these tribute missions on one hand indicate the Han court's increasing familiarity with the polities on its northwest frontiers, extending to parts of South Asia; on the other hand, they also reveal knowledge about Han markets, court policies, and political ideologies among the Jibin visitors.[7]

The establishment of the Kuṣāṇa Empire (c. 30–c. 375) in the first century CE by one of the branches of the Yuezhi people known in Chinese sources as Guishuang 貴霜 provided significant inputs to the circulation of knowledge between Han China and South Asia. The Kuṣāṇa Empire, which stretched from parts of Central Asia to the Gangetic region of South Asia, facilitated the movement of merchants and Buddhist missionaries through both overland and maritime routes.[8] These traders and Buddhist missionaries, not all of South Asian origin, emerged as the main transmitters of knowledge between South Asia and China for the next several centuries. Subsequently, Buddhist monks from China and the Korean Peninsula who traveled to South Asia also facilitated the circulation of knowledge.

The impact of Buddhist networking on the circulation of knowledge between South Asia and China during the first millennium CE was remarkable. The establishment of Buddhism in China, for example, triggered the desire among the Chinese to understand the geographical setting of places associated with the life and teachings of the Buddha. This led to the acquisition of knowledge about key urban centers, rivers, polities, inhabitants, and flora and fauna in several regions of South Asia. The descriptions of these sites in the travel records of Chinese monks and other works compiled by the Buddhists in China percolated to different genres of writing in China, including the dynastic histories.

Knowledge of languages was another important contribution of the Buddhist exchanges. The translation of Buddhist texts required training in Sanskrit and other Indic languages. While there were a few bilingual specialists, such as Kumārajīva (Jiumoluoshi 鳩摩羅什) and Xuanzang, the majority of the translations were done through teamwork.[9] These teams frequently included people from a third region, especially from Central Asia, and required wider knowledge of Indic scripts, grammar, mythology, and allegories. Thus, while very few Buddhist monks in China were versed in Indic languages and scripts, most were familiar, through these translated texts, with South Asian geography, polities, and society. At the same time, knowledge about ritual artifacts and practices, concepts of spiritual realms, and philosophical traditions all entered China with the rendition of Buddhist teachings. The spread of Buddhism also led to the diffusion of Indic painting techniques, methods of constructing temples and ritual spaces, patterns of musical tones, the technology to manufacture sugar, medical practices and prescriptions, and approaches to calculating astronomical phenomena.[10] Indeed, the agency of Buddhism in facilitating the circulation of knowledge between South Asia and China was complex, multifaceted, and encompassed aspects not always related to Buddhist teachings. Some of these wider influences of Buddhism on the transmission of knowledge between the two regions are examined later in this chapter.

Buddhism also made a significant contribution to the circulation of knowledge and information between China and South Asia. While sources from South Asia do not record in any detail what people in that region knew about China, the biographies and other notices of South Asian monks in Chinese sources indicate that these missionaries were aware of the routes, destinations, and cultural practices in China. Perhaps the most telling aspect in this regard was the knowledge among South Asian monks of Mount Wutai, which was considered to be the abode of the Buddhist divinity Mañjuśrī. Several Chinese sources from the seventh century onward mention the visits of South Asian pilgrims to the mountain (Sen 2003). There is also one document found in Dunhuang, cited below, that suggests that some of these monks even tried to learn the necessary Chinese phrases to find their way to Mount Wutai.

Letters exchanged between Xuanzang and his teachers and fellow students at Nālandā, preserved in Xuanzang's biography (Li 1995: 229–235), are also indicative of the circulation of knowledge and information between China and South Asia. After returning to Tang China in 645, Xuanzang settled in the capital Chang'an. Through diplomats and itinerant monks, Xuanzang was able to maintain contacts with his former teachers and colleagues at Nālandā. He informed these monks about the situation in Tang China and his translation activities, and he also discussed doctrinal issues with them. Indeed, these letters are evidence of the regular communication and exchanges that must have been taking place between the Buddhist communities in China and South Asia.

Furthermore, court representatives and itinerant traders transmitted knowledge about China to South Asia. It can be inferred from Chinese dynastic histories, for example, that South Asian rulers, such as Harṣa (r. 606–647), based in Kanauj, and Lalitāditya Muktāpiḍa (r. 724 CE–760 CE) of Kashmir, were aware of the military prowess of the Tang court and its activities in the Hindu-kush and the Tibetan plateau regions (Sen 2003). The Tang court maintained diplomatic ties with both of these South Asian polities and, at least in the case of Kashmir, established a strategic military partnership against the Tibetans in the eighth century (Sen 2004). Later, in the thirteenth century, diplomatic missions sent by the Yuan court to the polities located on the Coromandel and Malabar coasts seem to have informed the local officials and rulers about the situation in China under the Mongols. Thus, we find that in 1281, as detailed later in this chapter, one of the officials at the court of the Ma'bar polity sought asylum at the Yuan court because of irreconcilable difference with the rulers. The expeditions of Zheng He across the Indian Ocean in the early fifteenth century similarly contributed to the spread of knowledge about Ming China, especially, as discussed in chapter 3, its naval prowess, among South Asian polities.

The agency of traders in the circulation of knowledge between South Asia and China is somewhat neglected. In addition to ferrying goods between the two regions, traders were important suppliers of information about geography, routes of communication, political situations, and local produce and merchandise. They were also vital to the movement of Buddhist monks, who often hitch-hiked on the caravans or ships traveling between South Asia and China. Traders might have also contributed to the spread of culinary styles, medical cures, shipbuilding technologies, navigational skills, and the like. Unexamined is the role some of these itinerant traders might have played in introducing South Asian languages and scripts to China. The Song scholar Zheng Qiao 鄭樵 (1104–1162), who was concerned with various forms of knowledge and the ways of disseminating them (Bray 2007; Schäfer 2011), has a section in his encyclopedia titled *Tong zhi* 通志 (Comprehensive Records of the Institutions) that discusses the differences between Indian and Chinese languages. Although the focus of the discussion is primarily about Sanskrit and Chinese, the script that he uses in the text is South Indian Pallava script. A native of the port city Quanzhou, Zheng Qiao may have come into contact with the Tamil traders in the area and encountered the Pallava script (Mair [1993] 2013). A second example comes from the Ming source *Siyi guangji* 四夷廣記 (Extensive Records of the Four Barbarian [Regions]), where the record pertains to Bengali language and script (see figure 1.1). The Chinese pronunciations of over two hundred Bengali terms and a discussion on the language are provided in the text. This is the earliest extant Bengali–Chinese lexicon composed, it seems, by traders and interpreters engaged in commercial exchanges during the sixteenth century (Sen 2005; Sen 2016c).

It should be reemphasized here that the Buddhist, diplomatic, and commercial agents facilitating the circulation of knowledge between South Asia and China were not necessarily always from these two regions. In fact, in many cases those from neighboring (and intermediary) regions were important contributors. Thus, Iranian and Korean monks, Sogdian traders, and Southeast Asian diplomats frequently participated in the transmissions, or, at least in the case of the Śrīvijayans, in blocking the flow of knowledge. This role of intermediaries became more complicated with the arrival of European colonial polities in the sixteenth century and their subsequent domination of the routes that linked South Asia and China. The interactions between China, including the Republic of China, and colonial India are examined in the later chapters.

THE CIRCULATIONS OF GEOGRAPHICAL KNOWLEDGE

Three distinct phases in the circulation of geographical knowledge between South Asia and China can be identified before the sixteenth century. The period prior to the spread of Buddhism to China, when knowledge about the geographical contours circulated mainly through intermediaries, constituted the initial phase. During

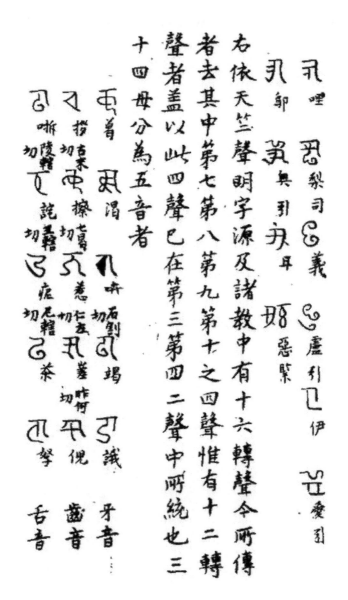

Figure 1.1. Bengali script and words, *Siyi guangji*.

this phase mutual knowledge seems to have been rudimentary, limited to areas in the frontier regions and a few urban centers and port towns. From about the second century CE to around the tenth century, which marked the second phase, Buddhist activities facilitated the circulation of detailed geographical knowledge, particularly about the hinterland regions. After the tenth century, due to the growth in maritime linkages, mutual knowledge about coastal regions became more widespread. These three phases were linked to overall changes in the nature of interactions between South Asia and China.

The *Shi ji* account of Zhang Qian learning about the region called Shendu in the markets of Bactria, mentioned above, indicates the fact that scribes at the Han court had started receiving information about certain regions of South Asia. Another noteworthy aspect of this account is the strategic knowledge Zhang Qian acquired about a route from the southwest frontier of the Han Empire through Shendu to Central Asia. Zhang Qian was later tasked to find this route. According to *Shi ji* (123: 3166; 116: 2995–2996), however, because of resistance from local people in the Sichuan-Yunnan region, Zhang Qian failed to accomplish his mission. Nonetheless, Zhang Qian was correct in his assertion about the existence of this so-called southwestern route, which linked the present-day provinces of Yunnan and Sichuan in the PRC to the Assam and Bengal regions of the ROI.[11] As discussed in the next chapter, the route and its various branches were used to supply cowries originating in the Maldives to the Yellow River Valley during the Shang period. Neither Zhang Qian nor the scribes at the Han court would have been aware of this fact.

It is also unlikely that the Han officials or scribes had any detailed knowledge about the area beyond the river Indus in the second century BCE. This is evident from the following brief description of Shendu in *Shi ji* (123: 3166):

> [Shendu] lies several thousand li southeast of Daxia. The people cultivate the land and live much like the people of Daxia. The region is said to be hot and damp. The inhabitants ride elephants when they go into battle. The kingdom is situated on a great river.

The "great river" mentioned here is most likely the Indus and not the Ganges, which had already emerged as the location of thriving urban life in South Asia in the sixth century BCE. Knowledge about the Gangetic region, which also included the leading Buddhist pilgrimage sites, seems to have only started filtering into Han China after the first century CE.

The period between the first century BCE and the end of the first century CE was the pivot to the subsequent expansion of geographical knowledge both in Han China and South Asia. The expansions by Han forces in Central Asia after the collapse of the Xiongnu confederacy contributed to a deeper Chinese understanding of the southern Hindukush (present-day Afghanistan-Pakistan) region. The *Han shu* (96a: 3884–3887), completed in the beginning of the second century CE, has a detailed account of the Jibin polity, including its geography, flora and fauna, political leadership, and economy. Such information was gathered not only from tribute carriers, as mentioned above, but most likely also from the military and espionage activities of the Han court in the region. The Han court tried several times to install a friendly regime in its Central Asian frontier region and also to extract tribute missions from polities located in the area (Yu 1992: 144–167). The *Han shu* does not mention the practice of Buddhism in Jibin, which was vibrant when the work was composed. It also does not record the presence of Buddhist practitioners in the Han capital at this time (Zürcher [1959] 1972; Sen 2012). These followers of Buddhism—Chinese and foreigners—emerged as the leading transmitters of information and knowledge between China and South Asia from the second century onward.

Knowledge of the Buddhist Heartland

In the first century CE, knowledge about the towns, ports, and markets of Han China, and the routes to reach these places, existed among several groups of merchants operating from South Asia. It was through these merchant groups that Buddhist ideas and images first reached Han China, a fact that can be discerned, for example, from the drawings engraved on the boulders of Mount Kongwang 孔望山 in northern Jiangsu Province. These images that date from the second century CE indicate the existence of seafaring traders from South or Central Asia who practiced Buddhism (Rhie 1999: 27–47; Sen 2014b). Additionally, textual records from third-century China indicate the presence of Sogdian merchants at Jiaozhi, in present-day northern Vietnam. These merchants are reported to have been sojourning between Jiaozhi and ports in South Asia and carrying out trade in commodities that included horses (*Gaoseng zhuan*, T. 2059: 325a13–14). Clearly, these seafaring traders were aware of the geographical contours of China in addition to the commercial demands and the supply routes.

For these traders, ports in Southeast Asia, especially those under the polity known in Chinese sources as Funan 扶南, must have been important sites for acquiring information about China. *Liang shu* (History of the Liang Dynasty), a seventh-century Chinese text, reports of a meeting between envoys representing the Wu polity 吳國, located in southeast China, and those from Tianzhu in Funan in the third century. From about the first to the fifth century, the ports of Funan were the main transit centers for traders traveling between the coastal regions of South Asia and China. *Liang shu* indicates that the representatives from the Wu polity, when in Funan, obtained information about South Asia's maritime links to Southeast Asian and on the spread of Brahmanism to the region (*Liang shu* 54: 787–793; Wang 1958: 31–45).

By the time the above-mentioned encounter between the representatives of Tianzhu (India) and the Wu polity took place in Funan, Buddhist doctrines had already made significant inroads into the Chinese hinterland. The number of Buddhist missionaries had gradually increased, images of the Buddha and other Buddhist divinities were being made locally, and, more importantly, a mechanism to render Buddhist texts into Chinese had been set up. The establishment of Buddhist networking between South Asia and China resulted in a significant increase in the flow of geographical information, including that about the terrains that lay between the two regions, the main transit centers, the major monastic sites, the key routes and pathways, and the modes of long-distance travel. Chinese sources indicate that access to such information was not limited to the local Buddhist community. Court scribes often used the information found in the translated Buddhist texts and in the travelogues of Buddhist monks to write official accounts of South Asian polities.

Translated Buddhist texts were one of the main conduits through which information about South Asian geography entered China. As Jan Nattier (2008, 2014) points out, "dozens (quite possibly hundreds)" of Buddhist texts were translated into Chinese between the mid-second century and the latter half of the third century CE. The translators of these texts were mostly natives of Central Asia, Parthians such as An Shigao 安世高 (fl. c. 148–180) and Indo-Scythians including Zhi Qian 支謙 (fl. 222–252). In almost every such translated work, polities, towns, and other geographical sites and terrains of South Asia, especially in the Gangetic region, are mentioned. These sites were all associated with the life of the Buddha, his sermons, or the places where he performed miracles. In most cases they are part of the opening passage that began with the formulaic stanza, "Thus I have heard, at one time the Buddha was at X." The polity of Śrāvastī (Sheweiguo 舍衛國) and the Jetavana park (祇樹給孤獨園, a literal translation of Jetavana-Anāthapindika), for example, are mentioned most frequently in these early texts. Also mentioned are places such as Rājagṛha (Wangshe guo/Wangshe cheng 王舍國/王舍城), Varanasi (Poluocha guo 波羅奈國), Champa (Zhanpo daguo 占波大國), Magadha (Moheti guo 摩竭提國), and Kapilavastu (Jiaweiluowei guo 迦維羅衛國). The sixteen great urban centers or *mahānagaras* (*shiliu daguo* 十六大國), the Gṛidrakuta mountain, and Mount Meru, as well as the Indic continent of Jambudvīpa are also included in these texts. Sometimes the names of towns and polities in South Asia are transcribed (such as those for Varanasi and Champa), and at other times they are translated (as for Rājagṛha). The designations for these sites often alter between *guo* 國 ("polity") and *cheng* 城 ("town"), indicating perhaps a confusion during the translation process.

These early translators (and even those of later times) of Buddhist texts had the challenging task of introducing foreign concepts and ideas to an audience that had very different worldviews and approaches to life. The rendering of foreign names for places and people on the one hand added to the complexity of geographical knowledge; on the other hand, it also generated interest in foreign teachings by sparking the imagination of unknown and exotic places. However, there does not seem to have been an effort made by the early translators to provide detailed information about the sites and places mentioned in the Buddhist texts. This changed in the fifth century when the Chinese monk Faxian 法顯 (337?–422?) traveled to South Asia and returned to write his travelogue titled *Foguo ji* 佛國記 (Record of the Buddhist Polities).[12]

Faxian embarked on his journey to South Asia in 399. By this time the route linking the urban centers of China and the Buddhist sites in South Asia were well known and frequently traversed by traders as well as by Buddhist missionaries from various parts of Asia. There may have been other Chinese monks prior to Faxian who attempted to visit the Buddhist holy land, but it is not clear if anyone before him successfully accomplished the journey. Faxian's *Foguo ji* was the first detailed Chinese account of the sacred Buddhist sites in South Asia. It also described the overland and maritime routes that connected China to the urban centers and ports in South Asia. More importantly, it provided inspiration to other Chinese Buddhists to make similar trips to the Buddhist holy land. At the same time, Faxian's work triggered a wider discussion among Chinese intellectuals about Indic culture and society vis-à-vis the Sinitic civilization, a dialogue that continued through to the twentieth century.

Faxian's purpose for visiting South Asia, as he explains in his travelogue (Li 2002: 163), was to bring back monastic rules (Ch. *lü* 律; *vinaya*) used in South Asia, only a few of which had been rendered into Chinese before he undertook the journey. For Faxian, South Asia was more than a repository of religious texts; it was also a sacred site containing the relics and traces of the Buddha and the commemorative monuments built by King Aśoka, the leading supporter of the doctrine. As a result, the geographical space he witnessed, experienced, and wrote about was viewed through the prism of a pilgrim visiting his holy land. His views were also framed by the descriptions of South Asia found in the translated Buddhist stories and teachings that he had read prior to embarking on his journey. However, Faxian added many details about the region that were not available in the Buddhist texts: the distances between various towns of South Asia, the mountains and rivers that lay in between, the layout and architecture of the cities, the beliefs and customs of the people, and the practice of Buddhism in monastic institutions. The Pamirs; the Himalayan ranges; the great Indus, Yamuna, and Ganges Rivers; cities such as Pāṭaliputra and Varanasi; and the port of Tāmralipta/Tāmralipti were all described in Faxian's record. He also recorded his travel by ship, first from Tāmralipta to Sri Lanka and then across the Bay of Bengal through Southeast Asia to China. For the readers of Faxian's travelogue in China, his descriptions confirmed the existence of the sites mentioned in the translated texts, corroborated the utopic nature of these places, and provided detailed information about a distant foreign land that had already entered the imagination of the Chinese.

The fact that Faxian's record was widely read in China is clear from the citations of his work in Buddhist and non-Buddhist works. Perhaps the most significant statement, based on Faxian's description, appeared in a sixth-century work called *Shui jing zhu* 水經注 (Commentary on the Water Classic) by Li Daoyuan 麗道元 (d. 527). Li noted,

> From here (i.e., Mathurā in northern India) to the south all [the country] is Madhyadeśa (Ch. Zhongguo 中國). Its people are rich. The inhabitants of Madhayadeśa dress and eat like the Middle Kingdom (Ch. Zhongguo = China); therefore they are called Madhyadeśa. (Petech 1950a: 20)

Faxian's use of "Zhongguo" may have been on one hand a translation of Madhyadeśa (Middle Country), but on the other hand it also was a subtle reference to the Central Plain in the Yellow River valley, considered by the Chinese as the center of the world. Indeed, the above statement of Li Daoyuan in the context of Chinese discourse on a foreign people, where comments on eating habits and the manner of clothing were usually associated with the level of sophistication of a non-Chinese culture, indicates that information provided by Faxian may have contributed not only to the expansion of knowledge about South Asian geography but also to an elevation of the Chinese perception toward South Asian society and culture (Sen 2003). Perhaps because of such eyewitness accounts by Chinese Buddhist monks, the court scribes in China became less ethnocentric in their description of South Asians than about other foreign regions and peoples.

In the period when Faxian composed his work to the mid-seventh century, when Xuanzang, the other renowned Chinese traveler to South Asia, gave a more detailed account of the Buddhist holy land, new knowledge circulation networks had emerged. The most important of these were the diplomatic channels. During this period between Faxian and Xuanzang, several diplomatic missions arrived from South Asia at the courts of Chinese rulers. The Chinese dynastic histories from this period have preserved two letters brought by representatives from the region the Chinese called "Zhong Tianzhu" 中天竺, or "Middle India." The first is found in *Song shu* 宋書 (97: 2384–2386), which covers the history of the Liu Song 劉宋 dynasty that ruled China from 420 to 477. Written by a ruler named Yueai 月愛 (Chandragupta II?) from a polity called Jiabili 迦毗黎, the letter was delivered to Emperor Wen 文帝 (r. 424–454) in the fifth year of the Yuanjia reign period 元嘉五年 (428). While it is evident that the court officials edited and embellished the original version according to Confucian protocols, including the passage on the submission of territories to the Chinese ruler, the letter nonetheless indicates the mechanism through which knowledge, including that related to geography, circulated between South Asia and China. The letter is translated in its entirety below:

> I have humbly heard that your polity rests on a river and is by the bank of a sea. Hills and streams surround and protect it. Everything [appears] marvelous and organized. It is magnificent and sparkling just like a magical city. The palaces and halls are imposing, the streets and alleys are all paved, [and] the people are content, happy, and joyful.
>
> When the sage king goes on excursions, the whole world follows him. He is wise and benevolent and does no harm to living creatures. All the neighboring [polities] obey him. [Your] polity is rich and prosperous like the ocean.
>
> The people of [your] polity revere and follow the true *dharma*. The great king is a benevolent sage who has transformed himself according to the Way. He is compassionate toward humankind and neglects none. The emperor cultivates the pure precepts. There are no paths that he has not trodden. With unsurpassed wisdom, he saves all from sinking [into distress]. All his ministers and officials are happy and have no resentment. Various gods protect him, the spirits stand on guard, and the evil demons have submitted to him. There are none who disobeys

[his command]. The king's body is majestic and radiant like the rising sun. Like a colossal cloud his benevolence and kindness benefits all. Saints and worthy men carry on their duties like the sun, moon and the Heaven. In your Cīnasthana 真丹, [you] are the most distinguished and worthy.

The place where this subject resides is called Jiabihe 迦毗河. It borders the sea in the east. The four walls of the city are all made of purple bricks. Under the protection of *Shouluotian* 首羅天, [my] polity is peaceful and free from evils. The kings succeed each other [to the throne] without break. The people of the polity cultivate good merits. When various polities gather here, they express their obedience to the *dharma*. The temples and cloisters [in the polity] are all shaped like the seven treasures 七寶. Everyone marvels and makes offerings [to them], just like the teachings of the previous kings. Your subject cultivates self-regulation and does not violate the prohibitions laid down by the *dharma*. Your subject is called Yueai, and he hails from the royal Qishi clan 棄世王種.

The only thing I can desire is [to wish] peace and harmony to the holy body of the great king, and peace and tranquility to all his subjects and officials. Now, all the subjects, officials and people, hills, streams and treasures of this polity belong to you, and with five appendages I prostrate myself at the feet of the great king. Since the mountains and seas stand as barriers, I am unable to pay homage and have an audience [with you] personally. To extend [my] admiration and reverence, I am sending an envoy to acknowledge vassalage.

The father of the Chief Envoy is called Tianmoxita 天魔悉達 (Devamahita? Dharmahita?), and the Chief Envoy is named Nituoda 尼陁達 (Nidatta?). As this person has all along been good, honest and faithful, I therefore send him to present this memorial in the capacity of an envoy. If the great king requires anything, precious objects or exotic goods, I shall offer them all. Let them be known to me. This land belongs to the king. The laws and decrees of the king are worthy to administer a polity, and thus can be enforced here. I wish that the exchange of letters and envoys between the two polities will continue without intermission. When this envoy returns, I hope that you would [re-

spond through] an envoy with your proclamations and orders so
that I can implement them correctly. I sincerely hope that the
envoy will not return empty-handed. I have stated all that I have
to say. I pray for more kindness and sympathy.

The second letter, preserved in the *Liang shu* (54: 799), which
follows the same template as above, dates from the early sixth
century and was sent by the ruler of Zhong Tianzhu named Quduo
屈多 (Gupta?). Later in that century, the Sui 隋 (581–618) court is
reported to have requested a Chinese monk named Yancong 彥琮
(557–610) to render two texts concerning the geography and Buddhist practices in Sui China into Sanskrit for readers in South Asia.
These two works were titled *Guojia xiangrui lu* 國家祥瑞錄
(Records of the Auspicious Signs in the Country) and *Sheli rui tu
jing* 舍利瑞圖經 (Illustrated Text of the Auspicious Signs Related
to the [Buddhist] Relics). It is not clear if they were delivered to
someone in South Asia or what impact they may have had with
regard to augmenting the existing knowledge about China.[13] But
this account from the Sui period indicates the transmission of information from China to South Asia and the possibility of groups of
people in the latter region having detailed knowledge of Chinese
geography.

It can be concluded from the above discussion that between the
fourth and the end of the sixth century, detailed information about
South Asian geography had entered China through monks, merchants, and diplomats. Based on this information the knowledge
about South Asia that was generated in China prior to Xuanzang's
visit can be summarized as follows: There were two distinctly separate geographical entities in the region, one of which was called
Tianzhu and the other Shiziguo.[14] The former, frequently associated with Zhang Qian's Shendu and the Buddhist sacred continent
known as Jambudvīpa, was divided into five parts, north, south,
east, west, and middle, and comprised several polities. The latter,
on the other hand, was an island. While Shiziguo was geographical-

ly distinct and sometimes politically autonomous, it was closely associated with Tianzhu, especially for the Chinese Buddhists.[15] The "Five Tianzhus," as the Chinese sources often termed the first entity, could be approached through land and sea routes. While great deserts and mountain ranges, the Pamirs and Snowy Mountain (i.e., Himalayas), had to be traversed to reach the borders of Tianzhu, vast seas needed to be navigated to arrive at the coastal regions of Tianzhu and Shiziguo. Until about the eleventh–twelfth centuries, as discussed below, the Chinese seem to have been more cognizant of the land routes rather than the sea routes connecting South Asia and China.

Within the Five Tianzhus, the Chinese knew about the existence of three large rivers, the Indus, Yamuna, and Ganges, as well as some of the urban centers in the hinterland, regional flora and fauna, climate, and social divisions. The readers of Chinese Buddhist works would also have been familiar with the locations of important Buddhist sites, monasteries, and places that housed sacred relics, histories and legends associated with some of the large towns, and the variations in languages and scripts in these five regions of Tianzhu. However, they must have also been confused about certain places in Tianzhu. Mount Meru/Sumeru, the imaginary mountain, for example, was described as part of Tianzhu's geography in Buddhist literature, but none of the Buddhist travelers to the region mention encountering the sacred site. Xuanzang describes the mountain in the following way:

> Mount Sumeru, meaning the Wonderful High Mountain, is composed of the four precious substances. It is located in the sea, standing on the golden wheel, under the illumination of the sun and moon in rotation, being the residence of heavenly beings, surrounded by a ring of seven mountains and seven seas. (Li 1996: 17)

The Japanese who drew maps of South Asia based on the descriptions of Xuanzang (see figures 1.2 and 1.3) were utterly baffled by this when they tried to plot the imaginary mountain. The same was true of the Koreans, who also attempted to reconcile the actual geographical layout of the Buddhist holy land based on the travel narratives of Chinese monks and the imaginary cosmic realm described in the religious texts. As seen from the maps of South Asia in figure 1.2, the Japanese and Koreans placed Mount Sumeru not on the sea, as suggested by Xuanzang, but in the region around the Himalayas.

Although it is impossible to similarly summarize the knowledge about China among South Asians, it can be conjectured that knowledge about China had also become relatively widespread there by the beginning of the Tang dynasty. Buddhist missionaries in the region, for instance, were aware of the routes to China, knew the location of key towns and monastic institutions, and were cognizant of the mountains, rivers, and the land beyond the region they called Mahācina. This knowledge of China was not limited to the Buddhists in South Asia. Chinese sources also report of several Brahmins who arrived in China expressly to transmit their religious beliefs (Sen 2003). Merchants engaged in long-distance trade, and also to some extent court officials in South Asia must have been acquainted with the political centers as well as the important ports and frontier markets in China. It is possible that some of these people, who had information about China, transmitted it to others in South Asia. The steady stream of Buddhist missionaries, traders, and tribute carriers from South Asia to China throughout the first millennium CE seems to confirm this.

The Augmentation of Knowledge Circulations

Interactions between South Asia and China from the seventh to the ninth centuries were more intensive than in any previous period. However, these three centuries also witnessed significant restructurings of the South Asia–China exchanges. Doctrinal input from South Asia to the Buddhist schools and practices in China saw

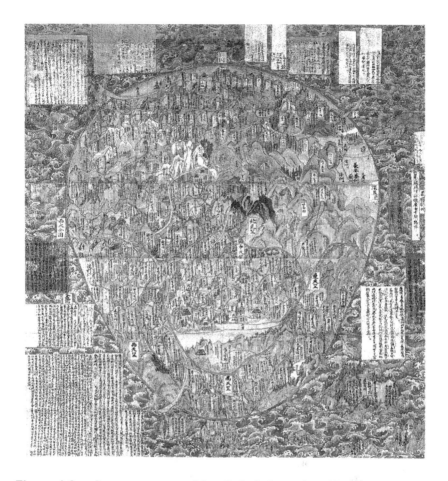

Figure 1.2.   Japanese map of South Asia based on Xuanzang's descriptions. Reprinted from Sen and Mair (2012)

appreciable decline, and the emergence of several powerful polities across Asia, including those established by the Tibetans, Arabs, and Śrīvijayans, exerted considerable impact on the diplomatic exchanges, while the spread of Islam and the establishment of networks by Muslim traders started transforming the commercial networks between the two regions. Some of these developments contributed to the deeper integration of South Asia–China exchanges into broader intra-Asian networks. As a consequence, the circula-

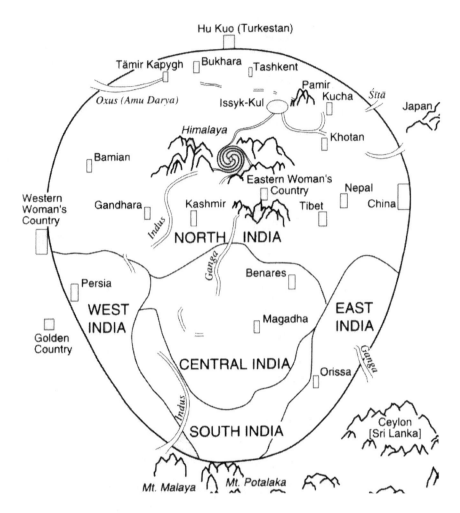

Figure 1.3.   Schematic rendering of the Japanese map of South Asia. After Rambelli (2014), reprinted from Sen (2014b)

tions of information and knowledge between the two regions became more diverse, complex, and confusing.

A closer examination reveals that the exchanges between South Asia and Tang transited through at least three phases. From the early seventh century until the death of Wu Zetian 武則天 (r. 648–705), Buddhism continued to be a leading factor in the interactions between the two regions. The period from the ascension in

712 of Emperor Xuanzong 玄宗 (r. 712–756) to the Huichang 會昌 persecution of Buddhism in 840 was highlighted by diplomatic overtures between the Tang court and the Karkoṭa polity (625–1003) in Kashmir as well as changes in the reception of Indic Buddhist ideas among the Chinese clergy. Finally, the period between 840 and the fall of the Tang dynasty in 907 witnessed the emergence of Muslim traders as the major players in the contacts between South Asia and China.

When Xuanzang returned to Tang China after a sojourn of about fifteen years, the reigning Tang emperor Taizong 太宗 (r. 626–649) asked him to write about his travels in foreign lands. The emperor is reported to have said, "The Land of the Buddha is far away. His holy traces and the teachings of his Dharma are not fully recorded in our historical works. Since the teacher has personally visited that land, an account of it should be written to inform those who have not heard about it" (Li 1995: 178). Thus, as Xuanzang set out to compose his travelogue, he knew that the main audience of his work would be the emperor keen to know about the bordering areas and foreign lands, not perhaps because of his interest in the Buddhist geography but because of his concern about the volatile borderlands of the empire. Although written from a Buddhist perspective, often highlighting the sacredness of the land he considered holy and exaggerating the political support Buddhism received from Indian rulers with the aim of enticing the Chinese emperor to support the Buddhist cause, Xuanzang was meticulous in describing the polities he visited.

Two aspects about South Asia stand out in Xuanzang's writing. First, in each chapter, Xuanzang provides basic information about the polities and towns he passed through (and even for those that he did not, such as Sri Lanka). The distance between places, the expanse of a particular region or polity, a description of the dwelling places of the people, the climate, the number of local Buddhist monasteries, and the related Buddhist legends associated with each site are narrated in great detail. While discrepancies and errors are evident in several places, modern archaeologists, most famously the British archaeologist Alexander Cunningham, the first director-general of the Archaeological Survey of India, have used his record as a manual to locate historical sites and ancient routes (Wriggins 2004: 212–213). The second noteworthy aspect is the comprehensive overview of South Asia that Xuanzang provides in the second chapter of his work. The Chinese monk argues that "Tianzhu,"[16] the usual Chinese term for the region, is confusing and incorrect. Rather, he proposes that the place should be called "Yindu," a name for India that is still in use in the modern Chinese language. However, his reasoning, instead of connecting the "correct" term to the river Indus (i.e., "Sindhu"), was that India should be compared to the moon (Ch. "Yindu"; Skt. "Indu") because

> it means that living beings live and die in the wheel of transmigration ceaselessly in the long night of ignorance without the rooster to announce the advent of the dawn. When the sun has sunk, candles continue to give light in the night. Although the stars are shining in the sky, how can they be as brilliant as the clear moon? (Li 1996: 49)

In the same section, Xuanzang also outlines the geography of Five Yindus 五印度, which according to him is "over ninety thousand *li* in circuit, with three sides facing the sea and the Snow Mountain at its back in the north" (Li 1996: 50). The measurement system, seasons, calendars, layout of cities, dresses and customs, languages, social divisions, and so forth are also methodically described.

The fact that Xuanzang's *Da Tang Xiyu ji* quickly became one of the most important reference works for geographical knowledge (and imagination) of India can be discerned from how it was employed by several contemporary writers. Daoxuan 道宣 (596–667), for example, used the information in the work to argue that South Asia, not China, should be considered the center of the world. He framed his conclusion not because the former was the source for

Buddhism in China, but from the study of geographical locations, including the positions of mountains and seas, found in *Da Tang Xiyu ji* (*Shijia fangzhi*, T. 2088: 949a–950c). Subsequently, during the Song dynasty, the Buddhist monk Zhipan 志磐 (fl. 1258–1269), as noted below, drafted a map of the Five Tianzhus based on Xuanzang's narrative. This idea of mapping Tianzhu based on *Da Tang Xiyu ji* was transmitted to Japan, where such drawings formed the source of Japanese imagination of South Asian geography until the seventeenth century (Rambelli 2014). The maps of South Asia, Rambelli (2014: 265) suggests, "may have been aids for the visualisation of mental trips to India, following the Chinese pilgrim, to the holy sites of the Buddha, to be used by Japanese monks who had given up the idea of real travel—or for whom, living in Edo period Japan, travel abroad was forbidden." The Japanese also created illustrations of various events described by Xuanzang, including his meeting with Silabhadra, the abbot of Nālandā, and the Buddhist procession organized by King Harṣa.

While Xuanzang traveled overland to South Asia and returned the same way, Yijing 義淨, who also visited Nālandā and wrote about the ways in which monastic rules were practiced in South Asia, journeyed by the maritime route. Yijing composed two works connected to his travels, *Nanhai jigui neifa zhuan* 南海寄歸內法傳 (A Record of Inner Dharma Sent Back from the Southern Seas)[17] and *Xiyu qiufa gaoseng zhuan* 西域求法高僧傳 (Biographies of Eminent Monks Who Went to the Western Regions in Search of the Dharma).[18] Both of these were completed in Palembang in Sumatra. The first work is perhaps the earliest comparative study of the customs and practices of Indians and Chinese, focused primarily on issues related to life in Buddhist monasteries. The latter is a biographical record of Chinese and Korean monks who traveled to South Asia during the seventh century.

There are several important details about South and Southeast Asian geography that Yijing provides as annotations to the *Nanhai jigui neifa zhuan.* For example, explaining the "frontiers" of Tian-zhu, he writes,

> All the places going eastward from Nālandā for five hundred post stops are known as the eastern frontier. At the extreme east there is the Great Black Mountain, which is, I reckon, the southern boundary of Tibet. It is said that it is southwest of Sichuan, from which one may reach this mountain after a journey of a little more than a month. Further to the south from here and close to the sea coast, there is the country of Srīkṣetra. Further to the southeast is the country of Lankasu. Further to the east is the country of Dvārapati. Further to the extreme east is the country of Linyi. (Li 2000: 12)

Since Yijing traveled by the sea route, his notice includes information about the maritime region between South Asia and Tang China. "In the Southern Seas there are more than ten countries," he reports and lists the islands of Malayu (which he says is now Śrīvijaya), Mohexin, Heling, Dada, Penpen, Poli, Kunlun, Bhoda-purea, Ashan, and Mojiaman. Yijing also provides the route, which merchants, and presumably he, took from Tang China to South Asia:

> Travelling due south on foot from Huanzhou for over a month, or for five or six high tides if going on board a ship, one may reach Bijing, and proceeding further south one arrives at Champa, that is, Linyi. . . . Travelling southwest for one month, one reaches the country of Banan, formerly called Funan. . . . This is the southern seaboard of Jambudvīpa; it is not an island in the sea. (Li 2000: 13)

Yijing's record is also important for extracting information about what people in South Asia knew about China. At one point, for example, he notes that, "In India it is said in praise [of the Chinese people] that as Mañjuśrī is now living in Bingzhou [in China], the people are blessed by his presence, and thus they should be admired and praised" (Li 2000: 146). Additionally, Yijing reports on the knowledge about Korea in Tianzhu. "The Cock-respecters is a name for the country of Korea used by the Indians, in whose language it is known as Kukkuṭeśvara, kukkuṭa meaning cock and Īśvara, respectable. It is said in India that cocks are respected as gods in Korea and that the people wear cocks' feathers by way of ornament" (Li 2000: 17).

Several Chinese sources corroborate Yijing's report about the knowledge of Bingzhou and Mount Wutai, the site of Mañjuśrī's reappearance, in South Asia. The most telling of these are the records by South Asian monks on pilgrimages to Mount Wutai located in the present-day Shaanxi Province. By the seventh century, Chinese Buddhist clergy, aided by their foreign collaborators, had manipulated Buddhist texts and commentaries and had promoted the idea of Mount Wutai as the abode of Mañjuśrī. Additionally, through the adornment of the mountain with Buddhist objects and paraphernalia, it was transformed into a sacred pilgrimage site within China. This belief spread rapidly to South Asia, attracting Buddhist monks who traveled to China expressly to pay homage to the Indian divinity purportedly living on a Chinese mountain (Sen 2003: 76–86).

The South Asian pilgrims to Mount Wutai went to China via both overland and maritime routes. To help these monks travel between the two regions, bilingual phrase books were composed. One such document (P. 5538, in Bailey 1938) was found in a Chinese border town called Zhangye 張掖 located in present-day Gansu Province. A dialogue provided in this phrase book, which appears in both Sanskrit and Khotanese, reads,

Whence have you come?
I have come from Khotan
When did you come from India?
Two years ago.
Where did you stay in Khotan?
I stayed in a saṅghārāma.

In which saṅghārāma did you stay? Did you duly see the king or not?
I duly saw him.
Now where are you going?
I am going to China.
What is your business in China?
I shall see the Bodhisattva Mañjuśrī.
When will you return here?
I shall see China and afterwards return.
(Bailey 1938: 528–529)

The above document is a rare non-Chinese-language source that confirms the diffusion of information from China to South Asia and suggests that knowledge about Chinese geography may have circulated as widely in South Asia as it did in the other direction.

Diplomatic exchanges between the Tang court and South Asian polities were frequent when Xuanzang and Yijing made their journeys. The multiple trips of the Tang diplomat Wang Xuance 王玄策 are the most notable, especially for the contributions they made toward the circulation of information and knowledge between China and South Asia. Wang had audiences with several South Asian rulers, he traveled to Nepal and Kanauj by the route through Tibet (something neither Xuanzang nor Yijing had done), and he took with him artists who sketched images of the Buddha and other Buddhist artifacts and drew maps of the regions the missions toured (Sen 2003). The maps and illustrations were included in a book titled *Zhong Tianzhu xing ji* 中天竺行記 (Records of Travels in Middle Tianzhu), which Wang composed in 666. While the book is now lost and none of the maps are any longer available, passages from his text are cited in several Chinese Buddhist works.[19]

Also lost are the maps that were drawn by Jia Dan 賈耽 (730–805), a high-ranking Tang official and one of the most prolific geographers of the period. Jia Dan, who held various offices and titles, including that of *youpushe* 右僕射, was known for his archery skills, love for hunting, and keen interest in geography. He made it a point to meet with foreign emissaries and made detailed inquiries about the topography, customs, and practices of their lands. He also examined the various routes between Tang China and foreign regions. Based on the information he collected, Jia Dan produced several geographical works and maps, including *Huanghua sida ji* 皇華四達記 (Records of Imperial Embassies to the Four Directions), *Hainei Huayi tu* 海內華夷圖 (Map of Chinese and Barbarian [Regions] within the Seas), and *Gujin junguo xiandao siyi shu* 古今郡國縣道四夷述 (Descriptions of Commanderies, Counties, Circuits, and the Four Barbarians from Past to Present). The *Hainei Huayi tu* was reportedly one of the largest geographical charts drawn in China. It may have depicted a large part of the Asian continent. Specifically pertaining to South Asia, Jia Dan drafted detailed itineraries from the Yunnan region to present-day Assam and the maritime route from the coastal region of Tang China to South Asia.[20]

Jia Dan's informants must have included Muslim traders from the Persian Gulf, a region that also formed part of his geographical works. These traders were gradually emerging as important intermediaries between China and South Asia. This is evident not only from Chinese sources but also from Arabic writings from the ninth century. Two such works are Ibn Khurdadhbih's (c. 820–c. 912) *Kitāb al-Masālik w'al- Mamālik* (The Book of Roads and Kingdoms), completed some time in 846–847, and *Akhbār al-Ṣin wa'l-Hind*, which forms part of Abu Zayd al-Sirafi's *Silsilat al-Tawarikh* (The Chain of Histories). Ibn Khurdadhbih and Abu Zayd collected their information about India and China from traders and sailors based in present-day Iraq. Similar to Jia Dan, Ibn Khurdadhbih wrote about the route between the Yunnan region and Assam, mentioning specifically the polity of Qamrun (Kāmarūpa, that ruled most of Assam), which according to him "adjoins China" and traded in rhinoceros horns and cowries (Ahmad 1989: 6, 27). Abu Zayd describes the sea route between Guangzhou and South Asia, which also parallels Jia Dan's record on the maritime connections.

Additionally, similar to Yijing, Abu Zayd provides a detailed comparison of the practices and customs of Indians and Chinese.

The works of Jia Dan, Ibn Khurdadhbih, and Abu Zayd point to two important changes taking place with regard to the circulations of information and knowledge between South Asia and China. First, the agency of Buddhism in these circulations was subsiding in the ninth century as Chinese monks composed no new descriptions of the Buddhist holy land. Second, maritime trade and connections between the coastal areas of the two regions became more vigorous after this period, leading to the emergence of seafaring traders as the main source of information and knowledge. As a result, the post-ninth-century circulation of geographical knowledge pertains mostly to the coastal regions. However, as is argued here, this took place at the cost of the loss of knowledge about the hinterland areas, which were the main focus of the Buddhist writers.

The Knowledge [Only] of the Coastal Regions

The above-mentioned transitions had a significant impact on the ways in which knowledge circulated between South Asia and China from the tenth century onward. Seafaring traders emerged as the main informants in the early second millennium, and, at the same time, some of the major works on foreign regions composed in China were written by officials and scholars based in the coastal regions. As a consequence, several differences can be discerned between the earlier Chinese records on South Asia and those that were composed after the tenth century. First, records on South Asia compiled between the eleventh and the mid-thirteenth century were based on secondhand accounts, collected, it seems, from West and Southeast Asian traders. These works mostly concentrated on the commercial aspects, often listing the main products produced and exported by these South Asian polities, with brief ethnographical overviews. Second, while the earlier records of the Buddhist travelers concentrated on the cities and towns in the hinterland areas, the later notices, even those that were composed by Chinese writers who visited South Asia after the mid-thirteenth century, focused primarily on the coastal regions. Third, as a result of this concentration on the coastal regions, several polities located on the Coromandel and Malabar coasts, such as Calicut and Cochin, appear disjoined from the rest of South Asia. In other words, the geographical locations of South Asian coastal polities vis-à-vis the hinterland regions were not clear to the Chinese writers. Fourth, there seems to have been significant confusion in the understanding of South Asian religions, especially Buddhism, in the later works. Brahmanical temples, for example, were frequently recorded in these sources as Buddhist monasteries.

Lingwai daida 嶺外代答 (Responses to [Questions about] the Land beyond the Passes) and *Zhufan zhi* 諸蕃志 (Records of the Various Barbarians) are two representative works from the Song period when the Chinese court actively promoted and administered maritime trade. The authors of these works had direct contact with foreign traders from whom they collected most of their information on foreign polities. Zhou Qufei 周去非, the author of *Lingwai daida*, served as the deputy governor of Guilin in southern Guangxi Province, and Zhao Rugua 趙汝适, who wrote *Zhufan zhi*, worked at the *tijushibo* 提舉市舶 (Bureau of Maritime Commerce) in Quanzhou in the early thirteenth century.[21] Completed in 1178, Zhou Qufei's *Lingwai daida* mentions the following South Asian regions and polities: Gulin 故臨 (Quilon/Kollam), Zhunian 注輦 (Chola), Xilanguo 錫蘭國 (Sri Lanka), and Xi Tian Nannihualuo 西天南尼華囉 (Veraval, Gujarat?). Gulin is noted as a place near Arabia, requiring about a seventy-day journey on ship from Song China through Lanli 藍里 (in present-day Sumatra). The people of the polity are described as worshipers of the Buddha, who rode elephants, while the rulers venerated cows. The work also points out that Chinese seafaring traders going to Arabia had to transfer to smaller ships at Gulin. Zhunian is reported as being part of "Nan Yindu" 南印度 (South Yindu) in "Xitian" 西天 (Western Heaven). According to Zhou, it could be reached on a boat from Gulin and also from Pugan 蒲甘 (Pagan, in present-day Burma). In the region called "Xitian zhuguo" 西天諸國 ("various polities of Western Heaven"), Zhou says there are several hundred polities, the most renowned of which were Wangshe cheng 王舍城 (Rājagṛha), Tian-zhu, and Zhong Yindu 中印度. He continues,

> Because it covers the sites where the Buddha clan was born, it has multiple names 蓋佛氏所生, 故其名重也. It is said that to its east are Heishui 黑水 (Black Water, i.e., Nu River), Yuhe 淤河 (Irrawaddy), and Dahai 大海 (Great Sea, i.e., the Bay of Bengal). Beyond these across the east [*sic*] are the regions of Xiyu 西域 (Western Regions), Tubo 吐蕃 (Tibet), Dali 大理, Jiaozhi 交趾. To its west is the Dong Dashi hai 東大食海 (Arabian Sea). Beyond it across the west are the various polities of Arabia 大食諸國. To its south there is an island called Xilanguo 細蘭國, which also has a sea called Xilan hai 細蘭海. Previously, the envoy Zhang Qian in Daxia heard that the Shendu polity was one thousand li southeast of Daxia. He also learned that from the polity of Dali to Wangshe cheng was no more than forty [days of] travel. According to Jia Dan's *Huanghua sida ji*, "Tianzhu is reachable from Annan." Additionally, Damo 達摩 (i.e., Bodhidharma) arrived [in China] through the seas to Panyu 番禺 (i.e., Guangzhou).

In another section of the book, Zhou records that the Tianzhu polity was a colony of the Daqin 大秦 polity (indicating, perhaps, the Ghaznavid Empire).

Zhao Rugua composed *Zhufan zhi* in 1225 and reproduced some of the information collected in *Lingwai daida*, frequently quoting the work verbatim. For instance, he also states that Tianzhu was subordinate to Daqin. "Its rulers are," Zhao adds, "all appointed by Daqin." The rest of the record on Tianzhu in *Zhufan zhi* is very confusing, often mixing information about Daqin and notices on

Tianzhu found in earlier Chinese sources. It says, for example, that Tianzhu traded with Funan, a polity that had ceased to exist by the eighth century. Separate entries are given for Nanpi 南毗, Gulin, Huchala 胡茶辣 (Gujarat), Maluohua 麻囉華 (Malwa), and Zhunian, without connecting them to the geography of Tianzhu.

Lingwai daida and *Zhufan zhi* reflect the beginning of confusion about South Asian geography that perplexed Chinese writers through to the late nineteenth century. Zhou Qufei and Zhao Rugua were evidently unable to reconcile the names for South Asian polities that had appeared in earlier Chinese sources with the information they were receiving in the thirteenth century. They did not have a clear sense of the similarities and differences between Xitian, Tianzhu, and Yindu. They were probably unable to verify the overall concept of Indian or South Asian geography from their informants who, on one hand, had no understanding of the terms employed in Chinese sources and, on the other, were themselves in contact with or represented a specific location or polity in South Asia. The use of Zhou Qufei and Zhao Rugua's jumbled descriptions of India and South Asian polities by later writers perpetuated this confusion. The report of the subjugation of Tianzhu by Daqin or of the Cholas by Śrīvijaya, which appears not only in *Zhufan zhi* but also in other Song sources,[22] may have resulted from the deliberate manipulation of information by the seafaring traders arriving in Song China from diverse regions of the Indian Ocean world, some with self-serving commercial and political agendas.

The fact that information about South Asia was deliberately manipulated can be discerned from the triangular contacts between Song China, Śrīvijaya, and the Chola polity. As the leading intermediary, the thalassocratic state of Śrīvijaya is reported in Chinese sources to have obstructed the flow of commodities from the Indian Ocean regions to Song China. It also seems to have supplied inaccurate information about its subjugation of the Cholas to the Song court. By portraying Chola as a vassal state, Śrīvijayan representatives would have been able to convince the Song officials to offer trade privileges and other benefits to their tribute carriers. The status of foreign polities, which entailed the privileges and benefits tribute carriers received from the Song court, was fixed based on their military prowess. The report on the subjugation of Tianzhu by Daqin in *Lingwai daida* and *Zhufan zhi* may also have resulted from similar attempts by traders and tribute carriers, who were often the same people (Hartwell 1989; Sen 2003), to obtain privileges at the Song court. Song scribes and officials at the coastal regions had no direct/independent sources with which to compare the information about faraway polities provided by these seafaring traders. In the case of Śrīvijaya, the flow of information about the South Asian polity in Song China continued to be monopolized by the Southeast Asians even after a massive naval raid on Śrīvijayan ports by the Cholas in 1025 (Sen 2009).

This confusion about South Asian geography during the Song period also extended to Buddhist authors. Zhipan, who between 1265 and 1271 composed the massive Buddhist historical work called *Fozu tongji* 佛祖統紀 (General Record of the Lineage of the Buddha), attempted to explain Buddhist cosmology and geography with the use of maps (Park 2010). The three maps included in his work, titled "Dong Zhendan dili tu" 東震旦地理圖 (Illustration of the Geography of China in the East), "Han Xiyu zhuguo tu" 漢西域諸國圖 (Illustration of the Various Polities in the Western Regions during Han), and "Xitu Wu-Yin zhi tu" 西土五印之圖 (Illustration of the Five Yindu in the Western Lands; see figure 1.4), made use of information about China as well as South, Southeast, and Central Asia available to Zhipan during the time of writing. However, Zhipan was unable to reconcile the differences between South Asian place-names used by Xuanzang in the seventh century and those appearing in the Song sources. As a result, he uses a combination of new and old designations, with the coastal regions named according to Song sources and the hinterland areas based on Xuanzang's text (*Fozu tongji*, T. 2035: 312a17–19). Thus, while knowledge about the costal polities of South Asia had clearly expanded during the Song period, Tianzhu, as a geographical entity, became a confusing concept among Chinese writers.

Even during the Yuan and early Ming periods, when interactions with South Asia were vibrant, with frequent visits to the region by traders and court officials from China, this inability to resolve the differences between the earlier records and the information entering through the maritime commercial and diplomatic channels continued. Wang Dayuan 王大淵, the author of *Daoyi zhilüe* 島夷誌略, traveled twice to South Asia with Chinese traders and completed this work in 1349 (Su 1981: 10). Although he records over twenty South Asian polities, several of which he visited personally, Wang was unable to link any of them to the larger entity Tianzhu found in earlier sources and also in his own work. The brief note on Tianzhu in *Daoyi zhilüe* is extremely vague. Wang reports that it was locat-

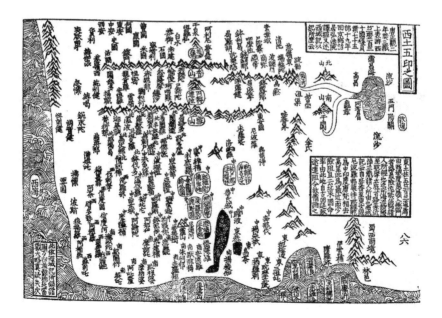

Figure 1.4.   The map of Five Indias, *Fozu tongji*.

ed to the "east of Arabia" 居大食之東, about 200 li from the sea, and had a "Qinwang" 秦王 as the ruler. Scholars have suggested that Wang was most likely indicating only the Sindh region in present-day Pakistan (Su 1981: 356–357). Qinwang, Su Jiqing (1981: 357) suggests, might indicate the Samma polity (c. 1351–c.1524) in that region.[23]

Within a century of the composition of Wang's book, several works associated with the expeditions of Zheng He appeared in Ming China. These include Ma Huan's 馬歡 (c. 1380–1460) *Yingyai shenglan* 瀛涯勝覽 (Overall Survey of the Ocean's Shores), written in 1433; Gong Zhen's 鞏珍 (fl. 1430s) *Xiyang Fanguo zhi* 西洋番國誌 (Records of the Barbarian Polities in the Western Oceans), written in 1434; and Fei Xin's 費信 (c. 1385–?) *Xingcha shenglan* 西洋番國誌 (Overall Survey of the Star Raft), composed in 1436. None of these works, or the related navigational chart known as the "Maokun map" 茅坤圖 or the "Zheng He hanghai tu" 鄭和航海圖 (Navigational Chart of the Zheng He Expeditions), deal specifically with Shendu/Tianzhu/Yindu. While several South Asian polities, regions, and towns, both in the coastal regions and in the hinterland, are recorded and sometimes indicated as part of one of the Five Yindus, there is no indication that these writers had a clear sense of the geographical contours of South Asia. Fei Xin's *Xingcha shenglan*, for example, places Bengal in Xi Tianzhu (West Tianzhu). Another Ming source, *Shuyu zhouzi lu* 殊域周咨錄 (Records of Inquiries about Faraway Regions), compiled by Yan Congjian 嚴從簡 (fl. 1530s–1570s) in 1574, confusingly writes about Bengal saying that it "was originally a prefecture of ancient Xindu 忻都, which is Xi Tianzhu. Tianzhu has five polities, this is the Dong Tianzhu polity, although some say that it is [actually] the Xi Tianzhu polity" (榜葛剌, 本古忻都州府, 即西天竺也。天竺有印度國五, 此東印度國, 或云此西印度國。). The *Huang Ming siyi kao* 皇明四夷考 (Examination of the Four Barbarians during the Imperial Ming), composed by Zheng Xiao 鄭曉 (1499–1566) in

1564, notes, "Western Heaven (Xitian 西天) has the Five Indian polities. Bengal is the East India[n polity]" (西天有五印度國。榜葛剌者, 東印度也。).

The above perplexities with the location of Bengal probably resulted from the continued misunderstanding of the nomenclature "Xitian," "Xi Tianzhu" (West India), "Tianzhu," and "Yindu" that was already evident during the Song period. Some writers seem to presume that "Xitian" was a contracted form of "Xi Tianzhu," and others believed that there were five "Tianzhu" polities, which together were called "Yindu." The fact that several southern polities, such as Guli 古里 (Calicut) and Kezhi 柯枝 (Cochin), are not mentioned in relationship to either Tianzhu or Yindu indicates that the Yuan and Ming writers were probably unaware of the exact location of these polities in the broader context of South Asian geography.

The concept of Tianzhu was baffling but was no longer really a concern for the Yuan and Ming writers as they were unable to empirically locate the entity. Court representatives traveled to South Asia through both maritime and overland routes, visiting not only the coastal regions but also places such as Delhi, Bengal, and the Buddhist pilgrimage site Bodh Gaya. In fact, during the early Ming period, the envoy named Hou Xian 候顯 (fl. 1403–1427) went to Bengal and Bodh Gaya by both the overland route through Tibet and the maritime route from Sumatra. However, since no one locally used the terms "Tianzhu," "Shendu," or "Yindu" (or "Sindhu," the original source of these words), these visitors, similar to the Yuan and Ming writers mentioned above, would have found it difficult to achieve any correlation between the subregional polities they encountered and the larger geographical entity named and constructed by the Chinese in the previous millennium.

It was only after the end of the Ming court's engagement with the maritime world that a serious attempt was made to understand the geographical contours of Shendu/Tianzhu/Yindu. Luo Yueji-

ong's 羅曰褧 *Xianbin lu* 咸賓錄 (Records of Tribute Guests), completed in 1591, has one of the most detailed description of Tianzhu
from the Yuan-Ming period. Luo Yuejiong's work, as Leo K. Shin
(2012: 289–290) has explained, was part of the sixteenth-century
interest in human diversity among Ming-dynasty scholars. It stands
out, as Shin points out, for the breadth of research, which included
consultation of 345 works and the description of over 100 foreign
groups and polities. Luo collates information on Shendu, Tianzhu,
and Yindu from various earlier sources, from *Shi ji* to the more
recent Ming records. He describes the visit of Hou Xian to Zhaona-
puer 詔納樸兒 (Jaunpur) as well as embassies that arrived at the
Ming court from Bengal in the fifteenth century. However, the
collating of records on Shendu/Tianzhu/Yindu does not seem to
have helped Luo resolve the earlier confusion among Yuan and
Ming writers. The opening passage in the section for Tianzhu, for
example, has the following description:

> Tianzhu, also called Shendu, is a large polity. It is over 30,000 li
> in area and is divided into the Middle, East, South, West, and
> North, the Five Tianzhu polities (Wu Tianzhu guo 五天竺國);
> that is, the so-called Five Yindus (Wu Yindu 五印度). Each
> polity has a king, and each place is several thousand li [in area
> or circumference?]. East Yindu neighbors Funan and Champa,
> but [is] separated by a small sea 小海. South Yindu borders a
> great sea 大海. West Yindu is connected to Jibin and Posi 波斯,
> [and] North [Yindu] is near the Snowy Mountain 雪山, with
> mountains on all four sides 四面皆山.

Luo clearly was unable to account for the political changes that
had taken place in South Asia and the neighboring regions over the
course of several centuries. He also could not explain the relationship between the subregional polities encountered during the Ming
period and the preexisting concept of dividing the larger region of
Shendu/Tianzhu/Yindu into five parts. Moreover, similar to the
Yuan and Ming writers before him, Luo did not know how to place

the coastal polities within the context of the fivefold division of Shendu/Tianzhu/Yindu. Luo also includes a very odd description of a place he calls "Poluomen" 婆羅門, a term that was used to refer to the Brahmins. "Poluomen," he explains, "is the ancient Shizi 師子國 (Sri Lanka) polity. It has been in contact [with China] since the Eastern Jin period, when it was a vassal state of Tianzhu."

Some of Luo's views were shared by Shen Maoshang 慎懋賞, who wrote the work titled *Siyi guangji* sometime after 1598.[24] The work is noteworthy, as mentioned above, because of the detailed discussion of Bengali script and the inclusion of a fairly accurate Bengali–Chinese lexicon. The information on Bengali language most likely came from one of the many translators/interpreters engaged in commercial exchanges between Bengal and Ming China (see the next chapter). However, Shen, similar to Luo Yuejiong, displays limited understanding of South Asian geography when he writes,

> The polity of Bengal, that is the Tianzhu polity, was the Shendu of Han [times]. Some say it is called Magadha and [some call it] Poluomen. To the east it reaches the sea and the border of Champa, to the west to Jibin and Posi, some say to the Jingangbaozuo 金剛寶座 (Vajrasena, i.e., Bodh Gaya) polity, which is also called Zhaonamoer 詔納模兒 (Juanpur). To the South it reaches the sea and north it extends to the Congling 蔥嶺 ranges. It is 30,000 *li* [in area] and is divided into East, West, South, North, and Middle, the Five Tianzhus.

Mathew Mosca in his extensive study of the Qing encounter with South Asian geography has pointed out the issue of "incommensurability" that resulted in the appearance of jumbled records on Shendu/Tianzhu/Yindu. "New sources constantly emerged," he writes (2013: 32), "giving more raw information about little-known parts of the outside world, but at the same time increasing the number of names and concepts with which geographers had to wrestle. As the numbers of variables increased within an intellectual environment that valued wide reading, there emerged a cacophony of conflicting opinions rather than a coherent synthesis." He rightly points out that the incommensurability among the Chinese accounts "rose simply from India's diversity" and because "information about India reached China after being encoded in different languages and intellectual traditions, and adjusted to meet the needs of competing religions and political loyalties" (2013: 64). However, the main problem with these later sources seems to be the valiant effort of the Chinese writers to preserve the earlier fivefold division of Shendu/Tianzhu/Yindu. No matter how much new information they received about South Asian polities, these writers, perhaps because of their attempt to understand the region through their logic of the administrative categories of a centralized state, tried to fit them all within that dated geographical construct. This also prevented them from placing politics such as Calicut and Cochin within this larger geographical entity. Finally, as noted earlier, the information system that was previously fostered by the traveling Buddhist monks and their writings ceased to exist by the tenth century, contributing to the confusion about South Asian geography. The new data, no matter how new or voluminous, only offered localized perspectives and not the larger viewpoint that the Chinese Buddhist monks strove to achieve when mapping their holy land.

No comparable tradition of mapping, gathering information, and writing accounts of foreign geographies seems to have existed in South Asia. As with the earlier periods, there are no notices of China and its geography during the first half of the second millennium. However, several tangential reports make it clear, as was the case previously, that knowledge about China was available to South Asian polities and merchant guilds. These polities and merchant guilds seem to have been aware of the markets in Song and Yuan China, the rulers of China, and the naval prowess of the early Ming court. It can be inferred that they also had knowledge of ports in China and the routes that led them to these places. Additionally, they were cognizant of the fact that intermediaries tried to obstruct direct trade with China. A Tamil inscription from a temple in Tanjavur, which records the Chola raid on Southeast Asian ports in 1025, is indicative of geographical knowledge of foreign regions available in South Asia. The inscription records that the Chola king Rājēndra,

> having dispatched many ships in the midst of the rolling sea and having caught Sanāma-vijayōttunga-varman, the king of Kaḍāram, together with the elephants in his glorious army, (took) the large heap of treasure, which (that king) had rightfully accumulated; (captured) with noise the (arch called) Vidyādharatōraṇa at the "war-gate" of his extensive city; Śri Vijaya with the "jewelled wicket-gate" adorned with great splendor and the "gate of large jewels"; Paṇṇai with water in its bathing ghats; the ancient Malaiyūr with the strong mountain for its rampart; Māyiruḍingam, surrounded by the deep sea (as) by a moat; Ilangāśōka (i.e., Lankāśōka) undaunted (in) fierce battles; Māpappāram having abundant (deep) water as defense; Mēviḷimbangam having fine walls as defense; Vaḷaippandūru having Viḷappandūru (?); Talaittakkōlam praised by great men (versed in) the sciences; Mādamālingam, firm in great and fierce battles; Ilāmuridēśam, whose fierce strength rose in war; Mānakkavāram, in whose extensive flower gardens honey was collecting; and Kaḍāram, of fierce strength, which was protected by the deep sea. (Nilakanta Sastri 1935: 1.254–255)

Several of the Southeast Asian ports mentioned in the above inscription were important transit centers for trade with Song China and were controlled by the Śrīvijayan polity, which, as mentioned above, may have been supplying false information about the Cholas to the Chinese court. Information about these ports and the role of Śrīvijaya in maritime trade with Song China would have been easily available to the Chola court through Tamil merchant guilds located in Southeast Asia. In fact, one of these guilds seems to have expanded into Quanzhou after the raid of 1025 (Sen 2009). A Tamil

inscription erected by members of this guild also corroborates the
fact that knowledge about China must have also existed in South
Asia. Dated 1281, it records,

> Obeisance to Hara (Śiva). Let there be prosperity! On the day
> (having) the Chitrā (asterism) in the month of Chittirai of the
> Śaka year 1203 (April 1281), the Tavachchakkaravatigaḷ *alias*
> Sambandhap-perumāḷ caused, in accordance with the *firman* of
> Chekachai-Khān, to be graciously installed the God Uḍaiyār
> Tirukkadalīśvaram Uḍaiya-nāyinār, for the welfare of the illus-
> trious body of the illustrious Chekachai-Khan. (Subramaniam
> 1978: 8)

"Chekachai-Khan" in the above inscription has been identified as
either Kublai Khan or his son Jurji (Karashima 1988).

   Knowledge about the political situation in China among South
Asians can be similarly extracted from Chinese textual records. In
the 1280s, an official of Ma'bar, a polity that replaced the Cholas
on the Coromandel coast, sought, and was subsequently given, asylum in Yuan China. The wish to defect to Yuan China by the
person named Buali 不阿里 (Abū 'Alī?) was related to a visiting
Yuan envoy to the Coromandel coast. The offer that Abū 'Alī made
to the envoy in exchange for asylum entailed submission, albeit
symbolically, of neighboring South Asian polities to the Yuan
court, something Kublai Khan had been trying to obtain in order to
demonstrate his status as the legitimate khan of the Mongol Empire
(Sen 2006b). Making the offer to the Yuan envoy, Abū 'Alī noted,

> When [they] heard that Celestial (that is, Yuan) envoys had
> come [to Ma'bar], the people were told to portray their kingdom
> (that is, Ma'bar) as poor and lowly. These are all lies. All the
> gold, pearls and precious objects of the Muslim kingdoms are
> produced in this country. Moreover, Muslim [merchants] all
> come here to trade. It is known that various kingdoms [in this
> region] are willing to submit [to the Yuan court]. If [the present
> ruler of] Ma'bar surrenders, my envoys, carrying letters [from

me], will go and summon these kingdoms. They can all be persuaded to submit [to the Yuan court].

Other sources from Yuan China, including the funerary inscription of Abū ʿAlī, confirm the validity of this episode (Liu n.d.; Sen 2006b).

Also apparent from this episode is the intra-Asian network of connections and movements. According to the funerary inscription of Abū ʿAlī, preserved in the fourteenth-century collection of epithets titled *Zhong'an ji* 中俺集 (Collection of [Records from the] Middle Hut), his family was originally from Helahedi 合剌合低 (Qalhat, Amman?). Abū ʿAlī's father migrated to the Coromandel coast and became one of the members of the ruling elite (Liu n.d.; Chen 1980). After Abū ʿAlī defected to Yuan China, the Yuan court rewarded him with a Korean wife named Cai 蔡 (Kor. Chʾae). This woman happened to be the daughter of the Korean official named Chʾae Inʾgyu 蔡仁揆/채송년, with whom Abū ʿAlī established contact by sending gifts through a tribute carrier in 1298. These connections across Asia in the thirteenth century through Abū ʿAlī and his family are recorded in the Korean works *Koryŏsa* 高麗史 (History of the Koryŏ [Kingdom]) and *Tongguk tʾonggam* 東國通鑑 (Comprehensive Mirror for the Eastern Kingdom), completed in 1451 and 1485, respectively. They report that,

[In the sixth lunar month of the twenty-fourth year of King Chʾungʾyŏl (Ch. Zhonglie) 忠烈 (i.e., 1298)], Pʾaehali, the prince of Maʾbar, sent an embassy to [the Korean court] to present a cap stitched with silver threads, handkerchiefs embroidered with gold, five *jin* thirteen *liang* (about seven pounds) of aloeswood, and two rolls of native cotton-cloth. Previously, the king had given the daughter of Chʾae Inʾgyu in marriage to [the Yuan] chief minister Sangha 桑哥. [After] Sangha was executed [by the Yuan court], the emperor (i.e., Qubilai Khan, r. 1260–1294) presented the woman Chʾae to Pʾaehali. [Because] Pʾaehali was at odds with the ruler of his country, [he] defected to Yuan [China] and has been residing in Quanzhou. And now,

because of [his marriage to] Ch'ae, [P'aehali] has sent an envoy
to [establish a channel of] communication with the Korean king.
(*Koryŏsa* 33: 676a; Sen 2006b: 315)

Similarly, intra-Asian, in fact Afroeurasian, connections can be
discerned from the travels and writing of Ibn Baṭūṭah. The Moroccan reached Delhi in 1333 after traveling through Mecca. He
worked at the court of the Delhi Sultanate from 1334 to 1341 before making a trip to China. His mission to China was in response
to an embassy from the Yuan court that had arrived in Delhi in
1340. Ibn Baṭūṭah suggests that people in South Asia were aware of
the maritime routes to Yuan China and that several people, including Islamic religious preachers, were frequently traveling between
the two regions (*The Travels of Ibn Baṭṭuṭa* 4: 894–895). The presence of such sojourning people and even Ibn Baṭūṭah's own journey from Delhi to Quanzhou, on which he embarked in 1341, demonstrates that geographical knowledge and information about China
existed in South Asia despite the lack of further extant written
evidence. The same would have been true a century later, when the
naval armada led by Zheng He sailed across the Indian Ocean. The
king of Bengal, aware of the naval prowess of the Ming fleet, is
noted to have sent a letter to the Yongle emperor requesting help in
a war against the neighboring polity of Jaunpur (Sen 2011). This
and other episodes related to Zheng He's expeditions are discussed
in chapter 3. It can be concluded, based on these tangential sources,
that during the first half of the second millennium, as in the previous centuries, knowledge circulated between South Asia and China
and that several groups of people in these two regions had some
basic understanding, distorted and confused as it may have been, of
the geographical contours, routes, and leading sites of interaction at
each place.

CIRCULATIONS OF TECHNICAL KNOWLEDGE

The circulations of geographical knowledge between South Asia and China during the first millennium, as evident from the above discussion, were intimately linked to Buddhist exchanges. Buddhism was also the main agency, as outlined in this section, through which the transfer of ideas and methods of astral science and medical cures took place. In addition, John Kieschnick (2003) has pointed to several objects, initially unfamiliar to the Chinese, that entered China with the spread of Buddhism. These included the monk's robe, the rosary, the chair, and, as discussed below, sugar. Kieschnick further explains the ways in which Buddhism contributed to the diffusion of bridge-building and tea-drinking traditions in China.[25] However, as emphasized earlier, this does not imply that Buddhism was the only conduit through which the transfer of knowledge and objects took place. Merchants, as discussed in the next chapter, from diverse ethnic backgrounds contributed to such circulations as well. Moreover, it is important to identify some of the non-Buddhist professionals from South Asia who were active in China, working as astronomers and physicians. This role of non-Buddhists, including Hindu and Islamic traders and preachers from Tamil lands, grew significantly after the tenth century, when Buddhism was no longer the main channel for the circulation of knowledge between South Asia and China.

Three aspects of the circulation of technical knowledge in specific fields are examined in this section. The first part focuses on the "sciences of the heavens," as Joseph Needham and Wang Ling (1959) terms them, which include the subfields of mathematics, astronomy, calendar making, and astrology. Also briefly outlined are the religious applications of knowledge associated with the study of the heavens appearing in stylistic images and representations. The second section examines the circulations of medical knowledge and healing practices. This includes the quest for South Asian immortality drugs and physicians by several Chinese rulers.

The final part of the section explores the transfer of three key
technologies that took place between South Asia and China prior to
the sixteenth century. These were the sugar-making technology that
was imported from Zhong Tianzhu during the Tang period, the
introduction of Chinese gunpowder technology into South Asia,
and the Chinese method of papermaking that reached South Asia in
the thirteenth–fourteenth centuries. Together these examples demonstrate the varied routes and agencies through which the circulations of knowledge, ideas, and techniques between South Asia and
China took place and the ways in which they were eventually incorporated into local traditions.

Computing and Representing the Heavenly Bodies

The transmission of Buddhism to China not only generated a need
to understand the geographical terrain of South Asia, as discussed
above, but also necessitated a comprehension of the cosmological
framework of the Buddhist teachings. In this process, people in
China, both Buddhists and non-Buddhists, encountered Indic notions of the terrestrial world, the planetary system, and the larger
cosmos that differed significantly from the ideas and beliefs existing in China. Texts and images entering China from South Asia,
and on some occasions from Central Asia, played a crucial role in
introducing Buddhist notions of the cosmos, which were connected
to the unique Indic concept of reincarnation. Indeed, Buddhism had
a tremendous impact on Chinese eschatological tradition, as the
idea of continuous rebirth and the existence of multilayered terrestrial and extraterrestrial realms made life after death a complex
issue. Fate prognostication, the connection between karma and rebirth, and the notions of paradise, heavens, and hells propagated by
the Buddhists all required knowledge and imagination of heavenly
bodies and realms.

The Buddhist notion of the cosmos was based on ancient Brahmanical views, which in places such as Gandhāra and Central Asia

mixed with Hellenistic concepts. After entering China, these ideas merged with local beliefs and practices. Thus, in some of the Buddhist texts and images, especially those associated with Tantric Buddhism, all three traditions (i.e., Indic, Hellenistic, and Chinese) can be discerned. This mixture of traditions also took place in the mathematical methods used to compute the movement of heavenly bodies for drafting calendars. The Chinese made a distinction between South Asians who were skilled at the empirical study of the heavens, those who propagated the extraterrestrial realms as part of Buddhist teachings, and those who were interested in the prognostication of fate through what Shigeru Nakayama (1969) and Nathan Sivin (1989) have called "horoscopic astrology."[26]

Niu Weixing (2004) has examined in detail the role of Buddhism in transmitting astronomical knowledge from South Asia to China. He does so through a detailed analysis of translated Buddhist texts that introduced Indic numerals; measurement systems; theories of the cosmos; the system of luminaries and lunar lodges; concepts related to the sun, moon, and planetary classifications; and the practice of calendar making. One of the earliest Buddhist texts that transmitted Indic ideas concerning the Seven and Nine Luminaries (*qiyao* 七曜/*jiuyao* 九曜; Skt. *saptagrahāḥ/navagrahāḥ*), twenty-eight constellations (Skt. *nakṣatra*), and seasonal variations was the *Modeng qie jing* 摩登伽經 translated by Zhu Lüyan 竺律炎 and Zhi Qian 支謙 in 230 (Schafer 1977a: 10). Explanations for lunar and solar eclipses and the names of zodiac signs were also available in some of the later translations. These translations seem to have played a salient role in informing the courts and calendar makers in China about Indic ways of observing and calculating the movements of heavenly bodies, which resulted in the introduction of new texts, several of them non-Buddhist, and the influx of specialists in the fields of astronomy and mathematics from South Asia to China during the seventh and eighth centuries.[27]

The *Sui shu* 隋書 (History of the Sui Dynasty) records several astronomy-related texts of South Asian origin that were circulating in Sui China. Only the titles of these works have survived. They include *Poluomen tianwen jing* 婆羅門天文經 in twenty-one *juan*, *Polumen Jiejia xianren tianwen shuo* 婆羅門竭伽仙人天文說 in thirty *juan*, *Polumen tianwen* 婆羅門天文 in one *juan*, *Poluomen suanfa* 婆羅門算法 in three *juan*, *Poluomen yinyang suanli* 婆羅門陰陽算歷 in one *juan*, *Poluomen suanjing* 婆羅門算經 in three *juan*, and *Jiejia xianren zhan meng shu* 竭伽仙人占夢書 in one *juan* (*Sui shu* 34: 1019). Although the titles indicate that these were mostly Brahmanical texts, Buddhist monks would have been involved in translating them. A South Asian monk named Damoliuzhi 達摩流支, for example, translated a text titled *Polumen tianwen* 婆羅門天文 in twenty *juan* for the Northern Zhou ruler Yu Wenhu 余文護. However, as this text did not belong to the Buddhist tradition, it was, according to the Buddhist catalog *Kaiyuan shijiao lu* (T. 2154: 544c29), not preserved in the canon (今以非三藏教故不存之).

Chinese Buddhist texts also describe the skills of Brahmins in the fields of astronomy and calendar making. Yang Jingfeng 楊景風, who held the post of *xiaguan* 夏官 (summer officer) during the reign of the Tang ruler Dezong and annotated the famous Buddhist astronomical text titled *Wenshushili Pusa ji zhuxian suoshuo jixiong shi ri shane xiuyao jing* 文殊師利菩薩及諸仙所說吉凶時日善惡宿曜經 (T. 1299), opined that "[t]hose who wish to know the positions of the five planets adopt Indian calendrical methods. One can thus predict what *xiu* a planet will be traversing" 凡欲知五星所在分者, 據天竺曆術; 推知何宿具知也 (T. 1299: 391c.3; Needham and Wang 1959: 202). It was perhaps because of such perceptions of Brahmins as specialists in mathematics and astronomy that the Tang court decided to employ South Asians at its Bureau of Astronomy.

According to Yang, these astronomers were from the Qutan 瞿
曇 (Gautama), Jiaye 迦葉 (Kāśyapa), and Jumoluo 拘摩羅
(Kumāra) families and served the Tang court for several generations. They made calculations of the movement of heavenly objects
and drafted calendars using Indic mathematical methods. The most
well known of these South Asian astronomers was a person named
Qutan Sida 瞿曇悉達 (Gautama Siddhārta), who not only attained
the highest position in the Tang Bureau of Astronomy but also
translated one of the important Indian astronomical treatises called
Navagrāha-siddhanta (*Jiuzhi li* 九執曆) into Chinese (Yabuuti
1979; Niu 2004).

More information is available about the Gautama family of
astronomers than the other two groups not only due to the high
position the members of the family attained at the Tang court but
also because of the controversies surrounding one of them named
Qutan Zhuan 瞿曇譔 (712–776). Fortunately the tomb and the accompanying epitaph of Qutan Zhuan have been excavated, giving
us details about the lineage, contribution, and the eventual assimila-
tion of the Gautama family into Tang society (Sen 1995). According to the epitaph, Zhuan's family was originally from Zhong Tianzhu. His great-grandfather named Yi 逸 (Ajita?) may have been the
one who first migrated to China. Zhuan's grandfather and the first
member of the family to serve at the Tang court was named 羅
(Rahula?), who held the position of the director of astronomy between 665 and 698 (Sen 1995: 201). The famous Gautama Siddhartha was Zhuan's father. Zhuan, the fourth son of Siddhartha, also
entered the Tang Bureau of Astronomy and rose to the position of
vice director. Zhuan married the daughter of a high-ranking Tang
official, belonging to the famous Wang clan of Langye 琅邪. He
died at the age of sixty-five *sui*, leaving behind his wife and six
children, all of whom, like him, had Chinese names.

The epitaph also hints at the controversy surrounding Zhuan. It
reports that "[i]n the beginning of the Guangde 廣德 period

(763–765), [because] Gautama made a mistake in his predictions, he was removed from his post. [But] not long thereafter, the Emperor returned to the capital after fleeing to Shan prefecture [from the Tibetan army]. Gautama's previous predictions were [hence] proven true" (Sen 1995: 206–207). This episode seems to have happened prior to 763, when Emperor Dezong 德宗 (r. 779–805) had to escape the invading Tibetan forces. In 733, Zhuan had accused the famous Buddhist astronomer Yixing 一行 of plagiarizing from *Jiuzhi li* when he drafted the Dayan calendar 大衍曆. The accusations were found to be false, and Zhuan was banished from the capital. In 758, Zhuan was recalled and reinstated at the Bureau of Astronomy. Three years later, in 761, Zhuan predicted a rebellion against the then emperor Suzong 肅宗 (r. 756–762). When two years had passed without any incident and a peaceful transition had taken place after the death of Suzong, the new emperor Dezong, believing that Zhuan's predictions about the rebellion were incorrect, dismissed him from the his post at the Bureau of Astronomy. The Tibetan invasion took place within a year of Zhuan's dismissal, which, as the epitaph suggests, vindicated his earlier prediction of an impending rebellion (Sen 1995).

These controversies associated with Gautama Zhuan, from his initial charge of plagiarism to the questioning of his skills, may have to do with the general differences between the South Asian and Chinese methods of astronomical calculations. Although the Chinese prized the South Asian method of predicting solar and lunar eclipses, neither Indic numerals nor the sine tables were employed in drafting calendars in China. The *Jiuzhi li* used the Indic method of calculation to predict astronomical phenomena in China. While the original text had the South Asian site Ujjain (in the present-day Madhya Pradesh state of the ROI) as the reference point, Siddhartha used for his calculations the Tang capital Chang'an. Thus, *Jiuzhi li* was not merely a translation of an Indic text but a composition intended to have relevance in Tang China.

The text included an Indic sine table, which Gautama Zhuan believed Yixing plagiarized to draft his Dayan calendar (Cullen 1982).

This episode also reveals the complexities of knowledge transfer from South Asia to China. Despite the fact that South Asian astronomers held high positions at the Tang court, it seems that only selective aspects of their findings and methods were employed, even though they may have been more advanced than those that existed in China. There could be several reasons for this. First, the Chinese seem to have been content with their own traditional ways of drafting calendars and only needed South Asian methods for calculating solar and lunar eclipses. Second, it is possible that they found the South Asian methods not applicable to the local situations and needs of the Chinese rulers. Third, it cannot be ruled out that there was intense competition between foreign and Chinese astronomers, as the Gautama Zhuan–Yixing episode indicates, and the latter did not want to allow the South Asian methods to dominate the local tradition. [28] No matter what specific reason led to such rejection, as Yabuuti Kiyosi (1979: 589), Needham and Wang (1959: 203), and others have pointed out, despite the translations of various texts and the presence of South Asian astronomers at the Chinese court, Indic astronomy and mathematics failed to have much impact on Chinese ways of interpreting the heavens.

Conversely, Pan Jixing (2012), following Needham and the examination of Arabic mathematics, has argued that the Chinese systems of calculations might have had a more significant impact on South Asia. Needham (1959: 146–150) has given several examples of how certain mathematical ideas found in Indic systems date from much later than their first appearance in Chinese records. The extraction of square and cube roots, for example, was, according to Needham, already "highly developed" in China in the first century CE, about five hundred years before its appearance in the work of the South Asian mathematician Brahmāgupta. [29] The influence of

Chinese mathematics, including replications of apparent errors, Needham suggests, are also found in the work of a ninth-century Indian mathematician named Mahāvīra. Similarly, Pan argues that some of the mathematical elements included in Arabic mathematical works originated in China and reached West Asia through South Asia. These arguments, as Needham acknowledges in a footnote (1959: 148n.a), are speculations based on the absence of earlier works from South Asia, "which may not have survived." Nonetheless, the transmission of Chinese methods to South Asia is a topic that has not been examined in much detail.[30] Clearly, like the Buddhist missionaries and pilgrims visiting Mount Wutai, mathematicians and astronomers in South Asia must have been aware of the opportunities in China. Other than the coincidental similarities, however, there is no evidence of translation projects that could have introduced Chinese mathematics and astronomy to South Asia.

Working in the same period as the above-mentioned South Asian mathematician-astronomers in Tang China was another group who, along with their Chinese collaborators and disciples, produced highly stylized illustrations of the sky, formulated horoscopic charts, and composed works in Chinese that framed the understanding of the cosmos within a Buddhist context (Yano 1986). The Chinese also had a preexisting tradition of representing the universe in the form of stylized diagrams that dates back to the Zhou period (Wu 2007). Some of these early Chinese diagrams of the universe were drawn on tomb ceilings and in shrines, as in the case of the tomb of the First Emperor (Qinshihuang 秦始皇) and the Wu family shrines from the Eastern Han period. Buddhist practices and ideas mixed with these preexisting traditions and resulted in astronomical drawings that were unique to East Asia.

The South Asian Tantric monk named Bukong 不空 (Amoghavajra, 705–774) was a notable figure who promoted texts and images of Buddhist cosmology. Arriving in Tang China in the early eighth century, Amoghavajra served several Tang rulers and established intimate relationship with members of the elite class (Chou 1944–1945; Goble 2012). Amoghavajra and his Tantric colleagues offered prognoses of fate and a spiritual connection to the Buddhist cosmos. A significant number of texts and images produced by Amoghavajra and his colleagues were associated with horoscopic astrology. These had much wider impact in China compared to the mathematical methods introduced by South Asian astronomers. While some of these texts were translations from Sanskrit, others were composed either in Central Asia or China. They all advocated the invocation of heavenly objects, lunar lodges, luminaries, and constellations in rituals and ceremonies related to fate prognostication, as well as for the protection of the state from natural calamities and foreign invasions.

Emerging shortly after the translation/composition of these texts were the cosmic diagrams known as *maṇḍala*s. These diagrams were employed in Tantric rituals and ceremonies and were intended to connect patrons to the intrinsic reality of the universe and allow them to attain, at some point, enlightenment. Also related to these practices were the horoscopic charts that allegedly helped foretell the future (Howard 1983; Yano 1986). These horoscopic charts and cosmic *maṇḍala*s circulated extensively in China and other parts of East Asia. They were used in Buddhist temples, households, and funerary art. In fact, the first illustrations of zodiac signs in East Asia come from the tombs of Han Chinese residents in the Khitan territories that were built, in the eleventh and twelfth centuries, according to a combination of Chinese funerary traditions and Tantric cosmological beliefs. They merged the earlier use of astronomical diagrams on tomb ceilings with the Buddhist cosmic *maṇḍala*s (see figure 1.5). They demonstrate the impact of Buddhist ideas of reincarnation, Tantric teachings, and Indic astronomical traditions on Chinese funerary rituals even after Buddhist philosophical input from South Asia had ended in the tenth century (Sen 1999, 2003).

Healing Bodies and Prolonging Life

There are many similarities between the transmissions of knowledge associated with astronomy and those related to medicine and healing from South Asia to China. Translated texts, as in the case of astronomy, also played a significant role in introducing several facets of South Asian medical practices to China. These included descriptions of diseases, symptoms, and possible cures. Frequently mentioned in these texts was the renowned South Asian physician Jīvika/Jīvaka (Ch. Qipo 耆婆), whose skills became well known in

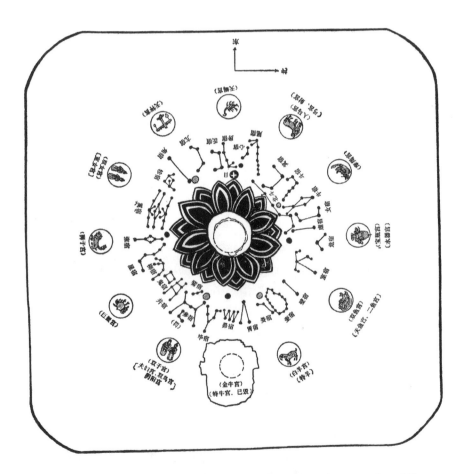

Figure 1.5.   Astronomical diagram from the Xuanhua tombs. After *Wenwu* **(1975: 8.44), reprinted from Sen (1999)**

China.[31] As a consequence, Indian physicians were invited by Chinese rulers to introduce specific methods of treatment. As with the diffusion of astronomy, diverse traditions and methods of Indic medicine reached China. This included the concocting of life-prolonging drugs by South Asian physicians who were specially invited to China. Moreover, South Asian cosmological beliefs and medical practices sometimes merged in China, especially when the causes and cures for disease were believed to be associated with cosmic forces.

It should be noted that the transmission of medical knowledge from South Asia to China might have been further facilitated by the fact that many Buddhist monasteries served as clinics for itinerant monks and merchants. Cures considered effective perhaps spread rapidly across the trade routes. Oasis and port towns were hubs of medical treatment as large numbers of travelers gathered at these sites. Documents concerning medical practices and cures from Dunhuang, for example, suggest that these places were storehouses of information that facilitated the circulation of medical knowledge in different directions (Cullen and Lo 2005; Chen 2005a, 2005b).

As outlined in the works of Chen Ming (2013) and C. Pierce Salguero (2014), the hagiographical accounts of Indian physicians, especially Jīvaka and Nāgārjuna (Ch. Longshu 籠樹), presented in Chinese Buddhist texts; the use of Indic medical practices by members of Chinese society; and certain compatibilities between aspects of Indic and Chinese medicines abetted the circulation of Indic medicine in China. C. Pierce Salguero (2009) has examined the representation of Jīvaka, the so-called Medicine King, in Chinese Buddhist sources by focusing on two early translated/composed texts, the *Āmrapālī and Jīvaka Avadāna Sutra* (*Foshuo Nainü Qiyu yinyuan jing* 佛說柰女祇域因緣經, T. 553) and the *Āmrapālī and Jīvaka Sutra* (*Fo shuo Nainü Qipo jing* 佛說柰女耆婆經, T. 554), that are often attributed to the Parthian monk-translator An Shigao. Salguero, and before him Kenneth Zysk (1998:

60), points out the incorporation of various Chinese medical practices and beliefs, such as acupuncture, into the biography of Jīvaka
found in these texts. The translations were amended, modified, and
recomposed with the aim of presenting Jīvaka as an "exemplary
Chinese physician" (Salguero 2009: 194–195). Several medical
episodes in these texts were also modified to fit the needs and
expectations of Chinese audiences. Ultimately, Jīvaka was a "won-
der-worker," on par with, if not better than, the renowned Chinese
physician named Bian Que 扁鵲.

These two texts are examples of translated and recomposed
Buddhist works that tried to legitimize Buddhist teachings, practices, and some of the important South Asian personalities in China. In fact, these texts played a significant role in promoting Jīvaka
and his healing abilities and spread beyond the Buddhist community in China. Jīvaka, for instance, is mentioned in the work of the
famous Tang physician Sun Simiao 孫思邈 (581–682) as well as in
several later Chinese and Japanese works. This demonstrates, as
Salguero (2009: 210) concludes, "Jīvaka's symbolic appeal to classical medical writers as a source of authority and efficacy, particularly useful for legitimizing the appropriation of Indian knowledge
into mainstream classical medicine."

A similar trajectory occurred with Nāgārjuna, another famous
South Asian physician, frequently associated with ophthalmology.
A hagiographical account of the healer appeared in a fifth-century
"translation" attributed to Kumārajīva. Titled *Longshu Pusa zhuan*
籠樹菩薩傳 (The Biography of Nāgārjuna, T. 2047), the text
records Nāgārjuna as a person from South Tianzhu, belonging to
the Brahmin caste, and as someone who was well versed in astronomy and geography and had various types of magical powers (*dao-
shu* 道術). Nāgārjuna's fame in China also spread with the translations of several other works bearing his name. These included, as
recorded in the bibliographical section of the *Sui shu*, *Longshu
Pusa yaofang* 籠樹菩薩藥房, *Lungshu Pusa he xiang fa* 籠樹菩薩

和香法, and *Longshu Pusa shixing fang* 籠樹菩薩食性方. During the later period, there were other texts such as *Lungshu Pusa yan lun* 籠樹菩薩眼論 and *Mi chuan yanke long mu zong lun* 秘傳眼科龍木總論. Nāgārjuna, his skills, and his works are also mentioned in the travelogues of Xuanzang and Yijing and in a poem by the Tang poet Bo Juyi 白居易 (772–846). *Longshu Pusa yan lun*, the treatise that Bo Juyi refers to in his poem, seems to have contained a list of thirty ophthalmic symptoms and their possible cures. Several of Nāgārujuna's treatises circulating in China dealt with glaucoma. This included the text titled *Longmu zong lun*, which explained the prognosis and treatment of glaucoma. *Longshu Pusa yan lun* and *Longmu zong lun* also recorded the surgical procedure for removing cataracts (Unschuld 1985: 144–148; Kovacs and Unschuld 1999: 43–48; Deshpande 1999).

The travel record of the Chinese monk Yijing, already mentioned above, is unique because of the comparative perspective it provides on the medical practices and remedies in South Asia and China. Yijing records, for example, the use of chew sticks and regular strolls in South Asia and their health benefits. While the use of chew sticks, he explains, prevented dental disease and cured toothache, regular strolls helped with digestion. These practices, he notes, were either not prevalent or not done properly in China. Yijing has several sections in his book that deal specifically with medical issues. These include "The Treatment of Disease," "Rules for Taking Medicine," and "Avoidance of Evil Drugs." In the section dealing with treating diseases, Yijing lists the eight branches of the science of medicine (*yiming* 醫明; Skt. *cikitsāvidyā*) that a physician in the "West" (*xifang* 西方) must be familiar with. These were "1) The treatment of all kinds of ulcers; 2) the treatment of ailments of the head by acupuncture; 3) the treatment of diseases of the body; 4) the treatment of illness caused by demons; 5) the treatment of sickness with *agada* (antidotal) medicine; 6) the treatment of children's diseases; 7) the art of longevity; and 8) the

method of strengthening the legs and body" (Li 2000: 119). These
eight arts of healing, he explains, were contained in the *aṣṭāṅga*
tradition of the Āyurveda. All physicians of the Five Tianzhus, who
were greatly honored and received official salaries, practiced their
craft according to these eight arts of healing.

Yijing also points out that the medicinal herbs of the "West"
were different from those used in "Dongxia" 東夏 (i.e., China).
Herbs such as ginseng, tuckahoe, Chinese angelica, polygala, acon-
ite, monkshood, Chinese ephedra, and *asarum*, considered some of
the best Chinese medicinal herbs, were, he reports, only found in
China and not in the West. He points out that several South Asian
herbs, such as *harītakī* (yellow *myrobalan*), turmeric, ferula, camphor, cardamom, and cloves, were needed in China. Acupuncture
and the skill of feeling the pulse, he writes, were found only in
China. In the section on the use of medicine, Yijing quotes the
Buddha as saying that ailments were caused by disorders of the
four elements, viz., (1) *guru* (indigestion), (2) *kapha* (phlegm), (3)
pitta (bile), and (4) *vata* (wind). These four, according to him,
corresponded to the Chinese concepts of (1) serious heaviness, (2)
phlegmatic illness, (3) yellow fever, and (4) the bursting of breath.
Yijing also recommends fasting and drinking tea as ways to prevent
illness (Li 2000: 121).

The translated Buddhist texts and the records of Chinese Buddhist travelers were instrumental in advancing Buddhist teachings,
rituals, images, and symbols that advocated disease prevention and
spiritual healing. Within this context, the Buddha was presented as
the "Supreme Physician," Bhaiṣajyaguru (Ch. Yaoshi rulai 藥師如
來) as the "Medicine Buddha," and Avalokiteśvara/Guanyin as the
bodhisattva with the power to heal diseases. Venerating, reciting
mantras/*dhāraṇīs* to, and invoking the names of these divinities
were recommended as some of the ways to cure ailments, especially those resulting from karmic consequences. The popular Lotus
Sutra was an important text, as Raoul Birnbaum (1989: 26) has

demonstrated, that promoted the belief in Buddhist healing deities. Birnbaum points out the powerful role of images of divinities, particularly that of the Medicine Buddha, in augmenting the influence of Buddhist spiritual healing in China. It is here that some of the astronomical ideas discussed in the previous section merged with healing practices. Venerating images of Buddhist divinities surrounded by celestial objects emerged in East Asia as a popular means to seek medical relief and cure. The image in figure 1.6 of Bhaiṣajyaguru surrounded by celestial objects is an example of the fusion of medical and astronomical beliefs in Buddhism. The spread of Tantric Buddhism in China also promoted healing practices that were connected to astrological beliefs.

While Buddhism introduced various aspects of Indic medical knowledge, there was also a belief in China, especially among the ruling elite, that South Asian physicians possessed the secret of longevity. This belief resulted in several attempts to fetch South Asian "longevity doctors" to China to concoct drugs for various emperors. The most famous episode related to a Brahmin physician named Naluoershapo[mei] 那羅邇娑婆寐 (Nārāyaṇasvāmin?) who

Figure 1.6.   The Bodhisattva Bhaiṣajyaguru with celestial objects. © **The Metropolitan Museum of Art, New York.**

was brought to Tang China by the diplomat Wang Xuance in 648. He also seems to have been in close contact with Xuanzang (Chen 2013: 325). Nārāyaṇasvāmin claimed to be over two hundred years old. He was housed in the Office of Precious Metals and given extensive support to produce longevity drugs for Emperor Taizong. Herbs and other rare objects were procured for the South Asian physician, and a high-ranking official was assigned to meet his needs. However, within a year after the arrival of Nārāyaṇasvāmin, Emperor Taizong died. Some court officials blamed the South Asian physician and the drugs he concocted for the death of the emperor. Although he was asked to leave Tang China, the interest in South Asian longevity doctors continued throughout the Tang period (Sen 2003; Chen 2013: 325–329). In 668, for example, a Brahmin named Lujiayiduo 盧迦溢多 (Lokāditya?) was appointed as the *huaihua da jiangjun* 懷化大將軍 (civilizing general) and ordered to produce "immortality drugs." This pursuit of South Asian longevity physicians indicates that the Chinese were cognizant of the existence of several different traditions of healing and longevity in South Asia.

Chen Ming, who has done extensive study on foreign medical knowledge in ancient China, points out that the translated Buddhist texts, in addition to introducing South Asian medical practices, were also instrumental in transmitting medicine and methods of treating ailments that originated in West Asia or those that belonged to the Greek tradition. This included the drug theriac (Greek *teriakos*), an antidote, which appears in some of the translated Buddhist texts (Chen 2013: 415–416). In the same manner, during the Yuan period, when Islamic medical methods entered China, Indian herbs were introduced through the so-called Huihui prescriptions (*Huihui fang* 回回方). One example of such an herb was that from the tree known as *terminalia chebula* (Skt. *harītakī*; Arabic *halīlaj*; Ch. *kezi*), a key ingredient in several of these Huihui prescriptions.

The herb was supposed to cure ailments ranging from coughs to tumors (Chen 2013: 479–482).

Chen and others have also pointed out the possible spread of Chinese alchemical products and practices to South Asia. David Gordon White (1996) suggests that the South Asian practitioners of *rasāyana* (elixir therapy) imported Chinese mercury. Moreover, according to the Sittar tradition in South India, the alchemist Bogar (also recorded as Pokar or Bhoga) may have traveled from China to South Asia sometime between the third and fifth centuries and introduced Daoist ideas related to producing elixir (Deshpande 1987; White 1996: 61–64). Some of these ideas of elixir therapy, as Chen Ming argues (2013: 295–296), reentered China through the translated Buddhist works. If verified, this would be an important example of the circulatory connections with regard to knowledge between South Asia and China.

Manufacturing Technologies and Know-How

Transfer of at least three important manufacturing technologies took place between South Asia and China prior to the arrival of European colonialism in Asia. The first was the transfer of South Asian know-how in terms of manufacturing sugar from sugarcane in the seventh century. The other two were the Chinese technologies of making paper and gunpowder, both of which reached South Asia during the first half of the second millennium primarily through the Islamic and Mongol networks. Two other technological transfers, that of South Asian steelmaking and Chinese shipbuilding techniques, are also briefly outlined in this section. Although somewhat speculative, the evidence for the spread of shipbuilding techniques corroborates the multilayered nature of the circulations of technical knowledge within broader intra-Asian interactions.

During the early Tang period, sweetened water was used in China to concoct medicines and also employed in Buddhist rituals. The water was sweetened with locally produced sweeteners, including juice extracted from sugarcane, and products imported from foreign regions. One of the foreign ingredients was known as *shimi* 石密, which, according to the *Hou Han shu*, came from Tianzhu. Christian Daniels (1996: 374n.3) has suggested that the term *shimi* initially referred to "concentrate sugar products made by a sun-drying process." Later, from the sixth century onward, it indicated sugar made by dissolving soft brown sugar (*shatang* 砂糖) in water and boiling. "The syrup," Daniels points out, "was then crystallised slowly by gentle stirring to produce a large-grained massecuite. Next the massecuite was placed in a utensil with a hole in the bottom. The solid sugar, *śarkarā*, remained in the utensil while the molasses passed below where it was collected" (Daniels 1996: 377). This later method of making sugar seems to have been brought from South Asia by Buddhist monks who accompanied a diplomatic mission from Tang China led by Wang Xuance to the court of King Harṣa in 647 (Daniels 1996; Ji 1997; Kieschnick 2003: 249–262; Sen 2003). The involvement of Buddhist monks suggests that the use of sweeteners in Buddhist rituals might have prompted the transfer of the technology from South Asia to China.

It is possible that the Chinese monk Xuanzang, who had returned to Tang China from South Asia just prior to the above mission, played some part in providing the initial information about the sugar-making method used in Middle India. In fact, one of the earliest reports on the procurement of the sugar-making technology during the Tang period comes from the biography of Xuanzang. Found in Daoxuan's *Xu gaoseng zhuan* 續高僧傳 (Continuation of the Biographies of the Eminent Monks), the record states,

> [King] Harṣa and the monks [from the Mahābodhi Monastery] each sent secondary envoys carrying various sutras and treasures to go afar and present [the gifts] to Dongxia. [The dispatch of] this mission was an accomplishment of [Xuan]zang [in his effort to] transmit the "August Plan" [of Emperor Taizong]. When [Harṣa's] envoys were about to return to the West, Wang

Xuance and twenty others were ordered to go towards Daxia along with them. Moreover, they (i.e., the envoys) were presented with more than a thousand bolts of silk. The king (i.e., Harṣa), monks, and others [with the mission] had their individual share. At the [Mahā]bodhi Monastery, the monks summoned the makers of sugar, and then sent two makers [of sugar] and eight monks to accompany [the Chinese embassy] to China. Shortly afterwards, an Imperial decree [from the Tang court] ordered [them] to proceed to Yuezhou. There, using sugarcane, they were able to make sugar. Everything was successfully accomplished. (T. 2060: 454c.22–29; Sen 2003: 38–39)

Without mentioning the role of the Buddhist monks, the *Xin Tang shu* (221a: 6239), the official history of the Tang dynasty, also records a diplomatic mission sent to the Mojietuo 摩揭陀 (Magadha) polity in Zhong Tianzhu to "fetch the method of boiling sugar." The method of making sugar imported by the Tang mission in 647 also seems to have been recorded on a document discovered in Dunhuang. The document, numbered P. 3303, dates from the ninth or tenth century and is important not only because it confirms the importation of the technology from South Asia but also because it mentions the application of the technology in China. It also suggests that the induction of the technology may have had an impact on sugarcane cultivation in China. The document, translated by Daniels (1996: 373–375, with slight modifications), reads,

Three types of sugarcane are produced in Wu Tianzhu of the Western Heaven. The first type has a stalk eight *chi* long and mostly not excellent for making *shatang*.

The second type is one or two *chi* shorter than [the first type] and makes [?] good *shatang* and makes excellent *shageling*. The third type is also good.

When making [sugar] first take the stalks of sugarcane, remove the tops and leaves, cut them into [lengths] of five *cun* and put them into a large wooden mortar. The oxen drags [the pestle] and the juice is pressed out.

The juice is received in an earthenware jar and is boiled in fifteen pans. Next drain [the boiled syrup] into a [cooling] pan and use chopsticks to add a little [. . .]. After being completely cooled beat [the sugar]. If it crystallises it is ready and forms *shatang*. If it does not crystallise it is still not ready and must be boiled again.

When making *shageling* return [the *shatang*] to the pan and after boiling it put it into a bamboo steaming bucket with seven holes in the base, and the molasses drains down into a receiving earthenware jar placed below. Keep the door [of the room in which the sugar in the bamboo steaming buckets are stored] closed for a full fifteen days [before] opening and removing. After the *shageling* has been drained out in the bamboo steaming bucket bring it together by hand and remove [any remaining molasses] by shaking. [This is] called *shageling*. The molasses that has been drained off is made into wine.

Stalks of sugarcane like panicum in Shazhou and Gaochang do not set seed [so] take a stalk one *chi* cut and bury it on ploughed ridges and it will grow. When planting sugarcane use the twelfth lunar month.

It is not clear if the import and use of the South Asian technology was in any way responsible for the subsequent popularity of sugar in China during the Song and, in particular, the Ming and Qing periods, when it became an important ingredient in Chinese cuisine (Mazumdar 1998). However, the method of making sugar continued to be that which was brought from South Asia in the seventh century.

There is an important aspect to this episode of the transmission of the sugar-making method that demonstrates the process of circulatory connections between South Asia and China. One of the objects that entered Tang China along with the sugar-making method was the "wooden mortar" mentioned in the above record from Dunhuang. The mortar described here is the South Asian animal-driven *kolhu*, used to extract juice from sugarcane. Several centuries later, most likely in the sixteenth century, the South Asian two-roller mill technology for sugar extraction also reached China.[32] The Chinese subsequently redesigned it, adding cog gears and adapting a vertical mode of roller mounting. This redesigned vertical two-roller mill technology was transmitted to South Asia in the seventeenth century, most likely through Christian missionaries (Daniels and Daniels 1988: 528).[33]

While the circulation of sugar-making technologies took place directly between South Asia and China, the diffusions of paper- and gunpowder-making technologies were a more complicated processes. Several different groups of people, mostly those associated with the expanding Mongol empire, may have been instrumental in introducing the two Chinese technologies into South Asia. The invention of paper in China is credited to Cai Lun 蔡伦, an official at the Han court during the second century CE. Archaeological evidence, however, indicates its existence at least two centuries prior to Cai Lun (Needham and Tsien 1985). In any case, by the middle of the first millennium, paper and its manufacturing technique had spread to parts of eastern Central Asia. Legend has it that the defeat of the Tang forces by the Arabs in the Battle of Talas in 751 resulted in the capture of Chinese prisoners skilled in the process who transmitted the technique to the Persian Gulf.

Whether the people of South Asia used paper before the Battle of Talas is a matter of controversy. Ji Xianlin ([1954] 2010), who wrote several articles on the transmission of Chinese papermaking technology to South Asia, points to Chinese Buddhist texts from the seventh century that mention four different Sanskrit words that he argues refer to paper. These were *kākali*, *kakali*, *kakari*, and *śaya*.[34] Additionally, the Chinese monk Yijing, who visited Nālandā in the seventh century, reports three different uses of paper. The first relates to the use of paper for making umbrellas, the second for its use in the toilet, and the third for printing Buddhist images. However, it is not clear if the monk was actually indicating the use of paper in South Asia or suggesting its application in

China. Thus, Irfan Habib (2011: 95–96) dismisses Ji's argument about the existence of paper in South Asia prior to the Battle of Talas, contending that "Chinese scholars using paper would naturally create Sanskrit words for it, though these did not occur in the Sanskrit texts themselves" (2011: 96)

Despite this skepticism it must be noted that paper was being used in Sogdiana prior to the Battle of Talas. Given the close cooperation between Sogdians and South Asian merchants since at least the fourth century CE, the introduction of the Chinese product earlier than the mid-eighth century cannot be completely ruled out. Moreover, the letters exchanged between Xuanzang and his teachers and fellow students at Nālandā, as noted above, must have been on paper. Thus, it is not impossible that paper, in some limited quantities, was circulating in South Asia when Yijing arrived in the region.

Irfan Habib contends that the spread of papermaking technology took place only during the first two or three centuries of the second millennium at various points of contact between Muslim merchants and marketplaces in South Asia, especially those located in Kashmir and Gujarat (Habib 2011: 96). The availability of paper in the territories belonging to the Delhi Sultanate in the thirteenth and fourteenth centuries is mentioned in local Persian-language sources. Irfan Habib argues that paper was "fairly abundant" in Delhi by the fourteenth century and widely used as packing material. Ma Huan, one of the envoys associated with the expeditions of Zheng He in the early fifteenth century, records "white paper" made from tree bark being available in the Bengal Sultanate. "It is," he writes, "glossy and smooth—like deer-skin" (Mills [1970] 1997: 165). For Habib this report indicates the possibility of a direct transmission of papermaking technology from Ming China to Bengal by the sea route. Joseph Needham and Tsien Tsuen-Hsuin (1985: 357), on the other hand, believe that papermaking may have entered Bengal through Tibet, which is also a possibility since Hou

Xian, the Ming envoy who visited Bengal multiple times, had at least once gone to the present-day Bihar-Bengal region by the land route through Tibet. Even with the introduction of paper and its widespread production under the Islamic sultanates, palm leaves remained popular with most South Asian scribes through to the early colonial period.

The lack of proper documentation prevents us from firmly establishing either the date or the route through which paper and paper-making technology entered South Asia. It seems clear that the agencies involved in introducing it included Buddhist monks, Muslim merchants, and Chinese diplomats. The routes through which they entered must have been equally varied: the land routes through Central Asia and Tibet and the maritime routes through Southeast Asia. It is also possible that paper entered South Asia in two different phases: the first may have been prior to the mid-eighth century, and the second in the twelfth and thirteenth centuries with the Muslim traders.

The transmission of gunpowder technology to South Asia was similarly a multipronged, complex process that is not easy to trace.[35] While it is clear that firearms, including guns with matchlocks and cannons, were in use in Gujarat and by the Mughals in the early sixteenth century, the earlier history of such weaponry in South Asia is unclear. As Jos Gommans (2002: 146) has noted, one of the main reasons for this ambiguity is "the complicated and ever-changing nomenclature of the weaponry involved. The distinction between so-called 'co-viative' throwers of projectiles and true guns—i.e. where a bullet or cannonball fills the bore of the barrel in order to use the maximum propellant force of the gunpowder charge—is not always evident from the terminology used in the primary sources." The primary sources that Gommans mentions are Persian records extensively studied by Iqtidar Alam Khan (1977, 1996, 2004). Based on these sources, both Gommans and Khan have suggested that the Mongols are to be credited with introducing

Chinese pyrotechnical devices, such as fire lances, grenades, and rockets, to South Asia.

The Persian writers Juwaini (in 1280) and Rashīd al-Dīn (in 1304–1305) indicate that soldiers in the Mongol Ilkhanate were using some of the above devices. Sometime around 1300, deserters from the Mongol armies entering South Asia may have introduced gunpowder and pyrotechnic devices to the region. It was also at this time that "fiery projectiles" emerged as weapons in the arsenal of the Delhi Sultanate. Khan (1996: 43) infers that the Delhi Sultanate might have already been using gunpowder in the middle of the thirteenth century. The Vijayanagara Empire (1336–1646), located in the Deccan area, seems to have had access to firearms by the middle of the fourteenth century. In fact, Burton Stein (1985) has argued that gunpowder played an important role in the establishment of the Vijayanagara Empire in 1336.

Khan's reference (1977: 26) to "guns" in Bengal in the early fifteenth century based on the record of Ma Huan is, however, problematic. This is because of the incorrect rendering of the Chinese terms by George Phillips (1895), which Khan cites to make his argument. The relevant passages in Ma Huan's records have the term "spears" in one edition and "bows and arrows" in another. Neither of these versions indicates a gunpowder-related device (i.e., "guns") in Bengal in the early fifteenth century. Similarly, the argument that gunpowder or firearms may have entered the Bengal region through Yunnan and Burma is also equally speculative. Although Sun Laichen (2011) has shown that gunpowder and firearms had spread among the Ahom people based in upland Southeast Asia by the Ming period, their role in introducing these items to South Asia is not substantiated in existing textual or archaeological sources.

There were several other technologies that spread between South Asia and China. This included the transmission of the so-called *bin* iron (*bintie* 鑌鐵), most likely high-quality steel, from the Afghanistan-Kashmir region to China. Donald Wagner (2008: 270) points out that in the sixth century, *bin* iron may have been imported into China "as a raw material rather than in finished products." Later, during the Yuan period, an office named *Bintie ju* 鑌鐵局 was established in China. While no details about this office are available, Wagner suggests that the name "probably reflects the idea that *bin* iron was an especially excellent steel, signaling that the office is concerned with an elite among the smiths." Wagner also proposes that the word *bin* might have originated from Sanskrit *piṇḍa*, meaning steel (2008: 270). Qian Wei (2007), on the other hand, argues that the Chinese character *bin* derived from the name of the polity Jibin ([罽]賓→鑌), which is mentioned in several Chinese sources as the place that produced *bin* iron.

Similarly, shipbuilding technology that uses nails to join together planks in building the hulls of ships is another method whose transmission into South Asia cannot be clearly tracked. Various sources indicate that South Asian ships, especially those from Sri Lanka, were active in Indian Ocean exchanges and frequented the Chinese coast during the first millennium CE. The Chinese developed the technology for oceangoing vessels only in the tenth and eleventh century, and it was not before the thirteenth century that Chinese-built ships started reaching the South Asian coastal regions.

Scholars such as Pierre-Yves Manguin (1980, 1996) have pointed out that the Chinese oceangoing ships, while using nails instead of coconut fibers to join wooden planks, were influenced in some ways by the designs of Southeast Asian ships. These were the so-called hybrid South China Sea junks. Despite the late development of the Chinese shipbuilding tradition, the presence of Chinese ships at South Asian ports, as recorded by Marco Polo and Ibn Baṭūṭah, became common during the thirteenth and fourteenth centuries. It is possible that some of these ships may have influenced the local shipbuilding tradition in coastal regions of South Asia. A shipwreck found in the Thikkal-Kadakkarappally region of the Malabar coast and dated to between the thirteenth and fifteenth centuries uses wooden planks that were joined using nails instead of the traditional coconut fibers (Tomalin et al. 2004). Some scholars have contended that the boat may have been built with Chinese technology. Even if true, the evidence, route, and method of such transmission are extremely vague.

KNOWLEDGE CIRCULATIONS AND ASIAN CONNECTIONS

The circulations of knowledge and technologies between South Asia and China discussed above were clearly part of broader intra-Asian interactions. Regions across Asia, from Persia to Japan, either facilitated these circulations or were at times the recipient of ideas that resulted from the mixing of South Asian and Chinese traditions. Indeed, most of Asia was integrated into the networks that connected South Asia and China through the movement of people, the translation of texts, the use of medical and astronomical knowledge, the reimagination/reinterpretation of knowledge, and, as examined in the next chapter, long-distance commercial activity. Intermediary regions, such as Central and Southeast Asia, were key to these circulations and interactions. Not only did they relay raw knowledge between South Asia and China, but they also often produced their own unique traditions that combined local ideas with those transmitted from South Asia and China. These regions were therefore important hubs for the diffusion of knowledge across Asia. Occasionally, China and regions of South Asia also served this role of hubs, diffusing knowledge to a third region. This was evident, for instance, in the discussion above of South Asian geography, knowledge of which was transmitted to Japan from China. In fact, the role of China was vital in the spread of Indic ideas, frequently interspersed with local traditions, to several regions of East Asia.

A second feature of Asian connections facilitating the spread of knowledge was the translation activities across several regions of Asia. Translated Buddhist texts and their role in introducing South Asian geography, astronomical ideas, and medical practices to China have been examined above. These translation projects undertaken in China were massive endeavors, requiring understanding of a range of foreign languages and scripts, as well as awareness of cultural practices, social norms, and in some cases specialized and technical knowledge. The participation of a diverse group of people, including Parthians, Sogdians, South Asians, and Chinese, underscored the intra-Asian nature of these translation projects. The Khitans, Tanguts, Uighurs, and Tibetans also employed similar mechanisms to render Buddhist texts into their own languages, some from Sanskrit originals and others (re)translated from Chinese. The sites for language learning to enable such translation work were not only located in South Asia or China. One could also study Sanskrit in Central Asia or, as the Chinese monk Yijing points out, in Palembang on the island of Sumatra.

Critical to the functioning of the networks of knowledge circulation was the movement of people from one region to another. These included itinerant traders and diplomats, pilgrims, military personnel, professionals and craftsmen who sought employment in foreign regions, and migrant populations. Some of these people wrote detailed accounts of their travels to foreign lands. This included Chinese Buddhist travelers to South Asia, Japanese monks who toured or studied in China, and Arab seafarers. A few professionals, such as the Moroccan Ibn Baṭūṭah, also penned descriptions of regions they visited. These travel accounts often circulated widely and formed the basis for knowledge about faraway places. In addition to travel accounts, these itinerant people often contributed to the diffusion of skills and knowledge in their area of expertise, ranging from foreign language learning to military strategy, image carving, and mathematics.

The circulations of geographical, mathematical, medical, and manufacturing knowledge between South Asia and China examined in this chapter are merely one facet of intra-Asian interactions. These circulations, as evident in the discussion above, were multifaceted and multidirectional, involved a multitude of people, and impacted societies and people in Japan, Korea, Southeast Asia, and West Asia. More importantly, they suggest remarkable connectivity and integration across several regions of Asia prior to the arrival of Europeans. Even the episodes of the distortion of information by intermediaries in South Asia–China exchanges mentioned in this chapter are indications of the integrated nature of intra-Asian connections.

NOTES

1. P. C. Bagchi ([1948] 2012) has pointed out that all three of these terms originated from the Indic name "Sindhu" and reached China respectively through Yuezhi "Induk(a)," Iranian "Hinduk(a)," and Kuchean-Tokharian "Indäk(a)."

2. In fact, an early connection between the Indic *nakṣatra* and the Chinese *xiu* (lunar lodges) systems cannot be fully ascertained. See Pankenier (2004: 12).

3. On the problems of equating the early Indian references of *cīna* with China, see *Arthaśāstra* 3.74–75.

4. The Zhang Qian episode is detailed in the Dayuan chapter of *Shi ji* (123: 3157–3169).

5. On the invention, evolution, and politics of the term "Silk Road," see Chin (2013).

6. On the location of Jibin, see Kuwayama (1990) and Enomoto (1994).

7. For a detailed study on Jibin's contacts with the Han Empire, see Kuwayama (1990).

8. Liu Xinru (1988) has discussed this early phase of South Asia–China interactions, including the role of the Kuṣāṇa Empire. On Yuezhi-Kuṣāṇa relations, see Liu (2001).

9. The best study on early Buddhist translation activity in China is Nattier (2008).

10. An overall survey of these aspects can be found in Bagchi ([1950] 1981).

11. On this route and its various branches, see Yang (2012).

12. A recent translation of Faxian's travelogue is by Li (2002). Max Deeg (2005) has done the most detailed annotation of the work.

13. *Xu gaoseng zhuan* (T. 2060: 437c.5–8). See also Forte (1984) and Chen (2002b: 85–86).

14. Nepal, as a separate political entity and not a part of Shendu/Tianzhu/Yindu, appears regularly from the seventh century.

15. On Sri Lanka in Chinese sources, see Sen (forthcoming).

16. The term was first used in the *Hou Han shu*. See Bagchi ([1948] 2012: 368).

17. The most recent translation of this work is Li (2000). Also important is the annotation by Wang (1995).

18. Lahiri's (1986) translation of this work has numerous errors. Wang Bangwei's (1988) detailed annotation remains the best reference work for this text.

19. Most of these passages were collected and translated into French by Sylvain Lévi (1900). Some of the new material, including inscriptions, can be found in Sun (1998).

20. These itineraries are studied in detail by Pelliot (1904). See also Park (2012: 31–36) and Sen (2003).

21. Rockhill (1913, 1914, 1915) has translated and provided extensive details on these and other related Chinese works on maritime connections.

22. For a study and translation of the Song sources on the Cholas, see Karashima and Sen (2009).

23. It is possible that this reference is to a comment in Zhao Rugua's work, citied above, which reports that its rulers (王) were "all appointed by Daqin."

24. On the author Shen Maoshang and his work, see Papelitzky (2015).

25. A more recent work outlining the impact of Buddhism on the tea-drinking tradition in China is Benn (2015).

26. Two classic works on Chinese astronomy and astrology within the context of broader Eurasian connections are Nakayama (1969) and Needham and Wang (1959). For the Tang period, the key study is by Schafer (1977a). For similar studies on South Asian astronomy and astrology, see the various writings of David Pingree, including Pingree (1963).

27. For an excellent study of the transmission of Indian astral science to China, see the recent works by Bill Mak (2015) and Kevin van Bladel (2014).

28. For similar discourse between Chinese and foreign experts on astronomy and cylindrical science, specifically that introduced by Jesuit missionaries, see Elman (2006).

29. A detailed study of Brahmāgupta's mathematical ideas and contributions can be found in Puttaswamy (2012: 161–208).

30. The only detailed study of such possibilities is Chatterji (1959).

31. On early South Asian medical practices, see Zysk (1985, 1993) and Meulenbeld and Wujastyk ([1987] 2001).

32. I would like to thank Chen Ming for providing me the references to this episode.

33. A related issue associated with the circulation of sugar is the term *cīnī* that is used currently for the product in various parts of South Asia, especially in many North Indian languages including Hindi and Bengali. It had been presumed that the term meant "Chinese" or "from China," implying that granulated white sugar might have entered South Asia from China. W. L. Smith (1984), however, has argued that *cīnī* initially stood for "white" and was associated not with sugar but with Chinese porcelain. It had nothing to do with place of origin but was used to describe a luxury product. "Most likely," he writes (1984: 232), "the term first appeared as *cīnī śakkar* or something similar and later the noun was dropped in the same way *cīnī* alone came to mean porcelain in Nepali and Gujarati."

34. Bagchi and Chatterji believe that the term *śaya* in Sanskrit may have been a loan word from Chinese. See Chatterji (1959: 96–97).

35. For a recent study of the history of gunpowder, see Andrade (2016). However, neither the introduction of the technology into South Asia nor its use by the Iranians is part of this study.

Chapter Two

The Routes, Networks, and Objects of Circulation

[T]hen Sarasvatī sat herself down
on the Çoṇa sands,
white, delicate as China silk,
rolling in waves, like a silken-soft bed.
—Bāṇa (fl. seventh century)

Archaeological evidence indicates that routes and networks of material exchange between parts of South Asia and the Yellow River Valley in China existed as early as the second millennium BCE. Cowries originating from the Maldive Islands in the Indian Ocean reached Anyang, the Shang capital, through these routes and networks that traversed the present-day regions of Bengal, Assam, Burma, and Yunnan (Vogel and Hieronymus 1993; Yang 2012). Various groups of people participated in relaying the commodity through a complex mechanism of exchange, networking, transportation, and profit making, much before the South Asians and the inhabitants of the Yellow River Valley became aware of each other's existence. This chapter analyzes some of these routes and networks that facilitated and sustained the circulation of material objects between South Asia and China. The first section outlines the routes that connected the urban centers, ports, and markets of the two regions. It also examines the traders and shippers who were involved in these interactions. The second section focuses on objects associated with Buddhism that constituted the principal items of trade and exchange between South Asia and China during the first millennium CE. The third section explores the tributary networks that contributed not only to the circulation of commercial goods and ritual objects, but also of exotic birds and animals. The fourth section examines the webs of commercial exchanges that linked South Asia and China. The concluding section underscores the wider impact of these circulations of material objects on pre-sixteenth-century intra-Asian connections.

Some overlaps occur through this chapter due to the fact that the exchange of objects took place with multiple aims and goals, including commercial, religious, and diplomatic, and those participating in these circulations frequently also assumed manifold roles. Traders, for example, were not only visiting markets in South Asia and China as profit seekers; they were also part of diplomatic/tributary missions and often the leading donors to monasteries and temples. Similarly, objects served diverse functions as tribute items, commercial merchandise, and religious adornments. Another point to note is that the networks between South Asia and China were not exclusive to one group of people, a single type of commodity, or a specific religious tradition. Furthermore, the circulation of objects through these routes and networks often formed part of the wider Afroeurasian "world system" that was connected through several interlocking circuits (Abu-Lughod 1989, and below). Indeed, as in the previous chapter, it is argued here that the interactions between South Asia and China must be understood in the larger context of intra-Asian, and sometimes Afroeurasian, connections that included contributions of people and objects from outside the two regions.

ROUTES AND NETWORKS

There are several conceptual issues about routes and networks that need to be clarified before examining the specific paths and routes through which material objects circulated between South Asia and China. First, as can be discerned from the dispersal of cowries, which is discussed in more detail below, the routes connecting South Asia and China passed through diverse terrains, including oceans, rivers, and mountains. They also involved a range of groups of people who participated in transporting, selling, purchasing, and retrading goods along these routes. Second, the use of the terms "routes" and "networks" usually presupposes that there was continuous, or at least regular, movement of people and goods through these conduits over centuries and millennia. However, climatic factors, availability of transportation facilities, safety, and supply-and-demand dynamics affected, and at times restricted, such movement. In fact, routes and networks shifted, changed, or declined over time depending on the alternatives available, cost considerations, advances in technologies, reallocations of markets, silting of harbors, changes in economic policies, and so forth. Third, almost all interregional routes were connected to the local market systems, through which foreign goods and objects entered into the hinterland areas and, in the same way, local products from the hinterlands streamed into the networks of interregional commerce. Fourth, political and imperialistic agendas, piratical activities, and rivalries among merchant groups also influenced the functioning of routes and networks. Finally, routes and networks required halting places, which provided medical needs, temporary accommodation, and repair and restocking facilities. Such places, which may not have taken part in commodity transactions, were nonetheless important for sustaining the circulation of objects over long distances.

Routes and networks were essentially interdependent entities established as a result of human connections. Human factors such as motivations and objectives, family concerns, linguistic abilities, cultural/religious interests, and political connections determined the extent, endurance, and impact of various routes and networks. Human factors also contributed to possible conflicts within the networks, promoted collaborations with other networks, and obstructed old routes and created new ones for the movement of people and objects. Commutable, secure, and navigable routes were imperative for the functioning of long-distance networks of merchants. They connected far-flung towns and ports as well as smaller pathways, river systems, and mountainous tracks. The leading urban/consumption centers and port towns across Asia, from which caravans and ships embarked on long-distance journeys, were linked through webs of roads linked to various production sites, markets, and transshipment locations. The effectiveness of routes and networks in commercial exchanges was dependent on the availability of transportation. The terrain through which routes traversed determined the appropriate modes for transporting commodities. Carts, donkeys, camels, boats, and ships were some of the common transportation means employed by itinerant traders. The specific geographical terrains and the corresponding modes of transportation often resulted in the formation of specialized networks involving specific groups of traders, caravan operators, or shippers.

The networks between South Asia and China discussed in this chapter were connected to several other regions of Asia. They involved either local merchant guilds or were operated by other Asian traders with extensive transregional connections. Some of these external traders conducted commercial transactions and at other times, as discussed below, represented South Asian polities as tribute carriers to the courts in China. All this made the networks that connected South Asia and China multifaceted, complex, and conducive to the long-distance circulation of objects and commodities across Asia.

The Routes between South Asia and China

The routes through which the Maldivian cowries reached the Yellow River Valley are early examples of the multifaceted long-distance commercial connections mentioned above. Although the specific pathways and methods of transporting the commodity are not recorded, some segments may have involved the routes mentioned by Zhang Qian and Jia Dan (see chapter 1 and below). Archaeological findings do however confirm some likely sites and regions through which cowries reached Anyang (Dikshit 1938; Heimann 1980; Peng and Zhu 1995; Biswas 2006). They were most likely imported through the ports in present-day Bengal and then carried overland via Assam and Burma into the Yunnan region. From Yunnan they would have been relayed to Anyang. Zhang Qian's report from the Han period suggests that products were also exported in the other direction perhaps along the same routes. Bamboo and cloth from the southwest region of the Han Empire, according to Zhang Qian, found their way to the markets of Bactria in Central Asia through South Asia.

Zhang Qian does not mention the operators of these early commercial networks who connected the Yunnan-Sichuan region to the markets in Central Asia. Most likely there were several groups of people responsible for transporting and trading these goods. It is not clear, however, if, similar to the trade in cowries, the supply of bamboo and cloth from the southwest regions of the Han Empire to Central Asia took place regularly. In fact, there are no records (or archaeological evidence) of trade in these commodities from the later periods when commercial activity along these routes apparently became more vibrant. The integration of the Yunnan, Burma, and Assam areas in the seventh and eighth centuries as a result of state formation, migrations, and religious exchanges led to increased trading activity and more detailed knowledge about specific routes and networks in the region (see figure 2.1). This is evidenced from Jia Dan's meticulous record of the routes that connected the Tang Empire to Assam. The starting points of Jia Dan's itineraries were Annan and Jiaozhi located in the coastal region of what is today northern Vietnam. The route described by Jia Dan then passed through the present-day Chinese provinces of Guizhou and Yunnan, across the upper reaches of the Red River, and into Burma and from there entered the polity of Kāmarūpa in Assam and continued to the urban centers of the Gangetic plains (Pelliot 1904).

The evidence from the cowrie trade, the report of Zhang Qian about bamboo and silk cloth in Central Asian markets, and the itineraries provided by Jia Dan suggest that the hinterland areas of China, the ports on the South China Sea, the urban centers of South

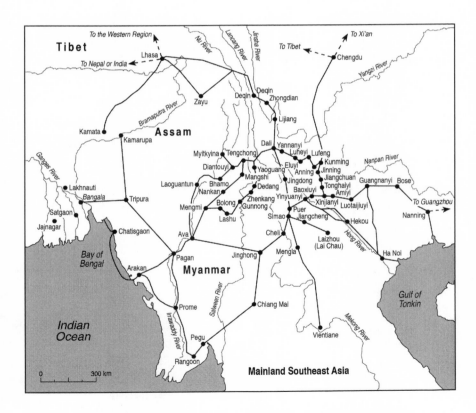

Figure 2.1.   The Yunnan–Burma–India routes. After Yang (2008)

Asia, and the markets in Central Asia were connected through multiple networks and the circulation of different types of commodities.[1] The same pattern is true of other routes and networks that linked South Asia and China. Through the maritime routes and networks, for example, semiprecious stones from Afghanistan, horses from Central Asia and Arabia, and porcelain from Chinese kilns circulated between ancient China and South Asia. The islands and ports of Southeast Asia and the networks of Southeast Asian sailors and traders were instrumental in such maritime circulations, which may have begun as early as the Neolithic period.

Peter Bellwood (1995, 2004) and Wilhelm G. Solheim (2006) have argued for the existence of extensive Neolithic migratory and trading networks of Southeast Asian inhabitants that stretched from the coastal regions of China across the Pacific to Madagascar in the Indian Ocean. The two scholars differ, however, on the origins, nature, and composition of these early networks. Bellwood has proposed that the Austronesians from Taiwan were responsible for colonizing the islands of Borneo, Sumatra, and Java, as well as the Malay Peninsula, by the second or first millennium BCE. Solheim's proposal is more controversial. The "Nusantao" people, Solheim (2006: 56) argues, who comprised Austronesian and non-Austronesian speakers, started establishing their maritime trading networks sometime around 5000 BCE. Originating from what is today eastern Vietnam, this "Nusantao Maritime Trading Network" encompassed "four lobes" or "subareas" and covered the vast region from Japan to Madagascar.

Even though Bellwood and Solheim differ on the specifics and origins of the early Southeast Asian networks, they agree that networks of maritime interactions originating in Southeast Asia connected and integrated various regions of the Pacific and Indian Oceans during the Neolithic period. Important archaeological evidence to support this argument comes from ceramics discovered on the Coromandel coast. The "carved paddle beating" technique, where a small wooden paddle is used by potters to give shape to pottery before firing, found in South Indian ceramic tradition, was imported, V. Selvakumar (2011: 207) contends, from Southeast Asia "either through the land via eastern India in the Neolithic period or through the coast route of Bengal or by overseas [*sic*]." Selvakumar (2011: 213) also suggests that the technique may have reached South Asia as part of long-distance trading activity.

Maritime contacts between South and Southeast Asia expanded rapidly during the last few centuries of the first millennium BCE. Based on archaeological finds in Thailand and Vietnam, Bellina and Glover (2004) have suggested that early commercial exchanges between Southeast Asia and South Asia can be divided into two distinct phases. The first phase covered the period from about the fourth century BCE to the second century CE, when there were "regular but less intense" contacts. The goods frequently exchanged between the two regions included glass and stone beads and ornaments, bronze containers, rouletted ceramic wares, and stamped wares. The second phase extended from the second century CE to the fourth century CE and was marked by "a lesser diversity but greater quality of goods" coming from South Asia. Many of the locally made ceramics in Southeast Asia were inspired by South Asian models, and while "glass and stone beads still came from India," local manufacturing "in an Indian tradition," Bellina and Glover (2004: 80) argue, is "beyond doubt."

Some of these commodities, either imports from South Asia or manufactured locally in Southeast Asia based on South Asian models, also reached the coasts of Han China. The items included semiprecious stones, glass beads, and gold jewelry, items which have been found in Western Han elite tombs in Hepu 合浦, Guangxi Province (Wu 2006; Xiong 2014). The emergence of the Funan polity in present-day Cambodia, which, as noted in the previous chapter, facilitated the circulation of geographical knowledge, also contributed to the expansion of commercial interactions. The port of Óc Eo was one of the main centers for long-distance commerce under the Funanese polity (see figure 2.2). Archaeological evidence not only indicates the presence there of commodities imported from South Asia, but also goods originating in China and even Rome (Hall 1985: 59–60; Higham 2002; Manguin 2004: 291–292, 298–300).

Sometime in the third century CE, Chinese texts inform us, Funan expanded its territories under a ruler named Fan[shi]man 范 [師]蔓, who built large ships and conquered several neighboring polities. Then, during the reign of Fan[shi]man's nephew Fan Zhan 范旃, Funan reportedly sent an embassy to Tianzhu. The embassy met a Tianzhu ruler, whose polity was located in the vicinity of the river Ganges. This Tianzhu ruler responded to the diplomatic mission by sending envoys to Funan together with four Bactrian horses as gifts (*Liang shu* 54: 798–799). The arrival of the embassy from Tianzhu in Funan coincided, as noted in the previous chapter, with a mission to this Southeast Asian polity from the Wu kingdom in China. The diplomats from the Wu polity named Kang Tai 康泰 and Zhu Ying 朱應 reportedly met their South Asian counterparts, whose names are rendered as Chen 陳 and Song 宋 in Chinese sources (*Liang shu* 54: 798–799). The purpose of this Chinese mission to Funan, as Vickery (2003: 112) explains, "was to explore a maritime route through Southeast Asia to acquire valued products from India and the Middle East at a time when the Wu dynasty in southeastern China was cut off by rival kingdoms from traditional overland routes." Funan not only facilitated such commercial interactions between Chinese polities and South Asia but was also one of the earliest Southeast Asian polities to participate in the circulation of Buddhist objects with courts in China. In 484, an embassy from Funan to the Southern Qi 南齊 (479–502) court in China included a Tianzhu monk named Najiaxian 那迦仙 (Nāgasena?), who had previously lived in China. On behalf of the king of Funan,

Figure 2.2.   Early Southeast Asian sites and polities. © Tansen Sen

Nāgasena presented Buddhist artifacts (*Nan Qi shu* 58: 1014–1017; Pelliot 1903: 257–261).

By the sixth century, the islands of Java and Sumatra in the Indonesian archipelago and Kedah on the Malay Peninsula were starting to replace Óc Eo and other Funan ports as the main transit centers of long-distance maritime trade. Commercial activity between South and Southeast Asia grew during the reigns of Gupta rulers in the Gangetic plains and under the Pallavas (fourth–ninth centuries) and Pandyas (sixth–tenth centuries) on the Coromandel coast. These commercial activities were further catalyzed by the development of shipbuilding and the shipping industry in Southeast Asia. Merchants and Buddhist monks are often noted as having traveled between South Asia and China on Southeast Asian ships known as "Kunlun bo" 昆侖舶. Additionally, because Southeast Asian ports provided facilities for repairing ships, they developed into important centers of transit trade with connections to both regional and long-distance intraregional networks. This gave Southeast Asian polities (as well as traders and pirates), such as Śrīvijaya, which replaced Funan as the leading maritime polity in Southeast Asia, significant control over the maritime trade between the Chinese coast and ports elsewhere in the Indian Ocean (see below).

The maritime route from the Chinese coast to South Asia is also mentioned in Jia Dan's work. According to Jia Dan, ships embarking from the Tang port of Guangzhou would pass Hainan island, the ancient port of Annan, the Malay Peninsula, Sumatra (or Java), the vicinity of Malacca, the Nicobar Islands, and Sri Lanka and from there would sail to the coastal regions of South Asia. Sailing to the ports of Kollam, the route continued to the Gujarat peninsula and all the way to Hormuz and Baghdad in the western peripheries of the Arabian Sea (Pelliot 1904). Two centuries later, Arab sources indicated a similar route from the western edges of the Indian Ocean to the coastal towns of China (see below). By the

Yuan and Ming periods, with these expanding connections, the Malabar coast ports emerged as the main transit point for Chinese traders, sailors, and government officials traveling to India and beyond. The expeditions of Zheng He in the early fifteenth century, discussed in the next chapter, used Calicut and Cochin as the hubs for their voyages across the Arabian Sea.

Chaudhuri (1985) and Abu-Lughod (1989) have proposed the idea of multiple interlocking, "circuits" as one way to conceptualize the patterns of connections across the Afroeurasian world. According to their model, there were two overlapping circuits between South Asia and China that converged in Southeast Asia. Geographical contours, monsoon winds, and the pattern of segmented trade facilitated the flow of people and goods between these two circuits. Linked to the Persian Gulf and the Mediterranean Sea through other circuits and networks, these two circuits formed part of the larger Afroeurasian network of interactions. Within these two circuits there were several types of networks that connected South Asia and China, including (1) networks of exchange among the polities skirting the Bay of Bengal, (2) networks that connected the areas around the South China Sea, and (3) networks of direct exchange between South Asia and China (see figure 2.3). These were not exclusively maritime or overland networks. With links to rivers and overland routes, these networks usually incorporated the hinterlands as well as the coastal regions. Commercial goods, Buddhist objects, and tribute items circulated through these connected yet self-contained networks.

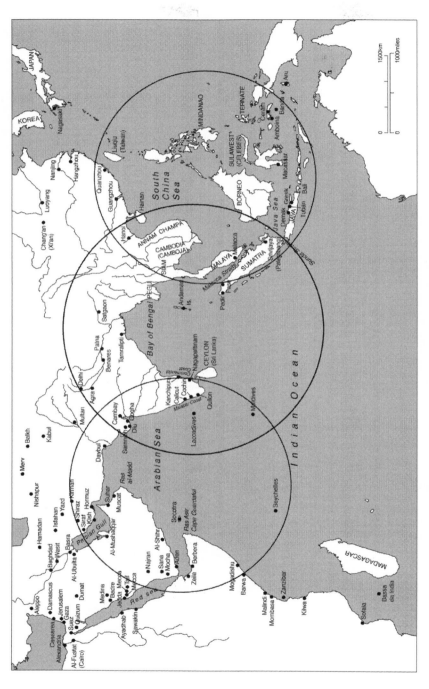

Figure 2.3. Afroeurasian interlocking circuits. After Abu-Lughod (1989)

The two circuits that connected South Asia to China were also linked to the networks of trade that extended to the Persian Gulf and the Mediterranean Sea. Starting from the late seventh century, commercial activity across the maritime circuits grew rapidly due to the participation of traders from the Persian Gulf. Mostly Arab and Persian Muslims, these traders increased their share in Indian Ocean commerce during the eighth century through their network of diasporic settlements that had spread to the ports in South Asia, Southeast Asia, and the coastal regions of China (Wink [1990] 1999). Because of the active involvement of these traders and their networks, maritime commercial exchanges between South Asia and China increased and diversified significantly, ushering in, according to some scholars, an "early age of commerce" in maritime Asia from the ninth century (Wade 2009).

The above-noted circuits of trade and interaction across the maritime world were connected to the Yunnan–Burma–Assam networks, discussed earlier, and also to the Central Asian caravan routes, famously called the "Silk Routes." Credit for establishing the so-called Silk Road is often given to Zhang Qian, but it is clear that the commercial exchanges and interactions in this region started long before his time. Detailed archaeological examination by E. E. Kuzmina (2008) indicates that commodities were circulating across the Eurasian Steppe zones and regions of present-day Xinjiang as early as the second millennium BCE. Advances in metallurgy, the domestication of horses, and the invention of wheeled vehicles facilitated these circulations. By the end of the Bronze Age, Kuzmina argues (2008: 114), caravan trade along the Eurasian routes had begun, and commodities, technologies, and belief systems were frequently circulating in the region.

The expansion of the Han Empire into Central Asia several decades after the failed mission of Zhang Qian was a significant factor in the emergence of silk as the leading export item from China. Initially, silk was used as a medium of payment to Chinese soldiers based at the military garrisons in the occupied regions of Central Asia and was also offered as a diplomatic gift to neighboring foreign rulers. It was subsequent to these "internal" circulations that silk eventually became a trading commodity and entered the stream of international commerce (La Vaissière 2005: 28–34). By the first century CE, silk was used to procure foreign luxuries such as precious stones and glassware, as well as Central Asian horses. These transactions made silk an important commodity in Eurasian commerce. In addition to its dispersal through the overland routes, silk was also brought from Central Asia to the South Asian ports in the Sindh and Gujarat, known to the Hellenistic mariners as Barbaricon (near present-day Karachi) and Barygaza (present-day Bharuch) respectively, and shipped to markets in the Mediterranean region using maritime routes (Raschke 1978; Liu 1996).

The earliest description of the Central Asian route from China to South Asia is found in the account of the Chinese monk Faxian, who embarked on his travels to the Buddhist holy land in the early fifth century. By this time, the oasis town of Dunhuang had emerged as an important halting place for those traveling between China and South Asia, and it was here that Faxian rested. Itinerant monks and traders often mingled at this location; it was also one of the greatest storehouses of Buddhist and non-Buddhist documents. From Dunhuang, Faxian journeyed through Shanshan, Agni, and Khotan. All of these were flourishing Buddhist communities and vibrant centers of intraregional trade. Crossing the Pamir Mountains from Khotan, Faxian eventually reached the banks of the Indus River (Li 2002; Deeg 2005).

Faxian did not return to China by the above overland route but instead traveled by sea from Tāmralipta, a port in the present-day Indian state of West Bengal, to Sri Lanka and from there through Sumatra (or Java) to China. The journey of Faxian by the overland and sea routes between China and South Asia (see figure 2.4) suggests the interconnectedness of these routes and also indicates that traders, pilgrims, and diplomats were aware of the fact that travel between the two regions was possible through multiple avenues. The choice of specific routes by these people most likely depended on opportunities available. Thus, Xuanzang in the first half of the seventh century visited South Asia by the overland route through Central Asia. Yijing, on the other hand, made his to-and-fro journey in the latter half of the same century by the maritime route. Similarly, individual merchants and trading guilds chose to use a specific route or at times were active across both the overland and maritime routes. The Sogdians, for example, had extensive maritime and overland trading networks that linked several parts of Asia. The Tamil merchant guilds operating from the Coromandel coast, on the other hand, established their influential maritime networks across the Bay of Bengal and South China Sea regions. The networks of these two groups of traders who connected South Asia and China are discussed below.

In addition to the Yunnan–Burma–Assam route, the maritime route through Southeast Asia, and the Central Asia routes, which were the three major conduits facilitating commercial, diplomatic, and cultural exchanges between South Asia and China, there were other important pathways. These included a route through Tibet that became popular in the seventh century as well as the several mountainous trails that connected the Swat region of Kashmir to Central Asia.[2] These were never detached or isolated pathways and trails. Rather they were part of the webs of interconnected routes and networks that provided several options to merchants, diplomats, and religious travelers to travel and move commodities and objects between South Asia and China.

Mercantile Networks between South Asia and China

Little is known about the networks of Austronesian mariners who already connected the coastal regions of South Asia and China during the Neolithic period. Oceanic currents and monsoon winds

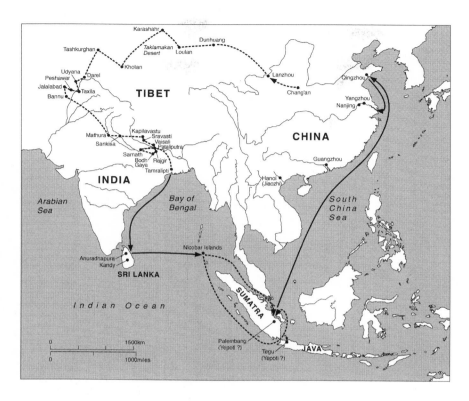

Figure 2.4. Faxian's itinerary between China and South Asia. © Tansen Sen

as well as knowledge about specific sites, local demands, and supply routes may have dictated these early maritime networks. Details about the operations and operators of some of the later mercantile networks are more readily available from textual records and archaeological sources. These sources reveal that Sogdians, Tamil merchant guilds, Śrīvijayan operatives, Muslim traders belonging to various ethnic groups, and Chinese seafarers and sailors were key participants in the circulation of material goods between South Asia and China from the early first millennium CE to the sixteenth century. Each of these groups networked across vast regions of Asia, maintained contact with political regimes, and cooperated or competed with the networks of rival merchant guilds. They not only facilitated the circulation of commercial merchandise but also helped in the movement of objects by missionaries, pilgrims, craftsmen, and diplomats. Some also participated in the expansionist schemes of political regimes and were frequently members of the diplomatic embassies exchanged between the Chinese courts and South Asian polities.

While the Austronesians contributed to the circulations of goods in the maritime regions, the migration of Indo-Europeans into the Indus region and Central Asia facilitated connections between South Asia and the Yellow River Valley region during the late second and early first millennium BCE through the overland routes. Unlike the early trade in cowries, there does not seem to be a single commodity that highlighted these overland connections until the advent of silk some time at the end of the first millennium BCE. Rather, the commodities that the nomadic tribes in Central Asia relayed between South Asia and the Yellow River Valley region might have included a large number of nonluxury items. This may have been the reason that certain agricultural goods with the prefix *cīna* appear in early Sanskrit literature—peaches (*cīnāni*), pears (*cīnarājaputra*), camphor (*cīnaka*), hides (*cīnasī*), and subsequently the luxury product *cīnāṃśuka* or *cīnapaṭṭa* (silk) (Thapliyal 1979; Rao 1993; Sen 2003: 184–185). Some scholars have argued that the use of the *cīna* prefix is not only indicative of South Asian knowledge about China but also evidence for direct contact between South Asia and China prior to the Common Era (Tan and Geng 2005: 43–44). As these terms appear in works whose dates of compilation could range from the second century BCE to the third or fourth century CE, and because no description of China is given in these sources, it is unlikely that either of these arguments is valid. Rather, the commodities circulating between the Yellow River Valley and areas of South Asia would have followed the pattern of cowrie trade, that is, being relayed through multiple routes and networks with little awareness among the consumers of the specific places of origin and the key transit centers.

Urban growth and economic expansion in the Gangetic region, the formation of the Achaemenid Empire in Persia, and the conquests of Alexander of Macedonia during the last half of the first millennium BCE facilitated the consolidation of existing Eurasian commercial networks and the establishment of several new networks. The discovery of South Asian silk fabric and Chinese goods from a fifth-century BCE tomb in Pazyryk (Bunker 1991), various types of South Asian beads and precious and semiprecious stones found in the maritime regions of Southeast and East Asia (Bellina and Glover 2004), and the excavations of Roman goods at Arikamedu on the Coromandel coast of South Asia (Bagley et al. 1996–2004) are indicative of the wide circulation of objects several centuries before the Common Era. It was also during this period that the long-distance trade in silk, particularly from the Central Asian garrisons of the Han Empire, began to take place. The expansion of the Han Empire created a demand for horses used for cavalry; it also resulted in an increased consumption of luxury goods by Han elites. Over the course of the following century or two, merchants from various regions of Asia started participating in these long-distance commercial exchanges, primarily in luxury products. These merchants formed their extensive trade networks, or what Philip D. Curtin (1984: 2–5) calls "trade diasporas," that connected several regions of Asia through settlements in foreign lands, collaborating with sojourning traders and transporters, and negotiating with host communities.

As can be discerned from the records of tributary missions in Chinese sources, merchants from the southern Hindukush region had already extended their trading networks to Han China during the first century BCE. Located north of this region, merchants from Sogdiana (Ch. Kangju 康居) most likely also had trading links with Han China during the same period. It was after the founding of the

Kuṣāṇa Empire in Central Asia and its expansion into the Gangetic plains during the first and second centuries of the Common Era that the role of Sogdian traders started expanding rapidly. By the fourth century, the Sogdian commercial networks dominated both the overland and maritime routes between South Asia and China. Sogdian and Sanskrit inscriptions found in the upper Indus region (i.e., sites around Gilgit) record the mercantile activities of the itinerant Sogdian traders (Sims-Williams 1994). Similarly, tombs and tomb inscriptions belonging to the members of the Sogdian community from China indicate the role of these traders in sustaining long-distance commercial exchanges through diasporic settlements. The Sogdian *Ancient Letters*, for example, provide details about the economic activities, everyday life, religious beliefs, and collaborations between Sogdian traders and other merchant groups, including those from South Asia (La Vaissière 2005: 71–84). The biography of a third-century Buddhist monk of Sogdian origin named Kang Senghui found in the Chinese text *Gaoseng zhuan*, on the other hand, demonstrates the existence of maritime networks involving Sogdian traders that connected South Asia and Jiaozhi (northern Vietnam). The ancestors of Kang, according to the biography, were from Kangju but lived in Tianzhu for several generations. Kang's father emigrated to Jiaozhi, the text points out, "in order to trade" (La Vaissière 2005: 71–72).

The above sources also make clear that Sogdians were not the only merchant group involved in the circulation of goods between South Asia and China. For instance, South Asian (including Sri Lankan) seafaring traders and sailors frequently traveled across the Bay of Bengal and the South China Sea to the coastal regions of China. In fact, the names of some of these traders have survived in Chinese Buddhist sources. The sixth-century Buddhist text *Chu sanzang ji ji* 初三藏記集 (T. 2145: 40c25–41a28) records an Indian trader in Guangzhou named Zhu Pole 竺婆勒, whose son, born in that port city, later became a monk. He was called Zhu

Nankang 竺南康, after his birth in the Nankang region (around present-day Guangzhou). A "ship owner" called Nanti/Zhu Nanti 難提 (Nandin?) from South Asia traveled frequently to China, not only to exchange commodities but also to ferry Buddhist monks and nuns between the two regions (Sen 2003: 162–163). It is possible that these traders were members of a South Asian diasporic community located in Guangzhou. A Chinese monk named Jianzhen 鑒真 traveling to Japan in the eighth century reports the presence of Brahmanical temples in Guangzhou (*Tō daiwa jōtō sei den*, T. 2089: 991c7–15; Wong 2014). Given that South Asian, especially Tamil, merchant guilds were already present at various locations in Southeast Asia, it is conceivable that traders from one of these guilds branched out onto the Chinese coast. Archaeological evidence from Quanzhou, which includes remains of a Brahmanical temple and a Tamil inscription, confirms that one such diasporic community of Tamil traders existed in that port in the twelfth–thirteenth centuries (Guy 1993–1994; Sen 2003: 227–231).

The Tamil merchant networks mostly operated from the Coromandel coast, northern Sri Lanka, and also ports in Southeast Asia. The networks and influence of Tamil merchant guilds, particularly the Maṇigrāmam and Ayyāvoḷe, expanded under the Chola rulers, mainly in the tenth and eleventh centuries. These two guilds not only monopolized the circulation of several South Asian commodities, such as pepper, but also pursued close associations with the ruling elites in South and Southeast Asia (Abraham 1988). Their presence in Southeast Asia, where they participated in the collection of local taxes from residents in port towns, made it possible for them to compete with local merchant communities, including those representing the thalassocratic polity of Śrīvijaya (Christie 1998, 1999). Merchants, sailors, and diplomatic representatives of Śrīvijaya formed a unique network of their own. While the functioning of the Śrīvijayan mercantile networks is not fully documented, it is clear that their reach extended from the Chinese coast to the Bengal and Coromandel regions (Sen 2003: 220–221).

The Śrīvijayan networks were built around three key elements: the strategic location of their base of activities, an advanced shipbuilding tradition, and vigorous diplomatic engagement. The shift of maritime traffic from the Isthmus of Kra to the Straits of Malacca in the sixth century led to the emergence of the Sumatran ports, such as Palembang, as the main transit centers for trade between the coastal regions of China and sites in the Bay of Bengal and beyond. The Śrīvijayans gained control of the earlier Funanese ports and, at least from the seventh century onward, monopolized commercial activity through the Straits of Malacca. By the tenth century, the Śrīvijayan networks dominated the trade in several commodities destined for Chinese markets. This included frankincense from Arabia, which had a huge demand in Song markets. The Śrīvijayans also charged special tolls on foreign ships passing through the Straits of Malacca and, according to Song sources, attacked those that refused to pay (*Zhufan zhi* 13; Sen 2003: 225).

The naval prowess of the Śrīvijayans would have developed from the existing advanced shipbuilding traditions in Southeast Asia. The Funan polity and local traders may have operated these vessels prior to the establishment of the Śrīvijayan Empire. Although none of these Funanese or Śrīvijayan ships has yet been excavated, their depictions at Angkor Wat and on Borobudur indicate the use of advanced shipbuilding technologies in the region (Manguin 1980). In addition to ships, Śrīvijayans also developed port facilities to support repair work and the replenishment of naval personnel and supplies. These maritime facilities were used by the Śrīvijayans to pursue strategic diplomatic interaction with the courts in China and those in South Asia. The Shailendra rulers of Śrīvijaya, for example, established intimate diplomatic connections with both the Song court in China and the Cholas in South Asia that incorporated geopolitical, commercial, and religious agendas.

An aspect of Śrīvijaya's diplomatic agenda may well have been control of the commercial networks between South Asia and China. Song sources, as outlined in the previous chapter, record the Chola polity as a vassal state of Śrīvijaya. This inaccurate information most likely came from Śrīvijayan merchants and representatives trying to receive preferential treatment at the Song Chinese court. The Śrīvijayan attempt to control the maritime networks between the Cholas and Song China appears to have resulted in a massive naval expedition by the South Asian polity against the Śrīvijayan ports in 1025 (see figure 2.5), illustrating the complexities and competition of the circulation of goods between South Asia and China. In addition to frankincense, the Śrīvijayan traders would have competed with their Tamil counterparts over the supply of pepper to Song China and the export of porcelain to South and West Asia.[3]

Persian and Arab traders and sailors were also part of this competition. Persian (*Posi* 波斯) mercantile ships, similar to the Kunlun vessels, are often mentioned as carriers of Buddhist monks between South Asia and China. The Tantric monk Vajrabodhi, for example, is known to have sailed on a Persian ship from the Coromandel coast to Java and subsequently to Guangzhou in the eighth century (*Zhenyuan xinding shijiao mulu*, T. 2157: 876a23–b9). With the spread of Islam in the eighth and ninth centuries, the networks of West Asian traders expanded significantly across the Indian Ocean, including in the South China Sea region. A ninth-century Arab dhow, with most of its cargo intact, discovered near the Indonesian island of Belitung reveals the frequent use of West Asian–made ships in these maritime connections. The cargo, consisting both of commercial-grade Changsha porcelain and luxury items made of gold and silver for diplomatic gifts, confirms the textual records about the participation of West Asian ships and sailors in the maritime networks between China and several regions of the Indian Ocean (Krahl et al. 2011).

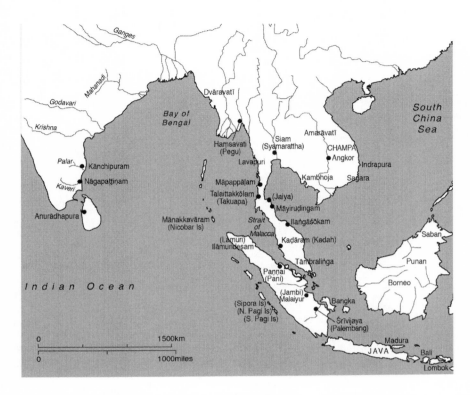

**Figure 2.5.   The sites of Chola raid on Śrīvijayan ports in 1025. ©
Tansen Sen**

These maritime networks of West Asian traders and sailors,
which included the South Asia–China sector, were fostered, as
noted above, through their diasporic communities. Especially after
the spread of Islam in the seventh and eighth century, Muslim
diasporic communities based in places such as Guangzhou and
Quanzhou seem to have been the most active in maritime commerce as well as diplomatic interactions. With the conversion of a
large number of South Asians to Islam, especially those based on
the Malabar and Coromandel coasts, the networks of Muslim traders became more vibrant. This also led polities such as Vijayanagar, Ma'bar, Calicut, and Bengal to engage in maritime commerce
more actively than at any time previously. The interlinked networks

of Muslim traders, now comprising West Asians, South Asians, and a few Southeast Asians, stretched from the Mediterranean region to the coasts of Song and Yuan China. They were involved in the circulation of Arabian horses, South and Southeast Asian spices, and Chinese porcelain. One of their main contributions was to integrate Chinese and South Asian markets into the larger Afroeurasian networks from the tenth to the fourteenth century. Indeed, the networks of Muslim traders, sailors, and navigators not only dominated the maritime routes and the circulation of goods between South Asia and China, but they also contributed to the globalization of the networks connecting the two regions.[4] The later Chinese and European maritime networks profited from the foundations for an Afroeurasian circulation of goods laid by these Muslim traders and sailors.

Arabian and Persian Muslim traders were also active on the overland routes between South Asia and China. Arabic sources indicate that they were involved in the trade through routes that linked the eastern regions of Bengal and Assam to Tibet and Yunnan. The establishment of various Islamic sultanates in the northern and eastern regions of India after the eleventh century and the founding of the Mongol Ilkhanate in Persia facilitated the growth and expansion of these overland networks of Muslim traders.[5] Thus, for over four centuries Muslim traders from West Asia and those who converted to Islam in South and Southeast Asia controlled much of the circulation of commercial goods between South Asia and China.

Existing records do not indicate the presence of Chinese trading or shipping networks in the Bay of Bengal region prior to the eleventh century. It was only after the development of Chinese shipbuilding technology, the emphasis on maritime trade by the Song court, and the spread of Chinese diasporic networks that commercial networks of traders and sailors from China started taking shape. By the late thirteenth century, Chinese traders and ships were the most prominent players in Indian Ocean commerce. This is reflected in the writings of Marco Polo and Ibn Baṭūṭah. Even the later Portuguese sources note the dominant status the Chinese traders enjoyed prior to European expansion. All these sources point to the presence of Chinese traders on the Coromandel and Malabar coasts and report on the superior Chinese ships that ferried people and commodities between the Chinese coast and South Asia.[6] Similar to the circulations of knowledge examined in the previous chapter, these networks indicate a clear preeminence of the maritime avenues over the overland routes in the circulations of commercial goods between the two regions during the thirteenth and fourteenth centuries.

Chinese naval power peaked in the early fifteenth century, when ships led by Admiral Zheng He made seven expeditions across the Indian Ocean. While the Ming armada is reported to have overseen trading activities at various South Asian ports, separate networks of private Chinese traders, many of whom operated from their bases in Southeast Asia, also existed. The Ming Hongwu 洪武 emperor's (r. 1368–1398) ban on foreign trade was one of the reasons for the emergence of distinct private and official networks of commercial transactions between China and South Asia. Perceiving the exuberant pursuit of commerce as immoral and perhaps not of benefit to the state, traders from Ming China were prohibited from dealing with foreigners (Li 2010). Instead, the Ming court, unlike the previous Song and Yuan dynasties, wanted to bring foreign trade under state control and highlight the tributary aspect of Ming-foreign relations.

As a result of these restrictions placed on foreign trade, merchants from Ming China who were engaged in foreign trade relocated to Southeast Asia, where several Chinese immigrant communities already existed by the early fifteenth century. For most of the fifteenth century, maritime commercial exchanges took place through Southeast Asia. Merchants from various regions of South

Asia, especially Bengal and Gujarat, also congregated at Southeast Asian ports, such as Malacca, to procure porcelain and other goods originating in China.[7] In return, these traders sold textiles and other South Asian products to their Chinese counterparts. This triangular trading system between South Asia and Ming China through Southeast Asia continued until European commercial enterprises, starting with the Portuguese, intersected with and eventually asserted their hegemony over the commercial networks in Asia.

THE CIRCULATION OF BUDDHIST OBJECTS

The spread of Buddhism to China in the first century CE resulted in the circulation of new types of objects between South Asia and China. Three categories of such objects are highlighted in this section. The first were images of the Buddha, Buddhist divinities, and leading devotees of Buddhism, as well as models of Buddhist monasteries. The second were objects used in Buddhist rituals and ceremonies, which ranged from the relics of the Buddha to ewers. The third type consisted of texts, primarily Buddhist sutras, but also non-Buddhist manuscripts. These objects were exchanged, gifted, traded, or even smuggled. Although the transmission of Buddhist teachings took place from South Asia to China, there were instances, as discussed below, when Buddhist objects moved in the opposite direction. During the first millennium CE, the circulation of objects associated with Buddhism may have dominated the material exchanges between South Asia and China. Various other regions of Asia, especially Central and Southeast Asia, were part of these circulations that resulted in the creation of a Buddhist cosmopolis, stretching from present-day Iran to Japan, integrated by the common belief in karmic consequences and connected through the movements and circulations of Buddhist missionaries, pilgrims, ritual objects, and texts.

Buddhist Images

Buddhist images played a critical role in the early spread of Buddhist doctrines. They were perhaps the first constituents of Buddhism to move over long distances even before the transmission of the doctrines and the exposition of relevant philosophical ideas occurred. These images included small, portable statues of the Buddha, Buddhist divinities, and models of renowned temples (such as the Mahābodhi Temple in Bodhgayā; see figure 2.6); talismans and votive tablets; and paintings that narrated the previous lives of the Buddha. Itinerant merchants, missionaries, pilgrims, and other travelers carried these items from one region to another. During the first and second centuries CE, members of the Sogdian and Parthian merchant communities, originating in present-day Tajikistan, Afghanistan, and Iran, were the leading carriers of Buddhist images to China. The establishment of the Kuṣāṇa Empire, which, as noted above, contributed to the formation of new merchant networks between South Asia and China, greatly facilitated the diffusion of Buddhist images and doctrines as well.

The most famous Chinese legend associated with the introduction of Buddhism into the Yellow River Valley revolves around a Han emperor's dream of a strange being. According to the legend, the Han emperor Ming 漢明帝 (r. 58–75) dreamed of a golden man with a halo around his head who flew into his palace. On inquiring, his officials explained to the emperor that the dream was probably about the Buddha, who was venerated in the "Western Regions." Emperor Ming soon dispatched envoys to bring to Han China people who could explain the teachings of this "sage of the West." The Han envoys returned in the year 67 CE with the first two Tianzhu monks, named Jiaye Modeng 迦葉摩騰 (Kāśyapa Mātaṇga?) and Zhu Falan 竺法蘭 (Dharmaratna?). These two monks are credited with initiating the translation of Buddhist texts at the imperially funded "first" Buddhist monastery in East Asia known as the White Horse Monastery 白馬寺. They are also reported to have brought

Figure 2.6. Replica of the Mahābodhi Temple. © Trustees of the British Museum

the earliest Buddhist images to China. This story of an official transmission of Buddhism was composed two to three centuries after Buddhist doctrines and images first entered Han China with the objective of legitimizing the transmission of the foreign religion by inventing a role for the Chinese emperor in the process (Zürcher [1959] 1972: 22).

Archaeological evidence suggests a more haphazard transmission of Buddhism and one that seems to have been more integrated with local beliefs from an early stage. The images found engraved on Mount Kongwang 孔望山 in the coastal area of Jiangsu Province are examples of this phenomenon. Dating from the second and third centuries, these images include various representations of the Buddha, in standing, seated, and *parinirvāṇa* postures. They are interspersed with traditional Chinese motifs and images of human figures wearing costumes that suggest their Central Asian origins (Rhie 1999: 27–47). Another early image of the Buddha, in a seated posture, is found in a cave-tomb at Mahao 麻浩 in Sichuan Province and also dates from the late second or early third century (Edwards 1954; Rhie 1999: 47–56; Sen 2003). The use of Buddhist images in Chinese tombs suggests the incorporation of Buddhist imagery in the local mortuary tradition. It is not clear, however, if the patron of the tomb was aware of the identity of the figure portrayed in the image or the teachings associated with Buddhism. In fact, Wu Hung (1986) has argued that these early images should not be termed "Buddhist" given the context within which they were used.

Despite this ambiguity in categorizing the use of images in the popular realm, it is evident that by the third century Buddhist objects were being used in veneration activities and rituals and for their perceived supernatural and miraculous powers. During the following few centuries, the usage of Buddhist objects in China became more widespread with the translation of Buddhist texts and the spread of Buddhist teachings to almost every level of Chinese society. The merits of making and venerating Buddhist images advocated in some of the translated texts contributed to this popularity. Additionally, images, especially paintings narrating the previous lives of the Buddha and representations of Buddhist hells and paradise, were employed to proselytize the basic teachings of Buddhism, particularly those related to the ideas of karma and retribution initially unfamiliar to Chinese audiences. These images, ritual objects, paintings, and texts all served to create a Buddhist world in China, the success of which resulted in the large-scale reproduction of these items, some of which were replicas and others made with local artistic features and aesthetics. While the induction of images played an important role in the early transmission of Buddhist doctrines, their reproduction locally accelerated the spread of Buddhism within China and also to places such as Korea, Japan, Vietnam, and the steppe regions of Mongolia and Central Asia. The demand for these objects also initiated the formation of new exchange and transportation networks and intensified the movement of people, including traders, monks, and diplomats.

The Buddhist images that initially reached China originated from different parts of South Asia, each having its unique stylistic features and motifs. Gandhāran, Gupta, Pala, and the artistic renditions from Nāgārjunikoṇḍa in south India were some of the major traditions that entered China. Styles that developed in Central Asia also had a significant impact on the making of Buddhist images in China. These images spread through different routes and means. There were instances, for example, when artisans from South Asia traveled to China expressly to make Buddhist statues and paintings. Indian painters named Shijiafotuo 釋迦佛陀 (Śākyabuddha?), Juecheng 覺稱 (Buddhakīrti?), and Tongzhi 童智 (Kumārabodhi?), during the Northern Wei period (386–534), are known to have done paintings that adorned several local Buddhist monasteries (Pelliot 1923: 238ff; Bagchi [1950] 1981: 195). Similarly, a Sri Lankan monk-artist in China during the Tang period made clay images of Buddhist divinities that were installed at monasteries in Luoyang (*Lidai minghua ji* 9: 298; Acker 1974: 255). On other occasions, Chinese monks and diplomats visiting South Asia returned with Buddhist images and other artifacts. The diplomatic mission sent overland to South Asia in 645 and led by the Tang diplomat Wang Xuance, for instance, included a Chinese artisan named Song Fazhi 宋法智, who drew several images of Buddhist figures that were subsequently replicated in China (*Fayuan zhulin*, T. 2122: 503a.6–12; Sen 2003: 38). Buddhist drawings, rubbings, and replicas were also brought to China from India by Xuanzang and displayed prominently at the Tang capital.

While there were times, such as during the Northern Qi (550–577) period in the sixth century, when attempts were made to closely copy Indic styles (Howard 1996, 2008), often Buddhist images produced in China followed local aesthetics. They were also made to serve political purposes, as can be discerned from some of the Buddhist statues created in the likeness of Empress Wu Zetian 武則天 (r. 690–705) who usurped the Tang throne in the seventh century (Karetzky 2002–2003; Rothschild 2015). Because of the efforts to produce localized forms of Buddhist art, China emerged, by the seventh century, as a leading producer and exporter of Buddhist images. Many of the images associated with Tantric teachings, which became popular in East Asia between the seventh and tenth centuries, originated in Tang China. The mandalic representation of the cosmos, the wrathful Tantric deities, and even the mantras (*dhāraṇīs*) written in Indic script combining Indic ideas and Sinitic forms were created in China. These were considered to be powerful and efficacious images and were employed in rituals, ceremonies, and mortuary practices in several regions of East Asia. Through the transmission of these and other images, China created its own sphere of Buddhist influence in East Asia that was actively promoted by the local monastic institutions and the state.

Some of the locally produced images were unique to the Chinese Buddhist pantheon. These included the representations of the Chan/Zen monk Bodhidharma (Jp. Daruma; see figure 2.7), the bodhisattvas Dizang 地藏 and Guanyin 觀音, and the so-called laughing Buddha named Budai (Jp. Hotei) 布袋. The image of the famous Buddhist divinity Mañjuśrī (Wenshushili 文殊師利) also may have originated in China and then successfully spread to all parts of the Buddhist world (see figure 2.8). In fact, even monks in South Asia believed that Mañjuśrī, the "bodhisattva of wisdom," lived on the Chinese mountain Wutai, and they traveled there expressly to pay obeisance. Paintings of Mañjuśrī and maps of Mount Wutai were produced for local consumption and for export to places such as Tibet, Japan, and South Asia. The widespread acceptance of Mount Wutai as the abode of Mañjuśrī validated the integration of China into the Buddhist realm and legitimized its status as one of the centers for the dissemination of Buddhist ideas and images (Sen 2003).

This role of China as the center for dissemination of new varieties of images across the Buddhist cosmopolis is clearly evident between the eighth and tenth centuries. Many of these images were inspired by Tantric texts translated or composed in Tang China.

Figure 2.7.   Image of the monk Bodhidharma. © Trustees of the British Museum

Figure 2.8.   The Buddhist divinity Mañjuśrī. © **Trustees of the British Museum**

Based on these texts, the Japanese, for example, developed unique ways of representing the Buddhist cosmos through paintings known as Star Maṇḍalas (Jp. *Hoshi mandara* 星曼陀羅) (see figure 2.9). Employed in Tantric Buddhist rituals, maṇḍalas are supposed to connect the patrons to the reality of the universe. The Star Maṇḍalas, which have representations of celestial objects, frequently in anthropomorphic forms, originated from Tantric texts that contain synthesized Hellenistic and Brahmanical ideas on astronomy and astrology. The Japanese diagrams entered the streams of Tantric circulations in East Asia, were transmitted back to the clergy in China, and had a significant impact on the lay believers of Buddhism. During the eleventh and twelfth centuries, images derived from these diagrams found their way into the tombs belonging to Han Chinese residents of the Khitan (Liao) Empire (Sen 1999). These tomb paintings (see chapter 1) are evidence of an enduring feature of East Asian Buddhist practices, starting from the Han tombs at Mahao, which saw Buddhist teachings melding with Sinitic mortuary traditions.

Unlike their Chinese and Korean counterparts, Japanese monks did not visit Buddhist sites in South Asia until the sixteenth century. However, their longing for the Buddhist holy land can be discerned from a series of images they created to visually represent the geography, peoples, and even the Chinese monks visiting the holy land in South Asia. By the fourteenth century, the Japanese, as pointed out in the first chapter, were making maps of India based on the seventh-century travel records of the Chinese monk Xuanzang. They also created visual representations of famous South Asian monks, including those who were active in China. The most intriguing of these are the images of the Tang monk Xuanzang's meetings with the South Asian ruler Harṣa and his teachers at Nālandā (see figure 2.10) (Rambelli 2014). All of these representations were imagined, often mediated through Chinese texts, and were an expression of the longing for and belonging to the Bud-

Figure 2.9.   Star Maṇḍala. © **Philadelphia Museum of Art**

dhist world. These representations, like the Star Maṇḍalas, are examples of images on the move, albeit not physically but as part of
the imagination of distant, yet connected, places within the Buddhist cosmopolis.

Almost at the same time as these cosmological images and
drawings of Buddhist maps of South Asia were circulating in East
Asia, Mongol Iran was intimately in contact with both South Asia
and China. The Ilkhanate official and prolific writer Rashīd al-Dīn
in his *Jami al-Tavarikh* included a section on the biography of the
Buddha. This "Life and Teachings of the Buddha" that he wrote

Figure 2.10. Xuanzang at Nālandā. After Rambelli (2014), reprinted from Sen (2014a)

was based on information provided by a Kashmiri monk named Kamalaśrī and two Chinese informants. One of the extant manuscripts of this work, dated 1314, has three images related to the life of the Buddha: the scene of temptation (see figure 2.11), where the evil Mara attempts to prevent the Buddha from attaining enlightenment; the Jetavana monastery, where the Buddha preached; and the holy site of Kuśīnagara, where the Buddha attained nirvana (Jahn 1965: xxi–lxxvii; Canby 1993; Akasoy 2013; Yoeli-Tlalim 2013). Two centuries later, paintings of the Buddha appeared in Hafiz-i Abru's *Majma al-Tavarikh* (Chronicles). While much of the information on the Buddha's life is copied from Rashīd al-Dīn's work, the illustrations, that of the birth of the Buddha, Buddha's meeting with a Brahmin, and his nirvana, are different in content and style when compared to the illustrated manuscript of *Jami al-Tavarikh*. They are, similar to the Japanese representations, also examples of the multicultural, interconnected, and imagined world of Buddhism.

The circulation of Buddhist objects did not cease with the colonization of Asia by European powers. In fact, in the late eighteenth and nineteenth centuries we still see Buddhist images from China being introduced into India by Chinese immigrants. These Chinese immigrants, as discussed in chapter 3, had settled primarily in Calcutta (now Kolkata), the capital of British India, and built several Chinese temples and shrines, including some dedicated to Guanyin. They also brought with them images of Ruan Ziyu 阮子鬱 (1079–1102) and Liang Cineng 梁慈能 (1098–1116), two localized (or "homegrown"[8]) Chinese Buddhist divinities whose temples originated in the Sihui region of Guangdong Province during the Song period, spread to present-day Malaysia in the late nineteenth century, and from there reached Calcutta (see figures 2.12 and

Figure 2.11.   Persian rendition of the temptation of Mara.

2.13). Members of the Chinese immigrant community also built temples in several other holy Buddhist sites in India and had statues of the Buddha and other divinities imported from China or Burma (Zhang 2014). Although non-Chinese Indians rarely frequent these Chinese Buddhist temples and shrines, they are nonetheless indicative of the continuing circulation of images and objects between South Asia and China.

Ritual and Ceremonial Objects

John Kieschnick (2003) has demonstrated in detail the significant impact Buddhism had on Chinese material culture. The spread of Buddhism not only introduced various Indic objects and artifacts, such as monk robes and rosaries, that had no previous place in Chinese society, but also indirectly led to the transmission of ideas

Figure 2.12.   The Ruan and Liang buddhas in Calcutta. © **Tansen Sen**

Figure 2.13.   Mummified body of Liang Cineng. © **Tansen Sen**

related to the establishment of monasteries, the construction of stupas, the building and maintaining of bridges, the use of chairs, and
the consumption of sugar and tea. Kieschnick also discusses the
role of relics of the Buddha, an important component of Buddhist
rituals and veneration in China. In many ways contradictory to the
Confucian teaching of separation of the living and the dead, the
venerated bodily remains of the Buddha, similar to some Buddhist
images, were also seen to have miraculous powers and served to
legitimize political authority. These relics ranged in size and shape
and were said to be various parts of the Buddha's body, including
his hair, teeth, finger bones, parietal bone, and so forth.

The story of King Asoka distributing the relics of Buddha was
well known in China from at least the third century (Zürcher [1959]
1972: 277). The story was sometimes used to trace and authenticate
relics "discovered" in China, and Asoka's act was also emulated by

Chinese rulers for religious and political purposes. Emperor Wu of the Liang dynasty and Emperor Wen of the Sui were two such Chinese rulers who undertook relic redistribution activities during their reigns (Sen 2003: 60–64). The spread of Tantric Buddhism, which emphasized the use of relics in various rituals and ceremonies, also had a considerable impact on the circulation of the bodily remains of the Buddha, or objects symbolically representing them, in China and elsewhere in East Asia (Sen 2003: 71–72). Similarly, both the Buddhist clergy and the rulers in China prized relics associated with the life of the Buddha, which included his alms bowl.

Chinese sources mention the procurement of the bodily remains and other Buddhist relics through purchase, gift giving, smuggling, or forced acquisition. The purchase of a relic of the Buddha, for instance, is mentioned in the context of the Tang diplomat Wang Xuance's visit to South Asia, from where he is reported to have paid four thousand bolts of Chinese silk to procure a relic (*Fayuan zhulin*, T. 2122: 497c28–498a2). Relics were also given as gifts to Chinese rulers by tribute carriers and presented to visiting Chinese monks by monastic institutions in South Asia, as was the case with Xuanzang. The most notorious episode of an attempt to smuggle a relic, the Tooth Relic of the Buddha from Sri Lanka, took place when a Chinese monk named Mingyuan 明遠 in the seventh century tried to hide it inside his thigh and bring it to China. According to the monk Yijing, the attempt failed (*Da Tang Xiyu qiufa gaoseng zhuan*, T. 2066: 3c2–c18). But several centuries later the Ming admiral Zheng He seems to have acquired the same relic after using military force against a local leader for the Yongle emperor (see chapter 3). Kublai Khan may also have had similar interests in acquiring Buddhist relics from South Asia through his representatives (Sen 2006b: 303n.11).

Not all relics circulating in China were brought from South Asia. Some appeared miraculously and became objects of widespread veneration. The most famous of such miraculously appearing relics was the finger bone of the Buddha housed at the Famen Monastery near Xian. The relic is reported to have appeared on the palm of a Chinese monk and was subsequently housed in the Famen Monastery. It was one of the few Buddhist relics that was "welcomed" into the palace of Tang rulers and venerated with lavish gifts and ritual performances. In fact, the veneration of this relic resulted in the circulation of several other ritual objects, including those made of gold and silver, imported glass, silk fabric, and other precious materials. Many of these were specifically made for donation to the Famen relic during the occasion of veneration ceremonies, which usually took place every thirty years (Sen 2003, 2014e). Indeed, relics also instigated manufacturing of certain ritual objects and building projects, such as relic coffers, stupas, ritual platforms, and underground chambers. The allure of the relics drew devotees and tourists, which not only resulted in donations and almsgiving, but also the establishment of marketplaces by traders to sell incense, talismans, images, and souvenirs. The circulation of relics, therefore, embodied the exchange of numerous other material objects, creating a market for goods and opportunities for various groups of traders.

The construction of stupas, as Liu Xinru (1988) has demonstrated, also had a similar impact on the circulation of material objects. The idea of *saptaratna*, or seven jewels, which usually included gold, silver, lapis lazuli, crystal, coral, pearl, and agate and was used to adorn Buddhist stupas, was promoted in Buddhist texts such as the Lotus Sutra as appropriate merit-making offerings for rulers and elites. Liu argues that the transmission of this belief and the construction of stupas in China resulted in the expansion of the trade in lapis lazuli, coral, pearls, and agate from foreign regions, including South Asia. During several phases of Chinese history, when rulers such as Emperor Wu of the Liang dynasty, Emperor Wen of the Sui, and Empress Wu Zetian used Buddhism to legitimize their political power, the importation of such goods through commercial and tributary channels increased significantly. In exchange for these items, Chinese silk, as Liu has also illustrated, was sent to South Asian markets and monasteries.

There were several other objects associated with Buddhist practices, veneration, and monument construction that also entered China from South Asia. These included miniature replicas of famous Buddhist monasteries and ritual implements such as ewers, incense burners, and the *vajra* scepter. Xuanzang, for example, in addition to carrying about 657 Buddhist texts and 150 grains of the "remains of the Buddha," is also reported to have brought back from India several gold, silver, and sandalwood images of the Buddha (Sen 2003: 206). Also used to decorate relic coffers, these imported items were placed on the statues of locally made buddhas and bodhisattvas, and functioned as wish-fulfilling jewels.

The demand for Buddhist objects and implements, according to Liu Xinru (1988), contributed to the growth and diversification of commercial exchanges between China and South Asia. Indeed, Buddhist goods dominated these commercial interactions through to the tenth and eleventh centuries (Sen 2003). During the tenth and eleventh centuries, despite the fact that the ideological connections between South Asian and Chinese clergies had declined, Buddhism became more intertwined with commerce. The belief in the eventual demise of Buddhist doctrine, followed by its regeneration at a future time, was an integral part of early Buddhism (Nattier 1991). Already during the seventh and eight centuries, reports about the abandonment of Buddhist monastic institutions in parts of India, which were linked to urban decay in the region, filtered into China through traveling monks. Buddhists in several parts of Asia associated the phenomena with Buddhist apocalyptic prophecies and started preserving Buddhist texts and artifacts. Their attempt sparked renewed demand for Buddhist texts, relics, and other paraphernalia that the Buddhist clergy in China and neighboring regions believed would be needed during the phase of the regenera-

tion of the doctrine. At the same time, parts of East Asia witnessed
the emergence of new polities established by previously seminomadic tribes. These polities started adopting Buddhism as state
doctrine, primarily to create their own ideological identities. South
Asian Buddhist paraphernalia reaching Song China were retransmitted to these new polities. Indeed, the Song court in China became an important participant in the circulation of Buddhist objects, as discussed below, by procuring them from South Asia and
then selling or presenting them to neighboring polities (Sen 2003:
117–118).

The impact of Buddhism was even greater during this period if
its contribution to the circulation of other related items is considered. The import of cotton from South Asia to China, for example,
may have started and was initially sustained due to the use of
monks' robes in China. Similarly, Chinese silk entered South Asia
in larger quantities because, as noted above, it was used to purchase
and exchange Buddhist items. Thus, it can be surmised that Buddhism was a dominating factor in the circulation of objects related
to Buddhist practices, rituals, and ceremonies as well as in the
circulation of the by-products of Buddhist exchanges between China and South Asia. While this domination by Buddhism clearly
lasted until the eleventh century, even later it continued to be a
factor through the early fifteenth century as can be discerned from
the interest in Buddhism and Buddhist relics during the reigns of
the Yuan emperor Kublai Khan and the Yongle emperor of the
Ming dynasty.

Buddhist Texts

Buddhist doctrines were transmitted from South Asia to China primarily through two means. First, individual monks or teams of
translators rendered texts in Indic languages into Chinese. Second,
some of the South and Central Asian monks in China recited texts
that they had memorized, which were then translated and written

down in Chinese. The Buddhist texts entering China were written on palm leaves and tied together with threads known as *sūtra* or *sūtram*, the name for ancient Indic manuscripts. These Buddhist texts were not only valued for the teachings contained within but were also perceived as sacred in themselves and on occasion venerated. The rendition of these Indic texts into Chinese meant that they were transferred onto paper, the widely used writing material in China by the time Buddhist doctrines penetrated Chinese society. Similar to the images and objects associated with Buddhism discussed above, Buddhist texts from South Asia also reached China through itinerant monks, merchants, and diplomatic missions. Some were also composed in China, but in order to legitimize the teachings contained in them, the Chinese clergy designated them as imports from South Asia.

The above-mentioned legend of the Han emperor Ming's dream also includes the narrative of the two Buddhist monks from South Asia bringing with them a text called *Sishier zhang jing* 四十二章經 (The Sutra in Forty-Two Chapters). The emperor, as noted above, housed the foreign monks at the White Horse Monastery in Luoyang, where this "first" Buddhist text was translated into Chinese. The legend, thus, not only attempted to legitimize the transmission of a foreign religion in China but also tried to give imperial sanction to the rendition of Buddhist teachings into Chinese. The transmission of Buddhist texts was not as organized as the legend suggests. Monks from different parts of the Buddhist world brought to China texts that had wide-ranging content. Initially, many of them contained basic Buddhist teachings (*abhidharmas*), stories of the Buddha's previous lives (*jatakas*), and tales of the leading supporters of the Buddha and his teachings (*avadanas*).[9] Since there was no systematic and coordinated effort to introduce Buddhism into China, certain important texts did not appear in Chinese for several centuries. The most pertinent of these were the *vinaya* texts, which contained monastic regulations. It was to obtain such missing texts that Faxian traveled to South Asia in the fifth century. Faxian, we are told in his travelogue, managed to get the *vinaya* texts from Sri Lanka, and some of these were translated into Chinese (Heirman 2007: 174).

In the early seventh century, the monk Xuanzang also decided to go to South Asia in search of Buddhist texts. Xuanzang was primarily interested in texts related to Yogacara teachings, which he learned was popular among contemporary South Asian monks (Kuwayama 1988). As noted above, Xuanzang procured over 650 Buddhist texts during his stay in South Asia. After returning to Tang China, Xuanzang translated several texts related to Yogacara teachings and tried to propagate them in China. He also maintained contact with his teachers and fellow students at Nālandā Mahāvihara through exchange of letters and gifts. In one of his letters, Xuanzang wrote that he had lost several texts while crossing a river on his way back to Tang China. He requested that his fellow students at Nālandā provide him with copies of these texts. Xuanzang noted that these could be sent through a Tang envoy then visiting South Asia (Li 1995: 233). Yijing traveled to South Asia a few decades after Xuanzang. Similar to Faxian, Yijing was interested in the monastic laws and observed the lives of Buddhist monks in Nālandā. He too brought back several *vinaya* texts and translated them into Chinese. About a century later, Amoghavajra, the South Asian Tantric master in Tang China, made a voyage to Sri Lanka to find an esoteric text unavailable to him in China (Sen 2014b).

Buddhist texts also formed part of the gifts exchanged between the Chinese court and foreign polities and were peddled by merchants to monasteries, courts, and individuals. Diplomatic missions from South Asia, for example, often brought Buddhist texts for presentation to Chinese emperors. Some of these texts, often considered sacred objects,[10] were decorated with jewels or gilded. Such diplomatic gifts of Buddhist texts witnessed a significant increase during the Song period, when the court actively sought to find Buddhist texts for translation and inclusion in the Buddhist canon. The Song court at times also bought and sold Buddhist texts and collections. It sponsored a special translation bureau in charge of translating Buddhist works, staffed it with South Asian and Chinese monk-translators, and asked them to produce translations of newly procured texts. The Song rulers offered these translated texts and printed collections to neighboring polities, such as Xi Xia and Koguryŏ, as part of their diplomatic overtures to prospective allies. The Song court's interest in procuring Buddhist texts resulted in merchants, some of whom also acted as diplomats, presenting a wide variety of manuscripts to the Chinese emperor in return for commercial favors (Sen 2003: 118–119).

The increased demand for Buddhist texts in East Asia during the Song period was also related to the fear, as mentioned above, of the predicted decline of Buddhism. Monastic institutions and polities that adhered to Buddhism made tremendous effort to acquire and preserve Buddhist texts in the tenth and eleventh centuries. The interest in Indic Buddhist texts at this time was primarily for their material value, intended for collections, preservation, sale, or gifts, rather than for use as sources of new or deficient teachings. This is not to say that the entire corpus of Song translations remained unutilized in Song China. The *dhāraṇīs* in particular were widely distributed and employed by the followers of Buddhism during this period.

The spread of Buddhism also facilitated the circulation of non-Buddhist texts. Various Brahmanical manuscripts on astronomy and medicine became, as outlined in the previous chapter, available in China. This included a few that were translated by Buddhist monks. It was also mentioned above that the Sui ruler Wen ordered the composition of texts in Sanskrit that described the geography and Buddhist practices in China. Additionally, an attempt was made to translate the Daoist work *Daode jing* into Sanskrit during the Tang period at the request of the king of Kāmarūpa. Xuanzang was asked to render the text into Sanskrit, but he is reported to have turned down the request, pointing out the difficulties associated with the incompatibility in the Indian and Chinese ways of thinking (Pelliot 1912; Sen 2003: 45–46). These episodes suggest the diversity of texts that were circulating between China and South Asia throughout the first millennium CE.

From about the twelfth century onward, however, with diminishing Chinese interest in importing Buddhist ideas from South Asia, the number of texts circulating between the two regions declined dramatically. This shift marked a watershed in China–South Asian interactions. The emergence of the coast as the main site of interactions between China and South Asia, as argued in the previous chapter, led to a decline in knowledge of the places that were formerly described in Buddhist (as well as Brahmanical) texts. The decline in the transmission of Buddhist texts was clearly one of the contributing factors in this loss of knowledge about the South Asian hinterland among the Chinese.

TRIBUTARY MISSIONS AND DIPLOMATIC GIFTS

The tribute system of the Chinese dynasties contributed significantly to the circulation of goods between China and South Asia. The system was rooted in the Confucian ideology of the Chinese emperor as sovereign head of all under heaven (*tianxia* 天下). According to this ideology, neighboring as well as distant polities were to send tribute to the reigning emperor in China in recognition of his sovereignty, endorsed by the Mandate of Heaven (*tianming* 天命). As acknowledgment for such "submission," the emperor offered return gifts and bestowed honorary titles on the foreign rulers who sent the tribute missions and rewarded those who carried these presents to the Chinese court.[11] In reality, however, the system largely functioned as a conduit for trading activities. Foreign traders frequenting China took on the role of tribute carriers, presenting tribute to the emperor but at the same time also selling part of the goods they brought in the local markets. The Chinese courts were aware of the commercial motives of the tribute carriers and at times tried to restrict or regulate their activities. While the Han, early Tang, and the Ming courts were particularly concerned about the integrity of the system, other dynasties were not very restrictive of the commercial activities of the tribute carriers. The tribute carriers themselves were cognizant of the differing attitudes of the Chinese courts and adjusted their approaches to the system accordingly.

The Dynamics of the Tributary System

The tribute system went through several modifications from the Han through to the Ming periods. The military strength of the specific dynasties, the diplomatic agenda and the economic policies instituted by the courts, and the fluctuations in commercial networks and exchanges beyond the frontiers of imperial China contributed to these modifications. The kinds of goods that circulated between China and foreign polities through the tributary system also varied depending on many factors, including the tribute carriers' intention to impress the Chinese emperor with the presentation of exotic goods as well as their plan to sell part of their consignment in local markets. The system included return gifts or titles given to the tribute carriers and the rulers who sent the missions. The return gifts and types of titles bestowed on foreign rulers also changed over time. As a result, the objects that circulated through the tribute system were extremely diverse and had a notable impact on cross-regional commerce as well as the fiscal considerations of several dynasties in China.

Confucian officials, mindful of the dual role of the tribute carriers, frequently voiced their displeasure over the commercial activities that took place after the tribute carriers entered China. During the Han dynasty, for example, an official named Du Qin 杜欽

criticized the polity of Jibin in the southern Hindukush region for sending profit seekers and not high officials with tribute to the court (*Hou Han shu* 3886–3887; Hulsewé and Loewe 1979: 108–112; Sen 2003: 4). Despite such complaints and attempts to restrict the involvement of "profit seekers" by court officials, the tributary system in imperial China remained largely a commercial venture. Nonetheless, the tribute system was meticulously organized. Audiences with the emperor were planned several months in advance; the expectations from near and distant polities were clearly outlined; templates for letters of "submission" from foreign rulers, with the interspersing of Confucian phrases, were carefully drafted; and the proper etiquette for appearing at court was conveyed to the tribute carriers.

Polities located in South Asia were grouped under the "distant regions" category. Compared to the East and Southeast Asian polities, the missions from South Asia to the courts in China were less frequent. While also overwhelmingly commercial in nature, the tributary missions representing South Asian polities frequently attempted to highlight the Buddhist heritage of the region. Thus, as mentioned above, they presented various Buddhist paraphernalia, in addition to exotic items, samples of local products, and goods in demand in Chinese markets. Before the twelfth century, it was rare for the Chinese dynasties to respond with their own official missions to South Asia. The few that were sent to South Asia in the first millennium CE were connected either to Buddhist undertakings or served the personal interests of a specific ruler in China. The missions from the Tang court to Middle India in the seventh century exemplified this rare interest in South Asia during the period. Initially, the emergence of Tibet as a powerful opponent on the frontier regions of Tang China may have prompted the court to send an embassy to the court of King Harṣa of Kanauj. The later Tang missions to the region, however, performed Buddhist activities or attempted to find longevity doctors for the Chinese emperors. Also during the Tang period, diplomatic missions were exchanged between the Karkoṭa polity in Kashmir and the court of Emperor Xuanzong in relation to the expansion of the Tibetans into the southern Hindukush region (Sen 2003: 30–34). One noteworthy aspect of these Tang missions, as with the earlier Sui attempt, was the courts' efforts to inform the South Asian rulers and people about Chinese geography, culture, and traditions. This may have been done to propagate Chinese culture to a region that had had a significant impact on China for several centuries and which seemed to be culturally on a par with Tang (and Sui) China.

During the Song dynasty, the court eventually recognized the economic potential of the tribute system and incorporated it into the government's fiscal policy. Acknowledging that the tribute carriers were merchants who traveled to China primarily to conduct commercial transactions, the Song court formally allowed them to sell goods they brought with them at Chinese markets. The Song court raised considerable revenue by imposing duties on the sale of such goods. At times, the court also sold items it received as tribute in order to add to its coffers (Hartwell 1989). Foreign traders settled in the coastal regions were instrumental in expanding the commerce-focused tribute system during the Song period. They often were the lead envoys or formed part of the foreign tribute missions visiting the Song court. The tribute mission from the Chola polity on the Coromandel coast to the Song court, for example, often included Muslim traders who were most likely based in either Quanzhou or Guangzhou (Hartwell 1989; Sen 2003: 166–168). By representing foreign polities, these traders not only profited from the sale of imported goods but also gained tax breaks and received honorary titles from the Song court in appreciation of their role in bringing tribute missions to China.

By the end of the Song period, a significant development had taken place with regard to the maritime connections between China and the foreign world. Advances in shipbuilding technology and the parallel spread of Chinese trading and shipping networks to the South China Sea and the Indian Ocean regions made it possible for the Yuan and Ming courts to frequently dispatch embassies to maritime polities to demand tribute submission.[12] As a consequence, the tribute system through the maritime realm during the Yuan and early Ming periods was transformed from a passive system of receiving symbolic acknowledgment of sovereignty to one that used the threat of punitive action to demand submission from foreign polities. Recognizing the naval power of the Yuan and Ming courts, the maritime polities in the South China Sea and the Indian Ocean regions also adjusted their relations with the Yuan and Ming courts. Some of them started pursuing strategic military alliances through the tributary missions in order to compete with local rivals. In other words, the tributary system during the Yuan and Ming periods was no longer merely a commercial venture but entailed strategic political considerations and, in some cases, military action.

A distinction, however, needs to be made between the Yuan court's revamping of the tribute system and what transpired during the early Ming period. While the Yuan court seems to have been forceful in its demand for submission and tribute missions, a policy most likely related to Kublai Khan's need to legitimize himself as the rightful khan of the Mongol world, it continued to encourage foreign trade, either as part of the tribute system or parallel to it. The Ming court, on the other hand, from the time of its founding under the Hongwu emperor, was aggressive in restoring the tributary system to its Confucian roots. In addition to placing strict restrictions on tribute carriers engaging in commercial activities, the Ming court also prohibited its subjects from engaging in foreign trade, prosecuting those who either illicitly took part in such activities or failed to report others who did not adhere to the court's directive (Li 2010).

The above changes were reflected in the diplomatic exchanges between several South Asian polities and the Yuan and Ming courts. The Yuan court under Kublai Khan, for example, had a special interest in Kollam, a port town on the Malabar coast that was a key transit point for ships traveling to the Persian Gulf. A Yuan emissary named Yang Tingbi 楊庭壁 was sent to Kollam on multiple occasions between 1280 and 1283 to solicit tributary missions. The Coromandel coast was also an important destination for the Yuan embassies. A Uighur person named Yiheimishi 亦黑迷失 (Yighmish) was dispatched to the Ma'bar polity located on that coast in 1272, 1275, and 1287. Perhaps as a result of these visits, 18 tributary missions are recorded to have arrived at the Yuan capital from the southern coastal regions of South Asia between 1274 and 1314 (Sen 2006b).

A memorial by a Uighur monk named Jialu'nadasi 迦魯納答思 (Karandas?), presented to the court sometime in 1278–1279, makes it clear that the Yuan missions to South Asia were connected to Kublai's overall strategy to persuade the rulers of maritime polities to submit and recognize him as the great khan of the Mongol Empire. The *Yuan shi* (134: 3260) reports that,

> [when] the [Yuan] court planned to embark on military operations against Siam, Lavo, Ma'bar, Kollam, Samudra, and other polities, Karandas memoriarized [saying]: "All these are petty and distant states. Although we can [easily] invade them, what can be gained [by belligerence]? The initiation of military operations will only lead to the destruction of people's lives. [It would be] better to send embassies [to these polities and] discuss the calamities [of warfare] and benefits [of submitting peacefully]. Attacking [those who] do not submit [peacefully] will not impede [the plan]. The emperor accepted his opinion [and] ordered Yuelayenu, Tiemie and others to proceed [to these polities] as envoys. [As a result,] the polities that surrendered [peacefully] were more than twenty. (Sen 2006b: 305–306)

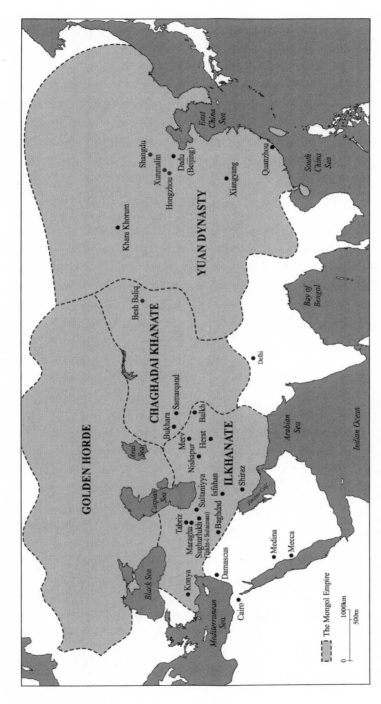

Figure 2.14. The Mongol Empire. © Tansen Sen

Diplomatic exchanges between the Yuan court and South Asia continued after the death of Kublai. Ibn Baṭūṭah reports that a Yuan embassy arrived in Delhi in 1340 carrying a bounty of gifts including slave girls, velvet cloth, musk, and other valuable goods. It was in response to this mission that Ibn Baṭūṭah was dispatched to Yuan China a year later. This exchange of embassies seems to be related to the shared military interest the Yuan court and the Delhi Sultanate had in the Himalayan regions, especially the areas of Khurāsān and Transoxiana (that is, present-day Afghanistan and western Central Asia respectively), which Muḥammad b. Tughluq planned to conqueror. The gifts that Ibn Baṭūṭah was supposed to carry to the Yuan in return for the presents made to the ruler of the Delhi Sultanate are detailed below.

The early Ming court continued the Yuan tradition of forcing maritime polities to send tributary missions to China. However, the Ming court was adamant, as noted above, about stopping (or at least bringing under court supervision) the commercial activities of the tributary carriers. The ideology that formed the basis of the Ming court's revamped tributary system is reflected in the following remark made by a Ming envoy to the ruler of Brunei during the Hongwu emperor's reign:

> Our emperor is the owner of everything under heaven and needs nothing from you. What we demand is your obedience, that you become a vassal state and join the "family." (*Huang Ming zhengyao* 皇明政要, 46, 20: 6a–b; translated in Li [2010: 26])

The Yongle emperor followed the framework of the tributary system instituted by the Hongwu emperor, but with more forceful intimidation in the form of the powerful armadas led by Admiral Zheng He. The seven expeditions of Zheng He not only demanded submission of foreign polities through tributary missions but also carried out regime changes when anyone refused to acknowledge the sovereignty of the Ming court (Wade 2005b; Sen 2014c). These aspects are evident from the activities of Zheng He and his entourage in various parts of South Asia, including on the Malabar coast and in Sri Lanka and Bengal. Each of these regions is recorded to have sent regular missions to the Ming court through the 1430s, when the Zheng He voyages ended (Sen 2016a). The Ming interest in South Asia through the expeditions of Zheng He is discussed in more detail in the next chapter.

The Ming court's interactions with Calicut, Cochin, Bengal, and Sri Lanka involved the dispatch of tributary missions by South Asian polities, but also military threat and actions taken by the Ming court. At the same time, the South Asian polities and Ming China were also linked through the commercial networks of Chinese merchants settled in Southeast Asia. The exchanges between Bengal and Ming China, for example, revealed the complex issues associated with the Ming tribute system, the motivations of foreign polities in sending embassies to the Ming court, and the role of traders in the web of connections between South Asia and Ming China in the early fifteenth century.

Several scholars (Bagchi [1945] 2012; Ray 1993; and Church 2004) have discussed the tributary exchanges between Bengal and Ming China and noted the disparity between the known reigning rulers of Bengal and those credited with sending these missions in the Ming sources. The ruler named Saifoding 賽弗丁, for example, is supposed to have sent embassies to the Ming court in 1412, 1414, and 1421. Identified as Saif-ud-din Hamza Shāh of the Ilyās Shāhi dynasty of Bengal, this ruler reigned for only two years, from 1411 to 1412, and thus could not have sent the latter two missions. Ray (1993) has explained this and other similar discrepancies between the Ming sources and the evidence from Bengal as mistakes on the part of the Chinese scribes who, in his opinion, were confused by the foreign names. Church, on the other hand, believes that the gap in time between when the missions were actually dispatched and their arrival at the Ming court, in addition to the extremely complex situation within Bengal, could account for these inconsistencies. Bagchi's argument was generally related to the latter point made by Church, but he contended that there was a dual government in Bengal, both of which were sending missions to Ming China.

The mention of ethnic Chinese representatives from Bengal in Chinese sources suggests the role of foreign traders in instigating some of the South Asian missions to the Ming court. The *Yingzong shilu* reports a Chinese merchant named Song Yun 宋允, who, as the deputy envoy of the mission from Bengal, visited the Ming court sometime in mid-1439. Song Yun, we are told, sought funds to repair his damaged ship and requested protection from the Ming ruler. "As Yun was Chinese and had been able to bring a foreign country to China," the *Yingzong shilu* records (*Ming shilu* 24: 1046; translated by Wade, 2005a, http://epress.nus.edu.sg/msl/entry/949, accessed 21 June 2016), "the Emperor approved both his requests." In a record dated 27 May 1446, the *Yingzong shilu* provides additional detail about this Chinese trader representing Bengal:

> The Ministry of Rites memorialized: "The Samudera person Aiyan 靄淹 has advised that his uncle Song Yun came to the capital to offer tribute to the Court in the first year of the Zhengtong reign (1436/37). However, he was murdered by the fan person Daxi 打昔 and others from the country of Java. Song Yun's wife Meimeidawai 眉妹打歪 complained to officials and Daxi was punished in accordance with the law. At this time, Meimeidawai, her female attendants (女使人) and so on are still residing in Guangdong (Alt: Guangxi) and, as they have no relatives, it is very difficult for them to clothe and feed themselves day by day. They are alone and have no one to depend on. It is requested that the three offices of Guangdong be instructed to have them sent back to their country." This was approved. (*Ming shilu* 28: 2783; translated by Wade 2005a, http://epress. nus.edu.sg/msl/entry/2059, accessed 21 June 2016)

Apparently Song Yun was a member of the Chinese diasporic network, the reach of which extended from Java to Bengal. He seems to have married a non-Chinese woman, who had at some point settled in Guangdong. The report of his murder explains why Song Yun, perhaps because of rivalry among seafaring traders, sought protection from the Ming court in 1439.

The *Yingzong shilu* also includes an entry regarding another Chinese person working on behalf of Bengal. The record reports that in the tenth lunar month of the third year of the Zhentong reign era (November 1438),

> [t]he Auxiliary Ministry of Rites memorialized: "The interpreter Chen Deqing 陳得清 and others from the country of Bengal have advised that they have long been travelling far away from their homes and that their bags are empty. They have thus requested that cotton clothing to protect them from the cold of winter be conferred upon them." As the Emperor felt that people from afar should be very well-treated, he ordered the Auxiliary Ministry of Rites to not restrict themselves to the regulations, but to confer on these people cotton clothing and other items for keeping out the cold. (*Ming shilu* 24: 916; translated by Wade 2005a, http://epress.nus.edu.sg/msl/entry/733, accessed 21 June 2016)

It is possible that Chen Deqing, like Song Yun, was a Chinese trader based in Southeast Asia involved in the tributary missions sent from Bengal to Ming China. Since both of these episodes took place after the cessation of the Zheng He voyages, it seems there was a transition in the South Asia–Ming China tributary relations sometime in the mid-fifteenth century. This transition was marked by the [re]emergence of private mercantile networks, especially those belonging to the Chinese traders in Southeast Asia, as the key link between the two regions.

The Circulation of Gifts

Marcel Mauss ([1954] 1990) has outlined the underlying functions and motives of gift giving and the corresponding "obligations" of return gifts in his seminal work *The Gift: The Form and Reasons for Exchange in Archaic Societies*. Mauss has explained, pointing to examples from several different societies and regions, the moral and social functions, the economic impact, and the political significance of the giving of gifts and the subsequent act of reciprocation. The Chinese tributary system was, as can be discerned from the above discussion, similarly complex and served several functions. It facilitated the circulation of goods between China and various regions of the world. Closely associated with commercial activity, the tributary system had economic impact on various groups of people, from producers and manufactures to merchant guilds and transporters. It contributed either directly or indirectly to the revenues collected by the polities involved. Foreign tribute items acquired by elites and high-ranking officials also augmented the social status of individuals in Chinese society, and in the same manner it elevated the position of foreign traders who received honorary titles as reward from the Chinese court. Additionally, the tribute system often facilitated political networking, peace negotiations, and military alliances between Chinese rulers and foreign polities/leaders.

Since the system promoted the idea of foreign regions as part of the Chinese emperor's realm, goods categorized as "local/native products" were the most frequent offerings by tribute carriers. Exotic items, including animals and birds, and even pygmies, were another category of tributary presents. Commodities that were in high demand in Chinese markets, such as precious and semiprecious stones, incense, and ingredients for medicines and cuisine, formed a substantial part of the gifts presented to Chinese emperors as well. Rituals objects, Buddhist texts, and other artifacts associated with Buddhism were gifted to Chinese rulers who seemed sympathetic to the Buddhist cause. The return gifts included cash, silk, and other artifacts; honorary titles; and tax exemptions. The choice of these return gifts often depended on the perceived strength and importance of the foreign polity.

The list of tribute gifts presented by missions representing South Asian polities and the return gifts they received followed the above pattern of the circulation of goods through the tributary system. The polities in the southern Hindukush region seem to have been the first to participate in the system. The Yuezhi polity is recorded to have gifted "divine incense" (*shenxiang* 神香) to the Han court in 98 BCE. Almost a century later, in 87 CE, Yuezhi sent a tributary mission with a lion and an animal, most likely a deerlike creature, known as *fuba* 扶拔 (*Hou Han shu* 3: 158). During the reign of Emperor He (89–105) the Tianzhu polity is reported to have sent "several" embassies carrying tributary gifts, which are not specified. Tribute missions from Tianzhu also arrived by the sea route during the second (159–160) and fourth years (161–162) of the Yanxi period under Emperor Huan (*Hou Han shu* 7: 306, 309), who is noted to have made "sacrifices" to the Buddha and Laozi.

After the fall of the Han dynasty, several of the succeeding regimes in a fragmented China continued to report the arrival of tributary missions from South Asia. The Yuezhi, for example, sent a mission to the court of the Wei emperor Ming in 229 bearing "native" gifts, for which the South Asian ruler was given an honorary title (*Sanguo zhi. Wei shu* 3: 97). Sometime in the second half of the fourth century, the Tianzhu polity presented asbestos (*huowanbu* 火浣布) to the court of the Former Qin (*Jin shu* 143: 2904). An envoy from King Yueai of the Jiabili polity offered several precious objects, including a *vajra*/diamond ring and a bracelet made of pure gold, to the Liu Song court in 428 (*Song shu* 97: 2386). Parrots, one red and the other white, were also part of the gifts offered. When the same polity sent another embassy in 466, the two lead envoys were given the honorary titles of *jianwei jianjun* 建威將軍 ("awe-building generals"). In 502, when Xiao Yan 蕭衍 (known as Emperor Wu) founded the Liang dynasty in southern China, Juduo, the ruler of Middle Tianzhu, sent a mission that offered a spittoon made of lapis lazuli 琉璃唾壺, assorted incense 雜香, and cotton (*Liang shu* 54: 799).[13] In 503, representatives from a polity referred to as Nan Tianzhu presented a relic of the Buddha to the Liang ruler (*Wei shu* 8: 196). Several other embassies from South Asian polities arrived at the Liang court in subsequent years, but the gifts presented by them were not always specified in Chinese sources.

In the fifth and sixth centuries, the polities located in northern China also received tribute from South Asia. In the 460s, the Northern Wei court hosted two missions from Jibin and two from a South Asian polity called Juchang 居常. The 460 embassy from Juchang presented three tamed elephants to the court (*Wei shu* 5: 119). In 509, the Northern Wei court received a white elephant with a bejeweled chamber (perhaps a howdah) sent by the Qianluo 乾羅國 polity (*Luoyang qielan ji*, T. 2092: 1012a). Between 500 and 515, representatives from a polity known to the Chinese as Poluo 婆羅 in South Tianzhu presented gold and silver objects, as well as horses (*Wei shu* 8: 204). Embassies from polities located on the island of Sri Lanka also appeared frequently in China. During the beginning of the Yixi period (405–418), for instance, a ruler from the island presented a jade image measuring four *chi* two *cun* (more than three feet) tall to the Jin court (*Nan shi* 78: 1964).

The reunification of China in 589 by the Sui dynasty did not result in any immediate tributary missions from South Asian polities. Rather, the Sui emperors Wen and Yang took initiatives to make contact with South Asian polities, most likely due to their attempts to legitimize the dynasty and their interest in Buddhism. While Emperor Wen is noted to have ordered the translation into Sanskrit of two books, Emperor Yang sent envoys Wei Jie 韋節 and Du Xingman 杜行滿 to South Asia. These envoys are recorded to have brought back from Jibin a carnelian cup (*manao bei* 碼磁 杯) and Buddhist texts from Wangshe City 王舍城 (Rājgṛha), as

well as ten dancing maidens 儛女, a lion skin 獅子皮, and the fur
of a "fiery rat" (*huoshu* 火鼠) from a polity called Shi 史國 (*Sui
shu* 83: 1841).

The seventh and eighth centuries witnessed a significant increase in the number of diplomatic exchanges between the Tang
court and polities in South Asia. These exchanges mostly took
place with the polities located in the southern Hindukush region,
Middle Tianzhu, and South Tianzhu. Political, religious, and likely
commercial motives were involved in the exchanges with Jibin,
Bolü, and Gushimi/Jiaxianmiluo (Kashmir) located in the southern
Hindukush; the empire of King Harṣa in Middle Tianzhu; and the
Chalukyas, Pallavas, and Rashtrakutas, which would have comprised the South Tianzhu region in Tang sources. Despite the diversity of the diplomatic exchanges, with regard to both destination
and purpose, the gifts presented to the Tang court by these South
Asian polities were not very different from the tribute offered during the previous periods. They also consisted of exotic items, luxury goods, and Buddhist paraphernalia. Exotic animals such as mon-
gooses, capable of healing snakebites, were given as tribute by
Jibin in 632 and 642 (*Cefu yuangui* 970: 11399a; 970: 11401a;
Schafer 1963: 91), and five-colored parrots were gifted twice in the
ninth century by the polity known as Kaliṅga,[14] which also presented a Kalaviṅka bird. Representatives from the South Tianzhu polity
gifted five-colored parrots, a leopard, and a "day-answering" crow
to the Tang court in 720 (*Cefu yuangui* 971: 11406b). Various types
of plants and plant products were brought to the Tang court by
envoys representing Magadha (*peepuls*), Jibin (saffron and *myrob-
alans*), Jiaxianmiluo (water lilies), and Nepal (spinach). The technology to make sugar from sugarcane, as discussed in chapter 1,
was transmitted from Kanauj to Tang China as part of diplomatic
exchanges between the two courts. Aromatics, drugs, and herbs
were presented by Kaliṅga, and also by envoys representing Kashmir, Jibin, and North Tianzhu at various times. Jibin (in 619), Sri

Lanka (in 746 and 750), and Kaliṅga (in 746) offered several types of jewels and precious stones, including pearls.

The embassies from the Tang court to South Asian polities, as noted above, often took silk with them to trade for goods and to offer as gift items. The missions led by Wang Xuance, for example, presented silk to the South Asian rulers and the Buddhist monasteries and used it to purchase Buddhist paraphernalia, including relics. Wang Xuance is reported to have also donated a silk robe to the Mahābodhi Monastery on behalf of the Tang ruler during one of his visits to Middle Tianzhu. Xuanzang's letters to his fellow students at Nālandā indicate that these embassies carried objects on behalf of Chinese Buddhist monks and monasteries to South Asia. Although the list of gifts to South Asian courts and monasteries is not recorded in detail, these examples suggest that the circulations of objects through the multiple Tang embassies would have been substantial. Wang Xuance himself received large pearls, metallic boxes, and reliquaries made of ivory and jewels from the monks at the Mahābodhi Monastery (*Fayuan zhulin*, T. 2122: 597b7).

The liberalized commercial policies of the Song court resulted in a revamping of the types of gifts presented as tribute by foreign delegations. Instead of exotic items that had little monetary value, the tribute carriers now regularly presented goods that were in high demand in Song markets. This was also reflected in the tribute presented by embassies representing South Asian polities. Frankincense, *putchuck*, cloves, rosewater, Barus camphor, pearls, rhinoceros horns, and elephant tusks, for example, were given as gifts to the Song court by embassies from the Chola polity. Those representing Tianzhu gave horses of "good" and "imperial" qualities, aromatics, and medicines. Many of these missions from Tianzhu also offered Buddhist texts and paraphernalia, which, as argued above, also had commercial value during the Song period (Hartwell 1989).

Exotic goods and native products reemerged as key tributary gifts during the reign of Kublai Khan as legitimization of political authority became a concern once again. The Ma'bar polity on the Coromandel coast and Julan (Kollam) on the Malabar coast, which had frequent diplomatic exchanges with the Yuan court, presented various "precious objects," including elephant tusks and rhinoceros horns (in 1279 and 1280). In 1282, Ma'bar offered native products and brought a letter written on gold leaf. Two years later, it gifted pearls, "rare treasures," and cotton textiles. In 1286, embassies from Ma'bar presented a bronze shield and a saddle. The following year, gifts received from the polity included an exotic animal with black fur and white stripes. Animals, two cows, a buffalo, and a tiger cat were again presented to the Yuan court in 1291. At the same time, the Yuan court dispatched envoys to bring local goods from various regions of South Asia. In 1285, for example, two officials were sent to Ma'bar with paper money to fetch "rare treasures." In 1287, a mission was dispatched to South Asia by the Yuan court commissioned to bring back the alms bowl of the Buddha (Sen 2006b). Three years later, in 1290, several Yuan officials were sent to fetch a "physician," probably a longevity doctor, from the region. In 1282, Kollam presented "valuable goods" and a black ape to the Yuan court, which responded by sending its own envoy the following year with gifts including bows, saddle, and a gold plaque for the South Asian ruler.[15]

As recorded by Ibn Baṭūṭah, one of the descendants of Kublai Khan sent a mission to the Delhi Sultanate. "The king of China," according to him, had sent "a hundred mamluks and slave girls, five hundred pieces of velvet cloth, including a hundred of those which are manufactured in the city of Zaitun and a hundred of those which are manufactured in Khansa, five maunds of musk, five robes adorned with jewels, five embroidered quivers, and five swords." Ibn Baṭūṭah (vol. 4: 773–774) then reports that the sultan of Delhi reciprocated with "even richer" gifts that included a hundred male slaves, a hundred Hindu singing- and dancing-girls, a hundred pieces of bairami cloth, which are made of cotton and are unequalled in beauty, each piece being worth a hundred dinars—a hundred lengths of the silk fabrics called juzz, in which the material of each is dyed with four or five different colours—four hundred pieces of the fabrics known as salahi, a hundred pieces of shirin-baf, a hundred pieces of shan-baf, five hundred pieces of mir'iz woolens, one hundred of them black and a hundred each in white, red, green, and blue, a hundred lengths of Greek linen, a hundred pieces of blanket-cloth, a seracha, six pavilions, four candelabra in gold and six in silver enameled, four golden basins with ewers to match, and six silver basins, ten embroidered robes of honour from the Sultan's own wardrobe and ten caps also worn by him, one of them encrusted with pearls, ten embroidered quivers, one of them encrusted with pearls, ten swords one of them with scabbard encrusted with pearls, dasht-ban, that is gloves embroidered with pearls, and fifteen eunuchs.

None of these gifts reached the Yuan court as, Ibn Baṭūṭah advises us, the ship carrying them sank near Calicut.

The ban on commercial interactions with foreign traders and an emphasis on the original intent of the tribute system by emperors Hongwu and Yongle of the Ming dynasty resulted in the domination of exotic goods as the main constituent of foreign gifts presented to the Chinese court in the late fourteenth and early fifteenth century. The polities located in the coastal regions of South Asia remained the main source of diplomatic exchanges with the Ming court as they were during the Yuan period. The polity called Suoli 瑣里, for example, sent several embassies between 1370 and 1403, with gifts that included letters written on gold leaf and black pepper (Wade 2005a, http://epress.nus.edu.sg/msl/entry/1035, accessed 30 October 2016). Presents from Calicut included horses and black pepper. Cochin, Bengal, and Sri Lanka, which also sent regular tributary missions to the Ming court, offered local goods and exotic items. The most remarkable of these gifts were the giraffes presented by the kings of Bengal in 1414 and 1438 (Church 2004). Polities from the western coastal regions of present-day India, such as Xialabi (Valabhi), Shelaqi (Surat), and Wushalati (Gujarat), are also reported to have sent tributary missions bearing gifts for the Ming rulers.

There are two noteworthy aspects to these tributary exchanges between the Ming court and the South Asian polities. First, during the Hongwu and Yongle reigns, the Ming court took an active role in urging foreign polities to send tributary missions. The steps taken by the Ming court were more extensive and forceful than those of the preceding Yuan period. In addition to the expeditions led by Zheng He, there were several other Ming emissaries (frequently eunuchs) who were sent to foreign lands to persuade and on some occasions personally bring tributary missions to the Ming court. In the case of South Asian polities, these representatives included Liu Shumian/Shumin 劉叔勉 sent to the Suoli polity in 1369, Yin Qing sent to Cochin in 1403, and Hou Xian and Hong Bao sent to Bengal in 1420 and 1432, respectively (Sen 2006a). In 1412, the Yongle emperor is also reported to have sent an unnamed envoy to Dili (Delhi). Second, as part of this policy to induce tributary missions, the Ming court gave generous return gifts to the tribute carriers and on some occasions allowed them to sell commodities in local markets without levying taxes. The latter, however, could only be done under state supervision. Brocades of several types, for example, were given to representatives and kings of Suoli, Cochin, Calicut, Delhi, and Bengal. The Zheng He mission to Sri Lanka in 1410–1411 made, according to a trilingual inscription erected on the island, lavish offerings to the Buddhist relics housed on the island (Nagel 2001). Tax exemptions were given to the Lani 剌泥 (most likely a polity in the Gujarat regions) envoys in 1403 for the sale of black pepper in Ming China (Wade 2005a, http://epress.nus. edu.sg/msl/entry/13, accessed 30 October 2016).

These tributary exchanges between the Ming court and South Asian polities ended by the middle of the fifteenth century. This cessation of tributary relations may have been connected to two key developments. First, the Ming court terminated the naval expeditions led by Zheng He and other eunuchs initiated by the Yongle emperor. This effectively ended the Ming court's role in actively seeking tributary missions from South Asian polities in the second half of the fifteenth century.[16] Second, foreign trade with China was increasingly carried out through Southeast Asian (including ethnic Chinese) intermediaries. As a result, foreign polities, especially those located further away from the Chinese coast, did not have to make direct contact with the Ming court to undertake commercial activity in China. For all intents and purposes, the traditional tribute system and the commercial ventures associated with it that had formed an important element of the circulation of goods between China and South Asia ceased by the mid-fifteenth century. However, tribute missions to the Ming court from the maritime polities in the South China Sea continued. It is possible that members of the South Asian trading guilds based in Southeast Asia sent some of the tributary missions to Ming China from places such as Malacca and Java in the late fifteenth and early sixteenth century. Moreover, as pointed out above, Chinese traders located in Southeast Asia continued to be active in the commercial exchanges between South Asia and China. Thus, the termination of Zheng He's voyages or the tributary missions from South Asian polities to the Ming court did not entail a cessation of the circulation of objects between China and South Asia.

THE WEBS OF COMMERCE

The circulation of Buddhist objects and tributary items were thus intimately associated with the commercial interactions taking place between South Asia and the regions controlled by the Chinese dy-

nasties. The routes and networks that connected these regions facilitated the movement of a wide variety of merchandise—Buddhist
paraphernalia, exotic animals, silk, porcelain, and the like—
through a range of geographical terrains and means of transportation. The trade in cowries and the networks of Austronesian sailors
indicate that such movement started several millennia before the
Common Era. They also demonstrate, more importantly, that the
commercial exchanges between South Asia and China were part of
a larger set of intra-Asian interactions that involved people from
several different regions. Polities in Southeast Asia, the oasis states
in Central Asia, nomadic groups, Sogdian traders, and Muslim merchants were all involved in these commercial circulations. This
broader context of the circulation of objects between South Asia
and China is analyzed in more detail in the concluding section of
this chapter.

Also evident from the above discussion is the fact that the nature
of objects circulating between South Asia and China, either as gifts
or commercial commodities, went through various changes over
time. While before the tenth century luxury goods and Buddhist
paraphernalia dominated the circulations, the post–tenth century
saw a significant influx of bulk goods such as spices and incense.
This noteworthy transformation was associated with the development of maritime linkages and shipping facilities, changes in the
nature of Buddhist contacts between South Asia and China, the
emergence of active networks of Muslim traders, the greater involvement of courts across Asia in promoting and profiting from
long-distance commercial activity, and shifts in the patterns of consumption and market demand. The initiation of the Buddhist phase
in the first century CE itself was a change from the prior period, in
the first millennium BCE, when smaller (and lighter) luxury products yielding higher profit margins were the mainstay of the relay
form of commercial activity between South Asia and China.

Indeed, since the main aim of itinerant traders was to maximize profits, goods that generated a high price and accounted for low transportation costs were the most common items of commercial exchange between South Asia and China in the early phases. Beads; precious and semiprecious stones such as carnelian, agate, and lapis lazuli; and pearls originating from various subregions of South Asia entered the Chinese markets. The demand for these goods was initially among the elites in China, and they were later also used for decorating Buddhist ritual items and monuments. As pointed out by Bellina and Glover (2004), some of the beads and semiprecious stones from South Asia were first processed in Southeast Asia and then traded on to China. This practice of modifying imported commodities for the purposes of reexporting was not limited to Southeast Asia. The oasis states of Central Asia are also known to have tailored and added motifs to silk fabrics originating in China according to the requirements of markets elsewhere.

These early patterns of commercial exchanges, and the monsoon winds which dictated the voyages across the Indian Ocean, thus resulted in the creation of interlocking trading circuits that integrated the Afroeurasian world. The fact that the commercial exchanges between South Asia and China were part of this integrated Afroeurasian trading system can be discerned from the trade in various commodities, where South Asian ports functioned as important relay centers. Roman glass objects found in the Hepu tombs were supplied through such relay ports. In the same way, Chinese silk products reaching South Asia were reexported to markets in the Red Sea region and beyond.

Both Roman glass and Chinese silk also enjoyed demand within South Asia. Chinese silk, for instance, was widely used by the elite members of the society. Although the exact volume of Chinese silk entering South Asia cannot be ascertained from present sources, works such as Bana's *Harṣacarita* that describes the court life of the seventh-century ruler Harṣa mention the use of the Chinese fabric (Liu 1996: 52–56). The development of the Byzantine silk industry in the fifth–sixth centuries and the local production of the fabric in South Asia seem to have reduced the trade in the commodity by the tenth century.[17] However, the procurement of foreign goods for both domestic consumption and transit trade gradually increased over time and seems to have dominated long-distance commerce after the tenth century. Porcelain emerged as such a commodity that was reexported in large quantities through South Asian ports to the Persian Gulf. At the same time, it was also in much demand within the Islamic sultanates of South Asia (Sen 2003).

Central Asian and Persian horses, and later Tibetan ponies and mounts, were imported in large numbers throughout most of China's imperial history. South Asia was an important part of this supply chain. Arabian horses were first exported to the Malabar coast from where they were transshipped to China. During the twelfth and thirteenth centuries, merchants from Kish in the Persian Gulf played an important role in supplying these Arabian horses to South Asia (Kauz 2006; Yokkaichi 2008). The lucrative nature of the trade in horses is underscored in the works of the Persian historian Waṣṣāf and the Italian traveler Marco Polo. The latter mentions that "some, indeed most of them, fetch fully two hundred pounds of Touraine apiece." Waṣṣāf reports that 1,400 horses were sold to the Pāṇḍyan ruler named Sundara on the Malabar coast by Arab traders at the price of 220 dinars of red gold each, including for those that might have been lost at sea. Waṣṣāf also notes that ten thousand horses were exported annually from the Persian Gulf during the reign of Atabeg Abu Bakr (r. 1226–1260) to ports in South Asia. The revenue from such exports, according to him, amounted to 2,200,000 dinars (Digby 1982: 148). Fei Xin confirms the continuation of this transit route two centuries later. According to him (Mills 1996: 69), horses were brought to the Malabar coast from

West Asia, bred locally, and "transferred" for onward sale to Ming China for hundreds or thousands of coins.

There was also another trading circuit through which horses were supplied to markets in China. The thirteenth-century Persian-language record from South Asia called *Tabaqāt-i Nāsirī* reports of trade in horses carried out by the Tibetans in Bengal and Kāmarūpa (the present-day Assam state of India). In the market town of Lankhnauti in northern Bengal, according to the work, about 1,500 horses were sold every morning (Chakravarti 1999). Some of these horses, it seems, were exported to China through the maritime routes that connected the Bay of Bengal ports to the coastal regions of China. Ming sources mention that representatives from Bengal often presented horses as tribute to the court. These representatives, in addition to presenting tribute, must have also sold some of the horses in local markets or at least informed the Ming court about their availability in Bengal. Since Bengal did not produce horses, the gifts brought to Ming China were most likely those that were procured in the markets of Lankhnauti.

The notices in the Song dynasty work *Zhufan zhi* also illustrate the vibrant long-distance commercial activity during the post-tenth-century period. In the first part of this work, which was discussed in the previous chapter, seven areas/polities of South Asia are recorded: Xilan 細蘭 (Sri Lanka), Nanpi 南毗 (Malabar), Huchala 胡茶辣 (Gujarat), Maluohua 麻囉華 (Malwa), Zhunian 注輦 (Chola), Tianzhu 天竺 (India), and Yantuoman 晏陀蠻 (Andaman Islands). Even though he did not travel beyond the Chinese coast, the author Zhao Rugua was aware of some of the important nodes of maritime commerce. Lanwuli 藍無里 (i.e., Lambri in northern Sumatra), for example, is mentioned as one of the transit places for ships sailing toward the Malabar coast (Hirth and Rockhill 1911: 89). Zhou Qufei's *Lingwai daida*, an earlier Song work, already reported in the twelfth century that merchants traveling to the Persian Gulf changed ships at Kollam on the Malabar coast (*Lingwai daida* 91).

Cat's-eye, red transparent glass, camphor, blue and red precious stones, cardamoms, "lulan" bark, and coarse and fine perfumes are noted in Zhao's work as items exported by Sri Lanka. Sandalwood, cloves, camphor, gold, silver, porcelain, horses, elephants, and silk stuff were, according to the work, offered in exchange for these Sri Lankan goods (Hirth and Rockhill 1911: 72–73). Most of the items listed in these exchanges came from the diverse regions of the maritime world, suggesting that commodities were traded several times before reaching their destinations. The presence of multiple commercial networks between South Asia and China, including those operated by Muslim, Tamil, and Southeast Asian merchants, indicates that the relay trade was highly profitable. The demand for a wide range of commodities, better transportation facilities, reduced risk factors, and the interest in raising revenue from long-distance trading activity may have been some of the main reasons for the popularity and success of this relay trade.

This complex nature of commercial activity was not always apparent to the scribes or even customs officials, as is evident from the second part of Zhao's book, which includes descriptions of various foreign commodities entering Song China. In this part of his work, Zhao Rugua rarely mentions South Asia as a place of origin for goods that obviously came from that region. Rather, Southeast Asian polities are reported as the source of several of these items. The reason for this discrepancy was clearly the nature of the relay trade, which prevented, sometimes deliberately, importers from knowing the ultimate sources of foreign goods. The active involvement of merchants and polities such as Śrīvijaya may have led to the misinformation Zhao gathered from his sources. Śrīvijaya, as noted earlier, controlled the Malacca Straits, a choke point in long-distance maritime commerce, and monopolized a number of foreign commodities destined for markets in Song China.

There were very few, if any, Chinese ships engaged in maritime commerce beyond the South China Sea region when Zhou Qufei and Zhao Rugua composed their works. The information reaching them, therefore, was primarily through foreign traders. By the late thirteenth century, however, Chinese traders and sailors started extending their own commercial networks to the coastal regions of South Asia, including the Coromandel and Malabar coasts and Sri Lanka. Wang Dayuan, who, unlike Zhou and Zhao, sailed in the Bay of Bengal and the Arabian Sea regions with Chinese seafaring traders in the early fourteenth century, produced a very different record of maritime commerce. For the first time commodities produced in and exported from South Asian coastal polities were detailed in his work. Wang provides records of at least twenty-five sites on the South Asian coast. For Bengal, for example, Wang writes that the polity produced fabrics such as *bibu* 芘布 (bairami/bafta), *gaonibu* 高你布 (kain cloth?), *tuluojin* 禿羅錦 (malmal), and kingfisher feathers. The Chinese traders, according to him, used "southern and northern [varieties of] silks, pentachrome taffetas and satins, cloves, nutmeg, blue and white porcelain, white tassels and such things [to trade with native merchants]" (*Daoyi zhilüe* 330). Wang's report not only suggests that textiles had become one of the leading commodities imported from South Asia into China, but also reveals the emergence of direct commercial exchanges between the two regions through the maritime routes.

Trade through the Central Asian routes also persisted between the tenth and fifteenth centuries. The formation of new polities that employed Buddhism as the state ideology, such as those established by the Uighurs, Tanguts, and Khitans, revitalized the demand for goods related to Buddhist rituals and ceremonies and prompted construction of Buddhist monuments (Sen 2003). Song China and the Korean Peninsula were the main suppliers of such Buddhist paraphernalia (see above). The establishment of the Mongol Empire in the thirteenth century not only boosted commercial exchanges along these Central Asian roads but also more intimately linked the overland and maritime routes. In fact, the Mongol period may have marked the peak of this integrated land-sea commercial activity because of the ease of travel by land routes and the advances in shipbuilding technologies. It also marked a period of direct commercial contacts between China and South Asia, laying the foundation for the circulation of objects and commodities between the two regions during the Ming and subsequent periods.

The expeditions of Zheng He were based on several developments that took place during the Mongol Yuan period, especially in knowledge about the Indian Ocean world. Traders and sailors from Yuan China had already established direct commercial and maritime networks between coastal China and the Coromandel and Malabar coasts. As a result, Ming subjects engaged in long-distance commerce were now cognizant of the markets, production sites, and transit places in the Indian Ocean. However, as outlined above, the Ming court under the Hongwu and Yongle emperors instituted restrictive policies on private trading ventures with foreign regions. At the same time, the Ming court introduced a new element to Indian Ocean commercial interactions. Through the Zheng He expeditions and its highly advanced ships and gunpowder-based weapons, the Ming court tried to control the circulation of commodities across the Indian Ocean world. Such hegemonic influence over the maritime routes, as will be detailed in the next chapter, did not exist previously. The Song court in China had encouraged Indian Ocean trade but had never actively participated in it; nor did it try to interfere in the commercial networks beyond its coasts. The Yuan court, under Kublai Khan, took punitive actions in several regions of the maritime world as part of its expansionist policy. It also actively sought tribute missions from maritime polities in South and Southeast Asia by sending diplomatic envoys, sometimes with threatening messages (Sen 2006b). However, it was never able to dictate the flow of goods or conduct trading activity across the entire Indian Ocean world. The Cholas from South Asia had also launched punitive naval raids on Southeast Asian ports (Sen 2009), but these raids did not have a lasting impact on the flow of commodities in the Indian Ocean.

Under the Yongle emperor, the Ming court tried to dictate the circulation of commodities in the Indian Ocean and perhaps even attempted to dominate the trading networks of Chinese traders operating from Southeast Asia. In fact, the massive Ming naval expeditions led by Zheng He between 1405 and 1433 had a significant impact not only on the circulation of commodities but also on the movement of people and animals throughout the Indian Ocean world (Sen 2016b). The specific methods the Ming court used to control these movements and especially the networks between China and South Asia are examined in the next chapter. Here it should be pointed out that for about three decades the Ming court seems to have monopolized and influenced the production and supply of several commercial goods. One such commodity was pepper.

Pepper, as T'ien Ju-kang (1981: 187) has pointed out, was an important commodity used by the Ming court to pay salaries to its officials. Both Ma Huan and Fei Xin, who, as noted in the previous chapter, accompanied Zheng He on some of his expeditions, report of the procurement of pepper from Samudera, Cochin, and Calicut by Ming court officials. These products were brought to China to meet local demand and were also used for trade with foreign polities in various regions of the Indian Ocean. Several other commodities, sandalwood from Southeast Asia, for instance, were similarly procured by the Ming naval representatives for consumption in China but were also used in trade with polities of the Persian Gulf (Sen 2016b). The list of commodities that circulated in multiple directions after their procurement by Ming officials included cotton textile items, semiprecious and precious stones, pearls, and kingfisher feathers. In fact, through these maritime expeditions, the

Ming court dictated not only the trade between South Asia and China but also much of the intra–Indian Ocean commerce.

Within a century of the cessation of the Ming expeditions, European enterprises entered and then dominated the commerce of the Indian Ocean and the South China Sea. Their entry into the Indian Ocean world was facilitated by the presence of existing nodes and networks, many of which were established during Zheng He's expeditions and even prior to this period. The entry of European enterprises led to the reemergence of Ming-style imperialistic control over the flow of goods. Unlike the Ming, however, the Europeans not only dominated the networks of exchange but also controlled the leading production sites in Asia (and Africa), with their own officials and military personnel expressly stationed in these regions to extract the necessary goods. While colonial expansion by the Europeans resulted in significant growth in the circulation of commodities, it also led to the exploitation of people and resources on a scale never witnessed before.

NETWORKS, CIRCULATIONS, AND THE AFROEURASIAN CONNECTIONS

The circulation of objects between South Asia and China and the networks that facilitated this were, as underscored above, part of a wider range of intra-Asian connections. From the relay trade in cowries to the export of pepper, the people, places, and transportation modes involved were all associated with these much broader exchanges across the Asian continent. The Austronesians, the Sogdians, the Tamil traders, the ports of Southeast and West Asia, and the oasis states of Central Asia, as well as Japan and Korea, formed integral components of circulations taking place between South Asia and China. Even the exchanges of Buddhist artifacts and paraphernalia involved people and places beyond South Asia and China. The routes and networks that facilitated the circulations of Buddhist artifacts and paraphernalia between South Asia and China were also associated with the movement of commercial items and tributary gifts. The people who operated these networks originated from different regions of Asia and relocated from one site to another depending on prospects for profit and livelihood. In other words, the circulation of material objects between South Asia and China reveals the interconnectedness of routes, networks, markets, and transit sites across Asia.

Buddhist images, relics, and texts that reached China did not all come from South Asia, nor were they brought exclusively by South Asians. The peoples of Southeast and Central Asia were intensely involved in the circulation of these goods, either trading on items manufactured in South Asia or creating their own versions of Buddhist images and paraphernalia. China also served a similar role, receiving, creating, and diffusing Buddhist artifacts to places such as Korea, Japan, and Persia. In fact, some of these Buddhist objects made in China, such as the images of Mañjuśrī, also traveled in the reverse direction and entered South Asia. The Buddhist cosmopolis, therefore, involved not only circulations of knowledge, as outlined in the previous chapter, but also the multidirectional movements of objects. These circulations and movements, and the notion of a Buddhist cosmopolis emphasized here, suggest the existence of a highly connected and integrated world of Asia in the first millennium CE.

The Buddhist connections and circulations had a significant impact on intra-Asian exchanges. They led to the introduction of and, subsequently, demand for new objects, which then became part of manufacturing industries, commercial activity, and cultural practices across most of Asia. The connections and circulations also resulted in the universal recognition of certain objects as sacred, ranging from the remains of the Buddha to monks' robes. This recognition triggered further circulations of objects that were used to venerate or were offered as donations to these sacred items.

Artistic traditions and the movement of artisans, the copying of images, the building of statues and temples, and the creation of proselytizing sites were all associated with and fostered by the circulations of Buddhist objects and artifacts. While local variations emerged as some of the imported items were continuously adapted to distinct cultural settings, the establishment of new centers of Buddhism, new temples, and even new political ideologies that attempted to use Buddhism to legitimize authority or a regime sustained the circulations of Buddhist objects and artifacts. This in turn prolonged the connections between various regions of Asia. Indeed, it can be argued that the economic, cultural, social, and even political history of Asia during the first millennium CE was intimately connected to the circulations of Buddhist objects.

The tribute system of the Chinese dynasties also had a substantial impact on Asian history. Since the system involved the participation of merchants from different regions of Asia, the connections between the Chinese court and foreign polities through this practice was extremely complex. Often it is not clear if the tribute carriers were in fact natives of the polities they are recorded to have represented. Indeed, in some cases, especially during the Song period, it is evident that several groups of foreign merchants settled in China's coastal ports vied with each other to appear at the Chinese court as foreign tribute carriers. Some, as in the case of a tribute mission designated as being from the Chola polity that reached the Song court in 1077, may have deliberately represented a foreign polity to obtain trading privileges or feed incorrect information to court officials. The most active group of people bringing tribute to the Chinese court was of West Asian origin. Several of these merchants also represented polities in South and Southeast Asia, offered goods that originated from various regions of Asia, and networked with other merchant communities in the coastal region of China. The tribute system, therefore, connected South Asia and

China not necessarily directly, but through people and places from different parts of Asia.

The objects offered as tribute to the Chinese court also reflect this wider involvement of other parts of Asia in the exchanges between South Asia and China. As noted above, the tribute objects ranged from exotic animals to commodities in demand in local markets. While some of these items were locally produced or manufactured in South Asia and offered to the Chinese courts by either native or foreign merchants, tribute missions representing South Asian polities often carried objects procured from a third region. This was especially true for items that had a high market value in China. Frankincense, for example, was offered by tribute missions from several different polities located in South and Southeast Asia, including the Cholas and the Śrīvijayans. The item was produced in the Persian Gulf and exported in large quantities to China. Similarly, the giraffes offered as tribute by Bengal to the Ming court came not from the local region but from Africa (see figure 2.15). In the same way, representatives of other Asian polities offered products and goods from South Asia, such as pepper and pearls, to the Chinese court.

The tribute system also facilitated the flow of objects from China to other parts of Asia. The return gifts and the regifting or sale of tribute items by the courts in China made the tributary system a circulatory process. The return gifts included Chinese products such as silk and other precious items. The court also "recycled" some of the foreign gifts, which were regifted to neighboring foreign polities, offered as rewards to court officials, or sold in local markets. The circulation of pepper during the Ming period discussed above (and in the next chapter) is an apt example of these multiple functions of tribute items, which were presented to the Ming court as gifts. The court then gave the spices to Ming officials as rewards and also sold or gifted them to foreign polities through officials accompanying Zheng He. It is evident, therefore, that the

Figure 2.15.   Tribute of giraffe, Ming Dynasty.

tributary system was one of the main facilitators of the circulation of objects across Asia. It functioned alongside the circulation of Buddhist objects and was closely connected to the commercial networks of diverse merchant groups.

Commercial networks formed the basis for the circulation of both the Buddhist objects and the tributary items that were discussed in this chapter. These networks of merchant communities either within a subregion or trading circuit or across Asian or Afroeurasian space facilitated the movement of various types of commodities. They also made it possible for Buddhist monks, tribute carriers, craftsmen, and artisans to move over long distances, carrying their own objects, artifacts, and expertise. These long-distance networks existed at least back to the Neolithic period and encompassed the South Asia–China segments as part of a wider network of commercial activity. There was diversity in the ethnic background of the merchants involved, in the ownership and operators of shipping and caravan networks, and in the kinds of objects that circulated between South Asia and China. Very few of the objects and people involved in these circulations may have intended to focus exclusively on the South Asia–China connections. The nature of routes, the modes of transportation, and halting places all ensured that these circulations involved multiple places, markets, and people.

Due to advances in shipbuilding technology, the appearance of polities that propagated long-distance commerce, and the establishment of the Mongol Empire, there was a rapid expansion of commercial activity in Asia between the tenth and fourteenth centuries. In fact, the webs of commerce after the tenth century became so distinctively complex, large scale, and multilayered that some scholars have identified the development of an early age of commerce and with it the initial stages of globalization (Stearns 2010: ch. 3). Intimately interconnected to the supply chains for bulk goods, economies of several polities within the Afroeurasian world depended on production and consumption trends in distant places. Consequently, the earlier pattern of relay trade developed into a more competitive and contested system, with several merchant groups and polities vying to profit from the lucrative long-distance commerce. The circulations of objects between South Asia and China became immersed within this global system that was indeed a precursor to the seventeenth- and eighteenth-century trade and exchanges under the European colonial states and enterprises. Commodities during the first half of the second millennium began circulating multiple times and in multiple directions. The people involved in these circulations increased and diversified significantly, and several maritime polities became intrinsically involved in promoting commercial activity primarily to add to their state revenues. This included the courts and merchants of Song China, Śrīvijaya, Chola, and the Abbasids.

The establishment of the vast Mongol Empire in the thirteenth century continued to foster this relationship between merchant communities and courts. It integrated more deeply the Afroeurasian world with regard to the circulations of objects and people—a development evidenced by the travels of Marco Polo and Ibn Baṭūṭah as well as the trade in horses. In fact, in many ways the Mongol period laid the foundation for the global circulation of goods that occurred during the colonial period. The overland and maritime routes became more intimately linked; knowledge about markets in Europe, Africa, and Asia became more widespread; shipbuilding and navigational skills improved significantly; and the Afroeurasian world became interdependent economically. Several Asian commodities entered European markets during the Mongol period, triggering an interest in African markets among the Europeans of the thirteenth and fourteenth centuries (Hodgett [1972] 2006).

The Ming expeditions under Zheng He were built upon earlier maritime exchanges and were a watershed moment in the history of Asian connections. The expeditions employed shipbuilding technologies and navigational skills that developed over several centuries among Arabs, South and Southeast Asians, and the Chinese. They also utilized the earlier nodes and networks of maritime interactions across the Indian Ocean. Even some of the political agendas were similar to those attempted by the Yuan court. At the same time, the expeditions inaugurated the phase of state-directed circulation of objects over the breadth of the Indian Ocean. The European colonial powers continued the monopolization of key commodities, but with significantly more violence and manipulation of resources. In fact, the colonial connections, discussed in the next chapter, were founded upon the routes, networks, technical knowledge, and exertion of naval power that had evolved over several centuries within Asia.

NOTES

1. On these interconnected routes, especially those centered on the Yunnan-Burma regions, see Yang (2004, 2012).

2. These routes are discussed in detail in Sen (2003: chapter 4).

3. For analysis of these episodes, see Sen (2003 and 2009). Earlier examinations include Nilakanta Sastri ([1958] 1975) and Spencer (1983).

4. Two important works that provide information about extensive West Asian and Muslim networks, both overland and maritime, are *Akhbār al-Ṣīn wa 'l-Hind* (An Account of China and India), compiled in 851, and *Kitāb al-Masālik wa l-mamālik* (The Book of Roads and Kingdoms), written around 870. Translations of the former work have been done by Ahmad (1989) and Mackintosh-Smith (2014).

5. Rashīd al-Dīn's *Jāmi'al-Tawārīkh* (Compendium of Chronicles) and Waṣṣāf al-Ḥaḍrat's *Tajziyat al-amṣār wa-tazjiyat al-a'ṣār* (The Allocation of Cities and the Propulsion of Epochs) are two sources for the later networks of Muslim traders that linked South Asia and China.

6. On the spread of Chinese maritime networks to South Asia during the thirteenth and fourteenth centuries, see Sen (2006b and 2011).

7. See the record of Malacca by the Portuguese apothecary Tomé Pires cited in the next chapter.

8. The popularity of stories related to the Chan Buddhist masters, such as Bodhidharma and Huineng, Peter D. Hershock (2005: 82) argues, led to the "advent of unprecedented 'homegrown' buddhas on Chinese soil." Ruan and

Liang, who are associated with the veneration of and stories related to the sixth Chan patriarch Huineng, are examples of such buddhas.

9. A detailed study of the early translations of Buddhist texts into Chinese is provided by Nattier (2008).

10. A detailed study of Buddhist texts as sacred objects and the cultic functions they served, especially in the South Asia context, is Kim (2013).

11. The classic work on imperial China's interactions with foreign polities within this ideological framework is Fairbank (1968).

12. On the development of shipbuilding technology during the Song and Yuan periods, see Lo (2012).

13. As mentioned in the previous chapter, both of these missions also carried letters to the courts in China.

14. Schafer (1963: 103–104) believes that Kaliṅga here indicates Indonesia and that the Kalaviṅka bird, a mythical bird often mentioned in Buddhist literature, is a drongo.

15. On the diplomatic exchanges between the Yuan court and the coastal polities in South Asia, see Sen (2006a).

16. Ming officials, including military personnel, were still visiting sites in Southeast Asia after the Zheng He voyages. An entry in the *Ming shilu*, dated 16 January 1484, for example, reports: "The Investigating Censor Xu Mao, regional inspector of Guang-dong, memorialized: 'As their ship had been damaged by the wind, 28 military personnel and civilians who had accompanied the envoy who was sent to Melaka, drifted to the country of Annam. Li Hao, the king of the country of Annam, provided them with grain and a ship and sent an envoy to escort them home. The language of his despatch is truly deferential and his words are all humble. His respect for the Court is obvious. This is respectfully advised.' The Emperor said: 'The king of the country of Annam has assisted in sending home military personnel and civilians who were drifting in the ocean. His loyalty and respect are pleasing. Swiftly instruct the Guang-dong Provincial Administration Commission to send a despatch advising the king of this.'" Wade 2005a, http://epress.nus.edu.sg/msl/entry/2788, accessed 11 June 2016.

17. But records of Ming naval expeditions in the early fifteenth century continue to mention the gift or sale of Chinese silk by Chinese court representatives visiting South Asia.

Chapter Three

The Imperial Connections

In the Ming the *sanbao* eunuch Zheng He
used a naval force to destroy Ceylon.
—Wei Yuan (1794–1856)

This and the following chapter demonstrate the extensive and diverse nature of connections between India and China during the
period between the fifteenth and the early twentieth century, a
phase that was marked by both Asian and European imperialism.[1]
The two chapters argue that these four and half centuries were
instrumental in creating new sites of interactions; generating distinctive perceptions, concerns, and knowledge; introducing new
commodities to the commercial exchanges between the two regions; and, perhaps more notably, fostering connections and relationships between various social groups ranging from court officials to indentured laborers. The connections between the two regions were intimately linked to the global circulations of people,
objects, and ideas that defined this period of imperialism. The silver mines in the Americas, the tea-drinking tradition in Europe, the
introduction of steamships, and the movement of plantation laborers to places such as Guiana and Mauritius all had a tremendous
impact on the connections between India and China.

Four hegemonic powers dominated the intra-Asian routes and networks during the period covered in these two chapters. In the early fifteenth century, the Ming court in China, primarily through the expeditions of Zheng He, influenced the politics, trade, and movement of people across the Indian Ocean world. The Ming court exerted its influence through the control of several "choke points" or "nodes of interactions" in the maritime region. In the sixteenth century, the Portuguese played a similar role, the Dutch did so in the seventeenth, and the British asserted their power over the intra-Asian networks during the eighteenth and nineteenth centuries.

The land routes that connected the inland areas of Asia, including those between India and China discussed in chapter 1, did not witness similar domination by imperial powers. The diverse and treacherous terrains through which these land routes extended, unlike the extensively charted and largely navigable maritime world of the Indian Ocean, may have created this difference. Consequently, more localized and less imperially controlled exchanges and communications took place through these overland routes, even though several European colonial powers (including Russia) vied with each other to control strategic routes and sites in this area. This is not to say that the Ming, Portuguese, Dutch, and British dictated every type of maritime interaction within Asia. The complexities of intra-Asian interactions during this phase of imperialism lay in the existence of various different contending regimes; the flourishing of a diverse group of traders, including Gujaratis, Parsis, Hokkiens, and the Portuguese; the networks of immigrant communities across several regions of the world; and the vibrancy of transport systems, including Tibetan mule caravans and private shipping services. The connections between India and China are examined within this context of a complex globalizing world being ushered in by Asian and European imperialism.

The extraction of resources and labor, and the trafficking of addictive products (such as opium, tea, and tobacco) by the colonial powers made this world of imperialism exploitative, destructive, and humiliating for Indians and Chinese as they interacted with each other in different parts of the globe. In the late nineteenth and early twentieth centuries, some of these episodes triggered nostalgic reminiscences of the historical interactions between "India" and "China" that, as discussed in the next chapter, became part of the anticolonial ideology known as Asianism or pan-Asianism (Ch. *fan Yazhou zhuyi* 泛亞洲主義). The advocates of this ideology stressed the notion of Asian universalism within which India and China were described as having a unique historical relationship that defined intra-Asian interactions and bonded the continent prior to the entry of European colonial enterprises. Yet this attempt to create Asian solidarity took place at the same time that Japan was rising as an imperial power, new prejudices were forming between Indians and Chinese, and, in the period following World War II, the need to demarcate border regions and assert territorial claims was becoming more imperative. As a result, when, in the middle of the twentieth century, India emerged as an independent nation-state and China a Communist country, the experiences, imaginations, treaties, and irreconcilabilities of the past became entangled with contemporary political and cultural intercourse between the two countries. In the final chapter of this book, some of the problems associated with this reconstructed notion of past interactions as part of the contemporary geopolitical agenda are examined.

In order to question the periodization of Asian history that emphasizes a watershed with the arrival of the European colonial powers, the first section of this chapter will argue that the seven maritime expeditions of Zheng He between 1405 and 1433 marked a significant transition from the earlier structures and methods of intra-Asian interactions. These expeditions were manifestations of Ming imperialism across the Indian Ocean that led to the creation of new ports and choke points, militarized the maritime realm, contributed to the formation of a dual system of court-controlled and private commercial connections, and dictated court-to-court interactions in the entire Indian Ocean realm. The second section examines the advent of early European imperial powers, who initially followed the networks and occupied the nodes created by the Zheng He expeditions. Subsequently, by the end of the seventeenth century, these colonial powers started dictating many of the interactions between India and China. The third and fourth sections explore the experiences, participations, perceptions, and interactions of select Indian and Chinese individuals and migrant groups living within the British colonial world. The writings and experiences of these individuals and groups are key to understanding the diversities and complexities of imperial connections between India and China noted above.

ZHENG HE AND THE RESTRUCTURING OF INTRA-ASIAN NETWORKS

Several aspects of Zheng He's expeditions, especially those pertaining to the circulations of knowledge and objects, have been mentioned in chapters 1 and 2. Here the emphasis is on the ways in which these Ming naval expeditions dictated and shaped the maritime connections between India and China in the early fifteenth century. The aim is to show that the maritime exchanges between India and China were already restructured prior to the arrival of the Europeans. This was done through the use of naval power, the creation of new nodes of interactions, and the establishment of allied and cooperative regimes by the Ming court at strategic sites in the Indian Ocean world. Later, the Portuguese, the first European colonial power to enter the Indian Ocean, would use these existing nodes to establish their authority in the region and gradually dictate the maritime exchanges between India and China.

Pointing out that the ships led by Zheng He carried tens of thousands of military men and outlining the possible "coercion" involved in forcing rulers of several Southeast Asian polities to travel to the Ming court to offer tribute to the Yongle emperor, Geoff Wade (2005b: 51) argues that the Zheng He missions were intended to "obtain control of ports and shipping lanes." He further explains (Wade 2005b: 51),

> It was not control of territory which was sought—this came with later colonialism. Rather, it was political and economic control across space—control of economic lifelines, nodal points and networks. By controlling ports and trade routes, one controlled trade, an essential element for the missions' treasure-collecting tasks. The colonial armies which manned these ships were the tools necessary to ensure that the control was maintained. In their method, the Ming through these maritime missions, were engaged in what might be called proto maritime colonialism. That is, they were engaged in that early form of maritime colonialism by which a dominant maritime power took control (either through force or the threat thereof) of the main port polities along the major East–West maritime trade network, as well as the seas between, thereby gaining economic and political benefits.

Employing M. N. Pearson's (1991) description of the Portuguese expansion into Asia during the fifteenth and sixteenth centuries, Wade outlines several similarities between the early European and the Ming Chinese techniques to assert power over maritime polities. These included the "tight connection between the Crown and trade," the use of "military coercion," and demand for tribute in exchange for protection. The examples of Zheng He's military interventions in Palembang, Java, Samudera, and Ayudhya that Wade provides are central to his arguments. Roderich Ptak (1991) and Robert Finlay (1992) have also drawn comparisons between the Zheng He missions and the early Portuguese activities in the Indian Ocean. Finlay perceives the Zheng He expeditions as hegemonic and indicative of Ming "maritime imperialism." He (1992: 230) points out that the Ming court "did not attempt to conquer overseas territories or to blockade key sea routes, it did not have to maintain a costly, permanent force of men and ships at enormous distance. In the face of it, then, China was in all respects far better suited than Portugal to pursue hegemony in the seas of Asia."

Finlay (2008) has further underscored the Yongle emperor's goal of controlling all aspects of maritime trade and exchanges. "The voyages of Zheng He," he writes (2008: 336), "may be regarded as Yongle's forceful attempt to reconcile China's need for maritime trade with the government's suppression of private foreign contact; or, to put it differently, they represented a deployment of state power to bring into line the reality of seaborne commerce with an expansive conception of Chinese hegemony." This state power was not only employed in coastal regions of Ming China and at the nearby polities in the South China Sea region, but also at foreign ports as far as the Swahili coast of Africa. In other words, the Ming court through the Zheng He expeditions exercised hegemonic power over much of the Indian Ocean world.

Unlike the European powers, the Ming did not launch large-scale occupations of foreign territories in the maritime realm. With its superior naval force the Ming court could intervene in the diplomatic, commercial, and cultural activities of foreign polities and also assert itself in the long-distance connections across the Indian Ocean without committing troops in alien territories. As Roderich Ptak (1991: 25) has pointed out, Ming naval superiority was a determinant factor in how foreign politics interacted with the Chinese court. "Some of the other maritime countries' ground troops probably would have outnumbered the Chinese marines in the battle field," he writes, "but foreign navies were definitely inferior to the Ming fleets, both in terms of quantity and quality; hence, in many parts of maritime Asia, Ming superiority was real and for a small and weak country it was certainly advisable to send tribute and acknowledge this superiority, rather than to risk a Chinese punitive campaign."

Indeed, the Zheng He expeditions brought about significant economic and political changes in the Indian Ocean world through coercion, shows of force, and military intervention. Perhaps the most important of these changes was the creation of alternative nodes of maritime connections, including the new port towns of Malacca, Cochin, and Malindi. They also had considerable impact on the commercial networks in the Bay of Bengal and the Arabian Sea regions and exerted influence over ports as far away as Hormuz (Sen 2016b). Additionally, the Ming court also tried to control prominent cultural artifacts and procure exotic animals as a demonstration of its expansive power both within China and beyond it shores (Sen 2016b, 2016c).

The Zheng He expeditions benefited from the precedents set during the previous Yuan period. The dispatch of court officials to foreign maritime polities and the use of naval force were some of the tactics employed by the Yuan court under Kublai Khan. Moreover, for Kublai Khan and the Yongle emperor, who initiated the Zheng He expeditions, political legitimacy was the common goal. While Kublai had to prove his status as the great khan among the contending descendants of Genghis, the Yongle emperor needed to legitimize his usurpation of the Ming throne.[2] In fact, it was within a year of his usurpation that the Yongle emperor ordered the building of a large number of oceangoing ships and chose Zheng He, a close aide who had served him since the age of ten, to lead the voyages.

The first naval expedition led by Zheng He embarked in 1405 with over 250 ships, including sixty large "treasure ships," and more than twenty-seven thousand personnel, of which twenty-six thousand were soldiers. By 1411 two additional expeditions had taken place. The destination of these three voyages was Calicut on the Malabar coast. It was during the fourth expedition, which left

Ming China in late 1412 or early 1413, that the naval armada for
the first time went beyond South Asia and reached Hormuz in the
Persian Gulf. The fifth, sixth, and seventh expeditions visited the
Swahili coast of Africa (see figure 3.1). The final expedition, which
set sail in 1431, came after a hiatus of almost a decade, a period that
witnessed the death of the Yongle emperor. Before his death, the
Yongle emperor had already decreed a temporary halt to the maritime expeditions on account, perhaps, of the expenses involved and
the burning of several buildings of the imperial palace being constructed at the new capital of Beiping (now Beijing). Some interpreted the latter episode as an omen, especially as a potent sign
against the maritime expeditions. The seventh and final expedition
was initiated by the Xuande emperor soon after the death of a
prominent minister in charge of finance and a critic of the maritime
expeditions named Xia Yuanji 夏原吉 (1366–1430).[3]

The first expedition, with its massive armada, must have made a
significant impression on various polities, merchant groups, and
pirates in the South China Sea, the Bay of Bengal, and parts of the
Arabian Sea. It was clearly a grand demonstration of Ming naval
power, expressed not only through the number and size of the ships
but also the advanced weapons, in the form of shipborne cannons,
and soldiers that the armada carried. Several sites at which the
Zheng He–led armada anchored during its first expedition were, in
fact, places previously visited by other eunuch representatives from
the Ming court. These included Palembang (known as "Old Port"
舊港 in Ming sources) and Calicut, which had already started sending tribute missions to the Ming court prior to the Zheng He expeditions. However, the arrival of the powerful naval fleet seems to
have resulted in an intense competition among several contending
rival polities and groups in the Indian Ocean that sought alliances
with the Ming court. This is evident from the situation at Palembang, where groups of Chinese merchant communities had settled
and wielded power over maritime commerce and interactions.

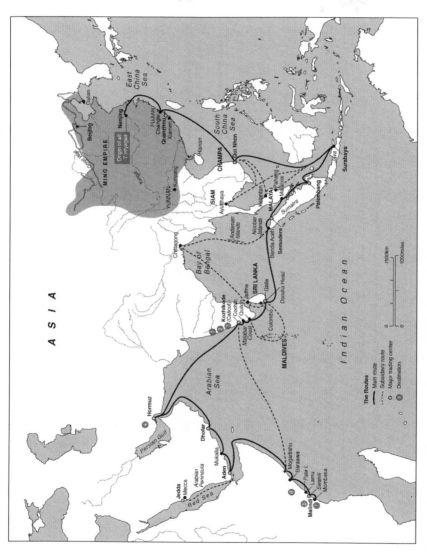

Figure 3.1.   Zheng He's maritime expeditions, 1405–1433. © Tansen Sen

The Ming sources record the presence of several "chieftains" in Palembang, all of Chinese origin, who seem to have migrated to the place after the "maritime ban" instituted by the founding Ming ruler Hongwu. The three chieftains mentioned prominently in Ming sources during the time of Zheng He's first expedition were Liang Daoming 梁道明, who is recorded as an "absconder" in the *Taizong shilu*; Chen Zuyi 陳祖義, described as a "pirate"; and Shi Jinqing 施進卿, the person the Ming eventually appointed as the pacification superintendent. In February 1405, several months before Zheng He embarked on this maiden voyage, the *Taizong shilu* reports that the Ming court dispatched officials to bring Liang Daoming to negotiated "pacification." These officials returned with Liang Daoming, who offered tribute of horses and was given paper money and silk products as gifts by the Ming court, in December of that year. It seems that whatever issues the Ming court had with Liang were settled after his appearance at the Ming court.

In August 1406, several months after the Zheng He armada passed through Palembang on its way to South Asia, a representative of Liang Daoming and the son of another chieftain of Palembang named Chen Zuyi presented tribute to the Ming court. It seems that a few months later another person from Palembang called Shi Jinqing went to the Ming court and reported on the "acts of savagery" committed by Chen Zuyi (Mills [1970] 1997: 100). On his way back to Ming China in October 1407, Zheng He anchored at Palembang and tried to negotiate with Chen Zuyi. The Ming sources report that Chen "secretly plotted to attack the Imperial army" (*Taizong shilu* 11: 987; Wade 2005a: entry 536). Knowing this, Zheng He led a counteroffensive, killing five thousand of Chen's men and capturing the "pirate." Chen was taken to the Ming court and beheaded. Shi Jinqing, who seems to have been at the Ming capital all this time, was appointed as the pacification superintendent of the Pacification Superintendency of Palembang. After Shi Jinqing's death, the Ming court appointed his son to the same post. This installation of a chieftain at Palembang gave the Ming court access to this important port in Southeast Asia that had commercial connections to the broader Indian Ocean world.

In the same year, 1407, the Ming court also started exerting control over Java's external networks. Java was closely integrated into the Indian Ocean commercial system as a hub for the export of commodities—including sappanwood, nutmeg, and sandalwood—produced in several Indonesian islands. During the fourteenth century, the Majapahit polity (1293–1527) located on the island exercised considerable power over several polities and ports in the South China Sea region. However, in the beginning of the fifteenth century a civil war weakened the polity and led to the contraction of its influence over places such as Palembang. Ming soldiers somehow got entangled in this civil war and were either deliberately or by mistake killed by one of the factions. A record dated 23 October 1407 in the *Taizong shilu* (11: 997–998; Wade 2005a: entry 553) reports that the king of Java sent an envoy to "admit guilt" for killing 170 Ming soldiers accompanying Zheng He who had gone "ashore to trade." The court chided the "Western king" of Java for killing the "Eastern king," both of whom the order noted were "enfeoffed by the Court," and demanded a compensation of sixty thousand *liang* of gold as atonement for the deaths of the Ming soldiers. The court order also warned that if the ruler failed to comply, there would not be any option "but to despatch an army to punish your crime. What happened in Annam can serve as an example." The Annam reference was to Ming China's successful invasion of Vietnam earlier that year.

The news of the Ming intervention in Palembang and the threat to Java would have spread quickly in the region. In 1408, when Boni 渤泥 (Brunei) reportedly sought Chinese help in ending the requirement to submit 40 *jin* of camphor each year to Java, the Ming court ordered the king of Java to cease this demand. A month later the king of Java, who had not paid the initial sixty thousand *liang* of gold as compensation, quickly sent an envoy with ten thousand *liang*. Within a few years of the launch of the Zheng He expeditions, the Ming court had clearly replaced the Majapahit as the main naval power in the South China Sea region.

Intervention in disputes between local polities and replacing existing maritime powers were common features of the Zheng He expeditions as the Ming court expanded its control over Southeast Asian ports and choke points. In 1415, Zheng He is credited with capturing the "leader" of a "bandit" group in Samudera by the name of Suganla 蘇幹剌 (Sekandar?). While Fei Xin describes Suganla as a "false king" who "robbed and usurped" the throne of Samudera, Ma Huan portrays him as someone trying to overthrow the reigning ruler. The *Taizong shilu* (13: 1869–1870; Wade 2005a: entry 914) has him as the younger brother of the former king plotting to kill the ruler. When Zheng He arrived in Samudera to bestow gifts from the Ming court on the reigning ruler, Suganla is recorded to have attacked the admiral's contingent with "tens of thousands" of soldiers. The [would-be] usurper was eventually defeated, taken to the Ming capital, and, according to Ma Huan, publicly decapitated. Scholars (Mills 1996: 58n.132; Wade 2005b: 50) have pointed out that this was a case of Ming intervention in domestic affairs, with the intention, most likely, of exerting influence and control over the area without having to occupy it with Chinese forces.

Another strategy that the Zheng He expeditions employed to accomplish the goal of exerting influence over strategic maritime choke points was to create alternative nodes in the Indian Ocean world. This is apparent in the emergence of Malacca as an important node in Indian Ocean interactions. Both Ma Huan and Fei Xin, who accompanied Zheng He on several expeditions, note that Malacca was not considered a polity, had no "king," and existed as a tributary region of Xianluo 暹羅 (Siam, present-day Thailand) prior to the fifteenth century. In 1403, the Ming court sent a eunuch envoy named Yin Qing 尹慶 to take an imperial proclamation to Malacca and perhaps to confer a title on the local chieftain, and by 1409, Malacca's status was raised to that of a "polity" (國), with the Ming court sending a stone tablet enfeoffing the western mountain of Malacca. Through this tablet the Ming court essentially brought the polity under its protection. The Ming court also established a *guanchang* 官廠 (government depot) on the island. This "official depot" was essentially a fortified Chinese cantonment and hub for Ming naval activity in the South China Sea (Wade 2005b: 47).

"Thereafter," Ma Huan notes (Mills 1997 [1970]: 109), Siam "did not dare to invade it [Malacca]." In fact, in 1431, when a representative from Malacca complained that Siam was obstructing tribute missions to the Ming court, the Xuande 宣德 emperor (r. 1425–1435) dispatched Zheng He carrying a threatening message for the Siamese king, saying, "You, king should respect my orders, develop good relations with your neighbours, examine and instruct your subordinates and not act recklessly or aggressively" (*Xuan-zong shilu* 20: 1762–1763). Obligated to the Ming court, the rulers of Malacca paid tribute to the Chinese emperor in person. In 1411, for example, King Bailimisula 白里迷蘇剌 (Paramesvara?) with his wife and more than 540 people visited the Ming court to express his gratitude. After Paramesvara, his son and grandson were also recognized as the kings of Malacca by the Ming court.[4]

The above patterns of intervention in local disputes and the creation of alternative nodes along the maritime routes by the Zheng He–led expeditions were also observed in South Asia (see figure 3.2). On the Malabar coast, the destination of Zheng He's first three voyages, the Ming court seems to have decided to support Cochin as an alternate hub instead of Calicut. Yin Qing, who was sent to Malacca prior to the Zheng He expeditions, also went to Cochin. Calicut, ruled by a Hindu king and a hub for commercial interactions controlled by Muslim merchants, already had the status of the leading emporium on the Malabar coast that monopolized the export of pepper. When Yin Qing and Zheng He reached the region, as a result of changes in the coastline, Cochin was only an emerging port site. The price of pepper was cheaper in Cochin than in Calicut, and it did not have an entrenched group of people controlling foreign trade. It was in this context that the Ming court seems to have decided to grant special status to Cochin and its ruler, Keyili 可亦里 (*Ming shi* 326: 8441–8442; Xu 2005: 83–85; Sen 2006a).

As part of his fifth expedition (1417–1419), Zheng He was asked to confer a seal upon Keyili and, similar to the case of Malacca, enfeoffed a mountain in Cochin and termed it the *zhengguo zhi shan* 鎮國之山 (mountain which protects the country). Other than Malacca and Cochin, only Japan (in 1406) and Brunei (in 1408) had received this privilege from the Ming court. "All were intended," as Wang Gungwu (1968a: 57) explains, "to commemorate the enfeoffment of mountains, and the sealing of closer relations between his empire and the four countries concerned." According to Wang (1964: 101n.4), the Yongle emperor enfeoffed the mountain in Japan "in recognition of Japan's help in curbing Wako piracy on the Chinese coasts." Brunei was given the honor because its ruler had come to the Ming court in person.

The ruler of Calicut seems to have taken issue with the decision of the Ming court to support his local rival. Diplomatic missions from Calicut to China declined after 1416, and it ceased to be one of the main destinations of Zheng He's remaining two expeditions. Only three Calicut embassies, in 1421, 1423, and 1433, seem to have been sent to the Chinese court after the seal was conferred upon the ruler of Cochin. Sources are ambiguous about Zheng He's visits to Calicut during his fifth and sixth expeditions. During his seventh and last expedition, Zheng He's entourage stopped at Calicut for only four days on the way to Hormuz. On its way back to China, however, the entourage stayed at the Indian port for about

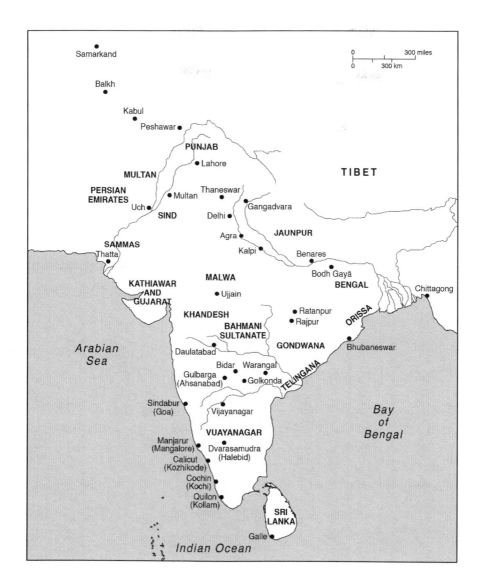

Figure 3.2.   Polities of South Asia during the Early Ming period. ©
Tansen Sen

nine days. In fact, some scholars have speculated that during this
expedition Zheng He was involved in a military skirmish between

Cochin and Calicut and died either on the Malabar coast or on his way back to China in 1433 (Ray 1993: 208–209; Lin 2005).

This, if true, would not have been the first time Zheng He engaged in a military conflict in South Asia. Every Ming source on the Zheng He expedition records a military conflict between the Chinese admiral and a Sri Lankan "ruler" in 1411. Passing through Champa, Java, Malacca, and Semudera, the ships led by Zheng He reached the southern coastal region of Sri Lanka in 1410. It was here (perhaps at Dondra Head) that Zheng He erected a trilingual inscription, indicating that the Ming representative was not only aware of the multiple stakeholders on the island but also its importance in maritime connections.

The *Taizong shilu* in an entry for 6 July 1411 gives a recounting of the events that transpired when Zheng He arrived in Sri Lanka:

> The eunuch Zheng He and others, who had been sent as envoys to the various countries in the Western Ocean, returned and presented Ya-lie Ku-nai-er, the captured king of the country of Sri Lanka, and his family members. Previously, [Zheng] He and the others had been sent as envoys to the various *fan* (i.e., foreign) countries. However, when they reached Sri Lanka, Ya-lie Ku-nai-er was insulting and disrespectful. He wished to harm He, but He came to know of this and left. Ya-lie Ku-nai-er also acted in an unfriendly way to neighbouring countries and repeatedly intercepted and robbed their envoys. All the *fan* countries suffered from his actions. When He returned, he again passed Sri Lanka and the king enticed him to the country. The king then had his son Na-yan demand gold, silver and precious objects, but He would not give these to him. The king then secretly despatched over 50,000 *fan* troops to rob He's ships. They also felled trees to create obstructions and impede He's route of return, so that he could not render assistance. He and the others found out about this and they gathered their force and set off back to their ships. However, the route had already been blocked. He thus spoke to his subordinates, saying: "The majority of the troops have already been despatched. The middle of

the country will be empty." He also said: "Our merchants and troops are isolated and nervous and will be unable to act. If they are attacked by surprise, the attackers will achieve their purpose." Thus, he secretly ordered persons to go to the ships by another route with orders that the government troops were to fight to the death in opposing the attackers. He then personally led 2,000 of his troops through a by-path and attacked the royal city by surprise. They took the city and captured alive Ya-lie Ku-nai-er, his family members and chieftains. The *fan* army returned and surrounded the city and several battles were fought, but He greatly defeated them. He and the others subsequently returned to the Court. The assembled ministers requested that the king be executed. The Emperor pitied the king for his stupidity and ignorance and leniently ordered that he and the others be released and given food and clothing. The Ministry of Rites was ordered to deliberate on and select a worthy member of the family to be established as the country's king in order to handle the country's sacrifices. (*Ming shilu* 12: 1477–1478; translated by Wade 2005a: entry 1778)

According to the above record, the "king of Sri Lanka" had "insulted" Zheng He when he reached the island during his first expedition to the Indian Ocean in 1405–1407. For his third voyage, Zheng He seems to have come prepared to battle Yaliekunaier/ Aliekunaier 亞烈苦柰兒/阿烈苦柰兒 (Alagakkonara or Alakéswara). The Sri Lankan was taken captive but was later released by the Ming court and eventually returned to his native country. Edward W. Perera (1904) has explained the extremely complex political situation in Sri Lanka when Zheng He landed in 1410. There may have been three principal contenders for power in Sri Lanka at that time. To complicate the matter further, there seems to be confusion about the person Zheng He actually captured and took to the Ming court (Somaratne 1975: 5). Somaratne (1975: 66–67) explains that the person Zheng He took captive was not the reigning ruler of Kotte, but a high official or minister holding the title of "*prabhuraja.*" This *prabhuraja* Alagakkonara was the one Zheng He met during his first visit to the island and came to know that he was not a supporter of Buddhism. Although Alagakkonara was pardoned by the Yongle emperor, the Ming court nonetheless appointed another person named Yebanaina 耶巴乃那 ([Parākramābahu] Apana?), who was in Ming China at the same time as Alagakkonara, to be the new "ruler."⁵ Apana, however, was murdered on the same day that he returned to Sri Lanka (most likely in 1414). Since the reigning ruler of Kotte was also named Parākramābahu (r. 1411–1466), the Chinese scribes mistook the two as the same person, and even the Ming court, Somaratne argues (1975: 74), continued to perceive him as their original "nominee of the Chinese emperor to the throne of Sri Lanka on account of their identical names."⁶ Somaratne further suggests, albeit speculatively, that Parākramābahu, aware of this confusion, maintained a strategic relationship with the Ming court by regularly sending tributary missions.⁷

There is another issue connected to this episode, which, despite the above-mentioned confusion about various personalities in Sri Lanka, suggests the Ming court's awareness of the importance of political legitimacy attained through the veneration of sacred objects. A note added to the Ming dynasty edition of the Buddhist monk Xuanzang's *Da Tang Xiyu ji* suggests that the military action undertaken by Zheng He in Sri Lanka in 1410–1411 was related to obtaining the famous Tooth Relic of the Buddha (later housed in Kandy). The note on the Tooth Relic is appended to the section where Xuanzang describes Sri Lanka. It now appears in the *Jiaxing zang* 嘉興藏 ("Jiaxing Tripiṭaka") composed in 1676, but it most likely originated from the *Ming beiben* 明北本 ("Ming Northern Edition") or the *Yongle beizang* 永樂北藏 ("Yongle Northern Tripiṭaka") edition compiled between 1421 and 1440 (Ji et al. 1985: 880n.5). Translated into English by Li Rongxi (1996: 353–355), it reads:

> The country of Siṁhala, known as the Land of Lions in olden times, and also called the Country of No Sorrow, is south of

India. As it produces plenty of rare gems, it is also named the Precious Island. Formerly, Śākyamuni Buddha transformed himself into a man named Simhala, and as he was a man possessing all virtues, he was made king by the people of the country. Therefore it was also called the country of Simhala. With his great supernatural powers, he destroyed the great iron city, annihilated the *rākṣasīs*, and rescued the victims who were in peril. Then he constructed a capital city and built towns to convert and guide the local people. After having propagated the right teachings, he passed away, leaving a tooth behind in this country. It is adamantine and will last for many *kalpa*s without being damaged. It issues a precious light like a brilliant star, like the moon shining in the night, or the sun brightening the daytime. Whenever a prayer is said to it, it responds as swiftly as an echo. In times of natural disaster, an earnest prayer will bring instant divine auspiciousness. What is now called the Mountain of Ceylon was the country of Simhala in ancient times. Beside the royal palace is a temple for the Buddha's Tooth Relic, decorated with various gems and shining with great brilliance. It has been worshipped from generation to generation without negligence. The reigning king A-lie-ku-nai-er[8] is a native of Soḷī. He worships heretics, does not venerate the Triple Gem, is a brutal and tyrannical ruler, has no feeling of pity for his people, and blasphemes the Buddha's Tooth Relic.

In the third year of the Yongle period (1405 C.E.) of the great Ming dynasty, the Emperor dispatched the eunuch Zheng He as an imperial envoy to send incense and flowers to that country and make offerings [to the Tooth Relic]. Zheng He exhorted King A-lie-ku-nai-er to respect Buddhism and keep away from heretics. The king was enraged and intended to kill the envoy. Having got wind of the intrigue, Zheng He went away. Afterward he was sent again to bestow gifts on various foreign countries, and he visited the king of the mountain of Ceylon, who was all the more arrogant and disrespectful, and attempted to kill the envoy. The king mobilized fifty thousand troops to fell trees to obstruct the road and sent a contingent to ransack the seagoing vessels. At that juncture a subordinate official leaked the secret, and Zheng He and his men, having realized

the situation, at once tried to return to their ships. As the road
had been cut off, they could only secretly send some men out,
but the captors of the ships would not allow them to go on
board. Zheng He, commanding three thousand soldiers, made an
assault by a shortcut at night and took possession of the royal
city.

The native troops who had captured the ships joined forces
with the native soldiers on land and launched a counterattack
from all four sides. They besieged the royal city with a tight
encirclement and fought for six days. Zheng He and his men
captured the king and opened the city gate, and after cutting
down trees to make a way, they moved away while fighting.
Going for more than twenty *li*, they reached their ships in the
evening. They brought the Buddha's Tooth Relic on board with
due ceremony. It emitted a brilliant light in a most unusual
manner as mentioned above, while a peal of thunder rumbled
with such a loud crash so that people at a great distance saw the
lightning and hid themselves. The ships sailed on the great sea
without encountering a windstorm, [and they were as safe] as if
they were walking on dry land. Ferocious dragons and mischie-
vous fishes emerged before the ships but caused no harm. All
the people on board the ships were safe and happy.

On the ninth day of the seventh month on the ninth year of
Yongle (1411 C.E.) they returned to the capital, and the Emper-
or ordered that a precious diamond seat be prepared in the imperial city for the Tooth Relic, in order to make offerings to it for
the benefit of living beings and the welfare of the people, so that
they might perform countless meritorious deeds. (T. 2087:
938c–939a)

Except for the concluding section describing the removal of the
Tooth Relic from Sri Lanka, the episode described in this commentary is remarkably similar to the *Taizong shilu* record cited above.
The relic part might be dismissed, as Edward Dreyer (2007: 68–70)
has done in his study of Zheng He, on the basis that it only appears
in a Buddhist source. However, a letter from the Yongle emperor to
the Tibetan lama Tsong-kha-pa (1357–1419) dated 11 March 1413

found at the Potala Palace in Tibet in the 1950s includes passages about Zheng He and his capture of the Sri Lankan relic that are exactly similar to the commentary found in the Ming edition of the *Da Tang Xiyu ji* quoted above (Su 1996: 213–214; Liu 2008).[9] The letter offers significant clues to the Yongle emperor's interest in employing Buddhism both for spiritual and political purposes (Sen 2016a).

The Sri Lankan Tooth Relic, which has been called the "relic on the move" by John Strong (2004, 191), is especially connected to political legitimization and to episodes of theft and cross-regional warfare. Strong points to the story in the thirteenth-century Pali text *Dāṭhavaṃsa* where the arrival of the relic in Sri Lanka is associated with its theft from Dantapura in ancient Kaliṅga (present-day Orissa). Rulers from other parts of Asia also wanted to obtain the Buddhist relic from Sri Lanka. Chinese sources mention an attempted theft by a monk in the seventh century. In the thirteenth century, the quest for the Sri Lankan relics, especially the Tooth Relic and the Buddha's alms bowl, seems to have become a widespread activity. It was said to have been captured and taken to South India by the Pāṇḍyan rulers; Candrabhānu, the ruler from Tāmbraliṅga, tried to procure it by launching naval attacks (Sirisena 1978: 36–57; Herath 1994: 107–109); and Kublai Khan sent missions to procure it in the 1280s. Later, in 1561, the Portuguese are reported to have taken it to Goa and destroyed it in a public ceremony. A few years later, the relic miraculously reappeared in Sri Lanka, only to be captured by the British in the early nineteenth century (Strong 2004: 195–197).

Strong (2004: 196) has also noted that the possession of the Tooth Relic was "viewed in Sri Lanka as an important symbol of sovereignty over the nation," and, as centers of power shifted, he writes, it "became a movable palladium of kingship."[10] The Yuan court, Herath (1994: 111) suggests, wanted to obtain the Sri Lankan relics "as the most effective means of enforcing their authority" over the island. The Yongle emperor, trying to legitimize his authority in China and demonstrate sovereignty over foreign lands as the heavenly mandated Son of Heaven, would have clearly recognized the power of an important cultural artifact.

A third site in South Asia—to which Zheng He did not travel and where no military conflict took place between the representatives of Ming and the local rulers—was Bengal. Nonetheless, a leading eunuch member of the expeditions named Hou Xian traveled to Bengal and accomplished his goal through the demonstration of military power. In 1420, by which time awareness of the naval prowess of the Chinese court must have circulated throughout the Indian Ocean world, the king of Bengal complained to the Yongle emperor that the forces of the neighboring Jaunpur polity had carried out several military raids on his territory. In response to the complaint, the Ming court dispatched Hou Xian and others "with Imperial orders of instruction for them (i.e., Bengal and Jaunpur), so that they would both cultivate good relations with their neighbors and would each protect their own territory" (*Ming shilu* 14: 2226; translated by Wade 2005a: entry 2690). The entourage led by Hou Xian arrived in Bengal in August or September 1420 and was welcomed with a grand reception. It was Hou Xian's second visit to the region, and this time he seems to have brought along Ming soldiers, who were all presented with silver coins by the ruler of Bengal. The entourage then proceeded to Jaunpur to convey the Yongle emperor's message and, according to the Chinese texts, resolve the territorial dispute peacefully (Sen 2006a).

Bengal's request that the Ming intervene in the local dispute and the Chinese emperor's swift response to the appeal demonstrates the influence that the Ming court seems to have had beyond its shores during the first half of the fifteenth century. Geoff Wade (2005b) has argued that such descriptions in Ming sources were simply self-validation for engagement in areas beyond Ming China. The rulers of Bengal undoubtedly knew about the Chinese military interventions in other Indian Ocean polities. Bengal had sent at least eight embassies to the Ming court before 1420, and the traders from the region were actively engaged in commerce across the Bay of Bengal. These Bengali diplomats and traders must have been familiar with the naval prowess of the Ming court. In 1406–1407, Zheng He had fought and defeated the "pirate" Chen Zuyi in Palembang; in 1411 the Chinese admiral, as outlined above, fought the battle in Sri Lanka; and in 1414 he defeated the "usurper" Sekander and "resolved a civil war" in Semudera. The court in Bengal may also have been aware of the Ming backing for Cochin in 1416, when the stele was presented to its king (Sen 2006a).

A significant political transition within the Bengal Sultanate could have been another reason that prompted the ruler of Bengal to seek help from the Yongle emperor. In fact, the military conflict between Bengal and Jaunpur had resulted from the usurpation of the throne by a local Hindu noble named Raja Ganesh. Probably a descendent of the former, non-Muslim ruling family of Bengal, Raja Ganesh deposed the Turko-Muslim ruler and, in 1415, installed his own twelve-year-old son as the new king. The son, because of pressure from the local Muslim nobility and the neighboring Sultanate of Jaunpur, converted to Islam and took on the name Jalāl ud-Dīn Muhammad. To seek recognition of his rule, Jalāl ud-Dīn is reported to have contacted the Timurid ruler Shah Rukh and the Abbasid Caliphate in Egypt. He seems also to have made a request—similar to the one made to the Ming court—that Shah Rukh help him fend off the military threat from Jaunpur (Eaton 1993: 50–63; Hussain 2003: 104–115; Sen 2006a).

Chinese sources do not specify whether the title of king was bestowed on the ruler of Bengal through the Hou Xian mission of 1420. However, an imperial edict, a strong contingent of Chinese soldiers, and precious gifts for the king, his family, and officials were part of the entourage. By dispatching this powerful mission to Bengal, the Ming court seems to have provided Jalāl ud-Dīn an opportunity to demonstrate his diplomatic capabilities and assure his wealthy Muslim citizens, many of whom were invested in maritime trade across the Bay of Bengal, that trading ties between Bengal and China would continue. Not only did Jalāl ud-Dīn successfully rule over Bengal for the next thirteen years, but diplomatic and commercial links between the two regions grew until the Ming court, in the mid-fifteenth century, decided to reverse its policies regarding the maritime voyages.

The military reach of the Ming court does not seem to have extended to the Persian Gulf and the eastern coast of Africa, although some sort of strategic partnership may have been established with the rulers of Hormuz (Lin 2005). Perhaps the fact that not all ships in the Zheng He–led armada were able to travel to the westernmost regions of the Indian Ocean prevented Zheng He from executing interventionist actions beyond the Malabar coast. Additionally, Chinese courts always distinguished between near and distant barbarians, and expectations of the two were different. It seems that the Malabar coast came within the realm of the "near" barbarians for the Ming court, where force could be used to extract submissions and assert suzerainty through naval might. For the distant barbarians, tribute missions would have sufficed. There could be a third explanation. Those places in which Zheng He intervened militarily or the new nodes that his expeditions created in the maritime realm were part of the Chinese mercantile network. These networks may not have been very extensive beyond the Malabar coast, primarily due to the dominance of South Asian and Arab merchant networks in those areas. The Ming court's primary interest, then, lay only in supervising these regions with Chinese diasporic trading communities, which the Yongle emperor could have perceived as possible hideouts of the deposed Ming ruler, as places for anti-Ming activities, or as a threat to state-directed commercial activity and the tribute missions from foreign polities.

However, a combination of reports of Zheng He's accomplishments and the imagination of exotic places that the voyages passed through eventually led to the compilation of a fictional work by Luo Maodeng 羅懋登 titled *Sanbao taijian xiyang ji* 三寶太監西洋記 (Records of the Eunuch Sanbao to the Western Oceans). In this book the violent aspects of the voyages are magnified and woven into the story as appropriate punishments for unruly barbarians. One of the stories pertains to the African coast, a place called Lasa 剌撒, where the Ming soldiers used "Huihuipao" 回回砲 or "Muslim cannons/catapults" to destroy the city walls. While this story may be a work of fiction, the visit of the Ming ships to Malindi in 1417–1418 may have resulted in the elevation of its status compared to that of Mombasa, which was the leading commercial port in the region. The lists of places Zheng He visited during his sixth and seventh expeditions do not mention Malindi as one of his destinations, but the port is noted to be the place of origin for one of the giraffes that reached the Ming court as tribute in 1415. It is possible that another giraffe reported to have been given by Bengal to the Ming court also originated in Malindi. Additionally, Ming-period porcelain, including some with imperial reign marks, found on the Swahili coast suggest that significant trade in commodities took place during each of the three Ming visits to the region (Qin 2015).

The impact of these Ming expeditions on Indian Ocean commerce was significant at several levels. First, the Zheng He voyages occurred with the backdrop of the Ming ban on foreign trade, which essentially prevented private Chinese merchants from trading to foreign lands. Instituted by the Hongwu emperor, this maritime ban policy continued during the Yongle period. As a result of this policy, Chinese merchants from some coastal regions migrated to various parts of Southeast Asia. These merchants established their own commercial networks in Southeast Asia, trading with Ming China, Ryukyu, Korea, and Japan as foreigners on the one hand and operating in the Bay of Bengal on the other. On occasion, such as the above-mentioned action against Chen Zuyi, the Zheng He expeditions seem to have tried to control these networks of Chinese traders functioning in the Indian Ocean world. It is also possible that some of these private Chinese traders benefited from the Zheng He expeditions. The opening of Malacca and Cochin, for example, were places these traders used to establish more profitable bases. When the maritime expeditions ended in 1433, these networks of Chinese traders continued to function and played a key role in the commercial activities of the region over the subsequent centuries.

Second, the Zheng He expeditions also helped to broaden the tributary trade aspect of commodity exchange. The Ming court not only received exotic animals and objects as gifts from foreign polities,[11] but it also obtained commodities such as pepper that were in high demand in China. Records indicate that tax breaks were given to some of the tribute carriers who brought commodities as tribute but who also wanted to sell in the local markets. The return gifts given by the Ming court were also significant and included silk, gold, and other products that were either presented to the tribute carriers or were conferred upon foreign rulers through the Zheng He missions.

Third, the expeditions had their own group of traders who conducted commercial transactions under the supervision of the Ming officials traveling with the fleet. The procurement of goods through the payment of copper coin or porcelain at foreign ports must have also contributed to the growth of commercial activity between 1405 and 1433. As will be seen below, many of these features of the Zheng He expeditions were similar to the activities of the European colonial powers subsequently between the sixteenth and twentieth centuries along the networks linking India and China.

Finally, the impact of the Zheng He expeditions on the price of pepper in Europe and its connection to the entry of the Europeans into the Indian Ocean region needs to be addressed. Arguing against the "persistent" view that the rise of the price of spices in Europe resulted in "Europe's oceanic expansion," Frederic C. Lane in an article written in 1968 demonstrated that the price of pepper in the Venetian markets actually declined in the fifteenth century. Lane contended that the Venetian example extended to most of Europe and that the Portuguese exploitation of the Indian Ocean spice trade in the early sixteenth century, instead of lowering the price of the commodity, actually increased it (Lane 1968: 596). Kevin H. O'Rourke and Jeffrey G. Williamson (2009), however, have demonstrated that the price of pepper was not universal across Europe. Rather, there were spikes and fluctuations in different markets. They (O'Rourke and Williamson 2009: 661) note that the price of pepper rose "steeply" in Austria, the Netherlands, Flanders, and England throughout the fifteenth century. Particularly between 1410 and 1414, there was a "spike" in the price of the spice across Europe, a fact also pointed out by Lane.

While Lane mentions the Zheng He expeditions only in passing, O'Rourke and Williamson (2009: 662–663) try to connect the pepper prices in Europe to the activities of Ming China in the Indian Ocean. They suggest that there may have been a "temporary Zheng He–induced shock" due to the disruptions "between the Indies and the Middle East" caused "most likely by the great Chinese armadas." Although this resulted in the "dramatic pepper price spike in Europe in 1411–22," the variations and increase in pepper prices, according to O'Rourke and Williamson, were still mostly internal to Europe. The varying inflation rates across regions and the poor integration of the European commodity market are the two factors they highlight. The connection between the Zheng He expeditions and the spike in pepper prices on European markets was more complex than what O'Rourke and Williamson propose.

The "disruption," which the Ming armada caused, was of a different nature than what O'Rourke and Williamson imply. There is no indication that the demand for pepper in Ming China was exceptionally high when the price of the commodity in Europe spiked. In addition to the frequent supply of pepper by foreign tribute missions, the Ming court by this time also had gained access to the pepper produced in Cochin. Zhao Zhongnan (2016: 111) has pointed out that the distribution of pepper (and sappanwood) as remuneration to Ming officials started in 1422 when the court took notice of the huge stockpile of the commodity and the depreciating prices. In other words, the consumption of pepper in China had nothing to do with the spike in prices in Europe. Instead, the connection to the Zheng He expeditions could have been with regard to the inflated price the Ming representatives paid to procure the commodity. Profit from commercial exchanges was not the primary goal of the Zheng He expeditions. Supplying commodities to foreign polities in order to showcase Ming imperial power was a more overriding objective. Thus, the procurement of pepper at high prices by the Ming court for redistribution in the Indian Ocean region, not "deflecting" the commodity away from the Levant and Europe (O'Rourke and Williamson 2009: 663), might account for the sudden spike in prices in Europe as well as in West Asia and Egypt.[12] As to the correlation between the demand for pepper (and other spices) in Europe and the "Age of Exploration" initiated by the Portuguese, C. R. Boxer (1969: 18) has pointed out that the search for spices may have been one among several reasons. Other motivations for the Portuguese entry into the Indian Ocean, according to Boxer, included the crusading zeal against the Muslims, the desire for Guinea gold, and the quest for Prester John.

THE ENTRY OF EUROPEAN COLONIAL POWERS

Soon after coming to the throne in 1451, the Ottoman ruler Mehmed II (r. 1451–1481) embarked on a series of conquests of places including Constantinople, the Balkans, and the Italian Peninsula that had a considerable impact on several aspects of world history, including the restructuring of maritime interactions in the Indian Ocean. Taxes imposed by the Ottomans on commodities originating in South Asia and China and destined for European markets, for example, may have compelled the Europeans to find direct routes to the sources of these goods, triggering the period of European "discovery" and expansion into the intra-Asian networks. The Ottoman involvement in the Arabian Sea region grew dramatically after the entry of the Portuguese into the region in the early sixteenth century. In fact, throughout the first half of the sixteenth century, first the Mamluks in Egypt and then the Ottoman Empire engaged in military conflicts with the Portuguese in the Arabian Sea arena. These military conflicts failed to curtail the rapid spread of Portuguese influences deeper into the Indian Ocean world, which by the end of the sixteenth century extended to the Bay of Bengal and the South China Sea. [13]

The Dutch, British, and other European colonial enterprises arrived subsequently and started to carve out their own colonies and niches with regard to the extraction of Asian commodities and exploitation of labor. By the end of the nineteenth century, the British dictated much of the commercial and diplomatic interaction between South Asia and Qing China. The focus below will be on this period of European expansion, that is, from the sixteenth to the late nineteenth century, and the impact it had on the connections between India and China.

In 1502, about four years after Vasco da Gama arrived in Calicut and inaugurated the European exploitation of the Indian Ocean commercial networks, a Syrian Christian from South India named Joseph of Cranganore wrote (Yule 1875: 2.391),

These people of Cathay are men of remarkable energy, and formerly drove a first-rate trade at the city of Calicut. But the King of Calicut having treated them badly, they quitted that city, and returning shortly after inflicted no small slaughter on the people of Calicut, and after that returned no more. After that they began to frequent Mailapetam, a city subject to the king of Narsingha; a region towards the East, . . . and there they now drive their trade.

The above reference to the "quitting" of the city by the "people of Cathay" may have been to the withdrawal of Chinese traders from the Malabar region following the skirmish between Cochin and Calicut in which Zheng He was likely involved. When the Portuguese reached the Malabar coast, the Chinese commercial (as well as shipping) network in the region was less active compared to two centuries before, and the ruler of Calicut had taken full control of Cochin. Similar to Zheng He, who intended to gain a foothold in the pepper-producing Malabar region, the Portuguese also became involved in the existing rivalry between Cochin and Calicut. This resulted in the establishment of Fort Emmanuel in Cochin in 1503, which was the first European fortification in the Indian Ocean world. By 1510, the Portuguese also gained footholds in Sri Lanka, Kollam, Diu, and Goa.

In 1511, the Portuguese led by Afonso de Albuquerque captured Malacca, a port that had emerged as a nodal port in Indian Ocean commerce. Chinese, Bengali, and Gujarati merchants, as well as ones from the Persian Gulf, congregated in Malacca. Due to the continued ban on foreign trade in Ming China, Malacca was one of the sites in Southeast Asia through which much of the commercial exchanges between India and China took place. Tomé Pires, a Portuguese physician who reached Malacca in 1512 and subsequently (in 1516) led an embassy from King Manuel I to the Ming court, remarked (2005: 287) that, "whoever is lord of Malacca has his hand on the throat of Venice." He also provides (2005: 268) a list of foreign traders from Asia and beyond active in Malacca during the early sixteenth century. He writes,

> Moors from Cairo, Mecca, Aden, Abyssinians, men of Kilwa, Malindi, Ormuz, Parsees, *Rumes*, Turks, Turkomans, Christian Armenians, Gujaratees, men of Chaul, Dabhol, Goa, of the kingdom of Deccan, Malabars and Klings, merchants from Orissa, Ceylon, Bengal, Arakan, Pegu, Siamese, men of Kedah, Malays, men of Pahang, Patani, Cambodia, *Champa*, Cochin China, Chi-

nese, *Lequeos*, men of Brunei, *Luçoes*, men of *Tamjompura*, Laue, Banka, Linga (they have a thousand other islands), Moluccas, Banda, Mima, Timor, Madura, Java, Sunda, Palembang, Jambi, Tongkal, Indragiri, Kappatta, Menangkabau, Siak, *Arqua* (*Arcat*?), Aru, Bata, country of *Tomjano*, Pase, Pedir, Maldives.

According to Tomé Pires, there were about a thousand Gujarati merchants and a similar number of Parsis and Bengali traders in the port. This presence of South Asian traders in Malacca and their involvement in carrying out trade across the Bay of Bengal could have been an additional reason for the contraction of private Chinese mercantile and shipping networks to the Malabar coast as noted above. Tomé Pires and other early European sources also underscore Malacca's status as a hub for commercial exchanges between Ming China and Southeast Asian ports. In 1515, an Italian named Andrea Corsali reported that "[t]he merchants of the land of China also make voyages to Malacca across the Great Gulf to get cargoes of spices, and bring from their own country's musk, rhubarb, pearls, tin, porcelain, and silk and wrought stuffs of all kinds, such as damasks, satins, and brocades of extraordinary riches" (Ferguson 1901: 423).

In 1517, a fleet of eight Portuguese ships carrying Tomé Pires arrived in Guangzhou from Malacca. One of the ships belonged to a Malaccan named Curiaraja, with ethnic Chinese as "pilots" of the fleet and a cargo consisting of pepper from the Malabar coast. The aim of the mission was to make contact with the Ming court and seek permission to trade in the coastal region of China. However, the mission failed to reach the Ming capital, and Tomé Pires died waiting (actually imprisoned in Guangzhou) to have an audience with the emperor. Nonetheless, by the 1540s the Portuguese managed to secure permission from the Ming court to conduct trade in Guangzhou. This decision by the Ming court paved the way for the Luso-Chinese agreement of 1554, which allowed the Portuguese to use Macau as their base starting in 1557. With the conclusion of this agreement, the Portuguese had essentially taken control of the commercial networks that extended from the Malabar coast to southern China and to the ports in Japan. The potential profit from selling Indian commodities, especially pepper, to the Chinese as well as from procuring goods from China for markets in India was frequently mentioned in the letters written by Asia-based Portuguese officials to the king of Portugal (Ferguson 1901: 433–436). According to these letters, the Portuguese repeatedly attempted to monopolize the supply of pepper from Cochin to China but failed (or achieved limited profit) due to accidents or blockades placed by Chinese fleets.

The Portuguese control of almost all leading nodes in the Indian Ocean world, from Malindi to Japan, and the connections of these places to the markets in Europe and silver mines in South America resulted in the establishment of the first global network of commercial exchanges that took place in multiple directions. Portuguese traders were not only engaged in the long-distance commercial connections across the Indian Ocean world but also participated in the exchanges taking place within the smaller intra-Asian circuits. While the trade in silver, which amounted to between six thousand and thirty thousand kilograms annually (Atwell 1982: 75), was indicative of the global reach of the Portuguese, their dealings in Southeast Asian spices, Chinese porcelain and silk, and Indian textiles demonstrated their wide involvement in several sectors of intra-Asian trade.

Om Prakash (1998: 50) has pointed out that the Portuguese occupation of Macau contributed significantly to the increase in commercial links between the Chinese coast and Indian ports. Indeed, in the sixteenth century, when the Ming court paid little attention to Indian Ocean exchanges, the Portuguese swiftly moved into the existing networks between India and China that were still operated by private traders. While the Portuguese may have used similar methods to the Ming under the Yongle emperor to control the key nodes of Indian Ocean interactions, they created a new method of dominating maritime space by colonizing several of these sites. The Portuguese occupation of Goa, Malacca, and Macau created a network of commerce and communication between India and China that was larger and more extensive, diverse, and contentious than any in the past.

Several ports in India, including Goa, Cochin, and Nagapattinam, were part of this extensive network (Malekandathil 2001; Subrahmanyam 2004). There was also a diverse range of traders who took part in these commercial exchanges. These included Portuguese officials and private traders, Gujarati and Tamil traders, and Chinese and Southeast Asian merchants and sailors. There were also Portuguese ships and Chinese junks that transported commercial goods and ferried missionaries across the Bay of Bengal and the South China Sea. These connections extended westward all the way to Lisbon, resulting in the integration of India–Ming China exchanges into the large-scale global system of trade that defined colonial interactions over the next several centuries.

The second half of the sixteenth century witnessed a sharp increase in the participation of private Portuguese traders, constituting the so-called Estado da Índia (the State of India). Highlighting the intensity of this intra-Asian commercial activity under the Estado da Índia, specifically by referring to the commodities reaching Bengal, J. J. A. Campos ([1919] 2000: 115) writes,

> The principal things they brought to Bengal were from Malacca, Sumatra and Borneo, such as "Brocades, Brocateles, Cloth, Velvets, Damasks, Satins, Taffetas, Tafiosinas, Tafissirias Escomillas or Muslins" of all colours but black, which colour was considered ill-omened in Bengal. From Malacca they also brought cloves, nutmegs, and mace; and from Borneo they brought highly prized camphor. They brought cinnamon from Ceylon and pepper from Malabar. From China they brought silks, gilt furniture such as bedsteads, tables, coffers, chests, writing-desks, boxes and very valuable pearls and jewels, for labour being

cheap in China "these were made in European style but with greater skill and cheaper."

Members of the Estado da Índia were clearly not simply trading goods from one location of Asia to another. They were also contracting manufacturers in Asia, as seen from the above description of furniture from China, to design and produce new types of goods.[14] Cochin and Goa were two other sites that were intimately associated with the China trade (Subrahmanyam 2004: 138–139). The fact that the commercial exchanges between the Indian ports and China were extremely lucrative to the Portuguese can be discerned from a remark made by a Portuguese official based in Goa. In the early seventeenth century, when the Dutch presence in the Indian Ocean was leading to the restructuring and contraction of Portuguese trading networks, the official noted that "the China trade is the principal activity on which the Portuguese in India exist, and without it the state would be destitute" (Disney 2010: 101).

The extensive commercial connections between South Asia and China that were created by Portuguese commercial networks and their gradual demise due to the intrusions by the Dutch are also reflected in the lamentations of a Flemish gem trader named Jacques de Coutre (c. 1572–1640). He reports,

> The Portuguese used to sell their textiles and buy spices and other commodities [in Malacca], and they used to load their ships and sail to Goa and Cochin. Over there they again used to pay their duties to Your Majesty; this apart from the two clove ships that used to come on the account of Your Majesty, and from there three or four ships that used to come to Goa every year from China, laden with raw and twisted silk, and many bolts of velvet, damasks, satin, taffetas, and many colchas, marquees, and silk hangings to decorate houses, and large quantities of musk, and seed pearls, and small pearls, and large quantities of gold, and camphor, and radix Chinae, and benzoin, and alum stone, and tintinago, Chinese porcelain, and sugar, and various

other commodities. Each of these carracks from China used to pay 50,000 to 60,000 pardaos at the customs and excise house in Goa as duties to Your Majesty. They then used to take these wares from Goa to the north: [to] Chaul, Cambay, Diu, Daman, Muscat, [and] Hormuz. . . . Your Majesty has lost all this trade; which is now in the hands of the [Dutch] rebels. They have grown rich with this commerce and by means of their robberies, and the Portuguese in India have become impoverished with this significant loss. This is why Your Majesty should help remedy that state in the manner that I have described, so as not to lose these lands and the many Christian communities over there. (Borschberg and Roy 2014: 270–271)

The "Christian communities" mentioned above by Jacques de Coutre were an integral part of the activities of the Estado da Índia as they supported the Portuguese venture in Asia through financial investments and proselytizing activities. The Portuguese Jesuit missionaries were the first group of European proselytizers who frequented the routes between South Asia and China. These Jesuits often used the maritime networks operated by the Portuguese state and private traders (Rule 2000). Francis Xavier, one of the earliest Jesuit missionaries in South Asia, for instance, traveled to China through Southeast Asia in the 1540s. There was also a Jesuit named Michele Ruggieri (Ch. Luo Mingjian 羅明堅), who lived in Goa for a year in 1578 and then went to Macau before reaching Guangzhou with Portuguese seafaring traders in 1580. Ruggieri described himself as a monk (*seng* 僧) from "West India" (Xizhu 西竺) and published a catechism in Chinese in 1585 with the title *Xinbian Xizhuguo Tianzhu shengjiao shilu* 新編西竺國天主聖教實錄 (Newly Compiled Records of Catholic [Teachings] of the Polity of Western India). He signed the translation as "Tianzhu guo seng" 天竺國僧 ("Indian monk") (Zhang 2015).

"Xizhu" at this time was used by the Jesuits to refer to Europe. However, they also often reported that they had reached Ming China through "Tianzhu" (i.e., India). This evidently led to confusion among the Chinese not only with regard to the two distinct places, but also with regard to the contemporary religious practices in India. The following passage from Cai Ruxian's 蔡汝賢 *Dongyi tuxiang* 東夷圖像 (Illustrated Accounts of the Eastern Barbarians), written in 1586, is indicative of this confusion:

> Tianzhu 天竺 [India] is ancient Sindu (身毒). There are five Sindu states, and they are located in the southwestern section of the sea, very far from China. Many of the people there worship the Buddha and become monks. They do not eat animal products and do not kill any living creatures. They go to worship once in seven days. They recite the scripture before a meal and recite it again afterward. They say this is to thank Heaven. . . . They put [images of] Tianzhu 天主 [the Lord of Heaven] all over their houses—on their chairs, beds, and utensils, in order to keep their minds focused. (Zhang 2015: 297)[15]

Cai also drew a portrait of the Virgin Mary and Jesus in his work titled *Tianzhu tu* 天竺圖 (Painting of India), which appeared in the form of a traditional Chinese painting of Guanyin in her "Giving Son" posture. The introduction of Catholicism into China was frequently credited to India since several Portuguese missionaries reached Ming China through Indian ports and used "Tianzhu" as their reference point for the transmission of Catholic teachings and images (Tang 2015: 218). Perhaps the latter was adopted deliberately because of the earlier Buddhist links between India and China, which had created a perception of India as a holy land among the Chinese.

Jesuit missioners also traveled between India and various regions of Qing China through the overland routes. In the early seventeenth century, Benedict Goes took the route through Afghanistan and across the Pamirs to China. In the 1620s John Cabral and Stephen Cacella trekked to Shigatse through Nepal and Bhutan, and in 1714 Manuel Freyre and the Italian Jesuit Ippoliti Desideri embarked on their journey to Lhasa through Srinagar and Leh. Similar to the earlier religious interactions between South Asia and China through Buddhism and Islam, the Jesuits also contributed to the circulation of objects and knowledge between the two regions. They were particularly involved, albeit with limited success, in the reconceptualizing of Asian geography in Qing China (Mosca 2013: ch. 3).

As noted above, the Portuguese involvement in intra-Asian trade was affected during the seventeenth century by the entry and subsequent expansion of the Dutch into the Indian Ocean world. Starting with the Dutch establishment of its factory at the Coromandel coast in 1605 and their subsequent assertion of authority in Batavia in 1609, commercial activity at several key centers of Indian Ocean commerce, including Sri Lanka, the Malabar coast, Bengal, and, eventually in the eighteenth century, Guangzhou, came under the dominance of the Dutch East India Company (Vereenigde Oost-Indische Compagnie; VOC). By the mid-seventeenth century, the Dutch had replaced the Portuguese as the leading hegemonic power in intra-Asian trade as well as in Asia's trade with Europe. Other European powers, including the British, were also part of the seventeenth-century networks of intra-Asian trade, but none were as dominant as the Dutch in the control of local production, transportation, and trade of Asian commodities.

In fact, the Dutch in the seventeenth century may have laid the foundation for the trade in several major products between India and China. These included silver, copper, textiles, tea, and opium. They also created and fostered a number of commercial networks between Indian and Chinese ports, either directly or through Southeast Asia. The Dutch operated from the Coromandel and Malabar coasts, Bengal, and Sri Lanka, with access to, or having exclusive rights at, ports in Taiwan, Japan, and Persia. Also through coordination undertaken from Batavia, the Dutch had access to several major production sites and markets in Asia for most of the seventeenth century. From Japan they obtained silver and copper, which were traded for silk, porcelain, tea, and sugar in China. They also monopolized the procurement of spices from the Indonesian islands and played a significant role in the growth and export of textiles from the Coromandel coast and Bengal. Specifically with regard to the exchange of commodities between Ming-Qing China and India, the Dutch were involved in both direct procurement and the sale of goods between the two regions as well as the complex circulatory trade that defined the intra-Asian commercial exchanges during the seventeenth century. Indian textile products, for example, were exchanged for Indonesian spices (principally pepper) and tin, which were then traded for Chinese silk, porcelain, bullion, and so forth. Chinese bullion was taken to Bengal and Coromandel to purchase the textiles that would then sustain the circulation of all these commodities (Prakash 1985: 16–18).

Similar to the earlier pattern of intra-Asian trade under the Portuguese, the commercial activity in the seventeenth century was conducted by an extremely diverse group of traders. These included people from Bengal and Gujarat, ethnic Chinese from Southeast Asia, and the Dutch. There were also smugglers and pirates who were involved in several of the smaller sectors of these vast intra-Asian and Eurasian trading networks. The land routes that connected Bengal to Yunnan through Burma were part of these exchanges as well. Chinese copper, Japanese silver, and Bengali textiles were the leading goods that were traded along these routes.

The Dutch were also involved in introducing two commodities to global trade in the seventeenth century that became the staples of India–Qing China commerce under the British. Tea and opium entered almost simultaneously, albeit through different networks and they were not initially exchanged for each other. The Dutch introduced Chinese tea to Europe in the early seventeenth century and then were influential in creating a market for the commodity in Europe. Under the "Seventeen Gentlemen," who comprised the governing body of the Dutch East India Company, the Dutch were the leading importer of tea during much of the eighteenth century. Because of the direct Guangzhou-to-Europe shipping system instituted by the "Seventeen Gentlemen," none of the tea shipments passed through the Indian ports.

Opium was already reaching the Chinese markets in the seventeenth century through the Dutch-held territories in Southeast Asia. The Dutch were using opium grown in Patna and Malwa to purchase other South Asian goods (Malabar pepper, for example). They also imported the commodity to Batavia and Java. Om Prakash (1985: 145–156) has demonstrated the gradual increase in the export of Bihar-grown opium through Bengal to Southeast Asia. The annual weight of the drug exported out of the Hugli port increased, he points out, from 77,000 ponds in 1698–1699 to 120,000 ponds in 1717–1718. This coincided with, on the one hand, the increase in consumption of opium in places such as Java (from 70,000 ponds in 1678 to 108,266 ponds in 1707) and, on the other, the decline in the price of the commodity due to the increase in the number of suppliers. The latter included smuggling of the commodity, which in 1676, for example, was recorded to be 140,000 ponds (Prakash 1985: 154).

In Batavia and other sites in Southeast Asia, the sojourning Chinese merchants emerged as one of the leading groups consuming the imported drug. In Batavia, opium was mixed with tobacco and smoked in pipes that were already in use in Ming-Qing China. "The Dutch seem to have been instrumental," writes Carl Trocki (1999: 35), "in bringing the habit of smoking opium to the Chinese, if not to China itself." Indeed, it was through the Chinese traders frequenting Southeast Asia that opium from South Asia started entering China in large quantities (Souza and Wade 2009). Already used as an ingredient in Chinese medicine and as an aphrodisiac, the new influx of opium was essentially for recreational use. The adverse social impact of the drug was evident to the Qing authorities, who instituted a prohibition on the sale of opium in China in 1729. By this time, however, opium had become one of the leading commodities in intra-Asian trade, particularly in the commercial exchanges between India and China.

Although Dutch control over intra-Asian and Eurasian trade was not always secure in the eighteenth century, primarily due to competition with other European enterprises and disputes and warfare with local polities, the VOC continued to be one of the main players in India–Qing China interactions until the second half of the eighteenth century. According to Om Prakash (1987: 185), "Amongst the European corporate bodies in trade in the Indian Ocean during the seventeenth and the eighteenth centuries, the Dutch East India Company was the most important in terms of both the volume and value of trade handled as well as the number of ports where trade was carried on."

The Dutch, and the Portuguese before them, had introduced fresh commodities, added new nodes of interaction, and fostered cultural connections between India and China. Compared to the Portuguese and the Dutch colonial powers, however, the involvement of the British in India-China interactions, starting from the second half of the eighteenth century, was considerably more substantial and consequential. This was not only because of the dominant role the British played in the trading exchanges between the two regions, but also due to their involvement in territorial negotiations, disputes, and expansions. In fact, as noted above, in many ways their multilayered and active role over the course of two centuries laid the foundation for contemporary India-China relations.

ENGAGING IN COLONIAL CONNECTIONS

There are numerous studies that have examined the relations between British India and Qing China. Most of them deal with the trade in opium and/or tea, the issue of Tibet, or territorial negotiations. The aim here is, instead, to examine less-researched aspects of British India–Qing China connections. Thus this section explores the experiences of three individuals: the first British traveler to Tibet, George Bogle (1746–1781); the Parsi opium and cotton trader Jamsetjee Jejeebhoy (1785–1859); and the first Qing official to visit British India, Huang Maocai 黃楙材 . Each of these individuals wrote about different facets of British India–Qing China connections. While Bogle's travel records and letters link with the British attempts to open the land route to China through Tibet, the correspondence of Jamsetjee Jejeebhoy concerns maritime commerce between British India and Qing China. The writings of Huang Maocai pertain to Qing China's predicament with the British rule of India. These individuals and their writings highlight the developments taking place during three different phases of British India–Qing China exchanges: the late eighteenth century, the early nineteenth century, and the post–Opium War period. Together, the experiences of these three individuals exemplify the complex and rapidly changing relationship between British India and Qing China during the late eighteenth and nineteenth centuries.

George Bogle and the Engagement with Tibet

The Battle of Plassey in 1757 and the Battle of Buxar seven years later set a new course for Indian history and brought about considerable structural changes to intra-Asian connections. The defeat of the nawab of Bengal Siraj ud-daulah by Robert Clive of the English East India Company (EIC) in the Battle of Plassey led to the establishment of British rule in Bengal and facilitated the company's subsequent expansion into India. It also resulted in the loss of territorial possessions in Bengal by other European colonial powers. This included the forfeitures by the French, who had allied with Siraj ud-daulah, and the Dutch, who had unsuccessfully tried to defend Chinsurah against the British. The British victory against the Mughal ruler Shah Alam II in the Battle of Buxar gave the

British the right to collect revenue (Diwani Rights) in Bengal and neighboring areas of eastern India. This penetration of the EIC into Bengal laid the foundation for their infiltration into Tibet, the establishment of tea gardens in Bengal and Assam, and the creation of an opium trade network between British India and Qing China.

Calcutta, the capital of British India until 1911, was to emerge as the key hub within the British Empire in Asia. It was from this port city that the British controlled the Straits Settlements in Southeast Asia between 1826 and 1867. It was also the place from where British Indian troops sailed to fight the Opium Wars and subsequent battles in Qing China. Indeed, as is evident in this and the next chapter, Calcutta, and Bengal in general, remained the main center of interactions between India and China through to the mid-twentieth century. The mission of George Bogle, the India trip of Huang Maocai, and the first Indian institution for the study of China (i.e., Cheena Bhavana in Shantiniketan) were all centered in Calcutta and its vicinity. Calcutta was also an important part of Jamsetjee Jejeebhoy's commercial enterprise. Particularly with regard to Tibet, several towns of Bengal, including Calcutta, Darjeeling, and Kalimpong, became important sites for political negotiations, espionage activity, and commercial transactions. These Tibet-related exchanges during the later periods were rooted in George Bogle's mission of 1774, which commenced from Calcutta.

Tibet has occupied an important position in the cultural and political interactions between India and China, as well as separately with each of these entities since the seventh century. Under Srong-btsan-sgam-po (r. c. 605–650), a unified Tibet emerged as a powerful empire that threatened the Tang dynasty in China and Nepal in South Asia and penetrated deep into the Taklamakan region. Srong-btsan-sgam-po is credited with the introduction of Brāhmī script into Tibet and the establishment of Buddhism in the region. Through to the mid-ninth century, Tibet remained a powerful empire, often in conflict with Tang China and polities in the southern

Hindukush region. This expansion of Tibet in some cases resulted in alliances between the Tang court and the rulers of Kashmir (Sen 2004), but at the same time the stability in the region facilitated the movement of Buddhist monks and court representatives between Tang China and the polities located in the Gangetic area (Sen 2003).

While Buddhist ideas entered Tibet from India and China, the sacred sites and monastic institutions in the Gangetic region attracted frequent Tibetan pilgrims and students. Under King Khri srong lde btsan (r. 755–794), intimate connections were also established with Buddhist monasteries located in Kashmir. The transmission of Tantric teachings from the monasteries in the Gangetic region and Kashmir sustained the connections between Tibet and India until about the thirteenth–fourteenth centuries. Pilgrimage activities to various parts of India persisted when Bogle embarked on his journey to Tibet.[16] Politically, however, Tibet came under the administration of the Mongols of Yuan China, instigating the later Chinese claim over the territory. Although Tibet became a fragmented state during most of the Ming period, it maintained political ties with the imperial court in Beijing through to the Qing period.

The eighteenth century was an eventful period in Tibetan history. The first half of the century witnessed internal political struggles, while the latter half, especially the final three decades, was marked by intense negotiations with two new powers to the south, the British in Bengal and the Gurkhas in Nepal. The period was also marked by the Qing court's assertion of power in Tibet, which it did by intervening militarily on three occasions: in 1720 against the Dzungars and their allies who had killed Lha-bzang Khan, a Qing appointee in Lhasa responsible for deposing the Sixth Dalai Lama, Tsangyang Gyatso; in 1750 to suppress an anti-Qing uprising; and in 1792 to drive out the Gurkhas who had invaded Tibet.

Throughout this period of turmoil, vibrant commercial networks connected Tibet to Qing China, the Russian Empire, Kashmir, Nepal, and various regions of northern and eastern India. People from diverse ethnic backgrounds operated these networks, but the Kashmiris and the Hindu wandering pilgrims known as Gosains were particularly active. In fact, Bogle compares the Kashmiris with the Jews in Europe and the Armenians in the Turkish Empire, who, he writes,

> scatter themselves over the eastern kingdoms of Asia, and carry on an extensive traffic between the distant parts of it, have formed establishments at Lhasa and all the principal towns in this country. Their agents, stationed on the coast of Coromandel, in Bengal, Benares, Nepal, and Kashmir, furnish them with the commodities of these different countries, which they dispose of in Tibet, or forward to their associates at Seling (i.e., Xining), a town on the borders of China. (Markham 1879: 124)[17]

As for the Gosains, he says,

> the trading pilgrims of India, resort hither in great numbers. Their humble deportment and holy character, heightened by the merit of distant pilgrimage, their accounts of unknown countries and remote regions, and, above all their professions of high veneration for the Lama, procure them not only ready admittance, but great favour. Though clad in the garb of poverty, there are many of them possessed of considerable wealth. Their trade is confined chiefly to articles of great value and small bulk. It is carried on without noise or ostentation, and often by paths unfrequented by other merchants. (Markham 1879: 124–125)

It was this lucrative commercial activity that enticed Warren Hastings (1732–1818), the governor-general of India from 1774 to 1785, to explore the possibility of access to markets in Tibet. Through the mission of George Bogle, Hastings perhaps also wanted to make direct contact with the Qing court, where no representative of the British colonial government had yet visited.

Although making commercial inroads into Tibet and diplomatic contact with the Qing court may have been the broader goals of the

Bogle mission, its origins lay in the EIC's involvement in a local dispute between the princely state of Cooch Behar (now in the state of West Bengal) and Bhutan. The EIC had previously tried to intervene in a civil war in Nepal, where the faction they supported eventually lost power to the Gurkhas. The Gurkhas in retaliation blocked the trade route that connected Bengal and Tibet through Nepal. The war between Bhutan and Cooch Behar meant that the alternate route to Tibet through Sikkim was also threatened. Expanding their commercial sphere beyond Bengal was one of the main reasons the EIC had initially inserted themselves in the local dispute. Siding with Cooch Behar, the EIC managed to defeat the Bhutanese military in 1773. However, the toll on the British soldiers was heavy, primarily because of the difficult terrain and the prevalence of malaria in the region (Cammann 1951: 27). Moreover, it was not certain that the victory would provide passage into Tibet for the EIC. It was at this time, not long after the battle had ended, that the Sixth Panchen Lama (Lobsang Palden Yeshe; called "Teshu Lama" in British sources) in Tibet offered to mediate between the British and the Bhutanese ruler.

The Panchen Lama, in a letter received by Warren Hastings on 29 March 1774, requested the British to "cease all hostilities" against Bhutan, "and in doing this," he added, "you will confer the greatest favour and friendship upon me" (Markham 1879: 3). Warren Hastings immediately used this opportunity to organize a mission to Tibet in order to explore the possibilities of reviving and expanding the trading relations between Bengal and Tibet. In a private communication to Bogle, Warren Hastings noted that one of the mission's tasks would be to "inquire what countries lie between Lhasa and Siberia and what communication there is between them. The same with regard to China and Kashmir" (Markham 1879: 8). Hastings also included a "Memorandum on Tibet" in his "instructions" to Bogle. In this document he outlined the history of Tibet, underscoring the fact that the region was under the subjugation of the Chinese Empire. Hastings was earnest in pointing out that he lacked knowledge about several issues, including the contemporary relations between Tibet and China. "I have been told," he wrote in the memorandum, "that a large river forms a boundary between China and Tibet, which was carefully guarded by the troops of both countries; and that Tibet received European commodities by the valley of Kashmir. But I have learned nothing satisfactory on these subjects, not so much as whether Kashmir and Lesser Tibet are at present dependent on Bhutan or Greater Tibet, or whether the Dalai Lama is still a vassal to China" (Markham 1879: 13).

The issue of Tibet's vassalage to China came up just before Bogle's mission reached the capital of Bhutan. In letters sent to Hastings and Bogle, the Panchen Lama urged that since Tibet was "subject to the Emperor of China, whose order it is that he shall admit no Moghul, Hindustani, Patan, or Fringy," the mission sent by the governor-general should return to Calcutta. Bogle, however, used the services of Purangir, a Gosain and a critical figure in the emerging Tibet–Qing court–British India relations, to convince the Panchen Lama to make an exception. Purangir seems to have successfully accomplished his task, but the site of the meeting between Bogle and the Panchen Lama was moved from Lhasa to Tashilhunpo (i.e., Shigatse).

Bogle's meeting with the Panchen Lama and the subsequent mission of Samuel Turner in 1783 have been studied in detail by scholars working on early British engagement with Tibet. Additionally, Matthew Mosca (2013) has demonstrated how the early encounters between Tibet and British India may have shaped Qing China's understanding and knowledge of South Asia. The aim here is not to explore these issues but to demonstrate the ways in which some of the individuals associated with this first British mission to Tibet experienced and participated in the developing connections between British India and Qing China during the late eighteenth century.

The first of these was George Bogle himself. As the examples from his writings cited below demonstrate, Bogle attempted to establish cordial relationships with the Tibetan and Qing authorities within the complex context of British colonial agendas, which sought to exploit commercial opportunities and expand territorial control. The second key individual was the Sixth Panchen Lama, an extremely knowledgeable monk whose connections extended from the Indian Gosains present in Tibet to the Qing emperor Qianlong 乾隆 (1735–1796). The third figure is the Indian Gosain Purangir, who played an important role in instigating the Bogle mission, made sure that the British emissary had an audience with the Panchen Lama, and continued to act as an intermediary between the British in India, the Tibetans, and the Qing Chinese after the deaths of George Bogle and the Sixth Panchen Lama.

Born to an elite Scottish family in Glasgow, George Bogle studied at Edinburgh University and worked at his brother's firm in London before joining the EIC in 1769. The following year he traveled to Calcutta, where he received a position in the EIC's Select Committee in charge of political affairs. He also started learning Persian, the language of official correspondence, soon after his arrival in India. Two years later, Bogle was appointed assistant secretary to the Board of Revenue and subsequently secretary to the Select Committee. It was during his tenure in these latter positions that Bogle started attracting the attention of Warren Hastings. On 13 May 1774, less than two months after the letter from the Panchen Lama arrived, Warren Hastings appointed Bogle as the envoy to the "Lama of Tibet."

Bogle's primary task, as noted above, was to explore the potential of reestablishing and expanding commercial connections between Bengal and its northern neighbors Bhutan and Tibet. Thus Bogle's writings focus on the routes and terrain that connected these places, the involvement of various traders and their networks, and the commodities that were and could be part of the transregional trade. On the future prospects of large-scale trading activity in the region, he makes the following insightful and critical observation (Markham 1879: 58–59):

> An open trade with Bhutan, Nepal, and Lhasa has been considered as an object worthy of the attention of Government, but the jealousy of the nation prevents this being obtained on pacific terms, and the natural strength and situation of these countries render it extremely difficult, if not impracticable, to do it by force. An open and unrestrained trade and intercourse with Assam, considered separately, is an object of much greater consequence; but when it is known that it will include all the advantages attending the other, it must of course become a much more desirable object. The Bhutanese, the inhabitants of the Gorkha Rajah's country, the natives of Lhasa, and of many other countries lying north-west of the Brahmaputra, carry on a constant trade to Assam. A settlement formed on the banks of the Brahmaputra, near the capital, would become the mart for supplying all the countries lying north-west of the Brahmaputra as well as those countries to the eastward of that river; it would open an ample field for commerce in general, and, considering its northern situation, would greatly increase the demand for European commodities, and particularly for broadcloths.

When describing the trading connections of Tibet, in addition to noting the existing networks of the Kashmiris and the Gosains, Bogle points out the presence of the Chinese traders in Lhasa, who, he says, were "engaged in an extended and lucrative commerce" (Markham 1879: 125). He stressed that most of Tibet's trade was with Qing China. Merchants participating in this trade included the Chinese, the agents of the Dalai Lama, and Kashmiris. Xining (in present-day Qinghai Province) was the main center of this commerce with China, where goods from Siberia supplied by Kalmyk traders were also available. He further reports that the expansion of the Gurkhas into the region was having an adverse impact on Bengal–Tibet trade.

To address the Gurkha issue, about which he entered into detailed discussion with the Panchen Lama, Bogle sought to formalize the trade through Bhutan and Sikkim. With help from the Panchen Lama, the Dalai Lama and his regent, Gesub Rinpoche, were also brought into this discussion. In fact, the Panchen Lama helped Bogle draft a letter to the Rinpoche stating, "I request, in the name of the Governor my master, that you will allow merchants to trade between this country and Bengal" (Markham 1879: 153). Bogle also investigated the possibilities of expanding the list of commodities traded between Tibet and Bengal. When the issue of gold was brought up in his conversation with a few Tibetan merchants, Bogle was told that the export of "extraordinary quantities" of the bullion to Bengal would displease the emperor of China, who, they noted, "was the sovereign of the country" (Markham 1879: 164).

George Bogle was successful in convincing the Bhutanese ruler Deb Rajah to sign an agreement with the British in 1778–1779 allowing trade between Bengal and Lhasa through Paro (Lamb 2002: 428–429). In April–June 1775, Bogle on his way back to Bengal from Tibet had a series of discussions with Deb Rajah that resulted in the drafting of this agreement. The agreement stated that,

> Whereas the trade between Bengal and Tibet was formerly very considerable, and all Hindu and Mussulman merchants were allowed to trade into Nepal, which was the center of communication between the two countries; and whereas, from the wars and oppressions in Nepal, the merchants have of late years been unable to travel into that country, the Governor as well as the Deb Rajah, united in friendship, being desirous of removing these obstacles, so that merchants may carry on their trade free and secure as formerly.

Two articles in this document clarified the groups of traders that could participate in this trade through Bhutan:

That the Deb Rajah shall allow all Hindu and Mussulman merchants freely to pass and repass through his country between
Bengal and Tibet.

That no English or European merchants shall enter the Deb
Rajah's dominions.

In his letter dated 9 June 1775, Bogle explained his reason for
including an article in the above agreement that barred Europeans
from engaging in the Bengal–Bhutan–Tibet trade. "In short," he
wrote, "I am convinced, if I had gone strongly upon the article of
Europeans, either in Tibet or at Tassisudon (i.e., present-day Thim-
phu), that I should have increased their jealousy, and have been
obligated to return without doing anything" (Markham 1879: 188).

The Deb Rajah was still not convinced of the provisions in the
document. However, the Panchen Lama, it seems, persuaded the
Bhutanese ruler to formalize the agreement (Lamb 2002: 321), and
as a result, a few years before the deaths of the Panchen Lama and
George Bogle, the 1788–1789 agreement was signed. The Panchen
Lama and Bogle also planned to convince the Qing emperor to
have direct communication with the British in India. The Panchen
Lama, wrote Bogle (Markham 1879: 199), had

> written to the Changay Lama, who is the high-priest at the Court
> of Peking, and in great favour with the Emperor, advising him to
> send his people to visit the temples in Hindustan. He has also
> promised to use his best offices with the Emperor of China to
> procure leave for the Company to send a deputation to Peking.
> The first, I am convinced, will take place; and although, from
> the cautious and jealous policy of the Chinese, I am not too
> sanguine as to the last, yet the advantage of opening even an
> indirect communication with the Court of Peking is, I humbly
> apprehend, an object of some importance to the Company.

Born near Tashilhunpo and appointed as the second-most-rever-
end figure when he was two years old, the Sixth Panchen Lama was
a remarkable figure with regard to his understanding of contempo-

rary geopolitics. For most of the 1760s and 1770s, when the Eighth Dalai Lama was still a minor, the Panchen Lama exercised significant influence over Tibet's commercial and diplomatic relations with neighboring polities. He was, as Petech (1950b: 333) remarks, "a most energetic and active ruler, always eager for information about countries outside Tibet." He interacted with powerful rulers such as Emperor Qianlong, the Gurkha Raja, and key religious leaders including the Changay Lama and had identified the incarnation of the Dalai Lama. He also met frequently with Muslim and Hindu merchants present in Tibet. Thus, when he met George Bogle in 1775, the Panchen Lama was aware of the various contending political forces and the competing commercial interests in the region. Furthermore, the fact that he could converse in Hindustani, Lamb (2002: 39–40) writes, "undoubtedly contributed to the creation of an extraordinary bond of friendship and understanding between the two men."

This "extraordinary bond of friendship" is apparent in Bogle's (Markham 1879: 132–133) description of the Panchen Lama:

> Teshu Lama is about forty years of age. He is of a cheerful and affable temper, of great curiosity, and very intelligent. He is entirely master of his own affairs; his views are liberal and enlarged, and he wishes, as every great man wishes, to extend his consequence. From his pacific character, and from the turn of his mind, naturally gentle and humane, he is averse to war and bloodshed, and in all quarrels endeavours by his mediation to bring about a reconciliation. In conversation he is plain and candid, using no flattery or compliments himself, and receiving them but badly if made to him. He is generous and charitable, and is universally beloved and venerated by the Tibetans, by the Kalmuks, and by a great part of the Chinese. The character I give of him may appear partial; but I received it in much stronger colours from his own subjects, from the Kashmiris, and from the fakirs; and I will confess, I never knew a man whose manners pleased me so much, or for whom upon so short an acquaintance I had half the heart's liking.

Indeed, from his correspondence with the British, records of the journey he made to the Qing court and the meeting with Emperor Qianlong, and other relevant sources on Bhutan and Nepal, it becomes clear that the Panchen Lama was well connected, respected, and a liked person. This enabled him to intervene in local disputes and to promote cordial interactions between various contending forces. His letter to Warren Hastings in March 1774, for example, indicated his influence over the ruler of Bhutan and his ability to mediate between the warring factions at the frontiers of Tibet. The letter also demonstrated his knowledge of the expanding authority of the British in India. Later, in order perhaps to fully understand the intentions of the Europeans in Asia, he requested George Bogle to compose an account of Europe. Alastair Lamb (2002: 193) points out that the Tibetan version of what Bogle wrote "appears to have been for many years the standard Tibetan account of Europe."

In addition to facilitating negotiations between the ruler of Bhutan and the British in Bengal, which eventually resulted in the above-mentioned trade agreement of 1788–1789, the Panchen Lama's most important contribution was his attempt to initiate the first official contact between the British in India and the Qing court. During one of his early conversations with Bogle, the Panchen Lama acknowledged his initial apprehensions about the British and his refusal to admit the mission sent by Hastings into Tibet. "I had heard also much of the power of the Fringies," he told Bogle (Markham 1879: 137–138), "that the Company was like a great king, and fond of war and conquest; and as my business and that of my people is to pray to God, I was afraid to admit any Fringies into the country." Then he added, "But I have since learned that the Fringies are a fair and a just people. I never before saw any Fringies, but am very happy at your arrival, and you will not think anything of my formal refusal."

Although the Panchen Lama, according to Bogle, had changed his views on the "Fringies," the Tibetan was always mindful about the suspicion the Qing court had about the British and other Europeans. He often reminded Bogle and Warren Hastings that the Qing court and their regent in Lhasa had a very different view on the British. "Gesub's apprehension of the English," he confided in Bogle (Markham 1879: 151), "rose not only from himself, but also from his dread of giving offence to the Chinese, to whose empire this country was subject and that he wished to receive an answer from the court at Peking." Later, in the summer of 1775 when Bogle had already left Tibet, he wrote, saying, "[A]s this country is under the absolute sovereignty of the Emperor of China, who maintains an active and unrelaxed control over all its affairs, and as the forming of any connection of friendship with Foreign Powers is contrary to his pleasure, it will frequently be out of my power to dispatch any messengers to you."

Despite these apprehensions and pessimisms, it was the Panchen Lama who volunteered to arrange a meeting between the British and the Qing emperor. When he came to know from Bogle that few if any British had gone into Qing China beyond the port of Guangzhou, the Lama said (Markham 1879: 168), "I will endevour through the means of the Lama at Peking, to get permission for the English to go to the Emperor; whether I shall be able to carry this point or not I cannot say, but I will afterwards write to the Governor how I have succeeded." This remark resulted in the Panchen Lama taking on the role of an intermediary between the British in India and the Qing court in China.

In April 1779, after the death of Gesub Rinpoche, Warren Hastings wrote to the Council of the EIC requesting permission to send George Bogle to Tibet for a second time. The aim was to "establish a free and lasting intercourse of trade with the Kingdom of Tibet and the other states to the northward of Bengal, to endeavor by the means of the Lamas of Tibet to open a communication with the Court of Peking and if possible procure leave to proceed thither" (Lamb 2002: 435). The Panchen Lama's willingness to facilitate the contact with the Qing court was highlighted in Hastings's note, but "he could not attempt it without great disadvantage while the Dalai Lama was a minor and Gesub in power" (Lamb 2002: 434). The council agreed to the proposal and provided funds for Bogle's second mission.

The Panchen Lama was summoned to the Qing capital in 1799, due to which Bogle's second mission had to be postponed. Bogle, pointing to this forthcoming mission of the Panchen Lama to the Qing court and the opportunity it presented in securing permission for him to travel to Beijing, wrote a memorandum in which he expressed his desire to reach the Qing court either by the overland route or through Guangzhou. Exuding confidence, he noted (Lamb 2002: 440), "If I succeed in procuring passports, I shall then be in a situation to urge any points at the Court of Peking with the greatest advantage. But even if I should be disappointed, I do not think it is possible for me to fail in procuring a channel of communication with the Court of Peking, and in finding some person stationed at Canton through whom representations can be made."

In what seems to be a coordinated effort to present the British case at the Qing court, Bogle in his memorandum suggested sending some presents to Beijing. These included large pearls, large coral, and Arabian horses. About a month later, Warren Hastings reported receiving a letter from the Panchen Lama along with 450 tolas of gold to purchase in India and send to Tibet the same objects mentioned by Bogle. Hastings quickly procured these objects and had the Gosain Purangir carry with him "two strings of coral and eight strings of pearls" and also "ordered some beautiful and swift Arab horses which will be worth presenting to the Emperor." In his note, Hastings wished that the Panchen's "journey to China and his interview with the Emperor be prosperous and auspicious" (Lamb 2002: 440–441).

The Panchen Lama and his delegation reached Chengde (Jehol), the site of the Qing summer capital, on 20 August 1780 (Cammann

1951: 69) and subsequently proceeded to Beijing. During his journey, the Panchen Lama seems to have regularly written to Bogle
(Lamb 2002: 443–444). At both Chengde and Beijing, the Panchen
had audiences with Emperor Qianlong. Whether the Panchen had,
as he had promised to Bogle, discussed the matter of a British visit
to Beijing with the emperor at these meetings is not certain. The
only report about such a conversation taking place between the
Panchen Lama and the Qianlong emperor comes from Purangir,
which has been dismissed as untrustworthy. The Panchen Lama
himself probably did not have an opportunity to write to Bogle
since he was infected with smallpox and died on 27 November.

Purangir was a fascinating figure associated with the Bogle mission and its aftermath. As Schuyler Cammann (1951: 145–146)
points out, he was "one of the most remarkable men of his time and
place, and deserves more recognition." The Indian Gosain was one
of the "floating" individuals who became common in India-China
interactions during the colonial period. Jamsetjee Jejeebhoy, discussed below, and later Raja Mahendra Pratap (Stolte 2014) are
two other examples of such well-connected individuals who operated between the two regions with ease.

The fact that Purangir was a trusted intermediary in the increasingly complex colonial connections can be discerned from his
interactions with the Sixth Panchen Lama as well as the British
officials in Bengal. The Gosain first appears as the carrier of the
initial letter from the Panchen Lama to Warren Hastings in March
1774. He then accompanied George Bogle on his trip to Tibet and
subsequently appears in all major communications between the
British government in Bengal and the Panchen Lama and his suc-
cessor. Purangir was also the person whom the Sixth Panchen
Lama entrusted to manage the estate Warren Hastings allocated to
the Tibetans visiting India on pilgrimage through Calcutta. Located
in Bhot Bagan, near the banks of the river Ganges, the site served

as a place of residence for Tibetan pilgrims visiting India (Bysack 1890).

The most controversial aspect of Purangir's role in these early British India–Tibet connections, as noted above, was his narrative of the Sixth Panchen Lama's visit to Beijing, during which, according to the Gosain, the Tibetan Lama discussed the developing contacts between Tibet and Bengal with Emperor Qianlong. The Panchen Lama reportedly mentioned the British presence in Bengal to the Qing ruler on two occasions. "In the country of Hindostan," he is supposed to have told Emperor Qianlong, "which lies on the borders of my country, there resides a great prince, or ruler, for whom I have the greatest friendship. I wish you should know and regard him also; and if you will write him a letter of friendship, and receive his return, it will afford me great pleasure, as I wish you should be known to each other, and that a friendly communication should, in future, subsist between you." The emperor responded by saying that it was "a very small" request, inquired about the details of this "friend," the "extent of the country," and the number of forces he had. Purangir answered the questions raised by the Qing emperor. "The governor of Hindostan was called Mr. Hastings," Purangir told the emperor, saying "that the extent of the country governed was not near equal to that of China, but superior to any other he knew, and that the troops of that country [sic] upwards of three lacks of horsemen" (Turner 1800: 463–464).

Later, during another meeting with the emperor, the Panchen Lama, according to Purangir, again brought up the issue of the British governor in India and the need for the Qing court to respond to him. The emperor assured the Lama that he would fulfill his wish of contacting the governor. He also asked the Lama if he should write a letter "immediately" or if he would prefer to carry the letter with him to Tibet and "forward it, in such a manner as he thought best." The Panchen Lama chose the latter option (Turner 1800: 468). Neither Chinese nor Tibetan sources that describe the

Panchen Lama's meetings with Emperor Qianlong mention this discussion on India or the British governor. As a result, scholars have doubted if the conversations on British India between the Panchen Lama and Emperor Qianlong were serious policy discussions. Perhaps, as one scholar remarks, this was no more than "a light-hearted conversation over tea" (Li 2012: 210). The seemingly minor status of Purangir, his language skills, and the Qing "court ritual and etiquette" have been noted as the reasons why either the conversations reported by the Gosain may have been exaggerations or not worthy of mention in Chinese sources (Li 2012: 211–213). "Purangir's report of personal participation in the Lama-Emperor meetings and conversations was a clear reflection," as Li Ruohong (2012: 215) concludes, "of his wishful thinking as influenced by the thinking of the EIC and its ambitious Governor."

Indeed, as with many narratives of personal contacts and conversations with royalty, Purangir most likely exaggerated his description of events, especially to maintain his close connections with Hastings and other British officials in Bengal. However, the questioning of his narrative does not explain why, according to a Tibetan biography of the Panchen Lama, Purangir was summoned a few days before the Lama's death and the two "conversed happily in the common speech of India" (Loo 1970: 141). It also fails to clarify the reasons why the regent of Tashilhunpo, Chungpa Hutukhtu; the Tibetan official Solpön Chenpo; and the new Panchen Lama employed Purangir in their interactions with the British in Bengal after the death of the Sixth Panchen Lama. In fact, Purangir continued to be an active participant in the interactions between Tibet and Bengal until his murder in Calcutta by robbers in 1795. Prior to his death, Purangir was also instrumental in the successful mission of Samuel Turner to Tibet in 1783. At least for the Tibetans and the British in India, Purangir seems to have been an important intermediary in the bilateral relations. Therefore, from the Sixth Panchen Lama's point of view, especially given his interest in the geopolitics of the region, Purangir's presence may have been necessary during the conversations with the Qing emperor when the matters related to British India.

The invasions of Tibet by the Gurkhas in 1788 and 1791 and the subsequent dispatch of Qing troops to the region, who quickly and overwhelmingly defeated the Nepalese, resulted in dramatic changes in the geopolitical situation of the regions bordering northern Bengal. The Qing presence in Tibet increased substantially, leading to polities such as Sikkim requesting protection by the Manchu court against local rivals (specifically the Nepalese). Additionally, trading activities through the overland routes between Bengal and Tibet were severely curtailed. These events in the Bengal-Tibet borderlands coincided with Lord Macartney's unsuccessful visit to the Qing court in 1793. As a result of these failures to penetrate Tibet and establish an overland route to the Qing hinterland, the focus of British India–Qing China interactions shifted to the coastal cities, primarily Guangzhou, Calcutta, and Bombay.

Jamsetjee Jejeebhoy and the Maritime Networks

The Qing general Fuk'anggan, who was responsible for routing the Gurkhas in Tibet, was able to establish the connection between the foreigners (*pileng* 披楞) at the borders of Tibet and those trading in Guangzhou. In his report to the Qing court after the war, Fuk'anggan wrote (Cammann 1951: 140–141),

> We humbly report as the result of investigations that the lands of the Moghul Emperor at Delhi are the most extensive of all the countries of India, and his vassals are very numerous. Calcutta is the largest of the Emperor's dependencies. It adjoins the southern boundary of the Gurkhas and is the extreme frontier of our outer borders. The barbarian people who live there trade at Canton, and we are under the impression that they are connected with the people from the countries of the West (Europe). When we, Fu-k'ang-gan and Sun Shih-i, were in Canton, we did not

know that there was a Calcutta tribe, nor had we any certain knowledge of their name, or from what part of the world they came.

When Bogle embarked on his mission to Tibet, private commercial activity of the British and Indian traders in Guangzhou was growing rapidly. In 1783 the tonnage of the private trade between British India and Qing China had reached forty-five thousand tons (Kumar 1974: 5). At the time, the American Revolutionary War and the Spanish involvement in it had hindered the supply for Spanish dollars used in intra-Asian trading activity (Kumar 1974: 5). As a consequence, commodities from British India became important media of exchange for Chinese tea, silk, sugar, and other goods, most which were procured for markets in Europe. Indian cotton and opium were two such commodities. In 1799–1800, the export of Indian cotton by private traders from Bombay totaled sixty thousand bales (Kumar 1974: 38). In the same year, despite Qing China's ban on the trade in opium issued in 1729 and again in 1799, 1,867 chests of opium were exported to Guangzhou from Bengal (Bakhala 1985: 45).

From the year 1800 onward, the export of cotton and opium primarily through Bombay and Calcutta to Guangzhou and Macau witnessed tremendous growth. Chinese tea, sugar, and bullion exchanged in return first reached Bombay, Madras, and Calcutta and were then transshipped to Europe. Singapore, Penang, Manila, and London were closely interlinked through this new network of global commercial activity. The fast-sailing Baltimore-built clippers, Chinese junks, private boats, ferries, and eventually steamships facilitated the movement of commodities across this vast network. The merchants involved in this partnership between private European companies and Chinese-Hong traders included Chinese, Indian, and British merchants, as well as Armenians, Arabs, Americans, and Portuguese. Several Indo-Portuguese were part of this opium-trading network as well in the early nineteenth century, including Roger de Faria, Jose Francisco Pereira, and Major António Pereira (Farooqui [2006] 2012: 21–24). Pirates and smugglers from various ethnic groups also tried to profit from these intensive trading exchanges. The EIC filled its coffers not by directly engaging in the trade between India and China. Rather, in the case of opium, for example, it derived revenue by monopolizing the production and supply of opium in Bihar and by imposing tariffs on private merchants. As Asiya Siddiqi (1982: 307) points out, "[t]he East India Company encouraged the trade but allowed it to remain largely in the hands of private merchants who were expected to hand over to the Company's Treasury at Canton, the proceeds of their Indian cargoes in exchange for bills of exchange on the Court of Directors or on the Indian government at Calcutta."

Let us now move to the network of the famous Parsi trader Jamsetjee Jejeebhoy through the study of the letters he wrote to his partners, financiers, British officials, and others. While much has been written about Jamsetjee and his trading network (see, for example, Subramanian 2012: 88–143; Palsetia 2015), the objective here is to demonstrate the complexity of British India–Qing China trade, especially during the first half of the nineteenth century, from the perspective of an individual trader. It is also intended to underscore the role of Indian merchants in the opium trade of the nineteenth century and their connections with European and Chinese traders, officials, and informants. The collection of Jamsetjee's correspondence used here is quite substantial. Now at the University of Mumbai, the collection includes hundreds of private and official letters he wrote to various partners and associates.[18]

Jamsetjee was one of the many Parsis involved in the opium and cotton trade with Qing China (Siddiqi 2005). There were several other Indians either sojourning in Guangzhou and trading with Calcutta or Bombay or operating their shipping and trading networks from one of these ports. There is mention, for example, of a Marwari merchant named Bahadur Mullshet who was known as the "prince of merchants of Hindoostan" and the "Rothschild of Malwa and Rajasthan." Mullshet exported about one million rupees worth of opium to China each year but did not trust European traders and instead wanted his own Marwari employees to be stationed in Guangzhou (Anon. 1834: 98–99). Jamsetjee adopted a different strategy and partnered with Scotsmen William Jardine and James Matheson, maintained regular commercial contacts with the Chinese Hong merchant Howqua (Wu Bingjian 伍秉鑑), and collaborated with several other Parsi traders involved in British India–Qing China exchanges. His letters demonstrate the cosmopolitan and highly interconnected world of the early nineteenth century that formed the foundation of a new maritime network across the Indian Ocean and particularly between British India and Qing China.

The two most impressive facets that are immediately apparent from the correspondence of Jamsetjee Jejeebhoy are the vastness of the network within which the Parsi trader operated and the rapid pace of the circulation of news and rumors between British India and Qing China. Both of these aspects were facilitated by the clippers, which linked the ports within Asia as well as those between Asia and Europe. There was also a significant number of people who traveled regularly between British India and Qing China, carrying with them commodities, artifacts, and news. Another feature revealed in the writings of Jamsetjee was the financial mechanisms through which bills of exchange, bullion, and credit circulated and were remitted from one global site to another. What also becomes evident from these letters is the emerging migrant community of Indians in Qing China. Guangzhou and Macau were two places where Parsi and Sindhi traders settled prior to the Opium War. Thereafter, subsequent to the signing of the Nanking Treaty in 1842 and the opening of treaty ports, migrants, professionals, and intellectuals from India also started living in places such as Shanghai and Hong Kong. This was also the period during which the Chinese started forming their own migrant communities in India, especially in Calcutta.

Jamsetjee visited China for the first time in 1799 as an accounts clerk of his cousin Merwanji Manockji Tabak, and his second voyage was as a partner of the firm belonging to his uncle Framji Nusserwanji Battliwala (Farooqui [2006] 2012: 27). In addition to his early trading activity in China, much of which is not recorded in detail, Jamsetjee also engaged in exporting cotton to England. During his fourth trip to China, when the French captured the ship he was traveling on, he met the Scottish surgeon William Jardine. It was, as noted above, in partnership with William Jardine and another Scotsman named James Matheson that Jamsetjee operated his trading network. Jamsetjee's initial contact with the Chinese merchant Howqua was, it seems, established through these two Scotsmen. While he focused on exporting cotton and opium, Jamsetjee on occasion also supplied other Indian commodities, such as pearls, to Guangzhou. He utilized the ports of Bombay, Calcutta, and Madras to ship these goods. From China, Jamsetjee acquired tea and sugar. Since shipping was an important component of his business, Jamsetjee emphasized the need for the returning ships to carry Chinese commodities for sale in India or transshipment to Europe. Asiya Siddiqi (1982: 311) has pointed out that Jamsetjee's income "was derived from five interlinked items: the profit of trade on his own account, the income from carrying freight on his ships, interest on loans to shippers, dividends on shares in marine insurance companies, and commission on the sale of his own bills."

Prior to the first Opium War, a significant number of Jamsetjee's private letters were sent to Guangzhou, where William Jardine, James Matheson, and Howqua were based. Together these four people operated the biggest opium cartel in Guangzhou and were influential on a global scale. Jamsetjee was knighted in 1842, while William Jardine and James Matheson played key roles in ending the EIC's trade monopoly in Guangzhou and were instrumental in triggering the Opium War, and Howqua was the single leading contributor to the compensation the Qing government paid to the British under the Treaty of Nanking. This global reach and influence of these four opium dealers originated from their ability to maintain close links with the producers, shippers, distributors, and financial institutions on the one hand and, on the other hand, their capacity to lobby and negotiate with relevant officials and political leaders. Through these contacts they were able to gather news and information on the vicissitudes in demand and supply of the commodities, the changes in official policies, and the movement of ships and troops. Such information, in turn, facilitated the calculation of goods intended for maximizing profits. They also used a range of financial instruments instead of depending on the sale of commodities in local markets. These aspects are all manifested in the collection of Jamsetjee's correspondence.

On 31 March 1831, for example, Jamsetjee wrote to Howqua about the prospects for cotton in the global market and indicated limited supply of the commodity from places such as Madras. "Our Cotton crop is rather late this season," Jamsetjee writes, "and account for England is favorable for this staple, consequently the price rise in the interim. The freight for England is scarce, and is not procurable @ 8£ per ton. This year the quantity of cotton will not exceed 90 to 100,000 Bales. No Cotton of Company's from Madras this [season?], and hope that some improvement will soon take place in your market, hoping long life and prosperity."

The following letter to Howqua in July 1831 is also remarkable because it indicates the diversity of commodities traded between British India and Qing China, the means through which letters were exchanged between traders, and the financial instruments these traders utilized to offer credit or receive payments:

In conformity with my letter to you of the 31st March per *Hannah*, and duplicate per *Golconda*, enclosing an invoice of Pearls, shipped by me, on your account and risk, on board the *Hannah*,

T. Jackson, Commander, I now hand you enclosed account Sales of your silk, and cassia, to my consignment, together with your account Current, (in which you will observe give you credit for one year's factory ground rent) exhibiting a balance in your favor of Bombay rupees Two thousand three hundred ninety two, two quarters and seventy two reas (Rs. 2392-2-72) which I have invested by a Bill of Exchange drawn by Saroopchund Hemchund in your favor for Spanish Dollars 1139–37 cents payable at 60 days sight and bearing interest at nine per cent per annum until paid, and which you [*sic*] have enclosed. This ac., the account Sales & ca. will I trust meet with your entire approbation.

In 1834, when the British government formally ended the EIC's monopoly of the China trade, Jamsetjee bitterly complained to Sir Charles Forbes, his principal London agent, about the intensifying competition and possible loss of profit. He argued in his letter that the China trade, especially with regard to imports, had already diminished and "our ships generally return empty, as there is no produce in China that answers the purpose and but little freight is procurable." He also pointed out the fact that while his ships were "shut out" from engaging in European trade, the "European sailors" were now allowed to enter the trade between India and China. Pointing to the problem of the influx of European cotton into India, he wrote,

To all this must be added the competition we now meet with in cotton from the great number of Liverpool and other agency houses established here, who sell Piece Goods, and other Europe staples at prices that cannot pay, in order to provide the means for their purchases of cotton, which I can assure are made without thought, and without calculation, the consequence naturally is that the holders of cotton will not listen to our reasonable offers and we are therefore precluded from providing cargoes for our ships, many of which this season, I fear, will be laid up, indeed the shipping interests of this Port have been utterly disregarded in all the late arrangements. We had all hoped that His

Majesty's Government, would instead of adding to the expenses incident to the China Trade, have tried to have obtained from the Chinese authorities some concessions but these hopes we must now abandon, and stand prepared for an increase instead of a diminution. (JJ to Forbes, London, 30 January 1834)

In the letter he also highlighted his experiences in Qing China and contended that the Chinese will not accept the new policy. "Perhaps you have not forgotten that I was four voyages to China [*sic*]," he noted rhetorically, "and I therefore speak from experience when I say that the new plans of the Home Government are not adopted to the Chinese. I know their manners and habits well, and I am sure they will not submit to the establishment of a Court of Law & ca. and I should not be at all surprised to see an early collision between the New Superintendent and the Chinese authorities" (JJ to Forbes, London, 30 January 1834).

The end of the EIC's monopoly ironically turned out to be extremely profitable for Jamsetjee as cotton and opium supplied by him to Jardine and Matheson were used to purchase tea meant for European markets. From these transactions the Parsi trader acquired the lucrative Court of Directors bills (Siddiqi 1982: 311; JJ to Matheson, Canton, 10 May 1834). As a result, Jamsetjee's dealings with Jardine and Matheson show a marked increase, from $536,000 in 1830 to $1.2 million in 1837. During the Opium War period, his business peaked at $2 million (Le Pichon 2006: 33).

Jamsetjee's persistent commercial success throughout the Opium War period may have been due to the contingency plans he put in place and which he fine-tuned as he received regular updates from Guangzhou regarding the strategy employed by Qing officials and the plans of the British government. When Lin Zexu 林則徐 (1785–1850) was appointed commissioner to Guangzhou to eradicate the supply of opium, for instance, the Hong merchants were consulted for options by the court officials. These Hong merchants in turn passed on the information to foreign traders. Thus, on 18

March 1839, when Emperor Daoguang 道光 (1820–1850) issued
an edict imposing severe penalties and punishments on opium traders, Jamsetjee was able to quickly move two of his ships, with
2,400 chests of opium, from Macau and Lintin. A few days later,
when Captain Charles Eliot agreed to surrender twenty thousand
chests of opium to the Qing authorities, Jamsetjee was one of the
traders who relinquished his holdings anticipating future compensation from the British. He later claimed that 1,118.5 chests belonged to his company (Anon. *Correspondence Respecting Compensation*: 5).

Jamsetjee continued to follow the events that transpired in Qing
China, not only adjusting his business decisions but also sharing his
views and anxieties with his partners and associates. In December
1839, for example, he wrote to James Matheson (JJ to James
Matheson, Canton, 8 January 1840), indicating, "if the British go to
war with the Chinese, I will take care respecting our shipping load-
ing with entire cargo of our own, with instructions to go direct to
Manilla and wait for your order whether to unload or to remain at
her anchorage until . . . adjustment made by the Authorities." In
February 1840, Jamsetjee communicated to his other partner
William Jardine in London (JJ to William Jardine, London, 27
February 1840), who was instrumental in convincing the British
government to use force in China, saying that "the Chinese people
never believe of the Edicts of Lin to Captain Elliott but our friend
resolved to act accordingly to avoid the risk. I am in hope that Mr.
Matheson could contract us our Teas to the consignment of F. F. &
Co. which will by new arrangement be made it over to you on safe
arrival."

Jamsetjee anticipated that the war would end quickly, with the
defeat of the Chinese, and that he and other Parsis would be com-
pensated either by the British or the Qing government for the
opium they had surrendered to Charles Eliot. In March 1840 he
wrote to Captain R. Cogan, saying, "[T]roops from Bengal are now

embarking for China and all the men of war on this station are hurrying to Calcutta where the Commodore Sir. . . . now is, with his Broad Pendant on board the *Wellesley*, 74, and I am in hopes that before the month of June expires, the Chinese will be made to feel the terrible power of the British arms" (JJ to Capt. R. Cogan, London, 25 March 1840).

The Parsi trader was correct. After defeats in key battles, the Qing government dismissed Commissioner Lin. Although the Qing did not officially surrender until the signing of the Treaty of Nanking on 29 August 1842, the outcome of the conflict was clear by the beginning of 1841 when the British forces captured strategic locations in the Pearl River delta. Jamsetjee's main concern during these several months of warfare and after the signing of the treaty was with regard to receiving indemnity for the opium he surrendered. He wrote widely and frequently to British officials, including Elliott; Lord Palmerston, the foreign secretary; and on 21 October 1842 the governor-general of India. His petitions yielded little results in securing the amount he demanded. Instead, in 1842 the British government knighted him.

Although the victory in the Opium War resulted in the opening up of the so-called treaty ports and an intensification of British India–Qing China trade during the second half of the nineteenth century, Jamsetjee's business did not benefit from any of these developments. In fact, he seems to have been adversely affected by them. The increased competition from the "free traders," the lack of return goods from Qing China, the influx of large quantities of cotton into India from Europe, and the introduction of steamships reduced Jamsetjee's profit margins with regard to both his trading and his shipping businesses. Many of these issues were not new, as reflected in his letters cited above, but the competition that he faced from private traders and shippers was significantly greater after the Opium War. *Charlotte* and *Bombay Castle*, two ships belonging to Jamsetjee, were burned, perhaps deliberately in order to claim insurance money (Siddiqi 1982: 319–324), essentially crippling his shipping business.

The collapse of Jamsetjee's commercial network marked the end of a phase of maritime commercial activity between British India and Qing China that was rooted in the collaboration between the EIC, a few Indian traders such as Jamsetjee, and private European merchants and Hong traders based in Guangzhou. This pattern of commercial activity was unsustainable in the aftermath of the Opium War with the opening of new Chinese ports for international commerce, the reduction in freight charges due to the oversupply of ships, and the institution, in 1854, of a tax collection system through the Chinese Maritime Customs Service. Additionally, the spread of migrant networks, the trade in indentured labor, and the introduction of a telegraphic system had a substantial impact on commercial activities across Asia. One of the consequences of this intensive commercial activity was the formation of Indian diasporic communities in Qing China and Chinese diasporic communities in India. While Indian traders were present in Guangzhou and a few Chinese had settled in Calcutta and its vicinity prior to the nineteenth century, their numbers increased significantly after the Opium War. This and other developments during the second half of the nineteenth century are further discussed below.

Huang Maocai and British India

The Opium War marked a watershed in British India–Qing China interactions. The second half of the nineteenth century and the early decades of the twentieth century witnessed the opening of treaty ports and an influx of Indian traders, soldiers, and professionals into these Qing cities. The migration of the Chinese to British India also increased significantly. Moreover, the British forced their way into Tibet in 1903–1904 with an expedition led by Francis Edward Younghusband (1863–1942). At the same time, Qing China's defeat in the Opium Wars and the subsequent signing of the Treaty of

Nanking triggered an interest in British India among Chinese intellectuals and officials. It had become clear to the Qing court that British India posed a threat to its territorial integrity and also mattered with regard to its internal socioeconomic affairs. It was due to such realizations that the need to gather information about British India and understand the reasons for the collapse of the "Indian civilization" became imperative. This interest in British India resulted in the production of new Chinese writings on the region that ranged from surveys undertaken by Qing officials to newspaper commentaries and stories that mocked the "failed" or "lost" Indian civilization.

Wei Yuan's 魏源 (1794–1857) *Haiguo tuzhi* 海國圖志 (Illustrated Records of Maritime Polities) and Xu Jiyu's 徐繼畬 (1795–1873) *Yinghuan zhilüe* 瀛環志略 (A Short Account of the Maritime Sphere) were works that were composed shortly after the signing of the Treaty of Nanking, in 1842 and 1850 respectively. These two works contain detailed geographical accounts of India, including, in the latter work, a history of the colonization of India by the British. Shortly thereafter, eyewitness accounts of India appeared in the works of Huang Maocai, Ma Jianzhong 馬建忠 (1845–1900), Wu Guangpei 吳廣霈, and Kang Youwei 康有為 (Lin 1991, 1993). The views of India presented in these works differed significantly from the earlier accounts of Chinese Buddhist pilgrims who saw India as a holy land. The Qing visitors to British India, except for Huang, whose views are discussed below, portrayed India as a failed state and criticized Indians for their inability to defend themselves again the British colonizers. Kang Youwei, for instance, noted, "Formerly, India was a celebrated nation in Asia, but she preserved her traditions without changing and so during the time of Qianlong [1736–1795] the British people organized a company with one hundred and twenty thousand gold as capital to carry on a trade with her and subjugated the five parts of India" (Teng and Fairbank 1954: 152).

Some of these views about India as a "failed" and "enslaved" country" percolated to Chinese newspapers and journals published in the early twentieth century. A Chinese journal published in Japan, for example, carried the following story about a fictional Chinese intellectual named Huang Shibiao who, in his dream, saw an old man and together they encountered in Shanghai foreign British troops led by a white person:

> Shibiao looked closely at these people and they all had faces black as coal. They were wearing a piece of red cloth around their heads like a tall hat; around their waists, they wore a belt holding wooden clubs. Shibiao asked the old man: are these Indians? The old man said, yes, the English use them as police. . . . Shibiao asked, why do they not use an Indian as the chief of police? The old man answered: who ever heard of that! Indians are people of a lost country; they are no more than slaves! (Karl 2002: 161)

The presence of Sikh policemen in the British conclave in Shanghai, as well as stories such as the one cited above, made it easier for the common Chinese to witness and understand the discourse on the capitulation of the "Indian civilization" to the European invaders.

These Chinese perceptions of India in the late nineteenth and early twentieth centuries must also be understood in the context of a globalizing world that the Chinese were confronting for the first time. India, occupied by the British, had suddenly emerged as China's leading trading partner and a region of concern because of its possible use as a staging ground for European colonial expansion. The latter fear came to pass in 1903 when Francis Younghusband invaded Tibet. Wei Yuan, Xu Jiyu, and other early Chinese writers were apprehensive about this predatory nature of the British. "The reason for her (i.e., Britain) becoming suddenly rich and strong, exerting political influence here and there beyond tens of thousand of *li*," Xu wrote, "is that in the west she obtained America and in the east she obtained the various parts of India" (Teng and Fairbank 1954: 42).

Within this new discourse on and concerns about British India in the aftermath of the Opium War, the writings of Huang Maocai offer the first detailed account of life, the economy, and the military and administrative arrangements of the British in occupied India. His eyewitness account of the region came after a hiatus of over four centuries, subsequent to the writings of those who accompanied Zheng He in the early fifteenth century. Huang's writings were also different from the later accounts of British India by Ma Jianzhong, Wu Guangpei, and Kang Youwei. Unlike them, Huang was impressed with the developments that had taken place in India under the British and occasionally recommended the need for Qing China to also induct some of the technologies available to the Indians. Huang was also not as critical of Indians as many other intellectuals and writers from his generation were for their inability to resist the British occupation.

Huang Maocai was sent to British India by Ding Baozhen 丁寶楨 (1820–1886), the governor of Sichuan Province, in 1878. Ding was concerned about the security of the western frontier regions of the Qing state not only with regard to the British but also the Russians and the Tibetans. The objective of Huang's mission was to collect intelligence and map the geographical contours of the regions bordering Sichuan. More specifically, Ding seems to have been interested in finding out if the British planned to invade through Burma and Yunnan. He requested and received formal approval from the Qing court to send the mission to British India. He also had the British mission in Beijing issue a passport to Huang Maocai.

Huang Maocai, who was acquainted with the writings of Wei Yuan and knowledgeable about the earlier interactions between China and South Asia, began his journey from Chengdu on 7 July 1878 with five other officials (Lin 1991: 18). The group had planned to take the route through Tibet and Sikkim into British India. However, they found the terrain difficult and perilous. Moreover, when they reached Batang 巴塘 in the border regions of Sichuan and Tibet, the local Tibetan groups reportedly prevented them from proceeding to India. As a result, Huang Maocai decided to opt for the route through Yunnan and Burma. Passing through Zhongdian, Lijiang, Dali, and Tengyue, Huang and his companions entered Burma. Taking a steamship downstream on the Irrawaddy River, the group eventually reached Rangoon (now Yangon). After sailing on a "large ship" for six days from the Burmese port, they arrived in Calcutta on 26 March 1879. The whole journey took them over nine months. It should be noted that this itinerary, from Yunnan to Calcutta through Burma, became a common route for many travelers from Qing (and subsequently Republican) China to British India as well as to Tibet.

Huang Maocai and his companions traveled extensively in British India after staying in Calcutta for about three months. The places they visited included Darjeeling, Assam, Manipur, Dhaka, Allahabad, Agra, Delhi, and Bombay. They took different modes of transportation, cars, trains, and steamships, during their travels. Local British officials, with whom they had several rounds of meetings and discussions, arranged most of the travels and lodgings for the Qing delegation. The group departed from Calcutta on 13 September 1879 and took the maritime route back to Qing China, which passed through Rangoon, Penang, Malacca, Singapore, and Hong Kong (Lin 1991: 19).

Upon his return to Sichuan, Huang Maocai produced several documents, books, and translations. He translated a catalog of Central Asian objects housed at the Indian Museum in Calcutta, drew maps of routes between Sichuan and Tibet and between Yunnan and Burma, and also reported on the situation in Central and Southeast Asia. Specifically on British India, he drafted a map of the "Five Indias" based on the maps he saw in India, maintained a diary with the title *Xiyou riji* 西輶日記 (Diary of the West[ward] Carriage), wrote two detailed accounts of the region titled *Yindu zhaji* 印度箚記 (Notes on India) and *Youli chuyan* 遊歷芻言 (My Travels), and even composed a poem titled *Yindu zaxing* 印度雜興 (Random Thoughts on India).

In all of his writings on India, including the poem, Huang expressed his nostalgia for the historical interactions between China and the land he visited. He was particularly drawn to the travels of the monk Xuanzang and the activities of the Tang diplomat Wang Xuance. The "Five Indias," he pointed out, were in ancient times known as Tianzhu and also called Shendu. This use of "Five Indias" by Qing writers often resulted in confusion between the earlier and contemporary geographical descriptions and place-names in India. This was true of Huang Maocai as well, who noted that North Yindu was Jibin of olden times, and West Yindu the ancient Yuezhi (*Youli chuyan* 432b). Huang was also influenced by some of the erroneous descriptions of Indian history found in the works of Wei Yuan and Xu Jiyu, whom Huang cities frequently in his writings. At the same time, however, Huang was cognizant about the difference between the earlier geographical narratives and what he found in India. In *Youli chuyan* he remarked that the situation in India was much changed from the times of the Han and Tang dynasties and also differed from what was recorded in *Haiguo tuzhi* and *Yinghuan zhi lüe*. This was, he explained, especially true of the place-names found in the earlier works. As a result, he decided to transcribe the English names for Indian cities and regions prevailing at the time of his visit (*Youli chuyan* 447a).

Huang's decision to use contemporary place-names helped clarify some of the confusions about the geography of British India that circulated in Qing China prior to his visit. "To the east the borders of Five Indias," he explains, "extend to Assam (Yashan 亞山) 23 degrees by the west, to the west it reached Afghanistan 48 degree by west, to the south it commenced from Cape Comorin at 7 degree north latitude, and in the north it extended to the Pamirs at 40 degrees north latitude" (*Yindu zhaji*). Huang points out that the British ruled over eighteen or nineteen of the several polities that existed within this region. His writing also offered a new conceptualization of the region as he described British India within the framework of the three "military jurisdictions" (*bingshuai suo xia* 兵帥所轄) or presidencies—Bengal, Madras, and Bombay, as well as the northwest provinces (*Xibei zhi sheng* 西北之省). The Bengal Military Jurisdiction was reported as the largest and included the Orissa, Bhopal, and Allahabad regions. The Deccan region and the Coromandel and Malabar coasts were placed within the Madras Military Jurisdiction, and areas between the Deccan and the Indus River were included within the Bombay Military Jurisdiction. Also described is the island of Sri Lanka, which Huang pointed out was originally under the Portuguese but was later occupied by the British. Huang delved into the relations between the various European colonial powers and noted how the British eventually gained control of much of India. He also paid particular attention to the presence of the Russians in the frontier regions of British India.

Huang gave the total strength of the British army in India as 212,000, with 30,000 British and 182,000 Indian soldiers (*Youli chuyan* 432a; Lin 1991: 22).[19] Huang described the administrative system of British India and writes that the top officials were sent from England at a young age, and they learned the local language and were then assigned various positions in the government (*Yindu zhaji* 442a; Lin 1991: 22). In summer and autumn, Huang pointed out, the top officials would move to the hill station of Shimla. He concluded that, since the route from Assam to Sichuan was difficult to traverse due to the perilous terrain and "angry barbarians," the threat from the British to Qing China actually came from the Darjeeling–Sikkim route. The British, he pointed out, had built a railroad to Darjeeling, constructed a fort there, and stationed troops in the region.

Calcutta was a place that clearly impressed him. "Calcutta," he wrote, "was the largest port in the western part of the Southern Oceans." The streets, the boats, the vehicles, and the cosmopolitan nature of the city all left a deep impression on Huang. In addition to people from various parts of Europe, he reported that there were over one thousand Cantonese settlers who had built temples dedicated to Guandi and Tianhou (*Yindu zhaji* 442a). He went on to describe the streetlamps, the availability of tap water, the customs formalities at the port, an art school, the Alipore zoo, the Indian Museum, and the botanical garden (*Yindu zhaji* 442b–443b; Lin 1991: 24–25). He was particularly fascinated by the railway system, which he suggested should also be constructed in Qing China (Lin 1991: 24), and the use of the telegraph to communicate orders when the leading government officials spent their summers in Darjeeling.

Within a few years of Huang Maocai's return, another delegation was sent to British India by the Qing court. Led by Ma Jianzhong and Wu Guangpei, the purpose of this delegation was to negotiate with British officials the issue of the trade in opium. The delegation arrived in Calcutta in July 1881 and stayed in India for about twenty-five days (Lin 1991: 55). Both Ma and Wu wrote of their impressions of the visit and the things they encountered in British India. Ma, who was well versed in English and French, met with and negotiated the export of opium with the top British officials, including Viceroy Lord Ripon (1827–1909) and a member of the governor-general's council, Steuart C. Bayley. Although also impressed with the urban developments in Calcutta and Bombay under the British, Ma and Wu, unlike Huang Maocai, were introspective about the colonization of India and its implications for Qing China. Both blamed Indians for the situation, with Ma chiding the "ignorant" natives "without sophisticated machinery" or rule of law and Wu impugning the "impotence" of the Indian government and the "cowardice" of its military. Both called on the Qing government to draw lessons from the Indian experience and failure (Lin 1991: 65–67). These views reflected the emergence of the discourse on India as a failed civilization and an enslaved country noted above. As Qing China tried to come to terms with its defeat in the Opium Wars, British India became a reference point, a region of concern and introspection, with a shared past but perhaps also a common traumatic future. Huang's writing in this context of anti-colonial discourse with India as a leading example of a capitulated and enslaved country was largely forgotten.

THE EXPANDED COLONIAL NETWORKS

The Central Asia oases and the ports of Southeast Asia were places where merchants, missionaries, and craftsmen from South Asia and China met and collaborated during precolonial times. The European colonization of Asia, Africa, and the Americas resulted in the creation of new sites of interactions, not only in the intermediary regions but also in places that were outside the Asian continent. While the new sites of interactions within Asia included Kashgar and Penang, the British Caribbean, Fiji, and Mauritius are examples of places outside the continent where people from colonized India and Qing China met and established unique relationships. This movement of Indians and Chinese to far-flung regions of the European empires formed an important element of the larger flows of people across the world instigated by the expansion of colonial networks, which included the movement of indentured labor; the transregional employment of soldiers, security personnel, and ship-builders; and the desire of individuals and groups to find places that offered better employment prospects, safety, or an opportunity to work for the cause of anti-imperialism. The encounters between Indians and Chinese within the larger British Empire leading to the formation of new migrant communities will be focused on below.

The Formation of Migrant Communities

In 1778, when William Hastings allocated land near the banks of the river Ganges in Calcutta to the Sixth Panchen Lama, he also gave a large area in the vicinity of the city to a Chinese trader named Yang Dazhao 楊大釗. Prior to this, Yang had met the governor-general and offered him Chinese tea.[20] While the quantity and the place of origin of this tea are not clear, Yang in return received a large land grant, where he established a sugar mill and brought laborers from China to work for him. Yang was nicknamed Atchew, and the area granted by Hastings later became known as Achipur (lit. "the town of Achi"). The granting of a large piece of land to Yang, in addition to the mission of Bogle (as well as that led by Samuel Turner) to Tibet discussed above, suggests William Hastings's broader interest in expanding commercial exchanges between British India and Qing China through both the overland and maritime routes.

Similar to the Gosain Purangir, Yang Dazhao maintained contacts with British officials. He approached the British authorities in Calcutta whenever he encountered problems running his business. In 1781, for example, he wrote a petition saying that the Chinese living in Calcutta were luring his workers away from the sugar mill in Achipur. The British Supreme Board, in response, immediately published a note in a Calcutta newspaper cautioning the involved persons (Bose 1934: 6; Zhang and Sen 2013: 206). The petition is important because it reveals the presence of Chinese in Calcutta by the time Yang received the land grant. In fact, an eyewitness account by a Vietnamese traveler named Ly Van Phuc 黎文額 (1785–1849) mentions that not only were there "several hundred" Chinese from Fujian and Guangdong regions residing in Calcutta, but the city also had temples dedicated to Chinese deities (Salmon 1999: 383–384; Zhang and Sen 2013: 206).

After the second Opium War, the Englishman Chaloner Alabaster ([1858] 1975), the person tasked with escorting the anti-British

Chinese official Ye Mingchen 葉名琛 (1807–1859) to his exile in Calcutta, reported in 1857 that there were about five hundred Cantonese and Hakka Chinese residing in the city. These people, according to him, were engaged in shoemaking, opium peddling, carpentry, and other activities. He also confirmed Ly's report about the existence of temples dedicated to Chinese deities, pointed to the presence of Chinese cemeteries, and described in detail the lives of the Chinese residents.

Some of the intriguing aspects mentioned by Alabaster include the work ethic of the Chinese, their perception of the natives, and their approval of British rule. About the Chinese shoemakers in the Calcutta, who were in high demand, he wrote ([1858] 1975: 384):

> They are not punctual, and their shoes are not lasting, but this is not their fault, being rather that of the ladies of Calcutta who, giving them so much more work than they can possibly get through, prevent their being the former, and by, in the same way, forcing them to employ native workmen and devote themselves to the simple superintendence, prevent their doing the latter. But with all their faults they are good citizens. Utterly as they are dependent on foreigners for their living, hating the natives in all the intensity of Chinese hatred; their only security is the maintenance of British power, and although they would not, unless paid for it, willingly shed their blood even for their native country, they would rather pay many dollars than that we should be driven hence. "The English Government is a very good one, it lets us manage our own affairs and helps us if any one else tries to injure us, its policemen leave us alone, and its Small Cause Court has been established specially for our convenience."

The number of Chinese in Calcutta mentioned by Alabaster is confirmed by the census report of 1871–1872, which records the presence of 574 Chinese in the city. Alabaster also describes the establishment of various institutions belonging to the community in the city. Several of the *huiguan*s (native-place associations), belonging to the people originally from the Yixing, Jiaying, and Siyi regions that he mentions, were established between 1838 and 1845. These *huiguan*s had either shrines dedicated to Guandi (the god of integrity and righteousness) or the bodhisattva Guanyin and served as both community and religious centers for the Chinese community living in the Bowbazar area of central Calcutta.

Alabaster's report on the support for British rule in India among the Chinese migrants differed significantly from the writings of Ma Jianzhong and Wu Guangpei mentioned above. For these migrants, whose movement out of China was facilitated by the British colonial network linking southern China to Bengal through Southeast Asia, the British customers provided job opportunities (in shipyards, for instance) and were better paymasters than the local Bengalis. In fact, the preference to work for the British in India continued to be expressed by Chinese migrants up through Indian independence (Zhang 2015), indicating the uncomfortable existence of the ethnic Chinese among the Indians, which, as chapter 5 will demonstrate, had an adverse impact on the community in the late 1950s and 1960s.

Calcutta was not the only place where the Chinese settled in British India. In 1871–1872, there were also 531 Chinese residing in Bombay. While the population of the Chinese in Bombay remained static through the beginning of the twentieth century, their numbers in Calcutta grew to 1,640. The reason for this increase was associated with the community facilities existing in Calcutta, such as the native-place associations, restaurants, and lodging places, that attracted new migrants. During this period, some Chinese also settled in the tea-producing areas of Assam and Darjeeling. The population of the Chinese community in India peaked at around fifteen thousand during World War II. Their situation in the twentieth century is discussed in the following chapter.

A similar trend with an increase in the number of Indians residing in China is also evident after the Opium Wars. Before the mid-nineteenth century, Indians, overwhelmingly traders, lived and worked in Guangzhou, Tibet, and Xinjiang. After the Opium Wars, not only did the number of Indians living in these places increase, but the newly opened treaty ports, especially Hong Kong and Shanghai, also witnessed an influx of people from different parts of British India. Unlike the Chinese in India, the Indian population was more diverse in terms of their places of origin (Markovits 2000: 61–68), as well as their activities and distribution in Qing China. During the second half of the nineteenth century, for instance, there were Parsi, Marwari, Kashmiri, and Sindhi traders; soldiers from different parts of India; and Sikh policemen and watchmen living and working in Qing China. More importantly perhaps was the fact that these migrant Indians had significantly more impact on the local economy and society than did the Chinese residing in British India.

Jamsetjee Jejeebhoy's correspondence and British documents include the names of several Parsi traders living in Guangzhou prior to the Opium War. The first Parsi to arrive in Guangzhou may have been a trader named Heerjee Jeevanjee Readymoney, who reached the port in 1756 (Guo 2005: 32). By 1837, according to the *Chinese Repository*, a periodical published in Guangzhou by the Protestant missionary Elijah Coleman Bridgman, of the 307 foreigners in Canton, sixty-two were Parsis and four were "Hindus" (Guo 2005: 193). The names of many of these Parsis appear on a pledge submitted to Commissioner Lin Zexu on 27 (or 25) March 1839. Of the forty-two foreign traders who signed the pledge not "to deal in opium, nor to attempt to introduce it into the Chinese Empire," twenty were Parsis (Guo 2005: 107–110). At least on one occasion the names of Parsis who worked as laborers in Guangzhou are revealed in some of these sources. This concerned the murder of a Dutchman in Guangzhou in 1830 by Framjee (Hualinzhi 化林治), Nowrojee (Niuluozhi 鈕羅治), and Jamsetjee (Renxiezhi 任些治). These three were servants of a Parsi merchant named Marvanjee

Hormajee. Despite the demand by the local Chinese authorities to surrender the accused and their threat to dispatch armed forces to retrieve them, the British decided to first keep the three Parsis in their factory and then move them to India for prosecution (Guo 2005; Thampi 2005).

The Parsis in Guangzhou had a "Parsi House" (*Basi guan* 巴斯館) as well as a cemetery for the community. However, unlike the Chinese in Calcutta who lived in the congested neighborhood of the city, the Parsis were largely segregated from the local population in Guangzhou. Yet they exerted a noticeable impact on the local society. This is evident not only from the influence of the opium they supplied but also from the ways in which they controlled the finances of some of the Chinese Hong merchants. Guo Deyan (2005) has pointed to several cases of bankruptcies among the Chinese trading houses that resulted from the failure to return loans or debts owed to the Parsi traders. Additionally, the Parsis were instrumental in financing the Opium War and renting their ships to the British forces.

Indian traders were also present on the western frontiers of the Qing Empire. Unlike in Guangzhou, trade in the Xinjiang region, because of the nature of the terrain and transportation facilities, rarely involved goods in bulk quantities. Additionally, since there were no designated areas for foreign traders to settle and trade, Indian merchants were found scattered in several towns of Xinjiang. In Kashgar and Yarkand, for example, merchants from Kashmir, Punjab, and Sind congregated and traded in products such as opium, sugar, and indigo from India and imported charas, silk, tea, gold, and silver from Qing China (Thampi 2005: 114–115). Initially most of these traders in the Xinjiang region were sojourners rather than residents of Kashgar and Yarkand. However, as the trading prospects increased and businesses expanded into the spheres of financing and real estate, some of these traders starting living in Xinjiang for longer durations, forming relationships with local women and bringing servants and even slaves from India. By the end of the nineteenth century, the number of these people had reached eight hundred (Thampi 2005: 116). Similar to the Parsis in Guangzhou, several Indian businessmen in Xinjiang exerted influence over the local economy through their involvement in money-lending and financing activities.

The increasing number of Indians in Xinjiang and disputes with the locals caused several problems for George Macartney (1867–1945), the British consul-general in Kashgar from 1890 to 1918. This included the issue of identifying people who should be considered as subjects of British India. Madhavi Thampi (2005: 129–130) points to a report by Macartney preserved at the National Archives of India (Foreign/Sec.-F/April 1903, NAI, 28–37), which notes,

> One of my duties here is to watch over the interests of British subjects in this country. But it is not always clear to me who those are that should be included under that denomination. Some persons originally from British Indian territory, have settled in the Yarkand district for a great many years, and now practically have no connection either with their country of origin or with the Indian trade. Others have executed bonds before the local authorities declaring themselves Chinese subjects, and have, in consequence, been admitted to privileges denied to ordinary foreigners, such as the owning of land, admission to administrative employ, etc. The whole situation is one of remarkable complexity. Yarkand appears to have always extended a special hospitality to all foreigners, and the result is that there are now amongst them several hundreds of Kashmiris, Baltis, Ladakhis, Gilgitis, and Indians, living in the country more as members of the native society than as sojourners. Such persons often apply, as British subjects, to me for protection, or assistance in litigation, whilst the local authorities, considering them as Chinese subjects, not unnaturally resent intervention. Again, the persons referred to have a tendency to proclaim themselves

British, or Chinese subjects, according to the convenience of the moment.

Claude Markovits (2000: 59) notes of a twentyfold increase in the Indian population in Shanghai between 1885 and 1919, then "doubling" in 1925–1935. The increase in the population of Indians at the treaty ports did not lead to the kind of complex intermingling mentioned above. There seems to have been clear distinctions with regard to both spatial and ethnic identities between the Indians and the natives at these places. Markovits (2000: 70) points out that the "Indian merchants tended to operate more in international trading or in certain kinds of specialised trade for a mostly European clientele, and they did not have very extended contacts with the Chinese trading communities." The fact that the natives at these treaty ports, unlike in Xinjiang, were Han Chinese may have also made a difference. Nonetheless, the Indians living, trading, and employed at the treaty ports also had considerable impact on the lives of the natives. The Armenian Sassoon family, with their base in Bombay, started as one of the opium suppliers in Shanghai but gradually emerged as a leading real estate company in the city with investments in hotels, residential buildings, and public utilities. Their involvement in the Shanghai real estate business was considerable as they owned some of the prime property in the city. The Sassoons also spread their company network to other cities in China (Thampi 2005: 94–95).

The Sikh guards and watchmen were ubiquitous in Shanghai from the 1880s as members of the city's municipal police force. They were often despised by the locals for the harsh treatment they meted out and were described in contemporary writings using the derogatory term *hongtou asan* 紅頭阿三 (lit. "red-turbaned number three"). Also described in Chinese literature from this period are the Parsis who had expanded their networks from Guangzhou to the various treaty ports. In 1870–1872, for example, Zhang Deyi 張德彝 (1847–1918), a student of English and later China's diplomatic representative to Britain, wrote about a group of Parsi traders he met on a boat between Shanghai and Guangzhou: "[a]ll with brown faces and black beard," he noted, with six-inch-tall white hats and able to converse in Chinese and English. He pointed out that these merchants, who had come from Bombay, traded in opium, cotton, and silk. Zhang asked them about their religion, which he noted was "called Zououlasitalan [Zoroastrianism], which [involves] the worship of the Sun, Moon, and the five planets. According to the people in the West, it has been over one hundred years since this religion degenerated." He then inquired of the Parsis about their language and provides the transcriptions of several Gujarati words (Guo 2005: 138–139).

The post–Opium War period also witnessed an influx of Indian soldiers, who took part in all major warfare undertaken by British-led forces in Qing China. In addition to the two Opium Wars, Indian soldiers also participated in the battles against the Taiping and Boxer rebels. In fact, "in 1841–2, 1857–60, 1900–1 and 1927," as Robert Bickers (2015: 62) points out, "the larger part of the British expeditionary forces sent to China came from British India." Of the seven thousand Indian troops sent during the first Opium War, 250 were killed. Some 3,300 Indian soldiers were dispatched to China during the second Opium War. The numbers increased dramatically by the end of the century, when over thirty thousand Indians troops and other personnel participated in the Boxer Rebellion in 1900 (Thampi 2005: 140–160; Bickers 2015: 62–63). Most of these soldiers served their duty and either returned to India or were sent to other British colonies, including Hong Kong.[21]

The participation of Indians in the British expeditionary forces bewildered the Chinese, who usually called them "*heigui*" 黑鬼 (black devils) or "*heiren*" 黑人 (black people). The Qing official Qiying, for example, wrote after the first Opium War about the "black" and "white" foreign soldiers who fought against the Chinese. Pointing out that the black soldiers came from Bengal and

Bombay, he wrote (trans. Mosca 2013: 254) that they were "very strong but with a stupid nature and do not know how to respond to the circumstances. The foreign leaders make them work like slaves or servants and rear them as one would a dog or a horse—and yet they willingly devote their lives to serve [their leaders]. This is also something that cannot be reasonably explained."

The fact that not all such troops "willingly devoted" themselves to the British masters is evidenced by the deserters and those who switched sides during the wars against the Chinese. There were also some exceptional soldiers for whom this phenomenon of colonized people fighting on behalf of the Europeans in other Asian countries led to agony and pain. This is reflected in the writing of a soldier from northern India named Gadhadhar Singh, who went to Qing China with the British troops in 1900 to fight the Boxers. His concerns, cited in the next chapter, are found in a Hindi-language book published in 1902 titled *Chin Meh Terah Mas* (Thirteen Months in China).

Out of Asia

The most significant aspect of British India–Qing China interactions during the nineteenth century in terms of human movement was the formation of sites outside the Asian continent where Indians and Chinese congregated. The colonization of Asia by European powers resulted in the emergence of Macau, Singapore, Penang, Hong Kong, and Tokyo as the new sites of interactions or "meeting grounds" for people from India and China. In the nineteenth century such sites extended to Africa, Europe, and the Americas. Some of the movement of Indians and Chinese beyond Asia was voluntary, mainly in search of better economic prospects. However, a majority of Indians and Chinese met at these sites as indentured laborers. British Guiana and Mauritius were two such places where Indian and Chinese congregated and worked on European colonial plantations.

The Wesleyan missionary Rev. H. V. P. Bronkhurst in 1883 wrote a detailed account of the indentured laborers from different parts of the world living in British Guiana. In 1881, according to a census cited by Bronkhurst, of the estimated total population of 252,186 in British Guiana, 69,554 were immigrants from India and China (1883: 26). Of these, the majority were Indians, numbering 65,161, while the Chinese formed a minority of only 4,393. The fact that most Chinese started arriving in the region only from 1853 accounted for their minority status. "Indian and Chinese Coolies," Bronkhurst wrote (1883: 99), "were the only class of people or immigrants that could suit as agricultural labourers and as settlers, and meet the requirements of the wealthy owners of sugar plantations in the Colony. Though the importation or introduction of these labourers from the distant East is very expensive on account of the means of communication, yet these Coolies or labourers alone have been the salvation of the Colony, and to them we are indebted for its present prosperous condition."

Bronkhurst's comparisons of the livelihoods and work ethics of the Chinese and Indian living in British Guiana provide important insights into the exchanges and intermingling that took place between the two migrant groups far away from their homelands. In fact, the connection to the respective homelands was a key aspect that Bronkhurst highlighted when comparing the two migrant communities. He noted, "The Chinese though they love their native land, and strongly desire at their death to be buried there, are yet a people who make themselves as happy and comfortable in foreign lands as in their own country. In this and other respects they are very unlike the East Indian Coolies. There is greater likelihood of the Chinese immigrant Coolies permanently settling in the Colony than the East Indian Coolies." He also points out that the British government's decision to provide free return passage to the Indians might have been a factor in this distinction and concludes that

"Chinese settlements will be far more preferable and advantageous than the Indian Coolie settlements" (1883: 107–108).

It is evident that the relationship between the Chinese and Indians living in British Guiana was more complicated than those residing in each other's country. The shortage of female immigrants among the Chinese was one of the causes of this complex relationship. In 1891, in British Guiana there were, as Bahadur (2013: 240) points out, "forty-three Chinese women for every 100 Chinese men and sixty-three Indian women for every 100 Indian men." This resulted in various social problems within and between the two communities, sometimes leading to violence against women suspected of "immoral" relationships. Such incidents seem to have been more frequent among the Indians than within the Chinese community, which resulted in the following perception expressed in the local *Royal Gazette* published in 1863: "Chinese females are chaste, the same cannot be said for the coolie women" (Bahadur 2013: 120). Yet there were episodes when Indian and Chinese men tried to address the issue of the shortage of women creatively. One such episode took place between a Chinese man who had escaped from China during the Taiping Rebellion and an Indian laborer. The two worked together in the plantation for several years. The Indian eventually decided to "loan" his wife to the Chinese so that he could have a child to "carry on his name." As Bahadur explains, this story "suggests an alternate way to understand the fluid, unorthodox sexual relationship during indenture. They may indicate accommodation, not immorality. Perhaps they were another improvisation, as when the indentured found ship sisters and ship brothers to replace families left behind" (Bahadur 2013: 121–122).

The above episode may have been an exception, but it was common in several sites outside Asia where the shortage of Chinese women, barred by the Qing government from being hired as indentured labor, resulted in the Chinese men marrying Indian women.

This happened, for example, in Mauritius, where by 1883 there were reportedly 415 Chinese men living with women of creole or Indian origin (Carter and Kwong 2009: 199). The census of 1921 indicated that there were 148 children "born from the union of Chinese men and Indian women" (Pineo and Fat 2008: 174). Unlike in British Guiana, the Chinese population in Mauritius in the nineteenth century was more diverse with regard to both place of origin of the migrant communities and the professions they engaged in. This resulted in the establishment of several different types of economic and social relationships, both competitive and cooperative, between the Chinese and Indian migrants.

While most Indian migrants reached Mauritius before the Opium War, a majority of the Chinese arrived between 1840 and 1844. These Chinese were not only from Qing China but also from the Straits Settlements and even British India (Carter and Kwong 2009: 33). The Chinese opened their shops and peddling businesses within the Indian settlement areas and sometimes leased lands from Indian landowners. The Hakka Chinese in Mauritius established business relations with the members of their community living in Calcutta, trading mostly in leather goods (Carter and Kwong 2009). Carter and Kwong point out that the relationship between some members of the Chinese and Indian communities in Mauritius was in fact established even before they reached the Indian Ocean island. "They frequently travelled together," they write (2009: 192), "with scores of Chinese arriving as paying passengers on the ships carrying Indian labourers to Mauritius from Calcutta and Bombay." After settling in Mauritius, the two immigrant communities formed intimate economic associations, especially within the expanding Hakka trading networks and in the cigarette-manufacturing business (Carter and Kwong 2009: 196–197). This collaboration between members of the Indian and Chinese migrant communities seems to have been so strong that some of the locals launched a sharp protest in 1848. Reflecting similar anti-immigrant sentiment, a local newspaper noted that "in the present day situation of the colony it is impossible to make one's fortune—the wholesale trade being in the hands of Asiatics from Calcutta, Bombay and Madras, and the retail trade in the hands of the children of the Celestial Empire" (Carter and Kwong 2009: 206).

While the Chinese and Indians also met in their respective homelands and at places in Southeast and Central Asia, their packaging together as foreigners in meeting grounds elsewhere was a rare phenomenon that became more frequent during the European colonial phase.[22] However, the situation and the nature of the interactions differed depending on the specific meeting ground. There were appreciable differences, for example, between the meeting grounds in Guiana, Mauritius, and Malaya. The distance between these sites and the respective homelands, which dictated the duration of one's stay in foreign areas, was perhaps an important factor that either augmented or lessened the opportunities for intermingling between the two communities. The makeup of the native population vis-à-vis the immigrant communities, with regard to both numbers and ethnicity, probably also mattered. Finally, the economic conditions and opportunities, which varied at each place, also must have determined the interactions between these two immigrant groups.

Each of the interaction sites or meeting grounds, in India or China, in the Straits Settlements, or in places outside Asia, offers a very different paradigm with regard to understanding the relationship between Indians and Chinese. In India and China, the foreigner-native divide was evident between the migrant communities and local residents through biases, stereotyping, and even segregation in economic and social activities. The shared experiences and the "packaging" together of Indian and Chinese immigrants as foreigners in the Strait Settlements,[23] Guiana, and Mauritius often resulted in the obscuring, but not necessarily total obliteration, of the "dividing lines" between the two groups of people that existed in their respective homelands. Racial and cultural prejudices remained, but practical social (the lack of a female population, for example) and economic necessities helped blur these divides between the Indian and Chinese communities. This not only resulted in the formation of new kinds of relationships between the Indians and Chinese in a global setting, but it also led to unprecedented circulations of knowledge and awareness, as well as the creation of a fresh set of misconceptions and prejudices, about each other. [24]

INDIA, CHINA, AND GLOBAL CONNECTIONS

Malacca was one of the first new sites of interactions between Indians and Chinese that emerged as a result of the expansion of imperial powers in maritime Asia. The Ming court's intervention in Malacca's relationship with Siam and the establishment of the "Official Depot" by Zheng He at the port created an alternate node for ships sailing between the Chinese coast and the Indian Ocean littoral. By the time the Portuguese entered the Indian Ocean world, Malacca was already a hub for Chinese and Indian traders operating their commercial networks that linked the South China Sea region to the Bay of Bengal and the Arabian Sea. The subsequent few centuries witnessed the emergence of Batavia, Singapore, and Penang as other such sites of interactions under the European colonial presence in Asia. New sites of exchanges and interactions also appeared in China and India. These included Calcutta, Bombay, Goa, Shanghai, Macau, Hong Kong, and Kashgar. Additionally, in the late nineteenth and early twentieth centuries, Tokyo became a center for intellectual discourse between Indian and Chinese scholars, some living there in exile. As argued in this chapter, perhaps the most notable development with regard to new sites of interactions was the advent of common meeting grounds for Indian and Chinese beyond the Asian continent. British Guiana and Mauritius were two such places highlighted in this chapter.

These new sites of interactions, which replaced the previous meeting grounds such as Dunhuang, Palembang, and Chang'an (present-day Xian), facilitated diverse forms of exchanges and circulations. Many of these sites were important nodes in the circulations of commodities such as opium, tea, and cotton. Others were created as plantation centers to serve the needs of European enterprises, governments, and consumers. Some were also political centers, from which the European powers administered their colonial empires. Each of these places fostered a wide range of interactions between Indians and Chinese. While in Calcutta the encounters took place between Chinese immigrants and local Bengali, Armenian, and Anglo-Indian communities, in Shanghai the Chinese confronted Indian soldiers and Sikh guards. In parts of the British Empire, the Malay world, British Guiana, and Mauritius, on the other hand, migrant Chinese and Indian laborers mixed and formed their own unique partnerships and relationships. The intermingling of Indians and Chinese at diverse places across the globe defined this phase of imperial connections.

These interminglings shaped positive and negative perceptions, led to the creation of new types of cuisines, and produced shared spaces where cultural traditions of the two groups of people were juxtaposed and sometimes merged. Some of the examples related to mutual perceptions were discussed above. With regard to cuisine, a distinct Chinese-Indian recipe developed in Calcutta and became part of Indian eating traditions. Similarly, in Southeast Asia, the intermingling contributed to the mixing of Indian and Chinese ingredients by newly formed communities such as the Baba Nyonyas in Malacca and Penang (Pampus 2017). The presence of Chinese temples in Calcutta, the Sikh *gurdwaras* in Shanghai, the erection of Hindu places of worship in close proximity to Chinese temples, and the placing together of Indian and Chinese divinities in roadside shrines in several Southeast Asian cities, on the other hand, exemplified the communal spaces of the Indians and Chinese in different settings. These were all the result of the connectivities—oppressive, exploitative, and humiliating as they may have been—that were formed by imperial expansions.

The shipyards in distant Baltimore that manufactured the fast-sailing clippers were also a part of these India-China connections. In the 1840s and 1850s these Baltimore clippers were in high demand from opium and tea dealers networking between India and China. Jamsetjee Jejeebhoy and the company of Jardine and Matheson, for instance, owned a few of these clippers. A specific clipper called *Frolic* exemplified the global connections within which interactions between British India and Qing China took place. Built in 1844, a 275-ton ship with the most advanced mechanical fittings, the best-quality masts, comfortable quarters for the crew, and two cannons, the *Frolic* reached Bombay on 28 March 1845. In early May of that year *Frolic* started its first run between Bombay and Guangzhou, carrying Malwa opium for the Bombay-based firm of Kessressung Khooshalchund. The *Frolic* completed the journey in a record thirty-four days (Layton 1997). Owned by Bostonian George Dixwell, the *Frolic* was crewed by Englishmen, Americans, Chinese, lascars, and Malays. The language of communication among these crewmen, as Layton (1997: 114) points out, was Portuguese, "the old trade language of western India, Malaysia, and Macao." The *Frolic* frequently sailed between the Chinese coast (Guangzhou and Shanghai) and the ports of Calcutta and Bombay until 1850, when it was reassigned to transport goods between California and China as part of the California gold rush. In the same year, when returning to America from Bombay through Hong Kong, the ship was wrecked near San Francisco. For what turned out to be the *Frolic*'s final journey, the clipper first carried Malwa opium from Bombay to Hong Kong and subsequently took on board 1,602 cases of objects from China that ranged from silk and Chinaware to four cases of oil paintings from the studio of the Chinese painter Tinqua, which produced landscape drawings in the style introduced to coastal China by the British painter George Chinnery (1774–1852).

Several individuals from Europe also made important contributions to India-China connections during this phase. The roles of George Bogle, James Matheson, William Jardine, and some of the Jesuit missionaries were noted above. There were a number of other Europeans who also made distinctive contributions as well. The above-mentioned George Chinnery, for example, lived in Madras and Calcutta during the first quarter of the nineteenth century and then worked in Macau and Guangzhou from 1825 to 1852 (Layton 1997: 134). Together with his Chinese student Lam Qua, the two produced portraits of the four leading individuals involved in the opium trade between British India and Qing China: James Matheson, William Jardine, Jamsetjee Jejeebhoy, and the Chinese Hong merchant Howqua. It is possible that the founding of the Sir Jamsetjee Jejeebhoy School of Art in Bombay in 1857 was an outcome of this relationship between the opium traders and the studio of Chinnery–Lam Qua in southern China.

Alexander Cunningham (1814–1893), the first director-general of the Archaeological Survey of India, initiated a different kind of connection. Using recently translated works of Xuanzang's travelogue, Cunningham traced several historical sites and monasteries mentioned by the Chinese traveler. He was also one of the first persons to map Xuanzang's itinerary in India (see figure 3.3). In 1848, in responding to questions raised about the value of Xuanzang's records, Cunningham wrote,

> The Itinerary of Hwan Thsang is the most valuable document that we possess for the history and geography of Ariana and India prior to the Mohamedan conquests. The minute accuracy of its details and the faithful transcription of the native names of men and places, give it a vast superiority over all the Mussalman works that I have seen, excepting only that of Abu Rihan. (Cunningham 1848: 476–477)

Cunningham's faith in the travelogue of Xuanzang and his sub-sequent archeological discoveries and identifications based on the narrative of the Chinese monk led to the incorporation of Chinese travel accounts into the study of Indian history. It also laid the foundation for the field of India-China studies in the late nineteenth and early twentieth centuries, which placed Xuanzang at its epicenter not only in order to highlight the historical connections between India and China, but also as contextual reference, as pointed out in the next chapter, to the contributions of later Chinese personalities to these exchanges.

This reconstruction of precolonial interactions was one of the main outcomes of the discourse that took place between Indian and Chinese intellectuals during the European colonial period. The common struggle against European imperialism rallied these intellectuals. Japanese expansion in the 1930s and 1940s further strengthened the collaborations that framed contemporary relations within a selective and often glorified narrative of past connections. Erased from this narrative was the Ming imperial expeditions under Zheng He, which were also coercive, exploitive, and violent. The overall narrative of India-China connections that emerged as a consequence, as noted in the introduction and detailed in chapter 5, was one that presented the phase of European colonialism as a dark age that came to an end only after the arrival of Rabindranath Tagore in Republican China in 1924.

The various sections of this chapter have demonstrated that such a reconstruction neglects the diverse and brisk connections that were established between India and China during the phase of imperialism. Several of the contemporary sites of interactions, (mis)perceptions and knowledge about each other, cultural practices, and connections to places outside Asia emerged during this phase. Rather than describing this as a "slow and sluggish" phase (Deepak 2001: 12), the period between the fifteenth and the late nineteenth centuries needs to be examined for the vibrancy and the

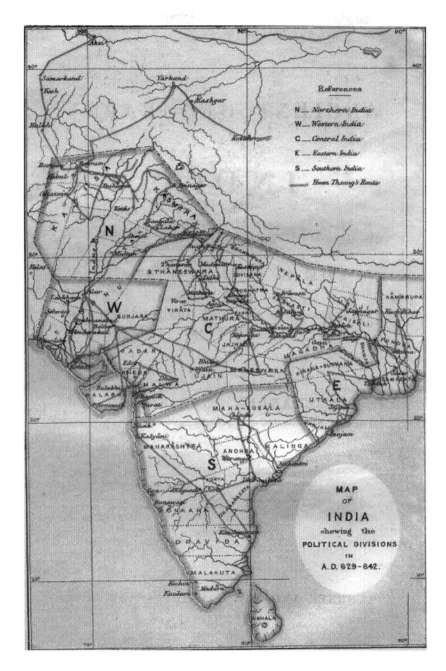

Figure 3.3. Alexander Cunningham's map of India with Xuanzang's itinerary. After Cunningham (1871), *The Ancient Geography of India*.

multilayered connections it created. In fact, the discussion above suggests that this period may have been a critical nexus between the pre-Ming phases of interactions and the contemporary bilateral relations between the Republic of India and the People's Republic of China.

NOTES

1. As noted in the introduction, in this chapter and the next the term "India" is used to describe the geographical area that now includes India, Bangladesh, and Pakistan. The term "British India" is also used for exchanges that pertain to the period between the mid-eighteenth century and Indian independence in 1947.

2. The exact reason for initiating the Zheng He expeditions, however, cannot be ascertained. The suggestions have included the possible search for the deposed emperor, who some believed had survived the assault on his palace and was in hiding among the Chinese overseas communities in Southeast Asia, the desire to assert the Ming court's supremacy in the wider world, and an investigation of the possible plan of the Mongol leader Temur to expand into Ming territories (Dreyer 2007). The *Ming shi* gives as the two motives the search for the deposed ruler and the Yongle emperor wanting to "display his soldiers in strange lands in order to make manifest the wealth and power of the Middle Kingdom" (Dreyer 2007: 187).

3. Dreyer (2007) and Levathes (1994) are two book-length studies on Zheng He. Detailed bibliographical references to other publications on Zheng He can be found in Liu et al. (2014).

4. On the various rulers ("kings") at Malacca at this time, see Wang (1968b).

5. On Yebanaina, see Karashima (1978).

6. Perera believes there were two persons named Alagakkonara, a petty official trying to manipulate the local political situation and a hero who had launched a battle against the Tamils in southern India. The official Alagakkonara, Perera (1904: 290–291) argues, was involved in creating a rift between the possible heirs to the throne in Kotte, with the aim of eventually becoming the ruler himself. When Zheng He reached the island on his first voyage, he may have met the hero Alagakkonara, who refused overtures from the Ming emissary and "defeated the Chinese in an engagement and beat them back to their ships" (Perera 1904: 291). Subsequently, the hero Alagakkonara became the king of Kotte and took the title Vijayabāhu VI. In 1410–1411, when Zheng He returned to Sri Lanka, the official Alagakkonara plotted with the Chinese to depose Vijayabāhu VI. On the pretext of entering the court to offer tribute, as *Rājāvaliya* reports, the Ming embassy captured Vijayabāhu VI and returned to China. Either when they realized that they had been tricked or because they were able to negotiate some sort of agreement with Vijayabāhu VI, the Ming court decided to let the Sri

Lankan return to his country. According to Perera (1904: 293), shortly after his return to Sri Lanka, Vijayabāhu VI was murdered by the usurper Alagakkonara, who was himself killed several months later.

7. This episode is discussed in the context of an earlier military action in South Asia by the Tang court in Sen (2014c). See also Karashima (1978) and Sen (2016a).

8. I have removed the identification of A-lie-ku-nai-er as Bhuvanaikabāhu V in the translation. As Somaratne (1975: 17ff) has argued, the two were not the same person.

9. Other than a few differences in the use of words, the two records of Zheng He obtaining the relic and bringing it to China are exactly the same. A detailed comparison of the two sources has been done by Liu (2008). Dreyer (2007) was not aware of this letter from Yongle; neither was Levathes (1994), who discussed the issue of the Tooth Relic in detail and also includes in her study other lesser-known Chinese sources on Sri Lanka.

10. On the political significance of the Tooth Relic, especially how it super-seded the earlier emphasis on the bowl relic, see Herath (1994: 92ff).

11. On the circulations of animals and various precious objects, see Sen (2016a, 2016b).

12. On pepper prices in Egypt and West Asia, see Ashtor (1976).

13. On Ottoman involvement in the Indian Ocean interactions, see Casale (2010).

14. European stimulation of Asian manufacturing industries can also be dis-cerned, as outlined below, from the developments in the South Asian textile industry during the later phase of colonial connections.

15. "Sindu" in the translation should read "Sindhu."

16. For a detailed study of the later Tibetan pilgrimage activities in India, see Huber (2008).

17. There are two important collections of the writings of George Bogle. The first is the volume compiled by Clements R. Markham of the Geographical Department of India Office in 1879. The scholar Alastair Lamb edited the second in 2002, which included several important correspondences of Bogle. Only one of the two planned volumes of the latter has thus far been published. Samuel Turner, who traveled to Tibet to see the Seventh Panchen Lama, also has impor-tant documents, especially the record of the conversation between the Sixth Panchen Lama and the Qing emperor, in his narrative (Turner 1800). Bogle's mission to Tibet is also narrated in Kate Teltscher's (2006) book *The High Road to China: George Bogle, the Panchen Lama and the First British Expedition to Tibet*. An earlier relevant work is by Diskalkar (1933).

18. Murali Ranganathan transcribed the private letters of Jamsetjee Jejeebhoy used in this section.

19. Huang reports that, of the 182,000, half were "Buddhists" and half Mus-lims, with their separate regiments intended to prevent them from unifying and rebelling against the British. The "Buddhist" here is clearly a mistake for Hindus.

20. Tea and sugar were at this time becoming important commodities of trade between British India and Qing China. In fact, Hastings was also interested in probing the possibility of planting tea in India.

21. There were also a few Indian soldiers who deserted or switched sides, especially during the Taiping Rebellion (Thampi 2005: 153–154).

22. On precolonial mingling, especially in Malacca, see Reid (2006).

23. This "packaging" also took place in French-occupied Vietnam, where the local Vietnamese opposed the Chinese and Indian economic domination with slogans such as "Send *Quan Công* (Guan Yu, indicating the Chinese) to his country and Buddha back to India!" and "Hit the *Chệc* (i.e., the Chinese) and expel the *Chà* (i.e., the Indians)!" (Pairaudeau 2016: 196–197).

24. A recent study of Indian and Chinese immigrant communities in comparative perspective is Bhattacharya and Kripalani (2015).

Chapter Four

Pan-Asianism and
Renewed Connections

Are not our three countries like a folding fan?
India is the paper; China is the bamboo frame; and
Japan is the pivot linking these two to the handle.
—Zhang Taiyan, 1907

The first half of the twentieth century was a crucial period in Asian history in that it witnessed the emergence of an Asian consciousness or "Asianism," fostered by the spread of ideas related to pan-Asianism that emphasized Asian unity and solidarity.[1] The advocates of this "Asianism" claimed that "Asia can be defined and understood as a homogenous space with shared and clearly defined characteristics" (Stolte and Fischer-Tiné 2012: 65). It was also an era during which nationalism, anti-imperialism, and independence movements bonded various regions of Asia. Influenced by these developments, people in Asia started perceiving and reconstituting their histories very differently than before. These reconstituted histories ranged from narratives about far-flung spheres of cultural influence exerted by certain "Asian civilizations" to those that underscored the peaceful and harmonious nature of intra-Asian interactions before European colonization. At the end of this period, however, with decolonization and the advent of independent nation-states with distinct political systems, it became evident that the ideas of pan-Asianism could not be easily implemented in a politically, culturally, and religiously diverse Asia.

By the 1920s, unity between India and China had become an integral part of this discourse on Asianism. Indian and Chinese intellectuals were quick to embrace the idea and called for political and cultural alliances between India and China. They frequently alluded to the historical precedents for such alliances and blamed the European colonial powers for interrupting the cordial relationships of the past. This narrative, as outlined below, began in the first decade of the twentieth century. It was subsequently fostered in the 1930s and 1940s at Cheena Bhavana, Visva-Bharati, in Shantiniketan, under the direction of the Nobel laureate Rabindranath Tagore (1861–1941) and the Chinese scholar Tan Yunshan 譚雲山 (1898–1983), as well as at the Maha Bodhi Society headquarters in Calcutta. It peaked during the period of the Japanese invasion of China, with a significant increase in publications and speeches that highlighted the need for cooperation and solidarity.

Asianism involved the use of the terms "India" and "China" for distinct, homogeneous, and politically identifiable units in historical periods when such geopolitical identities, as noted in the introduction, did not exist. The advocates of pan-Asianism employed these designations deliberately to accomplish their idealistic, political, or religious goals. As Sugata Bose (2006: 270) explains, the "nostalgia for the bonds of the past" during the early twentieth century was "very much part of a struggle in the present to try to influence the shape of a global future."

Chinese and Indian nationalists also trumpeted the precolonial connections between India and China. This was especially true of the works by scholars belonging to the Greater India Society, who aimed to "organize the study of Indian culture in Greater India, as well as in China, Korea, Japan and other countries of Asia" (Kwa 2013: xv). Indeed, Prasenjit Duara's (1995: 13) point about all good nationalisms having a transnational vision is apparent in these works. Buddhist connections offered a perfect paradigm for these writers, who used it not only to link India and China, but also, since Buddhism had spread to most parts of Asia, to demonstrate the universalism and homogeneity of Asian civilization.[2]

As India and China confronted British and Japanese imperialisms, internal political changes, and other realities of the colonial period, the rhetoric of friendship and bonding was often employed in international forums and bilateral diplomatic exchanges. In fact, it brought together a diverse group of people, Rabindranath Tagore and Jawaharlal Nehru (1889–1964) from India; Liang Qichao, Dai Jitao 戴季陶 (1891–1949), and Taixu 太虛 (1890–1945) from China; and individuals such as Tan Yunshan and Raja Mahendra Pratap (1886–1979), who moved between various Asian countries promoting their own versions of pan-Asianism. Some of these people were instrumental in nurturing the diplomatic relationship between the GMD and the Indian National Congress (INC) with the intent to create a joint front against Japanese military expansion and, in the process, realize the vision of India-China solidarity. On the verge of decolonization, however, the contentious issue of Tibet between India and China, which came to the forefront at the Asian Relations Conference held in Delhi in 1947, made it evident that the idealism of pan-Asianism could not resolve the problems of territorial sovereignty and border disputes.

This chapter examines three phases of India-China interactions during the first half of the twentieth century intimately connected to the ideals of pan-Asianism. The first three decades of the period witnessed the emergence of the discourse on pan-Asianism and its spread among Indian and Chinese intellectuals and political leaders. In the 1930s and the first half of the 1940s, pan-Asianist ideas, especially those that propagated India-China solidarity, were implemented at Cheena Bhavana in the Tagore-founded Visva-Bharati in an attempt to not only foster educational and cultural exchanges between Indians and Chinese but to also facilitate political connections between the GMD and the INC. The Maha Bodhi Society in Calcutta played a similar role when representatives from the Buddhist community in China visited, donated to the Buddhist cause, and forged cultural connections. The post–World War II period, from 1945 to 1950, saw major cracks in the idea of India-China solidarity as the GMD and Communist governments in China and the Indian leadership and intelligence community started to address complicated issues of Tibet and border demarcation. The concerns over Tibet and territorial demarcation defined the relationship between the Republic of India (ROI) and the People's Republic of China (PRC) during the second half of the twentieth century.

PAN-ASIANISM AND THE DISCOURSE ON INDIA-CHINA ONENESS

In 1900 an Indian solider named Gadhadhar Singh departed from Calcutta as part of a British regiment sent to fight the Boxer rebels in Qing China. He was one of the many Indians who served in the British army that fought wars in Qing China starting with the Opium War of 1839–1842. Thus, Singh was not unique in this respect. Rather, it was his diary detailing his experiences in Qing China within the context of British imperialism, written upon his return to India in 1901, that makes Gadhadhar Singh a noteworthy figure in India-China relations. Perhaps because the diary was written in Hindi, Singh's views and experiences have remained hidden until recently. In fact, his diary, titled *Chin Meh Terah Mas* (Thirteen Months in China), is part of a new genre of writings on China that appeared in Indian vernacular languages starting from the second half of the nineteenth century (Shen 2016).

In his detailed study of *Chin Meh Terah Mas*, Anand Yang has outlined Singh's perceptions on China, its humiliation by the European imperialists, and the affinity between the people of India and China. "To him," Yang writes (2007: 58) about Singh, "China and India were comparable and compatible because they were the two most ancient civilizations of the world." Indeed, at one point Gadhadhar Singh wonders,

> There was no need for us to feel compassion because we had come to fight the Chinese. But . . . seeing people of our same colour generated an "emotion" for them in our minds if not in actions. The Chinese are Buddhists. (I did not know about Confucianism at that time.) They share a religion with Hindustanis. As inhabitants of Asia they are also almost fellow countrymen. In complexion, tradition, and culture, too, they are not dissimilar. Why has God (Parameshwara) inflicted this distress on them! Did God not want to help them?
>
> A surge of sympathy [*sahanubhuti*] came to mind in seeing the plight of the Chinese. How innocent were our ancestors who fought with Lahore for Delhi or with Chittor for Jaipur! They fought the Rathors for Akbar and Ranjit[3] for the British. Why have their hearts and minds become worm-eaten? Then it occurred to me that probably God (Bhagavan) manufactured this delusion for the welfare of the Chinese. Were China to fall into the hands of our all-powerful government it would gain the calm and peaceful sleep that our holy Aryavarta is experiencing. That would be good news. Oh Lord—let it be so! Entrust China also to the great power [*shakti*] that Aryavarta has been! Establish a great Asian power by creating a "Hindu China" [India-China]! Amen! (Yang et al., forthcoming)

Anand Yang (2007: 60) explains that Gadhadhar Singh's tour in China "prompted him to interrogate Western civilization, whose forces looted and ransacked and filled like scavengers and hunted down people for sport. From such experiences developed subaltern sentiments about the empire and civilization he collaborated with and budding awareness of racial and cultural kinship between China and India—and even the rest of Asia—that anticipated the rising discourse about civilization and pan-Asianism in the decades to come."

The Japanese scholar Okakura Kakuzō formally inaugurated this discourse on pan-Asianism almost at the same time as Gadhadhar Singh's diary was published. In 1903, Okakura declared that Asia was "One," with India and China as the two "mighty civilisations" and Buddhism as the "great ocean of idealism, in which merge all the river-systems of Eastern Asiatic thought" ([1903] 1920: 1). This view was rooted in the scholarship and intellectual discourse related to Asian connections that emerged in the nineteenth century. The translations of the travel records of Chinese monks Faxian, Xuanzang, and Yijing published during the nineteenth century sparked an interest in the study of Buddhist connections in Asia and also inspired archaeological explorations of British India. Also in the nineteenth century, especially during the last quarter, the idea of *Ajiashugi* 亞細亞主義 (Asianism or pan-Asianism) started taking root in Japan. The idea was not only contextualized within the rising anti-imperialism and nationalistic sentiments across Asia but also grounded in the belief that Asian societies before European colonial expansion had interacted in peace and harmony. The historical interactions between India and China, as seen in the translated works of Chinese monks, were, according to these writers, evidence for the latter view.

The discourse on pan-Asianism occurring in Japan attracted several young Chinese and Indian revolutionaries, including Zhang Taiyan 章太炎 (aka Zhang Binglin 章炳麟; 1868–1936) and Taraknath Das (1884–1958). Zhang and Das believed that India and China should unite under the leadership of Japan, the only major Asian power at that time, to confront European imperialism. There were, however, already concerns and hesitations about the role and intentions of Japan. Even Okakura's emphasis on India and China was to highlight the role of Japan as the "sole heir" to the two ancient traditions in the realm of artistic tradition (Ninomiya-Igarashi 2010: 21). Distressed by such self-centered objectives of the Japanese, Zhang Taiyan, for instance, started stressing a China-India alliance instead of the China-Japan coalition that he had previously supported. "We can first unite India and China," he said of his vision in laying out the Charter of the Asiatic Humanitarian Brotherhood in 1907, "the two most ancient and largest lands in the East. If these two countries can achieve independence they will be able to form a protective shield over Asia and many countries will be the beneficiaries" (Cai 2011: 183). Zhang also wrote several articles highlighting the importance of India in Asia and the ancient connections between India and China.[4] This was the beginning of a genre of writing that framed the historical interactions between India and China within the pan-Asian context with the aim of bringing about Asian unity, or at least an alliance between contemporaneous India and China.

The pan-Asiatic ideas brewing in Japan also influenced Liang Qichao, who was initially critical of India's weak response to the British invasion but later became one of the leading advocates for India-China unity and the foremost scholar of the historical interactions between India and China. In 1921, he published an article titled "Zhongguo-Yindu zhi jiaotong" 中國印度之交通 (Communications between India and China), which listed some of the main episodes of historical exchanges between India and China. He noted in the article that "in the East, civilization originated in China and India" and that India and China were like older and younger brothers (*kundi* 昆弟). Three years later, when Rabindranath Tagore visited China, the "brotherly affinity" between India and China was more pronounced in Liang's speeches and writings. When welcoming Tagore in Beijing, in the talk cited in the introduction, he said, "Both in character and geography India and China are like twin brothers. Before most of the civilized races became active, we two brothers had already begun to study the great problems which concern the whole of mankind. We had already accomplished much in the interests of humanity. India was ahead of us and we, the little brother, followed behind" (Liang [1925] 2002: x). As to the earliest contacts between the two regions, Liang emphasized, "What we as historians are able to vouch for is that the first communication between us as brothers occurred in the first century of the era of Christ."

Liang's writings on the India-China exchanges were most likely influenced by his view of Chinese history as linear and progressive (Duara 1995: 33–36, 170–175) and his engagement with the discourse on civilization (Duara 2003: 89–103), which sought to respond to the civilizing missions of the Western colonial powers by highlighting the "civilized" state of Chinese and other Asian societies. In fact, as Duara (2003: 102–103) points out, "the rhetoric of Asian brotherhood was one of the civilizational narratives transcending the racial or ethnic nation that Chinese nationalists developed in order to integrate the populations of these vast outlying regions (constituting over half the present Chinese territory) into the Chinese nation."

Similar to Japan, Shanghai, during the early twentieth century, was also a hub for the interactions between Indian and Chinese intellectuals and revolutionaries.[5] One of the leading contributors to the discourse on pan-Asianism was the Indian sociologist Benoy Kumar Sarkar, who, based in Shanghai in 1916, wrote *Chinese Religions through Hindu Eyes: A Study in the Tendencies of Asiatic Mentality*. The book carried an introduction by the Qing, and later Republic of China, official, revolutionary, and Theosophist Wu Tingfang 伍廷芳 (1842–1911). A year later, Zhang Taiyan's close associate Taraknath Das published in Shanghai a collection of essays titled *Is Japan a Menace to Asia?* The first chapter of the book was devoted to an analysis of the political situation in China. Das's book included an introduction by Tang Shaoyi 唐紹儀 (1862–1938), who had briefly served as the prime minister of the Republic of China and had previously (in 1905) visited India. In the introduction, Tang highlighted the importance of India by stating, "Japan and China, if far-sighted, should not be unmindful of the problems of the people of India, because a strong, free India will be a source of strength to them."[6]

Sarkar, like Zhang and Das, was an avid supporter of the idea of Asian solidarity under Japan. Trying to give the idea a more philosophical grounding, he wrote that (Sarkar 1916: 276) although the "Asiatic mind" was one, Asian unity, especially between the peoples of India, China, and Japan (which he calls "San-goku" or the "Three Nations"), "rests on a common psychology supplying a fundamental basis." It is the "psychological groundwork," he explained (Sarkar 1916: 279–280), that "makes Asiatic Unity a philosophical necessity in spite of ethnological and linguistic diversities."

Rabindranath Tagore's visit to China in 1924 was instrumental in cementing the idea of the historical and psychological unity of Asia. Tagore already held the view that the Buddhist interactions between India and China stretched back to the first century CE. Speaking of the Buddhist missionaries and their contributions, he asked (Tagore [1925] 2002: 102) in one of his speeches in China, "Is it not marvelous how these men at all arrived, and having come, translated their metaphysical ideas into Chinese, a language so utterly different from Sanskrit that the difficulties thereby encountered were far more insurmountable than the mountains they climbed, the deserts they traversed, the seas they navigated?" And in order to revive these historical connections, he pleaded with his Chinese audiences, saying (Tagore [1925] 2002: 48), "My friends, I have come to you to re-open the channel of communication which I hope is still there; for though overgrown with weeds of oblivion its lines can still be traced. I shall consider myself fortunate if through this visit, China comes nearer to India and India to China—for no political or commercial purpose, but the disinterested human love and for nothing else."

To make this vision a reality, Tagore had already, before his trip to China, started the process of bringing to his base at Shantiniketan scholars from around the world to study ancient interactions between India and China (Das Gupta 2010). In 1902 Okakura had sent to Shantiniketan a Japanese Sanskritist named Hori Shitoku, who was tasked with collecting "Indian" texts from China and bringing them to India. Almost twenty years later, in 1921, the French Sinologist Sylvain Lévi (1863–1935) joined Visva-Bharati and inaugurated a department of Sino-Indian studies (Nag 1957: 10). In 1923, the Italian scholar of Buddhist art Giuseppe Tucci (1894–1984) arrived as a visiting professor. The same year saw the publication of *The Indian Teachers in China* by Phanindra Nath Bose (1923), a professor of history at Visva-Bharati, using many of the works of the nineteenth-century scholars. The following year, when Tagore visited China, the first Chinese-language courses were offered to the students at Visva-Bharati.

The efforts of the above intellectuals had a wider impact in the 1920s. In 1924, Sun Yat-sen 孫中山 (1866–1925) delivered a speech titled "Da Yaxiya zhuyi" 大亞細亞主義 (Greater Asianism) in Kobe, Japan. He started the speech by underscoring the importance of Asian civilization in world history. "We must first have a clear conception of Asia's place in the world," he wrote. "Asia, in my opinion, is the cradle of the world's oldest civilization. Several thousand years ago, its peoples had already attained an advanced civilization; even the ancient civilizations of the West, of Greece and Rome, had their origins on Asiatic soil. In Ancient Asia we had a philosophic, religious, logical and industrial civilization. The origins of the various civilizations of the modern world can be traced back to Asia's ancient civilization." After outlining the oppressions by European colonizers in Asia and criticizing their materialistic civilization, Sun noted, "If we want to realize Pan-Asianism in this new world, what should be its foundation if not our ancient civilization and culture? Benevolence and virtue must be the foundations of Pan-Asianism" (Brown 2011: 78–85).

Although ancient Buddhist links in Asia were not mentioned by Sun, they were part of the political discourse at the World Congress of Oppressed Peoples (also called the International Congress against Imperialism) held in Brussels in 1927. Funded by the Communist International, and perhaps the GMD as well as the Mexican government, the congress drew two hundred delegates from thirty-seven states (including colonized territories) and 134 organizations (Prashad 2008: 19). Jawaharlal Nehru represented the INC. In his report about the meeting to the All-India Congress Committee, Nehru pointed out that the strongest delegation in Brussels was from China. The delegates representing the GMD were, he writes, "the left wing of the party, cooperating with communists and near-communists abroad, that laid stress on this propaganda, both to strengthen China's national position abroad and its own position in the party ranks at home" (Nehru 1941: 124; Yang 1974: 11).

Nehru praised the Chinese for their revolutionary achievements, expressed his concerns about the British use of Indian soldiers in China, and noted the joint declaration that was worked out by the Indian and Chinese delegates. "Both the Chinese delegates and we felt it to be fitting," reports Nehru ("India in the Brussels Congress": 155), "to place on record our ancient intimate association from the days when the message of social emancipation which Gautama gave found such a ready welcome in China, and Chinese pilgrims and scholars came to India to learn of her wisdom, to the unhappy interruption of this intercourse at the beginning of British domination in India." Indeed, the joint declaration, perhaps the first such India-China joint political pronouncement at an international gathering, started with these words: "For more than three thousand years the people of India and China were united by the most intimate cultural ties. From the days of Budha [*sic*] to the end of the Mughal period and the beginning of British domination in India this friendly intercourse continued uninterrupted." Later, the declaration emphasized that India and China "must now resume the ancient personal, cultural and political relations between the two peoples. British imperialism which in the past has kept us apart and done us so much injury, is now the very force that is uniting us in a common endeavour to overthrow it" ("India in the Brussels Congress": 155–156). The joint declaration of the Indian and Chinese delegation resulted in an invitation from the INC to the GMD for a goodwill mission. Although the GMD selected a high-powered delegation led by Song Qingling 宋慶齡 (1893–1981), the wife of the late Sun Yat-sen, the trip never materialized because of the denial of visas by the British authorities.

The World Congress of Oppressed Peoples was Jawaharlal Nehru's first foray into implementing the ideals of pan-Asianism, something he would continue to attempt even twenty years later with the organization of the Asian Relations Conference in Delhi (see below) and his participation in the Bandung Conference in 1955 (see chapter 5). However, the limitations of the pan-Asian narrative appeared every time the operationalization of Asian union or unity was deliberated. This was already evident, for example, during the 1926 pan-Asiatic conference in Nagasaki. While Western colonial rule in Asia was the rallying cause among the delegates, the Japanese occupation of Korea and parts of China emerged as a matter of grave concern for those promoting Asian solidarity. There were other issues at the conference, such as the Japanese government's criticism of Asiatic projects and the lack of representations from nationalist movements in Asia, which, as Cemil Aydin (2007: 158) points out, "effectively demonstrated the weakness of pan-Asianism."

Concerns about the British employment of Indian soldiers and the Japanese military expansion into China led several advocates of pan-Asianism to instead focus on India-China unity, echoing, in some ways, Zhang Taiyan's call for an alliance between the two countries made in 1907. Throughout 1927, sympathetic sentiment about China among the public and political leaders had been growing in India. The main apprehension among various civil society groups and political parties was the British use of Indian troops in China, something Nehru highlighted in Brussels. Rabindranath Tagore, Mahatma Gandhi (1869–1948), Lajpat Rai (1865–1928), and other members of the INC made strong statements against the British policy of sending Indian soldiers to China. Public protests and condemnations by state legislatures occurred in Delhi, Madras (now Chennai), Calcutta, Lucknow, Aligarh, and other places. On 26 December 1927, the INC officially demanded the immediate recall of all Indian soldiers in China and protested the British Indian government's refusal to grant passports to the members of a medical mission that the INC had decided to send to China (Prasad 1979: 99–107; "The Indian National Congress" 1927: 378).

Similarly, Japan's invasion of Manchuria in 1931, its military expansion in Asia throughout the 1930s, and the imperial discourse advocating the establishment of a Greater East Asia Co-Prosperity Sphere (大東亜共栄圏 Dai-tō-a Kyōeiken) gave further impetus to those trying to emphasize the role of India and China in pan-Asianism. The Japanese aggression in China had also clearly divided the Indian pan-Asianists between those based in Japan, including Rashbehari Bose (1886–1945) and Taraknath Das, who continued to perceive Japan as the leader of the movement, and others, including Rabindranath Tagore and Mahatma Gandhi, who strongly condemned the Japanese invasion of China. The dilemma of the Indians as a result of the Japanese military actions is reflected in articles appearing in the *Modern Review* and the *Indian Annual Register*, two nationalistic Indian journals published in Calcutta, during the 1930s. In a 1933 issue of the *Modern Review*, for example, Dhirendra N. Roy (1933: 392), an Indian scholar based at the University of the Philippines, wrote that "[i]f China wins her case against Japan with the help of some Western nation, she may temporarily raise her position to some importance, but she would, I am afraid, hardly win that self-respect and self-confidence which Japan did by defeating Russia." The *Indian Annual Register*, in its January–June 1938 issue, summed up the changed feelings toward Japan over the course of thirty years in the following way:

> Time was, not thirty years back, when Japan was an inspiration to us in our fight for national freedom. It is on record that Okakura, author of *The Ideas of the East*, inspired with his presence, with his talks and writings the leaders of the Indian Nationalist Movement in the opening years of this century. . . . We came to regard Japan as the leader of the awakened Asia, as the shield and bulwark of Asiatic freedom. Since those days Japan has been a place of pilgrimage to Asiatic patriots, an asylum to exiles from the many lands of Asia. But those feelings are changed to-day. And Asiatic peoples, people in India, do feel that there is little to choose between imperialism, Western or Eastern. ("Indian Nationalism & Japanese Imperialism," 49)

To show solidarity with the Chinese, Subhas Chandra Bose (1897–1945), then the president of the INC, declared 18 June 1938 as All-India China Day. After over three decades of discourse on pan-Asianism and advocacy for India-China unity within that context, it was the attempt to jointly address the Japanese military threat, not the original anti–European imperialism stand, that gave birth to the most important symbol of "India-China oneness" in the twentieth century: the Cheena Bhavana, which opened at Visva-Bharati in 1937.

CHEENA BHAVANA: A NEW SITE OF INTERACTIONS

Unlike the new sites of interactions established during the period of European colonial expansion, Cheena Bhavana was a result of the attempts made by Indian and Chinese intellectuals to realize the ideals of pan-Asianism advocated by Gadhadhar Singh, Okakura, and others. In fact, because Cheena Bhavana tried to accomplish many of the goals set out by the pan-Asianists mentioned above, Brian Tsui (2010) has described its activities as "pan-Asianism in action." Cheena Bhavana attracted academicians as well as Buddhist monks and political leaders such as Chiang Kai-shek 蔣介石 (1887–1975), Nehru, and Zhou Enlai 周恩來 (1898–1976). From the time of its establishment, which happened to occur shortly before the Japanese launched a full-scale invasion of China, Cheena Bhavana (as well as Visva-Bharati) represented India-China and intra-Asian friendship and fraternity (Stolte and Fischer-Tiné 2012: 79). Until the late 1950s, it was the leading global center for India-China studies, which, while producing important scholarship on Buddhist interactions, romanticized the exchanges between the ancient Indian polities and the Chinese dynasties and placed them squarely within the vocabulary and framework of modern nation-states. Indeed, Cheena Bhavana seamlessly merged the earlier romanticism of Liang Qichao and Rabindranath Tagore, the political aspirations of pan-Asianism promoted by Nehru and Chiang, and the academic study of the historical interactions between India and China led by the Indian Sinologist P. C. Bagchi.

The main figure responsible for bringing the above three strains together at Cheena Bhavana was a Hunan native named Tan Yun-shan. Rabindranath Tagore met Tan, the future inaugural director of Cheena Bhavana, in Singapore in 1927 during his visit to Southeast Asia. Tan was then working as a teacher at a Chinese school in the colony. He frequently wrote articles on Chinese literary traditions in local newspapers and was also the founder of the Chinese-language newspaper *Xingguang* 星光 (Light of Singapore), which ceased publication within a year (Kenley 2003: 84–85). This was not the first time that Tagore had tried to recruit someone from the Chinese diasporic community. In 1924, on his way to China, Tagore was invited to a reception at a Chinese school in Rangoon (now Yangon). The principal of the school, named Lim Ngo Chi-

ang 林我將, who welcomed Tagore and his delegation and interpreted for Tagore, was the first Chinese-language instructor at Visva-Bharati from 1925 to 1926 (Nag 1945: 37, 52).[7] Later, in 1927,
Tagore also spoke to the Chinese community in Bangkok about his
desire to set up a China studies program at Visva-Bharati and requested their support. The community, according to the *Siam Observer*, agreed to form a committee to raise funds from the Chinese
in Malaya and Siam for a chair in Chinese language (Das Gupta
1961: 114).

Tan seems to have accepted Tagore's invitation and went to
Shantiniketan in 1928. It must have become clear to both Tagore
and Tan within the next few months that in order to establish an
institution dedicated to China studies, a large sum of funds would
be required. By late 1929, a promised donation from Aw Boon
Haw 胡文虎, a wealthy Singaporean Chinese, had not materialized
(Tan 1933: 30). The Chinese community in Bangkok most likely
was also unable to raise the funds for the planned chair in Chinese.
The extant, mostly hagiographical, accounts of Tan suggest that he
left Shantiniketan in 1930 to solicit funds from abroad.[8] However,
it is not clear why he decided to go to Burma and began working in
Rangoon as an editor of the newspaper *Xingshang Ribao* 行商日報
(Commercial Daily). Letters exchanged between Tan Yunshan and
V. Bhattacharya, a principal of Visva-Bharati, suggest that Tan's
departure from Shantiniketan in 1930 was not related to the issue of
raising funds from abroad (Tan 1933: 26–28). Tan most likely gave
up the hope of establishing a China studies center in Shantiniketan
due to a lack of funds and thus found new employment in Rangoon.[9]

By coincidence, when in Burma, Tan was introduced to Xie
Guoliang 謝國良, a representative of the GMD government, who
was on his way to meet the Thirteenth Dalai Lama in Tibet.[10] When
it was decided that Xie would travel to Lhasa through India, the
Chinese consul-general in Calcutta recommended that Tan Yun-

shan assist the aging and frail envoy. Tan agreed, and on 18 November 1930 he joined Xie in Kalimpong for their trip to Tibet. On the way, Xie died and Tan had to complete the mission. He also had to submit the official report about the mission to the GMD government, for which reason he returned to China in 1931 (Zhu 2006: 107–116; Tsui 2010: 357).[11] This episode brought Tan into direct contact with high-level GMD officials and eventually helped him secure funds for the establishment of Cheena Bhavana from the Nationalist government in China.[12]

Brian Tsui (2010) has demonstrated the political networking masterminded by Tan Yunshan that resulted in the establishment of Cheena Bhavana in 1937. But, as discussed below, Tan's Buddhist leanings and connections must also be taken into account when analyzing his role in procuring funds for and promoting India-China interactions through Cheena Bhavana. Before returning to China, Tan met Mahatma Gandhi and delivered a letter that the Dalai Lama had asked him to carry to the Indian leader. In China, Tan wrote several articles on Tibet, his travels in India, Gandhi, and Buddhism. By 1933, he was able to convince Dai Jitao, the then president of the Examination Yuan and a fellow Buddhist, to support closer ties between India and China. Dai not only accepted the position of "chief supervisor" of the Sino-Indian Cultural Society that Tan Yunshan initiated in Nanjing in 1933, but he also secured recurring funds and a large donation of Chinese books for the establishment of Cheena Bhavana. Tsui (2010: 360) has suggested that Dai's involvement in the projects initiated by Tan may have been connected to forging GMD alliances with members of the INC.

In 1934, Tagore drafted a concept note for building a "Chinese Hall" in Shantiniketan, in which he offered "hospitality" to the Sino-Indian Cultural Society at Visva-Bharati. "It is my hope," Tagore wrote, "that my Chinese friends will heartily welcome the Society and give generous help to my friend Prof. Tan Yun-Shan to realize the scheme of making it a permanent organisation for facilitating closer cultural contact between China and India" (see figure 4.1). Despite its claim to be "nonpolitical," the Sino-Indian Cultural Society, an Indian chapter of which was founded in 1934 with Rabindranath Tagore as the "founder-president," was, as Tsui (2010: 360) argues, "unmistakably a product of the vicissitudes of Asia's two biggest nationalist movements." The list of "honorary presidents" of the society included Mahatma Gandhi, Chiang Kai-shek, Jawaharlal Nehru, and Madame Chiang Kai-shek (National Archives, File 329-X, 1943). However, two other important members of the society were Dai Jitao and Chen Lifu 陳立夫 (1900–2001), who were not only members of the GMD but also advocates of the pan-Asianism ideology and civilizational dialogue. While the former had, in 1930, established an institute and a journal called *Xin Yaxiya* 新亞細亞 (New Asia) to advance the ideas of Sun Yat-sen,[13] the latter was the theorist of the New Life movement and promoted the idea of the "Great Unity" (*datong* 大同) of Asian and Western civilizations (Duara 2003: 102).

The Chinese government and individuals largely funded the Sino-Indian Cultural Society and the Cheena Bhavana. Chiang Kai-shek provided the seed money for Cheena Bhavana in 1935, on request from Dai Jitao, and gave further donations to the institution in 1942, 1945, and 1946. The government of China also contributed by sponsoring five "Chinese Culture Fellowships," and the Chinese Ministry of Education offered "special" three-year grants to the Cheena Bhavana and the Sino-Indian Cultural Society. Dai Jitao, H. H. Kung, and a Singaporean named Chen Yen-chien 陈延谦 gave individual donations. Indians, however, contributed only meager sums to the institution, with the industrialist J. K. Birla providing a few thousand rupees. Although deriving from Rabindranath Tagore's vision, Cheena Bhavana was clearly a Chinese-funded project. According to Tan (1998: 128), it was "a gift of the Chinese people to Gurudeva in response to his appeal and in appreciation of

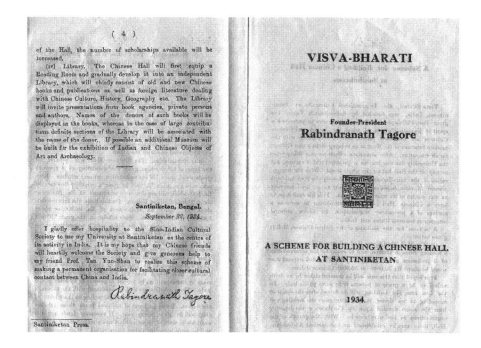

Figure 4.1. Cover page of Rabindranath Tagore's proposal for Cheena Bhavana.

his ideals for reviving the ancient Sino-Indian cultural relationship on one hand and to create new relations between the two countries on the other, and lastly to work together for world peace and fraternity mainly through cultural exchange."[14]

Jawaharlal Nehru was supportive of the project almost from its inception. In 1937, Nehru, who was then the president of the All-India National Congress, was invited to preside over the inauguration of the Cheena Bhavana. When he was unable to make the trip due to sudden illness, his daughter Indira Gandhi, a student of Visva-Bharati and later the prime minister of India, read the message from Nehru at the ceremony. Regretting that he was unable to attend the ceremony, Nehru stated, "I am ashamed that physical illness should incapacitate me from keeping my promise and being present at Shantiniketan tomorrow for the inauguration ceremony of the Chinese Hall." He continued, "I would join in the great ceremony, great in the memories of the long past that it invokes, great also in the promise of future comradeship and the forging of new links to bring China and India nearer to each other" (Tan 1957: 16). Two years later, in 1939, when Nehru visited China, he met Zhu Jiahua (Chu Jia-hua) 朱家驊 (1893–1963), a member of the Central Executive Committee of the GMD and the chairman of the Sino-Indian Cultural Society. The two discussed various ways in which India and China could cooperate in the fields of education, tourism, and industry. Zhu followed up this meeting with a letter to Jawaharlal Nehru in November 1939 in which he highlighted the initiation of the exchange of professors, who would hold chairs at various universities in the two countries; the exchange of students; and the translation and publication of various works in Chinese and Hindustani (Nehru [1958] 1960: 405–406). A month before he wrote to Nehru, Zhu had coauthored, with Chen Lifu, the then education minister of China and the standing director of the Sino-Indian Cultural Society, a letter to Chiang Kai-shek in which they noted that the Sino-Indian Cultural Society could be used as a "front organization" to promote contacts between the GMD and the INC "through seemingly benign religious, academic and education-al exchanges" (Tsui 2013: 242).

The Buddhist angle in the establishment of Cheena Bhavana and the India-China exchanges in the 1930s and 1940s was not as "be-nign" as Zhu Jiahua and Chen Lifu seem to be indicating to Chiang Kai-shek. Both Tan Yunshan and Dai Jitao were lay Buddhists and saw Buddhism, similar to the generation of pan-Asianists before them, as a key link to Asian unity. Sometime in the early 1920s, the Chinese Buddhist monk Taixu, who was to play a significant role in the revival of Buddhism in China and would, as discussed below, visit India on a "goodwill mission" in 1940, had "baptized" Tan Yunshan (Tsui 2010: 356). It is likely that Tan's decision to go to India in 1928 was connected to his religious faith,[15] which is evident in the two travelogues and several articles he wrote shortly after his pilgrimage to various Buddhist sites in India in 1930. His initial assessment of the Thirteenth Dalai Lama may also have been influenced by the shared belief in Buddhism. In an article published in August 1931, Tan wrote that he found the Dalai to be "both moderate and reasonable" and noted, "I will refuse to believe the allegation that his honeycoated words were designed to conceal his ill-natured heart." With regard to the relationship between Tibet and China, he wrote, "Rather than blame the Dalai Lama, we should blame the incompetency of our Government and officials for the past position of impasse." Tan further proposed that, "while on the one hand we should make every preparation on our part to take Tibet into our fold again, we must address the Dalai Lama a proposal agreeable to us and acceptable to Tibet on the other hand. I am decidedly of the opinion that the Dalai Lama will not offer any insurmountable difficulties in the way of a full reconciliation."[16] Later, when he settled in India, Tan was actively involved in the activities of the Maha Bodhi Society in Calcutta and at Sarnath and oversaw the construction and renovation of several "Chinese" Buddhist temples in India.

Dai Jitao was similarly an avid believer in Buddhism and often invoked the religion in diplomatic discourse with Tibetan leaders (Tuttle 2005: 172–176). In his letter to Rabindranath Tagore written from the Buddhist Association of China in Nanjing in 1933, Tan first informed the Nobel laureate of his success in procuring funds to establish Cheena Bhavana through Dai's help and then noted Dai's intention of building, with his own funds, a Buddhist temple in Rajgir with assistance from Shantiniketan. Dai Jitao, Tan wrote, "is a Chinese sage and great Buddhist scholar" (Hu 2012: 39). Together, Dai, Taixu, and Tan used Buddhism to foster political ties between the GMD and members of the INC and shared an interest in integrating Tibet (trips to which, it should be noted, frequently transited through British India and often involved negotiations with British officials) into the Chinese Republic. The three were also intimately involved in soliciting help from foreign governments in China's war against the Japanese.

Shortly after the Japanese launched a full-scale invasion of China, a few months after the inauguration of the Cheena Bhanava, Tan left for China. There, he seems to have been engaged in consultation with GMD leaders about gaining the support of the INC in the anti-Japanese war. Prior to his departure from India, Tan had already started communicating with Nehru and other Indian leaders about the need to jointly oppose Japanese imperialism. In early 1939, Tagore urged Tan to return to India. "The battle-field is hardly a place for a scholar," Tagore wrote in one of his letters to Tan, "and possibly you would be able to do greater service for the country by being in India and in disseminating true news about the Sino-Japanese conflict here, which is everyday becoming more and more necessary in view of the ever progressing Japanese propaganda" (Tan 1998: 135–136).

Tan Yunshan returned to India soon after he received this letter and started writing a series of articles in Indian newspapers and magazines underscoring the need for joint military action against the Japanese. Pointing to the "chaotic situation" in India caused by the anti-British Quit India Movement launched in 1942 by the INC, he wrote (Tan 1944: 38), "The present political and chaotic situation in India cannot in any case be any more prolonged and should not be allowed to last longer. It will do good to nobody but help the common enemy. It will serve neither the purpose of Great Britain nor the purpose of India, but will be a tempting invitation to the aggressive and avaricious Japanese Militarists." Additionally, Tan organized a series of photo exhibitions on Japanese atrocities in China.

Before joining Cheena Bhavana as the inaugural director and prior to Japanese military expansion in China, Tan actively expressed his views on Chinese society and politics, in addition to publishing essays on India, Visva-Bharati, and Buddhism. In an article published in 1930, for example, Tan was critical of the Chinatown in Calcutta, which, according to him, like other Chinatowns, portrayed an inaccurate and negative image of Chinese civilization (Tan 1930). Between 1931 and 1933, he wrote several essays on Tibet and at least one on Xinjiang, where he argued for the integration of these territories within the Chinese Republic. After joining Cheena Bhavana, however, Tan never expressed similar views in his lectures or writings; instead he focused on composing short articles and pamphlets on the ancient interactions between India and China and those that called for an India-China alliance against Japanese imperialism. Most of his publications in India (some of which were translated into Hindi and Bengali) were of a laudatory nature, inspired by the romanticism of pan-Asianism and influenced by civilizational discourse. They were primarily meant for general audiences and offered little critical analysis of sources or events. They presented the development of Buddhism in China as a consequence of the "dialogue" primarily between "Indians" and "Chinese,"[17] neglecting the agency of the Singhalese, Sogdians, and other groups of people in the transmission of Buddhist doctrines to Han and post-Han China. These writings also failed to effectively deal with the diversity of Buddhist practices and connections in areas such as the modern-day Xinjiang, Tibet, and Yunnan regions, important sites of interactions that mostly remained outside the control of the imperial courts located in the Yellow River Valley.

Tan's writings furthered the agenda of the pan-Asianists and the nationalists who wanted to promote the historical interactions among Asian societies within the nation-state framework. Additionally, because of his Buddhist and political networking, Tan was able to successfully transform Cheena Bhavana and Shantiniketan more generally into a site of educational, cultural, and diplomatic interactions between India and China. Visitors to Cheena Bhavana included Chiang Kai-shek; Dai Jitao; Taixu; W. Pachow 巴宙 (1918–) , a graduate of the Chinese-Tibetan Buddhist College in Shanghai; and several Buddhist monks, such as Wu Baihui 巫白慧 (1919–) and Fafang 法舫 (1905–1951), both disciples of Taixu. There were other Chinese students, teachers, and artists, including Xu Beihong 徐悲鴻 (1895–1953), who sought refuge during the Japanese invasion or were drawn to Shantiniketan because of the presence of Tan Yunshan and Rabindranath Tagore. The connections that Tan helped to nurture were not only with China but also extended to Burma, Singapore, and Sri Lanka.

Cheena Bhavana also facilitated a close collaboration between Sinologists and the members of the Greater India Society. Kshitimohan Sen (1880–1960) and Kalidas Nag (1892–1966), two scholars who had visited China in 1924 with Tagore, were close associates within the Greater India Society and friends of Tan Yunshan. Kalidas Nag in particular, a student of Sylvain Lévi and one of the founders of the Greater India Society, worked with Tan to promote interactions between India and China and wrote essays and articles on ancient India-China exchanges. In his edited volume *Tagore and China*, published in 1945 and dedicated to Chiang Kai-shek and his wife, Kalidas Nag wrote about a "Sino-Indian civilisation" of the past (Nag 1945: 31) and called upon Indians and Chinese to "exert themselves to the utmost cause of freedom for all mankind, for only in a free world," he wrote (Nag 1945: 34), "could the Chinese and Indian peoples obtain their freedom."

Like Nag, P. C. Bagchi had also received training in France under Sylvain Lévi and was a member of the Greater India Society.[18] His dissertation on two Sanskrit–Chinese lexicons was completed in 1926 at the University of Paris. A year later the first volume of his study of the Chinese Buddhist canon and translators of Indian Buddhist texts (Bagchi 1927–1938) was published in French. In the same year, he (Bagchi 1927) wrote an essay titled "India and China: A Thousand Years of Cultural Relations" for the

Greater India Society Bulletin. The article was later revised and published in book form in 1944, with several editions appearing thereafter. After working at the University of Calcutta, Bagchi joined Visva-Bharati in 1945 in a post that was funded by the government of China (Tan 1998: 120). In 1947, Bagchi went to China as a professor of Indology and worked at Peking University for about two years.

While Kalidas Nag's writings on India-China interactions were comparable in spirit and objective to those of Tan Yunshan, the publications of Bagchi differed from Tan's in at least two important ways. First, as a member of the Greater India Society, Bagchi often presented the interactions between ancient India and China within the ideological context of the organization. In 1944, for instance, he noted (Bagchi [1944] 2012: 179) that the "cultural expansion" of the Indian and Chinese "zones" of interaction "produced what may be called a Greater China (Maha-China) and a Greater India (Maha-Bharat)." Second, unlike Tan Yunshan, Bagchi published a significant number of academic books and articles on diverse topics. This latter aspect is also evident in the two very different types of journals that Tan and Bagchi launched in Shantiniketan. Tan's *Sino-Indian Journal*, "an organ of the Sino-Indian Cultural Society," sought to promote "understanding and co-operation" and "welfare" between India and China. Bagchi's *Sino-Indian Studies*, on the other hand, was a scholarly journal without any of the propagandist writings found in the former.[19] Although very different as far as their scholarly output and wider agendas were concerned, Tan and Bagchi concurred on the oneness of Asia through the union of India and China. Their contributions made Cheena Bhavana a site where the nationalistic, pan-Asiatic, anti-Japanese, Buddhist, and academic ideas and agendas of Indians and Chinese fused, evolved, and spread to different parts of the world.

The period between 1945 and 1949 was a decisive phase for advocates of pan-Asianism, especially those highlighting the role of India and China within it. Japanese imperialism had ended by this time, while India gained independence (in 1947) and the People's Republic of China was founded (in 1949). However, it was also a period marked by civil wars, border disputes, and struggles to resolve issues related to the sovereignty of regions that were previously located on the peripheries of empires. Under British imperialism and the threat of Japanese military expansion, the political leaders of the INC and the GMD were able to put aside contentious issues such as those related to Chinese-claimed sovereignty/suzerainty over Tibet. Scholars at Cheena Bhavana also avoided examining these controversial topics and declined to engage with writings and views, such as those of M. N. Roy (1887–1954), that dealt with the complex struggle between the Nationalists and the Communists in China.[20] Decolonization, the formation of territorialized nation-states, and the debates about national, cultural, and diasporic identities made the task of these idealistic political leaders and scholars more complicated and, eventually, untenable.

In the eight years of its existence, from 1937 to 1945, Cheena Bhavana produced several pamphlets (primarily written by Tan Yunshan) focusing mainly on historical interactions between India and China. Other than some essays about the situation during the Japanese occupation, nothing was written about the Chinese civil war between the GMD and the Chinese Communist Party.[21] Given the fact that Cheena Bhavana was funded by the GMD, it is not surprising that a detailed analysis of the topic was avoided. In the foreword to the inaugural issue of the *Sino-Indian Journal* in 1947,[22] Tan wrote (1947: ii), "We would like to publish from time to time articles of technical research and would also entertain thoughtful surveys, interpretations and critical estimates of current Sino-Indian problems of a non-controversial and non-political nature." Even in September 1949, when the brutal war between the Communists and the GMD was reaching its climax and sectarian violence between the supporters of the two factions disrupted the Chinese diasporic community in Calcutta (Zhang and Sen 2013: 223–224), Tan refused to discuss or take a stand on the civil war in China.[23] Instead, he produced a pamphlet titled "Ahimsa in Sino-Indian Culture." He noted (Tan 1998: 61) that the idea of *ahimsa* was "one of the cardinal virtues and doctrines" of China as it was with India.[24] In the same pamphlet, Tan (1998: 71) wrote that India and China "have never attacked or invaded any other country, never exploited any other people, though they have often been attacked, invaded and exploited by other warlike peoples."

Tan's role as a scholar was restrained not only because of the source of funding for Cheena Bhavana and his association with the leading members of the GMD government, but also because of his strong advocacy for friendly and cordial relations between India and China. The latter may also have been the reason he avoided writing about Tibet when in India. Moreover, increasingly after the end of World War II, his writings were influenced by his Buddhist faith. It is likely that Tan believed that he was continuing the work of Rabindranath Tagore and other pan-Asianists in establishing, as he wrote in his article on *ahimsa*, "a common culture called Sino-Indian Culture, entirely based on Ahimsa." Ultimately this common culture, he explained, would "lead the world to real and permanent peace, love, harmony, and happiness!"

Tan's writings and opinions may have been further complicated by the fact that in 1948 he was formally appointed as the "cultural representative" of China in India. According to Brian Tsui (2013: 231), "this allowed the idealistic academic to project his travels between India and China through the heavily contested geopolitical space of Tibet as instances of pure civilizational dialogue." Tsui also argues (2013: 231n.42) that Tan's official position was placed under the Ministry of Education rather than the Ministry of Foreign Affairs, "probably out of the consideration that a formal diplomatic appointment would have compromised Tan's apolitical identity."

The intelligence community in India (both during British rule and under the independent Indian government) was suspicious of the activities at Cheena Bhavana and especially the role Tan Yunshan had assumed. Already in 1925–1926, prior to the establishment of the institution, there had been a suspicion about Lim Ngo Chiang as "the link between revolutionaries of Bengal and China" (West Bengal State Archives, File 285A/25, Serial No. 117).[25] The Bengal Intelligence Branch had started compiling files on Cheena Bhavana (West Bengal State Archives, File 628/40, Serial No. 129) and Tan Yunshan (West Bengal State Archives, File 120/41, Serial No. 1) in 1940 and 1941, respectively. In 1945, one of the intelligence reports (West Bengal State Archives, File 1393/43, Serial No. 116, Part VI) noted that Tan had become a life member of the Maha Bodhi Society and observed that he appeared to be a "very definite politician." The report further commented, "[H]ere is a first class example of a man working for his government under the cloak of missionary or cultural activities."[26]

Another report expressed concern about the network of GMD offices in India and the activities of Chinese intelligence groups and pointed to the role of Tan Yunshan in establishing close cultural contacts between India and China. Nehru (1984: 462–463) responded to this report, saying that the GMD was an official organization of the Chinese and it was natural for them to organize branches across India. With regard to Tan Yunshan, he noted that "organizations to further Indo-Chinese relations have to be encouraged and have in fact been encouraged in the past. Professor Tan Yunshan has been prominent in these organizations and is the head of the China Hall in Shantiniketan. Dr. Rabindranath Tagore was a patron of this and I believe I am also a patron. In fact I performed the opening ceremony some years ago." Despite this statement, surveillance of Tan Yunshan and his family continued after the independence of India. In fact, the above intelligence file on him contains reports well into the 1960s.

RENEWING BUDDHIST CONNECTIONS

Cheena Bhavana was not the only organization in India that fostered interactions between Indian and Chinese intellectuals and facilitated anti-Japanese collaborations in the early 1940s. The Maha Bodhi Society, with its headquarters in Calcutta, also played an appreciable role in these interactions. This organization was specifically involved with the visit of two leading representatives from China in 1940, the monk Taixu and the GMD official Dai Jitao. These visits took place when the GMD was using diplomatic means to establish an anti-Japanese front in Asia. Indeed, the visits took place during the critical period for the Chinese and Indians in their respective struggles against imperialism. While Indians were trying to end almost two centuries of British rule, the Chinese found themselves facing brutal Japanese military expansion. In this period of anti-imperialism, Buddhism offered the possibility of reconnecting the two regions, which had witnessed vigorous cultural and commercial exchanges in the past. Although Buddhism had weakened in India and China several centuries earlier, the developing sense of Asianism in the early twentieth century, as pointed out above, resulted in the invocation of ancient Buddhist connections as a model for new Asia. It was within this context that Taixu led a goodwill mission to South Asia in early 1940, and in November–December of the same year, Dai Jitao toured several sacred Buddhist sites in India and met British officials and the leaders of the Indian National Congress.

It should be noted that the GMD also used Islamic networks to create an anti-Japanese coalition with countries in South, Southeast, and West Asia. The use of Islam was likewise an effort to consolidate the GMD's power within China, especially with the Muslim warlords, and to promote patriotism among the Muslim population within China (Mao 2011: 380–381). It was because of these considerations that the GMD quickly approved the 1937 proposal by Ma Tianying 馬天英, a Muslim businessman in China, to dispatch a "Chinese Muslim Delegation to the Near East." The delegation, consisting of five members, left Hong Kong on 8 January 1938 and traveled through Southeast Asia to Mecca, Egypt, Turkey, Lebanon, Syria, Iraq, Iran, and India. Already in Hong Kong, the delegation encountered the trans-Asian Indian Islamic network when the members attended a reception at a local mosque that was built by Indian migrants. They also note that they ate at an Indian Muslim restaurant in Saigon, met with members of the Indian Muslim Association in Sri Lanka, and had a discussion with an Indian Muslim leader in Mecca. It was on their way back to China that the delegation spent over one hundred days in India. Starting with Bombay, the members traveled by train to Agra, Lucknow, Patna, and Calcutta. They met several Muslim leaders, including M. A. Jinnah; held gatherings with various Islamic organizations across India; and visited the Chinese communities in Calcutta and Bombay. At all meetings with Indian Muslim organizations and leaders, according to the records compiled by Wang Zengshan 王曾善, the delegation received support for China's fight against Japanese imperialism and its calls for greater collaboration between the Muslim communities in the two countries (Wang 1997).

The goodwill mission of Taixu, however, involved an even greater engagement with Indian organizations and political leadership than did the above Muslim delegation. It also led to an intimate relationship between the Maha Bodhi Society and the Chinese Buddhist community through 1949. In fact, the attempt to renew the relationship between the Buddhist communities in India and China had started when Angarika Dharmapala visited China in 1893. Dharmapala, the Sinhalese founder of the Maha Bodhi Society, asked the Chinese Buddhists present at a meeting near Shanghai to show their "support and sympathy for the rehabilitation" of Buddhism in India. "India gave you her religion," he remarked, "now I appeal to you to help her in her hour of need" (Pittman

2001: 43). Yang Wenhui 杨文会 (1837–1911), Dharmapala's host and the future teacher of Taixu, in response suggested the possibility of recruiting Indian monks for studies in China, "in order to prepare them for subsequent mission work among their own people" (Pittman 2001: 44). Although such collaboration does not seem to have materialized, Dharmapala's visit to China eventually resulted in the establishment of contacts between the Maha Bodhi Society and members of the Chinese Buddhist community. Taixu, for example, became a member of the society in 1928 and subsequently a life member and a patron.

As a result of these past connections between the Maha Bodhi Society and the Chinese Buddhist community, Taixu's goodwill mission to India featured prominently in the *Maha-Bodhi: The Journal of the Maha Bodhi Society*. In its November 1939 issue, the journal announced the forthcoming visit by Taixu to Burma, India, Sri Lanka, and Siam. It included the following message by Taixu to the Chinese overseas communities in these countries:

> The visit has been planned at the request of the devotees of Buddhist shrines in China and the Chinese scattered overseas. We propose to visit Buddhist sites in Burma, Siam, India and Ceylon, to make contact with leaders of Buddhist thought in these various places and hold conferences for the study and discussion of Buddhism. We also hope to have opportunities to explain, according to views of Buddhism, how China is defending her independence and very existence; and how the Buddhists in China have achieved complete unanimity in regard to this struggle. I wish to add that through our co-operation in the national struggle Buddhism has won national esteem. This esteem is bound to result in positive gains on the day of victory.[27]

Although Taixu writes that the mission was "planned" by Buddhist institutions in China, it was in fact sponsored and instigated by the GMD government in order to garner support for the anti-Japanese war. The Chinese overseas were important contributors to the 1911 revolution led by Sun Yat-sen. The Chiang Kai-shek–led GMD government hoped to also receive financial and other logistical support from the diasporic communities in the war against the Japanese. Furthermore, the GMD government, and Chiang Kai-shek in particular, desperately wanted the leaders of the Indian freedom movement to support the Allied forces in World War II. Thus, in addition to visiting various Buddhist pilgrimage sites in India, Taixu made it a point to meet not only the members of the Chinese overseas communities but also the leaders of the Indian National Congress. He frequently updated the GMD government about these meetings and the progress of his goodwill mission.

On 17 October 1939, Taixu sent a letter to his disciple Tan Yunshan, informing him about his forthcoming visits to Burma and India. It is likely that Taixu's itinerary in India and his meetings with Indian political leaders, visits to Buddhist sites, and lectures may have all been arranged by Tan. On 2 January 1940, Tan wrote to Jawaharlal Nehru informing him of the arrival of Taixu and sought an appointment for the goodwill mission. Nehru responded three days later, saying that he would be willing to meet Taixu later that month in Allahabad. He added, "We hope that his visit to India will lead to a closer collaboration, cultural and otherwise, between our great countries. For him India can be no strange land for he comes to a country which is full of the sacred places and traditions of the great faith which he represents."[28]

On 6 December 1939, Taixu and his entourage arrived at Rangoon, Burma, through the Yunnan–Burma land road. In Burma, Taixu delivered lectures at various gatherings of Chinese overseas, met with members of the local Buddhist communities, visited sacred Buddhist sites, and also had discussions with Indian immigrants. Taixu stayed in Burma for a little over a month, during which time he held several consultative meeting with GMD representatives in Rangoon. At one of the meetings, a GMD representative expressed his hope that Taixu's trip would unify the Buddhist communities of India and Burma against the Japanese monks who had collaborated with the army and were "accessories to murder and killing of innocent people." Without mentioning the role of Japanese monks, Taixu responded by noting that the Buddhist community would do its utmost to bring "world peace" (*Taixu dashi quanshu* 19: 31).

On the morning of 9 January 1940, Taixu's delegation, consisting of five people, boarded a ship at Rangoon to travel to Calcutta. On the ship, Taixu met P. C. Bagchi, who was then returning from Rangoon. The two discussed the visit of Jawaharlal Nehru to Chongqing in 1939, the activities of the Indian medical mission led by Dr. D. Mukherjee, and various aspects of Buddhist teachings. Taixu noted that he had met Nehru and Mukherjee in China and hoped Bagchi could one day go there to teach.[29]

After three days of sailing, on 11 January, Taixu arrived in Calcutta. Several hundred people went to the harbor to receive the Chinese delegation, including the leaders of all major Buddhist organizations based in Calcutta, the Chinese consul-general and other officials from the Chinese consulate, heads of Chinese schools and associations, reporters, Tan Yunshan and his wife, and over two hundred members of the Chinese overseas community. Taixu was told that Mahatma Gandhi, Nehru, and Subhas Chandra Bose had sent welcome messages to the Chinese Buddhist delegation through Tan Yunshan.

During his forty-five-day stay in India (11 January–22 February), Taixu traveled to several cities and Buddhist pilgrimage sites, delivered lectures at key secular and religious institutions, and had in-depth discussions with political and Buddhist leaders of India. He spent the first week in Calcutta, followed by several days in Shantiniketan. At a talk that outlined the important doctrinal issues in Mahayana Buddhism, Taixu began his lecture by mentioning that

[t]he present century is the century of spiritual re-awakening of
India when the whole nation is reviving its ancient glory. Modern Indian culture is India's original culture infused with the
culture of the West and in my opinion Gurudeva is the best
representative of the culture and civilization of India to-day.
(Sarkar 1940: 315–316)

Between 24 January and 6 February, the delegation toured Buddhist pilgrimage sites at Bodh Gaya, Nālandā, Lumbini, Sarnath,
and Benaras. On 7 February, they arrived in Lucknow, from which
they proceeded to Agra, Mathura, Bhopal, and Sanchi, and they
reached Wardha on 12 February. After having an audience with
Mahatma Gandhi, the delegation went to Ajanta and finally to
Bombay (now Mumbai). After a weeklong stay in Bombay, on 23
February, the delegation departed for Sri Lanka to continue their
goodwill mission.

One of the first things the Chinese Buddhist delegation noticed
upon their arrival in Calcutta was the dearth of Buddhist monks and
monuments. Compared to Burma, the members exclaimed, "there
were very few Buddhist monks; it was also not easy to spot pago-
das and monasteries" (*Taixu dashi quanshu* 19: 39). Taixu and
other members of the delegation considered this clear evidence of
the demise of Buddhism in India. In almost every speech he delivered in India, Taixu made it a point to mention the status of
Buddhism in India and expressed his hope that the doctrine would
one day revive in its birthplace. In fact, on several occasions he
stressed that Chinese Buddhists had an important role to play in this
"revival" of Buddhism in India.

The themes associated with Buddhism in China, its revival in
India, the reestablishment of cultural interactions between India
and China, and the anti-Japanese war were the main elements of
Taixu's first speech in India.[30] It was delivered at a banquet organized by the Chinese overseas community in Calcutta at the Chinese Club on 12 January. The title of his talk was "The Present

Situation of Buddhism in China." Buddhism in China, Taixu explained, had declined under the Qing Empire. Since Buddhist monasteries and monks could not contribute to modern society, the doctrine was considered obsolete and irrelevant. People perceived monks as profit oriented and Buddhist teachings as mere superstitions. But Buddhism in China, he argued, was "back on the track of revival" because of appropriate propaganda work, renewed stress on the education of monks, the establishment of various Buddhist organizations, and participation of the *sangha* in social welfare. Taixu also credited the Nationalist government in China with protecting and supporting Buddhism, a point he made several times during his GMD-sponsored mission.

The idea of establishing a branch of the Chinese Buddhist Association in India, which was mentioned by the Chinese consul-general in his welcome address, was fully supported by Taixu in his speech. He noted that the establishment of such an organization would help the Chinese immigrant community improve their knowledge of Buddhism. He also pointed out that the Sri Lankans and Burmese had their own Buddhist organizations in India. A similar Chinese Buddhist organization, he suggested, could jointly work with these and other Indian Buddhist associations to improve the standing and image of Buddhism in the world.[31]

In his lecture at the Maha Bodhi Society in Calcutta the following day, Taixu noted that Buddhism in India was no longer flourishing as before, "but the spirit of Buddhism fills the hearts of every person. The Bengal Buddhist Association, the Maha Bodhi Society and others are making efforts to revive Buddhism." He added, "I think India will soon become the center of world Buddhism." He explained that while the Chinese clergy fully supported the efforts of the Maha Bodhi Society, they could not be of much help because China was going through a "difficult phase." The revival of Buddhism in China itself, he said, would have to wait until this "difficult phase" was over.[32] The reference here, no doubt, was to the Japanese invasion of China.

The reception at the Maha Bodhi Society was presided over by the mayor of Calcutta, N. C. Sen, who welcomed Taixu by pointing out the intimate cultural and spiritual contacts between India and China during the precolonial period. He also noted the fact that a medical mission had been sent by the Indian National Congress to help China in its war against Japan. The general secretary, Devapriya Valisinha, delivered the welcome address on behalf of the members of the Maha Bodhi Society. The address embraced Taixu "as one of us" and thanked him for his earlier donations toward the construction of the Mulagandhakuti Vihara in Sarnath. It also sympathized with the Chinese people during their period of crisis, expressing the hope that it "will soon be over and China will again be in a position to play her glorious part for the welfare of the entire human race." At the conclusion of the reception, Taixu presented a silver pagoda gifted by Chiang Kai-shek to the Maha Bodhi Society as "a token of China's Goodwill."[33]

Taixu attended several other receptions in Calcutta hosted by local organizations and had meetings with leading members of the society such as Maharaja Pradyot Kumar Tagore, Subhas Chandra Bose, and Jugol Kishore Birla. After these meetings, Taixu traveled to Shantiniketan to meet with Rabindranath Tagore. His next grand reception was in Benares, where he attended the Asoka Day celebrations with Jawaharlal Nehru on 31 January.

Taixu reached Benares on 29 January and was welcomed at the railway station by members of the Maha Bodhi Society, the Benares Congress Committee, and the Hindu Maha Sabha, in addition to other organizations and "hundreds of citizens."[34] The following day, Taixu and other members of the goodwill mission visited Sarnath, where he suggested the establishment of a committee to work toward the restoration of Buddhist sacred sites in India. On the same day, Taixu decided to become a life member of the Maha

Bodhi Society and promised to "continue to co-operate with the Society in its work for the resuscitation of Buddhism in India."[35]

On the morning of 31 January, Jawaharlal Nehru traveled from his residence in Allahabad to Sarnath to welcome the Chinese mission. Nehru and Taixu had a two-hour-long meeting that morning, during which the Buddhist monk stressed the fact that the Chinese did not have adequate knowledge of contemporary India. Taixu told Nehru that he hoped that some cultural aspects of modern India could be transmitted to China and at the same time Chinese Mahayana teachings could be translated and reintroduced to India. He added that the Chinese could also introduce to India the "spirit of anti-colonial war and nation building." Additionally, Taixu sought Nehru's support for the revival of Buddhist pilgrimage sites in India and the establishment of an international Buddhist university. These two ventures, Taixu pointed out, were closely linked to the future collaboration among Buddhist countries in Asia. Nehru responded by noting that the INC had in fact taken up the issue of reviving the Buddhist pilgrimage sites before the resignation of their members from the government (in protest at the unilateral British decision to announce India's participation in World War II). The Indian National Congress, he explained, had many other tasks at that time. There were also legal issues related to the ownership of property that had to be sorted out at some of the pilgrimage sites. With regard to the idea of an international Buddhist University, Nehru said that funds had to be raised first before establishing such an institution (*Taixu dashi quanshu* 17: 11–12).

Following the meeting, Nehru and Taixu traveled together to Benares to attend the Asoka Day celebrations. The *Maha-Bodhi* reports the grand reception the two received when entering the city:

It was truly a royal welcome that the citizens of Benares accorded to the Mission under the inspiration of Pandit Jawaharlal Nehru. From Dasasumedh Ghat the members of the Mission were taken to the Town Hall in a grand procession organised for

their welcome and for the observance of the Asoka Day. His
Holiness Tai Hsu and Pandit Jawaharlal Nehru sat in the same
carriage while the rest of the party as well as several prominent
citizens and Buddhist monks were also accommodated in other
carriages. Buddhist emblems, Congress flags, sayings of Asoka
written on placards and the yellow robes of the monks lent vivid
colour to the procession. His Holiness and Pandit Nehru were
profusely garlanded. The procession, after passing through various thorough-fares, entered the Town Hall grounds where arrangements had been made for a mass meeting. The roads
through which the procession passed and the shops on both sides
were decorated with triumphal arches and garlands. The crowds
were so dense that it was with difficulty that the procession
reached its destination where nearly 40,000 people were waiting
to take part.[36]

Acharya Narendra Dev, the president of the Town Congress
Committee; Nehru; and Taixu all gave speeches at the event. All
three emphasized the friendly relations between India and China in
the past and the need to strengthen them in the present. "The day is
not far distant," remarked Taixu as he thanked his hosts, "when the
cultural relations existing between India and China in the days of
Huen Tsang will be re-established between these two countries."[37]

Taixu repeated these words at a lecture he gave at the Benares
Hindu University the next day. Taixu noted that ancient India and
China had intimate cultural interactions, through which the Chinese
obtained in-depth knowledge of India. "But since there has been a
separation of around a thousand years," he said, "the Chinese need
to understand contemporary Indian culture." The Chinese should
also, he proposed, transmit back to India the teachings of
Nāgārjuna and others Buddhist philosophers that are preserved in
the translated texts (*Taixu dashi quanshu* 18).

The nostalgia for the ancient Buddhist links between India and
China and the prospects for reviving those links through the visit of
Taixu were apparent as the delegation toured various Buddhist

sites. Comparisons between Taixu's mission and the pilgrimage of Xuanzang in the seventh century were frequently drawn in welcome speeches and newspaper reports. Indeed, Taixu's journey through India was remarkably similar to that of Xuanzang in one aspect. Like Xuanzang, Taixu not only visited the sacred Buddhist sites but also had audiences with important Indian political leaders: Bose in Calcutta, Nehru in Benares, and Gandhi in Wardha. Xuanzang, for his part, was known for his intimate interactions with Harṣa, the king of Kanauj, and Bhāskaravarman, the ruler of Kāmarūpa. In addition, both Xuanzang and Taixu seem to have successfully accomplished their political pilgrimages and returned to China to promote Buddhist interactions between India and China.

On his way back to China, Taixu delivered a lecture in Singapore, where he summed up the aims and accomplishments of the goodwill mission that he had led in the following way:

> In Burma, we gave a detailed report on the situation in China with regard to the anti-Japanese war. This place (i.e., Burma) is intimately linked to the anti-Japanese war [effort]. International propaganda is either not easy or lacking. After our explanations, the Burmese have decided to form a delegation that will visit China. Later, after arriving in India, we undertook detailed discussion of cultural issues. I have now understood Indian culture and believe that Buddhism is the splendor of its ancient culture. But, in the midst of the past one thousand years, Indian culture witnessed a decline and we (i.e., China) also drifted afar, creating a deep divide between [the two countries]. . . . The aim to visit India was to study contemporary Indian culture and at the same time promote research of Chinese culture there. In Ceylon, the most important work of our Mission was to establish Buddhist links. . . . Ceylon is the thoroughfare to Europe and America and also a Buddhist country. In fact, since it is the best place to carry out international propaganda, there was a proposal to establish an International Buddhist Federation that would net-

work with the Buddhists in China. Preparations to start this [fed-
eration] have already begun. (*Taixu dashi quanshu* 18: 600)

Taixu ended his report by noting, "During this time of anti-
Japanese war, I hope Buddhist followers will greatly reform themselves, and, according to the needs of the times, support the government. After our victory against the Japanese, we can create a new
and invigorated nation and, at the same time, establish a new and
invigorated Buddhism. This will be of enormous benefit to our
people" (*Taixu dashi quanshu* 18: 601).

Indeed, the goodwill mission had significantly advanced many
of the objectives that Taixu was personally advocating in China:
making Buddhism relevant to contemporary domestic and international politics, creating an opportunity for Chinese Buddhist monks
to receive in-depth education about various societies and cultures,
and uniting the Buddhist community in Asia. Each of these aspects
continued to make progress after Taixu's return to China.

Less than nine months after the departure of the Taixu-led Chinese goodwill mission, Dai Jitao arrived in India. Dai was instrumental, as pointed out above, in raising funds for the establishment
of Cheena Bhavana that Rabindranath Tagore and Tan Yunshan
had envisioned. In fact, throughout the 1930s and 1940s Dai helped
find financial support for educational and Buddhist exchanges between India and China (Tsui 2010). He also made personal donations to various Buddhist institutions and organizations in India,
including the Maha Bodhi Society. Moreover, he played an important role in promoting political relations between the GMD and the
Indian National Congress.

Unlike Taixu's visit, Dai's trip to India was not an official
"goodwill mission," as was described in the Indian press (*Times of
India*, 30 November 1940).[38] In fact, there seems to have been
confusion among British officials about the purpose of his visit.
They were surprised and dismayed by the steps Tan Yunshan took
to arrange Dai's itinerary "from Madras to Kashmir" without con-

sulting either Dai or the Chinese consul-general in Calcutta. A confidential report by an agent of the Special Branch of the Calcutta police dated 29 October 1940 on Dai's planned visit pointed out that the consul-general was also upset with Tan's "unwarranted interference" in Dai's visit and even advised the Indian government to write and complain to the GMD government. The GMD authorities eventually clarified that Dai was going to India on his "own accord." On 3 December 1940, the Special Branch noted that Dai Jitao was "politely declining to answer questions of Press representatives at the Government House, Bombay, relating to the Chinese struggle, stating that the main object of his visit to India was to cement the bonds of friendship between China and India."[39]

Dai Jitao arrived in Calcutta on 3 November 1940 through Rangoon. In India he was enthusiastically received by the Indian Buddhist organizations, the intellectual community, and the members of the INC, including Mahatma Gandhi. On 14 November he traveled from Calcutta to Sarnath and then to Benaras, where Dr. B. V. Keskar welcomed Dai on behalf of the All-India Congress Committee. At a meeting in the city, Dai noted that "he was looking forward to meting [*sic*] the prominent people of India" and said that "he had brought a message of goodwill and friendship to the people of India and Congress from China."[40] On 15–16 November, Dai participated in a grand procession in Sarnath to mark the ninth anniversary of the establishment of the Mulagandhakuti Vihara.[41] After leaving Benares on 17 November, Dai reached Delhi via Agra. In Delhi, Dai and other members traveling with him met with Viceroy Victor Alexander John Hope, who invited him to a review and inspection of troops on 19 November and to the Legislative Assembly the following day. Dai also called on Muhammad Ali Jinnah and attended receptions organized by the Indian Religious Society and the local Chinese community. After Delhi, his itinerary included Wardha (where he met Gandhi), Bombay, Hyderabad, Ajanta, Ellora, Sanchi, and Darjeeling. In Shantiniketan he had an

audience with Rabindranath Tagore and visited the Cheena Bhavana (see figure 4.2). He could not, however, meet Jawaharlal Nehru,
who had been imprisoned by the British government. Even then,
Nehru issued a statement from prison for the Indian National Congress and other organizations to cordially receive the Chinese guest
(Bright 1947: 369–370). He also entrusted Dai with a letter for
Madame Chiang Kai-shek (Nehru [1958] 1960: 454–455).

At a reception organized in Bombay by the mayor of the city,
Dai described the "2,000-year-old relationship" between India and
China by noting that

> China was indebted to India not only for her religion and civil-
> ization but also for many other things. For instance, she learnt
> from India the system of phonetics, astrology, astronomy and

**Figure 4.2.   Dai Jitao in Shantiniketan. Courtesy of Rabindra-Bhava-
na Archives, Visva Bharati, Shantiniketan**

arithmetic. The people of both countries had, for centuries, braved the hazards of long journeys, and without any selfish motives, devoted their lives to cultivating friendship. Probably, the relationship between no other two countries had been so long and uninterrupted and amicable as between China and India. With improved facilities of communication, the friendship was bound to be more intimate." (*Times of India*, 30 November 1940: 10)

Dai returned to China on 14 December through Rangoon. On 26 December he sent a telegram from Rangoon thanking the All-India Congress Committee for hosting him at various Indian cities. He also expressed his regrets for not being able to meet Jawaharlal Nehru.[42]

Dai Jitao's mission cemented China's relations with the Maha Bodhi Society, helped the long-term finances of the Cheena Bhavana, and may have paved the way for Chiang Kai-shek's visit to India in 1942.[43] In fact, after Taixu and Dai Jitao's visits, Chinese monks, visitors, diplomatic representatives, and, in particular, Tan Yunshan became intimately involved with the activities of the Maha Bodhi Society. They frequently donated money to the organization, presided over various ceremonies, and contributed articles to the organization's journal, the *Maha-Bodhi*. In 1947, for instance, a few months before his death, Taixu wrote a letter to Ven. N. Jinaratana, the secretary of the Maha Bodhi Society, in response to the donations the latter sought to build an International Cultural Religious Center at the premises of the Maha Bodhi headquarters in Calcutta. The purpose of the center, Jinaratna explained, "was to accommodate those who engage in international cultural and religious activities and especially the professors, students etc. exchanged between India and China."[44]

Taixu informed Jinaratana that on his request, Chiang Kai-shek had agreed to donate Rs. 10,000 toward the cause. Recognizing his contribution, the Maha Bodhi Society decided to place a memorial tablet in honor of Taixu for its new annex building called the "China Block." The foundation-laying ceremony for the annex was performed by the Chinese consul-general, who noted that the "China Block will serve as a meeting place of Chinese and Indian scholars whereby the bond of friendship and cordiality existing between China and India will be further strengthened."[45] The ceremony took place six months after the death of Taixu. The Chinese monk was eulogized by the Maha Bodhi Society with several essays, including an obituary, dedicated to the life and contribution of Taixu in its May–June 1947 issue of the *Maha-Bodhi*.

For his part, Tan Yunshan continued to support Taixu's international mission by bringing several of his disciples to India. These included Fafang, Wu Baihui, and Zhou Xiangguang 周祥光 (1919–1963), all of whom studied and taught at Cheena Bhavana. All three seem to have been initially influenced by a speech Taixu delivered at the celebrations marking "India Day" in China on 17 March 1942. In the speech, Taixu outlined the ancient Buddhist links between the two regions, pointed to the exchanges between contemporary political leaders of the two countries, argued for the need to promote deeper understanding between the two peoples, and expressed his hope that after attaining independence, the two countries would together contribute to the betterment of the world (*Taixu dashi quanshu*). Fafang, Wu Baihui, and Zhou Xiangguang seem to have taken up this challenge of their master and traveled to India to fulfill his vision.

Similar to Tagore's visit to China in 1924, Taixu's goodwill mission to India in 1940 was an important event in the modern history of India-China interactions. While Tagore's visit contributed to the revival of cultural relations by triggering an interest in Indian literature in China, Taixu's trip helped revive the Buddhist links between the two countries. Many of Taixu's disciples were directly or indirectly responsible for fostering these links. They were, following Taixu's larger mission, trying to make Buddhism a socially and politically engaged religion. Indeed, in a vastly

changed world, when both India and China were occupied by imperial powers, Taixu had successfully presented Buddhism as a key
factor in fostering India-China relations and collaboration. These
exchanges, which not only involved the Buddhist communities but
also lay scholars and the political leaders of the two countries,
continued through to the establishment of the People's Republic of
China in 1949.

The fact that Taixu had left behind a deep impression on the
political leaders he met in India is clear from a letter Jawaharlal
Nehru wrote to his daughter Indira Gandhi a few days after his
meeting with Taixu in Sarnath. "Two hours were spent," Nehru
wrote, "in a laborious conversation with the mission and its leader,
the Rev. Abbot Tai Hsu. Laborious, because all conversations
through an interpreter are heavy and tiring. The old Abbot—but
was far from old looking—was delightful and had the face of a
cherub. The more I see of the Chinese the more I like them" (Nehru
1972: 651).[46]

TIBET AND THE FAILURE OF PAN-ASIANISM

The war against the Japanese, in addition to facilitating interactions
between the Buddhist communities in India and China, also resulted in closer cooperation between the INC and the GMD, fostered through the personal relationship between Jawaharlal Nehru
and Chiang Kai-shek. This rapport between the two leaders was
initiated in 1939, when Nehru visited Chongqing. The subsequent
visits of Taixu and Dai Jitao in 1940, and Chiang himself to India
in 1942, strengthened this relationship.[47] Even though Nehru and
Chiang had disagreements about the INC's support for the Allied
forces against the Japanese, the latter was a vehement advocate for
Indian independence (Yang 2015). This relationship started changing after the end of World War II. The disagreements over Tibet,
which emerged shortly after the war, made it difficult for the two to

jointly implement the ideas of Asian unity and solidarity, even though the rhetoric of India-China friendship continued. This discontent between India and China over the issue of Tibet and the problems of implementing the ideals of pan-Asianism were exposed at the Asian Relations Conference in 1947, organized at the behest of Jawaharlal Nehru and attended by Tan Yunshan as a representative of the Republic of China.

Between 1946 and 1949 there was a series of disagreements and contentions between the two governments about the issue of Chinese sovereignty over Tibet that indicated serious ruptures in the idealism underpinning pan-Asianism.[48] There were also major controversies involving alleged GMD spies, named as Ragpa Pandatshang (Goldstein 1989: 449–463) and F. M. Shen (West Bengal State Archives, File 923/44, Serial No. 302) based in Kalimpong in 1946–1947. This was perhaps one of the reasons the Intelligence Bureau was concerned about the activities of the Chinese in India, including those of Tan Yunshan. In fact, several Intelligence Bureau files, including that numbered 923/44, Serial No. 261, titled "Publication: Official. Tibetan Intelligence Report compiled by C.I.O. Assam," which extends to 1950, indicate that Tibet, the border areas between northeastern India and Tibet, and Chinese involvement in these regions were major concerns for the Indian intelligence community pre- and post-independence. This file is examined in detail later in this chapter.

On 25 December 1945, a few months after the defeat of the Japanese and the end of World War II, Nehru in a press interview indicated that he wanted to revive the idea of pan-Asian solidarity. He suggested that an "Asian Conference could be helpful to the understanding of Asia's problems and to the promotion of co-operation among Asian peoples" (*Asian Relations* 1948: 2). In fact, already in 1942, Nehru had envisioned a federation "which includes China and India, Burma and Sri Lanka, Afghanistan, and possibly other countries" (Green 1948: 14). In March 1946, after returning from a visit to Southeast Asia, Nehru (1946), in an article in the *New York Times* titled "Colonialism Must Go," wrote,

> A free India will link together the Middle East with China. India is so situated as to form the center of a group of Asian nations for defense as well as trade and commerce. Her cultural contacts with all these countries date back thousands of years. Already there is considerable talk about a closer union between the countries in the Indian Ocean region, which would include Australia and New Zealand. It has been proposed that a conference of representatives of Asian countries be held in India.

The Indian Council for World Affairs (ICWA), established in 1943 by a group of Indian intellectuals, was charged with organizing the conference (National Archives, File 62(6)-OSIII, 1947). [49]

In August 1946, the Executive Committee of the ICWA finalized the themes for the conference and sorted out the list of invitees. It decided to focus on five issues: national movements for freedom, migration and racial problems, economic development and social services, cultural problems, and women's problems. It also proposed to concurrently hold three exhibitions, one on inter-Asian art, one on science, and one on archaeology, as well as various cultural events. Mrs. Sarojini Naidu, the former president of the INC, was elected the chairperson of the organizing committee, and Jawaharlal Nehru was designated as the chairman of the working committee (*Asian Relations* 1948: 4–7). Initially the conference was supposed to be limited to Southeast Asian countries, but in the end the organizing committee chose to send invitations to all Asian countries, including Japan, and also to Egypt. Its most controversial decision, however, was inviting Tibet as an independent country to the conference.

A report from the British Foreign Office (FO 371/63539) noted that the Chinese initially selected Dai Jitao to lead the delegation. While the list did not include members of the Communist Party of China, Carsun Chang (Zhang Junmai 張君勱) and Mao Yihong 毛

以亨 of the Democratic Socialist Party were mentioned as possible members.[50] The same report also pointed out that the Tibetans had not responded to the invitation and that the organizing committee, in order to "avoid raising with China the question of Tibet's independence," had decided not to send a reminder. However, the Tibetans seem to have soon accepted the invitation, and as a result, according to Yang Yun-yuan (1974), Dai Jitao chose not to attend the conference. "He interpreted the separate invitation of Tibet," Yang (1987: 408) writes, "as an indication of Nehru having some ulterior motive in mind." In fact, the letters exchanged between Dai and Chiang Kai-shek about China's participation in the Asian Relations Conference indicate that some members of the GMD believed that Nehru wanted to use the gathering to "promote his personal prestige" (Dai [1946]1971).

The Chinese launched an official protest with the interim Indian government when they learned that representatives from Tibet had agreed to attend the conference. There were intense deliberations among the GMD officials about whether China should participate in the conference. Tan Yunshan was involved in these discussions, writing personally to Chiang Kai-shek on at least three occasions. In letters dated 29 September 1946, 19 November 1946, and 6 December 1946, he repeatedly noted that the Asian Relations Conference was "half academic, half social" (*yiban xueshu ban shehui xing* 一半學術半社會性), intended to promote cultural relations. He also suggested the various organizations whom the GMD could send to participate in the conference. With his third letter, Tan even attached a list of countries that were invited to the conference. The list, the source of which is not clear, did not include Tibet.[51]

Based on the above recommendations by Tan Yunshan, Chiang Kai-shek asked his officials to constitute a delegation to attend the Asian Relations Conference. However, he also noted that Tibet had received a similar invitation to the conference as had China. Tibet, he wrote in his memorandum, "is part of our territory." India, Chiang further pointed out, had always accepted China's sovereignty (*zongzhuquan* 宗主權) but not suzerainty (*zhuquan* 主權) over Tibet. This stand, he emphasized, "must be strongly criticized in writing."[52]

The GMD government wanted to make sure that "the question of Tibet's national status would not be raised at the Conference" and that the Tibetan representatives "should form part of Chinese delegation." The Chinese inquired if the Tibetans were invited as delegates or as observers (FO 371/63540/38). In response to these questions and concerns, Nehru "instructed" K. P. S. Menon, the Indian envoy in China, to convey the following to the Chinese: "[T]he Conference is not (repeat not) political though certain political aspects might come up for consideration in connexion [*sic*] with other matters. It will deal principally with cultural and economic matters and will not consider the internal situation in any country" (FO 371/63541/155–156).

An Indian official is said to have separately clarified that raising the issue of Tibet's national status would be "out of order." The official noted that Tibet had already accepted the invitation and that the seating arrangements were made according to alphabetical order, so the Tibetans "would therefore be separated from the Chinese." With regard to the status of the Tibetan delegation, the Indian official contended that since there were no cultural organizations in Tibet, the representatives could not be "linked" to the Chinese delegation (FO 371/63540/38).

On the Chinese side, Dai Jitao, in a letter dated 1 February 1947, strongly advocated China's participation in the Asian Relations Conference despite the reservations about the invitation extended to Tibet. He pointed out that it was premature to organize the conference when the situation in Asia was still unstable. He also lamented the fact that Nehru did not solicit China's input and organized the conference in haste. Nonetheless, Dai suggested that since the conference was going to take place in any case, China should send a delegation and ask the Tibetans to be part of it. He recommended Chen Daqi 陳大齊, the former acting president of Peking University, as the leader of the delegation, along with other scholars, including Tan Yunshan, as possible members. He further drafted a budget for each delegate, including for members from Tibet, as well as gifts they would carry to India.[53]

However, as late as 14 February 1947, the Chinese foreign ministry was not fully committed to sending a delegation to participate in the Asian Relations Conference. This was despite the fact that the Chinese ambassador in India had received personal assurance from both Nehru and Naidu that political and internal issues of participating countries would not be part of the agenda. The foreign ministry seems to have been particularly concerned about Tibetan delegates displaying their flag at the conference. They engaged in secret discussions with Naidu and other Indian officials about how this could be avoided. On 4 March 1947, the Chinese foreign ministry submitted to Chiang Kai-shek the names of possible Tibetan delegates, who, their note suggested, should seek international recognition of Tibet as part of China and demand that India return the Tibetan territories it had occupied.[54]

When the conference opened on 23 March at the Old Fort in Delhi, there were eight delegates from China led by Zheng Yanfen (Cheng Yin-fun) 鄭彥棻 (1902–1990). Tieiji Sambo (Sampho Theiji) of the Tibetan Foreign Office in Lhasa led the Tibetan delegation, which consisted of four people. Before their departure, Dai Jitao had tried to convince the Tibetans to travel together with the Chinese delegation and offered to pay for their travel expenses (Yang 1987: 408). The Tibetans may have been unwilling to accept this offer, and a similar one made directly by Chiang Kai-shek as noted below, because it seems Hugh Richardson, the British representative in Lhasa, had told them that the conference "would be a good opportunity publicly to demonstrate Tibet's de facto independence before all the neighboring Asian countries" (Goldstein 1989: 561).

Upon their arrival at the conference, the Chinese delegation became furious when they saw a map at the preparatory session showing Tibet as a separate country (see figure 4.3). Zheng Yanfen requested Nehru to remove the map. Although Nehru reluctantly agreed, the map continued to be displayed the following morning. George Yeh, another member of the delegation, warned Nehru that the Chinese delegates would withdraw if the map was not corrected. When Nehru consented to the Chinese demand, Yeh painted over "the Tibetan region in the same colour as that used for China" (Yang 1987: 408–409).[55]

Luo Jialun 羅家倫 (1897–1969), the Chinese ambassador in Delhi, invited the Tibetan delegation to the embassy and tried to convince them to let the Chinese speak for them. "We the Chinese," he is supposed to have told Teiji Sambo, "feel that it is better that you let us talk and handle the border issue. It will be more effective and more influential if we talk about it." The ambassador also insisted that they take funds personally sent by Chiang Kaishek for the delegation. Teiji Sambo refused to take the money and, on the ambassador's request, wrote a telegram to Chiang mentioning his decision (Goldstein 1989: 563).[56]

Jawaharlal Nehru chaired the session when Teiji Sambo gave his short speech. He thanked the Indian leaders for the invitation and stated, "We are a country which administers its subjects on the basis of religious aspirations and India being the motherland of Buddhism, we Buddhists and especially Tibet had friendly relations with India from ancient time. Therefore our Government have sent us here to attend this great Conference to maintain our peaceful relations based on religion" (*Asian Relations* 1948: 61).

After this opening statement, the Tibetan delegation rarely voiced their opinion in the conference deliberations.[57] The Chinese side, on the other hand, was vocal and participated in every panel.

Figure 4.3.   Map of Asia published in the Hindi newspaper *Hindustan*.

Tan Yunshan presented a paper titled "Inter-Asian Cultural Cooperation," in which he repeated his views about harmonious and peaceful relations among all "Asiatic Nations" in the past and that, after a hiatus of a few centuries, they must now "unite not only politically but culturally" (Tan 1998: 75–76). Tan did not publicly write anything about the dispute between the Indians and the Chinese over the Tibet issue at the conference despite the fact that he had been a strong advocate for the integration of Tibet. Kalidas Nag, who was invited to write a paper on the "Cultural Problems of Asia" for the conference and subsequently expanded it into the book titled *New Asia*, also avoided any mention of the contention

Figure 4.4. Maps of Asia for the Asian Relations Conference, 1947.
Times of India

between India and the Chinese delegates.[58] Tan and Nag also did not comment on the criticisms leveled against India and China by Southeast Asian delegates.[59] Some of these delegates expressed concern about the large number of Chinese and Indian migrants present in their countries. The Burmese delegate, for example, noted that his country was "frightened by the possibility that British imperialism may be substituted either by an Indian or by a Chinese imperialism" (*Asian Relations*, 1948: 96).

At the same time as the Indian and Chinese representatives tried to allay the fears of the Southeast Asian countries, the two sides were themselves having a contentious debate about the future of the forum and India's leadership in a planned pan-Asian organization (Green 1948: 85). A report on the conference by Nicholas Mansergh (1947: 303) noted that while India attempted to gain recognition "of her cultural leadership in Asia," the Chinese were opposed to this, and its "representatives lost no opportunity of saying that all nations in Asia were equal, that there was no question of leadership. . . . It was the Chinese view which prevailed."

The Chinese delegates also resisted the creation of a permanent "center of Inter-Asian relations" in India. They argued that "China was, and is, a centre of Asiatic culture, and that China, by its economic, political and geographical situation could facilitate the earlier economic and political development of Asiatic countries." And from this "the Chinese delegation reached the conclusion that if a centre of inter-Asian relations were to be set up, it should be located in China" (Platov 1947). After a protracted debate, according to Platov, "a provincial committee was set up for the organization of inter-Asian cultural relations and is to change its location annually." Other observers also reported this contention between Indian and Chinese delegates. For example, Virginia Thompson and Richard Adloff, representing the Institute of Pacific Relations in the United States, pointed out that in addition to China, the Southeast Asian countries and "those west of India" were also opposed to an organization dominated by India. "Actually," they wrote (1947: 99), "no group of delegates seemed vitally interested in establishing a permanent organization."

A decision was eventually made to set up an Asian Relations Organization, the aim of which would be to promote the study and understanding of Asian problems and relations in their Asian and world aspects, to foster friendly relations and cooperation among the people of Asia and between them and the rest of the world, and to further the progress and well-being of the peoples of Asia (*Asian Relations* 1948: 255).[60] Although, as a consolation to the Indian side, Jawaharlal Nehru was appointed as the president of the organization's Provincial General Council, the committee decided that the next conference, two years later, would be held in China. This was seen as a clear victory for the Chinese in their deliberations with the Indian side.

In 1949, after the Communists overthrew Chiang Kai-shek's government in China, the issue of the second conference was never brought up, and the Asian Relations Organization soon ceased to exist. Not only had Nehru failed to realize his dream of pan-Asiatic solidarity, but the conference in Delhi seems to have also sown a seed of distrust about India and Nehru among Chinese leaders. They were wary of Nehru's attempts to project himself as a pan-Asiatic leader, a belief that was reconfirmed during the later Bandung Conference of 1955 (Garver 2001: 118–120). More importantly, the Chinese became suspicious about Nehru's position on the status of Tibet, which was to be one of the key factors in the military conflict between India and China in 1962.[61] On 27 July 1949, Nehru noted that Tibet had never recognized Chinese suzerainty. In the latter half of 1949, after the fall of the GMD regime in Mainland China, the former Chinese ambassador to India Luo Jialun tried to warn that Nehru, in order to deny Chinese sovereignty over Tibet, might attempt to recognize the new government in China in exchange for their acceptance of the 1914 Simla Agreement. Signed between the British and Tibetans, with abstention from the Chinese, the agreement gave autonomy to the government in Lhasa. In one of his telegrams to Chiang Kai-shek, Luo cited Nehru saying, "In a vague sense we have accepted the fact of Chinese suzerainty, [but] how far it goes one does not know."[62] Such statements of vagueness by Nehru infuriated the Chinese, both GMD officials and Communist leaders. The official Communist publications swiftly called Nehru a "stooge" and "running dog" of British and American imperialists (Jain 1960: 7–19). The Asian Relations Conference in 1947, instead of bringing India and China together, had in fact made them more distant by highlighting the significant geopolitical differences between the two nations. The failure of the conference to unite the Asian countries made it clear that the idealism of pan-Asianism and the realpolitik of decolonized Asia could not converge.

EXPERIENCING NEW CONNECTIONS

There were several Indians who witnessed firsthand the collapse of the GMD regime in China and the founding of the People's Republic by the Communists led by Mao Zedong. This included government representatives such as K. M. Panikkar and K. P. S. Menon. While the former served as the Indian ambassador to both the Republic of China and the PRC, the latter was the agent-general for India in the ROC based at Chungking from 1943 to 1948 and subsequently became independent India's first foreign secretary. Also present in China before and after the 1949 divide was Frank Moraes, a war correspondent in China for the *Times of India* newspaper in early 1945, who subsequently visited the PRC as a member of an Indian delegation in 1952.[63] There were others who encountered the GMD and Communist factions in China prior to 1949 and wrote about Communist China without having the opportunity to visit the new state. M. N. Roy (1945, 1946), Ramnath Biswas (1941, 1943, 1944, 1949), and D. F. Karaka (1944) are a few examples of such individuals. The members of Indian communities living in places such as Shanghai and Kashgar were also witness to the transitional period but do not seem to have written accounts of their experiences living and working in the "two Chinas."

The political transition in China took place at the same time as an independent India was going through its own nation-building process. The departure of the British in 1947 entailed changes to the government bureaucratic system, especially at the top levels; the formulation of foreign policy goals; the creation of military services; and the consolidation of territory. Especially with regard to China, the Asian Relations Conference had highlighted a crucial area of concern for several branches of the Indian government. The status of Tibet was an issue that had to be dealt with not only by the political leadership but also by the ministries of foreign affairs, defense, and home affairs. Below we will examine some of the concerns of the Indian Intelligence Branch/Bureau (IB) with regard to Tibet as reported in one of its declassified files. Together with the writings of K. P. S. Menon and K. M. Panikkar, the reports in the IB file make it clear that the status of Tibet was one of the main impediments in the relations between India and China as the two countries attempted to form new connections in the mid-twentieth century.

On Two Chinas

Ramnath Biswas was a unique and important chronicler of China in the 1930s who continued to write about the country in the 1940s. However, he is rarely mentioned in the studies that deal with India-China connections during the first half of the twentieth century. This is primarily because he wrote in Bengali. Even among Bengali readers, Biswas is more famous for his globe-trotting adventures than as an observer of China.[64] In fact, Biswas wrote three books on China, the first of which was on his travels through the country in 1931–1932. The two later works expressed his sympathies and support for the Chinese Communist revolution in the 1940s. He seems to have been the only Indian writer in the 1930s who encountered and talked to a diverse group of people living in several different regions of a war-torn China. He met shopkeepers, farmers, bandits, GMD officials, Communist revolutionaries, and also Indians living in China. This diversity of Biswas's encounters in China resulted from the fact that he traveled across the country alone on his bicycle, passing through cities such as Guangzhou, Changsha, Hankou, Shanghai, Beijing, Tianjin, and the Japanese-occupied Manchuria.

Born in the region of Sylhet in what is present-day northeast Bangladesh, Biswas worked in the British army in West Asia. After leaving the army in 1924, he took up a clerical position in Persia and subsequently served as an interpreter in the marine court of Malaya. Charged with allegations of involvement with local revolutionaries, Biswas was fired from his job. It was from Singapore, starting on 7 July 1931, that he then embarked on his travels across

Eurasia on his bicycle (Ghosh 1987; Basu 2007: 487). His travel diary was serialized in the Bengali weekly *Desh* (The Nation). After his return to India in 1940, these episodes were published as a book with the title *Maranbijayi Chin* (Death-Defying China). An English version called *China Defies Death* appeared in 1944. In 1943, Biswas also published his second work on China called *Lal Chin* (Red China), which provided an overview of the country's history and society. Five years later, in August 1949, after the Chinese Communists took control of northern China, he published his third work titled *Mukta Mahachin* (Liberated Great China).

All three books by Ramnath Biswas indicate his strong support for the Communist movement in China and his equally fervent desire for the unity of Indian and Chinese people. In the preface (*amar katha*, i.e., "My Words") to the Bengali version of *Maranbijayi Chin*, he wrote,

> At last, as far as my experience in China has helped me to identify its true essence, I can say drawing on the basis of that— in the whole world if there is any nation, which is sympathetic to India that is China. (trans. Basu 2007: 498)

At a lecture he gave at Sun Yat-sen University in Guangzhou, Biswas noted,

> I ended by hoping that the sacrifices of the ancient peoples of the two great countries, India and China, would not be in vain, and that when we are both free and regenerated, we together would constitute a colossal force and contribute a tremendous wealth for the upliftment of all humanity.

And in the epilogue to the English version of the book, he rhetorically asks,

> Is it any wonder that I love China and feel proud of her? That I wish her a thorough-going victory? That I feel a burning desire

to see our people unite with her in the great fight for freedom and renaissance? (Biswas 1944: 176)

Biswas's "burning desire" reflected the sentiments of some of the advocates of pan-Asianism. But, unlike the pan-Asianists, Biswas clearly hoped that this unity would take place between the peoples of an independent India and a Communist China.

The overall context of *Maranbijayi Chin* was the tumultuous period in China, marked by civil war between the GMD and the Communists and the Japanese invasion of Manchuria. These two aspects are prominent throughout Biswas's book. When he arrived in Guangzhou, the locals mistook him for a Japanese and refused to give him lodging at any of the inns. In order to avoid this confusion, he attached a tag to his shirt that read in Chinese, "Hindu-Yangtze-Saikai" ("Hindu World Tourist").[65] Also during the early part of his travels in China, several people, especially government officials and American missionaries, cautioned him that the "Red bandits" had "been spreading dissension between rich and poor, dividing the nation and obstructing the consolidation of the Republic and the reconstruction of our national economy and national life" (Biswas 1944: 16–20). These "Red bandits," according to them, were also anti-foreigner and "live by banditry, only they are more godless, more ruthless than the regular bandits." Biswas called this "Red Phobia."

However, once he entered the Communist-held territories around Chalin (in Hunan), Biswas witnessed people living in clean villages, with the old and young all happy and busy at work, where "no one considered work a drudgery. No one grumbled or grudged" (Biswas 1944: 29). The poor farmers had in fact welcomed the "Red bandits," and "that's why they cast in their lot with the Reds, joined the Red Army and fought the whites with their lives! That's why the entire countryside wore a 'mobilising' air, to protect their Soviet land, their villages and farms, their newly acquired freedom" (Biswas 1944: 35). The Communists, he points out, were fighting against imperialism, trying to abolish feudalism, liberating the "toiling masses from capitalist exploitation," addressing the issue of "national oppression" (the right of self-determination of the national minorities in China, their right to separate and form independent states), eradicating illiteracy and ignorance, emancipating the women, and establishing a democracy of the workers, peasants, and toilers.

Biswas (1944: 44–53) also reports that the Communists were more committed to resisting the Japanese. In his view, the GMD government had made little effort in confronting the Japanese forces and was disliked by the ordinary folks. "Nanking," he writes (1944: 72), "truly was more busy in suppressing the Reds than defending Shanghai [from the Japanese]."

The contempt for the Japanese among the Chinese is described in several sections of *Maranbijayi Chin*. Biswas mentions, for example, a GMD solider who had a Japanese girlfriend but later realized that she was a supporter of the Japanese expansion in China. "From that day on," the solider told Biswas (1944), "my love for her turned into hatred for Japan. I cut myself off from her and joined the 19th Route Army to kill the Japanese and myself as an atonement for my having loved a Japanese girl." He also describes the resistance against the Japanese by the "patriotic women" from the Youth Association in Shanghai. Disguised as prostitutes, these "heroines of Chapei" managed to kill 1,500 Japanese soldiers.

When Biswas returned to China seven years later in February 1940, from the United States through Kobe, he found that the GMD and the Communist factions had united against the Japanese. He found Shanghai in dismal condition under the Japanese occupation and scorned their Greater East Asia Co-Prosperity Sphere propaganda by remarking, "This is 'Co-prosperity' indeed!" But he was optimistic about the united front put together by the GMD and the Communists. "Yes, the incredible unity had wrought an incredible transformation of the people too," he wrote (1944: 173); "even the downcast peasant is no longer downcast. He feels a warrior—a part of an invincible army."

Five years later when he wrote *Mukta Mahachin*, the war against the Japanese had ended, and the accord between the GMD and the Communists had collapsed. In fact, victory by the Communists in the reignited civil war seemed certain at this point. It was, he wrote in his third book on China, a "victory of the New Life Movement" and the defeat of the "blood thirsty Japanese" and the corrupt government of Chiang Kai-shek. "The People's Liberation Army has proved," he explained (1949: 107), "that the whole Chinese nation is Communist-minded—the direct result of New Democracy. It is because Mao's diplomacy has turned European Marxism into Asiatic Marxism—by bringing all the progressive people under one flag without introducing class war." In the concluding chapter of the book, written after the Communists had "liberated" Beijing and other northern regions of northern China, Biswas wrote (1949: 112), "the march of the Chinese communists is not just for liberation of China. It is, in all practical purposes, for the establishment of the great soul of Great China that would have far-reaching consequences."

Ramnath Biswas was not an eyewitness to the founding of the PRC in October 1949. But, as can be discerned from his above comments, he was clearly following the events. Reporting from China at this time of regime change were two representatives of the ROI: K. P. S. Menon and K. M. Panikkar. Menon had arrived in Chungking (now Chongqing) in September 1943 after a flight from Calcutta through Kunming.[66] Menon writes in one of his letters collected in a book titled *Twilight in China* that the diplomatic relations between British India and the ROC were established after several key developments in "Sino-Anglo-Indian history." This included Chiang's visit to British India in 1942, when he called for Indians to support the Chinese war against the Japanese; the British agreeing that Indians could appoint their first official representative to China; and the strong support the GMD expressed for the Indian independence movement and the contribution it made to famine relief activities in Bengal. Menon and Panikkar were considered the leading "China hands" in India and were close advisors to Nehru on matters related to foreign policy. Thus, their views on issues such as Tibet and territorial disputes between India and China prior to the establishment of the PRC, topics not mentioned by Ramnath Biswas, are important for understanding the period leading up to the conflict of 1962.

Menon reached Chungking just before Chiang took the title of chairman of the Nationalist government and president of the Republic of China. He formally met Chiang on the day of the inauguration, 10 October 1943, which coincided with the thirty-second anniversary of the founding of the ROC. Already at this time, Menon noted (1972: 11) the Chinese government's intention to consolidate its territories. In his first presidential address delivered in the same month, Chiang pledged that he would "endeavour to recover all 'lost territories.'" This idea of recovering the "lost territories" was not something that only Chiang idealized. It was also, as Menon found out, an aspiration of the common people. A survey conducted in 1943 found that a majority of female Chinese students wanted to contribute to the "restoration of all 'lost territory' including 'Korea, India-China and Burma which were formerly dependencies of China'" (Menon 1972: 13). Later, Menon (1972: 33) explains that "among the lost areas are Malaya ([lost in] 1896) and Hunza-Nagar tract in Kashmir ([lost in] 1890). Tibet, of course, is not 'lost territory,' but a province of China! Whatever Tolstoy and Dolan may say, I do not think it likely that China will use force against Tibet. She will probably wait with typical Chinese patience and pertinacity for Tibet to fall into her lap like Sinkiang."

At one point Menon explains the emphasis given to Tibetan studies in Sichuan and asks, "[I]ncidentally, isn't it worth our while to encourage Tibetan studies in some Indian universities? After all our cultural connection with Tibet is far closer than that of China." This observation of Menon with regard to Tibet's cultural connection with India subsequently became an important stance of the Indian government. John Garver (2001: 40), for example, points out that Indian president Rajendra Prasad, in response to the PRC's military action in Tibet in 1950, repeated this claim. "Tibet is not only a neighbor of India," the Indian president noted, "but has had close cultural and other ties with us for ages past."[67] In 1957, K. M. Panikkar also underscored a cultural affinity between India and Tibet in his book *India and China: A Study of Cultural Relations.* Later, as observed by Garver, "once China launched a systematic campaign against Tibet's traditional culture in 1959, there was an eruption of strong popular Indian sympathy for Tibet," leading a "secular" Nehru to also underscore "India's cultural interest in Tibet." In his speeches to the Lok Sabha in March and April 1959, Nehru said (cited in Garver 2001: 40–41),

> There is this feeling of a certain kinship, if I may use that word, cultural kinship between the people of India and the people of Tibet.
>
> We have no desire . . . to interfere in the slightest degree in Tibetan affairs. But we could not give up our interest, call it if you like sentimental interest . . . and you can observe for yourself the enormous feeling that has been roused in India by these recent developments in Tibet.

It was also in 1946 that Menon made a few other probing observations on Tibet, which appear in a report he submitted to the foreign secretary of the British government of India, Sir Hugh Weightman (FO 371/12168). Writing about a Tibetan mission that visited the GMD capital of Nanjing on 5 April and subsequently traveled to Shanghai, Menon chided the delegates for not having "the courtesy, or the courage, to call on the representative of the Government of India in China." It was significant, Menon notes, that the mission received little publicity compared to the visits by previous dignitaries. "Perhaps the reason," he writes, "is that the Chinese Government now feel little need for publicizing Tibetan loyalty to China; the Tibetan delegation themselves were prepared to show it by joining the National Assembly. There is little doubt that if the Assembly had not been postponed, the Tibetan delegates would have attended it; and this a Mission, which the Government of India welcomed as an assertion of Tibetan independence, would have turned out to be a demonstration of Tibetan dependence on China, as indeed it was meant to be by the genius who conceived it, namely Mr. T. L. Shen."[68]

Published in 1972, Menon's *Twilight in China* included an epilogue, which addressed the Tibetan issue in more detail, albeit with the hindsight of the India-China war of 1962. In 1950, K. P. S. Menon, then the foreign secretary of the ROI, was criticized for failing to take any action when People's Liberation Army (PLA) soldiers entered Tibet. Responding to these critics and those who blamed India for "giving away" Tibet to China, Menon (1972: 258) in the epilogue wrote that Tibet was not "India's to give away! The fact is that Tibet had never enjoyed an independent status in international eyes. Even Great Britain, which came nearest to the recognition of Tibet's independence, recognised it subject to China's suzerainty; and the USA always regarded Tibet as an integral part of China, until the Tibetan question became a convenient tool in the Cold War."

The PRC, Menon argues, not only reneged on its assurance to grant autonomy to Tibet but also gave India a "rude awakening" with regard to the border issue. He blames the PRC for deceiving Nehru on both instances. However, he (Menon 1972: 260) also explains that, "while China was thus primarily responsible for injuring the friendship between the two countries, we must ask ourselves whether we too have not unwittingly contributed to the deterioration of our relations with China." Menon cites the Indian government's decision to withdraw its ambassador from China during the aftermath of the war, the failure to renew the India–China Trade Agreement signed in 1954, the refusal to accept Zhou Enlai's proposal to swap the Aksai Chin region occupied by the PRC for China's recognition of the McMahon Line, and the "unhelpful" attitude of the legislature as examples of the ways in which the Indian side contributed to the deterioration of the ROI-PRC relations.

Just prior to the publication of Menon's book, the ROI, under Prime Minister Indira Gandhi, had achieved a decisive victory in the war against Pakistan, leading to the founding of Bangladesh as an independent state out of what was formerly East Pakistan. This victory had also propelled Indira Gandhi to sweep the state assembly elections in early 1972. These two developments, in Menon's opinion, placed India in a "better position to negotiate with China" with full backing of the Parliament and the state legislatures. "It may not be possible," he (Menon 1972: 264) concluded, "or even desirable, to reconjure the perfervid atmosphere of the days of Hindi-Chini Bhai Bhai, but there is a hope that in the not distant future our relations with China can be established on a friendly, sincere, good-neighbourly level."

Similar to Menon, K. M. Panikkar also experienced firsthand the political transition in China and the deterioration in relations between the ROI and the PRC. Also similar to Menon, he too was blamed for the ROI's failure to comprehend the "deceptive" plans of the Communist government in China with regard to Tibet and the ROI-PRC border. Panikkar arrived in China in April 1948, shortly after Menon had departed the country, to serve as independent India's first ambassador to the Republic of China. He also became the first Indian ambassador to the People's Republic of China after the ROI recognized the Communist state in 1950. Panikkar remained in the PRC until 1952, after which he served as ambassador to Egypt and then France. Prior to his appointment as the ambassador to the ROC in 1948, Panikkar was already an accomplished writer who wrote on the history of India and the Indian Ocean. He continued to write throughout the later stages of his life, with several of his books appearing posthumously. Panikkar's experiences in the ROC and the PRC are narrated in his book titled *In Two Chinas: Memoirs of a Diplomat*, which was published in 1955.

Panikkar's book covers several different aspects of his private and public life in the "two Chinas." They range from his dealings with GMD officials and the Indians living in the ROC to the situation in Nanjing during the Communist "liberation" of China to the relations between the ROI and the newly established PRC. Panikkar's opinion about ROC-India relations after the end of World War II can be discerned from the following passage in his book:

> It did not take me long to discover that the Kuomintang attitude towards India, while genuinely friendly, was inclined to be a little patronizing. It was the attitude of an elder brother who was considerably older and well-established in the world, prepared to give his advice to a younger brother struggling to make his way. Independence of India was welcome, but of course it was understood that China as the recognized Great Power in the East after the war expected India to know her place. (Panikkar 1955: 26–27)

This view of India as the younger brother reversed what Liang Qichao had expressed during Tagore's visit to the ROC in 1924. Calling India the elder brother, Liang had acknowledged the cultural debt that China owed to it. The above sentiments of the GMD, if true, suggest that geopolitical issues and anxieties had, by 1948, replaced the idea of cultural affinity emphasized during the struggle against colonialism and imperialism. Indeed, the geopolitical concerns were clearly on display at the Asian Relations Conference discussed above.

On 22 November 1948, Panikkar wrote a note titled "When China Goes Communist," in which he described how the impending political transition in China might affect India. The Communists, he suggested, would "follow a forward policy in Tibet" by employing Sun Yat-sen's doctrine of five races. "The independence of the five races and their voluntary union was Sun's formula," Panikkar pointed out (FO 371/75798: 38); "[t]he Communists can therefore claim that in establishing the republics of Manchuria, Mongolia, Sinkiang, and Tibet they are only carrying out the teachings of Sun Yat-sen." He continues (FO 371/75798: 39), "A China so organised will be in an extremely powerful position to claim its historic role of authority over Tibet, Burma, Indo-China and Siam. The historic claims in regard to these are vague and hazy, but at different times China did exercise authority over Tibet, Burma, Tonkin and Annam and claimed suzerainty over the Khmer kings of the present state of Siam." Explaining how the Chinese consolidation of Tibet might impact India, Panikkar wrote (FO 371/75798: 41), "Recent Chinese diplomatic action (e.g. the denunciation of the already invalidated treaty of 1908) shows clearly the direction in which a strong Central Government of China may move. Not only the McMahon Line, but the entire boundary from Ladakh to Burma may become a new area of trouble."

In his book, however, Panikkar is dismissive of Tibet becoming an issue of concern between the ROI and the PRC. He considered (Panikkar 1955: 112–113) the dispute over the "Chinese invasion of Tibet" in 1950 resolved after the two governments had made their respective views clear. It seems the Indian ambassador was more apprehensive about the criticism leveled against him for being "fooled" by the Chinese and not appropriately advising Nehru on the Korean conflict. Panikkar mentions the exchange of government communications between India and China that followed the announcement of the campaign on "Liberating Tibet." While the official communications were strongly worded, Panikkar pointed out that the Chinese were "determined to liberate Tibet by peaceful means" and that India had already "recognized Chinese sovereignty over Tibet." Two months later, he declared that "the stiffness which had entered into our relations with China as a result of the Tibetan controversy had by this time totally disappeared" (Panikkar 1955: 116).

Panikkar repeated his views about the peaceful liberation of Tibet by the PRC when he met a visiting Indian delegation in 1951. "The Liberation," as he reportedly informed the members of delegation, "was perfectly peaceful and Tibet today not only enjoys full religious and other liberties and internal autonomy, but also, as a part of the great People's Republic of China, is safe against aggression" (Sunderlal 1952: 57). Panikkar also told the delegation that the "Chinese have no aggressive or territorial designs against any other country" (Sunderlal 1952: 53). Perhaps because of such views, Panikkar continued to be optimistic about India-China relations later that year when he delivered lectures at the Maharaja Sayaji Rao University in Baroda. The "thousand years of contact" between India and China was a main theme of these lectures. After the colonial obstruction, he explained, "the lines of communication have been reopened. India and China confront each other in the modern age ready to learn from each other. This new period will no doubt produce results as glorious and as enduring as the previous confrontations of our two civilizations" (Panikkar 1957: 66).

Raja (G. P.) Hutheesing, the brother-in-law of Nehru and a journalist for the Press Trust of India, was one of the leading critics of Panikkar and his dealings with the Nationalist and Communist governments in China. Accusing the Indian ambassador of being easily manipulated by the Chinese, he wrote,

> In Chiang Kai-shek's China he was a believer in Kuomintang invincibility and from Nanking advised the government of India to enter into a defence pact with Chiang in 1948. When I met him in Peking in October, 1951, after a lapse of many years, I listened to his discourses on the achievement of the New Democracy only to find that all his "facts" were Chinese Communist propaganda. (Hutheesing 1953: 9)

A propagandist for Communist China was indeed one of the common criticisms leveled against Panikkar by critics of the PRC. He was also censured for accepting the ambassadorship to the PRC after serving in the same position in the ROC, accused of changing the word "suzerainty" to "sovereignty" with regard to Tibet's status vis-à-vis the PRC in an official Indian diplomatic communication, and slammed for his failure to make a strong case for the ROI with regard to the border and Tibet issues as the ambassador to the PRC. He was also accused of being gullible to PRC propaganda and someone "who too prided himself on being an historian" (Gupta 1987: 99). While Karunakar Gupta (1987) has demonstrated that all these charges were exaggerations, it is nonetheless clear that Panikkar shared Nehru's optimism about an enduring relationship between the PRC and the ROI founded on ancient linkages. This fundamental belief and faith in civilizational affinity might have prevented both Panikkar and Nehru from taking an aggressive or confrontational stand against the PRC throughout most of the 1950s.

The Concerns of the Intelligence Community

Both K. M. Panikkar and Jawaharlal Nehru were most likely aware of the concerns of the intelligence community in India about the rapid ascent of the Communists in China. The intelligence community was also apprehensive about the issues of demarcating the borders and the status of Tibet. Some reports of the IB have been declassified and are housed in the West Bengal State Archives in Calcutta. They include over one hundred files on the activities of the Chinese communities in West Bengal between 1914 and 1952. Reports have continued to be added to these files, as a result of which some of the documents in the files date from the 1960s. Anxieties about GMD activities in British India, the propaganda and espionage activities of the Chinese Communists, and the smuggling and other illegal undertakings of Chinese residents are frequently reported in these files. Issues with regard to intelligence gathering about the Chinese communities and the surveillance of a Chinese resident in Kalimpong accused of spying for the PRC are discussed in the next chapter. Analyzed here are the reports about Tibet found in a file titled "Tibetan Intelligence, Reports Compiled by C.I.O., Assam" (West Bengal State Archives File 923/44, Serial No. 302). The file was created in 1944 and spans six years, with the last entry dating from December 1950. It reveals the difficulties of collecting reliable intelligence about Tibet after the establishment of the Communist government in China. Perhaps because of this limited access to Tibet, the IB officers were also unable to appropriately assess the intelligence received from Tibetan groups and sources operating within the ROI, some of whom were working to resist the expansion of Chinese Communist forces into Tibet. The reports in this file also suggest a disconnect between the information collected and analyzed in the frontier regions and the policies and actions drafted by the government in Delhi with regard to both the newly founded Communist state in China and the as yet "unliberated" Tibet.

The file contains regular reports from IB informants based in Assam as well as input from officers located in Sikkim, Shillong, and, prior to 1949, Lhasa. It covers a wide range of topics, including Tibet's interactions with the GMD and Communist governments in China, Indian interests in Tibet, the economic conditions of the region, the key people involved in diplomatic and espionage activities, and the border issues between India and Tibet. It also has maps of the Tibet-India-Burma border region drawn in February 1947 that show the territorial claims of the GMD government. It is clear from the reports in this file that the intelligence community in India was aware of the ROC's intention to integrate Tibet into its territory as early as 1945. It is also evident that British Indian and subsequently ROI officials were cognizant of the possible conflict that might ensue between China and India over the status of Tibet and the demarcation of the border. Also apparent is the fact that both the GMD and the Communist governments were apprehensive about India's unclear role in and about the status of Tibet.

The McMahon Line, the main contested boundary between the ROI and the PRC, figures prominently in the intelligence reports. An intelligence report from 13 September 1944 points out that the Tibetan "Kashang" had issued secret orders to tax Walong and other villages south of the McMahon Line. This was, the report noted, "despite our attempts to occupy this area as far as the McMahon Line." Four years later, responding to a report about disruptions in the upper Pemako region north of the McMahon Line, H. E. Richardson, the officer in charge of the Indian mission in Lhasa, requested a clarification about the boundary. Dated 10 April 1948, Richardson's note stated (West Bengal State Archives File 923/44, Serial No. 302: 483), "If it is true that villages of Pemako from the North of the McMahon Line are rebelling against their officials and showing signs of anxiety to be included within the Tribal Areas of Assam I presume that no encouragement will be given to such tendency. We have assured the Tibetans that the Government of Indian [*sic*] would not advance even once beyond the McMahon Line."

Richardson was perhaps trying to underscore the importance of clearly demarcating the boundary between Tibet and the Indian territories. He might have made this recommendation due to the possibility of Tibet declaring independence and asserting its own territorial claims. In fact, in early 1947, the Tibetans sent a letter to Chiang Kai-shek "asking him to return to Tibet all the Eastern territories which are now under Chinese rule" (West Bengal State Archives File 923/44, Serial No. 302: 381). The Chinese National Assembly responded by noting that "these territories had been under Chinese Government rule for more than a century and at any rate Tibet itself was part of China. It was, therefore quite pointless in returning these territories to Tibet." The reply provocatively added, "However, if Tibet would claim those territories of hers which had been seized by the British and attached to India, such as Sikkim, Bhutan, Ladakh, Western Tibet, Towang and Dzayul, if these territories were returned[,] China would consider returning some of theirs too."

A year later, according to a report dated 30 June 1948, the GMD government offered Tibetans the opportunity to "accept autonomy under suzerainty." The report also described the "propaganda" that the GMD government was employing to convince the Tibetans to accept their proposal. "China and India are great friends," the proposal from the GMD pointed out, "and India will never interfere in the affairs of China. The British have left India and are far away to render any help to Tibet. The U.S.A., one of the greatest powers in the world, is China's great friend. Tibet's wisest course is to come under Chinese suzerainty, otherwise outside powers like Russia or Nepal may invade Tibet and conquer it." The proposal warned about the dire consequences of nonacceptance: "[I]f Tibet refuses to come under China—Generalissimo Chiang may order MA PU FENG, the Governor of Sinning (Chinghai) to invade Tibet as Ma PU FENG is reported to be very keen on it" (West Bengal State Archives File 923/44, Serial No. 302: 511).

Other reports discuss the possibility of Communist infiltration into Tibet. A report from Lhasa dated 16 January 1947 (West Bengal State Archives File 923/44, Serial No. 302: 9), for example, describes the presence of Communist agents in the region. In response to the threat from the Communists, Tibet at one point sought help from the United States and Britain to organize an army of fifty thousand troops (West Bengal State Archives File 923/44, Serial No. 302: 402). Soon after the establishment of the PRC, the Tibetans seem to have also contacted the Indian government. An entry dated 26 October 1949 records a meeting between the Indian political officer based in Sikkim and a representative of the "Tibetan Government." During the meeting the political officer reportedly "put up ten schemes for the defence of Tibet relating to the army, military stores, air bases and communication etc." A few weeks later, however, the political officer in Sikkim, having read the intelligence report, denied it, saying, "It is not correct that I proposed any schemes to the Tibetan Government for the defence of Tibet. The Tibetan Government have, however, made certain requests for help which have been referred to the Government of India." The political officer also denied a report that gave details about the visit of a Communist delegation to Lhasa to negotiate with the Tibetans. "I regard it as most unlikely," the officer wrote, "that any negotiations of the kind reported have taken place because the Tibetan Government have made fervent appeals to the Government of India for help against the Communists and have repeatedly affirmed their determination to resist the Communists by force" (West Bengal State Archives File 923/44, Serial No. 302).

The possibility of Indian help for the Tibetans is mentioned again in a report filed on 16 November 1949. Here it is noted that the deposed GMD government, then relocated to Taiwan, would join the Tibetans in the fight against the Communists with the help of India, America, and Britain. This report, however, was marked as "KMT Propaganda" in the file (West Bengal State Archives File 923/44, Serial No. 302).

While the above-mentioned reports from 1949 indicate a continuous flow of intelligence reports from Tibet, it is apparent that they were becoming hard to verify. As a result, words such as "unconfirmed" or "rumoured" were used to qualify these reports, especially those that related to Communist activities in Tibet. A communication dated 27 April 1950 notes an "unverifiable" meeting between Tibetan delegates and Communist representatives in Lhasa, during which the Communist representatives are said to have been willing to recognize Tibet's independence on two conditions. First, the Communist government would station five hundred people in Tibet as administrators, army officers, schoolteachers, and others "on a two years' scheme of development of Tibet." Second, it would send a force of five thousand "armed police" to "guard the borders of Tibet-India and Tibet-Nepal which would be withdrawn after two years should Tibet then prove capable of defending herself" (West Bengal State Archives File 923/44, Serial No. 302: 794). Another report, dated 21 September 1950, described the difficulties of gathering intelligence from Tibetans who spoke different dialects due to a lack of language competence. Additionally, there seem to have been rivalries among the IB officers located at different sites along the India-Tibet frontier region. One officer, for instance, complained after visiting Kalimpong, saying, "I gathered an impression that the S.I.B. (Special Intelligence Branch) staff at Kalimpong have some sort of veiled feelings of rivalry against my Frontier staff there. I think this is rather unfortunate as both the staffs are after all serving the same Government and the purpose behind the collection of Intelligence on the Indo-Tibetan frontier by both these staffs is also the same" (West Bengal State Archives File 923/44, Serial No. 302: 937).

The above confusions in intelligence reports originating from within Tibet and the border areas suggest deterioration in the intelligence gathering mechanism after 1949. The ability to penetrate the new regime in Beijing seems to have been lacking as well. Also absent were the facilities to exchange information between the IB officers in the frontier regions and the government in Delhi. The officers based in Kalimpong were aware, for example, in July 1950 that a Tibetan delegation led by Tsipon Shakabpa was traveling to Delhi to meet with Chinese embassy officials. But they do not seem to have received any information about the offer made by the Chinese government, through the embassy, to the delegation. According to a memoir later written by Shakabpa, the embassy official wanted Tibet to accept that it was part of the PRC and let Beijing be in charge of its defense, political, and commercial affairs. The ambassador is supposed to have added that "if Tibet accepted these points, there would be peaceful liberation; otherwise the PLA forces would liberate Tibet militarily" (Goldstein 2007: 46).

Shakabpa's meeting with the Chinese ambassador took place on 16 September 1950, and it was on 7 October that PLA forces entered Tibet. Even prior to these meetings, reports emitting from Hong Kong suggested an imminent military action in Tibet by the PLA. Indian officials, it was reported in the *Times of India* on 9 August, discounted such "stories" based on feedback from Ambassador Panikkar and the political officer in Sikkim. A few days later, "observers" in Kalimpong also confirmed that "there is no possibility of the Peking Government moving forces into Tibet in the next eight months" (*Times of India*, 17 August 1950: 9). Even after Chinese premier Zhou Enlai was quoted by *Pravda* on 1 October as saying that "China was fully determined to liberate the people of Tibet" (*Times of India*, 2 October 1950: 1) and the report from the New China News Agency on 7 October that the PLA had "liberated" Xinjiang and Tibet, neither the Indian intelligence community nor the Indian embassy in Beijing were able to confirm the event. No such confirmation came even after the *Times of India*, on 27 October, published a headline that read, "Delhi Awaits Report on Tibetan Situation: Urgent Communication Sent to Envoy at Peking," on its front page. The newspaper article noted that Indian officials were still waiting for "confirmation or elucidation" from K. M. Panikkar and "authentic information" from the political officer in Lhasa (*Times of India*, 27 October 1950: 1). This article appeared two days after Radio Peking had announced the liberation of Tibet.

B. N. Mullik, who became the director of the IB in 1950 and remained in that position until after the death of Nehru in 1964, has described the key problems in foreign intelligence gathering between 1947 and 1951. Under the British, he explains, the IB was responsible for internal affairs while London was in charge of collecting foreign and military intelligence. "When India attained in-

dependence," he writes, "whilst the Intelligence Bureau's respon-
sibilities increased greatly due to the integration of the States with
India, it still did not have any responsibility for foreign Intelligence." According to him, this responsibility was only allocated in
1951. "So," he points out, "up to that time the Intelligence Bureau's
work regarding external intelligence was directed at neutralizing
any threats to the internal security arising from the existence of a
hostile Pakistan and the emergence of a powerful China on the
borders" (Mullik 1971: 104).[69] In this context of the lack of proper
intelligence gathering, K. M. Panikkar's dismissive stand on the
PRC's unlikely military action in Tibet in 1950, which was noted
above, is perhaps understandable.

The IB file on Tibet discussed above clearly indicates the confusion about events transpiring in the region during the transition
phase between the GMD and the establishment of the PRC. Since
the Indian intelligence network was also going through a transition
during the same period, it is not surprising that such confusions
would have surfaced. More noteworthy perhaps is the fact that the
continuity in the file indicates a clear understanding of the issues of
contention between the ROI and the governments in China. The
intentions of the GMD and PRC governments to incorporate Tibet
had been known to Indian intelligence officers since 1945. The
territorial claims of the Tibetans, GMD, and PRC around the
McMahon Line area were also identified by the IB. Thus, by the
time the decade of "Hindi-Chini bhai-bhai" commenced, the potential areas of conflict and disagreement were well known to both the
ROI and the PRC.

INDIA, CHINA, AND THE SEARCH FOR ONE ASIA

The exchanges between Indians and Chinese intellectuals were one
of the most notable aspects of the Asian connections during the first
half of the twentieth century. These exchanges took place at multi-

ple levels and at different sites within the continent. They included leading figures in the intellectual histories of India and China, such as Liang Qichao, Rabindranath Tagore, Zhang Taiyan, Benoy Kumar Sarkar, and the monk Taixu. There were several others, such as Gadhadhar Singh, Ramnath Biswas, Tan Yunshan, and Dai Jitao, who also contributed to the discourse through their writings and speeches. Even the Japanese scholar Okakura Kakuzō played a role by highlighting the oneness of the Indian and Chinese civilizations. Indeed, the ancient connections between these two civilizations formed the core of the pan-Asianism ideology. The discourse on Asian solidarity served to coalesce anticolonial sentiments across Asia, promoted interactions among people living in different parts of the continent, and created a framework for conceptualizing Asia. This discourse took place in Tokyo, Shanghai, Calcutta, and Shantiniketan. Forums were even created in Europe, such as at the World Congress of Oppressed Peoples, where representatives of Asian countries, many of them still under colonial rule, met and forged plans for a common future in a decolonized world.

The spread of Japanese imperialism in the 1930s and early 1940s resulted in a deeper discourse between Indian and Chinese intellectuals. Political leaders such as Chiang Kai-shek and Jawaharlal Nehru became part of this conversation, as did the Buddhist and Islamic communities in the two countries. The period witnessed the exchange of goodwill missions and medical aid teams, military collaboration, and expressions of mutual sympathies with regard to Japanese and British imperialism. The goodwill missions from China, in particular, traveled to several places in Asia and tried to connect the continent through a common response to Japanese imperialism. This period was also marked by an increase in the migration of ethnic Chinese, not only from Mainland China but also from Southeast Asia, to India. During World War II, Chinese soldiers were stationed in various parts of Northeast India, where they received training from British and American military personnel. Also associated with the war against the Japanese was the construction of a supply road, known as the Stilwell Road (aka Ledo Road), which connected the Assam region of India to Yunnan through Burma.

The Asian Relations Conference of 1947 was the first convention for Asian intellectuals to gather and attempt to forge new connections at a moment in world history when Japanese imperialism had ended and European colonial powers were withdrawing from Asia. However, as discussed above, the conference revealed several fissures in Asian solidarity, including a key one between India and China. The vision of a unified Asia in the decolonized world and the oneness of India and China were found to be untenable and unrealistic. Further divisions were created with the rise of Communism in China and the fear of its spread elsewhere in Asia.

One of the institutions affected by the transition from GMD to Communist rule in China in 1949 was Cheena Bhavana. Not only did funding for the institution end, but Tan's "honorarium," which he received from the GMD government, also ceased. In 1951, Visva-Bharati became a central university. As a consequence, according to Tan Lee (1999: 9), a son of Tan Yunshan, "some of the primary goals of this unique institute charted by Tagore himself got lost in the euphoria of run-of-the-mill university expansion. This, no doubt, caused great disappointment for Tan. His strong discipline in the tenets of Buddhism, Confucianism and Taoism permitted Tan to endure this in silence." Perhaps to demonstrate his dissatisfaction, Tan Yunshan refused to take a salary from the university. By this time, Tan had brought all his family members from China to India and, in 1954, seems to have even applied for Indian citizenship (West Bengal State Archives, File 120/41, Serial No. 1).

Nevertheless, Jawaharlal Nehru's persistence with his attempt to establish Asian solidarity and forge friendly relations between the ROI and the PRC played an important role in ushering in a new phase of India-China oneness. This phase, as discussed in the next chapter, is usually described with the idiom "Hindi-Chini bhai-bhai." Some of the writings that appeared in the 1950s were reminiscent of the earlier works that emphasized friendly and cordial relations between India and China in the past and in the foreseeable future. In fact, in many ways the 1950s became an extension of the 1930s and 1940s with regard to cultural exchanges and attempts to forge ties of brotherhood between India and China.

Similarly, the attempt to reconnect Asian polities, the main objective of the Asian Relations Conference, continued into the 1950s and may have even been realized for some with the convening of the Bandung Conference in 1955. As outlined in the next chapter, the participating nations at the Bandung Conference were able to agree on the principles that would guide the future relationships between the decolonized and new regimes in Asia. While the attempt to unite Asian societies through the invocation of past cultural connections may have failed in 1947, the realistic approaches to interstate relations outlined in the principles formulated in Bandung seem to have brought about a consensus among the diverse nations of Asia.

There was, however, also a continuation between the pre- and post-1950 period of India-China connections with regard to the concerns about the status of Tibet and the demarcation of borders. The issue of Tibet came to the forefront during the Asian Relations Conference and was also expressed in the reports of intelligence officers that date from 1947 to 1950. As pointed out in the next chapter, this remained one of the most contentious aspects of ROI-PRC relations in the 1950s even though it was overshadowed by the euphoria over the call to brotherhood. In fact, the Asian Relations Conference may have instigated the feeling of mutual distrust and suspicion, which similarly extended through to the 1950s. These disputes eventually led to the armed conflict between the ROI and the PRC in 1962. It became apparent then that the brotherhood between India and China expressed in the 1950s was a facade and that the principles of Bandung made no difference to the possibility of achieving Asian solidarity. Although brief, the armed conflict fundamentally questioned the relevance of the rhetoric of brotherly affinity and a harmonious past that was promoted during the first half of the twentieth century. It demonstrated, as was clear during the earlier periods as well, the weakness of romanticized ideals of pan-Asianism and the political ambitions that were connected to the ideology. The Japanese military expansion in the 1930s had already severely diminished the model of pan-Asian unity; the Asian Relations Conference in 1947 and the subsequent 1962 war proved that ideals and intellectual aspirations for India-China solidarity were also immaterial and unrealistic in the context of territorialized nation-states involved in border disputes. Indeed, Asia was no longer, and perhaps never had been, one.

NOTES

1. For a good overview of pan-Asianism and a review of the salient writings, see Saaler and Szpilman (2011).

2. See Ninomiya-Igarashi (2010: 59–71) for how such views of ancient Buddhist linkages influenced Okakura Kakuzō 岡倉覚三 (1862–1913) in his formulation of ideas related to the oneness of Asia.

3. The reference here is to the great Sikh ruler of Punjab, Maharaja Ranjit Singh (1780–1839), and the Mughal emperor, Akbar (1542–1605). Chittor and Jaipur were seats of power for different Rajput clans; Rathors is the name of a Rajput clan. Different Rajput groups fought with one another and allied with the Mughals and other non-Rajput rulers at various times.

4. For some of these writings, see Shimada (1990: 76–83).

5. For details about the presence of Indian revolutionaries in Shanghai and other parts of China during this period, and especially the activities of the Ghadar Party, see Thampi (2005: 179–214) and Deepak (2001: 61–85).

6. Das's book drew criticism from Western writers. The *Far Eastern Review*, in particular, took a strong stand against the book and the introduction written by Tang Shaoyi. In May 1917 it published a pointed critique of the ideas presented in the work by noting (Okakura 1917: 448), "Whatever faults Occidental nations may have committed in China in the past—and Taraknath Das has not overlooked any of them in his Pan-Asian gospel—foreign intercourse, foreign commerce, even foreign rule in parts of Asia have raised that small element of the Asiatic people which can conspire to drive the foreigner out of Asia and has

the intelligence to conceive of such schemes as Pan-Asianism out of the old world darkness in which the Occident found them a few generations ago, and is still doing more to stimulate them to national feeling and national integrity than anything which any of these Oriental peoples have ever done for themselves. It is significant that even the Pan-Asian movement has not been bred in native trained minds, but is being promoted by the ultra-Occidental Chinese, Japanese and Indians who have had their training in the West and have found the nucleus of their scheme ready made for them there in the misconception that 'All Asia is One.'"

7. According to an intelligence report (West Bengal State Archives, File 285A/25, Serial No. 117), Lim was originally from Fujian Province, where he worked under General Chen Jiongming 陳炯明. Subsequently, he traveled to Guangzhou and then through the Straits Settlements reached Rangoon. He was appointed as the principal of the Chinese school that Tagore visited in 1923. Shortly after his meeting with Tagore, Lim was fired by the school's management committee because it found his work "unsatisfactory." Unable to find a job at the local university, the report states, he went to Calcutta and from there to Shantiniketan. During his stay in Shantiniketan, Lim (1925) contributed a short article to the *Visva-Bharati Quarterly* on early Chinese literature. Lim later received his PhD from the University of Chicago and taught in Hong Kong and Shanghai. In the 1950s, he joined Nanyang University in Singapore as one of its founding faculty.

8. See, for example, Tan (1999).

9. The "want of funds" was also the reason for the end of Lim Ngo Chiang's tenure at Visva-Bharati. See Lim's letter to the secretary of Visva-Bharati office, a copy of which is preserved in the West Bengal State Archives, File 285A/25, Serial No. 117.

10. The volatile situation in Tibet in the early 1930s, especially the armed conflicts between Tibet and the neighboring Xikang and Qinghai regions, see Lin (2006: 58–70).

11. The key points in Tan's report appeared in two articles that were published in 1931 (Anon. 1931a, 1931b).

12. In 1932, Tan (1932a) wrote an open letter to the Dalai Lama mentioning his meetings with GMD officials and members of the Buddhist community in China after returning from Tibet. The thrust of the letter was to emphasize the need for the political integration of Tibet.

13. Tan contributed several essays to this journal, including those dealing with his travels in India (1932c) and his views on the political integration of Tibet (1932a and 1932b).

14. The early history of Cheena Bhavana, including the aims, objects, and sources of initial funding, can be found in Tan (1957).

15. In an application to renew his permit to stay in India dated 14 August 1965, Tan, who at this point had a passport issued by the People's Republic of China, gave the purpose of his visit as follows: "First as a Buddhist pilgrim and also invited by Gurudeva Tagore to teach Chinese at Visva-Bharati, Shantinike-

tan." He also gave his nationality as "Chinese-Indian" (West Bengal State Archives, File 120/41, Serial No. 1).

16. The translation of Tan's article is included in the British Foreign Office file numbered FO 371/16188 and titled "Tibetan Affairs."

17. Robert Sharf (2002) has argued that this clearly was not the case with regard to the development of Buddhism in China.

18. For the impact of French Indology on Nag and Bagchi and the role of the Greater India Society in advancing academic study of India intertwined with nationalistic goals, see Bayly (2004, 2007) and Stolte and Fischer-Tiné (2012: 82–88).

19. Bagchi also edited the journal *Visva-Bharati Annals*, volume 1 of which, titled *Cheena Bhavana*, was published in 1945. It contained seven essays by Cheena Bhavana's researchers. In the introduction to the volume, Bagchi (1945: i–v) provides a report on the work carried out at Cheena Bhavana in 1945 with the support of the scholarships provided by the Chinese Ministry of Education. Volume 2 of the *Annals*, published in 1949, contained Sanskrit translations of three Chinese Buddhist texts.

20. M. N. Roy, the former representative of the Comintern in China in 1927, was vociferous in his criticism of the Nationalists and especially the Chiang Kai-shek regime. This was not only reflected in his *Revolution and Counter-Revolution in China* published in 1946, but also in an essay that appeared in the 1938 issue of the *Modern Review*, which was critical of the Nationalists for their failure to address the ills of Chinese society.

21. Tan mentioned the Chinese civil war in passing in his speech during the Vaisakha Day celebrations at the Maha Bodhi Society in Calcutta on 22 May 1948. Wars were still going on in various regions of Asia, he noted, including the one "between the Nationalists and the Communists who are backed by a new aggressive power of a country, in China" (Tan 1948: 238).

22. While *Sino-Indian Studies* edited by Bagchi was an academic journal, Tan's *Sino-Indian Journal* mostly propagated the views of the Sino-Indian Cultural Society in India. It is surprising that in his brief essay on the establishment of Cheena Bhavana, Bagchi ([1947] 2012) makes no mention of the contributions by Tan Yunshan.

23. Jawaharlal Nehru had taken a clear stand in 1945 when delivering the presidential address at the Fifth Annual Meeting of the Sino-Indian Cultural Society in Shantiniketan, noting, "In the midst of a great deal of civil conflict in China I do not think there is anybody who challenges the right of the Generalissimo to be the leader of China. Even those critics who might differ from him have to acknowledge that in the present circumstances he is the only possible leader, the one man to lead China out of chaos and confusion" (Nehru 1947: 3).

24. Perhaps Tan, influenced by Gandhism (Tsui 2010), was using the term "*ahimsa*" as, in Partha Chatterjee's ([1987] 2010: 51) words, "the moral framework for solving every *practical* problem."

25. A separate file on Visva-Bharati (West Bengal State Archives, File 285/25, Serial No. 69/1925) was initiated in 1925. On the compilation of intelligence reports, see also the next chapter.

26. Similar views are expressed in the reports of the External Affairs Department, government of India, in a confidential file dated 1943. Preserved at the National Archives in New Delhi, the file is numbered 329-X, 1943.

27. "Rev. Tai Hsu's Goodwill Mission," *Maha-Bodhi*, 47: 517–18.

28. Nehru Memorial Museum and Library, *Jawaharlal Nehru Correspondence*, vol. 98. Tan also wrote a telegram to Nehru on the 24th, asking, "[C]an Abbot Tai Hsu call on you on 31st or first."

29. On Nehru's visit to Chongqing, see Samarani (2005: 8–12). B. K. Basu (1986), a member of the medical team, has written a detailed account of the work of the medical mission in China. Bagchi eventually went to China as a professor of Indology in 1947.

30. "Chinese Buddhist Mission in India," *Maha-Bodhi*, 48: 85–91.

31. "Chinese Buddhist Mission in India," *Maha-Bodhi*, 48: 85.

32. "Chinese Buddhist Mission in India," *Maha-Bodhi*, 48: 86.

33. "Address Presented to His Holiness Tai Hsu," *Maha-Bodhi*, 48: 92.

34. "Chinese Buddhist Mission in India," *Maha-Bodhi*, 48: 87.

35. "Chinese Buddhist Mission in India," *Maha-Bodhi*, 48: 88.

36. "Chinese Buddhist Mission in India," *Maha-Bodhi*, 48: 88.

37. "Chinese Buddhist Mission in India," *Maha-Bodhi*, 48: 88–89.

38. It should be noted, however, that Chiang Kai-shek wrote letters to Gandhi, Tagore, and Nehru for Dai Jitao to carry to India. Dated 17 October 1940, the letters to Gandhi and Nehru mention China's anti-Japanese war and the need for India and China to jointly work toward a better Asia. Academia Historica (國史館), File 002000000625A, "Jiang Zhongzheng wei Dai Jitao fang Yin shoushu zhi Yindu Gandi, Taiger, Nihelu zhuyouren han."

39. West Bengal State Archives, Home/Political (Bhabani Dutta Lane Branch), File No. 457/40, Serial No. 309, "Arrangement in Connection with Visit to Calcutta of HE Dr. Tai Chi Tao, Member of the Council of State, China." The report was particularly rebuking of the letter Tan wrote to Jawaharlal Nehru on 16 October 1940 requesting that the Indian leader help him organize Dai's trip.

40. West Bengal State Archives, Home/Political (Bhabani Dutta Lane Branch), File No. 457/40, Serial No. 309.

41. "Ninth Anniversary of the Mulagandhakuti Vihara at Sarnath," *Maha-Bodhi*, 48: 460–463.

42. West Bengal State Archives, Home/Political (Bhabani Dutta Lane Branch), File No. 457/40, Serial No. 309.

43. Dai was invited to India again in 1946, when the Benares Hindu University decided to confer a degree of doctor of literature, *honoris causa*, on him. Dai, however, was unable to travel because of illness. He sent several goodwill messages, including one to the Maha Bodhi Society. See Tan (1948).

44. "Correspondence," *Maha-Bodhi*, 55: 210.

45. "Notes and News," *Maha-Bodhi*, 55: 219.

46. Through Tan Yunshan, Taixu sent a letter to Nehru from Bombay thanking the Indian leader for the "hospitality and kindness shown" to the Chinese mission. Nehru Memorial Museum and Library, *Jawaharlal Nehru Correspondence, 1903–1947*, vol. 98.

47. On Chiang's visit to India in 1942, see Yang (1974), Wu (1987), Samarani (2005), and Yang (2015).

48. On the Tibet issue between the interim and independent Indian governments and the Republic of China, see Li (1960), Goldstein (1989), Lin (2006), and Zhu (2006).

49. For recent studies on the conference and its legacy, see Abraham (2008a, 2008b) and Singh (2011).

50. Carsun Chang, however, was not part of the delegation that eventually arrived in India.

51. Academia Historica, File No. 001000005088A, "Fan Yazhou huiyi" 泛亞洲會議 (Pan-Asian Conference). At the bottom of the list, Tan noted that it included entities that were not nations and those that had not yet become nations.

52. Academia Historica, File No. 001000005088A.

53. Academia Historica, File No. 001000005088A.

54. Academia Historica, File No. 001000005088A.

55. Mao Yiheng (1947: 9), who wrote a diary on his participation in the Asian Relations Conference, points to various mistakes on the map displayed at the conference venue. Drawn, he says, by a professor at Calcutta University, it used the dated term "Manchukuo," portrayed Taiwan as an autonomous region, and separated Tibet from China with a distinct line. It was this line, he says, that Yeh painted over with whitener that he personally bought in Delhi.

56. There are two other accounts about the Tibetan delegation at the conference. One is by Sampho Tenzin Dhondup [Sambo Tenzin Dundrup] (1998), the son of Sambo Teiji, and the other is a joint report by Sambo Tenzin Dundrup and Kunga Tsidrung (1984) published in China. These accounts do not mention the episode at the Chinese embassy in Delhi. However, Dhondup (1998: 60) reports that the Tibetan delegation attended a "formal gathering" organized by the Chinese delegates, where the "chief of Chinese delegation" offered, on behest of Chiang Kai-shek, Rs. 10,000 to each of the two chief Tibetan delegates and Rs. 5,000 each to the other Tibetan members.

57. A central intelligence officer from Assam (West Bengal Archives, File 923/44, Serial No. 302, 389), however, cited a news item that appeared in the 4 April 1947 issue of *Dawn*, which quoted a Tibetan delegate as saying, "[W]e think that India refused to recognise the independent status of Tibet only because it did not like to antagonise Marshall Chiang Kai-shek."

58. The book was in 1957 incorporated in the voluminous work titled *Discovery of Asia*.

59. Indian intelligence, however, reported that Pachow, Tan's colleague at Cheena Bhavana, published an article in a Chinese paper printed in Guangzhou in which he wrote that "the action of the Indian authorities must be considered

unsound and shewing [*sic*] a lack of consideration. Tibet is an integral part of China, and if the presence of a Tibetan delegation was absolutely necessary, it should have participated as a wing of the Chinese delegation and not acted independently." The intelligence report, which is dated 10 June 1947, pointed out that the article was written with "Tan Yun-shan's blessing" and further noted that the essay described "how the wall map of Asia in Delhi Conference Hall shewed [*sic*] Tibet as a separate Asian unit, but on the Chinese delegation lodging a strong protest, the map was modified" (West Bengal State Archives, File 120/41, Serial No. 1, 130).

60. The *Hindustan Times*, in an editorial ("Asian Relations Organization"), remarked that the setting up of the organization was the "most outstanding result of the Conference." It also noted that "Asian unity can be truly founded only on the internal unity of India and China and a permanent friendship between the two." This article and a few others that appeared in the Indian press during the conference can be found in a file (62(6)-OSIII, 1947) at the National Archives in New Delhi. There are three other files at the archives that also pertain to the Asian Relations Conference: 10(29)-NEF, 1947; 12(5)-NEF, 1947; and 542(3)-CA, 1947.

61. See Garver's (2001) detailed study of the apprehensions between India and China with regard to Tibet prior to the 1962 war.

62. Luo's telegrams to Chiang Kai-shek were dated 18 November and 23 December 1949. These are preserved in the Chiang Kai-shek collection at Academia Historica. The file is titled "Geming wenxian: dui Ying, Yin waijiao" 革命文獻：對英、印外交, serial no. 002000000453A.

63. Frank Moraes's views on the PRC are discussed in the next chapter.

64. There were other Bengali globe-trotters similar to Ramnath Biswas. Tim Harper of the University of Cambridge, for example, is working on K. C. Banerjee, who like Biswas also traveled widely on a bicycle.

65. It is not clear what Chinese phrase is used here.

66. The writings of Menon and Panikkar are also discussed in Thampi (2014).

67. Garver (2001: 40) suggests that "Prasad's views were probably representative of non-elite Indian opinion."

68. T. L. Shen was the GMD's representative in Lhasa.

69. Mullik specifically points to (1971: 104–105) the steps taken, from as early as February 1949, to set up a surveillance system directed toward the Chinese residents in India. This issue is discussed in more detail in the next chapter.

Chapter Five

The Geopolitical Disconnect

The vaunted friendship of three thousand years vanished into thin air; and India and China became all but enemies.
—K. P. S. Menon

From the late eighteenth century, when George Bogle embarked on his mission to meet with the Sixth Panchen Lama, to the Asian Relations Conference of 1947, Tibet had remained a region of contention and concern for the governments in India and China. Although disagreements continued shortly after the founding of the PRC, the rhetoric of "Hindi-Chini bhai-bhai" and the celebration of "the vaunted friendship of three thousand years" (Menon 1972: 259) in the 1950s seem to have sidetracked the serious discussion needed to address the various impediments in the bilateral relations. Even the new means to attain Asianhood through the idea of "Panchasheel," or the "Five Principles of Peaceful Co-Existence," could not prevent the two countries from engaging in an armed conflict in 1962. Although brief, the war left a psychological scar on the Indian government and people, which continues to prove a major hindrance in settling the territorial dispute that centers on the southern region of Tibet, the Indian state of Arunachal Pradesh.[1]

It is not necessary here to analyze the details of the disputes over Tibet and border demarcation that form the undercurrent of contemporary ROI-PRC relations. Numerous publications in the past several decades have already done so. Rather, we will focus on the experiences and perceptions of individuals with the backdrops of the establishment of new nations in the late 1940s (the Republic of India in 1947 and the People's Republic of China in 1949), the celebrations of India-China brotherhood in the 1950s, and the aftermath of the India-China war of 1962. Some of these individuals were prominent figures in the relations between the two countries, while others were writers, journalists, and peace activists. There were also intelligence officers and informants, whose role can only be discerned through the study of confidential files. Indeed, a wide variety of sources on ROI-PRC connections emerged in the 1950s. They included travel diaries, memoirs, newspaper and magazine articles, intelligence reports, and government communications. These works and reports provide a distinct, often nonstatist perspective on the complex connections between the two countries influenced by rapid changes in bilateral political relations.

First, we will survey Indian writings during the 1950s that relate to views on the emerging Communist state in China. These works reveal fascination as well as apprehension among Indians about the regime established by Mao Zedong. Some of these writers were members of the cultural and scientific delegations exchanged between the two countries during the first decade of ROI-PRC relations. The India China Friendship Association (ICFA) in India and its counterpart, the China India Friendship Association (CIFA), in China nurtured and promoted many of these interactions.[2] The advocates of India-China solidarity, several Indian newspapers, and the Indian prime minister Jawaharlal Nehru believed that these exchanges and the civilizational bonds between India and China in general would triumph over the inconveniences of territorial disputes and the divergences in political systems. There were other writers, however, who expressed concerns about the PRC's policies on Tibet. Moreover, at the same time as Nehru advocated a "brotherly" relationship between the two countries, Indian intelligence officers were troubled by Chinese Communist actions in Tibet and the suspected pro-PRC activities of a few thousand ethnic Chinese living in India. This mixture of fascination, ambivalence, and suspicion, and not just the "bhai-bhai" catchphrase, defined the first decade of ROI-PRC interactions.

The impact of this complex relationship on ethnic Chinese migrants in the ROI also needs to be examined. The early migration of the Chinese to British India was outlined in chapter 3. Since most of these persons were undocumented migrants, their status remained ambiguous after Indian independence and became more complicated with the emergence of the PRC and Taiwan as contending political entities. In the late 1950s, when mutual suspicion, distrust, and the failure to resolve the border issue resulted in the deterioration of political relations and eventually armed conflict, several thousand ethnic Chinese living in India were arrested, interned, and deported. By scrutinizing the intelligence records on the surveillance, arrest, and deportation of a person named Chang Xiufeng 常秀峰, the ways in which individuals were caught in the vicissitudes of ROI-PRC relations will be explored. The case of an Indian resident of Shanghai named Makhan Lal Das during this period is also briefly discussed in this section.

The Delhi–Peking Friendship March of 1963–1964 is a neglected episode in India-China relations because of the extensive focus on the 1962 war. The planning, execution, and eventual failure of the march, which involved people from several different countries, negotiations with government officials and nongovernmental organizations, and the attempt to create awareness by an international group of peace activists, constitutes another illuminating vignette. The Friendship March reveals how members of civil society tried to intervene in the deteriorating relations between the ROI and the PRC and attempted to reconnect the people of the two countries. However, the failure of the march essentially ended the rhetoric of civilizational bonds and the advocacy of brotherhood between the two countries. The relations between the ROI and the PRC then entered a new phase that was marked by detachment, mutual distrust, and the inability to resolve existing problems.

This takes us into the ways in which the rhetoric of India-China bonding has been reemployed since the late 1970s to often distract from the highly charged geopolitical disagreements that emerged after the 1962 war. The ideas of "Chindia" and a "geo-civilizational" relationship, and even the invoking of shared "victimhood" experienced under colonial rule by the leaders of the two countries before and after the war (Miller 2013),[3] promoted a return to the cordial relationship of the first millennium of the Common Era by bypassing contemporary geopolitical disputes. The advocates of these ideas, who are mostly based in the ROI and the PRC, believed that there is an inherent affinity between Indian and Chinese that can overcome the temporary disputes over border issues and create a utopic state of "ZhongYin datong" 中印大同, or "Grand Harmony between India and China." With only incremental results in the border negotiations, the foreign ministries in the two countries have found these ideas useful for promoting cultural exchanges and bilateral collaboration, albeit the public faces of such events and projects are often more prominent than the actual accomplishments of these Chindian efforts.

To conclude, two cases of global connections in contemporary ROI-PRC interactions are examined. Similar to the peace activists involved in the Delhi–Peking Friendship March, the renowned British philosopher Bertrand Russell was involved in preventing the escalation of the armed conflict between the ROI and the PRC in 1962. His correspondence with Jawaharlal Nehru, Zhou Enlai, and other world leaders demonstrate the importance of examining the role and contributions of individuals, including those not from the two regions, in ROI-PRC relations. The emergence of multilateral government organizations, such as the East Asia Summit

(EAS) and BRICS (Brazil-Russia-India-China-South Africa) forums that facilitate and sustain the connections between the ROI and the PRC through wider global networks and the recent One Belt, One Road (OBOR) initiative of the PRC that attempts to revive the economic connections across the ancient trade routes, will also be briefly examined.

THE FASCINATION WITH AND
TREPIDATION OVER RED CHINA

The early 1950s witnessed a slew of publications by members of the Chinese and Indian delegations visiting each other's countries as part of an effort to promote bilateral friendship and understanding. These included the works of leading Indian journalists, activists, and intellectuals, which were mostly composed in English (Fisher and Bondurant 1956a), but some of which were also published in regional languages such as Bengali, Hindi, and Gujarati. Also appearing frequently were articles and commentaries in Indian newspapers and weeklies that concerned the new regime in China and the prospects of future cooperation between the two countries (Fisher and Bondurant 1956a). While a majority of these publications offered positive analysis, and some, such as the weekly *Blitz*, actively advocated cordial relations with the PRC, others warned about the rise of Communist power in China and its possible impact on other Asian countries.[4] The Indian intelligence community, whose reports are now partially declassified, was clearly more troubled by Communist China and the activities of its agents in the ROI. It seems to have cautioned the Indian prime minister about the possible territorial threat from the Communist regime soon after the founding of the PRC. Concerns relating to border demarcation and the status of Tibet are also reflected in the official communications exchanged between the governments of the ROI and the PRC. In other words, a wide range of opinions existed over ROI-PRC interactions during the early 1950s, which, when examined together, indicate a complicated relationship between the two countries and a complex perception of the PRC among Indians.

The Tibet and border issues came to the forefront in the mid-1950s and dominated the discourse for the remaining part of the decade. Intelligence reports and official communications exchanged between the Indian and Chinese governments reveal that the bilateral relations changed dramatically not long after Asian unity and solidarity was celebrated at the landmark Bandung Conference of 1955 held in Indonesia. Criticisms of the PRC's activities in Tibet and Nehru's foreign policies became common in newspapers and other publications. Reminisces and views about the latter part of the 1950s appeared in several books written after the war of 1962, which were significantly more critical of the PRC and Nehru. This included books by the former diplomats and intelligence chiefs T. N. Kaul (1982, 2000) and B. N. Mullik (1971), as well as the diplomat and subsequently Indian foreign minister Natwar Singh (2009). In the view of many such postwar Indian writers, including K. P. S. Menon, the former ROI ambassador to the PRC who is cited in the epigraph to this chapter, China's "strong, aggressive, ultra-nationalistic Government" was to be blamed for ending the "vaunted friendship" between the two countries (Menon 1972: 258–260).

It should also be mentioned in passing that Chinese publications on India also followed a similar trajectory. Several Chinese visitors to India in the 1930s and 1940s wrote about the Indian struggle against British imperialism. Tan Yunshan, Dai Jitao, and Taixu, as discussed in chapter 4, all sympathized with the Indian independence movement. Newspaper and magazine articles published in Republican China also conveyed the same sentiments. After the establishment of the PRC, members of the Chinese delegations visiting the ROI wrote travelogues that highlighted the friendly relations between the two countries and the historical ties that bound them. These included the works by Bingxin 冰心 (aka Xie Bingxin 謝冰心; 1900–1999), who was one of the leading translators of the writings of Tagore, and Yan Wenjing 嚴文井 (1915–2005), a famous author of children's stories. PRC newspapers such as the *Renmin Ribao* (People's Daily) and the *Guangming Ribao* regularly published news about the "friendly" exchanges between India and China. Additionally, Chinese magazines printed articles about India that were translations from Russian. Some of the books on Indian history published during this period were also translations of works originally written in Russian. Indian films, such as *Awara*, dubbed into Chinese, were a major source of imaginary connections to India for the Chinese (Hang 2013; Yuan 2014).

Critical news items and editorials, albeit not book-length studies, about India, its stand on Tibet, Nehru's China policy, and the border standoff started appearing in China from the late 1950s. *Qiaowu bao* 僑務報 (Overseas Chinese Post), a newspaper on and for the Chinese overseas, for example, published reports and interviews of the Chinese who were deported from the ROI. Books by individual authors blaming India for instigating the 1962 war and thus, ending the centuries-long friendly relations appeared in the 1970s. Also noticeable are the changes made to some of the new editions of books published after 1958. These included the collection of the composer He Lüting's 賀綠汀 musical lyrics for choruses titled *He Lüting hechang qu ji* 賀綠汀合唱曲集 (Collection of He Lüting's Music for Choruses). While the 1957 edition of the work included the "ZhongYin youhao ge" 中印友好歌 (India-China Friendship Song), the later reprints did not.

Additionally, Jin Kemu 金克木 (1912–2000), a famous scholar at Peking University and a product of Cheena Bhavana, having studied there between 1941 and 1946, wrote a book titled *ZhongYin renmin youyi shihua* 中印人民友誼史話 in 1957. The following year the book was translated into English and published by the

Foreign Languages Press in China as *A Short History of Sino-Indian Friendship*. The first Chinese and English editions of the book carried the following statement as the epigraph: "Chinese and Indians became friends and never waged war on each other" (1958: 5). In the subsequent editions and its translations into Indian languages done in China after 1962, however, this sentence was deleted from the book. Jin Kemu himself penned a stinging critique in the *Guangming Ribao* (4 May 1959) of the Indian government and a "small group" of Indian "adventurists" (*yexin jia* 野心家) working against the Chinese. Indians and Chinese were no longer friends or brothers by the time the 1950s came to an end, and the relations between the two countries became disconnected.

The Enigmatic Brother

In August 1949, when the victory of the Communists in the Chinese civil war was certain, the Indian prime minister Jawaharlal Nehru noted the lessons that could be drawn from the anticipated political change in China. "Mainly the rise of communism in China," he explained, "makes people think more in terms of economics. The revolution in China is primarily an agrarian reform movement—part of a centuries-old movement—part of a centuries-old dissatisfaction in Asia. Land reform is the great need throughout this part of the world—is long overdue. If we expect to cope with communism in India, we must anticipate its agitation for these land reforms" (Costello 1949). It was perhaps this acknowledgment of the Communist revolution in China as a movement of the people dissatisfied with the feudal order that paved the way for Nehru to recognize the PRC three months after its founding.

Nehru clarified that the decision to recognize the PRC had been made only after he was satisfied with the new government, which "had the support of the people and intended to work for the good of the Chinese people" (*Times of India*, 1 January 1950: 9). Despite his close relationship with Chiang Kai-shek and other GMD officials, Nehru was resolute in his belief that the Communists offered a better future for China. In a letter dated 1 July 1949 to Vijaya-lakshmi Pandit, his sister and at that time the Indian ambassador to the United States and Mexico, Nehru sharply criticized the GMD regime, pointing out that "[t]he Chiang Kai-sheks and their group have singularly failed in China, failed not because of military reasons, but essentially because of their other policies." He added, "[W]ith all my friendship for the Chiangs, I cannot as Prime Minister or Foreign Minister shut my eyes to facts and to my conviction" (Nehru 1991: 12.408).

On 29 November 1949, Tan Yunshan forwarded a copy of a telegram sent by Zhu Jiahua, the chairman of the Sino-Indian Cultural Society, to Nehru, to which he appended his own letter. Tan urged the Indian prime minister to mediate between Chiang Kai-shek and Mao Zedong, "not only for the good of China alone but of the whole Asia and the world at large." He even offered to meet with Chiang and Mao on behalf of Nehru. However, the main thrust of Tan's letter was to convince Nehru to not recognize the Communist regime in China in haste. "The real heart of China," Tan wrote, was with Chiang. The Communists, Tan pointed out, "are still far from capturing the heart of the people, still less the spirit of the nation." In response to Tan's letter, Nehru contended that his intervention would not make any difference. "The communists," he noted, "have said some very hard things about me. I do not mind this personally, though I regret it because this kind of thing produces wrong results anywhere. My appealing to the communists will not produce the slightest impression upon them. My appealing to the Generalissimo at this stage would have little meaning and would almost be discourteous." He added, "As for recognition, there is no doubt that recognition has to be given to a fact. We have not been in a hurry to recognize. . . . If a step has to be taken, it should be taken at the right time, neither too early nor too late. To do it too late means that it has been taken under compulsion" (NAI MEA/7 (1) P /1952/).[5]

The ROI became the first non-Communist state to recognize the PRC when it did so on 1 January 1950. By the end of year, however, it was clear that there were several impediments to ROI-PRC relations. Two of these, the ambiguous status of Tibet and the unsettled issue of border demarcation, were already apparent prior to the establishment of the PRC. With the victory of the Communists in China, apprehensions about the spread of Communist ideology to other parts of Asia emerged as the third key factor that had the potential to hinder relations between the two countries. These three impediments shaped the views and perceptions of several Indian journalists, intellectuals, and politicians in the 1950s, resulting in two very divergent views on the PRC in the ROI. One group was fascinated by the accomplishments of the Communist state and the Chinese leaders such as Mao Zedong. People belonging to this group promoted the idea of India-China affinity and brotherhood through the organization of various cultural activities and the publication of books, articles, and pamphlets. The other group was critical of almost every aspect of what the PRC did domestically and in the international arena. The latter group saw the ROI and the PRC as two distinct and contending political and ideological systems, the outcome of which, they professed, would define the soul of Asia.

Despite the bleak situation created by the entry of the PLA into Tibet in 1950, Nehru and Zhou Enlai were able to steer the relations between the two countries toward the utopic world of "Hindi-Chini bhai-bhai." This new concept differed from the earlier views of Liang Qichao, who recognized India as the elder brother, and that of Nationalist China, which considered itself as the senior sibling in Asian affairs. The idea of ROI-PRC brotherhood in the 1950s advocated egalitarianism between the two nations that had attained independence (for ROI) and liberation (for PRC) almost at the same time. The frequent exchanges of goodwill missions and cooperation in the fields of arts and sciences, the state visits by Nehru and Zhou, the signing of the Panchasheel Agreement, and the successful meeting of Afro-Asian countries in Bandung in 1955 suggested that the utopic world of "Hindi-Chini bhai-bhai" was on course for realization.

The first series of publications in India on the PRC in the early 1950s advocated the establishment of this world of brotherhood uniting Indians and Chinese. These writings continued some of the idealism expressed in the 1930s and 1940s, frequently emphasizing the historical connections and the shared struggle against imperialism. In 1953, for example, the minister of Parliament and member of the Socialist Party N. Sreekantan Nair wrote (1953: [v]),[6] "From early childhood, China has been the land of my dreams. The hectic struggles of Dr. Sun Yat Sen and his sudden and unexpected success created a thrill in the heart of youth all over India. The rape of China by Japan naturally created a righteous indignation in my heart and I started taking keen interest in the Chinese developments." Others, who had been supporters of the Communist movement, wanted to see the new state succeed. Russy K. Karanjia, the editor of *Blitz* who visited the PRC in 1951, for instance, described the country "steadily and sturdily marching towards a planned goal of scientific perfection." He also noted (1952: 409), "You have to go to China and see Chinese Communists at work to realise the vitality, dynamism and glory of Communism. They do not regard themselves as a privileged class, nor do they claim fat salaries and other unfair advantages over the people."

Karanjia was part of an "unofficial" delegation that visited the PRC in September–October 1951 at the invitation of the Chinese government.[7] Pandit Sunderlal, the leader of the mission and the chairman of the ICFA, noted that in response to the invitation, "effort was made to include persons of all shades of opinion and from all parts of the country" (1952: 2). The delegation, which eventually consisted of thirteen members, was called the "Indian Goodwill Mission to China." In addition to Sunderlal and Karanjia, it included Tripurari Chakravarti, secretary of the ICFA in Calcutta and a lecturer in Chinese history at Calcutta University; Mrs. Hannah Sen, president of the All-India Women's Conference; J. C. Kuarappa, director of Agrarian Research Center in Wardha; V. K. R. V. Rao, director of the Delhi School of Economics; Mulk Raj Anand, vice president of the All-India Peace Council; Mohammad Habib, professor of history and politics at Aligarh Muslim University; Nirmal C. Bhattacharya of Scottish Church College in Calcutta; Khwaja Ahmad Abbas of the All-India Peace Council; G. P. Hutheesing, mentioned in the previous chapter; Mohammad Mujeen of the Jamia Millia Islamia in Delhi; and Mata Din Bagheria, a journalist.

The delegation reached Guangzhou in three batches and subsequently traveled as a group to Beijing, Mukden (i.e., Shenyang), Tianjin, Nanjing, Shanghai, and Hangzhou. After returning to India, the members of the delegation wrote of their impressions of the PRC. Each also had their individual impressions summarized for Sunderlal's book titled *China Today*, which is a 701-page tome with detailed descriptions of the conducted tour in the PRC. Meetings with Chinese scholars and intellectuals; political leaders, including Mao Zedong; and factory workers and managers by the Indian ambassador K. M. Panikkar and other Indians living in China are narrated in the volume. Similar to the writings of Karanjia, this book offers an optimistic outlook on ROI-PRC relations and affirms the economic and social developments taking place in the PRC.

The two thousand years (alt. three thousand years) of "friendly relations" between the Indian and Chinese people was often stressed in the speeches and meetings organized during the visit of the goodwill mission, reminiscent of those made during the monk Taixu's visit to India in 1940 (see chapter 4). Sunderlal (1952: 8) wrote that members of the delegation "felt that friendship between India and China was something deeper than merely political. It had roots in the history, religion and culture of our two ancient nations as also in the hearts of our people." Elsewhere, Sunderlal (1952: 99) notes that he was "convinced that the Chinese, as a people, whatever the reason, do feel a sort of kinship with the people of India." Emphasized also are the improvements that had taken place in the Chinese economy, industries, judicial system, gender equality, rural development, and education policy after the Communist revolution. These views were summarized in the statement released by the delegation in Shanghai after four weeks of travel across the PRC. "The progress they have made," the statement read (Sunderlal 1952: 377), "in all fields of national reconstruction, within two years of Liberation, is a source of inspiration to all Asian countries." It ended with a note stating, "We go back now, and the only way we can express our gratitude is to convey to our people the goodwill that we, as their representatives, have received from the people and the leaders of New China, and the phenomenal, all-round progress we have observed, and thus to review and strengthen the silken bonds of friendship that have existed between our countries for well nigh two thousand years" (Sunderlal 1952: 378–379).

Sunderlal's book does not contain any reference to the impediments in ROI-PRC relations mentioned above. As Margaret W. Fisher and Joan V. Bondurant (1956a: 251) explain, Sunderlal was "an earnest and uncritical collector of data, setting down without question whatever he was told by his hosts (including Ambassador Panikkar), seemingly unaware that what he was reporting often possessed implications completely at variance with his own enthusiastic interpretations." They (Fisher and Bondurant 1956a: 253n.7) also point out that Sunderlal removed some of the criticisms of the PRC that the members of the delegation made in their contributions to the volume. J. C. Kumarappa was one such person who had used the word "evil" to describe the Communist regime in China and was critical of some of the policies of the PRC in his book titled *People's China: What I Saw and Learnt There*. However, his piece in Sunderlal's book did not carry any such comments or views.

Raja Hutheesing's short piece included in Sunderlal's book is also a positive appraisal of the PRC but very different from the critical views of the country he offered in his own book titled *The Great Peace: An Asian's Candid Report on Red China* (later reprinted with the title *Window on China*), published in 1953. "I, a visitor," he wrote (Hutheesing 1953: 6) about the conducted tour, "moved as an automaton directed about to see and to understand only that which redounded to the glory of a totalitarian state. I realized that communism was the new god of China, the Holy Dragon." He also reported that after returning from China he had sent a "personal note" to Nehru stating that there had been in China "little economic progress despite the claims of exportable food surplus" (Hutheesing 1953: 7–8). Hutheesing visited China a second time in 1952 as a representative of the Press Trust of India with an "official" Cultural Delegation led by Vijayalakshmi Pandit. His book is thus a reflection of his two visits, written with a very different agenda than Sunderlal, who intended to promote friendly relationship between the PRC and the ROI, most likely as part of the objectives for the India-China Friendship Association.

Hutheesing's antipathy toward the PRC is evident from the beginning of his book. He perceived the country from his anti-Communist viewpoint and was critical of almost all aspects of what he described as the "totalitarian" control by the state over the lives of the Chinese people. He argued that the "thought control" or "brainwashing" instituted by the Communists was to prevent individuals from having the right to think. There was, as a result, no liberty for individuals, no source of news other than the government, no freedom of movement, no voice for the people in the forming of policy, no rule of law (Hutheesing 1953: 234–239). Therefore, the "New

China" for him was "dogmatic, harsh and cruel" (Hutheesing 1953: 173–174), a "totalitarian dictatorship in which the Communists are its temporal and spiritual rulers" (1953: 240).

Hutheesing, while praising some of the developments that had taken place in the rural areas and the improvements in the lives of the peasantry, was unconvinced about the statistics provided by the PRC government about crop production and its ability to export surplus to foreign countries, including about five hundred thousand tons of rice and millet sent to India in 1951. "These exports," he wrote (1953: 86), "have been called political moves made at the expense of the Chinese consumers," and he pointed to reports from Hong Kong "stating that while there was famine in some areas in China, China was exporting food to India."

One of Raja Hutheesing's major concerns was Communist China becoming the new imperialist power in Asia and subsequently threatening its neighbors. Mao's aim, according to him, was to eventually create Asian unity by compelling "the submission of the world to the Sino-Soviet supremacy." Hutheesing suggests that the Chinese government might use its migrant population in Southeast Asia and India to accomplish this goal (Hutheesing 1953: 71). Specifically with regard to the ROI, he writes (1953: 72), "China, while outwardly paying tribute to a 'two-thousand-year-old friendship' and 'the interflow of culture,' has little consideration for the government of India or Indian interests." In fact, he argues (1953: 74) that the PRC with its "powerful army" did not intend "perhaps to attack, because aggression is not possible, but certainly to influence and promote the [Communist] 'liberation' of India."

Frank Moraes, who was a formal member of the 1952 delegation, had similar views about the danger that Communism posed to Asian peace in general and to the ROI in particular. Moraes had previously traveled to the ROC in 1944 as a war correspondent for the *Times of India*. As can be discerned from his book *Report on Mao's China*, Moraes was a close friend of Raja Hutheesing, often having conversations and visiting places together during their tour of the PRC in 1952. Similar to Hutheesing, he underlined the totalitarian form of government under Mao and pointed to the lack of individual freedom in the PRC. "In China," he wrote (1953: 53), "I discovered that a man's mind could be chained, tethered, and imprisoned." Moraes was more introspective about the two distinct forms of government that had emerged in Asia. "By a queer quirk of fate," he writes (1953: 207),

> Asia's two most densely populated countries, which are also neighbours, are the testing grounds for two differing and contending political philosophies. If China proves that her system of government ensures economic security to the vast mass of her people without detracting greatly from their sense of freedom, Asia will be lost to Communism. If India, on the other hand, demonstrates that democratic government can ensure not only economic security but individual liberty, then Asia will be won to democracy. What India and China are today in fact doing is wrestling for the political soul of Asia.

He adds later (Moraes 1953: 211), "The question our generation has to face is whether a war between Communism and democracy is inevitable. Can the two systems subsist side by side at peace with each other, or must they inevitably collide?"

Moraes likens the Chinese advocacy of "Asian peace and friendship" to the promotion of the Japanese idea of Asian Co-Prosperity, which he points out meant the prosperity of the Japanese alone. "The Chinese phrase," he argues (1953: 173), "carries much the same menace." Furthermore, he points to the "irredentist urge" in China for the recovery of lost territories and, similar to Hutheesing, suggests the possible recruiting of the Chinese overseas in order to achieve the goal (1953: 174). He gives (1953: 211) a dire warning to the leaders of the ROI:

> India has no illusions about Communism, though some of her leaders unfortunately cherish romantic notions on the country's

relationship with China. They like to idealise Mao as a benevolent Buddha eager for Asian peace and friendship. So he is—but on his own terms. Here India's danger lies in being an unconscious accessory to Communist China, in aiding and abetting her plans until the Chinese Frankenstein swallows up Asia, including India.

The divide among the Indians with regard to the newly founded PRC is evident from the above views of Karanjia, Sunderlal, Hutheesing, and Moraes. This rift was primarily along ideological lines, between those who sympathized with Communism and those who opposed it. It should be noted that the books by Raja Hutheesing and Frank Moraes were published in the United States. Although news about the rave reviews Moraes's *Report on Mao's China* received in the United States appeared in the Indian press, no Indian edition of either it or Hutheesing's *The Great Peace* was published locally. While Moraes's reflections of his trip were serialized in the *Times of India* in June 1952 under a column called "Journey to China," none of his ten contributions mention the potential threat Asia and India faced from the Communist PRC as he argues in his book. It was only at a talk Moraes delivered at the Rotary Club in Bombay on 25 June 1952 that he alluded to the looming conflict between the Communist and democratic systems, represented by the PRC and the ROI respectively, in Asia (*Times of India*, 26 June 1952: 5). It is possible that Moraes and Hutheesing primarily addressed American readers in their books and therefore gave greater coverage to the possible threat from a Communist China.

Writings in vernacular languages also followed this pattern of either expressing concern about or praising the PRC government. However, most avoided any mention of possible confrontation between the ROI and the PRC. While Brajkishore Shastri's *From My China Diary*, originally written in Hindi, has a critique of the PRC government similar to the views expressed by Hutheesing and Moraes, Manoj Basu's (1953) Bengali travelogue *Chin Dekhe Ealam* (Having Seen China) is an enthusiastic portrayal of the country. Basu was a member of the Indian Peace Delegation that visited the PRC in September–October 1952. His writings were initially serialized in the magazine *Desh* and later published in book form. This became one of the most popular works on the PRC among Bengali readers during the 1950s and was reprinted several times.

Almost all of the above writings, laudatory and critical, were by Indians who visited the PRC as part of delegations exchanged between the two countries or invited by the Chinese government. The ICFA, founded in 1951 and based in Bombay, with branches in several other Indian cities, and the CIFA located in Beijing played a critical role in organizing and managing several of these delegations (see figure 5.1). These two organizations also planned various cultural events, rallies, exhibitions, and lectures and held annual meetings. In fact, these events facilitated the circulation of knowledge about respective countries and were instrumental in propagating the message of "Hindi-Chini bhai-bhai" at the grassroots level. In October 1952, for example, the ICFA organized a "China Week" to mark the third anniversary of the founding of the PRC. Over one hundred thousand people were reported to have participated in the various events that included exhibition of Chinese arts and crafts, mass meetings, lectures, and cultural shows in and around Bombay (*Blitz* 11 October, 1952: 5). It is clear that these friendship/goodwill visits had a performative aspect.[8] The members of the visiting Chinese delegations delivered public lectures, participated in cultural performances, and wrote editorials in Indian newspapers that promoted India-China brotherhood. In other words, they were engaging with the common populace and enacting their parts in the demonstration of brotherhood between the Chinese and Indians.

Emerging out of these events and the efforts of the ICFA and CIFA was the "Hindi-Chini Poem," composed by the famous actor and member of Parliament Harindranath Chattopadhyaya, and the

Figure 5.1.   Event marking the founding of the China-Indian Friendship Association, 1952.

"India-China Friendship Song" written by the renowned composer He Lüting. The beginning lines of the "India-China Friendship Song" read as follows (He 1957: 62–63):

> The tall Himalayan mountains cannot split
> our friendship;
> The people of the two countries India and China
> have got along better than brothers.
>
> Along more than three thousand *li* of borders
> never has? there been a war
>
> The two thousand years of history
> have all been about cultural exchanges

The "Hindi Chini Poem" ended with the following stanza:

> Two great leaders having met
> Lo! the final dice is cast—
> An historic stage is set—
> From the first act to the last

> Human beings shall enact
> Such a dream as will bring
> Happiness from act to act,
> Let our Asian millions sing
> Tribute to the mighty pact
> Which shall ever be intact,
> Pandit Nehru, Chou En-lai
> Hindi-Chini bhai-bhai

Both of these adulatory pieces were composed in 1954 to com-memorate the signing of the "Agreement between the Republic of India and the People's Republic of China on Trade and Intercourse between Tibet Region of China and India" or the Panchasheel Agreement. The Chinese song was subsequently played at events organized by the ICFA and CIFA. Together the song and the poem epitomized the peak of "Hindi-Chini bhai-bhai" euphoria.[9]

A [Renewed] Sense of Asianhood

The signing of the Panchasheel Agreement on 29 April 1954 marked an important development in relations between the PRC and the ROI. Despite the exchanges of delegations and goodwill missions, the ROI and the PRC had not in any comprehensive manner addressed the impediments present in their relationship. The main outcome of the agreement was the formal recognition of the PRC's sovereignty over Tibet by the ROI. In fact, the preamble to the agreement declared that the two governments had "resolved to enter into the present agreement" based on the principles of mutual respect of each other's territorial integrity and sovereignty, mutual nonaggression, mutual noninterference, equality and mutual benefit, and peaceful coexistence.

The Panchasheel Agreement was widely applauded by the In-dian media. The *Times of India* contrasted the successful diplomacy between the ROI and the PRC with the "endless frustrations" of the Cold War among Western countries. "The Peking negotiations suc-ceeded," the editorial explained, "because both sides were realistic enough to take into account each other's special interests" (1 May 1954: 9; Fisher and Bondurant 1956a: 24). The *Deccan Herald*, often critical of Nehru, praised the government, saying that the agreement sought the "elimination of fear which is at the root of all present-day problems." It then commended Nehru by noting that the Agreement served "as an object lesson for other countries in that the Prime Minister claims it as the most important achievement of his foreign policy." A commentary in *Blitz* declared that the agreement was a "realistic approach to our Tibetan relations" (Te-jura 1954: 13). More laudatory comments appeared on the front page of *Blitz* on 28 June 1954, the day Zhou Enlai departed India after his four-day visit, including in an article written by R. K. Karanjia. The headline of the article read, "The Himalayas Fall as Nehru & Chou Meet to Usher in the Golden Age of Asia" (Karanjia 1954).

The Chinese premier had gone to the ROI directly from Geneva, where he attended a conference held to address the issues of Korea and Vietnam. The PRC was the sole Asian representative at the conference, but Zhou insisted in his speech that there must be a unified Asian voice on these matters. In a telegram written to Mao Zedong and Liu Shaoqi from Geneva, Zhou stated that his purpose in visiting India was to "conduct preparation work for signing some form of Asian peace treaty and to strike a blow at the Unites States' conspiracy to organize a Southeast Asia invasive bloc" (Zhou 1954). This decision by Zhou to visit the ROI directly from Geneva put the Indian press in a frenzy, with several commentators envi-sioning the realization of the dream of Asian solidarity. The posi-tive reviews of Zhou's visit were not limited to *Blitz*; the *Amrita Bazar Patrika*, putting to rest the concerns of Frank Moraes and Hutheesing, stated that "the gaze of the Prime Ministers of India and China in spite of their ideological differences is unfalteringly fixed on collective peace" (Fisher and Bondurant 1956a: 81).

Prime Minister Nehru's visit to China in October 1954 and the Bandung Conference in March–April 1955 also contributed to the belief in the 1950s that the "decade of Asia" had finally dawned. While the Soviet Union and the United States were carving the world into two military blocs, each armed with nuclear weapons, the Asian countries, led by the ROI and the PRC, were coming together despite differences in political ideologies and lingering distrust. The "Hindi-Chini bhai-bhai" idiom was no longer mere rhetoric, nor did the ideas of pan-Asianism and "Asianhood" seem unfeasible. G. P. Reddy (1954), the China correspondent for the *Times of India*, for example, summarized the impact of Nehru's visit as "going a long way in helping China develop a broader international perspective and think of peacefully co-existing with countries outside the Communist orbit. It would also help China develop a sense of 'Asianhood,' which began with Mr. Chou En-lai's visit to New Delhi, by co-operating with other Asian countries in building an area of peace in this continent." Nehru himself declared at a mass rally held in Calcutta after his return, "The people of China do not want war. They are busy constructing their country and working hard to remove poverty" (*Times of India*, 3 November 1954: 7).

The Panchasheel Agreement gave a significant impetus to the exchanges taking place between the ROI and the PRC. According to a report published in *Blitz* in 1958, forty Indian delegations visited China and thirty missions from the PRC arrived in India between 1954 and 1958 (Overstreet and Windmiller 1959: 431). Indeed, the concept of Panchasheel, in the middle of the 1950s, seemed a fitting solution for the divergent political systems, conflicting territorial claims, issues of nationality and citizenship among immigrant populations, and the Cold War between the Soviet Union and the United States that substantially divided a decolonizing Asia. Especially for the ROI and the PRC, the agreement of 1954 based on the Panchasheel principles had appreciable impact on curtailing the dispute over the status of Tibet. Similarly, the Panchasheel Agreement between the PRC and Burma, also signed in 1954, led to the demarcation of borders between the two nations. In 1956, the PRC and Nepal also concluded an agreement based on Panchasheel, ending, as the *Times of India* (1 October 1956: 6) reported, "the ambiguity in the relationship between Kathmandu and Peking, particularly after the change in the status of Tibet consequent on its closer integration with China."

Some even believed that Panchasheel was a model not only for Asia but for the entire world. The *Amrita Bazar Patrika* (2 April 1955; Fisher and Bondurant 1956a: 122), for example, proposed that a global catastrophe could only be avoided by "full and frank adoption of the five principles of co-existence—Panch Sila—which Asian statesmanship has offered to the world." The Bandung Conference in 1955 was a culmination of the discourse on Panchasheel, where great effort was made to resolve the fear of the spread of Communism, disagreements about territorial claims, and concerns over immigrant populations. Success at the meeting in Indonesia would then, as the participants at the Bandung Conference believed, lead to goals of "Asianhood."

The Asian Relations Conference, as discussed in the previous chapter, was a failure primarily because of the disagreements between the provisional Indian government and the ROC over the status of Tibet. Even though the ROC agreed to host the subsequent conference, it never made any attempts to follow through with the plans. At the Bandung Conference, however, the status of Tibet was never an issue, since it seems to have been settled with the signing of the Panchasheel Agreement of 1954. The fear of the Communist regime in China among various groups had also subsided with the visits of Zhou Enlai to the ROI and Nehru to the PRC in the same year. There was still trepidation about the PRC and its interests in Southeast Asia and the spread of Communism into that region, which were issues that Zhou Enlai addressed in his speeches at the Bandung Conference.

In his two speeches and his closing remarks, Zhou Enlai, without mincing words, directly responded to the concerns of some of the participating countries. In the speech delivered on 23 April 1955, Zhou said, "As for the so-called communist expansion and subversive activities, certain delegates seated here are very polite; they only talked about the Soviet Union and did not mention China. However, China is also a communist-led country. Therefore, we could not but think that these delegates also meant to include China. As for this issue, there needs to be an answer." Zhou then outlined seven guarantees with regard to relations with foreign countries: mutual respect for sovereignty and territorial integrity, mutual nonadoption of invasive actions or threats, mutual noninterference or nonintervention on internal affairs, acknowledging racial equality, acknowledging the equality of countries no matter their size, respecting that people of all countries have the right [and] freedom to decide their own lifestyle and political and economic systems, and mutual nondetriment. He added another point to the list, guaranteeing the use of peaceful methods to resolve international disputes. Here Zhou highlighted the role played by the ROI in the Korean dispute. "The Korean armistice," he noted, "received the support of many countries seated here, especially the promotion and support of India; this led to the possibility of a gradual diminishing of hostilities on the battlefield."

Zhou's speeches were widely applauded and his propositions credited for the success of the Bandung Conference. Members of the Indian media, some of whom were already familiar with the Chinese premier's diplomatic skills, declared Zhou as the "outstanding personality," a "hero" of Bandung (Fisher and Bondurant 1956a: 136). A columnist using the pseudonym "Onlooker" wrote for the *Times of India* (25 April 1955) that "Mr. Chou En-lai must have enjoyed himself hugely. Brought in as a rakish wolf amid a flock of embarrassed and suspicious sheep he succeeded by his lamb-like demeanour in making the rest look far more wolf-like than he." The *Hindu* (27 April 1955; Fisher and Bondurant 1956a: 138), on the other hand, summarized Zhou's contribution in the following way:

> Mr. Chou En-lai's assurances of China's peaceful intentions will no doubt pave the way for recognition of his Government by certain Arab States. . . . [His] offer [concerning Formosa] will, in any case, lower tension in the Far East and make it easier for the whole problem to be taken up when passions have cooled.

Several state leaders and the media representatives who were present at the Bandung Conference were convinced, as one reporter for the *Times of India* wrote (Reddy 1955), "of the common destiny and the basic unity of the Asian-African people." Even those who were consistently critical of the PRC also praised Zhou for alleviating the fears about the most powerful Communist state in Asia. In fact, the Chinese premier's performance at Bandung managed to unite the two most radical groups in India. *Janata* (Fisher and Bondurant 1956a: 139), a mouthpiece of the anti-Communist, anti-Nehru, Praja Socialist Party, heaped praise on the PRC by stating that

> Asian and African nations did not quite agree with the United States and her allies when they branded People's China as an aggressor sometime back. And now their stand has been vindicated at Bandung. People's China has once again, as she had done at Geneva, demonstrated her willingness to steer clear of the Moscow axis, at least in so far as Asian affairs are concerned.

New Age, the weekly of the Communist Part of India, reached the same conclusion (Fisher and Bondurant 1956a: 140):

The cornerstone of this new and mighty unity of the Asian and African Powers is the solid bond of friendship that unites Asia's two greatest Powers—India and China. It is this joining of hands across the Himalayas that gave the inspiring lead at Bandung, and upset all the calculations of Washington.

Finally, a commentary published in the *Times of India* (28 April 1955: 8; Fisher and Bondurant 1956a: 138) suggested that the Bandung Conference was an important step toward realizing Nehru's vision of Afro-Asian unity in a decolonized world. It noted,

Nehru was also playing for high stakes at Bandung—in a sense, higher stakes than Chou for his Afro-Asian strategy includes Chou. What Nehru is in effect attempting to do . . . is to create an Afro-Asian area of peace which would include China. In other words, China would be a member not of the Russian but of the Asian orbit with a Communist government owing neither allegiance nor subservience to Moscow but building up its own Marxist structure of society conditioned entirely by Chinese needs. The Chinese, Nehru believes, will always be Chinese.

The author of the above passage also felt that Nehru was attempting to reduce the apprehension among many political leaders and intellectuals in Asia about the prospects of two distinct political systems coexisting peacefully. "What Nehru appears to visualise," the author explained, "is an Afro-Asian world where democratic and communist governments co-exist in peace and progress." For many in India the ideals of pan-Asianism at this moment in time seem to have come to fruition.

The End of Brotherhood

Not everyone was confident about the success of the Panchasheel Agreement or the expressions of solidarity at the Bandung Conference. In *My Years with Nehru: The Chinese Betrayal*, B. N. Mullik, explaining the developments leading to the military confrontation between the ROI and the PRC in 1962, wrote (1971: 154) that the Intelligence Bureau was "disturbed" by the signing of the 1954 Panchasheel Agreement and felt that it "had gone entirely in favour of China and against the interests of India." The recognition of Tibet as a province of China under this agreement, he believed, not only prevented the ROI from expressing sympathy for the Tibetan people but also "shut India out from raising the question of Tibetan autonomy in the United Nations." He also argued that the agreement had no benefit for the ROI as far as trade was concerned and, in addition, gave the Chinese an opportunity to plant their spies in places such as Kalimpong through their trade agencies and support groups "who were hostile to the Government of India" (Mullik 1971: 155). On Zhou Enlai's performance at the Bandung meeting, Mullik suggests the Chinese premier's deficiencies in English-language skills led to disagreements with Nehru with regard to finalizing the declaration of the conference. "Throughout this period of 1952–58," he writes (1971: 161), "on the surface, Sino-Indian friendship was maintained," but while the ROI maintained no relationship with Taiwan, the PRC instigated "several cases of frontier violations" and used the time to "build a network of roads, both arterial and to our frontiers, and consolidating her position even in the remote parts of Tibet."

Mullik's assertion that Nehru was always aware of the Chinese threat is an oft-cited reference, especially for those advocating the launch of a "forward policy" by the ROI,[10] resulting in a military response by the Chinese in November 1962. Mullik alleges that as early as 1952 Nehru believed that the PRC intended to humiliate the ROI and quotes the Indian prime minster as saying,

China in the past had added vast territories to her empire and her maps still showed that she included portions or the whole of many present-day independent counties to be within that empire. She was not expecting to regain all the territory immediately and she was quite willing to wait, but nothing could swerve her from her final aim. China also felt that even apart from outright conquest, she could not just now even aspire for over-lordship; but she wanted to be treated as an elder brother—and in the Chinese society the elder brother was very important— and as China could not force the elder-brother theory on India, hence Indian influences had to be removed or liquidated. So by humiliating India, China warned the other countries that they should not also misbehave. (Mullik 1971: 455)

This claim of Nehru being aware of a Chinese threat is mentioned in several other sections of Mullik's book. In fact, he points out that in 1952, Nehru had also warned the IB to "never be deluded by Chinese assertions of friendship and we should always be prepared to counter Chinese claims against Indian territory" (1971: 179–180). He repeats (1971: 587–588) these views of Nehru again toward the end of the book, saying of the prime minister,

from the very beginning, when he started dealing with China, he had apprehensions that China could not be fully trusted though she was professing thousand year old friendship. He knew that in actual fact the two civilizations had been antagonistic to each other for those two thousand years; and now that the two eco-nomic systems were so much at variance, it was essential for China to humiliate India in the eyes of the non-communist world of Asia and Africa to prove not only the superiority of Chinese culture but also of the Chinese economic system

Mullik's descriptions of Nehru's assessments of the PRC in 1952 are difficult to confirm. In the aftermath of the war, Mullik was one of the people blamed for failing to provide proper intelli-gence to Nehru about the PRC and its activities in the border re-gion. What is certain, however, is the surveillance policy over the ethnic Chinese communities residing in the ROI, which Mullik instituted soon after he became head of the IB in 1950. He did this because of the suspicion of possible infiltration by the Chinese Communists into the ROI. This policy eventually led to the deportation and internment of Chinese residents as soon as relations between the two countries started deteriorating in 1959.

Some of the concerns of the IB, it should be noted, were not unique. As pointed out above, several writers continued to question the real intent of the PRC despite its promotion of Panchasheel as the solution to territorial and ideological disputes within Asia. Girilal Jain was a leading critic of the PRC and the Panchasheel treaties during the latter half of the 1950s. A reporter for the *Times of India* in the 1950s and subsequently the editor of the paper from 1978 to 1988, Jain wrote several books on the PRC between 1956 and 1960 that warned readers about the use of the Panchasheel Agreement by the PRC as a diversion to occupy territories in the ROI, Nepal, and Burma. In his *What Mao Really Means*, Jain detailed the ways in which Mao Zedong tried to exert dictatorial power within China and at the same time fight the imperialist powers internationally. The "emphasis on the solidarity of Socialist countries on the one hand of the Afro-Asian countries on the other" was, according to him, aimed at accomplishing that latter objective. Commenting perhaps on the Bandung meeting, Jain writes (1957: 72–73), "During the current phase, it is essential to isolate the imperialist countries from the newly-liberated countries of Asia and Africa. In the pursuit of this policy, it is necessary for the Chinese regime to give the impression of sweet reasonableness. Chou En-lai is ideally suited to play the role of a good friend."

Jain also authored a pamphlet titled *Chinese "Panchaseela" in Burma*, in which he argued that the agreement signed between the PRC and Burma in 1954 did not prevent the former from sending its troops into the territories of the Southeast Asian state. The aims of the PRC's military moves in Burma's frontier regions included, according to Jain (1956: 11), "attempts to disrupt the loyalty of the tribals in that part of the country, large-scale illegal immigration of Chinese and the financing of the activities of the local communists and allies." In 1960 he wrote another book titled *Panchsheela and*

After: A Re-appraisal of Sino-Indian Relations in the Context of the Tibetan Insurrection, in which he argued that his previous claims about the PRC's intentions had been vindicated. Nehru, he points out, had finally become aware of the fact that "people's faith in 'Panch Sheela' and Bandung principles has been shaken" (1960: 1). He contended that border incursions by Chinese troops in Indian territories began after the Bandung Conference because "the Chinese felt emboldened to pursue their objectives in a more forthright manner" (1960: 112). His main argument in the book was that "out of the policy of surrender in Tibet was born 'Panch Sheela.'"

By the time Girilal Jain wrote the above passages on the Chinese disregard of the 1954 agreement, the perceptions of the PRC in the ROI had turned considerably negative due to the armed conflict between PLA forces and the Tibetans in early 1959. The military confrontations forced the Fourteenth Dalai Lama to escape and seek exile in the ROI in late March–early April 1959. Concerned with these events, even the Communist Party of India (CPI) acknowledged in March 1959 that "all honest men in our country have been extremely pained by recent events in Tibet" (Anon. 1963: 1). But it continued to blame Western imperialists and the Chiang Kai-shek government in Taiwan for instigating the PRC's military action in Tibet in 1959. Only in October–November 1962 did the CPI unequivocally criticize "Chinese aggression." The resolution adopted by the National Council of the CPI on 31 October–2 November 1962 stated,

> The behavior of socialist China towards peace-loving India has most grossly violated the common understanding in the communist world arrived at in the 81 Parties' Conference in 1960 in relation to peaceful coexistence and attitude to newly-liberated countries and the question of war and peace. Socialist China has fallen victim to narrow nationalistic considerations at the cost of the interests of world peace and anti-imperialism, in its attitude towards India.

The watershed moment in the relations between the ROI and the PRC may have taken place prior to the military actions of the PLA forces in Tibet in 1959. The *Times of India* in early 1959 cited a report in the *Hong Kong Tiger Standard* which declared that "the year 1958 will probably go down in history as the time which marked India's disenchantment with Communist China" (*Times of India*, 5 January 1959: 7). The Hong Kong paper, which is now known as the *Standard*, cited several reasons for this "disenchantment." The effect of Chinese dumping of cheap textiles in Southeast Asian markets on Indian exports; the "aggressive policies" of the PRC in the South China Sea; the border disputes in the Ladakh, Northeast Frontier Agency (NEFA), and Bara Hoti regions; and internal problems caused by the failure of the Hundred Flowers movement were listed as the key reasons. Slogans like "Hindi-Chini bhai-bhai," the paper noted, "were today an almost dying echo."

Also in 1958, the Indian Ministry of Home Affairs seems to have issued an instruction to government officials asking them to "cut off all connections" with the ICFA (Letter from Nirmal Chandra Bhattacharyya to Pandit Sunderlal, File No. 49: 101, Pandit Sunderlal Papers). Additionally, in March 1958, Jawaharlal Nehru is supposed to have said the following to G. Parthasarathi, the Indian ambassador in China: "So, when has the foreign office told you Hindi-Chini bhai-bhai? Don't you believe it. I don't trust the Chinese one bit, despite Panchsheel [*sic*] and all that. The Chinese are arrogant, devious, hypocritical and thoroughly unreliable." These statements appear in the diary of G. Parthasarathi, released posthumously by the diplomat's son. The context does not seem to be any specific event in ROI-PRC relations but Nehru's doubts about V. K. Krishna Menon (*Indian Express*, 22 January 2010).[11]

The differences highlighted in the Hong Kong newspaper and whatever apprehensions Nehru might have had were amplified by Chinese military actions in Tibet in February 1959 and, more importantly, disagreements with regard to the border demarcation that started to come to the fore at the same time. The border issues were highlighted in newspapers and were raised in Parliament by members from every political party, and Nehru himself voiced his displeasure with the PRC. These concerns about the PRC had a significant impact on the work of the IB, which intensified its surveillance over the Chinese communities, members of the Communist Party of India, and those suspected of being "pro-PRC." At the same time, the general populace started becoming aware of the serious contentions over territorial claims between the ROI and the PRC through newspaper reports and the raucous parliamentary debates.

These reports and debates that portrayed the PRC as the aggressor and occupier of Indian territories did not subside even after Zhou Enlai's third visit to the ROI in April 1960. The talks between Zhou and Nehru were declared a failure, and border incursions continued to be reported by the two sides. The major armed conflict between ROI and PRC forces took place in November 1962, with Chinese troops easily penetrating deep inside Indian territories. The Indian defeat in the war was swift and overwhelming. It was humiliating not only for Nehru, who had defended the PRC throughout most of the 1950s, but also for the Indian armed forces and the intelligence apparatus. For the Indian public, who were nurtured through the rhetoric of India-China brotherhood, Asianhood, the ideals of Panchasheel, and the embellished images of the PRC presented in travel writings as well as through the performances of members of the goodwill delegations, the war came as a shock. The war was presented in government propaganda, newspapers, and magazines as a devious act, a betrayal of friendship and trust, and an invasion by a Communist and totalitarian state of a peace-loving India. The psychological impact of the event was so great that today the PRC remains one of the most untrustworthy countries for many Indians and several government ministries. This feeling extended not only to the PRC but also to ordinary Chinese persons living in the ROI.

CAUGHT IN THE CROSSFIRE:
THE CASE OF CHANG XIUFENG

Underneath the seeming "Hindi-Chini bhai-bhai" bonding, there were disconcerting political frictions, misunderstandings, and suspicions between the ROI and the PRC during the 1950s. The shock of the brief armed conflict and its lingering effects among Indians is primarily because of this exaggerated perception of "friendly relations," which were propagated by political leaders on both sides and accepted uncritically by the general populace and the media. The writings of Indian travelers to the PRC in the early 1950s also contributed to a perception that relations between the ROI and the PRC were cordial and that issues of disagreements could be resolved by invoking past civilizational connections. In other words, the psychological scar related to the PRC among Indians was a result not merely of the 1962 war but also of the hype of brotherhood that was created throughout the 1950s.

These frictions, misunderstandings, and suspicions were reflected in the opinions of B. N. Mullik cited above as well as in the famous letters of Sardar Patel, the then minister of home affairs, to Nehru in 1950 expressing his concerns about the threat from the PRC. These fears also appear in the reports of the IB, as discussed in the previous chapter. While the file examined in chapter 4 dealt with issues related to Tibet and the border, here the surveillance reports on a specific Chinese individual named Chang Xiufeng will be examined. The IB reports on Chang Xiufeng reveal that the surveillance over the Chinese communities was extensive, methodical, and often communicated to the Ministry of Home Affairs in Delhi. The cultural exchanges taking place between India and China centered in Shantiniketan was of special interest to the IB, with

Tan Yunshan as the main target. The general perception among intelligence officers seems to have been that Tan Yunshan, as well as the Chinese scholars, intellectuals, and monks visiting Shanti-niketan, had political agendas. Chang Xiufeng was one such person who studied art in Shantiniketan under the famous Indian artist Nandalal Bose.

The surveillance of the Chinese migrants living in India dates back to the early twentieth century. British officials were apprehensive about smuggling networks, the presence of illegal immigrants, and espionage and anti-British activities among these Chinese. Close watch was kept on events organized by the supporters of the GMD. Intelligence officers collected meticulous reports about these events and the activities of the Chinese communities in general. This monitoring of Chinese communities continued after India gained independence in 1947. In the 1950s, the IB was specifically apprehensive about the Chinese who had entered India illegally and those who were sympathetic to the Communist regime in China. It is clear from these records that the IB had sources from within the communities who supplied regular reports and information. The fact that some of the reports are contradictory suggests that these informants may have had their own agendas and intentions. The Guomindang-Communist divide that existed within the communities in the second half of the 1940s probably led to the composition of such contradictory, deliberately fabricated reports. Many of these aspects are evident from the reports on Chang Xiufeng, who was deported from the ROI in 1961.

Chang Xiufeng's experiences in India from 1947 to 1961 are reflective of the complex relationship between the ROI and the PRC in the second half of the twentieth century. Chang went to India drawn by the intellectual exchanges initiated by Rabindranath Tagore in the 1920s and subsequently became involved in the activities of the Chinese migrants living in West Bengal. Eventually, however, his life was traumatized because of the changes taking place in the political relations between the PRC and the ROI. Thousands of other ethnic Chinese living in India were interned and also deported. In China, on the other hand, Indian traders had to close their businesses and return to India. The Chinese also deported Indian nationals from the PRC, perhaps in retaliation for the expulsion of the Chinese from India. One such case is briefly outlined later in this section. The names of individuals, both Indians and Chinese, caught in the crossfire between the two countries often appear in official communications exchanged by the two sides. The intelligence reports and Chang Xiufeng's diary about his imprisonment in Darjeeling reveal the turmoil and tragedies that these individuals experienced as the ROI and the PRC moved closer to armed conflict.

Surveillance of the Chinese Communities

In 1947, when Chang Xiufeng arrived in India, there were already over fifteen thousand Chinese migrants in India, a number that did not include adult Chinese who had adopted Chinese nationality, Chinese children, deserters from the United States and Chinese forces that were stationed in India, and seamen "dumped in by the shipping companies" (Nehru 1984). West Bengal and Assam were the main regions where Chinese migrants had settled since the late eighteenth century. In Assam, a majority of these Chinese migrants were Cantonese, who worked as laborers, tea planters, and carpenters. In West Bengal, particularly in Calcutta and Kalimpong, the population was more diverse, with several sub-linguistic groups that engaged in distinct economic activities. The Hakkas were one of the four main groups of Chinese living in Calcutta, who had found their economic niche in shoemaking and the tannery businesses. There were also Cantonese, many of whom worked as carpenters, dentists from Hubei, and Shandong silk traders. There were several Chinese schools, temples, native-place associations, restaurants, clubs, and the like. Most of these were concentrated in two areas of the city, Bowbazar in central Calcutta and Tangra in the eastern suburbs. While those in the Bowbazar area were mostly Cantonese, the Chinese who settled in Tangra were overwhelmingly Hakkas from Meixian County in Guangdong Province (Zhang and Sen 2013).

In addition to these migrant groups, there were in Calcutta and elsewhere in India sojourning traders, school teachers, monks, intellectuals, and students from different regions of China. Some of them lived there for a short duration, and others, such as Chang Xiufeng, may have planned to stay and work in India for the long term. Only a few of the ethnic Chinese residing in India had proper immigration documentation. Those who came with passports issued by the GMD government found their status in limbo when the Communist government was established in China in 1949. After the recognition of the PRC government and the opening of the PRC embassy and consulates in the ROI, these and other people of Chinese descent were offered PRC passports. However, the Chinese communities, as noted above and below, were deeply divided between the supporters and opponents of the Communist regime. There were also divisions based on the linguistic/regional groups, between those who practiced endogamy and those who married locals or member of other Chinese groups, between the long-term residents and those who came for a shorter duration, as well as between different classes. Very few of them, even the later generations and the offspring of those marrying local Indians, had the option to become citizens of the ROI. Furthermore, the ROI government, including the intelligence agencies, failed to recognize this diversity and division among the ethnic Chinese. Especially for the intelligence agencies, almost every Chinese was potentially a government agent, a spy, or a propagator of Communist doctrines. Chang Xiufeng was a victim of this ideology.

The Chinese population in Kalimpong in the 1940s only numbered 281. This figure, however, might not reflect the fact that there were a considerable number of Chinese who passed through the town on their way from Lhasa to Calcutta. Indeed, Kalimpong was one of the important transit centers for itinerant traders, Buddhist monks, and missionaries. Some of these merchants were from Yunnan Province, who first traveled to Lhasa to trade in tea and horses and then trekked south through Kalimpong to Calcutta. One of the clauses of the Panchasheel Agreement was drafted to promote trade and facilitate pilgrimage activity through Kalimpong, where the PRC was allowed to set up a trade agency. The agreement also allowed pilgrims (Buddhists, Lamaists, and Hindus) to travel between Tibet and India through Kalimpong without "documents of certification."

The governments of the ROI and the PRC were aware of the international spying networks that existed in Kalimpong prior to the signing of the Panchasheel Agreement. In 1953, for example, Indian prime minister Jawaharlal Nehru called Kalimpong "a nest of spies" and remarked that "sometimes I begin to doubt if the greater part of the population of Kalimpong does not consist of foreign spies" (Maxwell 1970: 104). B. N. Mullik (1971: 183) wrote that "[b]y 1956, knowingly or unknowingly secret agents of America and Taiwan, operating mainly from Kalimpong, were engaged in the same activity as their counterparts from India and Russia—recruiting and arming Tibetan emigrés to organize a separatist rebellion in Tibet against the Peking administration, with the Khamba tribes in eastern Tibet providing the initial thrust." Mao Zedong and Zhou Enlai were also worried about the spies operating in Kalimpong. In 1956, Zhou Enlai complained to Nehru that American and GMD spies used the town as a base for anti-Chinese activities. Two years later, the Chinese government conveyed their concern to the Indian ambassador in China about the "stepped up" activities of these American and GMD spies. British Indian intelligence reports confirm the presence of GMD espionage activity in Kalimpong in the early 1940s. Mention, for example, is made of P.

Rapga, "a Tibetan exile and holder of a Chinese passport." Documents indicating his affiliation with the GMD were allegedly found during a search of his office. One of these documents indicated that the objective of Rapga and his associates was "to exert their efforts mainly for the liberation of Tibet from the existing tyrannical Government" (West Bengal State Archives 236/39[12], Serial No. 228). Rapga was deported from India in 1946. Another person, "strongly suspected" of being a Chinese agent in Kalimpong, was Shen Fumin, a teacher at the local Zhonghua Middle School (Zhonghua zhongxue 中華中學), where Chang Xiufeng eventually worked as the principal. [12]

During the 1940s and 1950s, there were sometimes violent rivalries between the GMD and Communist factions in India. These rivalries ranged from efforts to increase memberships for respective groups to attempts to control the Chinese schools and other community organizations in Calcutta and elsewhere. The British Indian and subsequently the ROI governments kept watch on these activities. During the 1950s, after the recognition of the PRC, the ROI government regularly opted to side with the Communist factions and even deported some of the prominent pro-GMD figures in Calcutta (Cohen and Leng 1972: 271; Zhang 2010).

Surveillance of the Chinese visiting Shantiniketan may have started in 1926, when the Chinese-language instructor Lim Ngo Chiang was suspected of having links with revolutionists in Bengal and China (see chapter 4). Subsequently, the IB closely monitored the activities of every Chinese living in Shantiniketan. Initially, given his close contacts with the GMD leaders and the fact that he had accompanied the official Chinese mission led by Xie Guoliang to Tibet in 1931, Tan Yunshan, as also pointed out in the previous chapter, was considered a Guomindang agent. Later, Tan allegedly switched his allegiance to the Chinese Communist Party and, according to one of the reports, "expressed his desire to support MAO TSE-TUNG" (West Bengal State Archives, File 120/41, Serial No.

1). All letters to Tan Yunshan were intercepted, translated, and sometimes investigated in detail.

Reports from field informants and officers in various districts of Bengal were collected and filed at the Calcutta branch of the IB. Often, the special superintendent of police (SSP) at the IB office in Calcutta solicited further information. Correspondence between field officers and the SSP was also recorded in the relevant files. These files were mostly categorized according to the state district (such as Darjeeling and Bolpur), but in some cases files were also devoted to specific institutions (Cheena Bhavana, for instance) or people (including those files on Chang Xiufeng and Tan Yunshan). Matters of importance were referred to the IB headquarters in Delhi. These exchanges with the Ministry of Home Affairs, as in the case of Chang Xiufeng, were also included in the files. Transcripts of interviews with people suspected of espionage, smuggling, crime, and illegally entering the ROI are found in these files, which also include copies of intercepted letters and excerpts from Chinese-language publications. In addition to the IB files, the Calcutta police also maintained surveillance over the Chinese communities in the city. The Calcutta police files usually concern the law-and-order situation in the Tangra and Bowbazar areas and the suspected criminal activities of the Chinese migrants. Together these files provide insights into the experiences of the Chinese in India, the concerns of the intelligence community, and the impact of ROI-PRC relations on the movement and livelihood of the largest foreign migrant group in South Asia since the late eighteenth century.

Chang Xiufeng's India-China Ordeal

Born in 1915 (other dates are 1919 and 1917) in Anhui Province, China, Chang Xiufeng studied art at Chongqing University under such famous artists as Chen Zhifo, Xu Beihong, and his uncle Chang Renxia. Xu Beihong and Chang Renxia had lived in Shantiniketan during the early to mid-1940s. In fact, it may have been because of Xu Beihong that Chang Xiufeng in 1947, two years after his graduation, decided to go to Shantiniketan for further studies. In an interview he gave to a Chinese journalist at the age of eighty-five, Chang (1999: n.p.), explaining his decision to go to India, said,

> I am a student of art and not someone who studies science and technology. India is one of the four ancient civilizations and its art is something that scholars must study seriously. Additionally, Uncle Chang Renxia (the former secretary to Zhou Enlai) was a professor at the Visva-Bharati University in India. [Thus,] because it was the right time, the right place, and the right people I decided to go to India.

As such, Chang Xiufeng was different from most other ethnic Chinese living in India. He did not belong to the four major immigrant groups and he came from an intellectual family. However, when he left China, Chang Xiufeng could not have imagined the tumultuous experience that awaited him in India. Throughout the vicissitudes of his life in India, Chang never stopped producing various forms of art that ranged from paintings to small bamboo baskets. Many of his paintings were later displayed in Hong Kong and Anhui. [13]

Chang Xiufeng's book on his experiences in India titled *Dajiling zhi qiu* 大吉嶺之秋 (An Autumn in Darjeeling), published in 1999, does not mention that before entering Visva-Bharati, he had worked as an art teacher at the Chinese Middle School in Calcutta. His uncle, Chang Renxia seems to have also taught at the same school. An intelligence report mentions that both Chang Xiufeng and Chang Renxia were members of the Chinese Democratic League in India. Written in 1951, the report further points out that the school committee suspected the two Changs of being "Pro-Communist and dispensed with their services with effect from January 1949" (West Bengal State Archives, File 2312/49 [1], Serial No. 274: 7–6 [*sic*]).

While Chang Renxia returned to China from India and joined Peking University, Chang Xiufeng went to Shantiniketan to study, "with," according to an IB report, "the assistance of Prof. Tan Yan-shen [*sic*]" (West Bengal State Archives, File 2312/49 [1], Serial No. 274). In his book, on the other hand, Chang Xiufeng writes that he received permission to study in India in 1946 and went on to work under Nandalal Bose, who had, in 1924, accompanied Rabin-dranath Tagore to China and was acquainted with some of Chang's teachers. It is not clear why Chang Xiufeng chose not to mention his work at the Chinese school in Calcutta. He notes that after graduating from Visva-Bharati in 1950 he received an invitation from the Chinese community to serve as the principal of Zhonghua Middle School in Kalimpong.

Chang Xiufeng's book is mostly about his experience in the jails in Kalimpong and Darjeeling. Suspected of being an agent of the PRC government, Chang was denied an extension of his stay in India. When he refused to leave by the deadline imposed by the ROI authorities, he and his wife were arrested for violating immi-gration laws. Although critical of the official who arrested him and the decision of the Indian government to deport him, Chang Xiu-feng often praised Indian culture, society, and the ancient cultural links between India and China. In the last chapter, for example, devoted to Tagore and Visva-Bharati, he enthusiastically describes the main characteristics of Tagore's writings and art, the peaceful and spiritual campus of Visva-Bharati, features of Indian paintings, and the intimate cultural exchanges between India and China be-fore the colonial period. He does not say much about his activities in Shantiniketan or his experience studying under Nandalal Bose. But these aspects of life can be seen from several works he painted in Shantiniketan (see figure 5.2). One of the paintings was of his teacher Nandalal Bose (see figure 5.3).

The IB reports are conflicting and ambiguous about Chang Xiufeng's involvement in espionage and other illegal activities in India. As noted above, the surveillance on him seems to have started in 1949, shortly after he began studying in Shantiniketan. It was also in that year that he married an orphan Chinese woman from Calcutta named Rao Huanying. The early IB reports portray Chang as someone who was involved in spreading Communist propaganda in India. A report dated 20 March 1951, for instance, suggests that in Shantiniketan Chang wanted to "get in contact with the Indian intelligentsia and graduates so as to form an Indian communist liaison office in future" (West Bengal State Archives, File 2312/49 [1], Serial No. 274). However, another entry filed three months later pointed out, on the contrary, that Chang was a very "reserved" person and was "seldom found to mix with Indian students nor with any professor intimately. Even he [*sic*] was not

Figure 5.2.   Painting by Chang Xiufeng at Visva-Bharati. Exhibition of Chang Xiufeng's Art, Anhui Provincial Museum, Hefei, 2008

Figure 5.3. Nandalal Bose painted by Chang Xiufeng. Exhibition of Chang Xiufeng's Art, Anhui Provincial Museum, Hefei, 2008

found to mix with his fellow countrymen who usually reside at Cheena Bhavan. He was often found to be absorbed in his painter's work." The report also notes that the IB person(s) watching him found nothing suspicious about his activities. "No information regarding his coming in contact with the Indian students and intelligentsia in Shantiniketan to form an Indian Communist Liaison Office there" came to the notice of these people. The last report from Shantiniketan indicated that Chang Xiufeng had left Shantiniketan for Calcutta in March 1950 "to take up the post of an Art teacher in a Chinese school."

After a gap of about seven years, in March 1958, a new report appeared in Chang Xiufeng's file. This report concerned a request Chang made to the local immigration office to extend his stay in India for another year. The report, filed by the superintendent of police, District Intelligence Branch in Darjeeling, pointed out that Chang was working as the "head master" of the Zhonghua Middle School in Kalimpong and recommended the approval of his application. The report also noted that there was "nothing adverse" against the applicant in the local office records (West Bengal State Archives, File 2312/49 [1], Serial No. 274). Based on this positive account, it seems, Chang Xiufeng's application was approved. Another application from Chang was submitted for a further extension of his stay in India "beyond 7.4.60."

Between 1958 and 1960, however, political relations between the ROI and the PRC were becoming contentious due to the situation in Tibet as well as border skirmishes. Especially because of Tibetan armed resistance against the PLA, Kalimpong and the activities of various foreign residents and organizations in the town became serious concerns for the IB. The town was already identified by the PRC government as the base for anti-China activities led by American and Taiwanese spies. In fact, already in 1956, when the Dalai Lama visited Kalimpong, the PRC government suspected that he was planning to seek asylum in India.[14] After getting Nehru's consent, the PRC government sent an aircraft to Siliguri to bring the Dalai Lama back to Tibet. Right around this time, in November 1956, the Zhonghua Middle School was set on fire. An arsonist supportive of the Tibetan cause was the main suspect. According to Chang Xiufeng (1999: 1), it was a year later that he was given the position of principal and asked to reestablish the school.

The Zhonghua Middle School was already under surveillance by the time Chang Xiufeng reached Kalimpong. The IB "Report Regarding the Activities of the Chinese in Kalimpong (Darjeeling)," dated 20 June 1959, states that there were three places in Kalimpong "which may be termed as Chinese Communist espionage centers" (West Bengal State Archives, File 2312/49 [1], Serial No. 274). These were the Chinese Trade Agency, the Ma Building at 10th Unite (the house belonging to the famous Ma family of traders in Kalimpong), and the Zhonghua Middle School. Another report, written three months later, alleged that Chang Xiufeng had been transferred to the Zhonghua Middle School in Kalimpong with the specific aim to "propagate Communist ideals among the students." In order to achieve this, he had revamped the curriculum. A third report from around the same time states that the reason Chang Xiufeng was the most trusted person within the PRC espionage network was because he was "in the confidence of the Chinese Consulate in Calcutta" (West Bengal State Archives, File 2312/49 [1], Serial No. 274).

On 29 November 1959, several months after the Dalai Lama fled to the ROI, the Darjeeling police interrogated Chang Xiufeng. The interrogators asked him about his family, which by this time included four children; the Zhonghua Middle School, which, Chang noted, had 192 students and 8 teachers; and his relationship with the Chinese Trade Agency, with which Chang answered he had limited contact. Within six months, the IB officers also collected information about Chang Xiufeng from a local source, in all likelihood a member of the GMD faction, who suggested that the Zhonghua Middle School was indoctrinating local students about Communism. Chang Xiufeng, the source suggested, was unqualified because he was "only an art teacher." He was appointed as the headmaster of the Zhonghua Middle School, the source further argued, because of his connection to the Chinese Consulate in Calcutta and to the Chinese Trade Agency in Kalimpong. The source also named several women who acted as agents for Chang Xiufeng in order "to collect information about the local non-Communist Chinese, Tibetans and others through the womenfolk of those people." The source finally accused Chang Xiufeng of importing and distributing banned publications on India-China relations with the aim of "rousing anti-Indian feelings amongst the students" (West Bengal State Archives, File 2312/49 [1], Serial No. 274).

Two weeks after the above report was filed, the IB formally concluded that Chang Xiufeng was "engaged in deeply anti-Indian activities" and should be deported at the earliest date. On 9 June 1960, the West Bengal state government informed the Ministry of Home Affairs about its decision to not renew the residential permits of Chang Xiufeng and his family. Acknowledging the receipt of this information, the ministry, in a letter dated 9 August 1960, also agreed with the decision. It requested the state government to order the Chang family to "leave Kalimpong within a specified period, which should not exceed one month." This "express letter" from the ministry further noted that "[a]n Order to this effect may therefore be served on them immediately and it be ensured that they carry it out. Thereafter, they should be served with a notice to leave the country within a period of one month and made to do so" (West Bengal State Archives, File 2312/49 [1], Serial No. 274). Subsequently, on 20 August 1960, the government of West Bengal, Home Department, issued an order stating that "Mr. CHANG HSIU FENG, son of CHANG CHIU HSIANG, a foreigner of Chinese nationality, shall not remain in Kalimpong after the expiry of 15 (fifteen) days from the date of service of this order on him." The superintendent of police, director of the intelligence bureau (DIB), Darjeeling, confirmed that the order was served to the Chang family on 30 August 1960 (West Bengal State Archives, File 2312/49 [1], Serial No. 274).

Life in Jail and Deportation

In 1958, when Chinese premier Zhou Enlai visited India, Chang Xiufeng was invited by the Chinese embassy to meet him. Chang (1999: 2) believed that this meeting might have triggered the view of his secret connections to the Chinese government among Indian intelligence officers. In his memoir, Chang refers to the Indian police and intelligence officers as "*diren*" 敵人 (enemies). In fact, several months before the order from the government of West Bengal was served on him, Chang knew that he was under surveillance by the IB. This surveillance, he writes, changed from covert reconnaissance in the initial stages to openly shadowing him. He reports that on one of the days leading up to his arrest, a few men appeared at his school on the pretext of protecting him from the anti-Chinese Tibetans living in Kalimpong whom, they alleged, were purportedly trying to kill him. These men then openly followed him everywhere he went. Chang also points out that one of the Nepali employees at the Zhonghua Middle School had been asked by the local police to report on his activities (West Bengal State Archives, File 2312/49 [1], Serial No. 274).

Chang Xiufeng was arrested because he refused to leave India after the order for him to leave the country was served on three occasions. On 5 December 1960, about a week after he received the third notice, Chang and his wife were detained. When Chang pointed out that his wife was ill and their youngest child still needed breast-feeding, they were told that a doctor would have to certify the illness. Leaving their children in the care of their Nepali nanny, Chang Xiufeng and his wife accompanied the policemen to the Kalimpong detention center (Chang 1999: 4–5). Chang's description of their first night at the detention center includes an account of how his wife was harassed by drunken policemen. Chang started by protesting vehemently and finally launched a punch at one of the drunken policemen harassing his wife. Reminiscing about his arrest and the experience at the jail, Chang wondered why a religious and democratic country like India could not be compassionate and humane (Chang 1999: 9).

The following morning, Chang Xiufeng and his wife were taken to the court. According to Chang, the judge, a Bengali, had strong anti-China views. The lawyer assigned to them, he pointed out, was the chairman of the anti-Chinese group in Kalimpong. The judge noted that the West Bengal state government had issued three orders asking him to leave Kalimpong, with the third order asking him to leave India with forty-eight hours. When the designated lawyer did not say anything in his defense, Chang started making his own case. The judge eventually offered to release Chang and his wife from detention if they immediately left India. When Chang Xiufeng refused to accept the offer, the judge ordered them sent back to the detention center. On the same day of his court hearing, the Indian newspaper *The Statesman* reported the sentencing of Chang Xiufeng and his wife. It noted that the two were arrested because of their refusal to leave India within the time specified by the government. "They were asked to leave," the newspaper reported, "some time ago for their undesirable activities. A local magistrate before whom they were produced today refused bail and remanded them to jail custody" (*The Statesman*, 6 December 1960).

The Changs were produced before the court a second time on 13 December. When asked to admit their guilt as a way to resolve the matter, the Changs once again refused to do so and were sent back to the detention center. Two days later, the consul-general of China in Calcutta wrote a letter to the West Bengal state government complaining that the local authorities had refused to release Chang Xiufeng and his wife on bail. Concerned about the two Chinese nationals, the consul-general sought permission for a Chinese diplomat to visit Kalimpong and meet with the Changs. The West Bengal state government almost immediately sent radiograms to the deputy commissioner of Darjeeling and the subdivisional offi-cer in Kalimpong asking them to facilitate the visit.

Chang Xiufeng (1999: 25) says that he was informed by one of the jail guards that a Chinese diplomat would be visiting him in the afternoon. Chang was extremely pleased to see the Chinese vice consul from Calcutta, who said that he was representing the consu-late-general and the Chinese community to inquire about the health of the two prisoners. The vice consul also assured the Changs that steps were being taken to have them released as soon as possible. A few days later, the Chinese representative from the Chinese Trade Agency also visited the Changs in prison. He informed Chang Xiu-feng and his wife that they would be shortly transferred to a jail in Darjeeling.

On 13 January 1961, while Chang Xiufeng was transferred to Darjeeling, his wife was released on bail. During his imprisonment in Darjeeling, Chang became friendly with one of the officers at the jail. Upon learning that Chang was an artist who had studied in Shantiniketan, the officer assigned him the task of making bamboo vases and other artifacts. The officer and Chang often talked about art, politics, and India-China relations. Once he is supposed to have told Chang (1999: 59) that the Indian president, prime minister, and industrialists such as the Birlas and the Tatas were responsible for the government's anti-Chinese policy. "The Indian people," he re-portedly told Chang, "were still friendly toward China. Even if you are in the prison, don't I still see you as a friend?" Chang Xiufeng responded by saying that he too saw the officer as a friend and he had great appreciation for Indian art and artists.

A little over a month later, Chang Xiufeng's wife was arrested again and sent to the prison in Darjeeling. One of the officials at the jail informed Chang and his wife that if they agreed to leave India within seven days, he was authorized to release them immediately. When Chang Xiufeng inquired who had made the decision of their release, the officer said that it was Prime Minister Nehru himself.

Chang and his wife, however, declined to sign the required documents without first consulting a representative from the Chinese diplomatic mission.

The jail officer seems to have made the above offer to the Changs based on an official order sent by the Ministry of Home Affairs in Delhi. On 30 March 1961, the ministry in an express letter to the West Bengal state government agreed to "remit the unexpired portions of the sentences (including unpaid fines, if any)" on the conditions that the Changs should leave India within seven days of their release and agree to the offer by signing a document (West Bengal State Archives, File 2312/49 [1], Serial No. 274). Four days after the jail official relayed the offer of the government of India to the Changs, the Chinese vice consul visited the Changs in Darjeeling jail. According to a report of the meeting by a surveillance officer, the vice consul told the Changs about the possible date of their release, and he also informed them about the whereabouts of their children.

Chang Xiufeng and his wife seem to have signed the documents and were released on 4 May 1961. After their release, the Changs first stayed in Siliguri and subsequently took a flight to Calcutta from Bagdogra. On the morning of 2 June, the family boarded a Union of Burma Airways plane to China (West Bengal State Archives, File 2312/49 [1], Serial No. 274). While a report by an IB officer says that the family left for China via Hong Kong, Chang Xiufeng in his book writes that they went to Kunming through Yangon. When they finally reached Beijing, the Chinese premier Zhou Enlai was at the airport to receive the Chinese couple. Such meetings took place with other prominent Chinese deported by the ROI. They were subsequently published in Chinese newspapers to illustrate the plight of the Chinese in India.

Chang Xiufeng and wife's detention was formally raised in a note dated 6 March 1962 from the Chinese Ministry of Foreign Affairs to the Indian embassy in China. The note criticized the

Indian government for prosecuting Chinese nationals, expelling by then one hundred such people, and subjecting them to "rude treatment." Pointing to the specific case of Chang Xiufeng and his wife, the ministry noted,

> In the case of Mr. Chang Sui-fung [*sic*], a Chinese national in Kalimpong, he was even denied legitimate defence before he was unjustifiably sentenced to imprisonment. His wife was first ordered to leave Kalimpong within a specified time limit, and then recalled to Kalimpong to be tried; under various means of persecution by the Indian authorities, she finally fainted at the court. Later the Indian authorities sentenced her to imprisonment, thus separating her from her four young children and a suckling baby and throwing the family into a miserable state where husband and wife and parents and children were separated. Are these the "humane and generous standards" the Indian Government boasted of in its memorandum? (*Notes* 6: 164)

The government of India responded as follows:

> The Chinese note refers to Mr. and Mrs. Chang Sui-fung. This couple had been served with orders on the 30th August 1960 to leave Kalimpong within a period of 15 days but as they did not comply with the order they were arrested on the 5th December 1960. The Court refused bail to Mr. Chang but allowed bail to Mrs. Chang on condition that she made arrangements to leave Kalimpong forthwith. Upon her refusal to do so, her bail application was rejected. But later, on the receipt of assurances on her behalf, she was released on bail on 17-12-1960. Mrs. Chang had been sentenced at her trial to two months simple imprisonment but in view of the special family considerations, the Government of India arranged to have the un-expired portion of the sentences on both Mr. and Mrs. Chang Sui-fung remitted and they were both permitted to leave the country. It will be seen from these facts that this Chinese couple had been released even before the expiry of their terms of imprisonment. Surely there was nothing inhumane about this. (*Notes* 6: 170)

Beyond this diplomatic squabbling and geopolitical confrontation, Chang Xiufeng and his family seem to have suffered both physically and mentally during the whole ordeal. It cannot be ascertained from any of the intelligence reports if he was actually propagating Communism in India or participated in any anti-Indian activities. No concrete evidence or specific cases are mentioned in the IB file, nor, it seems, were any such documents to prove the accusations produced at the court hearing. In fact, most of the reports on Chang Xiufeng's espionage, and even Communist, activities are based on secondhand sources and suspicion. [15]

As the above note by the PRC government indicates, the Changs were not the only Chinese living in the ROI who were arrested and deported. In fact, by the first half of 1963, around 2,500 Chinese had been asked to leave the ROI. This step was taken after the Defense of India Ordinance by the Indian president Radhakrishnan suspended certain individual rights. This was followed by changes to the Defense of India Act and the invoking of the Foreigners Act of 1946, which not only limited the movement of the Chinese in India but also led to the internment and deportation of these people (Cohen and Leng 1972: 271–272). Jerome Alan Cohen and Shaochuan Leng (1972: 275) argue that these measures were "an obvious manifestation" of Indian sentiment of shock, humiliation, frustration, and anger, "which also found expression in occasional anti-Chinese demonstrations and attacks on Chinese shops and nationals." Payal Bannerjee (2017) describes this as an episode of "ethnic nationalism." She (2017: 215) writes, "The Indian state systematically cultivated this ethnic nationalism and, in so doing, implemented a range of policies that discriminated against, disenfranchised and specifically targeted India's Chinese community—a community that included Indian citizens."

A note from the Ministry of External Affairs of the ROI to the embassy of the PRC in Delhi pointed out that 2,395 "persons of Chinese origin" had "opted" to go to China, and those who remained in detention did not want to leave. This was in response to a note from the Chinese embassy dated 31 July 1963 requesting permission to send a fourth ship "in order to rescue these victimized Chinese from their dire misery." The holding of "Chinese nationals," in what the embassy described as a "concentration camp," was "absolutely unacceptable to the Chinese Government" (*Notes* 10: 56–57).[16] One of these "concentration camps" was located in Deoli in Rajasthan. Many of the people, whom the ROI government indicated did not want to go to China, actually lived there for four to five years. All of their properties, homes, and businesses in places such as Calcutta, Kalimpong, and Assam were confiscated by the government or gradually occupied by the locals. When these internees were eventually released, they either struggled to rebuild their livelihood in the ROI, despite severe restrictions placed on them, or migrated to countries such as Canada or Australia.

The experiences of some of the people living in the Deoli camp have been recently published. One of these is a book titled *A Lost Tribe* by Ming-Tung Hsieh (2011: 189). Hsieh describes the situation at Deoli as follows:

> We didn't know if, when or where and how we were to get out of this horrible Camp, and if released, how & where to restart or live [*sic*], it was always a big question mark, everyone was worrying sick, the youngs [*sic*] and adolescents were more vulnerable.

Ming-Tung Hsieh was arrested on 20 October 1962, taken to Deoli, and eventually released on 30 August 1964, almost two years after the war. He reports the experiences of the Leong family who remained captive in the camp until the end of 1967.[17] The cases of Chang Xiufeng, Ming-Tung Hsieh, the Leong family, and many others indicate that the Indian government, as Payal Bannerjee (2017: 217) has noted, presented "every person of Chinese descent in India, regardless of settlement history, inter-marriage, or mixed

Indian ancestry over generations," as India's enemy. The Indian public followed this cue to inflict "public harassment, larceny, arson, physical assault, and even homicide" against the Chinese (Bannerjee 2017: 215). A handful of Chinese who had affiliation with the GMD and Taiwan tried to escape this treatment by describing themselves as patriotic residents of the ROI and raising funds to support the war against the PRC. However, Chinese communities in many places of India, including Kalimpong and Assam, either disappeared or dwindled to a few hundred in the aftermath of the India-China war. Many of them migrated to Canada, Europe, or Taiwan. It is now estimated that there are fewer than three thousand people of Chinese descent living in the ROI.

The Chinese in India were not the only ones to experience detention and deportation. Similar things were happening in China. A note from the Ministry of External Affairs to the embassy of China dated 14 October 1963 pointed out that five Kashmiri Muslims were arrested "on trumped up charges" by the local authorities in Tibet and awarded long term prison sentences without any trial. Two of these Kashmiris were sentenced to fifteen years of imprisonment (*Notes* 10: 88–89).[18] The *Times of India* on 7 December 1965 reported that eighteen Indians, mostly Sikhs who were engaged in dairy farming, petitioned the ROI government for the "repatriation of themselves and their families." They "pleaded that they and their families are being so systematically and relentlessly persecuted that the conclusion is inescapable that the Chinese intention is to hound them out of the country."

The most noteworthy of these cases of detention of Indians in the PRC was that involving a person named Makhan Lal Das. A resident of Shanghai since 1947 and trading in Indian condiments with his father who had lived in China from 1930, Das was arrested on 29 October 1963 by the Shanghai authorities on the charge of raping a Chinese woman. The ROI Ministry of External Affairs charged that the Chinese side was acting against international law by not allowing the Indian embassy in China to visit Das in prison, arrange for his defense, and be present at his trial (*Notes* 11). In a response dated 11 April 1966, the PRC Ministry of Foreign Affairs argued that the rape case against Das proceeded "in accordance with Chinese law" and "also in conformity with international practice." The ROI government, this response cautioned, was making a "fuss over this criminal case which is wholly within the sphere of Chinese sovereign rights." It threatened that "if the Indian Government continues to send notes to haggle unreasonably over the case, the Chinese Government will pay no attention to them" (*Notes* 13: 36). The ROI countered by noting, "the Chinese Government have been unable to refute the cogent evidence which the Government of India had listed in proof of the fact that M. L. Das's imprisonment and maltreatment in jail violates all well recognized principles of law and the ordinary canons of humanity" (*Notes* 13: 36). The *Times of India* reported on this case as well, mentioning that Das was sentenced to five years imprisonment without a public trial "on the grounds that the alleged victim of the criminal assault had given birth within three months to a child who very much resembled an Indian." Das was expelled from China in October 1968 only after serving the full five-year prison term (*Times of India*, 31 October 1968: 11).[19] No details about the case were released.

The experiences of Chang Xiufeng, Makhan Lal Das, and many other ordinary Chinese and Indians living in each other's countries during the late 1950s and early 1960s indicate a dramatic shift from the earlier phase of cultural bonding and brotherhood. Similar to the contention over Tibet at the Asian Relations Conference discussed in the previous chapter, these experiences suggest the fragile and contentious nature of the relationship between China and India from 1947 to the 1960s. This fragility was not necessarily due to the Communist government in China, as is sometimes suggested. Rather, it had to do with the failure of the respective governments, the government of independent India, the GMD, as well as the

Communists in the PRC, to confront and resolve the contentious issues with mutual trust and confidence. Indeed, the ordeals of Chang Xiufeng and Makhan Lal Das stemmed from the surfacing of mutual distrust and suspicion that seems to have existed since 1947.

FINDING AN ALTERNATE PATH TO PEACE

The three decades that followed the end of World War II witnessed several military conflicts in Asia, of which the wars in Korea and Vietnam involved countries outside Asia and were perhaps the most brutal. Wars also took place between the ROI and Pakistan, between the Arabs and Israel, and between the ROI and the PRC. Additionally, there were cross-border insurgencies, the rapid spread of espionage networks, and the emergence of revolutionary movements supported by foreign countries. All of these events occurred with the backdrop of the Cold War between the Soviet Union and the United States. The war between the ROI and the PRC in 1962 took place in this context of a politically unstable world divided into military and ideological alliances. In fact, it coincided with the Cuban missile crisis that may have brought the world to the brink of World War III.

After rapidly penetrating deep inside the territories of the ROI, the PRC unilaterally declared a cease-fire and withdrew its troops. As noted earlier, this armed conflict with the PRC had a profound impact on the psyche of the Indians despite its short duration. While the Indian government put constraints on visits by PRC nationals, curtailed investment by Chinese companies, and restricted the employment of ethnic Chinese residents in India, a strong anti-PRC sentiment developed among media outlets, leading scholars, and commentators, and even the common people expressed suspicion of the ethnic Chinese and sometimes launched violent protests.[20] Instead of a "brotherly" neighboring state, the PRC was henceforth perceived as a threat and an untrustworthy nation. In the PRC, on the other hand, the war was portrayed as an aggression against the Chinese launched by Nehru, the "running dog" of Western imperialists. However, despite frequent criticisms of Nehru and the ROI government in the leading newspapers, such as *Renmin Ribao* and *Guangming Ribao*, the Chinese populace was less informed and therefore ambivalent about the armed conflict. The impact of the war was clearly more widespread and profound in the ROI than in the PRC.

The lesser-known attempts by global peace activists to mediate between the ROI and the PRC during the aftermath of the 1962 war also require some attention. The aim of these activists was to promote the idea of goodwill and understanding among the citizens of the two countries by marching from Delhi to Beijing. The march plan brought together several organizations from across the world that advocated peaceful coexistence in the context of the Cold War; it also led to a joint effort by Sunderlal, the chairman of the ICFA, and J. P. Narayan, who had been a vocal critic of the PRC's policies in Tibet. While the organization of the march and its launch were remarkable demonstrations of global connections among peace activists in the 1960s, its failure was reflective, once again, of the disconnect that existed between the ROI and the PRC during the 1950s and early 1960s, much of which was overshadowed by the "Hindi-Chini bhai-bhai" euphoria.

The Idea of a Long March

In 1951, when Sunderlal led an Indian delegation to the PRC, Guo Moruo, then the vice premier and the chairman of the All-China Peace Committee, had advocated the establishment of a strong peace movement in Asia. "We think," Guo told the Indian visitor, "it is easy to have a strong Peace Movement in both India and China because the Asian people are all peace-loving people. It is out of good old tradition that we hate aggression and dislike war.

Asian countries, including India, have suffered at the hands of western imperialists. This is also one great reason why the Peace Movement can easily grow and prosper in Asia" (Sunderlal 1952: 65). However, when in 1963 attempts were made to contact the Chinese Peace Council to collaborate on the Delhi–Peking Friendship March by pacifists from around the world, it became clear that the PRC lacked a "strong Peace Movement." The inability to collaborate with the Chinese Peace Council was one of the many reasons that the Friendship March, which started on 1 March 1963 from Mahatma Gandhi's memorial in Rajghat, Delhi, failed. The marchers were unable, after walking all the way to Assam, to enter the PRC. Mutual distrust between the two governments, divisions among the peace activists themselves, and a lack of proper planning were some of the other important reasons the marchers were unable to accomplish their goal. The failure of the march also had significant repercussions on the Indian and world peace movements and the attempts to rebuild trust between the Indians and Chinese.

In 1960–1961, a pacifist group in the United States called the Committee for Nonviolent Action (CNVA) staged a six-thousand-mile San Francisco–to–Moscow March for Peace with the aim of promoting disarmament. Despite opposition, criticism, and threats in the United States, the marchers successfully organized vigils, distributed leaflets, and conducted rallies in large and small towns and at military bases. In Washington, D.C., they even had a meeting with presidential aide Arthur Schlesinger, who told the marchers that their position was "irresponsible and immoral." After the meeting, the marchers flew from New York to London, where several European volunteers joined the march (Wernicke and Wittner 1999). When obtaining visas to Eastern European countries and the Soviet Union emerged as the main obstacle to the march, the Reverend A. J. Muste, a leading activist in the United States, used his connections in the World Peace Council to contact Nikita Khrushchev, who agreed to allow the marchers to enter the Communist bloc countries. The peace committees of the Soviet Union, East Germany, and Poland also agreed to grant visas to the marchers.

On 7 August 1961, the marchers entered East Germany, where they faced significant opposition from local officials and anti-Western protestors. It was eventually on 15 September that the group reached the Soviet Union and on 3 October held a vigil in Moscow's Red Square. The Soviet peace committee helped arrange meetings with government officials, students, and common folk. The marchers secured an audience with Nina Khrushchev, the wife of the Soviet leader (Wernicke and Wittner 1999). It has been argued by Wernicke and Wittner (1999: 917) that the peace march may have made it possible for Khrushchev and other Soviet reformers to temporarily "break with the traditional authoritarian practices of Communist states." They add, "[T]he march shows that Western peace activists provided the crucial ingredient for a substantial act of political liberalization. Defying the odds and most expectations, they did succeed in lifting the Iron Curtain."

The Delhi–Peking Friendship March was proposed in this same spirit of defying the odds and expectations. In fact, the person who initially suggested the idea was twenty-eight-year-old Ed Lazar, a veteran of the San Francisco–Moscow March for Peace. In a note of 18 November 1962 that he wrote to fellow pacifists, Lazar outlined the events leading to the war between the ROI and the PRC; the broader geopolitical situation in the world, including the roles of the Soviet Union and the United States; and the status of the peace movement in the ROI. He attributed the PRC's attempt to seize "the leadership of the worldwide Communist revolution" and "qualify as the greatest Asian power by flaunting Chinese military might and by undermining the Indian economy" as the reasons for the war. However, he also blamed the West for failing to give the PRC the "desired recognition." The ROI, he contends, also added to the global tensions by confronting "weak Portugal" in Goa but "remaining friendly with its more threatening but larger neighbor,

China." Taking note of the reaction among the public after the border conflict, he wrote, "there is now a major attempt to create war fever in India. Students are demonstrating for war, sari-clad girls are training with rifles, gold bond issues are being supported to pay for arms, and army recruiting is being encouraged." Lazar's solution to end the hysteria and prevent an expansion of the conflict was to employ the San Francisco–Moscow walk model and approach the people directly. "It has become increasingly clear to me," he noted, "that the basic challenge for direct-action proponents is involvement in present day international conflict—such as Berlin, Cuba, and China-India. Through such involvement we help break down the dangerous concept of nationalism and help affirm the common humanity of man and our responsibility to the rest of life" (Lazar 1963: 1–5).

The following plan put forth by Lazar (1963: 5–6) eventually became the blueprint for the Delhi–Peking Friendship March:

> The direct action project which I am going to suggest amounts to an attempt to establish ties with the Chinese and Indian people; to challenge them to live up to the best in their own cultural heritage of past insights, wisdom, and tolerance. This action would first have to be discussed with Vinoba. It would be most encouraging if Vinoba would direct his walk through India, into the Ladakh area, across the Himalayas, and then into and across China. If Vinoba chooses not to do this, I feel that an international team built around a core of Indian shanti-sena and sponsored by the World Peace Brigade should undertake such a walk. This would be a venture at linking the finest aspects of two great cultures. It would be more a walk honoring the greatness of Indian and Chinese culture; emphasizing the values of nonviolence, wisdom, and tolerance which have played such an important role in these two rich cultures. The walk would be saying that the development of these values will be of great benefit to the people of both nations, and that prolonged hostilities will hurt all Asia. The walk might start in a gramdan village west of New Delhi, proceed through the capital, and go on to the

disputed area in Ladakh. On this phase of the trip, the nonviolent approach will be offered as a substitute for the war hysterics which are now being stimulated. A return to a willingness to arbitrate would be urged. Entering China should be significant in itself because this is the kind of contact the Chinese people need—encounter with an international group which has a real concern for the Chinese people, yet challenges Chinese militarism and aggression. (Americans on such a walk would of necessity be challenging our own government's ban on China travel.) The walk would continue across China to a small village east of Peiping. There would be no signs or leaflets on this walk— simply a group of men and women attempting to communicate with their action and lives.

The World Peace Brigade that Lazar recommended in his above note was one of several peace organizations that were active during the Cold War period. It was founded on 1 January 1962 with A. J. Muste, J. P. Narayan, and Michael Scott as the cochairmen. The Shanti Sena that he also mentions was an organization established in 1957 by the Gandhian Vinoba Bhave. After the World Peace Brigade and the Shanti Sena accepted Lazar's proposal, the two organizations sought help from the War Resisters' International, the World Peace Council, and individuals including Bertrand Russell, Martin Luther King Jr., and Anna Louise Strong. Most of these peace organizations had their own area of concentration, which included opposition to armed conflict, specific weapons, or policies (Carter 2014: 15–18). Some, such as the World Peace Council, were either pro-Soviet or pro-NATO; others were autonomous and avoided partisanship, especially in disputes between the Soviet Union and the NATO countries (Carter 2014: 14).

At the initial stages, Ed Lazar, A. J. Muste, J. P. Narayan, George Willoughby, and Devi Prasad focused on raising funds, organization, and coordination across three continents (Asia, Europe, and North America). It was decided that the World Peace Brigade would, at the invitation of the Shanti Sena, organize the

Friendship March. The Asian Regional Council of the World Peace Brigade was tasked with identifying potential marchers from Asia, Africa, and Australia; the European Regional Council selected representatives from Europe; and the North American Regional Council was to recruit people from the United States. The expenses for the march were to be borne by the march organizing committee, sponsoring organizations, or the participants themselves. It was planned that the marchers would start from Delhi and reach Calcutta through Agra, Allahabad, Varanasi, and Patna. From Calcutta the marchers anticipated traveling through East Pakistan (now Bangladesh) and Burma into China.

The organizers laid out the following as the four main objectives of the Friendship March (*Delhi–Peking Friendship March*):

1. Establish friendly relations between the people of India and China.
2. Urge peaceful solution of any disputes between the two nations.
3. Establish communication between the people of the two countries on a people to people level despite differences of viewpoint or ideology.
4. Propagate love as the fundamental basis of all human relationships.

They also clarified their stand on key issues that concerned the PRC by making the following statements:

> The group recognized that the Communist government of China is in fact the government of that country, and as such is entitled to take its rightful seat in the United Nations.
>
> While cognizant of the long historical relationship between Formosa and China we support the right of the people of Formosa to self-determination.
>
> The group deplored the use of violence by the Chinese authorities in Tibet. Irrespective of the question as to the claim of

Chinese suzerainty over Tibet, the group upholds the right of self-determination by the people of Tibet. (*Delhi–Peking Friendship March*)

By early 1963, the organizing committee had identified thirteen core marchers and seven short-term participants (see figure 5.4). The group included ten Indians, five Americans, two British, two Japanese, and one Austrian. The youngest member was twenty-two years old and the oldest sixty-eight. Pandit Sunderlal tried to recruit Tan Yunshan and wrote directly to Prime Minister Nehru, who was the chancellor of Visva-Bharati, to grant him leave. In fact, Tan was at Rajghat and walked about six miles on 1 March 1963, when the march formally started. One of the reasons for recruiting Tan was to seek his help in securing Chinese visas for the marchers. Siddharaj Dhadda, a member of Vinoba Bhave's Sarvodaya Movement and the secretary of the organizing committee noted that Tan Yunshan was personally acquainted with Mao Zedong and Zhou Enlai and had agreed to write to them directly. Dhadda wrote that "if necessary he may also go personally to China to explain matters" (West Bengal State Archives, File 120/41, Serial No. 1)

The Long March that Never Was

On February 28, Tan Yunshan visited the Chinese embassy in Delhi and requested that the officials issue visas to the marchers. However, he was told in no uncertain terms by the embassy representative that since J. P. Narayan was a "reactionary," he and others would not be allowed to enter the PRC (A. J. Muste Papers: Delhi–Peking Friendship March: Correspondence with Chinese Government Officials). As the marchers walked through various cities and villages in the northern areas of the ROI, the issue of Chinese visas became paramount among the organizers of the event. They wrote letters to Mao Zedong, Zhou Enlai, and Guo Moruo directly and also asked others, including Bertrand Russell, to write in support of their endeavor. The vast archival material on

Figure 5.4.   The Delhi–Peking Friendship March participants. After
Delhi–Peking Friendship March **pamphlet, A. J. Muste Papers,**
Swarthmore College Peace Collection, Swarthmore

the march does not indicate the receipt of a response from any of
the Chinese leaders. Rather, the march was criticized in the Chinese
newspapers, one of which described it as a "conspiracy by a group
of anti-PRC Indian reactionaries colluding with US imperialists"
(A. J. Muste Papers: Delhi–Peking Friendship March: Correspondence with Chinese Government Officials). The PRC also told the
Pakistani government that issuing visas to the marchers "would be
considered an unfriendly act" (*Hindustan Times*, 26 April 1963).
Unable to pass through East Pakistan, the marchers revised their
itinerary and planned to enter China through Burma.

The marchers walked an average of nine miles a day, starting
around 4:30 in the morning. Similar to the San Francisco–Moscow
Peace March, vigils and meetings were organized at several sites
for local people. The attendance at these public meetings ranged
between 1,500 and 4,500, with people joining the marchers as they

walked across their districts. Initially, the marchers received support and sympathy from Nehru and individual members of the Congress Party. The response was mixed from the Indian newspapers and the people. On 3 March 1963, the *Hindustan Times* published a cartoon (see figure 5.5), where it juxtaposed the marchers with the Tibetan refugees. Some directly challenged the marchers for not supporting India's war efforts. Black flag demonstrations by the Hindu Mahasabha often took place at these meetings. "The peace march," they contended, "is a fraud." There were also a few politicians in Uttar Pradesh who threatened to have the marchers arrested under the Defense of India Act. Even the antinuclear activist Gyotsu N. Sato of the Japan Buddha Sangha, in a letter to A. J. Muste dated 25 October 1963, criticized the march organizers for not understanding the Asian sentiments and the Indian pacifists for not standing up against Indian and American militarists. "The MacMahon Line is the delusion of the Indians," he wrote; "none had so far defined it. Better urge the Indian government to sit with the Chinese for the Peaceful negotiation, non-conditionally" (A. J. Muste Papers: Delhi–Peking Friendship March).

Despite these criticisms, the marchers persisted through the rough terrain, inclement weather, and internal differences. The main problem they often encountered was the anti-PRC feeling that had taken root within the Indian peace movement itself. The two leaders of Shanti Sena, Vinoba Bhave and J. P. Narayan, had taken a staunch partisan stand against China with regard to Tibet and the 1962 war. Vinoba Bhave, for example, in comments made in November 1962 described the Chinese as inherently expansionist and the Indians, on the other hand, as people with no expansionist ambition. "As a shanti sainik," Bhave noted, "my basic view that arms will do no good to the world or to anybody endures as ever. I cannot give up my opposition in thought and spirit to armed conflict. But, at the same time, I do feel that India never thought of fighting and was always prepared for peaceful negotiations. Even

Figure 5.5. **The Delhi–Peking Friendship March cartoon.** *Hindustan Times*, **A. J. Muste Papers, Swarthmore College Peace Collection, Swarthmore**

then China committed aggression" (*Times of India,* 6 November 1962: 6). Bhave continued his criticism of the PRC even after the marchers embarked on their trek across the ROI. On 12 May, he specifically noted the differences between the Indian and Chinese political and economic systems and insinuated that "China's challenge was directed mainly against India's efforts to build democratic socialism through peaceful means" (*Times of India,* 13 May 1963: 6). In fact, Bhave even emphasized that he was not against the use of force to resist "Chinese aggression on Indian soil." He stressed, "[W]hen India maintains an army, it has to be used to repel an armed attack" (Weber 1996: 81).

J. P. Narayan had already taken a much stronger anti-PRC stand in 1959–1960. At the inaugural address to the Bihar State Tibet Convention on 9 March 1959, he made his views on the issue of Tibet clear with the following opening passage:

> Tibet stands as on [*sic*] outstanding case of ruthless suppression of the freedom of weak and defenceless nations by strong and aggressive powers. Tibet is and has been throughout history a separate country and not the "Tibet region of China" as the imperialist formula goes, and the Tibetans are and have always been a distinct and separate nation. As such they are entitled, as any country and nation, to freedom and full sovereign rights. No moth-eaten page of imperialist history can controvert that truth or undermine that sovereign principle. (Narayan 2007: 7.399)

In April 1960, Narayan convened, despite opposition from Nehru, the Afro-Asian Convention on Tibet, which drew representatives from Sri Lanka, Indonesia, Japan, Thailand, Hong Kong, Malaya, Nepal, Sikkim, South Vietnam, Burma, Iran, Congo, the Philippines, Tibet, Kenya, Jordan, Turkestan, and Pakistan. In his presidential address, delivered on 9 April 1960, Narayan criticized the 1954 trade agreement between the ROI and the PRC as an attempt that "hushed up" the Chinese armed intervention in Tibet in 1950. He called (Narayan n.d.: 13) on the attendees to support the resolution to repudiate "the claim of China that she has a right to impose, by force, the so-called social, economic and scientific progress upon another nation, against its will, simply because she considers it backward and superstitious."

J. P. Narayan maintained his stand on Tibet during and after the armed conflict between the ROI and the PRC and even when the plans for the Delhi–Peking Friendship March were being discussed. On 1 December 1962, advocating a change in the ROI's Tibet policy, he noted, "India's policy of recognising Chinese sovereignty over Tibet was dictated by its friendship for China. Now that the two countries are at war, India's policy should change" (Narayan 2007: 8.274). Furthermore, in a speech titled "Sarvodaya Answer to Chinese Aggression" delivered at the Sixth Tamilnad Sarvodaya Conference on 24 May 1963, he outlined the evils of Communism and the urgent need to highlight *sarvodaya* ideals as an alternative to the "religion of Communism." The spread of Communism, Narayan argued (Narayan 1963: 32), is a mission of the PRC, and to accomplish it, "China will attempt by every means possible—violence, internal subversion, propaganda, bribery, by spending money—by every conceivable means; China will attempt to convert this whole region to Communism and it is this challenge which we have to answer."

The Western organizers and participants in the Delhi–Peking Friendship March were often concerned about these anti-PRC statements made by the leaders of the Indian peace movement, who were all key members of the march. Ed Lazar in a letter to Muste made the following critical comment (A. J. Muste Papers: Delhi–Peking Friendship March):

> The latest statements from Sarvodaya leaders in India have been quite distressing and prompt me to urge that the policy of such a walk be clarified at the beginning. It is my feeling that participants should stress the positive aspects of Chinese and Indian traditions and friendship; but it is essential that the walkers also

feel free to be critical of the actions of both the Chinese and Indian governments. Some Gandhians are now talking about the "just war" and not wanting to embarrass the Indian government. The myth of the "just war" must be exploded and the Indian contribution to the present tension must also be brought into focus, as well as the walkers speaking out against Chinese aggression.

Others were critical of J. P. Narayan. "If he can understand," one of them wrote, "that his statements often sound positively anti-communist and if he could cure himself from this allergy he is suffering from in his attitude to Communists, he would be a powerful force" (A. J. Muste Papers: Delhi–Peking Friendship March). Another letter written to A. J. Muste specifically pointed to the adverse impact Narayan's statements were having on the Friendship March. "The presence of JP highlighted the most complex question the group has faced thus far"; it summarized the various views Narayan had expressed with regard to Tibet, including the (later retracted) call for the Indian army to liberate the region from PRC control. As an example, the writer alluded to Sunderlal's query asking if the marchers would be promoting the ideas of Narayan and if so whether it could at all be called a "friendship walk." The impact of these statements against the PRC was evident, as the writer also mentioned, on the decision of the Chinese government to deny visas to the marchers. When a representative of the organizing committee went to the Chinese consulate to apply for visas, the writer noted,

> The information officer there looked at our literature and when he saw JP's name said "this man is guilty of subversive actions against China, he is the man behind Dalai Lama's flight, he calls for the liberation of Tibet; we consider him the number 1 enemy of China in India." The consulate man also referred to the Sarva Seva Sangh official statement which calls China the aggressor and says its sympathies are with India. (A. J. Muste Papers:

Delhi–Peking Friendship March: Correspondence with Chinese Government Officials)

Cognizant of the Chinese sentiments against the marchers, members of the organizing committee nonetheless made a global attempt to convince the PRC government to issue the visas. In addition to having prominent people write letters to the PRC leadership, they met with members of the Chinese Peace Council in London, contacted Buddhist organizations in Beijing, and traveled to Hong Kong and Japan to find ways to enter the PRC. They also planned to meet the Chinese representatives at the World Peace Council gathering at Warsaw, which was, to their dismay, eventually canceled. By the time the marchers entered Assam in November 1963, it had become clear that the PRC would not issue the visas. While some members suggested taking the path of civil disobedience and entering the PRC through the NEFA of the ROI, others advocated a final attempt to enter through Hong Kong.

In late September 1963, A. J. Muste wrote to the British Colonial Office in London requesting Hong Kong visas for the non-Commonwealth members participating in the march. The aim, he wrote in his letter, was to "establish contact and, hopefully, either to confer with Chinese peace committee leaders in Hong Kong or to gain admission to the Chinese People's Republic itself" (FO 371/170682). By the middle of October, the British government had decided not only to deny visas but also to prevent those marchers who belonged to Commonwealth countries from entering Hong Kong. This decision seems to have been based on the opinion of the British embassy representative in Beijing, who noted that "the Chinese government will be sensitive on this subject and I would think it much better to keep these people out of Hong Kong" (FO 371/170682). When the decision was communicated to Muste, a caveat stating that Hong Kong would allow the marchers to enter Hong Kong if a Chinese visa was granted was added. Almost at the same time, Nehru refused to let the marchers into the NEFA "unless China grants entry."

With no possibility of entering the PRC, the organizing committee of the Delhi–Peking Friendship March decided to end the march in the North Lakhimpur District of Assam, about 130 miles west of Ledo on the Burmese border. It was formally terminated at Rajghat on 30 January 1964. Prior to the termination, a conference was organized at the Maitri Ashram in Lilibari, Assam, on 16–20 January to discuss the achievements and failures of the march.

The problems with the international peace movement were apparent at the discussions that took place in Lilibari. While the coordination between the various peace organizations that made it possible to quickly organize the march indicated a noteworthy accomplishment for the international peace organizations, it was clear that they had failed to comprehend the situation in the PRC. As veterans of the San Francisco–Moscow Peace March, some of the participants seem to have expected a Khrushchev-like decision from the Chinese side, which would have allowed the marchers to enter the PRC. However, unlike the Cold War between the Soviet Union and the United States, the dispute between the ROI and the PRC concerned the demarcation of territory and a military conflict that had actually taken place. The fact that the leading organizers came from Western countries and their counterparts in the ROI were the leading critics of the PRC did not help the matter either. Additionally, the respective positions of the two governments as well as the stance of the Indian press and the public had created nationalistic fervor to such an extent that there was no scope to advocate Gandhian ideals so soon after the military conflict.

In his prognosis of the march, George Willoughby noted the failure of the organizers to pay attention to several issues that were connected to the India-China war. This included the treatment of the Chinese communities in the ROI, many of whom, as noted above, were either deported or interned. "The Friendship March," he concluded, "was an 'emergency project' hurriedly established to meet a particular situation; it drew upon the best manpower available." He then added, "Yet not one member of the March had any facility in the Chinese language or deep knowledge and understanding of China's long history and culture. If the nonviolent forces of India and the West are serious in pursuing the goal of friendship a start must be made now to enlist some young people who believe in nonviolence as a way and allow them to start on the intensive study of Chinese language and culture" (A. J. Muste Papers: Delhi–Peking Friendship March).

Willoughby's last statement is a reflection of yet another important, albeit overlooked, failure in ROI-PRC interactions during the 1950s. Beyond the missed opportunities to resolve the border and Tibet issues, the two countries, especially the ROI, failed to create either the knowledge base or a group of experts who could be consulted to clarify the doubts, misunderstandings, and issues related to Tibet when it was needed most. The record number of cultural and educational exchanges, celebrations of enduring friendship, the numerous writings about each other, and even the growing network of intelligence gathering did not translate into deeper understanding of the PRC. The period emphasized the performance part of the bilateral relations, perhaps intentionally to divert or delay the deliberation of contentious issues, rather than the laying of a foundation for serious academic discourse on the PRC. As K. P. S. Menon noted in his interview with the historian B. R. Nanda in 1976, it eventually dawned on Nehru that "Hindi-Chini bhai bhai might not be a practical policy" (Nehru Memorial Museum and Library, K. P. S. Menon Papers, Transcript 1976). However, this realization or the war itself had no impact on the ROI government with regard to devoting resources to studying Communist China. Rather, all avenues for accessing the PRC and having meaningful academic exchange between the scholars of the two countries were curtailed.

This is a policy that continues to this day, almost fifty-five years after the brief armed conflict of 1962 (Sen 2013).

The failure of the Friendship March had a significant impact on the two organizations involved in planning it. The Shanti Sena, as Thomas Weber (1996) has demonstrated, experienced a split because of the disagreements between Vinoba Bhave and J. P. Narayan. While the former advocated engagement within the ROI by focusing on land reform, the latter promoted a more active role in international peacekeeping. The World Peace Brigade also disintegrated not too long after the failure of the Delhi–Peking Friendship March. April Carter (2014: 247) argues that the World Peace Brigade "proved too grandiose in its ambitions, too lacking in resources and too reliant on key personalities in the USA and India (who had many other demands on their time): consequently, it faded away."

What did not fade away for a long time after the India-China war was the hatred, particularly with regard to how the Indian public perceived the PRC government. "Whatever legitimate steps the respective governments may take to safeguard their countries' interests," the souvenir of the *Delhi–Peking Friendship March* warned, "feelings of hatred, anger and vengeance must not be allowed to sway the peoples: for governments may come and go but the poison of hatred once generated in the hearts of the people dies hard." This hatred is now the main obstacle in contemporary ROI-PRC relations despite the record volume of trade, the frequent exchange of delegations and people, and the reemphasizing of India-China brotherhood.

AWAITING THE CHINDIAN UTOPIA

Similar to the multifarious literature on the India-China war that appeared in the 1960s and the 1970s, there has now emerged a genre of writing devoted to arguing a geo-civilizational relationship between the two countries, which reemphasizes the two-thousand-years-of-friendly-relations narrative and predicts a future marked by "Chindian" unity. Unlike the discourse of the 1950s, when similar nostalgia about past relations and hope for Asian brotherhood in the newly decolonized world kindled much of the writing, the more recent pronouncements are intended to divert attention away from contentious issues that have come to the forefront during the interim period. In both cases, as was pointed out in the introduction, these narratives of the past and predictions of the future have to do with the hopes and aspirations of a few writers rather than critical analysis of the past, present, and future. The historical interactions presented in these works are squarely placed in the framework of nation-states; they are unconcerned about the connections to and contributions of places and people beyond the borders of the ROI and the PRC, uncritical of the records found in Chinese sources, and selective of events and individuals that provide evidence of friendship and harmony. The objective is not to produce scholarly accounts of the past or a realistic prediction of the future, but to promote the idea of a harmonious and geo-civilizational relationship between the citizens of the ROI and the PRC, sometimes stretching to prehistoric times.

In 1979, an Indian Sinologist named Krishna Prakash Gupta (1979: 39) noted how in the post-1962 period of India-China relations "a reverential reference to the Buddhist connection has become standard practice. The image of cultural borrowings, exchanges and congruence provides a convenient backdrop to sorting out political obstacles to friendship between India and China." After pointing out that the reality of Buddhist exchanges between India and China may have been different from the perceived notions of mutual dialogue and accommodation, Gupta argues that "behind polite suggestions of friendly interaction in history lie two sharply opposed world views, and if these suggestions continue to this day with a tenacious force, it is only because they fulfill some necessary, even if self-contradictory, needs." He was especially critical of academics, whose approach, he writes, has "so far only served to reinforce these suggestions. The record of Buddhist interchanges has been so sanitized as to project images of two great nations in Asia, constantly living in peace, frequently learning from one another, and otherwise presenting an example of harmonious co-existence to the rest of the world. This record is dusted and displayed every time new moves are afoot to restore friendly relations between India and China."

The ideas of geo-civilizational and "Chindian" relationships are the latest manifestations of the attempt to "sanitize" the past for contemporary and future relations. In 2005, the politician Jairam Ramesh of the Congress Party (Indira) coined the term "Chindia," a conjugation of "China" and "India." In the preface to his book *Making Sense of Chindia*, which is essentially a collection of his columns published in the Indian newspaper the *Telegraph*, Ramesh (2005) clarifies that he is not as "romantic" as those who belong to the "civilizational school of 'India-China *wallahs*.'" Ramesh further notes that he does not believe "that conflict and confrontation is inevitable" between India and China. His notion of "Chindia," he explains, is associated more with the potential impact the two countries might have on global demographics, economics, and geostrategy in the future. "Ultimately," he writes, "there is truth in the next century being propelled by Asia and this is where understanding CHINDIA becomes important." Ramesh does not offer any detailed conceptualization of the term "Chindia," nor does he address the adverse impact the two countries, when taken together, would have on a range of environmental issues, including the emission of carbon dioxide, consumption of natural resources, and contribution to global warming.

In the subsequent decade, Chindia has attained a more utopic meaning than what Ramesh might have intended. It quickly became a catchphrase in the media and a symbol for India-China unity among the geo-civilizationalists. For instance, Tan Chung (2009), the leading advocate of the geo-civilizational idea, writes,

> I have discovered from Ramesh's conception an inspiration of Tagore and Nehru and an affinity with my father, Tan Yun-shan, and myself. I have translated it into Chinese as "Zhong-Yin datong" [*sic*] 中印大同 (literally "grand harmony between China and India"). . . . I conceive this Chindian "grand harmony" as one of the most powerful moral forces on earth. It was what Tagore and Nehru as well as other ancient and modern Indian and Chinese thinkers had dreamed of. I am confident that it will materialize with the joint efforts of the intellectual elites of the two countries.

Tan Chung's formulation of the geo-civilizational framework for contemporary ROI-PRC relations is intended to move away from what he calls (Tan 2009: 10) "the vicious circle of the geopolitical paradigm." India and China, he argues, are civilizational-states, not nation-states, with India emerging as a "united-states-of-Indian civilization" only in 1950 and China becoming a "united-states-of-Chinese-civilization" in 221 BCE with the Qin unification. "From a historical perspective," Tan explains (2009: 12), "the two civilizations stood as twin towers in the annals of human history because they were never competitive, but friends, companions and partners complementing one another." It is not clear what Tan implies by "civilization" in his arguments, as there is no consideration of the "civilizing" missions of various South Asian and Chinese polities (the Mauryans and the Han for example), while the role of Islam in connecting ancient India and China is neglected. The geo-civilizational concept also avoids discussion of the Chinese discourse on the failure of Indian civilization in the late nineteenth and early twentieth centuries. Furthermore, it makes forced and selective use of the past connections, which disregards contributions of people who did not live in areas that are now the ROI and the PRC.

This idea of civilizational friendship and the "sanitized" reconstruction of historical interactions are now common and oft-repeated jargon in the political discourse between the ROI and the PRC. In 2004, for example, the former Chinese premier Wen Jiabao noted that "China and India have enjoyed friendly relations for 2,000 years, which accounts for 99.9% of total time of our interactions. In terms of conflicts, it has lasted less than 0.1% of total time of our interactions." This statement, in fact, contradicts Mao Zedong's views in 1962, when he pointed out that the two countries previously fought "one-and-a-half wars" (Sun and Chen 1991: 97–98).[21] These episodes of military conflict between Indian polities and Chinese dynasties were rarely analyzed or mentioned in the reconstituted and imagined histories of India-China interactions during the 1950s by writers such as Jin Kemu, the contemporary proponents of Chindian and geo-civilizational unity, or those who profess a grand harmony between India and China ("ZhongYin datong") in the future. More notably, this friendship jargon is the foundation for several initiatives launched by the Indian and Chinese governments, including the building of a replica of the Sanchi Stupa at the White Horse Monastery in Luoyang by the Indian government, the construction of the memorial dedicated to the Chinese monk Xuanzang in Nālandā funded by the Chinese government, and the recent compilation of the *Encyclopedia of India-China Cultural Contacts* jointly sponsored by the foreign ministries of the two countries. The latter, in particular, is an example of the methods, implementation, and problems of highlighting the jargon of friendship.

The idea of compiling the encyclopedia was discussed during the former Chinese premier Wen Jiabao's visit to India in 2010 and mentioned in the joint communiqué between the ROI and the PRC released at the end of the trip. The objective of the project, as noted in the preface (Joint Compilation Committee 2014: xi) of the encyclopedia, was to make a "giant effort towards 'revitalising cultural rites' by revisiting, reviving and reemphasizing our shared cultural experience. It is expected to not only make the history of many centuries of India-China cultural contacts easily accessible to people of both the countries, but it is also expected to build popular consciousness about our common cultural heritage." The encyclopedia was published in 2014 to mark the "year of friendly exchanges between India and China" and officially launched in Beijing by Indian vice president Hamid Ansari and his Chinese counterpart Li Yuanchao in June 2014.

The Joint Compilation Committee working on the encyclopedia consisted of scholars and foreign ministry officials from the ROI and the PRC, with an eight-member (four each from the ROI and the PRC) Editorial Committee and Expert Group, as well as several contributors and editorial and research assistants from the two countries. The Editorial Committee and Expert Group met several times in Delhi and Beijing during the compilation of the encyclopedia before producing the two-volume work with seven hundred entries. However, contributions to the project were restricted to ROI and PRC citizens and only those residing in the two countries. No scholars from outside the two countries were asked to contribute to the volume, nor, it seems, was an attempt made to peer-review the entries or the volume overall.

Scholarship was clearly not the goal of this project, a characteristic shared by other such joint publications during the past two decades. The first line of the introduction makes this apparent. Invoking the oft-repeated cliché, it notes that "India and China are both ancient civilisations and as close neighbours there has been friendly intercourses and cultural exchange between their people for more than 2,000 years." A majority of the information included in the volumes, especially that related to Buddhism, is dated, having long been rejected by scholars. There are also numerous major and minor typographical and translation errors. The most glaring shortcomings are the lack of any critical analysis of primary sources, the absence of new research, and the use of modern national boundaries to reconstruct ancient interactions. Tibet, for example, is always taken to be a part of "China," as if it did not have any independent polities, diplomatic intercourse, or religious exchanges. This is clearly done to respect the territorial claims of the PRC. Similarly, no mention is made of the internment and deportation of ethnic Chinese from India, perhaps due to the sensitivities of the ROI government. Zheng He is described as "the envoy and commercial representative of the Chinese imperial court," who "gave gifts to the local rulers, established friendly relationships with them and made mutually beneficial trade at every stop" (846). The encyclopedia was evidently not meant to be an exercise in jointly advancing scholarship on India-China connections. Rather, it was intended to be an artifact, similar to the stupa in Luoyang and the memorial to Xuanzang, to showcase the success of ROI-PRC diplomacy in promoting collaborations between Indians and Chinese, when negotiations on resolving issues of contention have yielded no results, despite nineteen rounds of talks.

Writings that emphasize geo-civilizational interactions, together with state-sponsored publications and initiatives on India and China, usually have one common agenda, which is to connect past exchanges, especially those related to Buddhism, to contemporary ties as evidence of two thousand (or three thousand) years of friendship and harmony. Within this context, the armed conflict, the issues of mutual suspicion and distrust, the treatment of migrant communities, and the inability to resolve border disputes are considered irrelevant. Also ignored is the lesson learned in the 1950s that in an era of disconnect, trying to connect contemporary geopolitics to an imagined past does not lead to mutual understanding and peaceful coexistence.

The *Encyclopedia of India-China Cultural Contacts* is only one example of the failure of a bilateral initiative that placed people-to-people connections under the constrains of state agenda and deliberately curtailed multilateral collaboration in the field of academics. Pertinent also are the failures in advancing the innovative idea of establishing subregional collaboration in the region that connects the ROI, the PRC, Bangladesh, and Burma and the rejection of any Tibetan involvement in resolving problems that have ensued due to the defection of the Dalai Lama to the ROI and the presence of the government-in-exile of the Tibetans in Dharamsala.[22] While in the former case the ROI government seems to have stalled the progress due to concerns over economic and political domination in the subregion by the Chinese, the PRC government considers the participation of the Tibetans in geopolitical negotiations detrimental to its national integrity.

The BCIM Forum attempts to integrate the subregions of Bangladesh, China, India, and Myanmar/Burma through trade, tourism, transportation, and cultural connections.[23] The forum started as a "track-two diplomacy" initiative, with state and provincial governments, as well as the businesses in these regions, taking the lead. It has now morphed into a "track-one" initiative, expanding the involvement of the central governments. Despite several meetings and car rallies showcasing connectivity in the subregions during the past decade and a half, the forum has yet to produce any significant breakthroughs. The major hindrances to the integration of the subregion, which analysts suggest would benefit the local population through economic and infrastructure developments, have been the concerns about territorial integrity and mutual distrust. This is especially true of the proposed land and railway connections between the PRC's Yunnan Province and the West Bengal State of the ROI proposed by the forum. While the state governments and people in the Northeast Regions (NER) of the ROI are supportive of the connectivity element of the BCIM Forum, there are, it has been noted, "serious doubts" among the "Indian security and diplomatic establishments on the wisdom of opening up the volatile NER and partnering China in sub-regional development through the BCIM mechanism" (Uberoi 2016: 13). The lack of progress in this case is a demonstration of the ways in which bilateral concerns have become paramount to on-the-ground multilateral collaborations even though they could potentially benefit local regions, augment people-to-people connections, and promote mutual trust and confidence.

The issue of Tibet has been discussed in several sections of this book. The region had been an important part of India-China political discourse since Bogle's mission in the eighteenth century and emerged as a place of contention for contemporary governments from at least the 1940s. The ROI's ambiguity over the status of Tibet in the 1950s, the entry of the PLA into Tibet, the defection of the Dalai Lama, the fact that the key border dispute between the ROI and the PRC involves areas in and around Tibet, and the continuing protests and unrest in the region make it evident that Tibet is currently the most volatile crisis in ROI-PRC relations. The incorporation of Tibet into the PRC nation-state has negated any role the people living in the region or in exile could potentially contribute to resolving these disputes between the ROI and the PRC. Moreover, interactions between people belonging to the contested regions, Tibet in China and the Indian state of Arunachal, are curtailed because of the constraints placed by the contending nation-states, even when bilateral exchanges and collaborations are emphasized. Bilateralism thus comes with caveats and restrictions that are neither conducive nor constructive to normalizing relations between the ROI and the PRC.

GLOBAL CONNECTIONS IN AN ERA OF DISCONNECT

The disconnect between the Republic of India and the People's Republic of China emerged a few years before these two geopolitical entities were founded. After half a century of intellectual imagination and diplomatic collaboration, when Indians and Chinese were on the verge of declaring the attainment of the goals of pan-Asianism and the solidarity between the two states, the Asian Relations Conference of 1947 exposed one of the key issues that divided them. Tibet remained a concern throughout the 1950s, culminating in the defection of the Dalai Lama to the ROI in 1959. A disconnect also existed from almost the same time with regard to territorial claims, which led to the armed conflict in 1962. Together, the issues of Tibet and the border dispute defined ROI-PRC relations during the second half of the twentieth century. The regional and global connections of ROI-PRC relations were evident throughout that period. Neighboring states, such as Pakistan, Bhutan, and Nepal, were, and often still are, part of the political discourse and contention between the two countries. The United States and the Soviet Union (and later Russia) have been ingrained in the relations between the two countries since the late 1940s. The late 1940s was also the period in which the ROI became involved in the Korean dispute, when the Indian ambassador to Beijing, K. M. Panikkar, acted as the interlocutor between the Chinese and the United Nations. In the past two decades, the Bay of Bengal and the South China Sea regions have become new places of contention for "rising" India and China. Also during this period, Africa has emerged as a new site of interactions and competition for Indians and Chinese businesses and geopolitical agendas. The connections to all these regions were not new in the second half of the twentieth century; these places were all interlocked through trading networks in the nineteenth century. While commercial/financial motivations still link these places, geopolitical agendas have made the new connections significantly more restrictive, competitive, and contested than at any time in the past.

In concluding this chapter, it is perhaps appropriate to offer three examples of the global connections of the ROI-PRC relationship during the second half of the twentieth century and the first quarter of the twenty-first century that are associated with some of the geopolitical issues discussed above. Continuing with the emphasis on individuals and institutions in this chapter, the first pertains to the underappreciated role of Bertrand Russell in negotiating a peaceful settlement between the ROI and the PRC in the aftermath of the India-China war of 1962. The second relates to the formation of several regional and intraregional groupings that facilitate multilateral discourse between the ROI and the PRC. The third concerns the OBOR initiative (aka the Belt-Road Initiative, or BRI) launched by the PRC. These are examples of the wider global connections that are part of the contemporary relations between the two countries. Yet they are also instances of the geopolitical disconnect that has defined ROI-PRC relations since the late 1940s.

The Noble laureate Bertrand Russell supported both the cause of Indian independence and subsequently the PRC's membership in the United Nations. Unlike the organizers of the Delhi–Peking Friendship March, Russell was able to directly approach Zhou En-lai in 1962 and may have played a critical role in preventing an escalation of the armed conflict between the ROI and the PRC. He frequently communicated with Jawaharlal Nehru as well as with Indonesian president Sukarno, the Burmese UN secretary-general U Thant, President Kwame Nkrumah of Ghana, and the influential Sri Lankan political leader Sirimavo Bandaranaike on ways to mitigate the conflict between the two warring countries. Russell quickly established a cordial relationship with the Chinese premier Zhou Enlai and acted as an unbiased interlocutor. In fact, it was a day after Russell first wrote to Zhou that the Chinese suddenly declared a unilateral cease-fire and withdrew their troops after penetrating deep inside ROI territory. An astounded Russell (1963: 107) remarked, "I had thought it worthwhile to write to Chou En-lai as I had done, appealing for such magnanimous action on the part of the Chinese government, but I was taken by surprise, as was the rest of the world, that they believed sufficiently clearly and strongly that war must be avoided to take such extreme measures, to make such a sacrifice of their gains." It has been suggested that this action of the Chinese that followed Russell's letter to Zhou Enlai was a mere coincidence and not a result of Russell's intervention (Griffin 2001: 558).

Russell's above remark is nonetheless noteworthy because it indicates a significant shift in his opinion about the PRC. As Russell points out (1963: 86–87), he was "a lifelong friend of India," offering strong support for Indian independence and pursuing a close relationship with K. P. S. Menon and Prime Minister Jawaharlal Nehru prior to the ROI-PRC war. As with "almost everybody in the West," Russell writes (1963: 87), he had thought that "China was wholly in the wrong and had undoubtedly been the aggressor" in 1962. However, the unilateral withdraw of Chinese troops, his continued correspondence with Zhou and Nehru, and his detailed examination of documents produced by the ROI and the PRC representatives to make their respective arguments for territorial claims convinced Russell (1963: 131) that the "Chinese case was very much stronger" and that it was doubtful as to "whether the Chinese were the first aggressors." Russell was particularly dismayed by Nehru's talk about a "long war" with China, the ROI's insistence on the acceptance of its territorial claims as a prerequisite for peace negotiations, and also the "bellicose temper of the Indian public" (Russell 1963: 132). On the other hand, Russell found that the PRC was more willing to negotiate a peaceful settlement, magnanimous in accepting some of the demands made by the ROI government, and willing to let third parties meditate between the two contending nations.

Unable to travel to either the ROI or the PRC, Russell engaged in the complex and multisided negotiations from his home in England. After exchanging frequent messages with all relevant world leaders, Russell decided, in May 1963, to send his two assistants to meet with Jawaharlal Nehru in the ROI, Zhou Enlai in the PRC, and Sirimavo Bandaranaike in Sri Lanka. The latter had led a group of six nonaligned nations to draft the Colombo Proposal as a way to reach a tentative settlement on the border dispute between the ROI and the PRC.[24] Through his representatives Russell wanted to convince Nehru and Zhou to accept the Colombo Proposal and create an opportunity for the two sides, perhaps with mediation by an unbiased third party, to reach a final settlement on the contested borders.

Even though the proposal was more sympathetic to the demands made by the ROI, the Chinese accepted it in "principle" and agreed that it could be the basis for further bilateral negotiations. Nehru, however, wanted the Chinese to accept all provisions of the proposal "*in toto*," and not only as an interim solution but as a permanent settlement of the border issue (Griffin 2001: 568). Despite several concessions made by the PRC to accommodate the additional demands of the ROI, actions that were appreciated by Russell in his letter to Zhou Enlai dated 14 June 1963, Nehru was unable to write directly to the Chinese side confirming the acceptance of the Colombo Proposal as the basis for further negotiations and not a permanent settlement. In fact, the ROI government denied that Nehru had endorsed Russell's suggestion to begin the border negotiations on the basis of the Colombo Proposal (Griffin 2001: 571). This reaction by the Indian side eventually upset Zhou Enlai, who doubted Nehru's sincerity in resolving the border dispute. Zhou seems to have also become agitated with Russell's representatives, who could not relay more than a verbal commitment from Nehru (Griffin 2001: 569). This stalemate essentially ended the multilateral diplomacy and froze border negotiations between the ROI and the PRC until 1980, when representatives of the two countries met again in Beijing after a gap of seventeen years.

It was also in 1980 that the Chinese leader Deng Xiaoping laid the foundation for the contemporary relations between the ROI and the PRC. He essentially offered to the ROI the same proposal Zhou Enlai had made to Nehru in 1960, viz, Chinese recognition of the

McMahon Line in exchange for the status quo in the western (i.e., Aksai Chin) sector (Ramachandran 1980: 147; Garver 2001: 101). Deng is also reported to have suggested that "if the two countries cannot reach an accord," the "'issue can be put aside' as it need not 'hinder the development of relations between the two nations'" (Ramachandran 1980: 147). This set in motion, albeit only after the Indian prime minister Rajiv Gandhi's visit to PRC in 1988, several rounds of discussions on resolving the border dispute. However, following Deng Xiaoping's suggestions, the two sides have since then focused mainly on developing economic ties, which has resulted in a record volume of bilateral trade and the emergence of the PRC as the ROI's leading trading partner.

It is this focus on economic relations that also led to the ROI and the PRC's participation in several regional and transregional groupings. As Prasenjit Duara (2010: 974) has pointed out, during the post–Cold War period, nation-states and nationalism "have developed a new relationship to globalization. In this reconfiguration, regionalism has clearly strengthened, emerging as an intermediate zone between the deterritorializing impulses of capitalism and the territorial limits of nationalism." It is within this context that multilateral organizations, such as ASEAN, the EAS, and BRICS, have emerged. These groupings have created new intra-Asian and global linkages, integrated economies, triggered inter- and intraregional cultural circulations, and, as Duara (2010) has argued, brought about dramatic increases in interdependencies across Asia and the world.

For the ROI and the PRC, these multilateral organizations provide opportunities to collaborate in the fields of culture, science, and the environment, at the same time as they deepen their economic interdependencies. The collaboration at the East Asian Summit forum, for example, has resulted in the reestablishment of the Nālandā University, where Chinese monks such as Xuanzang and Yijing studied in the seventh century. Endorsed by the EAS countries, the largest foreign donor currently is the PRC. Similarly, the BRICS grouping has made it possible for five key developing countries to create a financial mechanism for economic and infrastructure development and to strengthen the information and technology sectors in each of the five countries involved.

The third example pertains to a multilateral initiative where the ROI and the PRC have not been able to work collaboratively due mostly to the territorial concerns of nation-states. Proposed by the Chinese president Xi Jinping in 2013, the One Belt, One Road initiative focuses on multilateral collaboration across the Eurasian landmass (the "Economic Belt") and the Indian Ocean maritime world (the "Twenty-First Century Maritime Silk Road"). Using the historical connections across these routes as metaphor, Xi Jinping (2017) at a recently concluded meeting of state leaders associated with the OBOR project noted that the initiative would promote the "Silk Road spirit" of peace and cooperation, openness and inclusiveness, mutual learning, and mutual benefit. Although emphasizing economic, especially infrastructure, development, Xi additionally pointed out that the initiative's goal was to also establish a "multitiered mechanism for cultural and people-to-people exchanges."

With a planned investment of $900 billion for the various projects within the scheme funded through PRC or PRC-initiated banks, such as the Asian Infrastructure Investment Bank (AIIB), the BRICS New Development Bank, and the China Development Bank, the OBOR initiative proposes to focus on infrastructure development ventures across the six "corridors" within the Eurasian landmass and the Indian Ocean world. These six corridors consist of the China–Mongolia–Russia Economic Corridor, extending from the northern PRC to eastern Russia; the New Eurasian Land Bridge Corridor, from western regions of the PRC to western parts of Russia; the China–Central Asia–Western Asia Corridor, which links western China to Turkey; the China–Indochina Peninsula

Corridor from Southern China to Singapore; the China–Pakistan Economic Corridor that connects the Xinjiang region of China to the Gwadar port of Pakistan in the Arabian Sea; and the Bangladesh–China–India–Myanmar Corridor (the above-mentioned BCIM project).

Two of the above corridors, however, have sites of intense territorial disputes. While parts of the South China Sea region, which forms the key maritime space within the China–Indochina Peninsula Corridor concept, are contested by the PRC, Taiwan, Vietnam, Brunei, Malaysia, Indonesia, and the Philippines, the upper regions of the China–Pakistan Economic Corridor are disputed territories between the ROI and Pakistan. It is due to this territorial dispute that the ROI decided not to attend the Belt and Road Forum for International Cooperation held in Beijing on 14 May 2017. Additionally, the ROI is the only major Asian country that has not formally endorsed the OBOR initiative. The territorial concerns that hinder the initiative once again illustrate the difference between historical connections and contemporary interactions constrained by the politics of nation-states. It also suggests that the legacy defining the contemporary ROI-PRC relationship is not the two thousand/three thousand years of friendly exchanges as highlighted by the proponents of geo-civilizational discourse, but the disconnect emerging out of the 1962 war and the persistent territorial dispute.

NOTES

1. A recent study of this Himalayan region in India-China relations is Guyot-Réchard (2016).

2. An excellent study of the interactions between the ROI and the PRC in the 1950s is Ghosh (forthcoming).

3. Manjari Chatterjee Miller (2013) has argued that "post-imperial ideology" (PII), which according to her emerged from a sense of victimhood inflicted by colonial powers (Europeans as well as, in the case of the PRC, the Japanese), influences "India's and China's international behavior," including ROI-PRC relations. This argument is not tenable when examined in the context of a broader

source material, such as the notes exchanged between the Indian and Chinese governments from 1954 to 1965, or in the view of the analysis of the "national humiliation" rhetoric of the PRC government undertaken by Julia Lovell (2011). Miller does not examine either of these sources. Miller also does not take into account the possible impact of the presence of the Dalai Lama as a political refugee in Dharamsala on the PRC's foreign policy toward the ROI.

4. On the views expressed in Indian newspapers and magazines, see Saksena (2005).

5. I would like to thank Atul Bharadwaj for sharing this document with me.

6. Nair wrote this book after his visit to the PRC in 1953 as a delegate to the Seventh Congress of the All-China Federation of Labour.

7. The delegation was designated "unofficial" because the Chinese embassy in New Delhi sent the invitations directly to various Indian organizations, including the India-China Friendship Association in Bombay. A comment by B. N. Mullik (1971: 147) indicates that the Indian government did not appreciate this action by the Chinese embassy.

8. Nakao Shimazu (2014), in her study of the Bandung Conference of 1955, has noted the performative aspect of intra-Asian/Afro-Asian diplomacy. "The Bandung Conference," she writes (2014: 231), "is a prima-facie case of how a diplomatic event can be highly significant without producing so-called concrete results." Shimazu adds (2014: 232), "The dramatization of diplomacy through performative acts can play a significant part in diplomacy, insofar as some diplomatic events are as much about public performances as they are about behind-the-scenes negotiations." The exchange of delegations between the ROI and the PRC, and even the mutual visits of Zhou and Nehru to the ROI and the PRC respectively in 1954, could be understood in this same context of serving performative roles rather than producing concrete results as far as solutions to the impediments in the bilateral relations were concerned.

9. The poet Yuan Shui-pai composed another poem dedicated to "China-India Friendship" after the signing of the Panchasheel Agreement. The poem appears in the commemorative volume published by the Foreign Languages Press for the Indian cultural delegation that visited China in 1955. See Anon. 1955.

10. On the "forward policy" of Nehru, see Maxwell (1970). More nuanced versions of Nehru's policies on China appear in Hoffmann (1990) and Raghavan (2006, 2010).

11. While this seems to be a similar sentiment that Nehru expressed to B. N. Mullik, the diary for G. Parthasarathi is not publicly available. The newspaper report is based on citations provided by Parthasarathi's son.

12. An IB file on Shen also exists at the West Bengal State Archives (File 816/46, Serial No. 261).

13. A collection of his paintings and calligraphy was published in 1998 by Xianggang suoyiyuan shufa xue hui as part of the exhibition in Hong Kong. The collection, after the exhibition, is titled *Chang Xiufeng yishu huigu zhan* 常秀峰藝術回顧展.

14. On this episode, see the recent narrative by Gyalo Thondup, the elder brother of the Dalai Lama. Gyalo Thondup (2015: 163) suggests that one of the objectives of Zhou Enlai's visit to India that year was to "force" the Dalai Lama to return to China. See also Pardesi (2011).

15. Unfortunately for Chang Xiufeng, who returned to his home province to teach at the Anhui Normal University and also to take up the post of the deputy director of the Anhui Provincial Museum, this ordeal did not end with his release from the Darjeeling jail. During the Cultural Revolution in China, he was accused of spying for the Guomindang. In fact, some of the Red Guards started questioning the reasons for his release from the Darjeeling jail and alleged that he was in fact spying for the Indian government. And when they discovered that he could speak Russian, Chang was branded a Soviet spy. After the humiliation in India and China, Chang eventually migrated to Hong Kong in 1982.

16. On the invocation of international law by the PRC government with regard to the internment and deportation of people of Chinese descent, see Cohen and Leng (1972).

17. Other narratives of the experience at the Deoli camp include Marsh (2012) and Li (2008). A detailed study of life at the camp is Li (2011).

18. The PRC in response argued that these people were not Indian nationals. However, the ROI communication insisted that these were all of "Indian origin" living and working in Tibet. "As the Indian laws are consistent with the recognized international principles of nationality," one of the communications from the Indian side argued, "the Government of India cannot accept any so-called law of nationality or executive decree of the Chinese Government which would deprive Indian nationals in Tibet of their nationality and citizenship" (*Notes* 11).

19. Das's parents were deported from Shanghai in 1964 (*Times of India*, 31 October 1968: 11).

20. The changed perception of the PRC in India is also apparent in Bollywood movies, which after 1962 started portraying China and the Chinese as villains and as untrustworthy. On the portrayal of the Chinese before and after the 1962 war, see Banerjee (2007).

21. The first military conflict between India and China, according to Mao, took place in 648, when a Tang envoy visiting the Kanauj region retaliated against a local ruler who had attacked him unprovoked. The second incident happened in 1398, when Tamerlane attacked the Delhi Sultanate. This was Mao's "half war" because he believed that Tamerlane was a Mongol (he was actually a Turk) and that part of Mongolia belonged to China. If India and China are taken as fixed geopolitical entities with bilateral relations stretching over two thousand years, as the pan-Asianists emphasize, then there were at least two additional military conflicts. During the second century BCE there were frequent battles between the Han Empire and the polity of Jibin (located in the present-day Afghanistan-Kashmir area), and in 1433 Admiral Zheng He, representing the Ming court, may have participated in a military conflict on the Malabar coast.

22. Also absent is any type of trilateral negotiations involving the ROI, the PRC, and Pakistan.

23. Also known as the Bangladesh, India, China, and Myanmar–Economic Corridor (BCIM-EC). The forum started as the "Kunming Initiative" in 1999.

24. On the Colombo Proposal, see Hoffmann (1990: 226–228).

Conclusion

Over 2,000 years ago, the Silk Road became a bridge of friendship linking our two ancient civilizations.
—PRC President Xi Jinping in the Pakistani Parliament
21 April 2015

Several aspects stand out in a study of the *longue durée* connections between the entities called India and China and their subsequent geopolitical incarnations, the ROI and the PRC. The contribution of Buddhism in connecting most of the Asian continent, the role of commercial exchanges in integrating the Afroeurasian region, the notable impetus to global circulations brought about by the expansion of imperial powers, and the disconnect that ensued through the creation of the nation-states in the mid-twentieth century are four such facets that have been discussed in this book. The people involved in these interactions included the family of the Sogdian monk Kang Senghui, the Arab merchant Sulaymān, the Moroccan traveler Ibn Baṭūṭah, the Portuguese missionaries, the Japanese scholar Okakura Kakuzō, and Nobel laureate Bertrand Russell. These facets and agents of connection suggest that elements of Indian, Chinese, overall Asian, and world histories have always been interlinked. The sites of interaction that brought Indians and Chinese together within and beyond Asia, the circulations of people and objects originating in different regions of the world that streamed through the networks connecting India and China, and even some of the factors that resulted in imagined realities made these connections vibrant and expansive.

The Buddhist exchanges, for example, created lineages across Asia, from Persia to Japan, by incorporating settled and seminomadic people, connecting varied polities, and facilitating the circulation of ideas and objects. The missionary and pilgrimage activities as well as the demand for Buddhist texts, translators, and ritual items sustained these connections over several centuries. Even the fear of an imminent demise of the Buddhist doctrine in the tenth and eleventh centuries prompted a common response by Buddhist clergies across Asia to collect and preserve Buddhist texts and artifacts. These all are indicative of a connected world of Buddhism for much of the first millennium CE.

Indeed, as argued in chapter 1, these Buddhist interactions created a cosmopolitan world across Asia, where diverse peoples and objects intermingled. The specific teachings and practices of Buddhism at each location differed to varying degrees, there were significant variations in the languages and scripts used by the communities involved, many places had their own pilgrimage centers, and there were also "homegrown" buddhas that had little or no connection to India or the doctrines that emerged out of that region. In fact, the physical connection to the Buddhist holy land was limited since very few people had the opportunity to travel to the pilgrimage sites associated with the life of Śākyamuni Buddha. Yet Buddhism facilitated the movement of people, not always to one specific destination, as the practice of Hajj did for the Muslims, but to many different sites of interactions. Some gathered at the learning centers in Nālandā, Palembang, and Chang'an, and others visited the monastic institutions and relics in Sri Lanka. People also met in Khotan and Dunhuang at the crossroads of Central Asia, traveled to Lhasa or to Persia, discussed anti-imperialism issues at the Maha

Bodhi Society in Calcutta, and took their personal Buddhist deities to Chinese diasporic locations in Southeast Asia. It was these circulatory connections, multidirectional movement, and multilocational engagement of many different people that made the Buddhist cosmopolis unique and fascinating.

Buddhist texts, relics, and other artifacts also moved in a similar, multidirectional way. Traders, pilgrims, missionaries, diplomats, migrants, and political leaders carried these objects from one place to another. These objects were used in rituals and ceremonies, in diplomatic exchanges, to legitimize political or religious authority, or as a means to earn profit. Some of these artifacts were also employed, as in the case of Mount Wutai, the cave temples of Central Asia and China, and Borobudur in Java, to create new spaces for Buddhist pilgrimage, veneration, and proselytizing activity. These artifacts, as they were copied, reshaped, and retransmitted, circulated widely throughout much of Asia, sustaining or creating new connections between places within the Buddhist cosmopolis.

These movements and circulations of people and objects associated with Buddhism contributed, as discussed in chapter 1, to the transmission of geographical and technical knowledge. While some of this knowledge was directly related to Buddhist teachings (such as the method of making sugar), others originated in Brahmanical tradition. The translation activities were the main conduits through which medical and astronomical traditions spread to China. However, not all of the medical and astronomical ideas and representations were devised in India. Hellenistic, Iranian, and Central Asian elements were also entangled in the process of rendering the texts or during the oral transmission of ideas. Certain medical prescriptions, the drawings of celestial objects, and the charts of horoscopic astrology produced in China demonstrated this mixture of different traditions that fused together in the course of the circulations.

The commercial networks connecting India and China were similarly part of wider linkages to markets elsewhere in the world. From Maldivian cowries and Arabian horses to South American bullion, the commodities involved in the commercial interactions between India and China often included goods that started their journeys from outside the two regions. Additionally, people from West Asia, Southeast Asia, and later Europe and America were involved in the exchange of goods between these two regions. Silk, porcelain, pepper, textiles, cotton, pepper, opium, and tea were some such goods that these traders procured and sold. Other parts of this trading system were caravan and ship operators, who ferried traders and commodities in many directions. While the trading system within which India-China commercial exchanges took place was already connected to the Mediterranean region in the early Common Era, by the nineteenth century, the long-distance commercial and transportation networks had extended to include markets in North America and mines in South America.

As noted in chapter 3, the early fifteenth century saw the intervention by the Ming state in the circulation of commodities not only between India and China, but also across the Indian Ocean world. The presence of operators representing a hegemonic state alongside the networks of private merchants became a common pattern with the subsequent arrival of the European colonial powers. Private Parsi and Kashmiri traders, Chinese Hong merchants, Dutch and EIC sailors, and the financial institutions in Europe all became entwined in the extensive commercial activities of the eighteenth and nineteenth centuries. At this time, profit came not only from directing the flow of commodities but also from the control of production sites and the exploitation of labor.

Diverse groups of people moved from one region to another either voluntarily or as part of the indentured labor circulations during the eighteenth and nineteenth centuries. This period also witnessed the formation of Chinese settlements in Calcutta and

Bombay as well as the establishment of Indian trading houses in Kashgar and, after the Opium War, in Shanghai. The key feature of this period was perhaps the creation of sites of interactions between Indians and Chinese outside the Asian continent, especially in the plantations in Guiana and Mauritius. New sites of interactions also emerged within Asia due to European colonial expansion. Thus, Macau, Penang, and Hong Kong developed into locations where Chinese and Indian traders, laborers, and intellectuals interacted and established social and cultural relationships. This intermingling among Indian and Chinese migrant communities across the colonial world resulted in new and complex forms of connections and circulations that are often disregarded in the nation-state-focused narratives of India-China interactions.

The nation-state-based histories of the past encounters between India and China enthusiastically include the activities of anticolonial revolutionaries and intellectuals in the diasporic settings of India or China. These undertakings are seen as joint efforts of Indians and Chinese against European and subsequently Japanese imperialism. The actions of the members of the Ghadar Party in China, for example, are usually part of these narratives. Excluded, however, is the study of the Chinese communities in Calcutta, who seem to have been too ordinary to merit a detailed examination in the context of India-China connections. In fact, in the early twentieth century, when the historiography of India-China connections developed as a consequence of the interactions between Indian and Chinese intellectuals meeting in China, India, and Japan, the roles of migrant communities were completely ignored. The intellectual discourse facilitated by the transmission of Buddhism during the first millennium CE was the main focus of this reconstruction/ reimagination of the past encounters. It was hoped that similar exchanges could be reestablished in the twentieth century. Within this imagination of past encounters and the anticipation of a future relationship between the two "civilizations," which is what the pan-

Asianist ideology essentially promoted, the subalterns did not seem to have any agency.

By the late 1940s when the Republic of India and the People's Republic of China were founded, this narrative of civilizational dialogue between India and China had taken deep root. It was quickly incorporated into the respective national histories, which merged groups of people and polities that previously had distinct identities, fused cultural diversities, removed episodes of military expansion, and created an impression that there had been no issues of contestation between India and China before the arrival of the Europeans. This included the promotion of Zheng He as a peaceful diplomatic envoy who connected the court of an "enlightened" Chinese emperor to the polities of India that were eagerly waiting to conduct trade relations with China. The fact that the Yongle emperor had usurped the throne and (along with Zheng He) been severely criticized by the later Confucian officials and that there were various accounts of the Ming admiral intervening in local disputes and abducting native rulers was found to be irrelevant to this discourse.

It was argued in chapter 5 that the emergence of the ROI and the PRC, each with their territorial delineations—however contested they may be—curtailed the earlier patterns of connections and interactions that had taken place between the regions now included within the borders of the two countries. The India-China war of 1962 further changed the nature of connections as the concerns became overtly bilateral and thus the way to address them could only be, in the opinion of the two governments, bilateral. It was within this context that the nation-state-based narratives of the past encounters once again became relevant. Unlike in the 1950s, these narratives are being produced today not only to celebrate the "ageless affinity" between India and China, but also to protect these nation-state-based and civilizational narratives from the "hijackers of the nobleness of civilization for evil purposes" (Tan and Geng 2005: 31). The two authors of the 547-page book titled *India and*

China: Twenty Centuries of Civilizational Interaction and Vibrations clearly lay out this agenda. "As the authors of this book," Tan and Geng write that they have "a lifelong commitment to upholding the goodness of civilization, hence the eagerness of this book in pumping fresh air to the heavily polluted atmosphere concerning civilization. It is hoped that by forcing good coins into this arena, bad coins may cease to circulate."

It is this incarcerating of the past connections within the framework of national and civilizational histories, or with the intention to advocate a particular agenda, that results in the failure to recognize the much broader and more complex connections that existed between India and China in the *longue durée*. These connections were not limited to two nonexistent nation-states or vaguely described civilizations, or even clearly demarcated geographical entities. Rather, multiple regions, peoples, objects, and even "civilizations" were part of the connections and circulations that defined and shaped the connected history of Asia and the world.

Within this broader context of intraregional connections, two strains of relationship between India and China can be surmised from the examination undertaken in this study. The first is that of Buddhism and trade-driven interactions. These interactions were multidirectional with the involvement of missionaries, pilgrims, traders, physicians, astrologers, craftsmen, and the like. The geographical space that separated the core polities in India and China restricted direct conflict. Thus, while changes in the policies and the desires of specific polities and rulers occasionally led to augmentation or termination of certain connections, the role of the state in the overall exchanges and interactions was limited.

The second strain is that of geopolitics, marked by competition, conquest, and territorial dispute, especially because of the increased participation of the state or other hegemonic powers. It began, as is argued in this book, with the Zheng He expeditions in the early fifteenth century, when the presence of the Ming fleet dictated commercial and diplomatic exchanges between polities in South Asia and the imperial court in China. The European colonial powers perpetuated and expanded this geopolitical strain through the exploitation of resources, people, and labor and the expansion and demarcation of territories. The Japanese, who occupied several regions of East and Southeast Asia, also implemented similar oppressive policies in the 1930s and 1940s. These imperial exploitations and expansions provoked nationalist sentiments among Indians and Chinese, leading to the emergence of anticolonial nationalist discourse and civilizational narrative, of which the book by Tan and Geng is a recent manifestation.

This civilizational narrative, which promoted the idea of harmonious connections among ancient Asian societies and avoided any mention of military expansions or cultural domination over peripheral societies prior to the arrival of the European colonial enterprises continued after decolonization. As the realities of competitive nation-states sharpened the geopolitical divides and triggered armed conflicts, the civilizational narrative became a refuge for those seeking alternatives to the discourse of rivalry and conflict. It also became an avenue for the states to promote cultural diplomacy through monitored, managed, and restrictive people-to-people connections. Deliberately sidestepped, however, was the fact that the earlier strain of interactions, even during the colonial period, flourished because of the free-flowing connectedness and interdependencies across Asia and other parts of the world.

The state-directed people-to-people exchanges and the propagation of civilizational dialogue also ignores the realities of contemporary India-China connections that can be discerned from the trading activity of several hundred Indian traders residing in places such as Keqiao 柯橋 in the Zhejiang Province of the PRC. The commercial and financial aspects involve markets, institutions, and consumers located in Southeast Asia, West Asia, and Africa. Rarely is this a direct trading affair between the PRC and the ROI.

Precisely because of the lack of state involvement and since this trade is not reflected in the statistics on bilateral economic relations, neither the ROI nor the PRC government acknowledges the importance of these multiregional ties and the contributions these traders make to the circulation of ideas, knowledge, and objects beyond India and China. The example from Keqiao also indicates, as Ka-kin Cheuk (2016) has demonstrated, the stereotyping of these traders as "evil Indians" by the locals because of their "questionable business ethics." Indeed, the data projected by the ROI and the PRC governments and the discourse of friendship and civilizational dialogue they advertise do not reflect the prevalent issues of stereotyping, trust deficits, or even racist viewpoints expressed by both sides on social media (Shen 2011).

India-China connections, therefore, have been, through history and during the contemporary period, a mishmash of complexities stemming from multiregional interconnectedness and indispensable interdependencies as well as detrimental perceptions and geopolitical antagonism. All these factors make the connections between India and China unique, noteworthy, and consequential given the *longue durée* and the broad geographical impact of the exchanges. The transmission of Buddhism, the circulations of knowledge and objects, the movement of people, and the appearance of India and China as neighboring nation-states shaped not only Asian history but also world history by creating Buddhist interactions in the first millennium; sustaining the colonial commercial connections in the seventeenth, eighteenth, and nineteenth centuries; generating the ideas of pan-Asianism in the early twentieth century; emerging as the key geopolitical rivals in Asia in the 1960s; and together offering tremendous potential for global finances, while at the same time raising concerns about their current and future impact on the ecology and the environment. At all times in the past, present, and it seems the foreseeable future, India-China connections have been and will remain intimately entangled with the rest of the world.

It is in the above context that even the territorial dispute, the main impediment to India-China relations today, may have to be settled through "neutral arbitration" rather than bilateral negotiations. Both President Kwame Nkrumah of Ghana and Bertrand Russell envisioned this solution in the aftermath of the India-China war of 1962. In a letter to Russell dated 30 November 1962, President Nkrumah suggested that the best course of action to resolve the dispute between the ROI and the PRC "might be the setting up of an impartial committee of experts respected by both sides, who can demarcate clear frontiers that can be recognized by India and China and become internationally acceptable" (Russell 1963: 126). On 13 December Russell conveyed a similar message to Nehru. "I cannot see that there is the faintest national humiliation in submitting legal questions to neutral arbitration," wrote Russell (1963: 127). He continued, "The whole legal position as to the frontier is tangled and obscure and controversial, and I do not see that either side has a right to insist upon its own interpretation as preliminary to negotiation or arbitration" (Russell 1963: 127–128). Russell made the same suggestion to the Chinese side. Given that the ROI and the PRC have been unable to settle their territorial dispute in over half a century since Nkrumah and Russell made their recommendations, and because several multilateral initiatives exist to enable neutral arbitration, it might be time for the two sides to relinquish the constraints of nation-state-derived bilateralism and allow an impartial committee to resolve the matter. Such a resolution will not only lead to a growth in people-to-people interactions between Indians and Chinese but also facilitate cooperation between the two countries with regard to global concerns. This was perhaps the kind of "responsibility" that Liang Qichao ([1925] 2002: xxx), when welcoming Rabindranath Tagore in 1924, thought India and China should "bear to the whole of mankind."

Bibliography

PRIMARY SOURCES

Chinese

Cefu yuangui 冊府元龜 (Outstanding Models from the Storehouse of Literature). Compiled by Wang Qinruo 王欽若 (962–1025) et al. Beijing: Zhonghua shuju, 1960.

Chu sanzang ji ji 出三藏記集 (Collection of Records Concerning the Translation of the Tripiṭaka). By Sengyou 僧祐 (443–518). T. (55) 2145.

Da Tang da Ci'ensi sanzang fashi zhuan 大唐大慈恩寺三藏法師傳 (Biography of the Master of the Tripiṭaka of the Great Ci'en Monastery [Compiled during the] Great Tang [Dynasty]). By Huili 慧立 (615–?) and Yancong 彥悰 (627–649). T. (50) 2053.

Da Tang Xiyu ji 大唐西域記 (Records of the Western Regions [Visited during the] Great Tang [Dynasty]). By Xuanzang 玄奘 (602?–664) and Bianji 辯機 (d. 649). T. (51) 2087.

Da Tang Xiyu qiufa gaoseng zhuan 大唐西域求法高僧傳 (Biographies of the Eminent Monks [who Traveled to the] Western Regions in Search of the Law, [Compiled during the] Great Tang [Dynasty]. By Yijing 義淨 (635–713). T. (51) 2066.

Daoyi zhilüe 島夷誌略 (Brief Record of the Island Barbarians). By Wang Dayuan 汪大淵 (c. 1311–?). Annotated by Su Jiqing 蘇繼廎 as *Daoyi zhilüe jiaoshi* 島夷誌略校釋. Beijing: Zhonghua shuju, 1981.

Fayuan zhulin 法苑珠林 (Pearl-Grove of the Garden of the Law). By Daoshi 道世 (d. 668?). T. (53) 2122.

Fozu tongji 佛祖統記 (General Record of the Lineage of the Buddha). By Zhipan 志磐 (fl. 13th century). T. (49) 2035.

481

Gaoseng Faxian zhuan 高僧法顯傳 (A Record of the Eminent Monk Faxian). By Faxian 法顯 (337?–422?). T. (51) 2085.

Gaoseng zhuan 高僧傳 (Biographies of the Eminent Monks). By Huijiao 慧皎 (497–554). T. (50) 2059.

Han shu 漢書 (History of the Han [Dynasty]). Edited by Ban Gu 班固 (32–92) et al. Beijing: Zhonghua shuju, 1996.

Hou Han shu 後漢書 (History of the Later Han [Dynasty]). Edited by Fan Ye 范曄 (398–445). Beijing: Zhonghua shuju, 1995.

Huang Maocai 黃楙材 . *Xiyou riji* 西輶日記 (Diary of the West[ward] Carriage).

———. *Yindu zhaji* 印度箚記 (Notes on India).

———. *Youli chuyan* 遊歷芻言 (My Travels).

Jin shu 晉書 (History of the Jin [Dynasty]). Compiled by Fang Xuanling 房玄齡 (579–658) et al. Beijing: Zhonghua shuju, 1974.

Jiu Tang shu 舊唐書 (Old History of the Tang [Dynasty]). Compiled by Liu Xu 劉昫 (887–946) et al. Beijing: Zhonghua shuju, 1975.

Jiye Xiyu xingcheng 繼業西域行程 (A Travelogue of [the Monk] Jiye to the Western Regions). Fan Chengda 范成大 (1126–1193). T. (51) 2089: 981b–982c.

Kaiyuan shijiao lu 開元釋教錄 (A Catalogue of [Texts Concerning] Buddhist Teachings [Compiled during the] Kaiyuan [Reign Period]). Compiled by Zhisheng 智昇 (fl. 8th century). T. (55) 2154.

Liang shu 梁書 (History of the Liang [Dynasty]). Compiled by Yao Cha 姚察 (533–606) and Yao Silian 姚思廉 (d. 637). Beijing: Zhonghua shuju, 1973.

Lidai minghua ji 歷代名畫記 (Records of Famous Painters through the Ages). Compiled by Zhang Yanyuan 張彥遠 (815–?). *Congshu jicheng* edition. Taipei: Shangwu yinshuguan, 1986.

Luoyang qielan ji 洛陽伽藍記 (Record of [Buddhist] Monasteries in Luoyang). Compiled by Yang Xuanzhi 楊衒之 (?–555). T. (51) 2092.

Ming shi 明史 (History of the Ming [Dynasty]). Compiled by Zhang Tingyu 張廷玉 (1672–1755). Beijing: Zhonghua shuju, 1974.

Ming shilu 明史祿 (Veritable Records of the Ming Dynasty). Taipei: Zhongyuan yanjiu lishi yuyan yanjiusuo.

Nanhai jigui neifa zhuan 南海寄歸內法傳 (Account of Buddhism Sent Home from the Southern Seas). By Yijing (54) 2125.

Nan Qi shu 南齊書 (History of the Southern Qi [Dynasty]). Compiled by Xiao Zixian 蕭子縣 (489–537). Beijing: Zhonghua shuju, 1974.

Nan shi 南史 (History of the Southern [Dynasties]). Compiled by Li Yanshou 李延壽 (d. c. 677). Beijing: Zhonghua shuju, 1974.

Pingzhou ketan 萍洲可談 (Talks from Pingzhou). By Zhu Yu 朱彧 (fl. 12th century). *Siku quanshu* 四庫全書 edition. Taipei: Shangwu yinshuguan, 1975.

Sanguo zhi 三國志 (Records of the Three Polities). Compiled by Chen Shou 陳壽 (233–297). Beijing: Zhonghua shuju, 1974.

Shi ji 史記 (Records of the Grand Historian). Compiled by Sima Tan 司馬談 (180–110? B.C.E.) and Sima Qian 司馬遷 (145–86? B.C.E.). Beijing: Zhonghua shuju, 1996.

Shijia fang zhi 釋迦方志 (Record of the Country of Śākya). Compiled by Daoxuan. T. (51) 2088.

Song gaoseng zhuan 宋高僧傳 (Biographies of Eminent Monks [Compiled during the] Song [Dynasty]). Compiled by Zanning. T. (50) 2061.

Song huiyao jigao 宋會要輯搞 (Collection of the Important Documents of the Song [Dynasty]). Compiled by Xu Song 徐松 (1781–1848) et al. Beijing: Zhonghua shuju, 1987.

Song shi 宋史 (History of the Song [Dynasty]). Compiled by Tuo Tuo 脫脫 (1212–1255) et al. Beijing: Zhonghua shuju, 1995.

Song shu 宋書 (History of the [Liu] Song Dynasty). Compiled by Shen Yue 沈約 (441–513). Beijing: Zhonghua shuju, 1974.

Sui shu 隋書 (History of the Sui [Dynasty]). Compiled by Wei Zheng 魏徵 (580–643) et al. Beijing: Zhonghua shuju, 1971.

Tang hui yao 唐會要 (Important Documents of the Tang [Period]). Compiled by Wang Pu 王溥 (922–982). Shanghai: Shanghai guji chubanshe, 1991.

Tangshuang pu 糖霜譜 (Treatise on Crystallized Sugar). Wang Zhou 王灼 (1105–1181). *Congshu jicheng* edition. Taipei: Xinwenfeng, 1985.

Tō daiwa jōtō sei den 唐大和上東征傳 (An Account of the Eastern Travels of the Great Tang Master). By Genkai 元開 (fl. 8th century). T. (51) 2089: 988a–995a.

Wang Zengshan 王曾善. 1997. *Zhongguo Huijiao Jindong youhao fangwentuan riji* 中國回教近東友好訪問團日記 (Diaries of the Chinese Muslim Goodwill Mission to the Near East). Kuala Lumpur: n.p.

Wei shu 魏書 (History of the Wei [Dynasty]). Compiled by Wei Shou 魏收 (506–572). Beijing: Zhonghua shuju, 1974.

Wenwu 文物. 1975. "Hebei Xuanhua Liao bihua mu fajue jianbao" 河北宣化遼壁畫墓發掘簡報 (Brief Record on the Excavation of Wall-Painted Tombs from Xuanhua, Hebei [Province]). 8: 31–39.

Xin Tang shu 新唐書 (New History of the Tang [Dynasty]). Compiled by Ouyang Xiu 歐陽修 (1007–1072) and Song Qi 宋祁 (998–1061). Beijing: Zhonghua shuju, 1975.

Xu gaoseng zhuan 續高僧傳 (Continuation of the Biographies of the Eminent Monks). Compiled by Daoxuan. T. (50) 2060.

Xu zizhi tongjian changbian 續資治通鑑長編 (Continuation of the Comprehensive Mirror for Aid in Government). Compiled by Li Tao 李燾 (1115–1184). Beijing: Zhonghua shuju, 1979–1995.

Youyang zazu 酉陽雜俎 (Miscellany of the Youyang [Mountain]). Compiled by Duan Chengshi 段成式 (c. 803–863). *Congshu jicheng* edition. Taipei: Shangwu yinshuguan, 1965.

Yuan shi 元史 (History of the Yuan [Dynasty]). Compiled by Song Lian 宋濂 (1310–1381). Beijing: Zhonghua shuju, 1976.

Zhenyuan xinding shijiao mulu 貞元新定釋教目錄 (Catalogue of the Buddhist Teachings Newly Compiled during the Zhenyuan [Reign Period]). Compiled by Yuanzhao 圓照 (719–800). T. (55) 2052.

Zhufan zhi 諸蕃志 (Description of the Barbarous People). By Zhao Rugua 趙汝適. Annotated by Yang Bowen 楊博文 as *Zhufan zhi jiaoshi* 諸蕃志校釋. Beijing: Zhoughua shuju, 1996.

Zizhi tongjian 資治通鑑 (Comprehensive Mirror for Aid in Government). Compiled by Sima Guang 司馬光 (1019–1086) et al. Beijing: Zhonghua shuju, 1992.

Non-Chinese Sources

Anonymous. *Correspondence Respecting Compensation for the Opium Surrendered at Canton in 1839.*

Arthaśāstra. By Kauṭiliya. Edited and translated by R. P. Kangle. 3 vols. Bombay: University of Bombay, 1963.

Asian Relations: Being a Report of the Proceedings and Documentation of the First Asian Relations Conference, New Delhi, March–April, 1947. New Delhi: Asian Relations Organization, 1948.

Beaumont, Joseph. 1871. *New Slavery: An Account of the Indian and Chinese Immigrants in British Guiana.* London: W. Ridgway.

Bronkhurst, Rev. H. V. P. 1888. *The Colony of British Guyana and Its Laboring Population.* London: T. Woolmer.

Delhi-Peking Friendship March pamphlet.

Harṣacarita. By Bāṇa. Translated by E. B. Cowell and F. W. Thomas. Delhi: Motilal Banarasidass, 1961.

Ibn Baṭṭūṭā, ʾAbū ʿAbd al-Lāh Muḥammad ibn ʿAbd al-Lāh l-Lawātī ṭ-Ṭanǧī. 1958–1994. *Rihla.* Translated by H. A. R. Gibb, *The Travels of Ibn Baṭṭūṭā, A.D. 1325–1354. Translated with Revisions and Notes from the Arabic Text Edited by C. Defrémery and B. R. Sanguinetti*, 5 vols. London: Hakluyt Society.

The Jamsetjee Jejeebhoy Papers. Mumbai Library. Transcribed by Murali Ranganath.

Koryŏsa 高麗史 (History of the Koryŏ [Kingdom]). Seoul: Asea Muhwasa, 1972.

Lamb, A., ed. 2002. *Bhutan and Tibet: The Travels of George Bogle and Alexander Hamilton, 1774–1777.* Vol. 1, *Bogle and Hamilton: Letters, Journals and Memoranda.* Hertingfordbury, Herts.: Roxford Books.

Marco Polo. 1938. *The Description of the World.* Translated by A. C. Moule and Paul Pelliot. 3 vols. London: Routledge.

Markham, Clements R. 1879. *Narratives of the Mission of George Bogle to Tibet and of the Journey of Thomas Manning to Lhasa.* London: Trübner.

Notes, Memoranda and Letters Exchanged and Agreements Signed between the Governments of India and China. Compiled by the Ministry of External Affairs, India.

Parliamentary Papers Relating to Opium Trade, 1821–1832. London: T. R. Harrison.

The Periplus of the Erytheaean Sea. Translated and edited by G. W. B. Huntingford. London: Hakluyt Society, 1980.

Pires, Tomé. 2005. *The Suma Oriental of Tomé Pires: An Account of the East, from the Red Sea to China, Written in Malacca and India in 1512–1515.* Edited by Armando Cortesao. 2 vols. New Delhi: Asian Educational Services.

Report of the Afro-Asian Convention on Tibet and against Colonialism in Asia and Africa, Held at Vigyan Bhavan, New Delhi, April 9–11, 1960. New Delhi: Afro-Asian Council.

Turner, Samuel. 1800. *An Account of an Embassy to the Court of the Teshoo Lama in Tibet; Containing a Narrative of a Journey through Bootan, and Part of Tibet.* London: W. Bulmer.

Waṣṣāf, ʿAbd-Allāh. 1966. *Tajziyat al-Amṣār wa-Tazjiyat al-A'sār.* Translated by H. M. Elliot and John Dowson, *The History of India as Told by Its Own Historians,* vol. 3, *Mohammadan Period.* London: Trübner.

ARCHIVAL DOCUMENTS

Academia Historica 國史館, Taipei, Taiwan

002000000453A, Jiang Zhongzheng zongtong wenwu 蔣中正總統文物 (President Chiang Kai-shek Collection). "Geming wenxian: Dui Ying, Yin waijiao" 革命文獻：對英、印外交 (Revolution Documents: Diplomacy with England and India).

002000000625A, Jiang Zhongzheng zongtong wenwu. "Jiang Zhongzheng wei Dai Jitao fang Yin shoushu zhi Yindu Gandi, Taiger, Nihelu zhuyouren han" 蔣中正為戴季陶訪印手書致印度甘地泰戈爾尼赫魯諸友人函 (Hand-written Letters by Chiang Kai-shek to Gandhi, Tagore, Nehru, the Various Indian Friends, for Dai Jitao to Carry to India). 17 October 1940.

001000005088A, 國民政府/外交 (Guomindang Government, Diplomatic Collection). "Wang Shijie cheng chuli Yindu guoji shishi yanjiuhui zhaokai Yazhou geguo guanxi huiyi ji wo zhu Yin dashiguan dian chen Yazhou huiyi kaihui qingxing, Dai Zhuanxian cheng Yindu faqi fanYa huiyi wo bixu canjia liyou, Wu Tiecheng cheng woguo canjia faYa huiyi jingguo jueding shixiang ji canjia renxuan" 王世杰呈處理印度國際時事研究會召開亞洲各國關係會議及我駐印大使館電陳亞洲會議開會情形，戴傳賢呈印度發起泛亞會議我必須參加理由，吳鐵城呈我國參加泛亞會議經過決定事項及參加人選 (Wang Shijie on the Organization of the Asian Relations Conference by the Indian Council of World Affairs and the Chinese Embassy in India's Report on the Opening of the Asian Conference; Dai Zhuanxian [i.e., Dai Jitao] on the

Reasons We Must Participate in the Pan-Asian Conference Initiated by India; Wu Tiecheng on the Decisions about Topics and the Selection of Participants from China for the Pan-Asian Conference).

British Foreign Office, London, UK

File FO 371/12168, "Report on China by the Agent-General for India in China."
File FO 371/16188, "Tibetan Affairs."
File FO 371/63539, "Inter-Asian Relations Conference, New Delhi, March–April 1947."
File FO 371/63540, "Inter-Asian Relations Conference, New Delhi, March–April 1947."
File FO 371/63541, "Inter-Asian Relations Conference, New Delhi, March–April 1947."
File FO 371/75798, "Memorandum by Sardar Panikkar on Developments in the Border Areas of China and Repercussions upon India of a Communist Regime in China."
File FO 371/170682, "Friendship March from New Delhi to Peking."

International Institute of Social History, Amsterdam, Netherlands

Devi Prasad Papers

Files 51–52: Documents Concerning the Delhi–Peking Friendship March, 1963–1964.

War Resisters' International Collection

File 436: File on the Asian Regional Council. India. 1962–1964; File on the Delhi–Peking Friendship March. 1962–1964.

National Archives of India, New Delhi, India

File 329-X, 1943, "Activities of Professor Tan Yun Shan of the Cheena Bhavana at Santiniketan and a prominent member of the Sino-India Cultural Association. His indiscretions in the field of Politics. Proposed organisation in India for the promotion of Indo-Chinese Cultural relations by the Formation of an extra-governmental body of recognised international Standing."
File 62(6)-OSIII, 1947, "Inter Asian Relations Conference Held at New Delhi in March & April 1947."
File 10(29)-NEF, 1947, "Visit of Tibetan Delegates at the Time of Inter-Asian Relations Conference. Return Presents from the Viceroy to the Dalai Lama, Regent and Kashag."

File 12(5)-NEF, 1947, "Request from the Inter-Asian Relations Conference for an Exact Description of the Official Flags of Tibet and Bhutan."

File 542(3)-CA, 1947, "Representation from China to Asian Relations Conference, New Delhi."

Foreign/Sec.-F/April 1903, NAI, 28–37.

NAI MEA/7 (1) P /1952/ Correspondence between Tan Yunshan and Jawaharlal Nehru.

Nehru Memorial Museum and Library, New Delhi, India

Jawaharlal Nehru Correspondence, 1903–1947.
Jawaharlal Nehru Papers.
K. P. S. Menon Papers.
Pandit Sunderlal Papers.

Swarthmore College Peace Collection, Swarthmore, USA

Asian Regional Council Papers.
Collection DG 50: A. J. Muste Papers, 1920–1967, Box 41.
World Peace Brigade. Delhi–Peking Friendship March: General.
————. Delhi–Peking Friendship March: Correspondence with Chinese Government Officials.
————. Delhi–Peking Friendship March: Correspondence with Marchers and with Personnel.
————. Delhi–Peking Friendship March: Policy and Strategy; Publicity; Response to Deo Statement; Vedchhi Statement.

West Bengal State Archives, Intelligence Bureau, Shakespeare Sarani, Calcutta, India

File 285A/25, Serial No. 117, "Instructions of Postmaster of Bengal regarding Foreign Correspondence with Santinekatan."

File 285/25, Serial No. 69/1925, "Note by Inc. Colson, Spl. Supert., IB on (a) Viswa-Bharati (b) Santiniketan."

File 236/39, Serial No. 228, "Chinese Nationals (Calcutta)."

File 628/40, Serial No. 129, "Schools: Cheena-Bhavana or 'Chinese Hall,' Viswa Bharati, Santiniketan, Birbhum."

File 120/41–120/41(1), Serial No. 1, "Prof. Tan Yun Shan, Professor of Chinese, Viswa Bharati University, Santiniketan, Bolpur, Birbhum."

File 1393/43, Serial No. 116, Part VI, "Publication/Official: Internal Interception Report (Weekly Interception), Issued by Chinese Intelligence Wing, Calcutta."

File 923/44, Serial No. 302, "Publication: Official. Tibetan Intelligence Reports Compiled by C.I.O. Assam."

File 816/46, Serial No. 261, "Shen Fu Min s/o Shen Shih Ching of Shansi Province, China—a Teacher in Kalimpong (Darjeeling) Chinese."

File 2312/49 (1), Serial No. 274, "Chang Hsiu Feng."

West Bengal State Archives, Home/Political, Bhabani Dutta Lane, Calcutta, India

File No. 457/40, Serial No. 309. "Arrangement in Connection with Visit to Calcutta of HE Dr. Tai Chi Tao, Member of the Council of State, China."

NEWSPAPER REPORTS

Blitz

11 October 1952. "100,000 Celebrate 'China Week': Many Facets of 7-Day Programme." 5.

The Indian Express

22 January 2010. "Don't Believe in Hindi-Chini Bhai-Bhai, Nehru Told Envoy."

Hindustan Times

4 April 1949. "Asian Relations Organization."

The Statesman

6 December 1960. "Chinese Arrested on Charge of Espionage."

Times of India

30 November 1940. "2000-Year Old Relationship: China's Cultural Ties with India."

1 January 1950. "Recognition of Red China: Pandit Nehru's Defence." 9.

9 August 1950. "Red's Two-Pronged Advance towards Tibetan Borders: Unconfirmed Reports." 1.

17 August 1950. "'Liberating Tibet.'" 9.

2 October 1950. "Tibet & Formosa to Be Freed: Chinese Premier's Pledge." 1.

27 October 1950. "Delhi Awaits Report on Tibetan Situation: Urgent communication Sent to Envoy at Peking." 1.

26 June 1952. "China Lacks Requisites of Democracy: Impressions of Mr. Moraes." 5.

1 May 1954. "Accord on Tibet." 6.

3 November 1954. "There is Revolution in Asian Continent: Mr. Nehru on National Reconstruction in China." 7.

25 April 1955. "The Practicability of Co-Existance." 5.

28 April 1955. "Chinese Premier's Offer 'Fair & Good': Mr. Nehru's Assertion in Calcutta, May New Avenues Opened." 1.

1 October 1956. "Nepal and China." 6.

5 January 1959. "'India's Disenchantment with Communist China.'" 7.

6 November 1962. "Expansionism & Not Communism: Bhave Criticises China." 6.

13 May 1963. "Bhave Criticises Chinese: Reds Disliked Our Way to Progress." 6.

7 December 1965. "Repatriation to India: Shanghai Sikh's Plea." 7.

31 October 1968. "Shanghai Indian Expelled after Release from Jail." 11.

SECONDARY SOURCES

Abraham, Itty. 2008a. "Bandung and State Formation in Post-Colonial Asia." In *Bandung Revisited: The Legacy of the 1955 Asian African Conference for International Order*, edited by See Seng Tan and Amitav Acharya, 48–67. Singapore: NUS Press.

———. 2008b. "From Bandung to NAM: Non-alignment and Indian Foreign Policy, 1947–65." *Commonwealth & Comparative Politics* 46.2: 195–219.

Abraham, Meera. 1988. *Two Medieval Merchant Guilds of South India*. New Delhi: Manohar, 1988.

Abu-Lughod, Janet L. 1989. *Before European Hegemony: The New World System A.D. 1250–1550*. New York: Oxford University Press, 1989.

Acker, William R. B. 1974. *Some T'ang and Pre-T'ang Texts on Chinese Painting*. Vol. 2, part 1. Leiden: Brill.

"Address Presented to His Holiness Tai Hsu." *Maha-Bodhi: Journal of the Maha Bodhi Society* 48.2–3 (February–March 1940): 92–93.

Ahmad, S. Maqbul. 1989. *Arabic Classical Accounts of India and China*. Shimla: Indian Institute of Advanced Study.

Akasoy, Ana. 2013. "The Buddha and the Straight Path. Rashīd al-Dīn's *Life of the Buddha*: Islamic Perspectives." In *Rashīd al-Dīn: Agent and Mediator of Cultural Exchanges in Ilkhanid Iran*, edited by Anna Akasoy, Charles Burnett, and Ronit Yoeli-Tlalim, 173–196. London and Turin: Warburg Institute and Nino Aragno Editore.

Alabaster, Chaloner. [1858] 1975. "The Chinese Colony in Calcutta." In *Calcutta: People and Empire; Gleanings from Old Journals*, edited by P. Chaudhury and A. Mukhopadhyay, 15–20. Calcutta: India Book Exchange.

Amrith, Sunil S. 2011. *Migration and Diaspora in Modern Asia*. Cambridge: Cambridge University Press.

Andrade, Tonio. 2016. *The Gunpowder Age: China, Military Innovation, and the Rise of the West in World History*. Princeton, NJ: Princeton University Press.

Anonymous. 1834. "The Opium-Dealers of Kotah." *The Asiatic Journal and Monthly Register for British and Foreign India, China and Australasia* 13 (January–April): 98–99.

Anonymous. 1931a. "Tan Yunshan tiaochen zhi Zang zhengce" 譚雲山條陳治藏政策 (Tan Yunshan's Memorandum on the Policy of Governing Tibet). *Yiyuan* 藝園 1.23: 252–253.

Anonymous. 1931b. "Zhengzhi: Tan Yunshan shangshu Guofu tiaochen zhi Zang celüe" 政治：譚雲山上書國府條陳治藏策略 (Politics: Tan Yunshan's

Memorandum to the Guomindang Government Regarding the Strategies of Governing Tibet). *Guanhai* 觀海 2: 38–40.

Anonymous. 1955. *The Indian Cultural Delegation in China, 1955.* Beijing: Foreign Languages Press.

Anonymous. 1963. *The India-China Border Dispute and the Communist Party of India: Resolutions, Statements and Speeches, 1959–1963.* New Delhi: Communist Party Publication.

Appadurai, Arjun, ed. 1986. *The Social Life of Things: Commodities in Cultural Perspective.* Cambridge: Cambridge University Press.

Aris, Michael. 1995. *'Jigs-med-gling-pa's "Discourse on India" of 1789: A Critical Edition and Annotated Translation of the* Lho-phyogs rgya-gar-gyi gtam brtag-pa brgyad-ki me-long. Tokyo: International Institute for Buddhist Studies.

Ashtor, E. 1976. "Spice Prices in the Near East in the 15th Century." *Journal of the Royal Asiatic Society* 108.1 (January): 26–41.

Atwell, William S. 1982. "International Bullion Flows and the Chinese Economy circa 1530–1650." *Past and Present Society* 95 (May): 68–90.

Aydin, Cemil. 2007. *The Politics of Anti-Westernism in Asia: Visions of World Order in Pan-Islamic and Pan-Asian Thought.* New York: Columbia University Press, 2007.

Bagchi, P. C. 1927. "India and China: A Thousand Years of Cultural Relations." *Greater India Society Bulletin* 2: 1–42.

———. 1927–1938. *Le Canon Bouddhique en Chine: Les traducteurs et les traductions.* 2 vols. Paris: Librarie Orientaliste Paul Geuthner, 1927–1938.

———. [1944] 2012. "Sino-Indian Spheres of Influences." In *India and China: Interactions through Buddhism and Diplomacy, A Collection of Essays by Professor Prabodh Chandra Bagchi*, compiled by Wang Bangwei and Tansen Sen, 179–183. Delhi and London: Anthem Press.

———. [1945] 2012. "Political Relations between Bengal and China in the Pathan Period." In *India and China: Interactions through Buddhism and Diplomacy, A Collection of Essays by Professor Prabodh Chandra Bagchi*, compiled by Wang Bangwei and Tansen Sen, 109–135. Delhi and London: Anthem Press.

———. 1945. "Report for the Year 1945." *Visva-Bharati Annals* 1: i–v.

———. [1947] 2012. "The Visva-Bharati Cheena Bhavana." In *India and China: Interactions through Buddhism and Diplomacy, A Collection of Essays by Professor Prabodh Chandra Bagchi*, compiled by Wang Bangwei and Tansen Sen, 199–201. Delhi and London: Anthem Press.

———. [1948] 2012. "Ancient Chinese Names of India." In *India and China: Interactions through Buddhism and Diplomacy, A Collection of Essays by Professor Prabodh Chandra Bagchi*, compiled by Wang Bangwei and Tansen Sen, 3–11. Delhi and London: Anthem Press.

———. [1950] 1981. *India and China: A Thousand Years of Cultural Relations.* Rev. ed. Bombay: Hind Kitabs Limited.

Bagley, Vimala, et al. 1996–2004. *The Ancient Port of Arikamedu: New Excavations and Researches, 1989–1992.* Pondichéry: Centre d'histoire et d'archéologie, École française d'Extrême-Orient.

Bahadur, Gaiutra. 2013. *Coolie Woman: The Odyssey of Indenture.* Chicago: University of Chicago Press.

Bailey, H. W. 1938. "Hvatanica III." *Bulletin of the School of Oriental Studies* 9.3 (1938): 521–543.

Bakhala, Franklin. 1985. "Opium and Sino-Indian Trade Relations, 1801–1858." PhD dissertation, University of London.

Banerjee, Payal. 2007. "Chinese Indians in Fire: Refractions of Ethnicity, Gender, Sexuality and Citizenship in Post-Colonial India's Memories of the Sino-Indian War." *China Report* 43.3: 437–446.

_____. 2017. "The Chinese in India: Internment, Nationalism, and the Embodied Imprints of State Action." In *The Sino-Indian War of 1962: New Perspectives,* edited by Amit R. Das Gupta and Lorenz M. Lüthl, 215–232. London and New York: Routledge.

Basu, Abhishek. 2007. "Performing Other-Wise: 'Death-Defying' China as Seen by Ramnath Biswas." *China Report* 43.4. (October–December): 485–499.

Basu, B. K. 1986. *Call of Yanan: Story of the Indian Medical Mission to China, 1938–43.* Bombay: All India Kotnis Memorial Committee.

Basu, Manoj. 1953. *Chin Dekhe Elam* (Having Seen China). Calcutta: n.p.

Bayly, Susan. 2004. "Imagining 'Greater India': French and Indian Visions of Colonialism in the Indic Mode." *Modern Asian Studies* 38.3: 703–744.

———. 2007. "India's 'Empire of Culture': Sylvain Lévi and the Greater India Society." In *Sylvain Lévi (1863–1935): Études Indiennes, Histoire Sociale Bibliothèque de l'Ecole des Hautes Études, Sciences Religieuses,* edited by L. Bansat-Boudon and R. Lardinois, 193–212. Turnhout: Brepols Publishers.

Bellina, Bérénice, and Ian Glover. 2004. "The Archaeology of Early Contact with India and the Mediterranean World, from the Fourth Century BC to the Fourth Century AD. In *South-East Asia: From Prehistory to History,* edited by Ian Glover and Peter Bellwood, 66–88. London: Routledge.

Bellwood, Peter. 1995. "Austronesian Prehistory in Southeast Asia: Homeland, Expansion and Transformation." In *The Austronesians: Historical and Comparative Perspective,* edited by Peter Bellwood, J. J. Fox, and D. Tryon, 96–111. Canberra: Australian National University.

———. 2004. "The Origins and Dispersals of Agricultural Communities in Southeast Asia." In *South-East Asia: From Prehistory to History,* edited by Ian Glover and Peter Bellwood, 21–40. London: Routledge.

Benn, James A. 2015. *Tea in China: A Religious and Cultural History.* Honolulu: University of Hawai'i Press.

Bhattacharya, Jayati, and Coonoor Kripalani, eds. 2015. *Indian and Chinese Immigrant Communities: Comparative Perspectives.* London: Anthem Press.

Bickers, Robert. 2015. "Britain and China, and India, 1830–1947." In *Britain and China, 1840–1970: Empire, Finance and War,* edited by Robert Bickers and Jonathan J. Howlett, 58–83. London: Routledge.

Bickers, Robert, and Jonathan J. Howlett, eds. 2015. *Britain and China, 1840–1970: Empire, Finance and War*. London: Routledge.

Birnbaum, Raoul. 1989. *The Healing Buddha*. Rev. ed. Boulder, CO: Shambhala.

Biswas, Anirban. 2006. *The Cowrie Currency and Monetary History of India*. Calcutta: CAMP.

Biswas, Ramnath. 1941. *Maranbijayi Chin* (Death-Defying China). Calcutta: Prajatak Prakasana Bhavan.

———. 1943. *Lal Chin* (Red China). Calcutta: Parjatak Prakasana Bhavan.

———. 1944. *China Defies Death*. Calcutta: Bose Press.

———. 1949. *Mukta Mahachin* (Liberated Great China). Calcutta: Bose Press.

Borschberg, Peter, and Roopanjali Roy, ed. and trans. 2014. *The Memoirs and Memorials of Jacques de Coutre: Security, Trade and Society in 16th- and 17th-century Southeast Asia*. Singapore: NUS Press.

Bose, Basanta Kumar. 1934. "A Bygone Chinese Colony in Bengal." *Bengal Past and Present* 47: 120–122.

Bose, Phanindra Nath. 1923. *The Indian Teachers in China*. Madras: S. Ganesan.

Bose, Sugata. 2006. *A Hundred Horizons: The Indian Ocean in the Age of Global Empire*. Cambridge, MA: Harvard University Press.

Boxer, C. R. 1969. *The Portuguese Seaborne Empire, 1415–1825*. London: Hutchinson.

Bray, Francesca. 2007. "Introduction: The Powers of *Tu*." In *Graphics and Texts in the Production of Technical Knowledge in China*, edited by Vera Dorofeeva-Lichtmann and Georges Métailié, 1–78. Leiden: Brill.

Bright, J. S., ed. 1947. *Important Speeches of Jawaharlal Nehru: Being a Collection of Most Significant Speeches Delivered by Jawaharlal Nehru from 1922 to 1946*. Lahore: Indian Printing Works.

Bronkhurst, H. V. P. 1883. *The Colony of British Guyana and Its Labouring Population: Containing a Short Account of the Colony, and Brief Descriptions of the Black Creole, Portuguese, East Indian, and Chinese Coolies, Their Manners, Customs, Religious Notions, and Other Interesting Particulars and Amusing Incidents Concerning Them*. London: T. Woolmer.

Brook, Timothy. 1998. *The Confusions of Pleasure: Commerce and Culture in Ming China*. Berkeley: University of California Press.

Brown, Roger H. 2011. "Sun Yat-sen: 'Pan-Asianism,' 1924." In *Pan-Asianism: A Documentary History*, vol. 2, *1900–Present*, edited by Sven Saaler and Christopher W. A. Szpilman, 75–85. Lanham, MD: Rowman & Littlefield.

Bunker, Emma C. 1991. "The Chinese Artifacts among the Pazyryk." *Source: Notes in the History of Art* 10.4 (Summer): 20–24.

Bysack, Gaur Das. 1890. "Notes on a Buddhist Monastery at Bhoṭ Bāgān in Howrah." *Journal of the Asiatic Society of Bengal* 59.1: 50–99.

Cai, Yuan P. 2011. "Zhang Taiyan and the Asiatic Humanitarian Brotherhood, 1907." In *Pan-Asianism: A Documentary History*, vol. 1, *1850–1920*, edited by Sven Saaler and Christopher W. A. Szpilman, 177–184. Lanham, MD: Rowman & Littlefield.

Cammann, Schuyler. 1949. "The Panchen Lama's Visit to China in 1780: An Episode in Anglo-Tibetan Relations." *Far Eastern Quarterly* 9.1 (November): 3–19.

———. 1951. *Trade through the Himalayas: The Early British Attempts to Open Tibet*. Westport, CT: Greenwood.

Campos, J. J. A. [1919] 2000. *History of the Portuguese in Bengal, with Maps and Illustrations*. Calcutta: R. N. Bhattacharya.

Canby, Sheila. 1993. "Depictions of Buddha Sakyamuni in the *Jami'al-Tavarikh* and the *Majma'al-Tavarikh*." *Muqarnas* 10: 299–310.

Carter, April. 2014. *Peace Movements: International Protest and World Politics since 1945*. London: Longman.

Carter, Marina, and Jamese Ng Foong Kwong. 2009. *Abacus and Mah Jong: Sino-Mauritian Settlement and Economic Consolidation*. Leiden: Brill.

Casale, Giancarlo. 2010. *The Ottoman Age of Exploration*. New York: Oxford University Press.

Chakravarti, Ranabir. 1999. "Early Medieval Bengal and the Trade in Horses: A Note." *Journal of the Economic and Social History of the Orient* 42.2: 194–211.

Chan, Albert. 1993. "Michele Ruggieri, S.J. (1543–1607) and His Chinese Poems." *Monumenta Serica* 41: 129–176.

Chang Xiufeng 常秀峰. 1999. *Dajiling zhi qiu: Chang Xiufeng lü Yin huiyi lu* 大吉嶺之秋：常秀峰旅印回憶錄 (The Autumn in Darjeeling: Memoirs of Chang Xiufeng's Travels in India). Beijing: Zhongguo wenlian chubanshe.

Chatterjee, Partha. [1987] 2010. "The Constitution of Indian Nationalist Discourse." In *Empire and Nation: Selected Essays*, edited by Partha Chatterjee, 37–58. New York: Columbia University Press.

Chatterji, S. K. 1959. "India and China: Ancient Contacts, What India Received from China." *Journal of the Asiatic Society, Calcutta* 1.1: 89–122.

Chaudhuri, K. N. 1985. *Trade and Civilisation in the Indian Ocean: An Economic History from the Rise of Islam to 1750*. Cambridge: Cambridge University Press.

Chen, Gaohua 陳高華. 1980. "Yindu Mabaer wangzi Bohali lai hua xinkao" 印度馬八爾王子孛哈里來華新考 (New Examination of the Arrival in China of the Prince Bohali [from the] India [Polity] of Ma'bar). *Nankai xuebao* 南開學報 4: 70–73.

Chen, Jian. 2006. "The Tibetan Rebellion of 1959 and China's Changing Relations with India and the Soviet Union." *Journal of Cold War Studies* 8.3 (Summer): 54–101.

Chen, Jinhua. 2002a. *Monks and Monarchs, Kinship and Kingship: Tanqian in Sui Buddhism and Politics*. Kyoto: Scuola Italiana di Studi sull'Asia Orientale.

———. 2002b. "Śarīra and Scepter: Empress Wu's Political Use of Buddhist Relics." *Journal of the International Association of Buddhist Studies* 25.1–2 (2002): 33–150.

Chen, Ming 陳明. 2005a. *Dunhuang chutu Huyu yidian "Jipo shu" yanjiu* 敦煌出土胡語醫藥典耆婆書研究 (Research on the Foreign Language Medical

Text *Book of Jīvaka* Excavated from Dunhuang). Taipei: Taipei xinfeng chu-banshe.

———. 2005b. *Sufang yiyao: Chutu wenshu yu Xiyu yixue* 殊方異藥：出土文書與西域醫學 (Special Prescriptions and Strange Medicines: Excavated Texts and the Medicine of the Western Regions). Beijing: Beijing daxue chu-banshe.

———. 2006. "The Transmission of Indian Ayurvedic Doctrines in Medieval China: A Case Study of Aṣṭāṅga and Tridoṣa Fragments from the Silk Road." *Annual Report of the International Research Institute for Advanced Buddholo-gy at Soka University* 9: 201–230.

———. 2013. *Zhonggu yiliao yu wailai wenhua* 中古醫療與外來文化 (English title: Foreign Medicine and Culture in Medieval China). Beijing: Beijing dax-ue chubanshe.

Cheuk, Ka-kin. 2016. "Everyday Diplomacy among Indian Traders in a Chinese Fabric Market." *Cambridge Journal of Anthropology* 34.2: 42–58.

Chin, Tamara. 2013. "The Invention of the Silk Road, 1877." *Critical Inquiry* 40.1: 194–219.

"Chinese Buddhist Mission in India." *Maha-Bodhi: Journal of the Maha Bodhi Society* 48.2–3 (February–March): 85–91.

Chou, Yi-lang. 1944–1945 "Tantrism in China." *Harvard Journal of Asiatic Studies* 8: 241–332.

Christie, Jan Wisseman. 1998. "The Medieval Tamil-Language Inscriptions in Southeast Asia and China." *Journal of Southeast Asian Studies* 29.2: 239–268.

———. 1999. "Asian Sea Trade between the Tenth and Thirteenth Centuries and Its Impact on the States of Java and Bali." In *Archaeology of Seafaring: The Indian Ocean in the Ancient Period,* edited by Himanshu Prabha Ray, 221–270. Delhi: Pragati Publications.

Church, Sally K. 2004. "The Giraffe of Bengal: A Medieval Encounter in Ming China." *Medieval History Journal* 7.1: 1–37.

Cohen, Jerome A., and Leng Shao-chuan. 1972. "The Sino-Indian Dispute over the Internment and Detention of Chinese in India." In *China's Practice of International Law,* edited by Jerome A. Cohen, 268–320. Cambridge: Cam-bridge University Press.

Conner, Patrick. 1993. *George Chinnery, 1774–1852: Artist of India and the China Coast.* Suffolk: Antique Collector's Club.

"Correspondence." *Maha-Bodhi: Journal of the Maha Bodhi Society* 55.9–10 (September–October 1947): 208–213.

Costello, William. 1949. "Chinese Red's Advance: India Unruffled." *Times of India,* 28 August: 8, 10.

Cullen, Christopher. 1982. "An Eighth Century Chinese Table of Tangents." *Chinese Science* 5.1: 1–33.

Cullen, Christopher, and Vivienne Lo. 2005. *Medieval Chinese Medicine: The Dunhuang Medical Manuscripts.* London: Routledge.

Cunningham, Alexander. 1848. "Verification of the Itinerary of Hwan Thsang through Ariana and India, with Reference to Major Anderson's Hypothesis of its Modern Compilation." *Journal of the Asiatic Society of Bengal* 17: 476–488.

———. 1871. *The Ancient Geography of India, the Buddhist Period, Including the Campaigns of Alexander and the Travels of Hwan-Thsang.* London: Trübner.

Curtin, Philip D. 1984. *Cross-Cultural Trade in World History.* Cambridge: Cambridge University Press.

Cutts, Elmer. 1942. "Chinese Studies in Bengal." *Journal of the American Oriental Society* 62.3 (September): 171–174.

Dai Jitao 戴季陶. [1946] 1971. "Dui Yindu Nihelu faqi zhaoji fan Yazhou huiyi zhi ganxiang" 對印度尼赫魯發起召集泛亞洲會議之感想 (Thoughts on the Pan-Asian Relations Conference convened by Nehru). In *Dai Jitao xiansheng wencun* 戴季陶先生文存 [Extant Writings of Dai Jitao], edited by Dai Jitao 戴季陶 and Chen Tianxi 陳天錫, 386–397. Taipei: Zhongguo Guomindang zhongyang weiyuanhui.

Daniels, Christian. 1996. "Agro-Industries: Sugarcane Technology." In *Science and Civilisation in China,* vol. 6, *Biology and Biological Technology,* part 3, "Agro Industries and Forestry," edited by Joseph Needham. Cambridge: Cambridge University Press.

Daniels, Christian, and J. Daniels. 1988. "The Origins of the Sugar-Cane Roller Mill." *Technology and Culture* 29.3: 493–535.

Das, Sisir Kumar. [1993] 2005. "The Controversial Guest: Tagore in China." In *India and China in the Colonial World,* edited by Madhavi Thampi, 85–125. New Delhi: Social Science Press.

Das, Taraknath. 1917. *Is Japan a Menace to Asia?* Shanghai: n.p.

Das Gupta, Shakti. 1961. *Tagore's Asian Outlook.* Calcutta: Nava Bharati.

Das Gupta, Uma. 2010. "Sino-Indian Studies at Visva-Bharati University: Story of Cheena-Bhavana, 1921–1937." In *Tagore and China,* edited by Wang Bangwei and Tan Chung, 53–68. Beijing: Zhongyang bianyi chubanshe, 2010.

Deeg, Max. 2005. *Das Gaoseng-Faxian-Zhuan als religionsgeschichtliche Quelle. Der älteste Bericht eines chinesischen buddhistischen Pilgermönchs über seine Reise nach Indien mit Übersetzung des Textes.* Studies in Oriental Religions 52. Wiesbaden: Harrassowitz Verlag.

Deepak, B. R. 2001. *India-China Relations in the First Half of the 20th Century.* New Delhi: A. P. H. Publishing.

Deshpande, Vijaya. 1987. "Medieval Transmission of Alchemical and Chemical Ideas between India and China." *Indian Journal of History of Science* 22.1: 15–28.

———. 1999. "Indian Influences on Early Chinese Ophthalmology: Glaucoma as a Case Study." *Bulletin of the School of Oriental and African Studies* 62.2: 306–322.

———. 2000. "Ophthalmic Surgery: A Chapter in the History of Sino-Indian Medical Contacts." *Bulletin of the School of Oriental and African Studies* 63.3: 370–388.

Deyell, John S. 1990. *Living without Silver: The Monetary History of Early Medieval North India*. Oxford and New Delhi: Oxford University Press.

———. 2010. "Cowries and Coins: The Dual Monetary System of the Bengal Sultanate." *Indian Economic and Social History* 47.1: 63–106.

Digby, Simon. 1982. "The Maritime Trade of India." In *The Cambridge Economic History of India*, vol. 1, *c.1200–c.1750*, edited by Tapan Raychaudhuri and Irfan Habib, 125–159. Cambridge: Cambridge University Press.

Dikshit, K. N. 1938. *Excavations at Paharpur, Bengal*. ASI Memoir 55. Delhi: Archaeological Survey of India.

Dirlik, Arif. 2008. "Timespace, Social Space, and the Question of Chinese Culture." *boundary 2: An International Journal of Literature and Culture* 35.1: 1–22.

Diskalkar, D. B. 1933. "Bogle's Embassy to Tibet." *Indian Historical Quarterly* 9: 420–438.

Disney, A. R. 2010. *Twilight of the Pepper Empire: Portuguese Trade in Southwest India in the Early Seventeenth Century*. New Delhi: Manohar.

Dreyer, Edward L. 2007. *Zheng He: China and the Oceans in the Early Ming Dynasty, 1405–1433*. New York: Pearson Longman.

Duara, Prasenjit. 1995. *Rescuing History from the Nation: Questioning Narratives of Modern China*. Chicago: University of Chicago Press.

———. 2003. *Sovereignty and Authenticity: Manchukuo and the East Asian Modern*. Lanham, MD: Rowman & Littlefield.

———. 2010. "Asia Redux: Conceptualizing a Region for Our Times." *Journal of Asian Studies* 69.4: 963–983.

———. 2015. *The Crisis of Global Modernity: Asian Traditions and a Sustainable Future*. Cambridge: Cambridge University Press.

Eaton, Richard M. 1993. *The Rise of Islam and the Bengal Frontier, 1204–1760*. Berkeley: University of California Press.

Edwards, R. 1954. "The Cave Relief at Ma Hao." *Artibus Asiae* 17: 5–28, 103–129.

Elman, Benjamin A. 2006. *A Cultural History of Modern Science in China*. Cambridge: Harvard University Press.

Enomoto, Fumio. 1994. "A Note on Kashmir as Referred to it in Chinese Literature: Ji-bin." In *A Study on the Nīlamata: Aspects of Hinduism in Ancient Kashmir*, edited by Ikari Yasuda, 357–365. Kyoto: Institute for Research in Humanities, Kyoto University.

Fairbank, John King, ed. 1968. *The Chinese World Order: Traditional China's Foreign Relations*. Cambridge: Cambridge University Press.

Fan, Ka Wai. 2005. "Couching for Cataract and Sino-Indian Medical Exchange from the Sixth to the Twelfth Century AD." *Clinical and Experimental Ophthalmology* 33: 188–190.

Farooqui, Amar. [2006] 2012. *Opium City: The Making of Early Victorian Bombay*. New Delhi: Three Essays Collective.

Ferguson, Donald. 1901. "Letters from Portuguese Captives in Canton, Written in 1534 and 1536." *Indian Antiquary* 30 (October): 421–451, 467–469.

Finlay, Robert. 1992. "Portuguese and Chinese Maritime Imperialism: Camões's *Lusiads* and Luo Maodeng's *Voyage of the San Bao Eunuch.*" *Comparative Studies in Society and History* 34.2: 225–241.

———. 2008. The Voyages of Zheng He: Ideology, State Power, and Maritime Trade in Ming China." *Journal of the Historical Society* 8.3: 327–347.

Fisher, Margaret W., and Joan V. Bondurant. 1956a. "Indian Views of Sino-Indian Relations." *Indian Press Digests 1* (February).

———.1956b. "Review Article: The Impact of Communist China on Visitors from India." *Far Eastern Quarterly* 15.2 (February): 249–265.

Forte, Antonino. 1984. "The Activities in China of the Tantric Master Manicinta-na (Pao-ssu-wei: ?–721 A.D.) from Kashmir and of His Northern Indian Collaborators." *East and West*, n.s., 34.1–3 (September): 301–347.

Garver, John W. 2001. *Protracted Contest: Sino-Indian Rivalry in the Twentieth Century*. Seattle: University of Washington Press, 2001.

Ghosh, Arunabh. Forthcoming. "Before 1962: The Case for 1950s China-India History." *Journal of Asian Studies*.

Ghosh, Supriya. 1987. "Ramnath Biswas, 1893–1955." In *Banglar Manisha*, edited by Sudhirkumar Gangopadhyay, 201–204. Calcutta: Sarat Publishing House.

Goble, Geoffrey C. 2012. "Chinese Esoteric Buddhism: Amoghavajra and the Ruling Elite." PhD dissertation, Indiana University.

Goldstein, Melvyn C. 1989. *A History of Modern Tibet, 1913–1951: The Demise of the Lamaist State*. Berkeley: University of California Press.

———. 2007. *A History of Modern Tibet, Volume 2: The Calm before the Storm: 1951–1955*. Berkeley: University of California Press.

Gommans, Jos. 2002. *Mughal Warfare: Indian Frontiers and High Roads to Empire, 1500–1700*. London and New York: Routledge.

Grant, Joan. 1978. "The China Connection: Indian Nationalist Relations with China, 1880–1950." Unpublished MA thesis, Monash University.

Green, John Park. 1948. "The Inter-Asian Relations Conference of March–April 1947." Unpublished MA thesis, University of Chicago.

Griffin, Nicholas, ed. 2001. *The Selected Letters of Bertrand Russell: The Public Years, 1914–1970*. London: Routledge.

Guo Deyan 郭德焱. 2005. *Qingdai Guangzhou Basi shangren* 清代廣州巴斯商人 (English title: Parsee Merchants in Canton during the Qing Period). Beijing: Zhonghua shuju.

Gupta, Karunakar. 1982. *Spotlight on Sino-Indian Frontiers*. Calcutta: New Book Center.

———. 1987. *Sino-Indian Relations, 1948–52: Role of K. M. Panikkar*. Calcutta: Minerva Associates.

Gupta, Krishna Prakash. 1979. "The Making of China's Image of India." *China Report* 15.2 (March–April): 39–50.

Guy, John. 1993–1994. "The Lost Temples of Nagapattinam and Quanzhou: A Study in Sino-Indian Relations." *Journal of the Institute of Silk Road Studies* 3: 291–310.

Guyot-Réchard, Bérénice. 2016. *Shadow States: India, China and the Himalayas, 1910–1962*. Cambridge: Cambridge University Press.

Gyalo Thondup (Rgya-lo-don-grub, Lha-sras), and Anne F. Thurston. 2015. *The Noodle Maker of Kalimpong: The Untold Story of My Struggle for Tibet*. New York: PublicAffairs.

Habib, Irfan. 2011. "Non-Agricultural Production." In *History of Science, Philosophy and Culture in Indian Civilization*, vol. 8, part 1, "Economic History of Medieval India, 1200–1500," edited by Irfan Habib, 85–103. New Delhi: Centre for Studies in Civilizations.

Hall, Kenneth R. 1985. *Maritime Trade and State Development in Early Southeast Asia*. Honolulu: University of Hawai'i Press.

Hang, Krista van Fleit. 2013. "'The Law Has No Conscience': The Cultural Construction of Justice and Reception of *Awara* in China." *Asian Cinema* 24.2: 141–159.

Hartwell, Robert. 1989. "Foreign Trade, Monetary Policy and Chinese 'Mercantilism.'" In *Collected Studies on Sung History Dedicated to James T. C. Liu in Celebration of His Seventieth Birthday*, edited by Kinugawa Tsuyoshi, 453–488. Kyoto: Dohosha.

Hay, Stephen N. 1970. *Asian Ideas of East and West: Tagore and His Critics in Japan, China, and India*. Cambridge, MA: Harvard University Press.

He, Lüting 賀綠汀. 1957. *He Lüting hechang ji* 賀綠汀合唱集 (Collection of He Lüting's Chorus Songs). Shanghai: Shanghai yinyue chubanshe.

Heimann, James. 1980. "Small Change and Ballast: Cowry Trade and Usage as an Example of Indian Ocean Economic History." *South Asia: Journal of South Asian Studies* 3.1: 48–69.

Heirman, Ann. 2007. "Vinaya from India to China." In *The Spread of Buddhism*, edited by Ann Heirmann and Stephan-Peter Bumbacher, 167–202. Leiden: Brill.

Herath, Dharmaratna. 1994. *The Tooth Relic and the Crown*. Colombo: n.p.

Hershock, Peter D. 2005. *Chan Buddhism: Dimensions of Asian Spirituality*. Honolulu: University of Hawai'i Press.

Hettiaratchi, S. B. 2003. "Studies in Cheng-Ho in Sri Lanka." In *Zheng He xia xiyang guoji xueshu yantaohui lunwen ji* 鄭和下西洋國際學術研討會論文集 (Collection of Essays from the International Workshop on the Zheng He's Expeditions to the Western Oceans), edited by Chen Xinxiong 陳信雄 and Chen Yunü 陳玉女, 91–109. Taipei: Daoxiang chubanshe.

Higham, Charles. 2002. *The Civilization of Angkor*. Berkeley: University of California Press.

Hindi-Cheeni. 1955. *Indian View of China before the Communist Revolution*. Cambridge: Center for International Studies, Massachusetts Institute of Technology.

Hirth, Friedrich, and W. W. Rockhill, eds. and trans. 1911. *Chau Ju-kua: His Work on the Chinese and Arab Trade in the Twelfth and Thirteenth Centuries, Entitled Chu-fan-chih*. St. Petersburg: Printing Office of the Imperial Academy of Sciences.

Hodgett, Gerald A. J. [1972] 2006. *A Social and Economic History of Medieval Europe*. Oxon, OX: Routledge.

Hoffmann, Steven A. 1990. *India and the China Crisis*. Berkeley: University of California Press.

Howard, Angela. 1983. "Planet Worship: Some Evidence, Mainly Textual, in Chinese Esoteric Buddhism." *Asiatischen Studien* 37.2: 104–119.

———. 1996. "Buddhist Cave Sculpture of the Northern Qi Dynasty: Shaping a New Style, Formulating New Iconographies." *Archives of Asian Art* 49: 6–25.

———. 2008. "Pluralism of Styles in Sixth-Century China: A Reaffirmation of Indian Models." *Ars Orientalis* 35: 67–94.

Hsieh, Ming-Tung. 2011. *A Lost Tribe*. Central Milton Keynes: AuthorHouse UK.

Hu Lingling 胡鈴鈴. 2012. "Huaxia zhi xin dianran Tianzhu zhi deng: Tan Yunshan de bufan rensheng daolu" 華夏之心點燃天竺之燈：譚雲山的不凡人生道路 (The Chinese Heart that Kindled the Indian Lamp: The Remarkable Life of Tan Yunshan). In *Tan Yunshan* 譚雲山, edited by Tan Chung 譚中 and Yu Longyu 郁龍余, 1–151. Beijing: Zhongyang bianyi chubanshe.

Huber, Toni. 2008. *The Holy Land Reborn: Pilgrimage and the Tibetan Reinvention of Buddhist India*. Chicago: University of Chicago Press.

Hulsewé, A. F. P., and M. A. N. Loewe. 1979. *China in Central Asia , the Early State: 125 B.C.–A.D. 23, an Annotated Translation of Chapters 61 and 96 of the History of the Former Han Dynasty*. Leiden: Brill.

Hussain, Syed Ejaz. 2003. *The Bengal Sultanate: Politics, Economy and Coins (AD 1205–1576)*. New Delhi: Manohar.

Hutheesing, Raja. 1953. *The Great Peace: An Asian's Candid Report on Red China*. New York: Harper.

Hyman, Malcolm D., and Jürgen Renn. 2012. "Survey: From Technology Transfer to the Origins of Science." In *The Globalization of Knowledge in History*, edited by Jürgen Renn, 15–44. Berlin: Edition Open Access. http://www.edition-open-access.de/studies/1/5/index.html.

"India in the Brussels Congress." *Indian Quarterly Register* 1–2 (1927): 152–159.

"The Indian National Congress." *Indian Quarterly Register* 1–2 (1927): 353–419.

"Indian Nationalism & Japanese Imperialism." *Indian Annual Register* 1 (January–June 1938): 43–50.

Jahn, Karl. 1965. *Rashīd al-Dīn's History of India. Collected Essays with Facsimiles and Indices*. The Hague: Mouton.

Jain, Girilal. 1956. *Chinese "Panchsheela" in Burma*. Bombay: Democratic Research Service.

———. 1957. *What Mao Really Means*. Delhi: Siddhartha Publications (Private) Ltd.

———. 1960. *Panchsheela and After: A Re-Appraisal of Sino-Indian Relations in the Context of the Tibetan Insurrection*. Bombay: Asia Publishing House.

Jan, Yün-hua. 1970. "Nāgārjuna, One or More? A New Interpretation of Buddhist Hagiography." *History of Religions* 10.2 (November): 139–155.

Ji Xianlin 季羨林. [1954] 2010. "Zhongguo zhi he zaozhi fa shuru Yindu de shijian he didian wenti" 中國紙和造紙法輸入印度的時間和地點問題 (The Issue of the Time and the Site of the Spread of Chinese Paper and Papermaking Technology to India). In *Ji Xianlin quanji* 季羨林全集 (Complete Works of Ji Xianlin), vol. 13: 59–90.

———. 1997. *Wenhua Jiaoliu de Guiji: Zhonghua zhetang shi* 文化交流的軌跡：中華蔗糖史 (The Tracks of Cross-Cultural Intercourse: The History of Chinese Cane Sugar). Beijing: Jingji ribao chubanshe, 1997.

Ji Xianlin 季羨林 et al. 1985. *Da Tang Xiyu ji jiaozhu* 大唐西域記校注 (Annotation of the Records of the Western Regions [Visited during] the Great Tang Dynasty). Beijing: Zhonghua shuju.

Jin Kemu 金克木. 1957. *ZhongYin renmin youhao shihua* 中印人民友好史話 (History of Friendship between the Chinese and Indians). Beijing: Zhongguo qingnian chubanshe.

———. 1958. *A Short History of Sino-Indian Friendship*. Beijing: Foreign Languages Press, 1958.

———. 1959. "Tongchi ganshe zhe" 痛斥干涉者 (Denouncing the Interventionist). *Guangming ribao*, 4 May: 4.

Joint Compilation Committee. 2014. *Encyclopedia of India–China Cultural Contacts*, 2 vols. New Delhi: MaXposure Media Group (I) Pvt. Ltd.

Karaka, D. F. 1944. *Chungking Diary*. Bombay: Thacker.

Karanjia, Russy K. 1952. *China Stands Up and Wolves of the Wild West*. Bombay: People's Publishing House.

———. 1954. "The Himalayas Fall as Nehru & Chou Meet to Usher in the Golden Age of Asia." *Blitz*, 28 June.

Karashima Noboru 辛島昇. 1978. "The Yeh-pa-nai-na Problem in the History of Sri Lanka: A Review Based on New Chinese Sources." In *Senarat Paranavitana Commemoration Volume*, edited by Leelananda Premayilleke, Karthigesu Indrapala, and J. E. van Lohuizen-de Leeuw, 98–106. Leiden: Brill.

———. 1988. "Jūsan seikī matsu ni okeru mīnami Indo to Chūgoku no aida no kōryū: Senshu Tamirugo kokubun to 'Genshi' Bahachijiden o megutte" 十三世紀末における南イソドと中國の間の交通—泉州タミル語刻文と元史馬八兒伝をめぐって (Relations between South India and China at the End of the Thirteenth Century: On the Quanzhou Tamil Inscription and Descriptions of Ma'bar in the *History of the Yuan*). In *Enoki hakushi shōju kinen Tōyō shi ronsō* 榎博士頌壽紀念東洋史論叢, edited by Enoki hakushi shōju kinen Tōyō shi ronsō hensan iinkai, 77–105. Tokyo: Kyūko Shoin.

Karashima, Noboru, and Tansen Sen. 2009. "Appendix II: Chinese Texts Describing or Referring to the Chola Kingdom as Zhu-nian." In *Nagapattinam to Suvarnadwipa: Reflections on the Chola Naval Expeditions to Southeast Asia*, edited by Hermann Kulke, K. Kesavapany, and Vijay Sakhuja, 292–315. Singapore: Institute of Southeast Asian Studies.

Karetzky, Patricia E. 2002–2003. "Wu Zetian and Buddhist Art of the Tang Dynasty." *T'ang Studies* 20–21: 113–150.

Karl, Rebecca E. 2002. *Staging the World: Chinese Nationalism at the Turn of the Twentieth Century*. Durham, NC: Duke University Press.

Kaul, T. N. 1982. *Reminiscences, Discreet and Indiscreet*. New Delhi: Lancers.

———. 2000. *A Diplomat's Diary: The Tantalizing Triangle: China, India, and USA*. Delhi: Macmillan.

Kauz, Ralph. 2006. "The Maritime Trade of Kish during the Mongol Period." In *Beyond the Legacy of Genghis Khan*, edited by Linda Komaroff, 51–67. Leiden: Brill.

Kenley, David L. 2003. *New Culture in a New World: The May Fourth Movement and the Chinese Diaspora in Singapore, 1919–1932*. New York: Routledge.

Khan, Iqtidar Alam. 1977. "Origin and Development of Gunpowder Technology in India: A.D. 1250–1500." *Indian Historical Review* 4.1: 20–29.

———. 1996. "Coming of Gunpowder to the Islamic World and North India: Spot on the Role of the Mongols." *Journal of Asian History* 30.1: 27–45.

———. 2004. *Gunpowder and Firearms: Warfare in Medieval India*. New Delhi: Oxford University Press.

Kieschnick, John. 2003. *The Impact of Buddhism on Chinese Material Culture*. Princeton, NJ: Princeton University Press.

Kieschnick, John, and Meir Shahar, eds. 2014. *India in Chinese Imagination: Myth, Religion, and Thought*. Philadelphia: University of Pennsylvania Press.

Kim, Jinah. 2013. *Receptacle of the Sacred: Illustrated Manuscripts and the Buddhist Book Cult in South Asia*. Berkeley: University of California Press.

Kitson, Peter J. 2013. *Forging Romantic China: Sino-British Cultural Exchange 1760–1840*. Cambridge: Cambridge University Press.

Kovacs, Jürgen, and Paul U. Unschuld, trans. 1999. *Essential Subtleties of the Silver Sea: The Yin-Hai Jing-Wei; A Chinese Classic on Ophthalmology*. Berkeley: University of California Press.

Krahl, Regina, John Guy, and Julian Raby, eds. 2011. *Shipwrecked: Tang Treasures and Monsoon Winds*. Washington, D.C.: Smithsonian Books.

Kumar, J. 1974. *Indo-Chinese Trade, 1793–1833*. Bombay: Orient Longman.

Kuwayama, Shōshin 桑山正進. 1988. "How Xuanzang Learned about Nālandā." In *Tang China and Beyond: Studies on East Asia from the Seventh to the Tenth Century*, edited by Antonino Forte, 1–33. Kyoto: Istituto Italiano di Cultura Scuola di Studi sull'Asia Orientale.

———. 1990. *Kāpiśi = Gandhāra shi kenkyū* カーピシー＝ガンダーラ史研究 (Research on the History of Kāpiśi, i.e., Gandhāra). Kyoto: Institute for Research in Humanities, Kyoto University.

Kuzmina, E. E. 2008. *The Prehistory of the Silk Road*. Philadelphia: University of Pennsylvania Press.

Kwa, Chong-Guan, comp. 2013. *Early Southeast Asia as Viewed from India: An Anthology of Articles from the* Journal of the Greater India Society. Delhi: Manohar Publishers.

La Vaissière, Etienne de. 2005. *Sogdian Traders: A History*. Leiden: Brill.

Lahiri, Latika. 1986. *Chinese Monks in India: Biography of Eminent Monks Who Went to the Western World in Search of the Law during the Great T'ang Dynasty*. Delhi: Motilal Banarsidass.

Lai, Walton Look. 1993. *Indentured Labor, Caribbean Sugar: Chinese and Indian Migrants to the British West Indies, 1838–1918*. Baltimore, MD: Johns Hopkins University Press.

Lane, Frederic C. 1968. "Pepper Prices before da Gama." *Journal of Economic History* 28: 590–597.

Latour, Bruno. 2005. *Reassembling the Social: An Introduction to Actor-Network-Theory*. London: Oxford University Press.

Layton, Thomas N. 1997. *The Voyage of the Frolic: New England Merchants and the Opium Trade*. Stanford, CA: Stanford University Press.

Lazar, Ed. 1963. "Across National Barriers." *MANAS* 16.3 (16 January): 1–13.

Le Pichon, Alain, ed. 2006. *China Trade and Empire: Jardine, Matheson & Co. and the Origins of British Rule in Hong Kong, 1827–1843*. Oxford: Oxford University Press.

Lei, Wan. 2010/12. "The Chinese Islamic 'Goodwill Mission to the Middle East' during the Anti-Japanese War." *Divan Disiplinlerarasi Calismalar Dergisi* 15.29: 133–170.

Leoshko, Janice. 2003. *Sacred Traces: British Explorations of Buddhism in South Asia*. Aldershot: Ashgate.

Levathes, Louise. 1994. *When China Ruled the Seas: The Treasure Fleet of the Dragon Throne 1405–1433*. New York: Simon and Schuster.

Lévi, Sylvain. 1900. "Les missions de Wang Hiuen-ts'e dans l'Inde." *Journal Asiatique* 9.15: 297–341, 401–468.

Li, Kangying. 2010. *The Ming Maritime Trade Policy in Transition, 1368 to 1567*. Wiesbaden: Harrassowitz Verlag.

Li, Kwai-Yun. 2008. *The Last Dragon Dance: Chinatown Stories*. New Delhi: Penguin.

———. 2011. "Deoli Camp: An Oral History of Chinese Indian from 1962 to 1966." Unpublished MA thesis, University of Toronto.

Li, Rongxi, trans. 1995. *A Biography of the Tripitaka Master of the Great Ci'en Monastery of the Great Tang Dynasty*. Berkeley: Numata Center for Buddhist Translation and Research.

———, trans. 1996. *The Great Tang Dynasty Record of the Western Regions*. Berkeley: Numata Center for Buddhist Translation and Research.

———, trans. 2000. *Buddhist Monastic Traditions of Southern Asia: A Record of the Inner Law Sent Home from the South Seas*. Berkeley: Numata Center for Buddhist Translation and Research.

———, trans. 2002. "The Journey of the Eminent Monk Faxian." In *Lives of Great Monks and Nuns*, 155–214. Berkeley: Numata Center for Buddhist Translation and Research.

Li, Ruohong. 2012. "Aspects of the Contact between the Sixth Panchen Lama and the British East India Company." *Frontiers of History in China* 7.2: 198–219.

Li, Tieh-Tseng. 1960. *Tibet: Today and Yesterday.* New York: Bookman Associates, 1960.

Liang Qichao 梁啟超. [1921] 1990. "Zhongguo-Yindu zhi jiaotong" 中國印度之交通 (Communications between India and China). *Yinbingshi Foxue lun ji* 飲冰室佛學論集 (Collected Works on Buddhism by Liang Qichao), edited by Liang Qichao, 103–136. Shanghai: Jiangsu guangling guji.

———. [1925] 2002. Introduction to *Talks in China*, edited by Rabindranath Tagore, vii–xxx. New Delhi: Rupa.

Lim, Ngo-Chang. 1925. "A Brief Review of Early Chinese Literature." *Visva-Bharati Quarterly* 2 (January): 396–402.

Lin, Chengjie. 1991. "Ma Jianzhong and Wu Guangpei's Visit to India and Their Diaries." *Asia-Pacific Studies* 1991: 55–72.

———. 1993. *ZhongYin renmin youhao guanxi shi* 中印人民友好關係史 (History of the Friendly Relations between the Peoples of China and India). Beijing: Beijing daxue chubanshe.

Lin, Hsiao-Ting. 2006. *Tibet and Nationalist China's Frontier: Intrigues and Ethnopolitics, 1928–49.* Vancouver: UBC Press.

Lin Meicun 林梅村. 2005. "Zheng He jiri ji shenhou shi" 鄭和忌日及身後事 (The Day Zheng He Died and Related Problems). *Jiuzhou xuelin* 九州學林 3.2: 2–27.

Liu, Xinru. 1988. *Ancient India and Ancient China.* Delhi: Oxford University Press, 1988.

———. 1996. *Silk and Religion: An Exploration of Material Life and the Thought of People.* Delhi: Oxford University Press, 1996.

———. 2001. "Migration and Settlement of the Yuezhi-Kushan: Interaction and Interdependence of Nomadic and Sedentary Societies." *Journal of World History* 12.1 (Fall): 261–292.

Liu, Ying, Zhongping Chen, and Gregory Blue, ed. 2014. *Zheng He's Maritime Voyages (1405–1433) and China's Relations with the Indian Ocean World: A Multilingual Bibliography.* Leiden: Brill.

Liu Yingsheng 劉迎勝. N.d. "Cong 'Buali shendao beiming' kan nan Yindu yu Yuan chao ji Bosi wan de jiaotong" 從不阿里神道碑銘看南印度與元朝及波斯灣的交通 (The Interactions between Southern India, the Persian Gulf and the Yuan Dynasty as Seen from the Funeral Inscription of Buali). *Lishi dili* 歷史地理 7: 90–95.

———. 2008. "Xilanshan bei de shiyuan yanjiu" 錫蘭山碑的史源研究 (Research on the Historical Sources for the Sri Lankan Stele). *Zheng He yanjiu* 鄭和研究 72.4 (2008): 45–52.

Lo, Jung-pang. 2012. *China as a Sea Power, 1127–1368: A Preliminary Survey of the Maritime Expansion and Naval Exploits of the Chinese People during the Southern Song and Yuan Periods.* Singapore and Hong Kong: NUS Press and Hong Kong University Press.

Loo, Margaret M. Shu-yi. 1970. "The Biography of the III Panchen Lama, Blo-bzang-dpal-ldan-ye-shes-dpal-bzangpo, Examined in the Light of the Sino-Tibetan Relations during the Late Eighteenth Century." PhD dissertation, University of Washington.

Lovell, Julia. 2011. *The Opium War: Drugs, Dreams and the Making of China.* London: Picador.

Mackintosh-Smith, Tim, trans. 2014. "Abū Zayd al-Sīrāfī, Accounts of China and India." In *Two Arabic Travel Books*, edited and translated by Tim Mackintosh-Smith and James E. Montgomery. New York: New York University Press.

Mair, Victor H. [1993] 2013. "Cheng Ch'iao's Understanding of Sanskrit." In *China and Beyond: A Collection of Essays by Victor H. Mair*, edited by Rebecca Shuang Fu, Matthew Anderson, Xiang Wan, and Sophie Wei, 185–206. Amherst, NY: Cambria Press.

———. 2004. "Foreword: The Beginnings of Sino-Indian Cultural Contact." *Journal of Asian History* 38.2: 81–96.

Mak, Bill. 2015. "The Transmission of Buddhist Astral Science from India to East Asia: The Central Asian Connection." *Historia Scientiarum* 24.2: 59–75.

Malekandathil, Pius. 2001. *Portuguese Cochin and the Maritime Trade of India, 1500–1663.* New Delhi: Manohar.

Manguin, Pierre-Yves. 1980. "The Southeast Asian Ship: An Historical Approach." *Journal of Southeast Asian Studies*, 11.2: 266–276.

———. 1996. "Trading Ships of the South China Sea: Shipbuilding Techniques and Their Role in the History of the Development of Asian Trade Networks." *Journal of the Economic and Social History of the Orient* 36.3: 253–280.

———. 2004. "The Archaeology of the Early Maritime Polities of Southeast Asia." In *Southeast Asia: From Prehistory to History*, edited by I. C. Glover and P. Bellwood, 282–313. Singapore: NUS Press.

Mansergh, Nicholas. 1947. "The Asian Conference." *International Affairs* 23.3 (July): 295–306.

Mao Yiheng 毛以亨. 1947. "Fan Yazhou huiyi riji: Yi" 泛亞洲會議日記（一） (Diary of the Pan-Asian Conference: Part 1). *Zaisheng zhoukan* 再生週刊 160: 8–9.

Mao, Yufeng. 2011. "A Muslim Vision for the Chinese Nation: Chinese Pilgrimage Missions to Mecca during World War II." *Journal of Asian Studies* 70.2: 373–395.

Markovits, Claude. 2000. "Indian Communities in China, c. 1842–1949." In *New Frontiers: Imperialism's New Communities in East Asia, 1842–1953*, edited by Robert Bickers and Christian Henriot, 55–74. Manchester: Manchester University Press.

Markovits, Claude, Jacques Pouchepadass, and Sanjay Subrahmanyam, eds. 2003. *Society and Circulation: Mobile People and Itinerant Cultures in South Asia, 1750–1950.* Delhi: Permanent Black.

Marsh, Yin. 2012. *Doing Time with Nehru: A Memoir of Yin Marsh.* Crockett: Sugartown Publishing.

Mauss, Marcel. [1954] 1990. *The Gift: The Form and Reason for Exchange in Archaic Societies*. London: Routledge.

Maxwell, Neville. 1970. *India's China War*. London: Jonathan Cape.

Mazumdar, Sucheta. 1998. *Sugar and Society in China: Peasants, Technology, and the World Market*. Cambridge, MA: Harvard University Asia Center, 1998.

Menon, K. P. S. 1972. *Twilight in China*. Bombay: Bharatiya Vidya Bhavan.

Meulenbeld, G. Jan, and Dominik Wujastyk. [1987] 2001. *Studies in Indian Medical History*. Delhi: Motilal Banarsidass.

Miller, Manjari Chatterjee. 2013. *Wronged by Empire: Post-Imperial Ideology and Foreign Policy in India and China*. Stanford, CA: Stanford University Press.

Mills, J. V. G., trans. [1970] 1997. *Ma Huan Ying-yai sheng-lan: "The Overall Survey of the Ocean's Shores" [1433]*. Bangkok: White Lotus.

———, trans. 1996. *Hsing-ch'a sheng-lan: "The Overall Survey of the Star of the Raft by Fei Hsin."* Wiesbaden: Harrassowitz.

Mitra, Rajendralala. 1878. *Buddha Gaya: The Hermitage of Sakya Muni*. Calcutta: Bengal Secretariat Press.

Moraes, Frank. 1953. *Report on Mao's China*. New York: Macmillan.

Mosca, Mathew. 2013. *From Frontier Policy to Foreign Policy: The Question of India and the Transformation of Geopolitics in Qing China*. Stanford, CA: Stanford University Press.

Mullik, B. N. 1971. *My Years with Nehru: The Chinese Betrayal*. Bombay: Allied Publishers.

Nag, Kalidas. 1945. *Tagore and China*. Calcutta: Prabasi Press.

———. 1957. *Discovery of Asia*. Calcutta: Institute of Asian African Relations.

Nagel, Eva. 2001. "The Chinese Inscription on the Trilingual Slabstone from Galle Reconsidered: A Case Study in Early Ming-Chinese Diplomatics." In *Ancient Ruhuna: Sri Lankan–German Archaeological Project in the Southern Province*, vol. 1, edited by H.-J. Weisshaar, H. Roth, and W. Wijeyapala, 385–468. Mainz: Verlag Philipp von Zabern.

Nair, N. Sreekantan. 1953. *The Chinese Puzzle*. Bombay: Progressive Publications.

Nakayama, Shigeru. 1969. *A History of Japanese Astronomy*. Cambridge, MA: Harvard University Press.

Narayan, Jaya Prakash. 1960. "Chairman's Address." In *Report of the Afro-Asian Convention on Tibet*, 19–32. New Delhi: Afro-Asian Council.

———. 1963. *Sarvodaya Answer to Chinese Aggression*. Thanjavur: Sarvodaya Prachuralaya.

———. 2007. *Jayaprakash Narayan: Selected Works*. Vol. 7 (1954–1960), vol. 8 (1960–1966). Edited by Bimal Prasad. Delhi: Manohar.

Nattier, Jan. 1991. *Once upon a Future Time: Studies in a Buddhist Prophecy of Decline*. Berkeley, CA: Asian Humanities Press.

———. 2008. "The Meanings of the Maitreya Myth: A Typological Analysis." In *Maitreya, the Future Buddha*, edited by Alan Sponberg and Helen Hardacre, 25–32. Cambridge: Cambridge University Press.

Needham, Joseph, and Tsien Tsuen-Hsuin. 1985. *Science and Civilisation in China*, vol. 5, *Chemistry and Chemical Technology*, part 1, "Paper and Printing." Cambridge: Cambridge University Press.

Needham, Joseph, and Wang Ling. 1959. *Science and Civilisation in China*, vol. 3, *Mathematics and the Sciences of the Heavens and the Earth*. Cambridge: Cambridge University Press.

Neelis, Jason. 2010. *Early Buddhist Transmission and Trade Networks: Mobility and Exchange within and beyond the Northwestern Borderlands of South Asia*. Leiden and Boston: Brill.

Nehru, Jawaharlal. 1941. *Toward Freedom: The Autobiography of Jawaharlal Nehru*. New York: John Day, 1941.

———. 1946. "Colonialism Must Go." *New York Times*, 3 March: SM5.

———. 1947. "India and China." *Sino-Indian Journal* 1.1 (July): 1–4.

———. [1958] 1960. *A Bunch of Old Letters, Written Mostly to Jawaharlal Nehru and Some Written by Him*. London: Asia Publishing House.

———. 1972. *Selected Works of Jawaharlal Nehru*. Vol. 10. New Delhi: Orient Longman.

———. 1984. "Chinese Activities in India." In *Selected Works of Jawaharlal Nehru*, 2nd ser., edited by S. Gopal, vol. 2: 462–463. New Delhi: Oxford University Press.

———. 1991. *Selected Works of Jawaharlal Nehru*. 2nd ser. Edited by S. Gopal. Vol. 12. New Delhi: Oxford University Press.

Nightingale, Pamela. 1970. *Trade and Empire in Western India, 1784–1806*. Cambridge: Cambridge University Press.

Nilakanta Sastri, K. A. 1935. *The Cōḷas*. Madras: Madras University Press.

———. [1958] 1975. *A History of South India: From Prehistoric Times to the Fall of Vijayanagar*. Delhi: Oxford University Press, 1975.

Ninomiya-Igarashi, Masumi. 2010. "Drawn toward India: Okakura Kakuzō's Interpretation of Rájendralála Mitra's Work in His Construction of Pan-Asianism and the History of Japanese Art." PhD dissertation, University of North Carolina at Chapel Hill.

"Ninth Anniversary of the Mulagandhakuti Vihara at Sarnath." *Maha-Bodhi: Journal of the Maha Bodhi Society* 48.12 (December): 460–463.

Niu, Weixing. 2004. *Xiwang Fantian: Hanyi Fojing zhong de tianwenxue yuanliu* 西望梵天: 漢譯佛經中的天文學源流 (Gazing toward the Brahma Heaven: The Spread of Astronomical Studies Seen from the Translated Buddhist Texts). Shanghai: Shanghai jiaotung daxue chubanshe.

"Notes and News." *Maha-Bodhi: Journal of the Maha Bodhi Society* 55.9–10 (September–October 1947): 219–220.

Okakura Kakuzō. [1903] 1920. *The Ideals of the East, with Special Reference to the Art of Japan*. New York: Dutton.

————. 1917. "The Pan-Asian Movement: A Pro-German, Anti-British, Anti-American Propaganda Calculated to Harm the Orient More than the Occident." *Far Eastern Review* 13.12 (May 1917): 446–451.

O'Rourke, Kevin H., and Jeffrey G. Williamson. 2009. "Did Vasco da Gama Matter for European Markets?" *Economic History Review* 62.3: 655–684.

Overstreet, Gene D., and Marshall Windmiller. 1959. *Communism in India.* Berkeley: University of California Press.

Pairaudeau, Natasha. 2016. *Mobile Citizens: French Indians in Indochina, 1858–1954.* Copenhagen: NIAS Press.

Palsetia, Jesse S. 2015. *Jamsetjee Jejeebhoy: Partnership and Public Culture in Empire.* New Delhi: Oxford University Press.

Pampus, Mareike. 2017. "Heritage Food: The Materialisation of Connectivity in Nyonya Cooking." Paper presented at the International Conference on Traveling Pasts: The Politics of Cultural Heritage in the Indian Ocean World, 18-19 May 2017, Halle, Germany.

Pan Jixing. 2012. *Zhongwai kexue jishu jiaoliu shi* 中外科學技術交流史 (History of Scientific and Technological Exchanges between China and Foreign [Regions]). Beijing: Sheke wenxian chubanshe.

Panikkar, K. M. 1955. *In Two Chinas: Memoirs of a Diplomat.* London: Allen and Unwin.

————. 1957. *India and China: A Study of Cultural Relations.* Bombay: Asia Publishing House.

Pankenier, David W. 2004. "A Brief History of Beiji 北極 (Northern Culmen), with an Excursus on the Origin of the Character di 帝." *Journal of the American Oriental Society* 124.2: 211–236.

Papelitzky, Elke. 2015. "An Introduction to *Siyi guangji* 四夷廣記." *Crossroads* 11 (April): 85–95.

Pardesi, Manjeet S. 2011. "Instability in Tibet and the Sino-Indian Strategic Rivalry: Do Domestic Politics Matter?" In *Asian Rivalries: Conflict, Escalation, and Limitations on Two-Level Games,* edited by Sumit Ganguly and William R. Thompson, 79–117. Stanford, CA: Stanford University Press.

Park, Hyunhee. 2010. "A Buddhist Woodblock-Printed Map and Geographic Knowledge in 13th Century China." *Crossroads* 1: 55–78.

————. 2012. *Mapping the Chinese and Islamic Worlds: Cross-Cultural Exchange in Pre-modern Asia.* Cambridge: Cambridge University Press.

Pearson, M. N. 1987. *The New Cambridge History of India,* vol. 1, part 1, "The Portuguese in India." Cambridge: Cambridge University Press.

————. 1991. "Merchants and States." In *The Political Economy of Merchant Empires: State Power and World Trade, 1350–1750,* edited by James D. Tracy, 41–116. Cambridge: Cambridge University Press.

Pelliot, Paul. 1903. "Artistes des Six Dynasties et des T'ang." *T'oung Pao* 22: 215–291.

————. 1904. "Deux itineraires de Chine en Inde à la fin du VIII e siècle." *Bulletin de l'École française d'Extrême-Orient* 5: 131–413.

———. 1912. "Autour d'une traduction Sanscrite du Tao Tö King." *T'oung Pao* 13 (1912): 351–430.

———. 1923. "Notes sur quelques artistes des Six Dynasties et des T'ang." *T'oung Pao* 22: 215–291.

Peng, Ke, and Zhu Yanshi. 1995. "New Research on the Origin of Cowries Used in Ancient China." *Sino-Platonic Papers* 68: 1–26.

Perera, Edward W. 1904. "Alakéswara: His Life and Times." *Journal of the Royal Asiatic Society (Ceylon)* 55.18: 281–312.

Petech, L. 1950a. *Northern India according to the Shui-ching-chu*. Roma : Is-MEO.

———. 1950b. "The Missions of Bogle and Turner According to the Tibetan Texts." *T'oung Pao* 39.4–5: 330–346.

———. 1972. *China and Tibet in the Early XVIIIth Century: History of the Establishment of Chinese Protectorate in Tibet*. Leiden: Brill.

Phillips, George. 1895. "Mahuan's Account of the Kingdom of Bangala (Bengal)." *Journal of the Royal Asiatic Society*, 523–535.

Pineo, Ly-Tio-Fane, and Edouard L. Fat. 2008. *From Alien to Citizen: The Integration of the Chinese in Mauritius*. Rose-Hill, Mauritius: Éditions de l'océan Indien.

Pingree, David. 1963. "Astronomy and Astrology in India and Iran." *Isis: A Journal of the History of Science* 54: 229–246.

Pittman, D. A. 2001. *Toward a Modern Chinese Buddhism: Taixu's Reforms*. Honolulu: University of Hawai'i Press.

Platov, I. 1947. "The Results of the Inter-Asian Conference." *Soviet Press Translations II* 2: 95.

Prakash, Om. 1985. *The Dutch East India Company and the Economy of Bengal, 1630–1720*. Princeton, NJ: Princeton University Press.

———. 1987. "The Dutch East India Company in the Trade of the Indian Ocean." In *India and the Indian Ocean, 1500–1800*, edited by A. Das Gupta and M. N. Pearson, 185–200. Calcutta: Oxford University Press.

———. 1998. *The New Cambridge History of India*, vol. 2, part 5, "European Commercial Enterprise in Pre-Colonial India." Cambridge: Cambridge University Press.

Prasad, Birendra. 1979. *Indian Nationalism in Asia (1900–1947)*. Delhi: B. R. Publishing.

Prashad, Vijay. 2008. *The Darker Nations: A People's History of the Third World*. New York: The New Press.

Prazniak, Roxann. 2010. "Siena on the Silk Roads: Ambrogio Lorenzetti and the Mongol Global Century, 1250–1350." *Journal of World History* 21.2: 177–217.

———. 2013. "Tabriz on the Silk Roads: Thirteenth-Century Eurasian Cultural Connections." *Asian Review of World Histories* 1–2: 169–188.

———. 2014. "Ilkhanid Buddhism: Traces of a Passage in Eurasian History." *Comparative Studies in Society and History* 56.3: 650–680.

Ptak, Roderich. 1987. *Portuguese Asia: Aspects in History and Economic History (Sixteenth and Seventeenth Centuries)*. Stuttgart: Steiner Verlag Wiesbaden GMBH.

―――. 1989. "China and Calicut in the Early Ming Period: Envoys and Tribute Embassies." *Journal of the Royal Asiatic Society of Great Britain and Ireland* 1: 81–111.

―――. 1991. "China and Portugal at Sea: The Early Ming System and the Estado da Índia Compared." *Revista de Cultura/Review of Culture* 13–14:21–38.

Puttaswamy, T. K. 2012. *Mathematical Achievements of Pre-Modern Indian Mathematics*. London: Waltham.

Qin Dashu 秦大樹. 2015. "Kenniya chutu Zhongguo ciqi de chubu guancha" 肯尼亞出土中國瓷器的初步觀察 (Archaeological Investigations of Chinese Ceramics Excavated from Kenya). In *Ancient Silk Trade Routes: Selected Works from Symposium on Cross Cultural Exchanges and Their Legacies in Asia*, edited by Qin Dashu and Yuan Jian, 87–109. Singapore: World Scientific.

Raghavan, Srinath. 2006. "Sino-Indian Boundary Dispute, 1948–60: A Reappraisal." *Economic and Political Weekly* 41.36 (9–15 September): 3882–3892.

―――. 2010. *War and Peace in Modern India*. New York: Palgrave Macmillan.

Ramachandran, K. N. 1980. "Sino-Indian Relations." *Strategic Analysis* 4.4: 147–150.

Rambelli, Fabio. 2014. "The Idea of India (*Tenjiku*) in Pre-Modern Japan: Issues of Signification and Representation in the Buddhist Translation of Cultures." In *Buddhism across Asia: Networks of Material, Intellectual and Cultural Exchange*, edited by Tansen Sen, 259–290. Singapore: Institute of Southeast Asian Studies.

Ramesh, Jairam. 2005. *Making Sense of Chindia: Reflections on China and India*. Delhi: India Research Press.

Rao Zongyi [Jao Tsung-i] 饒宗頤. 1993. "Shubu yu Cīnapatta" 蜀布與 *Cīnapatta* (Sichuan Cloth and *Cīnapatta*). In *Fanxue ji* 梵學集 (A Collection of Studies on India), edited by Rao Zongyi, 223–260. Shanghai: Shanghai guji chubanshe.

Raschke, M. G. 1978. "New Studies in Roman Commerce with the East." *Aufstieg und Niedergang der römischen Welt*, vol. II.9.2: 604–1378.

Ray, Haraprasad. 1993. *Trade and Diplomacy in India-China Relations: A Study of Bengal during the Fifteenth Century*. New Delhi: Radiant Publishers.

Raychaudhuri, Tapan. 1962. *Jan Company in Coromandel, 1605–1690: A Study in the Interrelations of European Commerce and Traditional Economies*. The Hague: Martinus Nijhoff.

Reddy, G. P. 1954. "Nehru Convinced China Does Not Want War." *Times of India*, 31 October: 9.

―――. 1955. "Astounding Success of Bandung Meet: New Pattern Set for Co-existence." *Times of India*, 26 April: 1.

Reid, Anthony. 2006. "Hybrid Identities in the Fifteenth-Century Straits of Malacca." Asia Research Institute Working Paper Series 67. http://www.ari.nus. edu.sg/wps/wps06_067.pdf.

Renn, Jürgen, ed. 2012. *The Globalization of Knowledge in History*. Berlin: Edition Open Access. http://www.edition-open-access.de/studies/1/toc.html.

"Rev. Tai Hsu's Goodwill Mission." *Maha-Bodhi: Journal of the Maha-Bodhi Society* 47 (November 1939): 517–518.

Rhie, Marylin M. 1999. *Early Buddhist Art of China and Central Asia*, vol. 1, *Later Han, Three Kingdoms, and Western China in China and Bactria to Shan-shan in Central Asia*. Leiden: Brill.

Rockhill, W. W. 1913. "Notes on the Relations and Trade of China with the Eastern Archipelago and the Coast of the Indian Ocean during the Fourteenth Century." *T'oung Pao* 14.4: 473–476.

———. 1914. "Notes on the Relations and Trade of China with the Eastern Archipelago and the Coast of the Indian Ocean during the Fourteenth Century, Part I." *T'oung Pao* 15.3: 419–447.

———. 1915. "Notes on the Relations and Trade of China with the Eastern Archipelago and the Coast of the Indian Ocean during the Fourteenth Century, Part II.IV." *T'oung Pao* 16.4: 435–467.

Rothschild, N. Harry. 2015. *Emperor Wu Zhao and Her Pantheon of Devis, Divinities, and Dynastic Mothers*. New York: Columbia University Press.

Roy, Dhirendra N. 1933. "With the Hero of Woosung Forts." *Modern Review* 53.4 (April): 391–395.

Roy, M. N. 1938. "The Structure of Chinese Society." *Modern Review* 64.2 (August): 200–203.

———. 1945. *My Experience in China*. Calcutta: Renaissance Publishers.

———. 1946. *Revolution and Counter-Revolution in China*. Calcutta: Renaissance Publishers.

Rule, Paul. 2000. "Goa-Macao-Beijing: The Jesuits and Portugal's China Connection." In *Vasco da Gama and the Linking of Europe and Asia*, edited by Anthony Disney and Emily Booth, 248–250. New Delhi: Oxford University Press.

Russell, Bertrand. 1963. *Unarmed Victory*. New York: Simon and Schuster.

Saaler, Sven, and Christopher W. A. Szpilman, eds. 2011. *Pan-Asianism: A Documentary History*. 2 vols. Lanham, MD: Rowman & Littlefield.

Saksena, Shalini. 2005. "Indian Perceptions of the Emergence of the People's Republic of China." In *India and China in the Colonial World*, edited by Madhavi Thampi, 199–223. New Delhi: Social Science Press.

Salguero, C. Pierce. 2009. "The Buddhist Medicine King in Literary Context: Reconsidering an Early Medieval Example of Indian Influence on Chinese Medicine and Surgery." *History of Religions* 48.3 (February): 183–210.

———. 2010–2011. "Mixing Metaphors: Translating the Indian Medical Doctrine *Tridoṣa* in Chinese Buddhist Sources." *Asian Medicine* 6: 55–74.

———. 2014. *Translating Buddhist Medicine in Medieval China*. Philadelphia: University of Pennsylvania Press.

Salmon, Claudine. 1999. "Bengal as Reflected in two South-East Asian Travelogues from the Early Nineteenth Century." In *Commerce and Culture in the Bay of Bengal, 1500–1800*, edited by Om Prakash and Denys Lombard, 383–402. Delhi: Manohar.

Samarani, Guido. 2005. "Shaping the Future of Asia: Chiang Kai-shek, Nehru and China-India Relations during the Second World War Period." Working Paper 11. Centre for East and South-East Asian Studies, Lund University, Sweden.

Sambo Tenzin Dundrup 桑颇·登增顿珠, and Kunga Tsidrung 贡噶坚赞. 1984. "Xizang daibiaotuan chuxi fan Yazhou huiyi zhenxiang" 西藏代表團出席泛亞洲會議真相 (The True Story about the Participation of the Tibetan Delegation in the Asian Relations Conference). *Xizang wenshi ziliao* 西藏文史資料 2: 12–18.

Sampho Tenzin Dhondup [Sambo Tanzin Dundrup]. 1998. "Inter-Asian Conference." *Tibet since the Asian Relations Conference*, edited by Tsering Tsomo and Shankar Sharan, 59–61. New Delhi: Tibetan Parliamentary & Policy Research Centre.

Sarkar, Benoy Kumar. 1916. *Chinese Religion through Hindu Eyes: A Study in the Tendencies of Asiatic Mentality*. Shanghai: Commercial Press.

———. 1940. "Tai Hsu on India and Buddhism." *Calcutta Review* (March): 315–316.

Schäfer, Dagmar. 2011. *The Crafting of the 10,000 Things: Knowledge and Technology in Seventeenth-Century China*. Chicago: University of Chicago Press.

Schafer, Edward H. 1963. *The Golden Peaches of Samarkand: A Study of T'ang Exotics*. Berkeley: University of California Press.

———. 1977a. *Pacing the Void: T'ang Approaches to the Stars*. Berkeley: University of California Press.

———. 1977b. "*T'ang*." In *Food in Chinese Culture: Anthropological and Historical Perspectives*, edited by K. C. Chang, 85–140. New Haven, CT: Yale University Press.

Scott, James C. 2009. *The Art of Not Being Governed: An Anarchist History of Upland Southeast Asia*. New Haven, CT: Yale University Press.

Selvakumar, V. 2011. "Contacts between India and Southeast Asia in Ceramic and Boat Building Traditions." In *Early Interactions between South and Southeast Asia: Reflections on Cross-Cultural Exchange*, edited by Pierre-Yves Manguin, A. Mani, and Geoff Wade, 197–220. Singapore: ISEAS Publishing.

Sen, Narayan. 2005. "Accounts of Bengal in Extensive Records on Four Foreign Lands." In *Hawai'i Reader in Traditional Chinese Culture*, edited by Victor H. Mair et al., 505–513. Honolulu: University of Hawai'i Press.

———. 2007. "China as Viewed by Two Early Bengali Travellers: The Travel Accounts of Indumadhav Mullick and Benoy Kumar Sarkar." *China Report: A Journal of East Asia Studies* 43.4 (October–December): 465–484.

Sen, Tansen. 1995. "Gautama Zhuan: An Indian Astronomer at the Tang Court." *China Report: A Journal of East Asian Studies* 31.2: 197–208.

———. 1999. "Astronomical Tomb Paintings from Xuanhua: Mandalas?" *Ars Orientalis* 29: 29–54.

———. 2003. *Buddhism, Diplomacy, and Trade: The Realignment of Sino-Indian Relations, 600–1400.* Honolulu: University of Hawai'i Press.

———. 2004. "Tang China, Kasmir, and Muktapida Lalitaditya's Ascendancy over the Southern Hindukush Region." *Journal of Asian History* 38.2: 141–162.

———. 2006a. "The Formation of Chinese Maritime Networks to Southern Asia, 1200–1450." *Journal of the Economic and Social History of the Orient* 49.4: 421–453.

———. 2006b. "The Yuan Khanate and India: Cross-Cultural Diplomacy in the Thirteenth and Fourteenth Centuries." *Asia Major* 19.1–2: 299–326.

———. 2009. "The Military Campaigns of Rajendra Chola and the Chola-Srivijaya-China Triangle." In *Nagapattinam to Suvarnadwipa: Reflections on the Chola Naval Expeditions to Southeast Asia*, edited by Hermann Kulke, K. Kesavapany, and Vijay Sakhuja, 61–75. Singapore: ISEAS Publishing.

———. 2011. "Maritime Interactions between China and India: Coastal India and the Ascendancy of Chinese Maritime Power in the Indian Ocean. *Journal of Central Eurasian Studies* 2: 41–82.

———. 2012. "The Spread of Buddhism to China: A Re-examination of the Buddhist Interactions between Ancient India and China." *China Report: A Journal of East Asian Studies* 48.1–2: 11–27.

———. 2013. "Is There a Need for China Studies in India?" *Economic and Political Weekly* 48.29 (July 20): 26–29.

———, ed. 2014a. *Buddhism across Asia: Networks of Material, Intellectual and Cultural Exchange.* Vol. 1. Singapore and Delhi: Institute of Southeast Asian Studies and Manohar Publishers.

———. 2014b. "Buddhism and the Maritime Crossings." In *China and Beyond in the Mediaeval Period: Cultural Crossings and Inter-Regional Connections*, edited by Dorothy Wong and Gustav Heldt, 39–62. Amherst and Delhi: Cambria Press and Manohar Publishers.

———. 2014c. "Changing Regimes: Two Episodes of Chinese Military Interventions in Medieval South Asia." In *Asian Encounters: Networks of Cultural Interactions*, edited by Upinder Singh and Parul P. Dhar, 62–85. New Delhi: Oxford University Press.

———. 2014d. "Maritime Southeast Asia between South Asia and China to the Sixteenth Century." *TRaNS: Trans-Regional and -National Studies of Southeast Asia* 2.1: 31–59.

———. 2014e. "Relic Worship at the Famen Temple and the Buddhist World of the Tang Dynasty." In *Secrets of the Fallen Pagoda: Treasures from Famen Temple and the Tang Court*, edited by Alan Chong, 27–49. Singapore: Asian Civilisations Museum.

————. 2015. "Chinese Sources on South Asia." In *Beyond National Frames: South Asia Pasts and the World*, edited by Rila Mukherjee, 52–73. New Delhi: Primus Books.

————. 2016a. "Diplomacy, Trade, and the Quest for the Buddha's Tooth: The Yongle Emperor and Ming China's South Asian Frontier." In *Ming China: Courts and Contacts, 1400–1450*, edited by Craig Clunas, Jessica Harrison-Hall, and Luk Yu-Ping, 26–36. London: British Museum.

————. 2016b. "The Impact of Zheng He's Expeditions on Indian Ocean Interactions." *Bulletin of the School of Oriental and African Studies*, 79.3: 609–636.

————. 2016c. "Taixu's Goodwill Mission to India: Reviving the Buddhist Connections between India and China." In *Buddhism in Asia: Revival and Reinvention*, edited by Upinder Singh and Nayanjot Lahiri, 293–322. New Delhi: Manohar.

————. Forthcoming. "Serendipitous Connections: The Chinese Engagements with Sri Lanka." In *Connectivity in Motion: Island Hubs in the Indian Ocean World*, edited by Burkhard Schnepel and Edward A. Alpers.

Sen, Tansen, and Victor H. Mair. 2012. *Traditional China in Asian and World History*. Ann Arbor: Association for Asian Studies.

Sharf, Robert. 2002. *Coming to Terms with Chinese Buddhism: A Reading of the Treasure Store Treatise*. Honolulu: University of Hawaiʻi Press.

Shastri, Brajkishore. 1954. *From My China Diary*. Delhi: Siddhartha Publication.

Shen Dansen 沈丹森 (Tansen Sen). 2016. "Daoyan" 導言 (Introduction). In *ZhongYin guanxi yanjiu de shiye yu qianjing* 中印關係研究的視野與前景 (Conceptualizing and Re-Examining India-China Connections), edited by Shen Dansen and Sun Yinggang, 1–12. Shanghai: Fudan daxue chubanshe.

Shimada Kenji. 1990. *Pioneer of the Chinese Revolution: Zhang Binglin and Confucianism*. Translated by Joshua A. Fogel. Stanford, CA: Stanford University Press.

Shimazu, Naoko. 2014. "Diplomacy as Theatre: Staging the Bandung Conference of 1955." *Modern Asian Studies* 48.1: 225–252.

Shin, Leo K. 2012. "Thinking about 'Non-Chinese' in Ming China." In *Antiquarianism and Intellectual Life in Europe and China, 1500–1800*, edited by Peter N. Miller and Francois Louis, 289–309. Ann Arbor: University of Michigan Press.

Siddiqi, Asiya. 1982. "The Business World of Jamsetjee Jejeebhoy." *Indian Economic and Social History Review* 19.3–4 (July–December): 301–324.

————. 2005. "Pathways of the Poppy: India's Opium Trade in the Nineteenth Century." In *India and China in the Colonial World*, edited by Madhavi Thampi, 21–32. New Delhi: Social Science Press.

Simon Shen. 2011. "Exploring the Neglected Constraints on Chindia: Analysing the Online Chinese Perception of India and Its Interaction with China's India Policy." *China Quarterly* 207 (September): 541–560.

Sims-Williams, Nicholas. 1994. "The Sogdian Merchants in China and India." In *Cina e Iran: Da Alessandro Magno alia Dinastia Tang*, edited by Alfredo Cadonna and Lionello Lanciotti, 45–67. Firenze: Leo S. Olschki Editore.

Singh, Natwar. 2009. *My China Diary, 1956–1988*. New Delhi: Rupa.

Singh, Sinderpal. 2011. "From Delhi to Bandung: Nehru, 'Indianess' and 'Pan-Asian-ness.'" *South Asia: Journal of South Asian Studies* 34.1: 51–64.

Sirisena, W. M. 1978. *Sri Lanka and South-East Asia: Political, Religious and Cultural Relations, A.D. c. 1000 to c. 1500*. Leiden: Brill.

Sivin, Nathan. 1989. "Chinese Archaeoastronomy between Two Worlds." In *World Archeoastronomy: Selected Papers from the Second Oxford International Conference on Ascheoastronomy Held at Merida, Yucatan, Mexico, 13–17 January 1986*, edited by Anthony R. Aveni, 55–64. Cambridge: Cambridge University Press.

Smith, W. L. 1984. "Chinese Sugar? On the Origin of Hindi *Cīnī*, 'Sugar.'" *Indologica* 12: 225–232.

Solheim, Wilhelm G. 2006. *Archaeology and Culture in Southeast Asia: Unraveling the Nusantao*. Manila: University of Philippines Press.

Somaratne, Gintota Parana Vidanage. 1975. *The Political History of the Kingdom of Kotte, 1400–1521*. Colombo: n.p.

Souza, George Bryan, and Geoff Wade. 2009. "Identifying Hokkien (and Other) Merchants in VOC-ruled Batavia: Data from the Ci Ji Stele (1697) and the Financial Records of the Amfioen Sociëteit, 1745–1785." Occasional Paper 2, November. Center for the Study of the Chinese Southern Diaspora, Australian National University.

Spencer, George. 1983. *The Politics of Expansion: The Chola Conquest of Sri Lanka and Sri Vijaya*. Madras: New Era.

Stearns, Peter N. 2010. *Globalization in World History*. New York: Routledge.

Stein, Burton. 1985. "Politics, Peasants and the Deconstruction of Feudalism in Medieval India." *Journal of Peasant Studies* 12.2–3: 54–86.

Stolte, Carolien. 2014. "'Enough of the Great Napoleons! Raja Mahendra Pratap's Pan-Asian Projects (1929–1939)." *Modern Asian Studies* 46.2: 403–423.

Stolte, Carolien, and Harald Fischer-Tiné. 2012. "Imagining Asia in India: Nationalism and Internationalism (c. 1905–1940)." *Comparative Studies in Society and History* 44.1 (January): 62–92.

Strong, John S. 2004. *The Relics of the Buddha*. Princeton, NJ: Princeton University Press.

Su Bai 宿白. 1996. *Zangchuan fojiao siyuan kaogu* 藏傳佛教寺院考古 (Archaeology of Tibetan Buddhist Temples and Monasteries). Beijing: Wenwu chubanshe.

Su, Jiqing. 1981. See *Daoyi zhilüe*.

Subrahmanyam, Sanjay. 1990. *The Political Economy of Commerce: Southern India, 1500–1650*. Cambridge: Cambridge University Press.

———. 1997. "Connected Histories: Notes towards a Reconfiguration of Early Eurasia." *Modern Asian Studies* 31.3: 735–762.

————. 2004. *Explorations in Connected History: From the Tagus to the Ganges*. New Delhi: Oxford University Press.

————. 2005. *Explorations in Connected History: Mughals and Franks*. New Delhi: Oxford University Press.

————. 2016. "One Asia, or Many? Reflections from Connected History." *Modern Asian Studies* 50.1: 5–43.

Subramaniam, T. N. 1978. "A Tamil Colony in Mediaeval China." In *South Indian Studies*, edited by R. Nagaswamy, 1–52. Madras: Society for Archaeological, Historical and Epigraphical Research.

Subramanian, Lakshmi. 2012. "Jamsetjee Jeejeebhoy: The First Parsi Baronet." In *Three Merchants: Doing Business in Times of Change*, by Lakshmi Subramanian, 88–143. New Delhi: Allen Lane.

Sun, Laichen. 2011. "Chinese-Style Gunpowder Weapons in Southeast Asia: Focusing on Archaeological Evidence." In *New Perspectives on the History and Historiography of Southeast Asia: Continuing Explorations*, edited by Michael Aung-Thwin and Kenneth R. Hall, 75–111. London and New York: Routledge.

Sun Xiao 孙晓 and Chen Zhibin 陈志斌. 1991. *Ximalaya shan de xue: Zhong Yin zhanzheng shilu* 喜馬拉雅山的雪：中印戰爭實錄 (Snows of the Himalaya Mountains: Records of the China-India War). Jinan: Beiyue wenyi chubanshe.

Sun Xiushen. 1998. *Wang Xuance shiji gouchen* 王玄策史述鉤沉 (Trawling the Historical Achievements of Wang Xuance). Urmuqi: Xinjiang renmin chubanshe.

Sunderlal, Pandit. 1952. *China Today: An Account of the Indian Goodwill Mission to China, September–October 1951*. Allahabad: Hindustani Culture Society.

Tagore, Rabindranath, ed. [1925] 2002. *Talks in China*. New Delhi: Rupa.

Taixu 太虛. *Taixu dashi quanshu* 太虛大師全書 (Complete Works of Taixu). Vols. 17–19. http://www.nanputuo.com/nptlib/html/200707/1812143485802.html.

Tan, Chung, ed. 1999. *In the Footsteps of Xuanzang: Tan Yun-shan and India*. New Delhi: Gyan Publishing House and Indira Gandhi National Centre for the Arts.

————. 2009. "Towards a Grand Harmony." *IIC Quarterly, India China: Neighbours Strangers* 36.3–4: 2–19.

Tan, Chung, and Geng Yinzeng. 2005. *India and China: Twenty Centuries of Civilizational Interactions and Vibrations*. History of Science, Philosophy and Culture in Indian Civilization Series, vol. 3, part 6. Delhi: Center for the Studies in Civilizations.

Tan, Lee. 1999. "Life Sketch of Tan Yun-shan." In *In the Footsteps of Xuanzang: Tan Yun-shan and India*, edited by Tan Chung, 1–12. New Delhi: Gyan Publishing House and Indira Gandhi National Centre for the Arts.

Tan Yunshan 譚云山. 1930. "Yindu Jia'ergeda zhi Huaqiao" 印度加爾各答之華僑 (Overseas Chinese in Calcutta). *Dongfang zazhi* 東方雜誌 (Eastern Miscellany) 27.11 (June): 23–30.

———. 1932a. "Xizang zhi santiao lu" 西藏之三條路 (Three Options for Tibet). *Xin Yaxiya* 新亞細亞 3.4: 158–160.

———. 1932b. "Zhi Dalai Lama shu" 致達賴喇嘛書 (A Letter to Dalai Lama). *Xin Yaxiya* 新亞細亞4.5: 147–150.

———. 1933. *Yindu zhouyou ji* 印度周遊記 (Records of Travels around India). Nanjing: Xin Yaxiya xuehui.

———. 1944. *China, India and the War (Part I)*. Calcutta: China Press Limited.

———. 1947. "Foreword." *Sino-Indian Journal* 1.1 (July): i–ii.

———. 1948. "Vesak Address." *Maha-Bodhi: Journal of the Maha Bodhi Society* 56 (July): 231–241.

———. 1957. *Twenty Years of the Visva-Bharati Cheena-Bhavana, 1937–1957.* N.p.: The Sino-Indian Cultural Society of India.

———. 1998. *Sino-Indian Culture*. Calcutta: Visva-Bharati.

Tang, Kaijian. 2015. *Setting Off from Macau: Essays on Jesuit History During the Ming and Qing Dynasties*. Leiden: Brill.

Tejura, D. K. 1954. "India-China Pact on Tibet Opens Pathway to Peace." *Blitz*, 15 May: 13.

Teltscher, Kate. 2006. *The High Road to China: George Bogle, the Panchen Lama and the First British Expedition to Tibet*. London: Bloomsbury.

Teng, Ssu-yü, and John K. Fairbank. 1954. *China's Response to the West: A Documentary Survey, 1839–1923*. Cambridge, MA: Harvard University Press.

Thampi, Madhavi. 2005. *Indians in China, 1800–1949*. New Delhi: Manohar.

———. 2014. "Window on a Changing China: Diplomatic Musing of India's Envoys to Republican China, 1943–9." *China Report: A Journal of East Asian Studies* 50.3: 203–214.

Thapliyal, Uma Prasad. 1979. *Foreign Elements in Ancient Indian Society*. New Delhi: Munshiram Manoharlal.

Thompson, Virginia, and Richard Adloff. 1947. "Asian Unity: Force or Façade?" *Far Eastern Survey* 16.9: 97–99.

T'ien, Ju-Kang. 1981. "Cheng Ho's Voyages and the Distribution of Pepper in China." *Journal of the Royal Asiatic Society of Great Britain and Ireland* 2: 186–197.

Tomalin, Victoria, et al. 2004. "The Thaikkal-Kadakkarappally Boat: An Archaeological Example of Medieval Shipbuilding in the Western Indian Ocean." *International Journal of Nautical Archaeology* 33.2: 253–263.

Trocki, Carl A. 1999. *Opium, Empire and the Global Political Economy: A Study of the Asian Opium Trade, 1750–1950*. London: Routledge.

Tsui, Brian. 2010. "The Plea for Asia—Tan Yunshan, Pan-Asianism and Sino-Indian Relations." *China Report: A Journal of East Asian Studies* 46.4 (November): 353–370.

———. 2013. "China's Forgotten Revolution: Radical Conservatism in Action, 1925–1949." PhD dissertation, Columbia University.

Tuttle, Gray. 2005. *Tibetan Buddhists in the Making of Modern China.* New York: Columbia University Press.

Uberoi, Patricia. 2016. "Moving Forward on Parallel Tracks? A New Perspective on the BCIM Initiative." Working paper. Institute of Chinese Studies, Delhi, September.

Unschuld, Paul U. 1985. *Medicine in China: A History of Ideas.* Berkeley: University of California Press.

van Bladel, Kevin. 2014. "Eighth-Century Indian Astronomy in the Two Cities of Peace." In *Islamic Cultures, Islamic Contexts Essays in Honor of Professor Patricia Crone*, edited by Asad Q. Ahmed, Behnam Sadeghi, Robert G. Hoyland, and Adam Silverstein, 257–294. Leiden: Brill.

van der Geer, Alexandra. 2008. *Animals in Stone: Indian Mammals Sculptured through Time.* Leiden: Brill.

van Schendel, Willem. 2002. "Geographies of Knowing, Geographies of Ignorance: Jumping Scale in Southeast Asia." *Environment and Planning D* 20.6: 647–668.

Vickery, M. 2003. "Funan Reviewed: Deconstructing the Ancients." *Bulletin de l'École française d'Extrême-Orient* 90–91: 101–143.

Vogel, Hans Ulrich, and Sabine Hieronymus. 1993. "Cowry Trade and Its Role in the Economy of Yunnan: From the Ninth to Mid-Seventeenth Century. Part 1." *Journal of the Economic and Social History of the Orient* 36.3: 211–252.

Wade, Geoff, trans. 2005a. Southeast Asia in the Ming Shi-lu: An Open Access Resource . Singapore: Asia Research Institute and the Singapore E-Press, National University of Singapore, http://epress.nus.edu.sg/msl.

———. 2005b. "The Zheng He Voyages: A Reassessment." *Journal of the Malaysian Branch of the Royal Asiatic Society* 78.1: 37–58.

———. 2008. "Engaging the South: Ming China and Southeast Asia in the Fifteenth Century." *Journal of the Economic and Social History of the Orient* 51.4: 578–638.

———. 2009. "An Early Age of Commerce in Southeast Asia, 900–1300 CE." *Journal of Southeast Asian Studies* 40.2: 221–265.

Wagner, Donald. 2008. *Science and Civilisation in China*, vol. 5, *Chemistry and Chemical Technology*, part 11, "Ferrous Metallurgy." Cambridge: Cambridge University Press.

Wang Bangwei 王邦維 (Annotation of the Biographies of the Eminent Monks who went to the Western Regions in Search of the Law During the Tang Dynasty). 1988. *Da Tang Xiyu qiufa gaoseng zhuan jiaozhu* 大唐西域求法高僧傳校注. Beijing: Zhonghua shuju.

———. 1995. *Nanhai jigui neifa zhuan jiaozhu* 南海寄歸內法傳校注 (Annotation of a Record of Inner Dharma Sent Back from the Southern Seas). Beijing: Zhonghua shuju.

Wang, Gungwu. 1958. "The Nanhai Trade: A Study of the Early History of Chinese Trade in the South China Sea." *Journal of the Malayan Branch of the Royal Asiatic Society* 31.2: 1–135.

————. 1964. "The Opening of Relations between China and Malacca." In *Malayan and Indonesian Studies*, edited by John Sturgus Bastin, 87–104. Oxford: Clarendon Press.

————. 1968a. "Early Ming Relations with Southeast Asia: A Background Essay." In *The Chinese World Order: Traditional China's Foreign Relations*, edited by John K. Fairbank, 34–62. Cambridge: Harvard University Press.

————. 1968b. "The First Three Rulers of Malacca." *Journal of the Malaysian Branch of the Royal Asiatic Society* 41.1 (July): 11–22.

Wang Jiawei and Nyima Gyaincain. 1997. *The Historical Status of China's Tibet*. Beijing: China Intercontinental Press.

Weber, Thomas. 1996. *Gandhi's Peace Army: The Shanti Sena and Unarmed Peacekeeping*. Syracuse: Syracuse University Press.

Wernicke, Günter, and Lawrence S. Wittner. 1999. "Lifting the Iron Curtain: The Peace March to Moscow of 1960–1961." *International History Review* 21.4 (December): 900–917.

White, Gordon David. 1996. *The Alchemical Body: Siddha Tradition in Medieval India*. Chicago: University of Chicago Press.

Wink, André. [1990] 1999. *Al-Hind: The Making of the Indo-Islamic World*. vol. 1, *Early Medieval India and the Expansion of Islam, 7th–11th Centuries*. Leiden: Brill.

————. 1997. *Al-Hind: The Making of the Indo-Islamic World*, vol. 2, *The Slave Kings and the Islamic Conquest, 11th–13th Centuries*. Leiden: Brill.

————. 2004. *Al-Hind: The Making of Indo-Islamic World*, vol. 3, *Indo-Islamic Society, 14th–15th Centuries*. Leiden: Brill.

Wong, Dorothy. 2014. "An Agent of Cultural Transmission: Jianzhen's Travels to Japan, 743–63." In *China and Beyond in the Mediaeval Period: Cultural Crossings and Inter-Regional Connections*, edited by Dorothy C. Wong and Gustav Heldt, 63–99.

Wriggins, Sally Hovey. 2004. *The Silk Road Journey with Xuanzang*. Boulder, CO: Westview.

Wu, Chen-Tsai. 1987. "Chiang Kai-Shek's Visit to India and the Indian Independence." *Chinese Studies in History* 21.1: 2–38.

Wu, Hung. 1986. "Buddhist Elements in Early Chinese Art (2nd and 3rd Centuries A.D.)." *Artibus Asiae* 47.3–4: 263–316.

————. 2007. "Picturing or Diagramming the Universe." In *Graphics and Text in the Production of Technical Knowledge in China*, edited by Francesca Bray, Vera Dorofeeva-Lichtmann, and George Métailié, 191–216. Leiden: Brill.

Wu Zhuanjun 吳傳鈞, ed. 2006. *Haishang Sichou zhilu yanjiu: Zhongguo Beihai Hepu haishang Sichou zhilu shifagang lilun yantao lunwen ji* 海上絲綢之路研究：中國合浦海上絲綢之路始發港理論研討會論文集 (Research on the Maritime Silk Road: Collection of Papers from the Workshop on the Theory of Hepu, China, as the Earliest Port on the Maritime Silk Road). Beijing: Kexue chubanshe.

Xi Jinping. 2017. "Work Together to Build the Silk Road Economic Belt and the 21st Century Maritime Silk Road." http://news.xinhuanet.com/english/2017-05/14/c_136282982.htm.

Xiong, Zhaoming. 2014. "The Hepu Han Tombs and the Maritime Silk Road of the Han Dynasty." *Antiquity* 88: 1229–1243.

Xu Yuhu 徐玉虎. 2005. "Zheng He xia Xiyang yu zhu fanguo leshi libei xinkao" 鄭和下西洋於諸番國勒石立 碑新考 (New Examination of the Erection of Engraved Stone Tablets at Various Foreign Polities [during] Zheng He's Expedition along the Western Oceans). In *Zheng He yuanhang yu shijie wenming: Jinian Zheng He xia Xiyang 600 zhounian lunwen ji* 鄭和遠航與世界文明: 紀念鄭和下西洋600周年論文集 (Zheng He's Maritime Expeditions and World Civilization: Collection of Essays Marking the 600th Anniversary of Zheng He's Expedition to the Western Oceans), edited by Wang Tianyou 王天有, Xu Kai 徐凱, and Fang Ming 方明, 68-96. Beijing: Beijing daxue chubanshe.

Yabuuti, Kiyosi. 1979. "Researches on the Chiu-chih li: Indian Astronomy under the T'ang Dynasty." *Acta Asiatica: Bulletin of the Institute of Eastern Culture* 36: 7–48.

Yang, Anand. 2006. "Travel Matters: An Indian Subaltern's Passage to China in 1900." *Education about Asia* 11.3: 12–15.

———. 2007. "(A) Subaltern('s) Boxers: An Indian Soldier's Account of China and the World in 1900–1901." In *The Boxers, China, and the World*, edited by Robert Bickers and R. G. Tiedemann, 43–64. Lanham, MD: Rowman & Littlefield.

Yang, Anand, et al. Forthcoming. *An Annotated Translation of Thakur Gadadhar Singh's* Chin Meh Terah Maas. New Delhi: Oxford University Press.

Yang, Bin. 2004. "Horses, Silver, and Cowries: Yunnan in Global Perspective." *Journal of World History* 15.3: 281–322.

———. 2008. *Between Winds and Clouds: The Making of Yunnan.* New York: Columbia University Press.

———. 2012. "The Bengal Connections in Yunnan." *China Report: A Journal of East Asian Studies* 48.1–2: 125–145.

Yang, Tianshi. 2015. "Chiang Kai-shek and Jawaharlal Nehru." In *Negotiating China's Destiny in World War II*, edited by Hans van de Ven, Diana Lary, and Stephen R. MacKinnon, 127–140. Stanford, CA: Stanford University Press.

Yang, Yun-yuan. 1974. "Nehru and China, 1927–1949." PhD dissertation, University of Virginia.

———. 1987. "Controversies over Tibet: China versus India, 1947–49." *China Quarterly* 111 (September): 407–420.

Yano Michio 矢野道雄. 1986. *Mikkyō senseijutsu: Sukuyōdō to Indo senseijutsu* 密教占星術: 宿曜道とインド占星術 (Esoteric Buddhist Astrology: The Japanese Sukuyōdō School of Astrology and Indian Astrology). Tokyo: Tokyo Bijutsu.

Yoeli-Tlalim, Ronit. 2013. "Rashīd al-Dīn's *Life of the Buddha*: Some Tibetan Perspectives." In *Rashīd al-Dīn. Agent and Mediator of Cultural Exchanges in*

Ilkhanid Iran, edited by Anna Akasoy, Charles Burnett, and Ronit Yoeli-Tlalim, 197–211. London and Turin: Warburg Institute and Nino Aragno Editore.

Yokkaichi, Yasuhiro. 2008. "Chinese and Muslim Diasporas and the Indian Ocean Trade Network under Mongol Hegemony." In *The East Asian Mediterranean: Maritime Crossroads of Culture, Commerce and Human Migration*, edited by Angela Schottenhammer, 73–102. Wiesbaden: Harrassowitz Verlag.

————. 2009. "Horses in the East–West Trade between China and Iran under the Mongol Rule." In *Pferde in Asien: Geschichte, Handel und Kultur* (Horses in Asia: History, Trade and Culture), edited by Bert G. Fragner, Ralph Kauz, Roderich Ptak, and Angela Schottenhammer, 87–97. Wien: Verlag der Österreichischen Akademie der. Wissenschaften.

Yu Taishan 余太山. 1992. *Saizhong shi yanjiu* 塞種史研究 (Research on the History of the Śakas). Beijing: Zhongguo Shehui kexue chubanshe.

Yuan Qingfeng 袁慶豐. 2014. "Yindu dianying zai Zhongguo de shisu chuanbo he wenhua yingxiang: Yi 20 shiji 70 niandai mo chongxin gongying de 'Liulang zhe' wei lie" 印度電影在中國的世俗傳播和文化影響：以20 世紀70 年代末重新公映流浪者為例 (English title: Secular Spread and Cultural Impact of Indian Movies in China: A Case Study of *Awaara* Re-leased in the Late 1970s). *Wenhua yishu yanjiu* 文化藝術研究 7.4: 116–124.

Yule, Henry. 1875. *The Book of Ser Marco Polo the Venetian Concerning the Kingdoms and Marvels of the East*. 2 vols. London: John Murray.

Zhang, Qiong. 2015. *Making the New World Their Own: Chinese Encounters with Jesuit Science in the Age of Discovery*. Leiden: Brill.

Zhang, Xing. 2010. *Preserving Cultural Identity through Education: The Schools of the Chinese Community in Calcutta, India*. Singapore: ISEAS Publishing.

————. 2014. "Buddhist Practices and Institutions of the Chinese Community in Kolkata." In *Buddhism across Asia: Networks of Material, Intellectual and Cultural Exchange*, vol. 1, edited by Tansen Sen, 429–457. Singapore: Institute of Southeast Asian Studies.

————. 2015. *The Chinese Community in Calcutta: Preservation and Change*. Halle: Universitätsverlag Halle-Wittenberg.

Zhang, Xing, and Tansen Sen. 2013. "The Chinese in South Asia." In *Routledge Handbook of the Chinese Diaspora*, edited by Tan Chee-Beng, 205–226. London and New York: Routledge.

Zhao, Zhongnan. 2016. "The Gradual Termination of the Early Ming Voyages to the 'Western Ocean' and Its Causes." In *Ming China: Courts and Contacts, 1400–1450*, edited by Craig Clunas, Jessica Harrison-Hall, and Luk Yu-Ping, 106–112. London: British Museum.

Zhou, Enlai. 1954. "Cable from Zhou Enlai, 'Premier's Intentions and Plans to Visit India,'" 22 June 1954, History and Public Policy Program Digital Archive, PRC FMA 203-00005-01, 3–4. Translated by Jeffrey Wang. http://digitalarchive.wilsoncenter.org/document/112437.

Zhu Lishuang 朱麗双. 2006. "Zai zhenshi yu xiangxiang zhi jian: Minguo zhengfu de Xizang teshimen (1912–1949)" 在真實與想像之間：民國政府的西藏特使們 (Between Truth and Imagination: Special Envoys on Mission to Tibet during the Period of Republican China, 1912–1949). PhD dissertation, Chinese University of Hong Kong.

Zürcher, Erik. [1959] 1972. *The Buddhist Conquest of China: The Spread and Adaption of Buddhism in Early Medieval China.* 2 vols. Leiden: Brill.

Zysk, Kenneth. 1985. *Religious Healing in the Veda: With Translations and Annotations of Medical Hymns in the Ṛgveda and the Atharvaveda and Renderings from the Corresponding Ritual Texts.* Philadelphia: American Philosophical Society.

———. 1993. *Religious Medicine: The History and Evolution of Indian Medicine.* New Brunswick: Transaction Publishers.

———. 1998. *Asceticism and Healing in Ancient India: Medicine in the Buddhist Monastery.* Delhi: Motilal Banarasidass.

Index

About the Author

Tansen Sen is director of the Center for Global Asia and professor of history at NYU Shanghai and Global Network Professor at NYU. He received his MA from Peking University and his PhD from the University of Pennsylvania. He is the author of *Buddhism, Diplomacy, and Trade: The Realignment of Sino-Indian Relations, 600–1400* (2003, 2016) and *India, China, and the World: A Connected History* (2017). With Victor H. Mair he has coauthored *Traditional China in Asian and World History* (2012). He has edited *Buddhism across Asia: Networks of Material, Cultural and Intellectual Exchange* (2014). Currently he is working on a book on Zheng He's maritime expeditions and coediting (with Engseng Ho) the *Cambridge History of the Indian Ocean*, volume 1.

Made in the USA
Middletown, DE
19 December 2021

56564793R00331